"This lady is organized . . . well-researched guide."
San Francisco Chronicle Book Review

". . . almost overwhelmingly full of detailed information. Excellent."
San Diego Tribune

"We had a great time on our California vacation. *Weekend Adventures* was essential both during planning and execution. Thank you for a wonderful guide!"
Joleen Chambers, parent, Annapolis, MD

"Ms. Meyers has left no stone unturned in researching the recreation opportunities available in the northern half of the state."
Travelin' magazine

"Carole Terwilliger Meyers writes intelligently about family fun. She finds places kids like that adults can stomach. And vice versa."
Alice Kahn, author

"The guide is very well organized . . . Highly recommended."
Pacific Sun

". . . a gold mine of travel tips."
The Montclarion

"Carole's weekly family outing suggestions are welcome reminders of what a wonderful area of the world we live in. Sometimes all we need is another's enthusiasm to put sparkle in our day!"
C. J. Bronson, Bay Area radio personality

"Whenever we need a break from the city routine, I reach for my copy of *Weekend Adventures*. It's the greatest guidebook around for families who want to explore Northern California."
Dixie Jordan, Editor, Parents' Press

"Enjoyable to read . . . and loaded with photos."
Small Press magazine

". . . easy-to-follow format."
Booklist

Also by Carole Terwilliger Meyers:

The Family Travel Guide: An Inspiring Collection of Family-Friendly Vacations (Editor)

Miles of Smiles: 101 Great Car Games & Activities

San Francisco Family Fun

How to Organize a Babysitting Cooperative and Get Some Free Time Away From the Kids

Eating Out With the Kids in San Francisco and the Bay Area

Getting in the Spirit: Annual Bay Area Christmas Events

Eating Out with the Kids in the East Bay

Weekend Adventures

in Northern California

6th Edition

by Carole Terwilliger Meyers

CAROUSEL PRESS

Berkeley, California

Published by: **CAROUSEL PRESS**
P.O. Box 6038
Berkeley, CA 94706-0038
(510) 527-5849

Distributed to the book trade by Publishers Group West

Library of Congress Cataloging-in-Publication Data:
Meyers, Carole Terwilliger.
    Weekend adventures in northern California / by Carole Terwilliger
Meyers. -- 6th ed.
      p.   cm.
    Rev. ed. of: Weekend adventures for city-weary people. 5th ed.
c1993
    Includes indexes.
    ISBN 0-917120-15-9
    1. California. Northern--Guidebooks. 2. Family recreation-
-California. Northern--Guidebooks. I. Meyers, Carole Terwilliger.
Weekend adventures for city-weary people. II. Title.
F867.5.M48 1997
917.9404'53--dc21   96-47236
                                         CIP

The information in this book was correct at press time. However, the author and publisher hereby disclaim any liability due to changes, errors, or omissions, and cannot be held responsible for the experiences of readers while traveling. Specific prices are gathered in the year before publication and are mentioned only to give an approximate idea of what to expect; phone numbers are included so that readers can call to determine current rates. All establishments listed in this book are mentioned to alert the reader to their existence; they are endorsed by neither the author nor publisher. No business has paid to be included.

Reader Feedback: Please let us know if any place listed in this book doesn't live up to your expectations. The author will look into the situation on your behalf and adjust any misinformation in the 7th edition of *Weekend Adventures*. Please also alert us to any exciting discoveries.

Special Sales: Bulk purchases of Carousel Press titles are available to corporations at special discounts. Custom editions can be produced to use as premiums and promotional items. For more information, call (510) 527-5849.

Manufactured in the United States of America

 Printed on recycled paper

10 9 8 7 6 5 4 3 2

for Gene

Contents

Introduction

We residents of the Bay Area are fortunate to live within easy driving distance of a wealth of exciting vacation possibilities—mountains, ocean, rivers, snow. Our biggest recreational problem is deciding, from among the many possibilities, where we should go and what we should do.

The destinations in this book radiate out from San Francisco. Most make good weekend trips, and all can be adapted easily to longer stays.

Because it is frustrating to discover after you're home that an area where you've just vacationed had an interesting attraction you didn't know about, and because it also isn't much fun finding out too late that there was a better or cheaper (depending on what you're after) lodging you could have booked into . . . or a restaurant you would have enjoyed trying, this book is designed so that you can determine quickly what is of special interest in the area you are planning to visit. Listings are selected based on the fact that they are in some way special—bargain rates, welcoming of families, aesthetically pleasing, historically interesting, etc. Phone numbers necessary for obtaining further information are included, and toll-free 800 numbers are provided when available. (I have found that writing for information is slow and unreliable, so I recommend that you instead always call for a brochure or to make a reservation.)

Parents especially need to have this information in advance. I know because one of the worst trips I ever experienced was the first trip my husband and I took with our first baby. I hadn't planned ahead. We took off for the Gold Rush Country and went where the winds blew us—just like before we were parents. That was a mistake. We wound up in a hotel that had no compassion for a colicky baby or his parents, and we ate a series of memorably bad meals. Now my husband and I can laugh about that trip, but at the time it wasn't funny. That fateful trip turned me into a travel writer. After that I never went anywhere without exhaustively researching it beforehand. And truthfully I've never had a bad trip since that I can blame on lack of knowledge.

With all of this in mind, I've written this book to help make your trip-planning easier, allowing you to get the most out of your weekends away.

This 6th edition of *Weekend Adventures* reflects a name change from the previous title: *Weekend Adventures for City-Weary People: Overnight Trips in Northern California*. At one time this book included information only about trips away from the Bay Area, hence the "city-weary" part of the title. However, in recent years people have shown an interest in not traveling so far afield for a getaway. Catering to this desire for more close-in vacations, this edition has added chapters on San Francisco as well as on destinations in Marin County, the Peninsula, and the East Bay. This edition also reflects a merging with another of my books, *San Francisco Family Fun*, which will no longer be updated.

Credits

Book design and typesetting: Betsy Joyce
Maps: Eureka Cartography
Computer wizardry: Gene Meyers
Printing: McNaughton & Gunn, Inc.
Photos:
Cover: top to bottom, left to right: California Department of Parks and Recreation; Royal Gorge Nordic Ski Resort; Balloon Aviation of Napa Valley, Redwood Empire Association; Carol Piechocinski, Spanish Springs Ranch; Carl Wilmington, San Francisco Convention & Visitors Bureau; Lake Tahoe Visitors Authority; Great America; Ansel Adams, Redwood Empire Association; Wilderness Adventures.
Inside pages: p.8: San Francisco Convention & Visitors Bureau; *p.9:* George Olson, Dudell & Associates; *p.11:* Alameda Naval Air Station Public Affairs Office; *p.12:* Arne Folkedal, San Francisco Ballet; *p.15:* Hotel Diva; *p.23:* Park Hyatt San Francisco; *p. 26:* The Mansions Hotel; *p.28:* Fortune Public Relations; *p.47:* Katy Greene; *p.51:* Robert Stinnel, Red & White Fleet; *p.55:* Herb Bettin, San Francisco Convention & Visitors Bureau; *p.56:* San Francisco Convention & Visitors Bureau; *p.58:* Haas-Lilienthal House; *p.60:* Richard Barnes, SFMOMA; *pp.61 & 62:* San Francisco Maritime National Histoical Park; *p.63:* Susan Middleton, California Academy of Sciences; *p.64:* Nancy Rodger, Exploratorium; *p.69:* San Francisco Convention & Visitors Bureau; *p.70:* San Francisco Recreation and Park Department; *p.72,top:* Michael Shay, San Francisco Zoological Society; *p.72, bottom:* San Francisco Zoological Society; *p.73:* Ron Scherl, Steve Silver Productions; *p.75:* Ghirardelli Square; *p.76:* Hanford Associates; *p.77:* Edelman Public Relations; *p.85:* Terry Pimsleur & Co.; *p.87:* California State Department of Parks and Recreation; *p.92:* Santa Cruz Beach & Boardwalk; *p.95:* Janet Anderson; *p.96:* Shadowbrook; *p.102:* Jerry Lebeck, Monterey Peninsula Visitors & Convention Bureau; *p.103:* Monterey Bay Aquarium; *p.105:* Pete Amos, California Department of Parks and Recreation; *pp.116, 117, & 121:* California Department of Parks and Recreation; *p.124:* Ken Raveill, Hearst San Simeon State Historical Monument; *p.127:* Theodore Osmundson, California Department of Parks and Recreation; *p.128:* John Kaestner, California Department of Parks and Recreation; *pp.133 & 134:* California Department of Parks and Recreation; *p.137:* Clerin Zumwalt, Audubon Canyon Ranch; *p.140:* Redwood Empire Association; *p.142:* Osmosis; *p.143:* Sharon Taussig, Sonoma County Convention & Visitors Bureau; *p.147:* Ansel Adams, Redwood Empire Association; *pp.151 & 155:* Redwood Empire Association; *p.168, top:* Paramount Parks; *p.168 bottom:* Great America; *p.169:* Rosicrucian Egyptian Museum; *p.170:* Winchester Mystery House; *p.173:* Valley Guild, Steinbeck Library; *p.179:* Carole Terwilliger Meyers; *p.182:* Jane Oka, Marine Mammal Center California; *p.184:* Michael Morgan, Sea Trek Ocean Kayaking Center; *p.193:* Paladino Agency; *p.194:* Scott Hess, Petaluma Area Chamber of Commerce; *p.206:* Carole Terwilliger Meyers; *p.215:* Redwood Empire Association; *p.218:* Vichy Springs Resort; *p.221:* California State Department of Parks and Recreation; *p.224:* Pat Cudahy, Gingerbread Mansion Inn; *p.226:* California State Department of Parks and Recreation; *p.228:* Eureka Inn; *p.229:* Eureka/Humboldt County C.V.B.; *p.230:* California State Department of Parks and Recreation; *p.240:* Roaring Camp & Big Trees Narrow-Gauge Railroad; *pp.243 & 246:* Hal Schell; *p.251:* Carole Terwilliger Meyers; *p.254:* Gundlach-Bundschu Winery; *p.256: Sonoma Index-Tribune,* Sonoma Valley Visitors Bureau; *p.258:* Smothers Winery; *p.272:* Penn, Dr. Wilkinson's Hot Springs; *p.276:* Redwood Empire Association; *p.281:* Gold Prospecting Expeditions; *p.284:* City Hotel; *p.285:* Larry Paynter, California Department of Parks and Recreation; *p.286:* Moaning Cavern; *p.287:* 39th District Agricultural Association; *p.295:* Larry Paynter, California Department of Parks and Recreation; *p.298:* California Department of Parks and Recreation; *p.305:* Yosemite Concession Services; *p.307:* John Michael Flint, Oakwood Lake Resort; *p.308:* Yosemite Concession Services; *p.311:* John Poimiroo, Yosemite Concession Services; *p.312 top:* Yosemite Resources Library; *p.312 bottom:* John M. Giosso, San Francisco Recreation and Park Department; *p.314:* Sanger District Chamber of Commerce; *p.329:* East Bay Regional Parks District; *p.330 top:* Jon Winet, Pacific Film Archive; *p.330 bottom:* California Alumni Association; *p.331:* Peg Skorpinski, Lawrence Hall of Science; *pp.332 & 333:* Marine World Africa USA; *p.334:* Harre W. Demoro; *pp.335 & 340:* California Department of Parks and Recreation; *p.349:* Travel Systems Ltd.; *p.350:* Lake Tahoe Visitors Authority; *p.353:* Northstar-at-Tahoe; *p.357:* Greater Reno Chamber of Commerce; *p.358:* Carole Terwilliger Meyers; *pp.361, 367, & 370:* John F. Reginato, Shasta-Cascade Wonderland Association; *p.376:* Bob Everson, Alpine Meadows; *p.379:* Yosemite Concession Services; *p.381:* Paul Herzoff, Royal Gordge Nordic Ski Resort; *pp.382 & 383:* Yosemite Concession Services; *p.384:* California Department of Parks and Recreation; *p.387:* Shasta-Cascade Wonderland Association; *p.388:* Rapid Shooters, Mariah Wilderness Expeditions; *p.389:* Shasta Llamas.
Back cover: author photo by David Sanger.
Acknowledgments: Special thanks to Keith Walklet at Yosemite National Park and Malinee Crapsey at Sequoia and Kings Canyon National Parks for their extensive help in updating the information in the chapters pertaining to their areas.

Guidelines for Interpreting Listings

This book is organized by geographical area. Each chapter has the following subsections:

A LITTLE BACKGROUND: Historical and general background information about the area; what kinds of activities to expect.

VISITOR INFORMATION: Address and phone number of Chamber of Commerce or Visitors Bureau.

GETTING THERE: The quickest, easiest driving route from San Francisco; scenic driving routes, other transportation options.

STOPS ALONG THE WAY: Noteworthy places for meals or sightseeing.

ANNUAL EVENTS: The area's best events; in chronological order. When no phone number is listed, contact the Chamber of Commerce or Visitors Bureau for information.

WHERE TO STAY: Select lodging facilities, listed alphabetically and including the following information when available: Street address, toll-free 800 reservations number, phone number (area code appears immediately under city heading), fax number for reservations. Number of stories; number of rooms; number of non-smoking rooms; price range per night for two people (see price code below); if there is a minimum stay of more than 1 night. Months closed. Policies regarding children (if children stay free in parents' room; if facility is unsuitable for children under a specified age). If no TVs are available; if VCRs are available; if kitchens, gas or wood-burning fireplaces, or wood-burning stoves are available; if any baths are shared. What recreational facilities are available: pool, hot tub, sauna, health spa, fitness room, parcourse, tennis courts, golf course. If there is a complimentary afternoon or evening snack; if there is a complimentary breakfast (continental or full); if there is a restaurant, room service (if there are children's items). If pets are welcome. If there is a parking fee.

$=under $50 $$=$50-$99 $$$=$100-$149 $$$+=over $150

WHERE TO EAT: Worthwhile restaurants, listed alphabetically and including the following information when available: Address, phone number, fax number. Meals served (B, L, D, SunBr), days open; price range (see price code below). Availability of highchairs, boosters, booths, child portions or menu. If it is 100% non-smoking. If reservations are advised, accepted but not usually needed, or not accepted. Credit cards accepted (see code below). If parking is difficult, whether a validated parking lot or valet parking are available.

$ = inexpensive. Dinner for one adult might cost up to $15.
$$ = moderate. Dinner for one adult might cost from $15 to $30.
$$$ = expensive. Dinner for one adult might cost over $30.

Projected costs are based on dinner prices and are exclusive of drinks, dessert, tax, and tip.

Credit Cards: American Express (AE), MasterCard (MC), Visa (V)

WHAT TO DO: Activities and sights in the area that are of special interest, listed alphabetically and including the following information when available: Address, phone number. Days and hours open. Admission fee.

Note that some restaurants and attractions are closed on major holidays. Always call to verify hours.

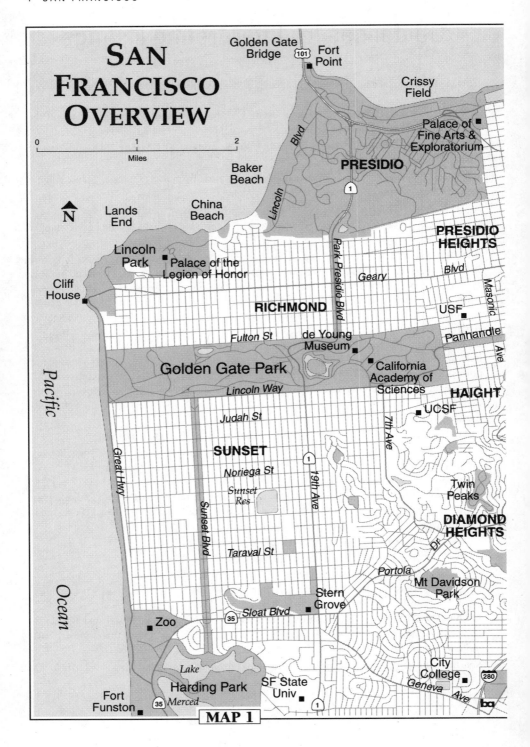

SAN FRANCISCO OVERVIEW

Golden Gate Bridge

101 Fort Point

Crissy Field

Palace of Fine Arts & Exploratorium

0   1   2
Miles

Lincoln Blvd

PRESIDIO

Baker Beach

N

Lands End

China Beach

Park Presidio Blvd

1

PRESIDIO HEIGHTS

Lincoln Park

Palace of the Legion of Honor

Geary

Blvd

Masonic

Cliff House

RICHMOND

USF

Fulton St

de Young Museum

Panhandle

Ave

Pacific

Golden Gate Park

California Academy of Sciences

HAIGHT

Lincoln Way

UCSF

Judah St

7th Ave

SUNSET

Noriega St

1

Sunset Res

19th Ave

Twin Peaks

DIAMOND HEIGHTS

Great Hwy

Sunset Blvd

Taraval St

Portola

Dr

Mt Davidson Park

Ocean

Stern Grove

35 Sloat Blvd

Zoo

Lake

Harding Park

Fort Funston

35 *Merced*

SF State Univ

1

City College

Geneva Ave

280

MAP 1

Map 1 5

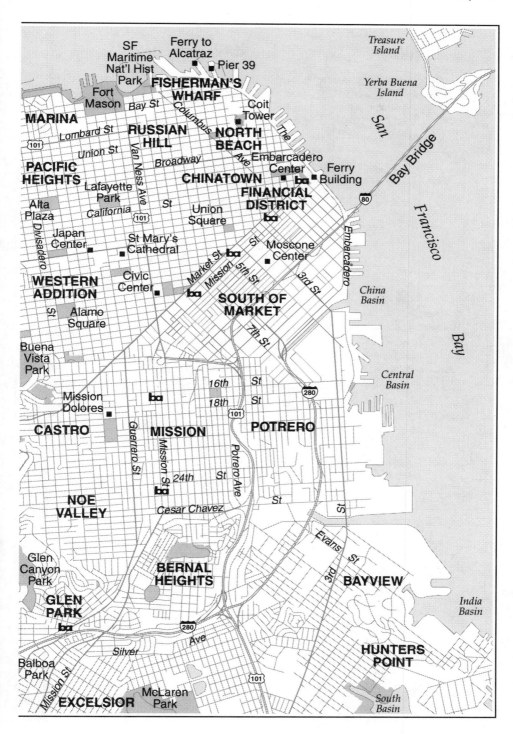

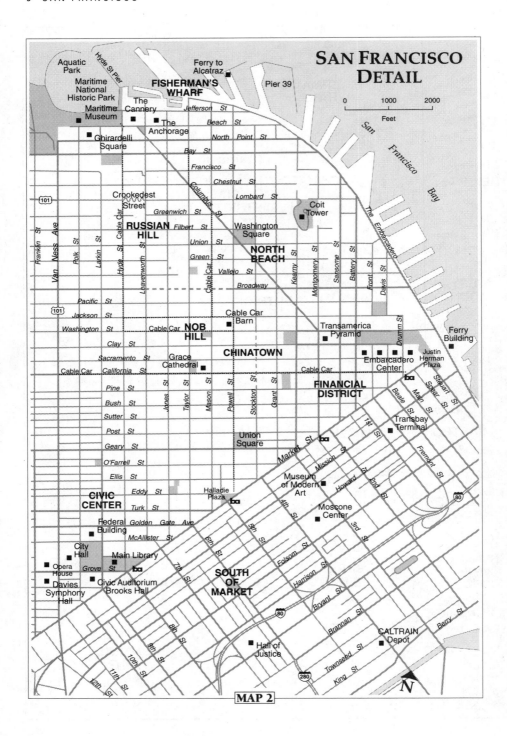

SAN FRANCISCO
DETAIL

MAP 2

(Area Code 415)

A LITTLE BACKGROUND

"You wouldn't think such a place as San Francisco could exist. The wonderful sunlight there, the hills, the great bridges, the Pacific at your shoes. Beautiful Chinatown. Every race in the world. The sardine fleets sailing out. The little cable-cars whizzing down the city hills. The lobsters, clams, & crabs . . . Every kind of seafood there is. And all the people are open and friendly."

—Dylan Thomas

"San Francisco has only one drawback. 'Tis hard to leave."

—Rudyard Kipling

Though the quotes above are not heard often, the saying attributed to Mark Twain, "The coldest winter I ever spent was a summer in San Francisco," is familiar to most people. Scholars dispute that the words were Twain's, but no one who has spent a summer in San Francisco will dispute the comment.

This city is known for its morning and evening fog in summer. Locals coming in from the suburbs have learned to always bring along wraps. In summer it is easy to spot tourists. They are the ones wearing shorts . . . or white shoes, another no-no among locals. Perhaps these visitors are confusing San Francisco with the image of Southern California's warm beaches. That is a mistake.

In general the climate is temperate, ranging between 40 and 70 degrees. The best weather usually occurs in September and October.

VISITOR INFORMATION

San Francisco Convention and Visitors Bureau *P.O. Box 429097, San Francisco 94142-9097, 391-2000.*

Send $2 for a copy of *The San Francisco Book*. It is filled with sightseeing, shopping, and dining information. *The Lodging Guide* will also be included.

Upon arrival, stop at the **Visitor Information Center** *(Halladie Plaza, Market St./Powell St., 391-2000. M-F 9-5:30, Sat 9-3, Sun 10-2.)* to get oriented.

For a recorded listing of the day's events, call 391-2001. For the same information in French, call 391-2003; German 391-2004; Spanish 391-2122; Japanese 391-2101.

ANNUAL EVENTS

JANUARY

Chinese New Year Celebration & Parade *Or in February or March, depending on the lunar calendar.* *391-9680. Free.*

First held in 1851 and held again every year since, this popular event is composed of a beauty pageant, an outdoor carnival in Chinatown, and the famous Golden Dragon Parade featuring the spectacular block-long golden dragon. (The parade is one of the few illuminated night parades in the U.S.)

FEBRUARY

Pacific Orchid Exposition *Or in March. Fort Mason Center; 665-2468. $5-$8.*

Thousands of gorgeous blooming orchid plants are on display at this stunning show, which displays both amateur and professional collections. It is the largest of its kind on the West Coast. Many plants are entered for judging and show only, but hundreds more are available for purchase. Lectures by international orchid experts are scheduled. Sponsored by the San Francisco Orchid Society.

MARCH

St. Patrick's Day Parade *467-8218 or 467-6426. Free.*

This traditional parade has been held annually for over 80 years.

APRIL

Cherry Blossom Festival *563-2313. Free.*

Japanese cultural events at this elaborate celebration of spring include traditional dancing, martial arts demonstrations, taiko drum and koto performances, and tea ceremonies. A Japanese food bazaar operates continuously, and demonstrations of the Japanese arts of doll-making, calligraphy, and flower arranging are usually scheduled. The festival culminates with a colorful two-hour Japanese-style parade.

San Francisco Decorator Showcase *221-9295. $15.*

Strict quality control gives this show house a reputation for being the best in the West—perhaps even the best in the entire country.

San Francisco International Film Festival *929-5000. $4.50-$20.*

Known for honoring the finest in cinematic achievement, North America's oldest film festival presents recent productions from around the world. Some children's films are usually included.

MAY

Bay to Breakers *(415), (510), or (408) 808-5000 x2222. Entry fee $15.*

The world's largest, and perhaps zaniest, footrace is usually routed through the Financial District, up the Hayes Street hill, and on through Golden Gate Park to the Great Highway. Outrageous outfits are de rigueur and in the past have included everything from a set of crayons to Humphrey the Whale. All participants receive a commemorative t-shirt and a follow-up postcard with their finishing time and ranking. Sponsored by the *San Francisco Examiner*.

Carnaval *824-8999. Free.*

This spectacular Mardi Gras-like revel is a multicultural celebration of life. It includes a parade and a two-day outdoor festival.

Cinco de Mayo Festival *826-1401. Free.*

Commemorating the Battle of Puebla, Mexico on May 5, 1862, which marked the defeat of the powerful French Napoleonic Army by a small, poorly equipped Mexican force, this is the largest such festival in the U.S. It attracts visitors and performers from throughout Latin America and includes a parade, the Healthy High Five race, and a two-day festival.

JUNE

Cable Car Bell Ringing Championships *Union Square; 392-4880. Free.*

Competition is held in both pro and amateur divisions. The previous year's champion defends his title, and amateurs (who include some well-known Bay Area personalities) ring on behalf of non-profit organizations. Judges are selected from among the area's musical and theatrical elite.

North Beach Festival *403-0666. Free.*

This granddaddy of street fairs, said to be the very first in the country, features Italian foods, sidewalk cafes, traditional Italian sword fighting demonstrations, bocce ball games, and a variety of entertainment.

Stern Grove Midsummer Music Festival *Through mid-August. 19th Ave./Sloat Blvd.; 252-6252. Free.*

Featuring the finest of Bay Area performing arts, this program has been held in the Grove's natural outdoor amphitheater each summer since 1938. It is the country's oldest continuous free summer music festival. It is traditional to bring a picnic lunch and the Sunday paper and to spend the pre-performance wait indulging in food, drink, and relaxation. Also bring a blanket to sit on, and dress for warm weather, but bring wraps in case it turns chilly.

The city's **croquet lawns** are available here year-round for play; for more information, call 776-4104.

JULY

Fourth of July Waterfront Festival *777-8498 or 777-7120. Free.*

Beginning in the early afternoon, a variety of music and entertainment is presented continuously. A highlight is the Sixth Army's traditional 50-cannon salute to the nation. The celebration culminates with a fireworks spectacular after sunset. Sponsored by the *San Francisco Chronicle.*

AUGUST

ACC Craft Fair *Fort Mason Center; 896-5060. Adults $7, under 12 free.*

Produced by the American Craft Council, this is the largest juried craft fair on the West Coast. It features the latest work of over 350 of the nation's premier craft artists.

SEPTEMBER

San Francisco Blues Festival *Great Meadow at Fort Mason; 979-5588. $17-$20.*

Known for its all-star lineup, this upbeat affair has been called "one of the best blues events in the world." It also features a breathtaking background view of the Golden Gate Bridge.

OCTOBER

Columbus Day Celebration *467-8218. Free.*

San Francisco's is the only Columbus Day celebration in the country that includes a re-enactment of Columbus's landing in San Salvadore. When landing at Aquatic Park, the person acting as Columbus wears a handmade Italian replica of the great navigator's clothing. The **Blessing of the Fishing Fleet** takes place the next day at Fisherman's Wharf, and the **Italian Heritage Parade** usually takes place the next weekend.

Festa Italiana *Pier 45; 673-3782. Free.*

This celebration of everything Italian includes big name entertainment, bocce ball tournaments, and cooking demonstrations, plus plenty of food and arts and crafts booths.

Fleet Week *981-8030. Free.*

To celebrate the anniversary of the Navy's birthday, the City of San Francisco throws a gigantic birthday party each year and the public is invited. In the past there have been demonstrations of high-speed boat maneuvering, parachute drops, and a fly-by of World War II vintage aircraft. **The Blue Angels**, the Navy's precision flight demonstration team, also perform in a breathtaking culmination. Viewing is best from Crissy Field, the Marina Green, Aquatic Park, Pier 39, and the Marin Headlands. As part of the celebration, all Navy ships moored at the piers are usually opened for public visits.

Grand National Rodeo, Horse, & Stock Show *Cow Palace; 469-6058. $7.50-$20.*

This is the largest such show held west of the Mississippi. The rodeo and horse show are scheduled each evening in the arena. Ticket-holders are invited to come early to enjoy a variety of related activities: dairy animal auctions; judging contests; displays of unusual breeds of livestock, including tons of premium steers, woolly sheep, and prime swine. A special White Line Tour leads kids in to see the baby animals.

NOVEMBER

San Francisco Bay Area Book Festival *Concourse Exhibition Center; 861-BOOK, fax 861-2670. $2.*

Always featuring an impressive line-up of author appearances, this gathering of the area's literati, publishers, and bookstores is positively exhilarating.

DECEMBER

A Christmas Carol *Geary Theater; 749-2ACT. $14-$47.50.*

Dickens' popular seasonal ghost tale, which celebrates the rebirth of the human spirit and the death of indifference, is sure to rekindle any lagging Christmas enthusiasm in grumpy holiday Scrooges. ACT's lively, colorful production enhances the story with a musical score of carols, songs, and dance. It is interesting to note that Dickens' story is credited with actually reviving the celebration of Christmas, which at the time his book was published in 1843 had slipped to the status of a quaint, almost obsolete, custom. It is also considered responsible for some English social reform. Fortunately for all of us, his story still manages to wake up the spirit of human kindness. Performances run almost two hours with no intermission.

Golden Gate Park Christmas Tree Lighting *Golden Gate Park; 666-7024. Free.*

San Francisco's official Christmas tree, a 100-foot Monterey Cypress located at the east entrance to Golden Gate Park, is decorated each Christmas season with over 3,000 lights. The mayor is usually present to flip the switch. Santa also makes an appearance, and the audience is led in singing carols.

Guardsmen Christmas Tree Sale *Fort Mason Center; 781-6785.*

Claiming to have the largest enclosed Christmas tree lot in Northern California, the Guardsmen sell approximately 5,000 trees each year. This sale is famous for having the best selection of Noble Firs but also stocks a variety of other trees, including Douglas Fir, Frazer Fir, and Scotch Pine. Just visiting the lot is a thrill—it resembles a small forest—and imagine how nice it is on a rainy day. Trees range from table-top size to 14 feet and cost from $10 to $200. Garlands, wreaths, holly, mistletoe, and ornaments are also on sale. All purchases are tax-deductible, and proceeds fund camperships and educational programs for underprivileged Bay Area children.

The Nutcracker *War Memorial Opera House; 865-2000. $7-$100.*

The San Francisco Ballet has been presenting its delightful and festive version of *The Nutcracker* since 1942, when it blazed the path for all subsequent U.S. Nutcrackers by dancing the first full-length production. It has always been an extravagant interpretation, with hundreds of thousands of dollars worth of scenery and handmade costumes. Each performance features a cast of over 177 dancers that includes the company's principal dancers plus children from the Ballet School. A spectacular growing Christmas tree and a cannon that uses real gunpowder and makes a loud, smoke-producing boom are also featured. (The cannon once not only boomed but self-destructed!)

Sugar Plum Parties follow some matinee performances. They are held in the downstairs cafeteria. Guests are served sugary goodies (cookies, candy, soda), and the costumed cast

members are available for autographs. Proceeds benefit the Ballet School. Purchase party tickets at the same time as purchasing Nutcracker tickets.

Union Square Window Displays.

Each year the biggest department stores—Macy's, Saks Fifth Avenue, Neiman-Marcus—treat the public to elaborate window decorations, some with moving mechanical displays. A visit to Macy's commercial, but gorgeous, seventh-floor Christmas wonderland, known as Bayberry Row, is a treat; Santa is also found here. The lobby of the St. Francis Hotel is also worth a walk-through. Street entertainers, vendors, and carolers provide further diversion.

WHERE TO STAY

According to a 1996 survey, the average hotel room in San Francisco costs $120 a night.

UNION SQUARE

This is a choice area to stay in, especially if traveling without a car. (Hotels listed here charge between $14 and $26 per day for parking.) All of these hotels are within a few blocks of downtown, the theater district, and the cable car line. Many are quaint establishments that provide an European-style small hotel experience.

Canterbury Hotel *750 Sutter St./Taylor St., 3 blocks from Union Square, (800) 652-1614, 474-6464, fax 474-5856. 10 stories; 250 rooms; $$. Children under 18 free. Restaurant, room service. Self-parking 1 block away, $14.*

The **Lehr Brothers Grill** *(740 Sutter St., 474-6478, fax 474-0831. B, L, D daily; $$-$$$. Highchairs, boosters. Reservations advised. AE, MC, V. Validated parking.)* operates adjacent. Situated within the enormous room that formerly housed the popular Lehr's Greenhouse restaurant, the grill enjoys natural light. A cook's garden, with oversize cooking utensils providing whimsical decoration, is seen on two sides. The menu promises "American classics with an attitude" as well as retro touches such as classic martinis. Among the starters are delightful rock shrimp and wild rice fritters with an orange marmalade-horseradish sauce, and fresh potato gnocchi prepared with toasted pine nuts and a light curry cream sauce. The varied main dishes include fresh fish, house dry-aged steaks, and a tasty roast rack of lamb with medjool date demi-glacé. Among the "Code Blue" desserts prepared by well-named Noah Butter are a rich chocolate crème frâiche gateau and a refreshing trio of sorbets served in a crisp and delicious tuile Florentine. After-dinner cigars and digestifs can be enjoyed in the adjoining **Cigar and Cognac Lounge**. A more informal bistro, with a different but equally interesting menu, operates in front.

Cartwright Hotel *524 Sutter St./Powell St., 1 block from Union Square, (800) 227-3844, 421-2865, fax 398-6244. 8 stories; 114 rooms; 82 non-smoking rooms; $$$-$$$+. Children free. Afternoon tea, continental breakfast. Parking $16.*

Built in 1914 for the Panama-Pacific Exposition, this hotel is conveniently located on a fashionable shopping street. Its pleasant rooms are furnished distinctively with antiques, and fresh flowers and floral wallpaper add to the cozy, European ambiance. A complimentary tea is served each afternoon in the pleasant lobby, and guests have free use of a fitness facility located ½ block from the hotel.

The Clift *495 Geary St./Taylor St., 2 blocks from Union Square, (800) 65-CLIFT, 775-4700, fax 776-9238. 17 stories; 329 rooms; 13 non-smoking floors; $$$+. Some VCRs. Fitness room. 2 restaurants, room service (child items). Pets welcome. Valet parking $23.*

Beautifully decorated rooms with high ceilings can be enjoyed in this luxury historic hotel dating from 1915. Hefty rates put this hotel on the list of the world's rich and famous: Mick Jagger, Madonna, and former President Jimmy Carter have all stayed here. Service is high priority for the staff, and everyone gets the royal treatment—celebrity or not. Even kids. A family plan includes two connecting rooms charged at the single occupancy rate so that children can have a separate room. Toys are available for toddlers, magazines for teens, and children's books and board games can be checked out from the desk. VCRs are in all suites, and Nintendo games and children's movies can be borrowed from the desk. Bedtime snacks such as cookies and milk or popcorn and soda are available from room service. The concierge has loaner strollers and can help plan family sightseeing trips.

The Redwood Room *(L daily)*, a classic art deco cocktail lounge, features its original 1933 redwood panels—it was built from a single 2,000-year-old giant redwood tree—and immense Gustav Klimt prints. Highly acclaimed, **The French Room** *(B daily, D Tu-Sat, SunBr; $$-$$$. Highchairs, boosters, child menu. Reservations advised. AE, MC, V.)* serves sophisticated cuisine prepared with the finest ingredients. Elegantly appointed with Louis XV-style furnishings, crystal chandeliers, and tall potted palms, this sophisticated spot treats children equally as well as adults. While adults choose beautifully presented items such as tender peppered veal with lemon-sauced angel hair pasta or grilled sea bass with delicate Chardonnay sauce, children choose from their own moderately-priced menu such favorites as a peanut butter & jelly sandwich, a hot dog, or a hamburger. Breakfast is a particularly pleasant time to dine here; a traditional Japanese breakfast is among the selections.

The Donatello *501 Post St./Mason St., 1 block from Union Square, (800) 227-3184, 441-7100, fax 885-8842. 15 stories; 94 rooms; 79 non-smoking rooms; $$$+. Children under 18 free. Hot tub, 2 saunas, spa services, fitness room. Restaurant, room service. Valet parking $19.*

Named after the Italian Renaissance sculptor, this European-style luxury hotel is said to have the largest standard guest rooms in town. The 15th-floor Penthouse Club Room and Spa has a wood-burning fireplace and a wraparound terrace with sweeping city views; it is stocked with snacks and reading material and is available at no charge to guests. More than 300 pieces of original art decorate the hotel. The lobby features 18th- and 19th-century antiques, imported Venetian chandeliers, and Italian marble quarried from the same site where Michelangelo selected the marble for his statue of David.

Grand Hyatt San Francisco *345 Stockton St./Post St., on Union Square, (800) 233-1234, 398-1234, fax 391-1780. 36 stories; 693 rooms; 503 non-smoking rooms; $$$+. Children under 18 free. 6 VCRs. Fitness room. 2 restaurants, room service (child items). Parking $24.*

In a prime location, this hotel is well known locally for its Ruth Asawa-designed bronze fountain depicting scenes of San Francisco. Room amenities include two phones and a TV in the bathroom. Guests have privileges at the San Francisco Tennis Club, which also has a steam room, sauna, and hot tub. The Camp Hyatt childcare program sometimes operates.

The Handlery Union Square Hotel *351 Geary St./Powell St., 1/2 block from Union Square, (800) 843-4343, 781-7800, fax 781-0269. 8 stories; 376 rooms; 225 non-smoking rooms; $$-$$$+. Children under 14 free. 2 kitchens. Heated pool, sauna. Restaurant, room service. Parking $17.*

Built in 1908, this hotel offers the best rate in the area for parking a car.

Under separate management, **New Joe's at Union Square** *(347 Geary St., 989-6733. B, L, & D daily; $-$$. Highchairs, boosters, booths, child portions. Reservations advised.)* has a mesquite grill. The menu offers pastas and pizzas as well as more sophisticated fare such as seafood risotto and a spinach-stuffed cannelloni.

Holiday Inn Union Square *480 Sutter St./Powell St., 1 block from Union Square, (800) 243-1135, 398-8900, fax 956-1004. 30 stories; 400 rooms. Children under 19 free. Fitness room. Restaurant, room service. Parking $19.*

Built in 1973, this is a modern high-rise.

Not to be missed is a visit to the **S. Holmes Esq. Public House and Drinking Salon** on the 30th floor, where a magnificent view can be enjoyed along with a pretty good drink and light snacks. Special non-alcoholic cocktails are available for children. Additionally, there is a mini-museum of Sherlock Holmes paraphernalia to peruse. Carrying this theme yet further, the hotel doorman dresses in Sherlock Holmes regalia.

Hotel Diva *440 Geary St./Mason St., (800) 553-1900, 885-0200, fax 885-3268. 7 stories; 108 rooms; $$$. Children under 12 free. All VCRs. Fitness room. Continental breakfast; restaurant, room service (child items). Valet parking $17.*

Built in 1913, this hotel features a modern Italian hi-tech decor. Each room is decorated in neutral black, white, and grey—snazzed up with touches of chrome. Throughout, lacquered furnishings complement the contemporary design and lighting. The two-room suites are especially comfortable and well-priced for families. Each has a wall bed in the living area. Teens might especially enjoy the punkish feel of the decor and the four TVs mounted on the wall behind the artsy check-in desk in the stark lobby. A **Sidewalk of Fame** in front bears the handprints of famous divas that include Lily Tomlin, Angelica Huston, Carol Channing, and Mary Martin.

The airy, pleasant **California Pizza Kitchen** *(563-8911. L & D daily; $. Highchairs, boosters, booths. AE, MC, V.)* operates as the hotel restaurant. The specialty is a large selection of pizzas and pastas with unusual toppings.

Hotel Monaco *501 Geary St./Taylor St., 2 blocks from Union Square, (800) 214-4220, 292-0100, fax 292-0111. 7 stories; 201 rooms; 140 non-smoking rooms; $$$-$$$+. Children under 18 free. 34 VCRs. Hot tub, sauna, fitness room, health spa. Evening snack; restaurant, room service. Valet parking $20.*

Built in 1910, this landmark American beaux-arts building has been completely renovated. The inviting lobby has high, high ceilings with hand-painted domes, as well as an impressive two-story French inglenook fireplace and grand staircase with the original bronze filigree railing and marble steps—both remains from the hotel's prior incarnation as the Bellevue Hotel. Each sumptuously decorated room features a canopy bed

The magnificent 1920s-1930s-style **Grand Cafe** *(292-0101, fax 292-0150. B, L, & D daily; $$-$$$. Highchairs, boosters, booths. Reservations advised. AE, MC, V.)* operates within the prior hotel's restored turn-of-the-century ballroom. It features an immense, high-ceilinged dining room, with ornate columns and majestic art deco-style ceiling lamps, original murals, and fanciful decorative art. Seating is in intimate booths, arranged in asymmetrical formations that give all diners a good view. The menu offers European-inspired classics and comfort foods, including items such as cassoulet, duck confit, and saffron paella.

Hotel Nikko San Francisco *222 Mason St./O'Farrell St., 2 blocks from Union Square, (800) NIKKO-US, 394-1111, fax 394-1106. 25 stories; 523 rooms; $$$+. Children under 18 free. 3 kitchens. Indoor heated pool, hot tub, sauna, fitness room. Restaurant, room service. Small dogs welcome. Parking $26.*

Featuring clean architectural lines and a slick, marble-rich decor, this luxury hotel has San Francisco's only atrium-style glass-enclosed pool.

Hotel Rex *562 Sutter St./Powell St., 2 blocks from Union Square, (800) 433-4434, 433-4434, fax 433-3695. 7 stories; 94 rooms; some non-smoking rooms; $$$-$$$+. Evening wine; room service. Self parking $18.*

Designed as a focal point for the arts, this theme hotel has a clubby, writer-friendly ambiance. It aspires to become the Algonquin Hotel of the West Coast. Sketches of Martha Graham in the '30s hang in the lobby, which is furnished with period pieces, and literary events are regularly scheduled in the wood-paneled **Lobby Bar**, where appetizers and drinks are served each evening.

The Bookstall *(570 Sutter St., 362-6353, fax 362-1503. M-Sat 11-6.)*, an antiquarian bookstore specializing in books for the collector, has a particularly good section on California and the West. It is located just across from the lobby.

Hotel Triton *342 Grant Ave./Bush St., 3 blocks from Union Square, (800) 433-6611, 394-0500, fax 394-0555. 7 stories; 140 rooms; 80 non-smoking rooms; $$$-$$$+. Children free. 7 VCRs. Fitness room. Evening wine; restaurant, limited room service. Valet parking $20.*

Situated across the street from the dragon-gate entrance to Chinatown in the heart of the "French Quarter," this playfully decorated hotel is sophisticated, casual, amusing, and chic all at the same time. Original art adorns public areas and guest room walls, much of it painted by local artist Chris Kidd, and bathrooms are positively slick. The Carlos Santana Suite sports hand-painted angels on the ceiling and concert posters and photos of the musician on the wall; it is stocked with meditation candles, incense, and a prayer pillow. Suites honoring Jerry Garcia and artist Wyland are also available, and another very special suite has an in-room hot tub. A must-have souvenir rubber ducky inscribed with the hotel logo is for sale in the room honor bar.

Casual **Cafe de la Presse** *(352 Grant Ave., 398-2680. B, L, & D daily; $. Highchairs, boosters. AE, MC, V.)* is located adjacent to the hotel. With large windows offering views of the sidewalk, it is the place to head for breakfast. The menu offers continental items such as croissants and lattes, as well as waffles, pancakes, and hot oatmeal. In addition, international newspapers and magazines are for sale. French is often heard spoken by patrons, as this area is filled with French cafes and has become popular with French visitors.

Hotel Union Square *114 Powell St./Ellis St., 1 block from Union Square, (800) 553-1900, 776-1876. 6 stories; 131 rooms; $$-$$$. Children under 12 free. Continental breakfast; restaurant, room service. Valet parking $17.*

Situated just steps from the cable car turnaround, this comfortable hotel is decorated in a tailored contemporary style. It is where Dashiell Hammett wrote *The Maltese Falcon.*

The Inn at Union Square *440 Post St./Powell St., ½ block from Union Square, (800) AT-THE-INN, 397-3510, fax 989-0529. 7 stories; 30 rooms; 100% non-smoking; $$$-$$$+. 2 wood-burning fireplaces. Afternoon tea, evening snack, continental breakfast. Parking $20.*

This small, narrow, European-style hotel pampers guests with terry cloth robes, down pillows, evening turndown, complimentary overnight shoe shines, and a morning newspaper at the door. It is the first hotel in San Francisco to introduce a no tipping policy (employees are paid more to make up for income lost by not receiving tips). One suite is available with a private hot tub, another with a private sauna.

Kensington Park Hotel *450 Post St./Powell St., 2 blocks from Union Square, (800) 553-1900, 788-6400. 12 stories; 83 rooms; $$$. Children under 12 free. Afternoon tea, continental breakfast; room service. Valet parking $17.*

Built in a Gothic style of architecture in 1924, this tastefully decorated hotel provides terry robes, free shoe shines, and phones in every bathroom. A pianist entertains during afternoon tea in the attractive lobby, and breakfast is set up conveniently on each floor level.

Theatre on the Square *(433-9500)* operates on the hotel's second floor.

The King George Hotel *334 Mason St./Geary St., 1 block from Union Square, (800) 288-6005, 781-5050, fax 391-6976. 9 stories; 143 rooms; 70 non-smoking rooms; $$$. Children under 12 free. 2 kitchens. Room service (child items). Self parking $16.50.*

Built in 1914, this pleasant hotel has thick walls and is very quiet. Thomas Edison was an original investor, and it was he who convinced management to switch from gaslight to electricity. A large bowl of complimentary apples is always available at the desk.

Guests (and non-guests) can enjoy a continental breakfast or afternoon tea in **The Bread & Honey Tea Room** *(B daily, tea M-Sat 3-6:30; $. No reservations. AE MC, V.)*. Reached via either a narrow, winding marble stairwell or a vintage elevator, this second-floor balcony tea room offers a cozy respite. Simple teas consist of a choice of ten kinds of tea and either a crumpet, a giant house-made muffin, a raisin scone, fruit and custard tarts, or traditional finger sandwiches. A larger tea service includes several of these items plus such additional goodies as a quail egg and preserved kumquat on a pick, or a blackberry trifle infused with sherry. A rich chocolate layer cake and sherry and port are also available.

Room service is provided by **Lori's Diner** *(336 Mason St., 392-8646. $. Other nearby locations: 500 Sutter St./Powell St., 981-1950; 149 Powell St./O'Farrell, 677-9999.)*, located next door. Featuring a '50s decor and dispensing the likes of burgers, fries, shakes, and onion rings, Lori's never closes.

Monticello Inn *127 Ellis St./Cyril Magnin, 2 blocks from Union Square, (800) 669-7777, 392-8800, fax 398-2650. 5 stories; 91 rooms; 69 non-smoking rooms; $$-$$$. Children under 12 free. 1 wood-burning fireplace. Afternoon wine, continental breakfast; restaurant, limited room service. Parking $16.*

Built in 1906, this hotel is furnished in an unusual (for the West Coast), but comfortable, Colonial American decor. Rooms are large and many have beds with canopied headboards.

The Pan Pacific Hotel *500 Post St./Mason St., 1 block from Union Square, (800) 327-8585, 771-8600, fax 398-0267. 21 stories; 330 rooms; $$$+. Children under 18 free. Restaurant, room service. Valet parking $24.*

The luxurious rooms in this hotel feature marble bathrooms with TVs and terry bathrobes. Glitzy window-walled elevators traverse the inside levels, and complimentary transportation via Silver Shadow Rolls Royce is provided within the city.

The acclaimed hotel restaurant, **Pacific** *(929-2087. B & L M-Sat, D daily, SunBr; $$-$$$. Reservations advised. AE, MC, V.)*, is situated off the sedate marble lobby. Elegant marble columns grace the attractive space, and fresh orchids decorate each table. Unusual, well-executed dinner items have included grilled squab with truffled risotto and a delicious filet mignon topped with enoki mushrooms. Brunch items have included a delightful eggs Benedict topped with the freshest of crabmeat, an omelette made with choice of filling (Egg Beaters are an option), and waffles with fresh berries, pecans, and whipped cream. Presentations are gorgeous. A special pastry chef turns out a satisfying array of endings—sometimes sprinkling the plates with crystallized sugar drops mimicking diamonds.

Petite Auberge *863 Bush St./Mason St., 4 blocks from Union Square, (800) 365-3004, 928-6000, fax 775-5717. 5 stories; 26 rooms; 100% non-smoking; $$$-$$$+. Some fireplaces. Afternoon tea, continental breakfast. Valet parking $19.*

Located on the lower slopes of Nob Hill, this small, ornate, baroque-style building now operates as a B&B. Rooms are furnished with French country antiques, and breakfast is served in a cheery room decorated with a wrap-around painted mural depicting a French market scene and sporting a little garden view. Special features include a beveled-glass door leading to the entry, curved bay windows, and an unusual vintage elevator. A sister property, The White Swan Inn, is just a few doors away.

San Francisco Hilton and Towers *333 O'Farrell St./Mason St., 2 blocks from Union Square, (800) HILTONS, 771-1400, fax 771-6807. 46 stories; 1,900 rooms; 1,285 non-smoking rooms; $$$+. Children free. 1 kitchen; 2 gas fireplaces. Heated pool, sauna, fitness room. 3 restaurants, room service. Parking $24.*

Occupying a full block and incorporating three buildings, this is the largest hotel on the West Coast. It features a dramatic sunken marble lobby.

The St. Francis *335 Powell St./Geary St., on Union Square, (800) 228-3000, 397-7000, fax 774-0124. 32 stories; 1,192 rooms; 715 non-smoking rooms; $$$+. Children under 18 free. 1 gas fireplace. Fitness room. 3 restaurants, room service (child menu). Dogs welcome; other pets upon approval. Valet parking $24.*

Built in 1904, this classy landmark hotel has a superb location opening right onto Union Square. It consists of both an older 12-story section and a newer 32-story tower with an outside glass elevator that goes non-stop from the lobby to the glitzy 32nd-floor night club disco, **Oz**, in less than 30 seconds. This is the only hotel in the world that washes its money—literally—a custom the hotel began in 1938 to keep women's white gloves from being soiled by dirty coins. Upon check-in, children 12 and under get a free Westin Kids Club packet filled with an assortment of age-appropriate amenities, and strollers, cribs, highchairs, bottle warmers, potty seats, and step stools can be placed in the room at no additional charge.

Dewey's *(774-0169. B & L daily; $. Highchairs, boosters. No reservations. AE, MC, V.)* sports bar offers a casual, clubby, pub-like atmosphere and a make-your-own-sandwich and soup buffet lunch. The cable cars are visible from most tables. In the evening, light snacks are available. A revitalizing tea can be enjoyed seated among the staid, plush, Old World splendor of the elegant room housing **The Compass Rose** *(774-0167. Tea daily 3-5; complete service $15.95. Highchairs, boosters. Reservations advised. AE, MC, V.)*. Diners choose from nine kinds of tea, plus two relaxing herbals. The complete tea service includes a scone, several delicate tea sandwiches sans crust, fresh berries topped with Grand Marnier cream, and several petit fours. These items can also be ordered a la carte. And all the while a violin-bass-grand piano trio provide relaxing musical background. Lunch and evening snacks can also be enjoyed here daily. The more trendy **St. Francis Cafe** *(774-0264. B & D daily; $$. Highchairs, boosters, booths. Reservations accepted. AE, MC, V.)* features comfortable booths and artsy tableware and offers a menu that includes an appetizer salad of flavorfully dressed baby lettuce topped with six perfect barbecued shrimp, and entrees such as a fresh grilled red snapper with a full-flavored dried tomato-fennel-spinach sauce, and a homey, tender oven-braised veal shank. Among the house-made desserts are a strawberry-rhubarb pie with lemon mascarpone cream and a trio of profiteroles stuffed with Ben & Jerry's ice cream.

Villa Florence *225 Powell St./Geary St., 1 block from Union Square, (800) 553-4411, 397-7700, fax 397-1006. 7 stories; 180 rooms; 118 non-smoking rooms; $$-$$$+. Children under 12 free. Evening wine; restaurant, limited room service. Parking $17.*

Built in 1908, this hotel is in a highly convenient location. Its colonnaded entrance has a Giotto-style wishing fountain, and the lobby is decorated with a rare 17th-century velvet tapestry and a trompe l'oeil mural depicting 16th-century Florence. A Medici-style wood-burning fireplace warms guests in the lobby, and a piano player entertains there nightly.

A popular restaurant, **Kuleto's** *(221 Powell St./Geary St., 397-7720, fax 986-7050. B, L, & D daily, Sat & SunBr. Highchairs, boosters, booths. Reservations advised. AE, MC, V.),* operates off the lobby serving superb northern Italian cuisine in elegant surroundings. Should tables be filled, a seat at the counter can often be had at the last minute, providing the additional treat of watching the skilled kitchen staff in action. Grilled items are particularly good, including appetizers of red potatoes and eggplant with an aioli sauce, and desserts are exceptional. A good souvenir is the 100-percent cold-pressed extra-virgin California olive oil used in the restaurant and attractively bottled to take home.

White Swan Inn *845 Bush St./Mason St., 4 blocks from Union Square, (800) 999-9570, 775-1755, fax 775-5717. 4 stories; 26 rooms; 100% non-smoking. Children under 5 free. All fireplaces. Afternoon tea, full breakfast. Valet parking $19.*

Built after the 1906 earthquake in 1915, this charming hotel resembles an English manor house, with curved bay windows, warm dark woods, and handsome antique furnishings. The cheery reception area, cozy living room, and book-lined library all have fireplaces and are inviting places to relax. The large guest rooms each have a separate sitting area and are individually decorated with English floral wallpapers. Each is furnished with a mahogany bed fitted with a warm European wool mattress cover. Amenities include terry robes, evening turndown service, and a morning newspaper. Breakfast is served in a dining room just off a tiny English garden. A sister inn, Petite Auberge, is just a few doors away.

SOUTH OF MARKET

*Referred to by old-timers as "South of the Slot," signifying its location south of the street car tracks on Market Street, this colorful area was city center in the mid-1800s. Rapidly being refurbished, it is now home to many art museums and to the **Moscone Convention Center**.*

Ana Hotel San Francisco *50 Third St./Market St., (800) ANA-HOTELS, 974-6400, fax 543-8268. 36 stories; 667 rooms; 220 non-smoking rooms; $$$+. Children under 18 free. 2 saunas, fitness room. Restaurant, room service. Parking $24.*

Each room in this sleek contemporary hotel is equipped with three phones. A floor equipped with "Green Suites"—which use recycled paper goods, all natural amenities, and state-of-the-art air and water filtration systems—is available. All guests have complimentary access to the San Francisco Tennis and Health Club.

San Francisco Marriott *55 Fourth St./Mission St., (800) 228-9290, 896-1600, fax 896-6177. 39 stories; 1,500 rooms; $$$. Indoor pool & hot tub, 2 saunas, fitness room. 3 restaurants, room service (child items). Valet parking $25.*

Referred to by locals as the "Jukebox" Marriott in recognition of its distinctive design, this mega-hotel opened at 9 a.m. on October 17, 1989. It closed at 5:04 on the same day, just after the strongest earthquake since 1906 hit this city. Fortunately, it sustained only cosmetic damage. Most rooms have sweeping views of the city, and panoramic views are available from the 39th-floor **View Lounge.** Occasionally one of the hotel's restaurants will offer the Golden Gate Spectacular—an impressive and award-winning dessert designed by the hotel's pastry chef that reconstructs the famous span in chocolate and cream.

Sheraton Palace Hotel *2 New Montgomery St./Market St., (800) 325-3535, 392-8600. 8 stories; 500 rooms; $$$+. Indoor pool. Restaurant. Valet parking $20.*

When this grande dame hotel opened in 1875, it was the largest and most luxurious in the world. Though that original hotel burned to the ground after the 1906 earthquake, it was rebuilt in 1909 as the present structure. A dubious claim to fame from its past is the fact that this was where President Harding, who was staying in the Presidential Suite, died in 1923. Nowadays anyone with $2,600 can stay in the Presidential Suite, and the list of those who have includes Sophia Loren and Whoopi Goldberg. **Tours** are given through the public rooms by City Guides (see page 50); make reservations through the hotel by calling 557-4266.

One of the most elegant public rooms is the **Garden Court**. Filled with tall columns and potted palms, its most glorious feature is its 25,000-pane skylight said to be worth over $7 million, and it is the only *room* on the National Register of Historic Places. **Afternoon tea** *(546-5010. Daily 2:30-5; $15.95.)* here is an elegant affair, with a classical harpist providing background ambiance. A special **Princess Tea** *(W-Sat 2-4:30; $12.95/child.)* welcomes children; each young attendee is presented with a crown or scepter, and kid-friendly food—including hot chocolate and peanut butter & jelly finger sandwiches—is served. The **Pied Piper Bar** holds three noteworthy murals: Maxfield Parrish's "Pied Piper" and two Antonio Sotomayors depicting famous San Franciscans—one of Mark Twain and the other of madam Sally Stanford.

NOB HILL

After its steep slopes were conquered by Andrew Hallidie's development of the cable car in 1873, Nob Hill became one of the city's most exclusive residential areas. It was known as the "Hill of Palaces" because it held so many opulent mansions. Unfortunately, all of them burned down in the fire that followed the 1906 earthquake, save the brownstone shell of what is now the private Pacific Union Club. Because of its spectacular views and steep streets, Nob Hill has been the setting for many films. Most memorable, perhaps, is Bullitt *with Steve McQueen.*

Fairmont Hotel *950 Mason St./California St., (800) 527-4727, 772-5000, fax 772-5013. 24 stories; 596 rooms; 476 non-smoking rooms; $$$+. Fitness room. 5 restaurants, room service. Valet parking $27.*

Situated at the top of one of San Francisco's highest hills, this elegant landmark hotel welcomes guests with a gargantuan lobby filled with marble columns and a valuable art collection. The hotel has hosted many heads of state, including President Clinton, and international celebrities, and it has starred in many movies—*Vertigo, Shoot the Moon, Sudden Impact.* Its lobby and grand staircase were the setting for the *Hotel* TV series. Guest rooms are spacious, with goose-down pillows, terry cloth robes, and twice-daily maid service, and the cable cars, which stop in front of the hotel, can be heard from some. The hotel's crown is the historic eight-room Penthouse Suite—the most opulent and expensive in the U.S. It rents for $6,000 per night and features a two-story circular library, a game room with a stained-glass skylight, and 24-karat gold-plated bathroom fixtures.

The **Lobby Lounge** is the perfect place to relax over **afternoon tea** *(M-Sat 3-6, Sun 1-6.)* accompanied by live classical string music. In the **Tonga Room and Hurricane Bar**, *(ext.5278. D daily)* simulated tropical rainstorms occur every 40 minutes in a Tiki-hut atmosphere—making it the place to stop in the evening for an exotic drink; it also has a great **happy hour buffet** *(daily 5-7).* A live dance band floating aboard a boat in the room's indoor lagoon (a converted swimming pool dating from 1929) entertains. And the famous glass elevators are always ready to whisk diners up to enjoy the breathtaking views in the lavish **Crown Room** *(ext.5131. Cocktails daily from 11am. D buffet daily, SunBr; $34, under 12 $16.50.)* situated atop the hotel.

Mark Hopkins Inter-Continental *One Nob Hill, California St./Mason St., (800) 662-4455, 392-3434, fax 421-3302. 18 stories; 392 rooms; 168 non-smoking rooms; $$$+. Children under 14 free. Some VCRs; 2 wood-burning fireplaces. Fitness room. 2 restaurants, room service. Parking $23.*

Built on the spot where once stood the mansion of Mark Hopkins, who founded the Central Pacific Railroad, this hotel opened in 1926. Combining an architectural style that is part French château, part Spanish Renaissance, it has a central tower and two wings affording spectacular city views.

The tower is crowned by **The Top of the Mark** bar *(ext. 6916. Tea M-F 3-5; $20; reservations advised. Cocktails daily from 3. SunBr 10-2; $39, under 13 $21. Reservations advised.)* which has a 360-degree view of the city and features live jazz. It is said that proposing marriage by presenting a diamond engagement ring in the bottom of a drink glass is played out more frequently here than anywhere else in the world.

Nob Hill Lambourne *725 Pine St./Stockon St., 3 blocks from Union Square, (800) BRITINN, 433-2287, fax 433-0975. 3 stories; 20 rooms; 100% non-smoking; $$$-$$$+. All VCRs & kitchens. Evening wine, continental breakfast. Valet parking $20.*

Sitting pretty in a residential area mid-way up Nob Hill, this intimate, contemporary hotel offers guests a quiet, posh retreat with easy access to downtown sights. Designed primarily for the business traveler, each room has personalized voice mail and a fax, and laptop computers with Internet access can be borrowed. In the interest of having guests feel healthier when they leave the hotel than when they arrived, each of the six suites here is outfitted with an instrument of torture, otherwise known as an exercise machine, and turndown brings an antioxidant supplement and inspirational quote. The mini-bar is stocked with vegetarian chili, organic wine, and even a healthy version of those famous black and white cookies, and music is piped from a radio in the bedroom into the bathroom. A dedicated spa room for treatments is on the main floor (packages are available), and just outside are the Joice steps up to California Street, which could easily qualify as Satan's StairMaster north (the more famous southern version is in Santa Monica). Carrying the theme yet further, wellness videos can be borrowed from the front desk, as can a great selection of movies filmed in San Francisco.

The Ritz-Carlton *600 Stockton St./California St., (800) 241-3333, 296-7465, fax 986-1268. 9 stories; 336 rooms; 284 non-smoking rooms; $$$+. Children under 17 free. 42 VCRs. Indoor heated pool, hot tub, 2 saunas, fitness room, health spa. 2 restaurants, room service (child items). Valet parking $27.*

Occupying a full square block about halfway up Nob Hill, with the California Street cable car line stopping at the corner, this branch of the classy chain is set within a restored neoclassical landmark building built in 1909. The completely new interior features Italian marble, silk wall-coverings, Bohemian crystal chandeliers, Persian carpets, and antique furnishings. A museum-quality collection of 18th- and 19th-century European and American art and antiques is displayed throughout. Room amenities include a morning newspaper, terry robes, and twice-daily maid service.

The Courtyard offers the only outdoor hotel dining in San Francisco. In fair weather, its dressy al fresco Sunday jazz brunch *(Adults $42, 5-12 $21)* is sublime. Diners sit on a red brick courtyard that is surrounded by a colorful flower garden and protected on three sides by the building's "U" shape. Inside, a battery of buffet tables offer delicacies that include a variety of caviars, smoked salmon, imported cheeses, fresh fruits, tasty cold salads, and hot entrees such as eggs Benedict, blintzes, and fish and meat courses. There is also a heavily laden pastry table, and a killer dessert table. Coffee and freshly squeezed orange juice are included. Everything is carefully prepared and elegantly presented by a well-trained kitchen staff. **The Dining Room** *(D daily; $$$. Highchairs, boosters, booths, child menu. Reservations advised. AE, MC, V.)* is considered one of the city's top restaurants, and a relaxing **afternoon tea** *(Daily 2:30-5; $14-$22. Reservations advised.)* is served daily in **The Lobby Lounge.** Two special teas for children are held annually: The **Easter Bunny Tea,** when the Easter Bunny serves tea, and **Teddy Bear Teas** during the weeks leading up to Christmas.

Stanford Court Hotel *905 California St./Powell St., (800) HOTELS-1, 989-3500, fax 391-0513. 8 stories; 402 rooms; 200 non-smoking rooms; $$$+. Children under 18 free. VCRs available; 2 kitchens; 10 gas fireplaces. Fitness center. Restaurant, room service (child items). Pets welcome. Valet parking $24.*

Built on the site where Leland Stanford's mansion once stood—it was described as "a mansion that dominated the city like the castle of a medieval hill town"—this grand old hotel is blessed with striking turn-of-the-century detail, a beaux-arts fountain in the carport, and a lobby dome of Tiffany-style stained glass. Its elegant lobby is furnished with fine antiques, including Baccarat chandeliers and an 1806 grandfather clock once owned by Napoleon Bonaparte. Guest room pampering includes marble bathrooms with heated towel racks, complimentary coffee and newspaper delivered to the room in the morning, and a complimentary overnight shoeshine. Complimentary limousine service is available to downtown.

Among the lobby shops is **John Small Ltd.** A small shop indeed, specializing in traditional British regimental items, it was the hotel's first shop. Among the many treasures dispensed here is an authentic Metropolitan brand bobby whistle imported from England.

The celebrated **Fournou's Ovens** *(989-1910. B, L & D daily, Sat & SunBr; $$-$$$. Highchairs, boosters, child menu. Reservations advised. AE, MC, V.)* is known for its massive, beautifully tiled European-style roasting ovens and intimate, finely appointed dining rooms. Specialties are roasted meats and seafood. The wine cellar holds more than 10,000 bottles and has one of the country's largest selections of California wines. In the **Lobby Lounge,** live piano music accompanies afternoon tea and evening cocktails.

FINANCIAL DISTRICT/THE EMBARCADERO

Harbor Court Hotel *165 Steuart St./Mission St., (800) 346-0555, 882-1300, fax 882-1313. 8 stories; 131 rooms; 24 non-smoking rooms; $$$-$$$+. Children free. Indoor heated pool, hot tub, sauna, fitness room, health spa. Evening wine; restaurant, room service. Parking $19.*

Featuring an Old World flavor, this historic 1907 landmark building offers some rooms with spectacular views of the bay and Treasure Island. Guest facilities include a basketball court, a racquetball court, and a running track.

Lively **Harry Denton's** *(161 Steuart St., 882-1333, fax 979-0471. B & L M-F, D daily, Sat & SunBr; $$. Boosters, booths. Reservations advised. AE, MC, V.)* features an upscale American menu with a classic San Francisco saloon atmosphere. Desserts are a high point: white chocolate banana cream pie, cranberry-apple crisp. Monday through Saturday evenings, the bar has live entertainment, with dancing from 10:30 p.m. to 2 a.m.

Hyatt Regency San Francisco *5 Embarcadero Center/Market St., (800) 233-1234, 788-1234, fax 398-2567. 17 stories; 805 rooms; 670 non-smoking rooms; $$$+. Children under 18 free. 2 restaurants, room service (child items). Parking $25.*

Built in 1973, this elegant hotel resembles a pyramid, and every room has a view of either the city or the bay. Nifty glass elevators run the height of the hotel's magnificent 17-story atrium interior.

Mandarin Oriental, San Francisco *222 Sansome St./Pine St., (800) 622-0404, 885-0999, fax 433-0289. 48 stories; 158 rooms; 78 non-smoking rooms; $$$+. Children under 12 free. 2 VCRs. Fitness room. Restaurant, room service (child items). Valet parking $21.*

Located in the heart of the Financial District, this luxury hotel occupies the first two floors of a skyscraper with its lobby, lounge, and two restaurants. Then it shoots up into the air and places guest rooms in twin towers on the top 11 floors of the 48-story building. This translates into stupendous views and quiet rooms. Furnishings are tasteful, contemporary, and a bit oriental. A pot of hot jasmine tea is delivered to the room upon check-in, and bathrooms are stocked with fine English soaps and lotions.

Appointed sumptuously, with art created especially for the restaurant, **Silks** *(986-2020. B & D daily, L M-F; $$-$$$. Highchairs, child menu. Reservatons advised. AE, MC, V. Valet parking.)* offers an excitingly sophisticated menu of California cuisine with an Asian accent. Sample starters include an unusual chicken and shitake spring roll with Vietnamese salad, and a mild celeriac and roasted garlic soup with grilled bay scallops. Entrees are items such as seared lobster and scallops with spinach risotto cake and lemon-herb essence, and teriyaki salmon with carrot and daikon sprout salad and a smoked salmon-avocado roll. Desserts include the familiar—a banana split—and the wild—a gooey chocolate cake served with a raspberry truffle swirl ice cream sandwich.

Park Hyatt San Francisco *333 Battery St./Clay St., (800) 323-PARK, 392-1234, fax 421-2433. 24 stories; 360 rooms; 300 non-smoking rooms; $$$+. Children under 12 free. 50 VCRs; 1 kitchen; 1 wood-burning fireplace. Continental breakfast; restaurant, room service (child items). Parking $24.*

Built in 1989, this hotel is conveniently located across the street from the upscale Embarcadero Center shopping complex. Luxurious in every way, its public areas are decorated

with fine art. Each room has a bay or city view, fresh fruit, and terry cloth bathrobes. Guests get complimentary shoe shines and have a Mercedes Benz available to shuttle them around. Camp Hyatt operates for ages 3 through 15 on weekends year-round and daily during summer and holiday periods; sometimes cooking lessons in the hotel's kitchen are part of the fun.

CHINATOWN AND NORTH BEACH

Royal Pacific Motor Inn *661 Broadway/Columbus Ave., (800) 545-5574, 781-6661. 5 stories; 74 rooms; 18 non-smoking rooms; $$. Children under 16 free. Sauna. Free parking.*
    Situated on the Chinatown-North Beach border, this bargain motel is right in the thick of it.

The Washington Square Inn *1660 Stockton St., (800) 388-0220, 981-4220, fax 397-7242. 2 stories; 15 rooms; 100% non-smoking; $$-$$$+. Some shared baths. Afternoon tea, continental breakfast. Valet parking $20.*
    This charming North Beach gem features a super location that permits late-evening coffee-house-hopping, and it is just a few blocks from an uncrowded cable car stop. Each room is individually decorated and furnished with English and French antiques. Several choice rooms in the front have bay windows overlooking Washington Square Park and the beautiful **St. Peter & Paul church**, the bells from which can be heard tolling the hour. Amenities include terry cloth robes, down pillows and comforters, and a morning newspaper delivered to the room. Tea is served in the cozy lobby, and breakfast is delivered to the room.

FISHERMAN'S WHARF

This is a very popular area to stay. The major chains are well represented.

Dockside Boat & Bed *Pier 39, (800) 432-2574, 392-5526, fax (510) 444-0420. 13 yachts; $$$+. All VCRs & galleys. Continental breakfast. Self parking $8.*
    Spend the night on a yacht anchored near Fisherman's Wharf. All yachts have separate state rooms; most have two or three. Catered candlelight dinners can be arranged, and the Snooze and Cruise package brings a captain on board to take you for a ride.

Holiday Inn Fisherman's Wharf *1300 Columbus Ave./North Point St., (800) HOLIDAY, 771-9000, fax 771-7006. 4 stories; 585 rooms; 351 non-smoking rooms; $$$-$$$+. Children under 17 free. Heated pool. Restaurant. Self parking $10.*

Hyatt at Fisherman's Wharf *555 North Point St./Jones St., (800) 233-1234, 563-1234, fax 749-6122. 5 stories; 313 rooms; 168 non-smoking rooms; $$-$$$+. Heated pool, hot tub, sauna, fitness room. Restaurant, room service. Valet parking $16.*
    Built on the site of an historic marble works building and incorporating that façade into its new architecture, this attractive hotel has been constructed using some of the original bricks recycled into a modern interpretation of the building's inceptive design. Rooms are decorated in Victorian style, and washers and dryers are located on each floor.

Hyde Park Suites *2655 Hyde St./North Point St., (800) 227-3608, 771-0200, fax 346-8058. 3 stories; 24 suites; 4 non-smoking suites; $$$+. Children under 12 free. All kitchens. Afternoon snack, evening wine, continental breakfast. Parking $15.*
    In this small building it is possible to feel like a local rather than a visitor. In addition to offering most of the comforts of home, the lodging is located across the street from Ghirardelli Square, is right on the Hyde Street cable car line, and is very close to the best aspects of the Fisherman's Wharf area. It also has a rooftop sun deck with a spectacular view of the Golden Gate Bridge, and a newspaper is delivered to the door each morning.

Ramada Plaza Hotel at Fisherman's Wharf *590 Bay St./Jones St., (800) 228-8408, 885-4700, fax 771-8945. 3 stories; 232 rooms; 155 non-smoking rooms; $$$-$$$+. Children under 18 free. Parcourse. Restaurant, room service (child items). Parking $8.*

This motel claims to have the largest guest rooms at Fisherman's Wharf. A sun deck and jogging track are among its amenities.

San Francisco Marriott Fisherman's Wharf *1250 Columbus Ave./Bay St., (800) 228-9290, 775-7555, fax 474-2099. 5 stories; 256 rooms; $$$-$$$+. Children under 18 free. Restaurant, room service. Valet parking $17.*

Plenty of comfortable public spaces enhance the comfort of this posh hotel, and guests have privileges at a nearby health club.

Sheraton at Fisherman's Wharf *2500 Mason St./Beach St., (800) 325-3535, 362-5500. 4 stories; 525 rooms; $$$-$$$+. Children under 17 free. Heated pool. Restaurant, room service. Self parking $12.*

This huge, contemporary-style hotel features that rarest of San Francisco amenities—a heated swimming pool.

Travelodge at the Wharf *250 Beach St./Powell St., (800) 255-3050, 392-6700, same fax. 4 stories; 250 rooms; $$-$$$+. Children under 18 free. Heated pool. Restaurant. Free parking.*

An outdoor pool is located within the enclosed, landscaped courtyard of this modest lodging, and some rooms have bay views from their balcony.

Tuscan *425 North Point St./Mason St., (800) 648-4626, 561-1100, fax 561-1199. 4 stories; 221 rooms; 155 non-smoking rooms; $$$+. Children under 17 free. 34 VCRs; 1 wood-burning fireplace. Evening wine; restaurant, room service. Pets welcome. Valet parking $15.*

Combining the best features of a small hotel with many of the conveniences of a motel, this comfortable, pleasantly appointed lodging is reputed to be popular with filmmakers.

The appealing **Cafe Pescatore** *(2455 Mason St./North Point St., 561-1111. B, L, & D daily, Sat & SunBr; $-$$. Highchairs, boosters, booths, child menu. Reservations advised. AE, MC, V.)* has windows that open to the sidewalk in warm weather and a menu of fresh fish, house-made pastas, and pizza baked in a wood-burning oven.

JAPANTOWN

Surprisingly, this quiet part of town is just ten blocks from Union Square. Both of these hotels have an oriental flavor.

Miyako Hotel *625 Post St./Laguna St., (800) 333-3333, 922-3200, fax 921-0417. 13 stories; 218 rooms; 97 non-smoking rooms; $$$-$$$+. Children under 19 free. Fitness room. Restaurant, room service. Valet parking $15.*

Opened in 1968, this hotel has fully traditional Japanese-style rooms with futon feather beds on tatami mats, as well as western-style rooms with oriental touches. Most of the serene rooms have deep furo bathing tubs, and some suites have a private redwood sauna. The tasteful lobby overlooks a Japanese garden where guests can stroll.

The hotel's restaurant, **Yoyo Tsumami Bistro** *(1611 Post St., 922-7788 , fax 921-0417. B, L, & D daily; $$. Reservations advised. AE, MC, V.)*, specializes in small plates of Franco-Japanese cuisine. The menu changes regularly but might include such items as ginger-pickled salmon or roast halibut with green papaya salad.

Miyako Inn *1800 Sutter St./Buchanan St., (800) 528-1234, 921-4000, fax 923-1064. 8 stories; 125 rooms; $$-$$$+. Children under 18 free. Restaurant. Self parking $7.50.*

Sixty rooms in this contemporary hotel have a private steam bath, and many have dramatic views of the southwestern portion of the city.

PACIFIC HEIGHTS

El Drisco Hotel *2901 Pacific Ave./Broderick St., (800) 634-7277, 346-2880, fax 567-5537. 4 stories; 42 rooms; 100% non-smoking; $$-$$$+. Continental breakfast; restaurant. No parking.*

Built in 1903, before the '06 quake, this Edwardian-style building is in a quiet residential neighborhood. It maintains its original dark-wood interior trim and is elegantly decorated and furnished. Turn-of-the-century millionaires are said to have kept their mistresses lodged here. Rooms are spacious and comfortable, and most have good views.

The Mansions Hotel *2220 Sacramento St./Laguna St., (800) 826-9398, 929-9444, fax 567-9391. 3 stories; 21 rooms; 100% non-smoking; $$$-$$$+. Children under 6 free. Full breakfast; restaurant, limited room service. Self parking $15.*

This unusual hotel consists of two Victorian houses joined together by a covered walkway. Guests staying in the hotel's original beautifully restored 1887 twin-turreted Queen Anne Victorian have use of a billiard table located in an authentic Billiard Room decorated with pig murals and a mini-museum of memorabilia. They are free to wander through the house and admire a large Turner oil painting, a wall-size turn-of-the-century stained glass mural, and an impressive collection of Beniamino Bufano sculptures. According to owner Robert Pritikin, cousin of the diet guy and author of *Christ Was an Ad Man,* there are approximately 100 tons of Bufano art scattered throughout the house and surrounding garden. "It is the largest definitive collection ever displayed," he says. Maids and butlers here are dressed spiffily in black and white attire. Though this hotel is located in a fashionable residential neighborhood, a cable car stop is just four blocks away.

A campy **Magic Concert** *(Daily. $15; $5 with dinner. Reservations advised.)* is scheduled in a theater room located in the second mansion. On Friday and Saturdays it can include a special fixed-price dinner *($47)* in the inn's elegant restaurant; Sunday through Thursday a regular a la carte menu is available. Both the magic show and restaurant are open to non-guests as well.

HAIGHT-ASHBURY/GOLDEN GATE PARK

Stanyan Park Hotel *750 Stanyan St./Waller St., 751-1000. 3 stories; 36 rooms; 18 non-smoking rooms; $$-$$$+. Children under 3 free. 6 kitchens. Continental breakfast. No parking.*

Located at the park's edge, this 1904 Victorian mansion survived the great quake of '06. It has been renovated and tuned into a pleasant hotel with attractively decorated rooms.

BY THE SEA

Ocean Park Motel *2690 46th Ave./Wawona St., in the Sunset, 566-7020. 2 stories; 24 rooms; 28 non-smoking rooms; $-$$. 8 kitchens. Hot tub. Dogs welcome. Free parking.*

Located near the ocean and just a block from the zoo, this art deco-style motel dates from the '30s, when it was San Francisco's first motel. Maintaining its original nautical decor, some windows are shaped as portholes. Rooms are attractive and homey, and several spacious family suites are available. Amenities include a playground, barbecue area, and several gardens.

MISCELLANEOUS

The American Property Exchange *(800) 747-7784, 447-2000, fax 440-1008. 1-30 stories; 400 units; 320 non-smoking units; $70-$250. All VCRs & kitchens; some wood-burning & gas fireplaces. Some pools, hot tubs, saunas, fitness rooms, & tennis courts. Some free parking.*

Live like a native. This service offers lodging in interesting residential areas. Among the possibilities are a cottage with a garden and view of the Golden Gate Bridge, and a penthouse with city views. According to this office, "We have it all—just call."

Bed & Breakfast International.

See page 391. Most of the San Francisco host homes listed with this reservations service cannot accommodate more than two people in a room, but at least a dozen are appropriate for families.

Hostels *In Union Square area: 312 Mason St./Geary St., 788-5604, fax 788-3023. 230 beds; couples rooms avail. At Fort Mason: Bay St./Franklin St., Bldg. 240, 771-7277, fax 771-1468. 150 beds; no private rooms.*

The hostel in Union Square is well-located and in a good area. The one at Fort Mason—a former Civil War barracks—is situated on a peaceful knoll with a magnificent view of the bay. It is the largest and busiest hostel in the country. See also page 391.

Motel Row

A plethora or lodgings line the 20-block corridor stretching along Lombard Street from Van Ness Avenue to the Presidio.

WHERE TO EAT

There are far too many good restaurants in San Francisco to permit listing them all here. Those that are included are excellent in some way. Don't be afraid to try places discovered while wandering. If the people dining inside look happy and animated, give it a try. I am continuously amazed at how infrequently I experience a bad meal in this food-fanatical town. Even hotel restaurants, which are often best overlooked in other places, are usually good here. Many are described in the "Where to Stay" section. More restaurants are also listed in the "Shopping" section. They don't call San Francisco "Food City" for no reason. In fact, there are said to be more restaurants per capita in San Francisco than in any other city in the U.S.

And do try some of the local food products. The for-
tune cookie, Irish coffee, and martini were all invented
here. One unusual drink, Pisco punch, which is made
with Peruvian brandy, dates back to the Gold Rush.
Sourdough bread is credited to Isidore Boudin, a French
immigrant who in 1849 got some sourdough from a gold
prospector and mixed it in with his French bread to pro-
duce the world's first sourdough French bread. (Look
around town for Boudin cafes, where soups and stews are
served in hollowed-out bread rounds.) Dry salame is
made by several local companies, including Molinari and
Cariani, which both date back to the 1890s. Until recent-
ly, the original Swensen's ice cream shop still operated at
Hyde and Union streets. It's It—an ice cream sandwich
made with oatmeal cookies, vanilla ice cream, and a coat-
ing of chocolate—was developed in 1928 at now-gone
Playland-at-the-Beach; they are sold now in grocery

stores. Double Rainbow is the ice cream of choice, Anchor Steam the beer, Calistoga (from the Wine
Country) the mineral water, Ghirardelli the chocolate, and Tom's the cookie.

Note that a city ordinance forbids smoking in all San Francisco restaurants. At the owner's dis-
cretion, smoking is still permitted in bars. A state law has been passed that will make smoking in
any public place of business illegal; its implementation date is in limbo.

Betelnut *2030 Union St./Buchanan St., 929-8855. L & D daily; $-$$. Highchairs, boosters. Reservations*
advised. AE, MC, V. Validated parking.

With a menu of native dishes from throughout Asia and a streamlined, exotic interior featuring lacquered walls and some very comfortable half-moon booths, this casual spot is always
bustling. A favorite area to sit is in the bar, where large windows overlook the sidewalk traffic.
Though most dishes are full-flavored and satisfying, truly exceptional items include minced
chicken in lettuce cups, red-cooked pork in a spicy-sweet sauce, and tea-smoked duck. Portions
are small and meant to be shared tapas-style. Modeled after the beer restaurants found in Asia,
it accordingly offers a selection of brews. Prime is the ice-cold house rice ale, which is perfect
with a plate of sun-dried anchovies, peanuts, and chilies to munch on. An assortment of
unusual mixed drinks is also available. Desserts are limited, but an unusual Chinese tea can provide a satisfying conclusion.

Boulevard *One Mission St./Stewart St., on the Embarcadero, 543-6084, fax 495-2936. L M-F, D daily; $$$.*
Highchairs, boosters, booths. Reservations advised. AE, MC, V. Valet parking $6.

Co-owned by chef Nancy Oakes and acclaimed local restaurant designer Pat Kuleto, this
sumptuous restaurant offers a feast for both the palate and the eyes. Diners enter the gorgeous
1889 French-style building via a revolving door. The belle epoque-style interior features stun-
ning mosaic tile floors as well as sensuous blown-glass light fixtures and pressed tin and iron-
work accents. Some tables have three-landmark views—of the Ferry Building, Embarcadero
Center, and the Bay Bridge. Large, serious forks foreshadow the exciting, full-flavored dishes to
follow. One flawless meal here began with a Chinese-seasoned appetizer of two perfect prawns
intertwined over a plump rock shrimp dumpling. The entree was a delicious, thick honey-cured
pork loin served with roasted potatoes and baby spinach. A pear tart with caramel sauce and
vanilla bean ice cream provided the perfect finish.

Buca Giovanni *800 Greenwich St./Columbus, in North Beach, 776-7766. D Tu-Sun; $$$. Boosters. Reservations advised. AE, MC, V.*

Operating in a cozy, subterranean space, this cave-like restaurant has a loyal local following. The rustic, Tuscan-style food includes an extensive variety of rabbit dishes and some excellent pastas. Among the desserts are a gelato, a chocolate hazelnut tart, and tiramisu.

Buena Vista *2765 Hyde St., near Fisherman's Wharf, 474-5044. Daily 9am-1:30am. No reservations. No cards.*

In 1952 the owner of this legendary bar challenged local travel writer Stanton Delaplane to help him re-create the Irish coffee served at Shannon Airport in Ireland. The biggest deterrent to success was getting the cream to float. Once mastered, the result is history. It is de rigueur to stop at this cozy spot and find out what all the fuss is about. Casual meals are also served.

Cadillac Bar *1 Holland Ct./4th St., South of Market, 543-TACO. L & D daily; $$. Highchairs, boosters. Reservations advised. AE, MC, V.*

Sporting a Mexican cantina atmosphere that feels authentically south of the border (well it *is* south of Market), this cheery spot has a large, high-ceilinged dining room. Margaritas and sunrises are dispensed at a massive bar, helping to ease any wait, and are best enjoyed along with an order of queso flameado (a baked cheese dip flavored with chorizo and fresh chiles). A mesquite grill produces fresh fish and marvelous fajitas. Fish entrees, cabrito (milk-fed kid), and carnitas are also available on the creative menu. Loud thumps are heard throughout a visit here. They are "poppers"—glasses of tequila and 7-Up that are slammed on the table and then swallowed macho-style in one gulp.

Cafe Bastille *22 Belden Pl./Bush St., near Union Square, 986-5673, fax 986-1013. L & D M-Sat; $. Reservations advised for D; no reservations for L. AE, MC, V.*

Located in the middle of a quaint alley in the "French Quarter," this Very French bistro provides a quick fix for Francophiles. The entry bar is often packed with European-style smoking patrons surveying the hip scene. Seating is at a long row of tight tables with a wall bench on one side and a chair on the other, or in the Bohemian atmosphere of the crowded cellar. In warm weather, tables are made available outside in the alley. The Americanized menu includes salads, sandwiches, crêpes, and more substantial entrees such as Boudin noir (black sausage) and quiche. Authentic French desserts include crème caramel, crêpes Suzette, and chocolate mousse. Live music is performed upstairs Tuesday through Saturday.

Cafe de Paris L'Entrecote *2032 Union St./Buchanan St., 931-5006. L M-F, D daily, Sat & SunBr; $$-$$$. Highchairs, boosters. Reservations advised. AE, MC, V. Valet parking at D.*

Situated within the shell of the first mansion built west of Van Ness Avenue, which was also the home of the dairy that gave the name "cow hollow" to this district, this authentic French bistro opened on Bastille Day in 1983. In a bow to history and city dictates, an unusual sort of greenhouse cafe was built around a glass-encased palm tree planted in front of the house in 1867; it is a great room to be in during daylight, as views of the sidewalk parade are prime then. The restaurant's signature dish is a charbroiled New York steak served with their 12-ingredient secret sauce (made downstairs, out of sight even of the chef!), a flawless butter lettuce salad, and crisp pommes frites. The menu also holds seasonal surprises such as a deep-fried soft shell crab appetizer (the French would definitely love this) and house-smoked salmon. Crêpes and omelettes, a hamburger, and several daily specials are also available. A full-flavored tarte tatin— sort of a French apple pie with caramelized apples—is the dessert specialty of the house. Other endings include peache Melba, profiteroles with chocolate sauce, and the classic crème brulee.

Both the secret steak sauce and salad dressing are available bottled to take home. On weekend evenings, live music is scheduled in the bar until 2 a.m. A Cafe de Paris also exists in Geneva, and a L'Entrecote de Paris in Paris.

Cafe Trieste *601 Vallejo St./Grant Ave., in North Beach, 392-6739. Daily 6:30am-11pm; $. No reservations. No cards.*

This Very Cool coffeehouse was a favorite hangout with the Beat Generation and was once frequented by Jack Kerouac, Allen Ginsberg, and friends. In traditional Italian style, the owners perform live opera every Saturday afternoon.

California Culinary Academy *625 Polk St./Turk St., (800) BAY-CHEF, 771-3536. Reservations required. AE, MC, V.*

Founded in 1977, this training school for professional chefs operates two very different restaurants, both of which are completely student-run while overseen by chef-instructors. **The Academy Grill** *(L M-F, D buffet M-F; $)* offers a casual setting and features American specialties. **The Carême Dining Room** *(L M-Thur, F buffet; D M-W, Thur & F buffet; $$.)* is more formal and serves a modern classical continental cuisine. An European buffet lunch is served on Fridays and a French buffet dinner on Thursdays. Its famous Grand Buffet, a fabulous showcase of student work, has been presented every Friday night for 20 years. At all other times the menu is a la carte. **The CCA Store** *(M-F 6:30am-7pm, Sat 8-4)* sells house-made sandwiches, salads, and pastries as well as logo apparel and cooking utensils.

Calzone's Pizza Cucina *430 Columbus Ave./Green St., in North Beach, 397-3600, fax 397-3446. L & D daily; $-$$. Highchairs, boosters, booths, child menu. Reservations accepted. AE, MC, V.*

Reflecting the colors of the Italian flag, walls reaching to a high ceiling are painted dark green and lined with colorful Italian cooking ingredients. Diners seated at the small Formica tables downstairs enjoy superb views of sidewalk traffic; some upstairs diners are entertained by overviews of the downstairs diners. Meals begin with a crusty hunk of Italian bread. A favorite appetizer is the light and crunchy deep-fried calamari served with a tangy basil pomodoro sauce. Crisp-bottomed pizzas prepared in a wood-fired brick oven include a delicious number topped with prosciutto, roasted garlic, fresh tomato, marinated artichoke hearts, fresh herbs, and melted mozzarella. Contrary to what one expects given this restaurant's name, only a few calzones (pizza turnovers) are available. However, they are unusual and delicious, especially the version made with salami, sweet onions, jalapeño Jack cheese, and basil vinaigrette. Fresh fettuccine, linguine, and angel hair pastas are prepared with a variety of interesting toppings, and homemade lasagna and tortellini are also on the menu. (Note that a free limo shuttle operates from downtown for lunch; call for details.)

For dessert, **Stella Pastry** is just next door.

Capp's Corner *1600 Powell St./Green St., in North Beach, 989-2589. L M-F, D daily; $$. Highchairs, boosters, booths, child portions. Reservations advised. AE, MC, V. Validated parking.*

The fun begins here as soon as you walk through the saloon-style swinging doors. Reputed to be the liveliest and noisiest of the North Beach family-style restaurants, this popular spot is usually crowded. When there is a wait for a table, a seat at the Victorian-era bar can make the time fly. In the cozy, friendly interior dining room, photos of prior happy diners decorate the walls, and noisy family groups rub elbows with swinging singles while enjoying the hearty Italian food. The bountiful six-course dinner includes minestrone soup, a green salad, pasta, sautéed vegetables, an entree (steak, roast duck, chicken breast picatta, ossobuco, lasagna, seafood cannelloni, etc.), and spumoni ice cream.

Cha-Am *701 Folsom St./3rd St., 546-9711, fax 546-0354. L M-Sat, D daily.*
For description, see page 321.

Chinatown Restaurants. See page 53.

The Cliff House *1090 Point Lobos Ave., in the Outer Richmond. B, L, & D daily; $$. Highchairs, boosters, booths. No reservations. AE, MC, V.*
Perched solidly at the edge of the ocean on a piece of the city that is bedrock, the Cliff House has been around for quite some time. Since 1850 to be exact, but in three different versions, having twice burned to the ground. The most recent version was constructed in 1909. Though it has gone through many changes, it has always been a restaurant. Since 1977 it has been part of the National Park Service's Golden Gate National Recreation Area. Diners choose between two dining rooms and a bar—all with magnificent views of the ocean and adjacent **Seal Rocks**. Downstairs, **Phineas T. Barnacle** *(386-7630)* serves a casual menu of soups, salads, and sandwiches, as well as snacks and mixed drinks. Next door, the **Seafood & Beverage Co.** *(386-333)* serves a more formal menu of fresh seafood. The informal atmosphere and cozy decor in **Upstairs at the Cliff House** *(386-3330)* makes it the best dining choice for families. On a menu offering 30 different omelettes, the tastiest just could be a combination of spicy linguica sausage, mashed avocado, tangy tomato chunks, and melted Swiss cheese. Other menu items include both hot and cold sandwiches, a Louis salad, chile, and a hamburger. At dinner, the menu adds pasta and seafood entrees and becomes more pricey. See also page 54.

dallaTorre *1349 Montgomery St./Union St., in North Beach, 296-1111, fax 982-2055. D daily; $$-$$$. Reservations advised. AE, MC, V. Valet parking $5.*
Situated atop Telegraph Hill, in one of the city's most hidden and splendidly scenic locations, this is a redo of the German Old World-style Shadows, which opened here back in 1923. Much brighter, with stone floors and an open gabled ceiling in the main dining room, this restaurant's name translates as "at the tower." It has a Mediterranean feel, with walls painted warm Tuscan colors and windows looking out upon gardens or the bay. The third-floor Rooftop Room overlooks a multicolored slate roof with a spectacular bay view beyond. The perfect time to dine here seems to be as soon as the restaurant opens at 5 p.m., when the light permits seeing the panorama at its clearest, but most diners arrive much later in favor of seeing the even more romantic evening lights. While diners peruse the Italian menu, delicious olives are brought to nibble on. Delicacies include sophisticated items such as prosciutto-wrapped roasted quail on polenta, lobster risotto with cherry tomatoes and leeks, and house-made gnocchi with Fonduta cheese and black truffles. Dessert here comes in three courses. First, one from the menu—perhaps a chocolate Nutella bread pudding or a tiramisu—with a leisurely coffee. Second, a climb up the **Filbert Steps**, which pass by the restaurant's front door and terminate near Coit Tower. Third, a viewing of *Dark Passage,* the 1946 classic with Humphrey Bogart and Lauren Bacall that was filmed in the art deco building across the street.

Dim Sum.
Translated variously as meaning "touch of heart," "touch your heart," "heart's desire," and "heart's delight," dim sum items were originally served for breakfast during China's Tang Dynasty (618 to 907 A.D.) A meal of these appetizers makes an interesting change of pace for breakfast or lunch, and there is no better place to try the cuisine than here: There are said to be more dim sum parlors in San Francisco than in any other city in the U.S.
The varieties of dim sum are seemingly endless and include steamed buns, fried

dumplings, and turnovers, as well as delicacies such as steamed duck beaks and feet. It is great fun to pick and choose from the items brought around to the tables Hong Kong-style on carts or trays that circulate non-stop. Just flag down the servers as they pass. Be aware that in crowded restaurants it can be difficult to get a server to describe what a particular item is composed of, and sometimes they don't speak or understand English very well.

Tea is brought automatically. The three most common kinds are mild green, semi-fermented oolong, and strong fermented black. Chrysanthemum combines black tea with dried flowers; jasmine combines oolong with dried flowers. To get a tea refill, do as the Chinese do: Signal the waiter by turning over the lid on the tea pot. Some, but not all, establishments offer other drinks.

Note that although crossed chop sticks are usually considered an omen of bad luck, in dim sum houses they signal the server that the diner is finished.

Though this quaint custom is rapidly dying, the bill in some restaurants is determined by how many serving plates are on the table at meal's end. (This concept reminds me of the little hill town of San Gimignano in Italy, which was once filled with 70 bell towers. A family's wealth there was measured by the height of its bell tower.) To keep a running tab, just make a stack of the serving plates and steamers as they are emptied. Most teahouses charge about $1.50 to $2.25 per plate, and tips are usually divided by the entire staff.

• **Fountain Court** *354 Clement St./5th Ave., in the Richmond, 668-1100. Daily 11-3; $. Highchairs, boosters. Reservations advised. AE, MC, V.*

Unusual items served at this authentic Shanghai-style restaurant include bowls of savory soy bean milk seasoned with hot chile-sesame oil and topped with floating slices of Chinese doughnut; pan-fried turnip rice cake; pan-fried pork buns wrapped in fried, then steamed, bread dough; marinated pig ears; eel noodle soup; and braised boneless pig's feet. Though there are some more usual dishes, such as pot stickers and beef chow fun, this is definitely a spot for the dim sum adventurer.

• **Gold Mountain** *644 Broadway/Stockton St., in Chinatown, 296-7733. Daily 8-3; $. Highchairs, boosters. Reservations advised. AE, MC, V.*

Dim sum is served on floors two and three of this gigantic, bustling restaurant, which is so big that the waiters use walkie-talkies to communicate. Though floor two alone seats 280 people, there still is usually a wait. Once seated, if carts don't arrive fast enough, flag down someone who looks in charge and order directly from the kitchen. Crisp taro balls and roast duck are particularly good here.

• **Harbor Village** *Four Embarcadero Center, lobby level, 781-8833. Daily 11-2:30, Sat & Sun from 10:30; $. Highchairs, boosters. Reservations accepted for M-F. AE, MC, V. Validated parking in center garage.*

It is worth the wait generally required to dine on the upscale dim sum served at this Hong Kong-style spot. The back room, with its large windows overlooking the treetops to the Vaillancourt Fountain and Ferry Building, is choice. Special touches include doilies and pretty blue-patterned dishes that actually match. The selection of delicious items brought around on carts changes daily. They are made with impeccably fresh ingredients, and a tasty complexity characterizes many of the refined renditions.

• **King of China Restaurant** *939 Clement St./11th Ave., in the Richmond, 668-2618. Daily 9-3; $. Highchairs, boosters. No reservations. AE, MC, V.*

In this gigantic second-floor dining room, with an entire mirrored wall making it appear even larger, attracting a serving cart can be similar to hailing a cab in New York City. However, the wait to get in tends to be short, and the food quality rivals the best found in Chinatown.

Favorites here are deep-fried taro balls, delicate steamed shrimp dumplings, succulent roasted duck, and finger-licking-good foil-wrapped chicken.

Another busy dim sum parlor, the **Tong Palace** *(668-3988)*, is just next door.

• **Lichee Garden.** See page 53.

• **New Asia** *772 Pacific Ave./Stockton St., in Chinatown, 391-6666. Daily 8:30-3; $. Highchairs, boosters. No reservations. MC, V.*

Even with a reputed 1,000 seats, this elegant spot usually requires a wait for seating in its popular ground level dining room. However, immediate seating is often available upstairs. Head servers here use walkie-talkies to communicate across the huge, noisy interior. Hesitation when offered a choice of eight teas usually is translated by the server into "green," because that tea is the most popular. Deep-fried shrimp toast topped with a tiny quail egg, deep-fried taro balls filled with sweet poi, and cloud-like pork bows are all especially good. A busy dim sum-to-go counter operates by the waiting area.

• **Pearl City** *641 Jackson St./Grant Ave., in Chinatown, 398-8383. Daily 8-2; $. Highchairs, boosters. No reservations. MC, V.*

The front room here is chilly and quiet, the back room warmer and noisier. Items are brought around on platters rather than carts. Excellent choices include many delicate shrimp items and very good steamed custard buns.

• **Ton Kiang** *5821 Geary Blvd./22nd Ave., in the Richmond, 387-8273. Daily 11-3; $. Highchairs, boosters. No reservations. MC, V.*

Operating on two floors, this attractive spot specializes in Hakka-style cuisine. Among the exemplary dim sum items: deep-fried taro croquettes, miniature egg-custard tarts, chives with shrimp dumplings, and foil-wrapped chicken.

A branch is located at 3148 Geary Boulevard *(at Spruce St., 752-4440).*

• **Yank Sing** *427 Battery St./Clay St., near the Embarcadero, 362-1640 or 781-1111. M-F 11-3, Sat & Sun 10-4; $. Highchairs, boosters. Reservations advised. AE, MC, V.*

In 1957, when it opened in a previous location on Broadway in Chinatown, this was the first dim sum parlor in the city to serve the cuisine as it was known in Hong Kong. Two big reasons to forsake tradition and visit this now upscale parlour at it location outside of Chinatown are that they take reservations and that the parking is easier. The tasteful, brightly lighted upstairs interior here is a labyrinth of dining rooms. Downstairs, tables are separated by etched-glass partitions and a peaceful bamboo fountain sets the tone. Tablecloths, cloth napkins, and fresh flowers grace each table. Soft drinks, and ever Perrier, can be ordered. Servers are friendly and can usually answer questions. Top items include cloud-soft rice noodles stuffed with a variety of meats, succulent stuffed black mushroom caps, deep-fried crab claws, sweet deep-fried taro balls, wedges of orange peel filled with shimmering orange Jell-O, and flaky-crusted custard tarts.

It is a Cantonese custom to introduce a new baby to family and friends at a Red Egg and Ginger Party. Named for some of the food items included in the luncheon menu, these parties are catered here and set menus are available.

A branch is located at 49 Stevenson Street *(at 1st St., 495-4510).*

Doidge's Kitchen *2217 Union St./Fillmore St., 921-2149. B & L daily; $-$$. Boosters. Reservations advised. MC, V.*

Breakfast here is a winner, and it's available all day. Eggs are cooked to order and served with toast and a side of either cottage fries or sliced tomato. Eggs Benedict, omelettes, pancakes, house-made granola, and French toast made from a choice of six different breads are among the other items available. Don't miss the Motherlode bacon—a flavorful honey-cured variety made without preservatives. And then there are the fresh-squeezed orange and grapefruit juices, and hot chocolate made with milk. For lunch it's a variety of hamburgers, sandwiches, house-made soups, and a beautiful fresh fruit salad. Often there is a wait for seating in the cozy dining room. However, there is usually room at the counter, where the bonus is watching the busy, colorful cooks.

Elite Cafe 2049 Fillmore St./California St., in the Upper Fillmore, 346-8668. D daily, SunBr; $$. Highchairs, boosters, booths. No reservations. AE, MC, V.

Parties of four get the best seats here—enclosed wooden booths left from the restaurant's prior life as an old-time Chinese restaurant. In addition to Cajun martinis and other exotic bar drinks, and appetizers such as Cajun popcorn, the menu offers a selection of authentic spicy Creole and Cajun dishes.

El Mansour 3123 Clement St./32nd Ave., in the Outer Richmond, 751-2312, fax (510) 669-0444. D daily; $$. Child portions. Reservations advised. AE, MC, V.

Upon entering the double doors of this Moroccan restaurant diners are encased in another world. Cloth is draped from the ceiling of the intimate dining room, giving occupants the illusion of being inside a sultan's tent. Adding to the sensuous feeling are pink walls, floors covered with plush oriental carpets, and seating on hassocks at low tables of inlaid wood. After diners choose an entree from the fixed-price menu, a waiter dressed in a long caftan appears to perform the ritual hand-washing. Hands are gathered over a large silver pot placed in the middle of the table, where they are splashed with warm water. When the first course, a tasty lentil soup, arrives, diners drink it right from the bowl, since no eating utensils are provided here. A bland Moroccan bread is offered to accompany it. The next course is a salad plate of spicy marinated rounds of carrots and cucumbers and a wonderful mixture of tomatoes and green peppers meant to be scooped up with the bread. Then comes a bastela—a fragrant pie containing a sweet chicken and almond mixture wrapped in filo pastry and sprinkled with powdered sugar. Entree choices include seafood, rabbit, couscous, and a flamboyantly served shish kabob. Both succulent roasted chicken and tender stewed lamb are offered with a choice of toppings such as almonds, honey, or prunes. Dessert is fried bananas with honey and a repeat of the hand-bathing ritual. And finally the waiter pours mint tea, skillfully and beautifully, from up high. Belly dancers perform nightly.

Enrico's 504 Broadway/Kearny St., in North Beach, 982-6223, fax 397-7244. L & D daily; $$. Highchairs, booths. Reservations advised; accepted for same day only. AE, MC, V. Valet parking $7.

Though no longer run by Enrico Banducci—the well-known original owner, who now operates a hot dog cart in Richmond, Virginia—this landmark restaurant was the city's first coffeehouse. Informal coffee and snacks are still served on the outdoor patio, which is heated in cool weather and is one of the best spots for people-watching around. More substantial meals can also be ordered there, or in the large interior room where paintings by local artists adorn the walls and jazz is performed nightly from 9 p.m. The dinner menu offers a large selection of tapas, as well as several soups, salads, pastas, and pizzas. More substantial entrees include delicious items such as salmon coated with a fruit mustard and served with garlic mashed potatoes, and a surprisingly flavorful top sirloin served with a braised onion and perfect oven-roasted potatoes. Accomplished house-made desserts, such as malt ice cream in a chocolate cookie sandwich with toasted pecans, are hard to resist. Special events are sometimes scheduled.

Epplers Bakery *3465 California St./Laurel St., 752-0825. Tu-Sat 7-7, Sun & M 8:30-6; $. 1 highchair. MC, V. Free parking lot adjoins.*

This bakery is famous for its extensive assortment of baked goods, including cakes, pastries, tortes, petit fours, cookies, muffins, and tea cakes. Specialty cakes include a Grand Marnier and Black Forest. All stops are pulled out for Christmas, when specialty items include gingerbread, marzipan, fruit cakes, mincemeat and pumpkin pies, several kinds of bûches de noël, and elaborate gingerbread houses. A variety of candies are also available. Though there is no table service, a sit-down area invites relaxing over a bakery selection with some tea or coffee.

More Epplers are located at 750 Market Street near Union Square *(392-0101)*, at Stonestown *(731-5544)*, and at Embarcadero Center *(982-5383)*. The main bakery is at 1301 17th Street *(431-2032)*.

The Fly Trap Restaurant *606 Folsom St./2nd St., South of Market, 243-0580. L M-F, D M-Sat; $$. 1 highchair, boosters. Reservations advised. AE, MC, V. Valet parking $3-$4.*

Once, long ago, in a former incarnation, the restaurant in this spot solved its fly problem by putting fly paper on the tables, prompting the GIs of the 1898 Spanish-American war to refer to it as the "fly trap." The flies stuck and so did the name. When the original owner's cousin reopened the restaurant after the 1906 earthquake and fire, he irreverently named it "The Fly Trap Restaurant," and it is still called that today. A replica of Louie's Restaurant, a turn-of-the-century Market Street eatery, it has a spiffy updated interior that features high ceilings and a bank of small tables perfect for those who are dining alone. Some unusual items are found on the menu. Among the starters are several soups, including a chilled vichyssoise, and a variety of salads, including a tasty celery Victor. House specialties include an exquisite chicken coq au vin, the hard-to-find Hangtown fry, and an Old World wiener schnitzel. Steaks, seafood, pastas, and a hamburger are also available. Each entree is accompanied by thick, crispy house-made ridged potato chips. The rich house-made desserts range from a banana split to a chocolate torte with marscapone cream, and intriguing drinks such as the Fly Trap Coffee, prepared with Godiva and Frangelica liquors, are also available.

Fior D'Italia *601 Union St./Stockton St., in North Beach, 986-1886, fax 986-7031. L & D daily; $$-$$$. Highchairs, boosters, booths. Reservations advised. AE, MC, V. Valet parking $6-$9.*

Opened in 1886, when great sailing ships were seen in the bay and goats roamed Telegraph Hill, this venerable traditional northern Italian restaurant is the oldest in the U.S. The small dining area in the bar is graced with a large composite mural depicting the Church of St. Francis of Assisi in Tuscany, while the spacious main dining area in back is decorated with historic San Francisco memorabilia and offers plenty of comfortable oversize booths. Experienced servers, attired in traditional black and white uniforms, offer expert assistance in navigating the extensive menu. Always a good choice is the four-course fixed-price dinner; main courses include seafood, veal, and chicken. Additionally, the regular menu offers fresh pasta, risotto, and polenta. Desserts include the classic tiramisu, fresh berries, and sometimes a delicious poached pear in caramel sauce and cream.

Fringale *570 Fourth St./Brannan St., South of Market, 543-0573. L M-F, D M-Sat; $$. Reservations advised. MC, V.*

Cheery yet intimate, this bright, very popular spot is owned by French-Basque chef Gerald Hirigoyen. He offers a seasonal menu of light Franco-California bistro fare that American's can recognize. Appetizers might include a soup du jour of creamy fava bean purée, house-cured salmon, foie gras medallions, and a mashed potato croquette. Dinner entrees have included delicate steamed salmon topped with threads of deep-fried onions and served on a bed of tart braised leeks, a lemon-chicken breast with a side of couscous and dates, and a marinated roast rack of lamb. Among the possible desserts are a tangy lemon tart with fresh raspberries and a wonderful clafouti made with toasted almond slices and fresh raspberries. In French "fringale" means "the urge to eat," and that urge is delightfully satisfied here.

Gabbiano's *One Ferry Plaza, on the Embarcadero, 391-8403, fax 391-1617. L & D daily, SunBr; $$-$$$. Highchairs, boosters, child menu. Reservations accepted. AE, MC, V. Valet parking $4.25.*

The main reason to dine here is for the incredible view of Treasure Island and the Bay Bridge afforded from the second-floor dining room, where all seats are good seats. Fortunately, the food is tasty as well. The menu is eclectic, with an extensive selection of sandwiches and salads on the lunch menu. Items such as crab cakes and oysters on the half shell are among the appetizers, and paella and lobster in puff pastry are among the dinner entrees. The Sunday champagne brunch extravaganza should please anyone. Note that weekend lunch is served only on the first floor.

Golden Turtle *2211 Van Ness Ave./Vallejo St., 441-4419; D Tu-Sun; $$. Highchairs, boosters. Reservations advised. AE, MC, V.*

Decorated with hand-carved wooden scenes and light sconces constructed from tree branches, and featuring a goldfish pond at the entrance, this elegant, sedate Vietnamese restaurant serves a cuisine that is a cross between Cantonese and Szechwan Chinese. A good starter is the crisp-fried imperial rolls, which are stuffed with a pork-seafood mixture and served with thin rice noodles, lettuce, and a mild dipping sauce. More dramatic appetizers include barbecued quails flambè and sizzling rice soup. Main dishes include a tasty grilled beef kabob; spicy, aromatic lemon grass curry prawns; steamed whole sea bass in a subtle ginger sauce; and fresh catfish in a clay pot. The Seven Jewel beef dinner consists of seven special beef dishes served in a specific order; each dish can also be ordered separately. Tea comes with the meal, and a sweet, fresh-squeezed lemonade is also among the drink selections. For dessert, don't miss the spectacular presentation of the bananas flambè.

Greens *Laguna St./Marina Blvd., in Fort Mason Center, 771-6222. L & D Tu-Sat, SunBr; $$. Highchairs, boosters. Reservations essential. MC, V. Free parking lot adjoins.*

With high ceilings, large windows framing the Golden Gate Bridge, and colorful modern art hanging on the walls, this trendy, all-vegetarian restaurant packs 'em in. Starters on the ever-changing menu might include a fragrant and flavorful black bean chile or a delicate watercress salad with pears and walnuts. Entrees include items such as tofu brochettes, spinach salad, and refined pizzas. Desserts are uncomplicated but delicious—perhaps a pear-almond upside down cake or a Meyer lemon tart. On weeknights, cafe-style dinners are served; on Fridays and Saturdays, a fixed-price, five-course dinner. The brunch menu is a la carte. Greens is run by the San Francisco Zen Center, and many of the fresh herbs and vegetables are grown at the center's West Marin farm.

Greens To Go *(771-6330, fax 771-3472. M-F 8am-9:30pm, Sat 8-4, Sun 9-3:30.)* dispenses many menu items as well as their delicious breads and an assortment of pastries and desserts.

Hamburger Mary's *1582 Folsom St./12th St., South of Market, 626-1985. L & D daily; $. Highchairs, boosters. Reservations advised. AE, MC, V.*

With a sound system rivaling that of the Hard Rock Cafe and a decor as eclectically mixed as the clientele it serves, this funky spot dishes up its signature charbroiled hamburger until the wee hours in a very relaxed atmosphere. The menu also offers a variety of sandwiches and salads, and breakfast is served all day. Ten beers are on draft, and the cream pitcher is a baby bottle. In sum, it's the kind of place that would make Dorothy say to Toto, "We're not in Kansas anymore!"

Hard Rock Cafe *1699 Van Ness Ave./Sacramento St., 885-1699. L & D daily; $-$$. Highchairs, boosters, booths, child portions. Reservations accepted Sept-May. AE, MC, V.*

Sitting in one of the roomy booths positioned on raised platforms around the perimeter of the cavernous room here—which was formerly a new car showroom—allows first-rate people-watching. Bizarre wall decorations include half a Cadillac convertible, Elvis's rhinestone-bedecked white cape, and Kurt Cobain's guitar. And, as might be expected from the name, rock & roll blasts out at ear-splitting levels. Considering the sensory overload and the fact that many people come here to look and to be seen, it is impressive that the American-style food is quite good, the service attentive, and the prices reasonable. The house salad is crisp, cold romaine lettuce, and the house-made Thousand Island dressing is tangy with fresh onion. Hamburgers are served on whole wheat sesame buns and are just plain good. The menu also offers an assortment of sandwiches, house-made chile, grilled fresh fish, and rich, old-fashioned desserts. A plethora of souvenir items can be ordered at the table and added to the tab.

Hornblower Dining Yachts *Pier 33/Bay St., on the Embarcadero, 394-8900. L, call for schedule, $26; D daily, $61-$74; Sat & SunBr $36-$41; children 4-12 half price, under 4 free. Reservations required. AE, MC, V.*

Cruises board 1/2-hour before departure. Diners are seated as they board, and the maitre d' announces to each table when it is their turn to visit the groaning board of tasty brunch buffet items. Magnificent views of San Francisco and the bay are enjoyed as the boat goes out under the Golden Gate Bridge, past Sausalito and Angel Island, and beside Alcatraz. Live music plays in the background, and the Captain makes the rounds to greet everyone. After dining, there is time to tour the vessel. Special events are often scheduled. Note that though highchairs and booster seats are not available, parents are welcome to bring strollers with wheel locks on board, and children are given crayons and coloring books to keep them busy.

House of Prime Rib *1906 Van Ness Ave./Washington St., 885-4605. D daily; $$$. Highchairs, boosters, booths, child portions. Reservations advised. AE, MC, V. Valet parking $4.*

The specialty of the house in this posh spot is the finest aged prime rib—served right from the cart and carved to order table-side. (In fact, the only other entree on the menu is grilled fresh fish.) Choose a City Cut (for small appetites), an English Cut (several thin slices), or a King Henry VIII Cut (for those with king-size appetites). The complete dinner includes a chilled green salad prepared at the table and presented with *chilled* forks, bread and butter, either mashed potatoes and gravy or a baked potato, fresh horseradish sauce, creamed fresh spinach, and Yorkshire pudding. Come here hungry.

Hunan Restaurant *924 Sansome St./Broadway, 956-7727. L & D daily; $-$$. Boosters. Reservations accepted. AE, MC, V.*

Once upon a time this was a tiny, obscure restaurant located in Chinatown. It seated 29 people. Then it was described in *The New Yorker* as "the best Chinese restaurant in the world." Lines formed, and it was no longer possible to just saunter in and sit down at one of the few tables or at the counter, where half the pleasure was in watching the cooks in action. To satisfy demand, the restaurant moved to this huge warehouse, which seats 314. The kitchen uses unsaturated oils, lean meats, and skinned chicken, and it uses no MSG or sugar; salt-free dishes are also available. Soft drinks are served in the can with a glass full of ice. Appetizer dumplings here are like pot stickers only spicy hot; the unusual Diana's Special consists of a spicy meat sauce and lettuce sandwiched between two deep-fried flour pancakes. Harvest pork (a traditional dish fed to farm workers and pallbearers to give them strength), hot and sour chicken, and bean sprout salad are all especially good, as is the cold chicken salad mixed with shredded cucumbers and shiny noodles tossed with peanut dressing. Specialties include excellent fresh seafood dishes and unusual house-smoked ham, chicken, and duck—all smoked over hickory wood, tea leaves, and orange peels. The distinctive hot bean sauce—a combination of fermented black beans, powdered red peppers, garlic, oil, and vinegar—is available to go. With some of this sauce and a souvenir copy of the owner's book, *Henry Chung's Hunan Style Chinese Cookbook*, which is also sold on the premises, it is possible to try out more of these unusual dishes at home.

Branches are located at 1016 Bryant Street *(at 8th St., 861-5808. L & D M-Sat.)* and 674 Sacramento Street *(at Kearny St., 788-2234. L & D M-F.)*.

Jackson Fillmore *2506 Fillmore St./Jackson St., in the Upper Fillmore, 346-5288. D daily; $$. Highchairs, boosters. Reservations advised; accepted only for 3+. AE, MC, V.*

Those who show up without reservations usually find themselves standing in a line that stretches out the door. Even those with reservations can find themselves sitting at crowded tables or on a stool at the counter. However, the exceptional antipastos and pastas make it all worthwhile. Exceptional cloud-like gnocchi, fresh fish items, and truffle dishes are also served, and a classic zabaglione provides the perfect dessert.

Japanese Restaurants. See page 76.

John's Grill *63 Ellis St./Powell St., near Union Square, 986-DASH. L & D M-Sat; $-$$. Highchairs, boosters, booths. AE, MC, V.*

One of the settings in Dashiell Hammett's *The Maltese Falcon*, this restaurant's cozy interior features its original gaslight fixtures, some original period furnishings, and mahogany-paneled walls covered with photos of famous patrons and old San Francisco scenes,. The lunch menu offers a variety of salads as well as a hamburger, several pastas, and that hard-to-find Hangtown fry (an early California dish prepared with oysters and eggs). Dinner brings on extensive seafood selections. One of the most popular dishes is straight-out-of-the-book Sam Spade's Chops (broiled rack of lamb with a baked potato and sliced tomatoes). The bar is worth checking out from 5 to 7, when complimentary hors d'oeuvres are served.

Just Desserts *248 Church St./Market St., 626-5774. Daily 8am-11pm; $. Booths. No reservations. MC, V.*

Bakery cases here are filled with goodies such as almond croissants, black-bottom cupcakes, chocolate chip cookies, and a variety of pastries, muffins, cheesecakes, and pies. Personal favorites are the cakes, which include such wonders as carrot cake with cream cheese frosting, chocolate fudge cake with a rich fudge frosting, lemon cake topped with a choice of lemon or bittersweet chocolate glaze, exquisite German chocolate cake, and sublime weekend cake—devil's food with cream cheese frosting. And on and on. And although they *are* fattening, they are made *without* preservatives, artificial colorings, or artificial flavorings.

Branches are all over town: Three Embarcadero Center *(421-1609)*; 836 Irving Street *(at 10th Ave., in the Sunset, 681-1277)*; 3735 Buchanan Street *(at Marina Blvd., near Fort Mason, 922-8373)*; 1750 Fulton Street *(at Masonic Ave., 441-2207)*; 1000 Cole Street *(at Parnassus Ave., in the Haight-Ashbury, 664-8947)*.

Khan Toke Thai House *5937 Geary Blvd./24th Ave., in the Richmond, 668-6654. D daily; $. Boosters. Reservations advised. AE, MC, V.*

Diners remove their shoes in the entryway before entering a maze of lushly decorated small dining rooms. Most diners sit on floor pillows at richly embellished tables; some tables are also available with wells in the floor underneath, into which legs can dangle. Many of the unusual Thai herbs used in preparing dishes for the extensive menu are grown in a courtyard behind the restaurant. An all-inclusive dinner includes an appetizer of fried fish cakes, spicy and sour shrimp soup, a green salad, a choice of two entrees, either a pudding or fried banana, and hot tea or coffee.

Kirin *6135 Geary Blvd./26th Ave., in the Richmond, 752-2412. L & D Tu-Sun; $. Highchairs, boosters. No reservations. MC, V.*

This unpretentious restaurant is yet another example of the axiom that some of the best Chinese restaurants in San Francisco are not in Chinatown. The Mandarin and Szechwan dishes served here are complex combinations of spices and ingredients and a pleasure to both eye and palate. All meals include a complimentary bowl of kimchee—a Korean dish of bok choy marinated in hot oil. Recommended menu items include a fragrant and tasty shredded pork with fish flavor and garlic sauce (pork bits, woodear, hot red peppers, bits of crunchy water chestnut, and green onion), chewy dry-fried beef (batter-dipped pieces of meat, deep-fried and served in a delicious thick sauce), and crunchy, flavorful dry-sautéed string beans. Hot braised fish a la Kirin—a specialty—consists of crispy-fried whole rock fish in a dark sauce of ginger, green onions, and garlic. Handmade noodles are mixed up with plum sauce or fried chow mein-style, and house-made chow fun noodles are available off the menu.

La Taqueria *2889 Mission St./25th St., in the Mission, 285-7117. L & D daily; $. Highchairs. No reservations. No cards.*

To experience fast food Mexican-style, step through one of the two arches here and head to the counter to place an order. Then pick a table, and sit back until the right number is called. Entertainment is provided by a colorful folk mural decorating one wall, by cooks in the open kitchen busily preparing orders, and by a jukebox featuring Mexican music. The menu is simple. Choose between tacos made with two steamed corn tortillas and burritos made with chewy flour tortillas. Fillings are a choice of superb pork (carnitas), beef (carne asada), sausage (chorizo), chicken (pollo), or cheese (queso). Pinto beans and fresh tomato salsa round things out; avocado and sour cream cost a bit more. Depending on the season, house-made fresh fruit juices include strawberry, cantaloupe, orange, banana, and pineapple.

Walk-away desserts can be picked up next door at **Dianda's Italian-American Pastry**, *(647-5469)* where everything is made from scratch and the cannolis are particularly good.

Leon's Bar-B-Q *2800 Sloat Blvd./46th Ave., 681-3071. L & D daily; $. Highchairs, boosters, booths. No reservations. AE, MC, V.*

Located across the street from the zoo, this tiny, extremely casual spot is known for delicious, messy pork ribs slathered with a tangy sweet sauce. Good beef ribs, hot links, and barbecued chicken are also available. Meals come with a corn muffin and choice of baked beans, spaghetti, potato salad, or coleslaw. The menu is rounded out with a half-pound hamburger, house-made chile, and tiny pecan or sweet potato pies. Everything can be prepared to go, and the picnic area in the zoo or the nearby beach are both good places to take it.

A branch is located at 1913 Fillmore Street *(at Bush St., 922-2436)*.

LuLu Restaurant *816 Folsom St./4th St., South of Market, 495-5775. B, L, & D daily; $$. Highchairs, boosters. Reservations advised. AE, MC, V. Valet parking at D $6.*

Outrageously popular, this casual restaurant operates in the large, open, high-ceilinged room of a converted 1910 warehouse. The house specialty is simply-prepared foods of the

French and Italian Riviera served family-style. Tasty items include almost anything from the wood-fired rotisserie or oven, especially the rosemary-scented roast chicken and the crisp, delicate fritto misto with artichokes. Among the unusual nightly specials are suckling pig on Friday and air-dried duck on Saturday.

An adjoining cafe serves the same menu but takes no reservations.

MacArthur Park *607 Front St./Jackson St., 398-5700. L M-F, D daily; $$. Reservations advised. AE, MC, V.*
For description, see page 162.

Mama's Girl *1701 Stockton St./Filbert St., in North Beach, 362-6421. B & L daily; $$. Highchairs, boosters. No reservations. No cards.*
Located on a corner of Washington Square, this cozy, cheery, often crowded spot has cafeteria-style service. Breakfast choices include blueberry pancakes, thick French toast made from various breads, a variety of omelettes, and fresh-squeezed citrus juices. Lunch brings on salads, sandwiches, hamburgers, hot dogs, and a zucchini and cheese frittata. Delicious desserts and fresh strawberry creations—even out of season—are a house specialty.

Masa's *648 Bush St./Powell St., in Hotel Vintage Court, near Union Square, (800) 258-7694, 989-7154, fax 989-3141. D Tu-Sat; $$$. Reservations essential. Valet parking.*
This highly acclaimed, elegant, and very expensive restaurant serves a menu of classic French cuisine at tables set with Hutschenreuther china and Christofle silver. Guests are expected to dress accordingly, with men in coat and tie. Menu highlights include shellfish and game dishes—such as lobster salad with truffle vinaigrette, and roast breast of pheasant with morels and pears—and a dessert tasting platter. Adding a little intrigue, the restaurant bears the name of its founding chef, who was murdered long ago in a still unsolved case.

Max's Diner *311 3rd St./Folsom St., South of Market, 546-MAXS. L & D daily; $$. Boosters, booths. Reservations accepted. AE, MC, V.*
Specializing in serving large portions of '50s food, this popular spot continues the theme with lots of chrome and Formica, miniature tabletop jukeboxes filled with '50s tunes, oversize vinyl booths that offer privacy to families, and waitresses dressed in black-and-white uniforms and bobby socks. The extensive menu offers crispy-coated chicken-fried steak, New York deli-style sandwiches, a gigantic hamburger with bacon and cheese, and a blue plate special of well-seasoned, moist meatloaf served with made-from-scratch mashed potatoes indented with a gravy-filled crater. A few appetizers and side dishes are a meal in themselves: country-style ribs, sliders (baby burgers), spicy chicken wings with blue cheese dip, giant onion rings, a salad (a wedge of iceberg lettuce topped with house-made dressing), slaw, and tasty house-made chile. Among Max's famous gargantuan desserts are a tapioca pudding layered with strawberries and topped with whipped cream, a bread pudding with vanilla sauce, a delicious seven-layer cookie topped with hot fudge and ice cream, and a large selection of ice cream concoctions. To top it all off, each diner receives a piece of Bazooka bubble gum with the check.

Across town, **Max's Opera Cafe** *(601 Van Ness Ave./Golden Gate Ave., 771-7300. L & D daily; $$. Boosters, booths. No reservations. AE, MC, V.)* offers similar fare but with the added bonus of talented servers who also take turns serving entertaining stints singing at the mike between 7 and 11 p.m.

McCormick & Kuleto's Seafood Restaurant *900 North Point, in Ghirardelli Square, 929-1730. L & D daily; $$-$$$. Highchairs, boosters. Reservations advised. AE, MC, V. Validated parking in Ghirardelli Square garage.*
Spectacular views are available from most tables in this splendidly appointed seafood

restaurant, though the half-circle booths on the second of three tiers are choice. High ceilings, floor-to-ceiling leaded glass windows, and fantastical light fixtures add to the overall elegant ambiance. The extensive menu is designed to please every appetite. Starters include tiny, but delicious, crab cakes; sweet, crisp rock shrimp popcorn; and a satisfying, nicely seasoned clam chowder. Among the many seafood dishes, which are fresh whenever possible, are an excellent pan-fried petrale sole with caper-lemon butter and a delicious blackened sea bass with a side of homey mashed potatoes. Pastas, salads, and a variety of meats round things out. Desserts— among them a plate-size fresh peach tart with a flaky crust and crème frâiche topping—are not an afterthought.

The restaurant's more casual **Crab Cake Lounge** offers the same incredible view with a less expensive, less extensive menu and the additional options of pizza and a hamburger.

Mel's Drive-In *2165 Lombard St./Fillmore St., 921-2867. B, L, & D daily; $. Highchairs, boosters, booths, child menu. No reservations. No cards. Free parking lot adjoins.*

When Mel's was a *real* drive-in, carhops brought trays out to clamp on windows for in-car dining. Now the eating goes on inside the restaurant. Seating is at a long counter, in booths, or at tables with chairs. Most seats are within reach of a computerized mini-jukebox where an oldie but goodie can be played for two bits. (An interesting aside: Jukeboxes were invented in San Francisco in 1888.) Dress is just-off-the-jogging-trail casual. Menu items include the Famous Melburger with all the trimmings, a variety of veggie burgers, fries with the skins still on, and, of course, big onion rings. All this, plus salads, soups, and sandwiches galore. For more substantial appetites, the menu also offers a chicken pot pie, meat loaf served with lumpy mashed potatoes and gravy, and the day's blue plate special. Among the drinks are flavored cokes and thick, old-fashioned milkshakes made with Carnation deluxe ice cream and served in the mixer tin. Desserts include chocolate fudge cake, banana cream pie, and a banana split. Teens call this place "cool."

A branch at 3355 Geary Boulevard *(at Stanyan St., 387-2244)* is the exact location of one of the three original Mels.

Mike's Chinese Cuisine *5145 Geary Blvd./16th Ave., in the Richmond, 752-0120. D W-M; $$. Boosters. No reservations. MC, V.*

Located far from the crush of Chinatown, this is one of the best Chinese restaurants in town. Tables are covered with white linens, and the tastefully decorated, well-insulated down-stairs dining room keeps the noise level low. House specialties include crispy chicken, shredded barbecued chicken salad (cold smoked chicken with chopped almonds, lettuce, and a mustard dressing), and Peking duck (order one day in advance). More winners include a spicy, fragrant hot and sour soup, an incredible smoky and tender Mongolian beef served on a bed of crispy rice noodles, and a large selection of colorful sweet and sour dishes and pan-fried chow mein noodle items that are popular with children.

Mission Rock Resort *817 China Basin Rd./3rd St., 621-5538. B & L daily, SunBr; $. Boosters. No reservations. AE, MC, V.*

Known mainly to people who work in the area and to boaters who dock in front while stopping to eat, this unpretentious spot is a relaxing find. The weathered deck is choice when the sun is shining. Seated there on one of the funky chairs, diners can view gigantic cargo ships docked nearby and gaze across the bay to Oakland. A small indoor dining/bar area is cozy in inclement weather. The simple menu consists of a variety of omelettes and sandwiches, as well as a hamburger and fish & chips.

Moose's *1652 Stockton St./Union St., in North Beach, 989-7800. L M-Sat, D daily, SunBr; $$$. Highchairs, boosters. Reservations advised. AE, MC, V. Valet parking $7.*

A reincarnation of the owner's popular former restaurant, this version is just as popular but feels much less cramped. A large, open room makes most tables good ones, and carpeting keeps the din to a minimum. Live piano music in the evenings adds to the inviting atmosphere. Appetizer selections from a recent intriguing menu included a delightful salad of watercress, candied pecans, Stilton cheese, and perfect summer peaches; and a trio of crostini—little open-faced sandwiches on toasted bread. Entree selections included both an exotically flavored chicken breast on fruited couscous with a Madras curry sauce, and a special of ahi with herbed mashed potatoes and a flavorful reduced wine sauce. (Pastas, pizzas, and Mooseburgers are also available.) Desserts didn't disappoint either. Among the choices were a perfect fresh peach baked in brioche and served with olallieberry sorbet, and an unusual flourless carrot cake served with corn ice cream.

North Beach Pizza *1499 Grant Ave./Union St., in North Beach, 433-2444. L & D daily; $. Boosters, booths. No reservations. AE, MC, V.*

Lacking pretension and finesse, this restaurant serves an unfussy kind of pizza in a relaxed, easy atmosphere. The pepperoni and cheese and the spicy-hot sausage versions are both particularly tasty, with an excellent chewy crust, and the delicious antipasto salad tossed with the tasty, creamy house Italian dressing is the perfect accompaniment. An outstanding cannelloni is among the pasta choices, and barbecued ribs or chicken and a submarine sandwich are also on the menu.

A branch is one block up the street at 1310 *(433-2444).*

North China *315 Van Ness Ave./Green St., 673-8201. L & D M-Sat; $$. Highchairs, boosters. Reservations advised. AE, MC, V. Validated parking.*

Tastefully decorated with crisp tablecloths and fresh flowers, this restaurant produces superior cuisine that draws diners back again and again. Excellent appetizers include dramatically served sizzling rice soup, spicy hot and sour soup, exceptionally good pot stickers, and a cold appetizer plate with honey-glazed spareribs, chicken salad with sesame dressing, spiced slices of beef, fried and baked prawns, and smoked fish. Other great dishes include dry-braised beef (dipped in egg batter and then flash-fried), mu-shu pork, spicy kung pao shrimp, Szechwan beef (tender bits of beef mixed with crunchy shreds of celery and carrots and tossed with a slightly hot sauce), and smoked tea duck.

One Market Restaurant *1 Market St./ Steuart St., 777-5577, fax 777-4411. L M-F, D daily, SunBr; $$$. Highchairs, boosters. AE, MC, V. Valet parking $6.50.*

Situated in a corner of an attractive historic building dating from 1917, just across from the bay, this popular restaurant is co-owned by celebrity chef Bradley Ogden. On his all-American menu, appetizers include items such as crab cakes and barbecued oysters. For entrees, the changing menu might offer tender Yankee pot roast with roasted turnips and potatoes, or succulent rosemary-roasted chicken breast with three kinds of garlic mashed potatoes and wild mushrooms. For dessert, new takes on old favorites appear: strawberry shortcake with orange ice cream, peach cobbler topped with a dab of fresh peach sorbet. A Sunday jazz brunch offers a menu of breakfast favorites, and the kitchen makes English muffins from scratch for the eggs Benedict.

Oritalia *1915 Fillmore St./Bush St., in the Upper Fillmore, 346-1333. D daily; $$. Booths. Reservations advised. AE, MC, V.*

Positioned in the thick of a trendy shopping neighborhood, this always-bustling restaurant has particularly comfortable booths and offers a unique "grazing" menu of Oriental-Italian "small plates." Among the items on the changing menu are superb, crispy fried shrimp and pork dumplings with a cilantro-mint sauce, local dungeness crab cakes topped with several kinds of colorful caviar and surrounded by a red pepper-curry cream moat, a complex arrangement of house-smoked trout on a sea of cucumbers with dabs of red onion and green wasabi, and cloud-soft potato gnocchi in a sauce of ginger cream with cilantro and rock shrimp—topped with a sprinkling of caviar. Desserts are artfully presented—fresh lemon soufflé is served on an oversize, colorfully rimmed plate with a vertical cookie "hook" holding a ring of candied orange peel. The gooey center chocolate cake with espresso bean gelato is just plain fantastic.

Palomino *345 Spear St./Steuart St., in Hills Plaza, on the Embarcadero, 512-7400, fax 512-0648. L & D daily; $$-$$$. Highchairs, boosters. Reservations advised. AE, MC, V. Validated parking.*

Offering a great view of the bay and Bay Bridge, this bustling "Euro-bistro" offers a raised seating area, unusual glass lighting fixtures, and interior palm trees that echo the palm trees lining the street outside. Kids get a color-in place mat to occupy them while the adults contemplate the menu. All dinners start with a crusty loaf of bread and a delicious crushed tomato-Feta-kalamata spread. A choice appetizer is the crisp hearts of romaine salad, which is deliciously tossed with a creamy herb vinaigrette, toasted pine nuts, and gorgonzola. Pizza with cracker-thin crust is prepared in an apple wood-fired oven, and a variety of panini, pasta, fish, and spit-roasted meat items round out the menu. Sixteen beers are on tap, and a large selection of wine varietals are available by the glass.

Pasand *1875 Union St./Laguna St., 922-4498. L & D Tu-Sun; $. Highchairs, boosters.*

For description, see page 324.

Picnic Pick-Ups.

• **Andronico's** *1200 Irving St./Funston Ave., near Golden Gate Park, 661-3220. Daily 7am-11pm. MC, V.*

For description, see page 324.

• **Lucca Delicatessen** *2120 Chestnut St./Steiner St., 921-7873. M 10-6:30, Tu-F 9-6:30, Sat & Sun 9-6. No cards.*

Owned by the same family since 1929, this deli prices its made-to-order sandwiches by weight. House-made salads, handmade breadsticks, and a large selection of Italian wines are also available.

• **Macy's Cellar** *170 O'Farrell St., on Union Square, 397-3333. Hours vary.*

This food court in Macy's basement dispenses great house-made salads and prepared dishes. Wolfgang Puck's pizza is also available, as are Boudin sourdough items, Tom's Cookies, and a large assortment of specialty candies. Small, crowded tables permit eating on the premises.

• **A North Beach Picnic.**

Florence Italian Delicatessen & Ravioli Factory *(1412 Stockton St./Vallejo St., 421-6170. M-Sat 7-6, Sun 9-3. AE, MC, V.)* is a traditional Italian deli that has been in business since the 1920s. Across the street, **Panelli Bros. Italian Delicatessen** *(1419 Stockton St./Vallejo St., 421-2541. M-Sat 7:30-5:30, Sun 8:30-2:30.)* has been around almost as long. Either can provide the makings for a great picnic. Dash into one of the Chinese markets for some fresh fruit, and into **Victoria Pastry Co.** *(1362 Stockton St./ Vallejo St., 781-2015. M-Sat 7-6, Sun 8-5.)* for a dessert—perhaps a cannoli or their unique zuccotto cake—and that's picnicking North Beach-style!

• **Say Cheese** *856 Cole St./Carl St., in the Haight-Ashbury, 665-5020. M-Thur 10-7, F & Sat 10-8, Sun 10-5. AE, MC, V.*

Hot soup and a variety of sandwiches, salads, and cheese spreads are available. More selections include over 200 kinds of cheese, a variety of pâtés and crackers, and fresh cookies.

• **Shenson's Kosher Style Delicatessen** *5120 Geary Blvd./15th Ave., 751-4699. Daily 8-5:45. Highchairs. MC, V.*

This fragrant spot has been making picnickers happy since 1933. Among the offerings are blintzes, pastries (including a delicious cherry strudel), house-made Kosher dill pickles and pickled tomatoes, and a great corned beef with coleslaw and Russian dressing on rye.

• **Stoyanof's** *1240 9th Ave./Lincoln Ave., near Golden Gate Park, 664-3664. L & D Tu-Sun 10-9. Highchairs, boosters. AE, MC, V.*

This small, pleasant Greek restaurant has cafeteria-style service but will pack anything to go. For an unusual picnic try a tiropetes (flaky filo triangle stuffed with cheeses) or a dolma (grape leaf stuffed with rice). Add a traditional Greek salad and, for dessert, a flaky baklava. Everything is made in-house.

• **Sweet Things** *3585 California St./Spruce St., in Cal-Mart in Laurel Village, 221-8583; M-Sat 8-7, Sun 9-6.*

For description, see page 188.

• **Vivande Porta Via** *2125 Fillmore St./California St., in the Upper Fillmore, 346-4430. Daily 10-10. AE, MC, V.*

All items here are prepared in the heavenly smelling open kitchen and are, in keeping with the literal meaning of the deli's name, "food to carry away." The Italian fare varies, but main dishes might include succulent roasted chicken, mushroom or chicken turnovers in a flaky crust, or torta Milanese (a tall pie layered with ham, spinach, and cheese). Salads include cannellini beans and caviar, caponata (eggplant with raisins and pine nuts), and several fresh pastas. Sandwiches are made to order with freshly baked breads, and tempting dolci (sweets) beckon from a display case. Comfortable seating is available on the premises.

Polly Ann Ice Cream *3142 Noriega St./39th Ave., in the Outer Sunset, 664-2472. Daily 11-10, F & Sat to 11; $. No cards.*

Claiming to be the only ice cream store in the world where dogs and babies get a free ice cream cone, this small shop is notable for yet other reasons. Where else is there a constantly changing choice of over 425 flavors of ice cream? Where else does the owner make all of his own ice cream and smile happily as he declares, "Tonight I think I'll make watermelon"? At least 52 flavors are available every day. Some are seasonal, and some are trendy—like Batman (black vanilla with lemon swirl) and E.T. (dark green vanilla with Reeses Pieces). Among the many unusual flavors are sunflower seed, vegetable, red bean, chocolate peanut butter, and American beauty (made with rose petals). Believe it or not, some very traditional flavors are also available, and vanilla is always the number one best seller. According to the owner, "Anything is possible."

Postrio *545 Post St./Mason St., in the Prescott Hotel, near Union Square, 776-7825. B & L M-F, D daily, Sat & SunBr; $$-$$$. Highchairs, boosters, booths. Reservations advised. AE, MC, V. Valet parking $7.*

Owned by Los Angeles celebrity chef Wolfgang Puck, and referred to inelegantly by some as Puck's Place, this grand spot is entered via a dramatic staircase leading down to an attractive contemporary dining room. It is a place to see, to be seen, and to enjoy a fabulous meal. Among the California-style cuisine, with Mediterranean and Asian accents, are such specialties as fried quail with pineapple glaze and Chinese-style duck with mango sauce. Desserts are generally excellent. As would be expected in any restaurant owned by Mr. Puck, a bar menu with great pizzas is also available. And don't overlook enjoying a power breakfast here. The menu then features fresh crab omelettes, sourdough waffles, and breakfast pizzas.

Prego *2000 Union St./Buchanan St., 563-3305. L & D daily. Highchairs, boosters; $$-$$$. Reservations advised. AE, MC, V.*

Said to have originally introduced to the San Francisco restaurant scene such now-standard items as tiramisu and buffalo mozzarella, this popular spot also seems to be a magnet for celebrities. Any of the various dining rooms seem choice: The bustling bar area has some tables with a great view of the sidewalk scene, while several other rooms have comfortable booth seating. A great way to start is with several antipasti—perhaps a Parma prosciutto with fruit, or deep-fried eggplant with garlic and tomato sauce. In fact, the assorted appetizer platter can satisfy as a light meal. Contorni such as roasted Yukon Gold potatoes with rosemary and garlic, polenta, and pan-braised greens are also available. Pastas here are house-made and exceptional, with wonderful renditions such as fazzoletti al salmone (large green and white-striped raviolis filled with fresh salmon, mozzarella, and arugula and topped with a delicate tomato cream sauce) and mezzelune alle melanzane (half-moon spinach pockets filled with ricotta and topped with grilled eggplant, fresh tomato, and fresh basil). Pizzas and calzone, as well as fresh fish and assorted meat dishes, round out the menu. Among the desserts is a plate of house-made cookies that are perfect with a cappuccino.

Red Crane *115 Clement St./12th Ave., in the Richmond, 751-7226, 386-5979. L & D daily; $. Highchairs, boosters. MC, V.*

Good service and delicious interpretations of Chinese vegetarian and seafood dishes makes this otherwise simple neighborhood restaurant quite popular. Menu winners include the vegetarian pot stickers, the excellent hot braised string beans in a tasty sauce, and the wonderful Szechwan eggplant. Gluten and bean curd substitute for meat in many dishes, and there is an extensive seafood menu.

Rendezvous du Monde *431 Bush St./Grant St., near Union Square, 392-3332. L M-F, D Tu-Sat, SatBr; $-$$. Reservations advised for D, not accepted for L. AE, MC, V.*

Seated in either a cozy sidewalk-side cubicle in the front room or at a table in the line-up tucked away in the cave-like back room, which mimics a weathered Parisian alley, diners at this family-run bistro in the "French Quarter" are in for a surprisingly satisfying experience. The menu features an innovative Mediterranean cuisine, with many French and Italian specialties. Starters include the unusual—marinated red and gold beets mingled in a colorful circle with ruby grapefruit and topped with a fragrant mixture of fresh parsley and mint—and the expected—a Caesar salad, a goat cheese salad. For the main course, a highly spiced roasted Moroccan chicken breast, served atop a flatbread with caramelized carrots and balsamic onions, is superb. The house-cured pork chop, house-made chicken-apple sausages, and cheeseburger on house-made focaccia are also good choices. The menu changes to take advantage of the chef's whim and the local bounty, and several vegan and vegetarian options are always available. Among the generally delightful desserts—all of which are made by Mom Mogannam—is a to-die-for warm, dense, brownie-like chocolate cake topped with caramel gelato. The homey pear skillet cake isn't too shabby either. Save room.

Rubicon *558 Sacramento St./Montgomery St., in the Financial District, 434-4100. L M-F, D M-Sat; $$$. Reservations advised. AE, MC, V. Valet parking at D $6.*

With celebrity investors including Robin Williams, Francis Ford Coppola, and Robert DeNiro, this bustling, sophisticated spot seems to have no choice but to be a hit. The two-level dining area is tucked between attractive brick walls decorated with modern art, and beams crisscross near windows as an earthquake safety measure. Full-flavored dishes include items such as rock shrimp ravioli, pan-roasted chicken on garlic mashed potatoes, and tasty grilled quail. Exceptional desserts are prepared by a special pastry chef and include such tempting delights as coconut cake topped with mango ice cream, or cookies and house-made cherry ice cream..

Sears *439 Powell St./Sutter St., just off Union Square, 986-1160. B & L W-Sun; $. Boosters. No reservations. No cards.*

Known for its extensive menu, this downtown institution is always busy. A wait in line is usually required before being seated at one of the tables covered with lacy crocheted cloths under protective see-through plastic. Breakfast is available all day and includes items such as silver dollar pancakes, crisp waffles, French toast served with homemade strawberry preserves, banana nut bread, an imposing fresh fruit bowl (a must in summer), a huge baked apple with cream, and house-made yogurt.

South Park Cafe *108 South Park Ave./2nd St., South of Market, 495-7275. B, L, & D M-F; on Sat D only. Highchairs, boosters. Reservations accepted for D. AE, MC, V.*

With large windows overlooking the large and popular park that fills the center circle of this unique street, this is a great place to sit down for a continental breakfast or simple lunch. Somehow reminiscent of a New York City cafe, it is actually French-owned.

Just a few doors down, **Lumbini** *(156 South Park Ave., 896-2998, fax 896-2995. M-F 9:30-6.)* purveys an eclectic collection of unusual accent items for the home.

Speckmann's *1550 Church St./Duncan St., in Noe Valley, 282-6850. L & D daily; $-$$. Boosters. Reservations advised. AE, MC, V.*

If someone were dropped into this restaurant blindfolded, they very well might be convinced they were in Germany when the blindfold was removed. Waitresses wear lacy tops and white aprons, tables are covered with red-and-white-checked cloths, and some of the patrons converse in German. When additionally offered a menu with a variety of Very German items, it isn't a stretch to imagine being in Germany itself. Diners can sit in either the restaurant-like winestube in front or in the more informal bierstube adjacent to a bar in back. Menu choices include Ungarisches goulasch (Hungarian goulash with spatzle), sauerbraten (marinated beef with potato pancakes), an assortment of schnitzels, and several wursts (sausages). Imported and draft beers are, of course, available. The dessert tray is heavy with strudels and rich pastries, including a traditional Black Forest cake. A take-out delicatessen also operates on the premises.

Spuntino *524 Van Ness Ave./McAllister St., in Civic Center, 861-7772. B M-F, L & D daily; $. Highchairs, boosters. AE, MC, V.*

Since its name means "snack" in Italian, it isn't surprising to find a menu of inexpensive a la carte items at this informal, cheery contemporary cafe. Fortunately for diners, portions tend to be much larger than snack size. Panini (sandwiches) and yeasty-crusted pizzette are perfect at lunch. At dinner, a heartier pasta such as the delightful fresh vegetable pasta primavera might be more satisfying. Orders are placed at the counter and when ready delivered by staff to the table.

Stars *150 Redwood Alley/Polk St., in Civic Center, 861-7827. L M-F, D daily; $$$. Highchairs, boosters. Reservations advised. AE, MC, V. Valet parking at D $6.*

Owned by celebrity chef Jeremiah Tower, who was on the staff of Berkeley's legendary Chez Panisse when California cuisine was born, this popular upscale hangout offers a grand dining room that spills into the bar. The menu of American bistro fare changes daily and includes items such as butternut squash soup with candied ginger, and roasted lamb sirloin with polenta. Though simpler, the bar food is also very good—even the hamburger and hot dog.

St. Francis Fountain *2801 24th St./York St., in the Mission, 826-4200. L & D daily; $. Boosters, booths, child portions. No reservations. No cards.*

Run by the same family since 1918, this informal coffee shop features old-time wooden booths and a counter with swivel stools. It was last decorated in 1949 and claims to be the oldest ice cream parlor in San Francisco. Patrons can try any of the 20 flavors of house-made 14 percent butterfat ice cream in such delights as triple-scoop milkshakes, served in an old-time metal canister, and giant double-dip sodas. Sundae syrup toppings are house-made, too. There is even an authentic New York egg cream and a root beer made from house-made syrup. In fact, most items are made from scratch, including the soups, salads, sandwiches, mayo, and potato salad. At a candy counter in front, made-on-the-premises candy

includes peanut brittle, old-time German-style fudge, and rum truffles. Best sellers are rocky road (they make the marshmallow up fresh, too, of course) and coconut clusters.

The Stinking Rose *325 Columbus Ave./Broadway, in North Beach, 781-ROSE, fax 403-0665. L & D daily; $$. Highchairs, boosters. Reservations advised. AE, MC, V.*

A warren of unusual rooms awaits garlic-lovers here, as does some delicious food made with as much garlic as possible. A don't-miss item is the bagna calda, which consists of tender, soft, almost sweet cloves of garlic served with bread for spreading. Among the winning dishes are a wild mushroom-roasted eggplant lasagna, a delectable thick-cut pork chop served with garlic relish and garlic mashed potatoes, and 40-clove garlic chicken. For dessert the truly adventurous can try garlic ice cream! For those who still haven't had enough, a tiny shop in front sells all things garlic.

Straits Cafe *3300 Geary Blvd./Parker Ave., in the Richmond, 668-1783, fax 668-3901. L & D daily. Highchairs, boosters. AE, MC, V.*

In a nod to the tropics, columns have been turned into pseudo palm trees in this airy, casual cafe. The delicious Singaporean cuisine is a complex, refined, and aromatic combination of Malaysian, Indonesian, Chinese, and Indian cuisines. It seems impossible to order wrong. However, particularly tasty items include murtabak (Indian bread stuffed with spiced minced beef), achar (cucumbers in a spicy-hot peanut sauce), basil chicken, green bean sambal (long beans stir-fried with chiles), and chile crab. Meats are cooked slowly and literally fall off the bone. The mixed bar drinks are outstanding—Raffles punch, Singapore sling, Midori margarita —and some are available in frozen versions. Great smoothies and a variety of luscious fruit syrup sodas are also available.

Taiwan *445 Clement St./6th Ave., in the Richmond, 387-1789.*

For description, see page 326.

T.G.I. Friday's *685 Beach St./Hyde St., at Fisherman's Wharf, 775-8443.*

For description, see page 158.

Tommaso's *1042 Kearny St./Broadway, in North Beach, 398-9696. D Tu-Sun; $$. Highchairs, boosters. No reservations. AE, MC, V.*

In 1935, when this spot was known as Lupo's, it was the first restaurant to bring pizza from New York City to the West Coast. (Pizza was introduced to the U.S. at the Lombardy Pizza Restaurant in New York City in 1905.) And for quite a while it was the only restaurant in the entire U.S. to prepare all of its baked foods in a genuine oak wood-burning brick oven. (In fact, world-renowned Chez Panisse in Berkeley used this oven as a model for their own, which then began producing a trend-setting gourmet mini pizza.) Truly a family operation, the owner is a waiter, his sister is hostess, his mother and another sister are cooks, his father keeps the books, and his wife does a little bit of everything. Movie director Francis Ford Coppola has been known to dash in from his nearby office—sometimes to chow down from the menu, other times to whip up his own creations in the kitchen. Seating in the dimly-lit cellar consists of both a large community dining table and smaller tables in semi-private compartments separated by wooden partitions. Murals depicting scenes of Naples and the Amalfi Coast decorate the walls. A delightful starter is any of the marinated salads—broccoli, string beans, or roasted peppers. Use the crusty bread to soak up the excess marinade. Almost 20 kinds of pizza are made with a superb thin, crisp-yet-chewy crust. Several calzones—a sort of pizza turnover—are also available, as are pastas, seafood, veal, and chicken entrees. For dessert there's a cannoli, spumoni ice cream, and a house-made tiramisu.

Tommy Toy's *655 Montgomery St./Washington St., in Washington and Montgomery Tower, in the Financial District, 397-4888, fax 397-0469. L M-F, D daily; $$$. Reservations advised. AE, MC, V. Valet parking $3.50.*

It's hard to imagine a more elegant, more romantic restaurant than this well-established hideaway. After passing through the dark entry, diners are greeted by the striking sight of giant goldfish in a tank and then seated in a refined room displaying authentic Asian antiques. The pampering service begins immediately and doesn't stop. To begin, diners are offered the chance to order delicious crisp drinks from the bar to enjoy while perusing the menu. Specializing in cuisine Chinoise, the specialty here is a blend of classic Chinese cuisine with traditional French presentation. The amazing fixed-price Signature Dinner *($48)* includes: minced squab Imperial; seafood bisque in a coconut shell crowned with puff pastry; an artistically presented whole fresh Maine lobster, shelled and sautéed with pine nuts and fresh mushrooms in a peppercorn sauce and served on a bed of angel hair crystal noodles; Peking duck wrapped in lotus buns; tender wok-charred medallion of beef with garlic and wine, served with four-flavors fried rice; and peach mousse in a strawberry compote beautifully swirled with hearts. The elaborate, elegant presentations are served on oversize plates, and a fresh hot finger towel is offered after each course. Chopsticks appear only by request.

Tuba Garden *3634 Sacramento St./Spruce St., 921-TUBA. L M-F, Sat & SunBr; $. Highchairs, boosters. Reservations advised. AE, MC, V.*

Located within an old Victorian on a low-key, high-quality shopping street, this pleasant spot offers comfortable indoor tables as well as outdoor seating in a garden, weather permitting. The work of local artists colorfully decorates the premises. Lunch items include smoked trout, soothing polenta spiced up with a pepper sauce, and a great hamburger served with house-made potato chips and sides of perfectly dressed shredded carrot and coleslaw. At brunch, the menu changes to cheese blintzes, Belgian waffles, and fresh seafood. The tempting desserts, which usually include an array of cakes, are all house-made.

Yet Wah *2140 Clement St./23rd Ave., in the Richmond, 387-8040. L & D daily; $$. Highchairs, boosters. Reservations advised. AE, MC, V.*

Once just a little hole-in-the-wall at a different location on the same street, this modest establishment has blossomed into something more. The long menu lists over 200 dishes, and the quality is generally good. Favorites include hot and sour soup, fried won tons stuffed with Chinese sausage, pot stickers, mu shu pork, Szechwan spiced beef, and ginger-garlic lamb. Explore the menu and enjoy the adventure of trying something new. How about dragon's eye fruit for dessert?

Branches are at 5238 Diamond Heights Boulevard *(at Clipper St., 282-0788)* and Pier 39 *(434-4430)*.

WHAT TO DO

GUIDED TOURS

– By Boat –

• **Blue and Gold Fleet Bay Tours** *Depart from Pier 39, 705-5444. Daily from 10am; from 11 in Jan & Feb. Adults $16, 62+ & 5-18 $8.*

This 1¼-hour narrated cruise of the bay goes out under the world's most beautiful bridge—the Golden Gate—and the world's longest bridge—the 8¼-mile-long San Francisco/ Oakland Bay Bridge. It also passes close to Alcatraz Island. A three-hour dinner cruise with live music is available in summer.

• **Red & White Fleet** *Depart from Pier 41 or Pier 43½, Fisherman's Wharf, (800) 229-2784, 546-2628. Schedules & prices vary.*

Tours by boat and bus are scheduled for San Francisco, Tiburon, Sausalito, Muir Woods, Angel Island, and the Wine Country, as well as further away to Monterey, Carmel, and Yosemite National Park.

• *Ruby* **Sailing Yacht** *At foot of Mariposa St./near 3rd St., 861-2165. Daily at 12:30 & 6. Adults $30, under 10 $15. Reservations required.*

Captain Joshua Pryor built the 64-foot steel sloop *Ruby* himself in 1979. He also sails her himself. On the lunch cruise, guests can dine on deli sandwiches either on the deck or below deck in the salon. The 1½-hour trip circles Alcatraz. An evening trip, lasting 2½ hours and including hors d'oeuvres, sails to Sausalito. Beer and wine are available at additional charge.

• **Whale-Watching Tours** *Depart from Fort Mason, (800) 326-7491, 474-3385. Sat, Sun, & some F; Jan-Apr only. $46-$48. Children must be at least 10. Reservations required.*

Sponsored by the non-profit Oceanic Society Expeditions, these all-day trips have two professional naturalists on board to explain all about the whales and interpret their behavior. Half-day trips depart from Princeton-by-the-Sea (see page 83).

Farallon Islands Nature Cruises *(Sat, Sun, & some F; June-Nov only. $58. Children must be at least 10. Reservations required.)* take participants 25 miles across the Pacific Ocean from the Golden Gate Bridge to this National Wildlife Refuge. These islands support the largest seabird rookery in the eastern Pacific south of Alaska and are the habitat to 200,000 nesting sea birds— including tufted puffins, loons, and auklets—plus sea lions and seals.

– By Bus –

• **Gray Line Tours** *(800) 826-0202, 558-9400. Fares vary; children under 5 free when sitting on parent's lap. Reservations required 1 day in advance.*

Day tours are available of San Francisco, Muir Woods/Sausalito, and the Wine Country. Dinner tours of San Francisco and other Bay Area locations are also scheduled. The deluxe San Francisco tour is enjoyed aboard a red double-decker, London-style bus.

• **3 Babes and a Bus** *552-CLUB. F & Sat 9:30pm-1:30am. $30. Must be 21 or older. Reservations advised.*

These babes and their bus pick up guests and take them out to party in the city's hottest dance clubs. The price includes pick-up, all cover charges, and priority entry. There is no need to worry about parking, taxi fares, or drinking and driving, and a variety of venues are experienced.

– By Car –
• **49-Mile Drive.**

This planned driving route through San Francisco hits most of the high points. For a free map of the route, contact the Convention & Visitors Bureau (see page 7).

– On Foot –
San Francisco is a walker's paradise. The city's naturally intriguing streets become even more interesting when walked with a knowledgeable guide. Even natives have been known to learn something new on such as tour.
• **Chinatown Walks.** See page 52.
• **City Guides** *557-4266. Free.*

Sponsored by the San Francisco Public Library, these informative tours last approximately 1½ hours and cover most of the city: Alamo Square, City Hall, Coit Tower, Haight-Ashbury, Historic Market Street, Jackson Square/Portsmouth Square, Japantown, Mission Murals, Montgomery Street, Nob Hill, North Beach, Pacific Heights Victorians, Presidio Museum, San Francisco Fire Department Museum, Union Square . . . and more! For a free schedule, send a stamped, self-addressed envelope to: City Guides, Main Library, Civic Center, San Francisco 94102.
• **Dashiell Hammett Tour** *939-1214. Sat at noon, May-Aug; by appt. rest of year. Adults $10, under 15 free. Meet at NW corner of Main Library, 100 Larkin St./Fulton St.*

While dashing off trivia and anecdotes, guide Don Herron leads walkers to landmarks from *The Maltese Falcon* and to all Hammett's known San Francisco residences. Herron, who is always appropriately attired in trench coat and fedora, has operated this tour since 1977. It is said to be the longest ongoing literary tour in the country. The tour lasts four hours and covers approximately three miles.
• **Golden Gate National Recreation Area** *923-WALK. Most are free. Reservations often required.*

A variety of ranger- and docent-led walks are scheduled in this expansive area.
• **Golden Gate Park Guided Walking Tours.** See page 71.
• **Mission Mural Walk** *348 Precita Ave./Folsom St., 285-2287. Sat at 1:30. Adults $4, under 18 $1.*

This two-hour tour begins at the **Precita Eyes Mural Arts Center** with a slide show and talk by a professional muralist, and is followed by a walk to view some of the 200-plus murals found in the Mission District.
• **Pacific Heights Walking Tour.** See page 58.
• **Wok Wiz Chinatown Tours** *(800) 281-9255, 355-9657, fax 355-5928. Daily at 10am. $35 with lunch, $25 without lunch; discounts for 62+ & under 12. Reservations required.*

Led by cookbook author Shirley Fong-Torres and her staff, these easy tours (no hills) take participants behind the scenes in this colorful and historic neighborhood. A dim sum lunch is optional.

– Factory Tours –
• **Anchor Steam Brewery** *1705 Mariposa St. /DeHaro, on Potrero Hill, 863-8350. M-F at 11 & 2; by appt. Free.*

The locally popular ale that is produced here at San Francisco's only remaining brewery is distributed to almost every state. After the hour-long tour, participants are treating to a generous tasting. Children are welcome but get only water at the end.

• **Basic Brown Bear Factory.** See page 74.

HISTORIC SITES

Alcatraz Island *(800) BAY-CRUISE, 546-2700, fax 541-2623. Daily departures; call for schedule. Adults $10, 62+ $8.25, 5-11 $4.75; includes audio tour; less expensive no-audio option avail. Reservations advised.*

Before Alcatraz was opened to the public in 1973, it served as a fort in the 19th century and as a federal penitentiary from 1934 to 1963. It was occupied by Native Americans from 1969 to 1971. During the time it was a maximum security prison, it was home to some of the country's most hardened criminals: Al Capone, George "Machine Gun" Kelly, Robert "Birdman of Alcatraz" Stroud. Now it is run by the national park service as part of the Golden Gate National Recreation Area—the largest urban park in the world. And it is as good as it's cracked up to be—the boat ride, the tour, and the 360-degree bay view. Boats from the Red & White Fleet are boarded at Pier 41, and after a short, scenic ride to this infamous island, visitors follow a self-guided tour. Several ranger-led tours are also scheduled each day on special topics. A top-notch audio tour of the cell block, narrated by former inmates and guards, is optional but highly recommended. It is interesting to note that the still-operating 214-foot-tall lighthouse here was built in 1854, when it was the first on the West Coast. No picnicking is permitted. Wear comfortable shoes, dress warmly, and expect cool, windy weather—even in summer.

Cable Cars *673-6864. Daily 6am-1am. Adults $2, 5-17 $1.*

These beloved objects have operated since 1873 and were designated the country's first moving National Historic Landmark in 1964. Before they were developed by Andrew Hallidie, horses had to pull carts up the city's steep hills. Many died in the process. Now 26 "single-enders" operate on the two Powell Street routes and 11 "double-enders" operate on the California Street run. Catch the Powell-Hyde line at the turnaround located at the base of Powell Street and ride it up and over the hills all the way to Aquatic Park. This line goes down the steepest hills and affords the most breathtaking views. The Powell-Mason line ends at Bay Street, about three blocks from Fisherman's Wharf. The less used California Street line begins at Market Street and runs along California Street, passing Chinatown and then climbing over Nob Hill, ending at Van Ness Avenue. Ticket machines are provided at turnarounds, but riders can also board at designated stops along the routes and pay the conductor.

Chinatown *Bounded by Broadway, Bush St., Kearny St., & Powell St.*

The most memorable way to enter Chinatown is on foot through the ornate dragon-crested archway located on Grant Avenue and Bush Street. Designed to the Taoist principles of Feng Shui, the gate features Foo dogs to scare away evil spirits, dragons for fertility and power, and fish for prosperity. Many visitors miss this unique experience in favor of driving to the heart of the action. Either way, a walk along pedestrian-crowded Grant Avenue, the city's oldest street, is quite an experience. With a population of approximately 80,000 residents and covering 24 square blocks, San Francisco's Chinatown is the largest Chinese community outside of Asia. For good souvenir hunting, stop in one of the many shops. Favorite items with children include golden dragon-decorated velvet slippers, rice candy in edible wrappers, and silk coin purses.

At 600 California Street, **Old St. Mary's Church** *(288-3840)*, which was built of brick in 1853, is the West Coast's first Roman Catholic cathedral. Half-hour chamber music concerts occur after noon mass every Tuesday and Thursday at 12:30; suggested donation is $3.

• **Chinese Culture Center** *750 Kearny St./Washington St., 3rd fl. in Holiday Inn, 986-1822, fax 986-2825. Tu-Sun 10-4; closed last 2 weeks in Dec. Free.*

This two-room gallery has a permanent exhibit of historical and contemporary Chinese art by both native Chinese and Chinese-Americans.

Cultural and culinary tours of Chinatown sponsored by the Chinese Culture Foundation are scheduled year-round; all require reservations. The **Culinary Walk** *(W at 10:30am. Adults $30, under 12 $15.)* introduces Chinese cuisine with stops in markets, at a fortune cookie factory, at an herb shop, and at a tea shop. It concludes with a dim sum lunch. The **Heritage Walk** *(Sat at 2pm. Adults $15, under 18 $5.)* stresses the history and cultural achievements of the area. Stops might include a Chinese newspaper office, a Chinese temple, and a historical society. **Chinese New Year Walks** *(Adults $15, under 18 $10. Reserve several months in advance.)* are given only during that time of year. A history of the holiday is presented, and all participants sample special Chinese sweets from a "Tray of Togetherness."

• **Dim Sum.** See page 31.

• **Fortune Cookie Factories.**

Always fun after a Chinatown meal is a walk through the narrow streets and alleys to find a fortune cookie factory. Though workers aren't often pleased to see tourists, it is usually possible to get at least a glimpse of the action by peeking in through a door or window. Proprietors are usually glad to sell cookies, and bags of broken "misfortune" cookies can be picked up at bargain prices.

• **Golden Gate Fortune Cookie Company** *56 Ross Alley/Washington St., 781-3956. Daily 10-7.* Tucked away in a picturesque alley in the heart of Chinatown, this factory also sells delicious mini-almond cookies.

• **Mee Mee Bakery** *1328 Stockton St./Broadway, 362-3204. M-Sat 10-4.* Located at the border of Chinatown and North Beach, this factory has been baking fortune cookies longer than anyone else in town. They also sell X-rated cookies, mini-almond cookies, and both chocolate and strawberry fortune cookies.

• **Grocery.**

May Wah Trading Co. *(1230 Stockton St./Pacific St., 433-3095.)* is well-stocked and provides a good browse. Exotic items to pick up for the home kitchen include powdered lemon grass, tiny containers of coconut milk, and exotic instant ramens.

• **Herb Shop.**

Superior Trading Co. *(837 Washington St./Grant Ave., 982-8722, fax 982-7786. Daily 9:30-6:30.)*, an interesting and somewhat mysterious shop, measures out aromatic herbs on scales. Unless actually planning to purchase something, it is best just to peek in the window.

• **Restaurants.**

Though locals often claim good Chinese restaurants aren't in Chinatown, in reality some are.

• **Far East Cafe** *631 Grant Ave./Sacramento St., 982-3245. L & D daily; $$. Highchairs, boosters. Reservations advised. AE, MC, V.* Looking much as it did when it opened in 1920, this intriguing restaurant has 30 private wooden booths with curtains for a door. These wonderful, cozy enclosures provide the ultimate in privacy. The extensive a la carte menu includes sizzling rice soup, fried won tons, cashew chicken, deep-fried squab, and a variety of chow mein and chop suey, and the family-style Cantonese dinner is always a good choice. Exotic shark's fin, bird's nest, and seaweed soups are also available.

• **Kowloon Vegetarian Restaurant** *909 Grant Ave./Washington St., 362-9888. L & D daily; $. Boosters. Reservations advised. MC, V.* This atmosphere-free cafe serves up some tasty gluten puffs and tofu-based dishes, as well as a large selection of dim sum. For an appetizer, don't miss the charming "bird nest" made with taro and filled with minced tofu, mushrooms, and vegetables. The house brown rice goes great with fake meat dishes such as sweet and sour "pork" and roast "goose." For dessert, step up to the counter and pick from not-too-sweets such as giant almond cookies, and exotics such as custard balls mimicking the look of a hard-boiled egg.

• **Lichee Garden** *1416 Powell St./Vallejo St., 397-2290. Dim sum daily 7-3; L & D daily; $. Highchairs, boosters. Reservations advised; accepted for dim sum 1 day in advance. AE, MC, V.* Located on the North Beach side of Broadway, this family-style restaurant is known for its exceptional soups, its Hong Kong-style crispy noodles, and its crispy Peking-style spareribs. It's a good idea to come here with a large group: Seating is at mostly large round tables, portions are generous, and sodas are served in their original large plastic containers.

• **Lotus Garden** *532 Grant Ave./California St., 397-0707. L & D Tu-Sun; $. Highchairs, boosters. Reservations taken. AE, MC, V.* This simple restaurant is noteworthy because of its wide selection of vegetarian, vegan, and imitation meat items.

• **Lucky Creation** *854 Washington St./Grant Ave., 989-0818. L & D Thur-Tu; $. Boosters. No cards.* In the sparest of atmospheres, this all vegetarian restaurant dishes up some of the most fabulous veggie dishes in town. Among the many choices are won tons and a stunningly presented sautéed black mushrooms with baby bok choy. Clay pot dishes, noodle dishes (including wonderful chow fun items), and rice plates are available, as are imitation meat dishes made with gluten.

• **New Woey Loy Goey Cafe** *699 Jackson St./Grant Ave., 399-0733. L & D daily; $. Highchairs, boosters, booths. No reservations. No cards.* This subterranean diner has a Cantonese menu. Comfortable seating is provided in booths and at a counter. But the name alone is reason enough to dine here.

• **The Pot Sticker** *150 Waverly Pl./Washington St., 397-9985. L & D daily; $. Highchairs, boosters. Reservations taken. AE, MC, V.* Situated in a picturesque alley famous for its historic buildings sporting ornate painted balconies, this spot is known for its lightly spiced Mandarin-style cuisine and handmade noodles and dumplings. Dishes tend to be lightly sauced with lots of vegetables. Good choices include hot and sour soup, Mongolian beef, and princess chicken. Dramatic Hunan crispy whole fish is served with hot sauce.

• **Sam Wo** *813 Washington St./Grant Ave., 982-0596. L & D daily; $. No reservations. No cards.* People once came here for the experience of being insulted by, and to watch the reaction of others being insulted by, Edsel Ford Fong—the infamous waiter who once reigned over the second floor. Unfortunately, for those of us who actually became fond of him, Fong passed away in

1984. It is doubtful a replacement could ever be found. So now the main reason to come here is for the fresh homemade noodles and the unusual layout of the tiny dining rooms. Entering this "jook joint" through the cramped and busy kitchen and climbing the narrow stairs to the second and third floors is not unlike entering a submarine, only going up instead of down. Diners sit on stools at tables unexpectedly topped with real marble. Waiters shout orders down an ancient dumbwaiter by which finished dishes are later delivered. The house specialty, noodle soup, is available in 12 varieties. Won ton soups and chow fun dishes are also on the menu. The cold roast pork rice noodle roll is especially good. No soft drinks, milk, or coffee are on the menu, and no fortune cookies arrive with the amazingly inexpensive check. It is worth knowing this place stays open until 3 a.m.

> • **Taiwan.** *289 Columbus Ave./Broadway, 989-6789.* For description, see page 326.

• **Temples.**

> Though there are many temples in Chinatown, only one seems to welcome visitors: **Tin How Taoist Temple** *(125-129 Waverly Pl./Washington St., 391-4841. Daily 10-5 & 7-9pm.).* Located in the heart of Chinatown on a lane known for its ornate, colorfully-painted balconies, this temple is easy to find. Just follow the scent of incense up the narrow wooden stairs to the fourth floor. Built in 1852, it is the oldest Chinese temple in the U.S. Though there is no charge to visit, donations are appreciated and an appropriate reverent behavior is expected. Bear in mind that the temple is still used for worship.

City Lights Book Store *261 Columbus Ave./Broadway, in North Beach, 362-8193, fax 362-4921. Daily 10am-midnight.*

> Founded in 1953 by beatnik poet Lawrence Ferlinghetti, who still looks after the business, this multi-level bookstore is said to be the first in the country to specialize in paperbacks. Many obscure titles are in its eclectic collection, providing great browsing. Not content to just sell books, the proprietors published Allen Ginsburg's *Howl* and continue to publish unusual books.

Cliff House Visitors Center *Point Lobos Ave./48th Ave., 556-8642. Daily 10-4. Free.*

> Learn the history of the Cliff House area from the 1890s to the present. Adjacent **Sutro Baths**, once the world's largest indoor swimming pool complex, was filled with ocean water via an ingenious system developed by Adolph Sutro. The pools could hold 10,000 swimmers and 7,500 observers! Free ranger-led tours of the ruins are scheduled each month. See also page 31.

• **Musee Mecanique** *386-1170. Daily 11-7; in summer 10-8. Free admission.*

> Located across from the visitors center, this "mechanical museum" is filled with old arcade games, some dating from the 17th century. It is said to be the world's largest collection of antique coin-operated machines. For just a quarter it is possible to operate a miniature steam shovel and collect 90 seconds worth of gumballs, or to see naughty Marietta sunbathing in 3-D realism. Highlights include a player piano, a mechanical horse ride, and Laughing Sal and her original soundtrack—both rescued from the Fun House at the now torn-down Playland-at-the-Beach. Beeping modern video games are in the back, where they belong.

• **Giant Camera Obscura** *750-0415. Daily 11-sunset, weather permitting. Adults $1, 2-12 50¢.*

> Also nearby is this reproduction of Leonardo daVinci's 16th-century invention. The personalized tour is entertaining and educational.

• **Seal Rocks.**

> Barking sea lions and brown pelicans share space on these historic rocks. They can be seen with just the naked eye or through an antique telescope.

Coit Tower *At top of Lombard St., in North Beach, 362-0808. Daily 10-6. Adults $3, 63+ $2, 6-12 $1.*

Located atop fashionable Telegraph Hill, this 210-foot-tall tower (approximately 18 stories) offers magnificent 360-degree views. Colorful painted murals on the ground floor walls date from 1934. Depicting area activities during the Depression, they were controversial at the time because of left-wing political content. The fee includes an attendant-operated elevator ride to the top. Parking is extremely limited. Visitors who walk or take the 39 Coit bus up, can then walk down the **Filbert Street Steps**, past the **Grace Marchant Garden**, to Levi Plaza, located near Battery Street.

Crookedest Street in the World *Lombard St. between Hyde St. & Leavenworth St.*

This famous curvy street is one-way downhill. Drivers must maneuver over a bumpy brick-paved road with eight tight turns while trying not to be distracted by the magnificent view. Get here by driving up the steep incline on the west side of Lombard Street, or, for an easier time of it, drive up from the south side of Hyde Street.

The **other crookedest street** is Vermont Street, between 20th and 22nd streets on Potrero Hill. Though it has only six turns, they are said to be tighter than Lombard's.

The city's **steepest streets** are said to be Filbert Street between Hyde and Leavenworth streets (with a 31.5 percent grade), 22nd Street between Church and Vicksburg streets (with a 31.5 percent grade), and Jones Street between Union and Filbert streets (with a 29 percent grade).

Fort Mason *Laguna St./Marina Blvd., 441-3400.*

In addition to housing the park headquarters for the GGNRA (see page 68), this complex of buildings houses theaters, art galleries, museums, and myriad other facilities. Highlights include:

• **Book Bay Bookstore** *Bldg. C, 771-1076. Tu-Sun 11-5.*

Thousands of bargain books, as well as records and tapes, await. The West's largest **Used Book Sale** is held each September. Proceeds benefit the library.

• **Greens** restaurant. See page 36.
• **The Mexican Museum.** See page 60.
• **Museo Italo-Americano.** See page 60.
• **San Francisco Craft & Folk Art Museum.** See page 66.
• **Young Performers Theatre.** See page 74.

Fort Point National Historic Site *Located directly under the south anchorage of the Golden Gate Bridge; take Lincoln Blvd. to Long Ave., turn left, at bottom follow road along water to fort; 556-1693. W-Sun 10-5. Free; audio tour: adults $2.50, children $1.*

Built in 1861, this is the only Civil War-era fort on the West Coast. Its four tiers were once home to 126 cannon. Each winter **Candlelight Fort Tours** *(Nov-Feb; 6:30-9pm. Participants must be 15 or older. Reservations required.)* are scheduled. Participants see the fort from the viewpoint of a Civil War soldier. What was it like in the 1860s to live in drafty quarters heated by fireplaces and lighted by candles? What kind of food was eaten, and how was it prepared? These questions and more are answered on the fort tour and following walk through the 1870 gun emplacements located south of the fort.

Golden Gate Bridge.

Once called "the bridge that couldn't be built," this magnificent example of man's ingenuity and perseverance is one of San Francisco's most famous sights. Measuring 6,450 feet, it is the longest suspension bridge in the world, and its 746-foot-high towers are the tallest ever built. Many people are disappointed to discover that the bridge is not a golden color. In fact, it is painted with a protective dull red-orange coating. The color, known officially as International Orange, was chosen by the bridge's architect, Irving Morrow, to make it visible in dense fog. Crossing it is a must—by car, foot, or bicycle. The round-trip is about two miles, and views are breathtaking. It is interesting to note that bungee-jumping is said to have originated here in 1979.

Grace Cathedral *1100 California St./ Taylor St., 749-6300. Daily 8-6; tours available. Free.*

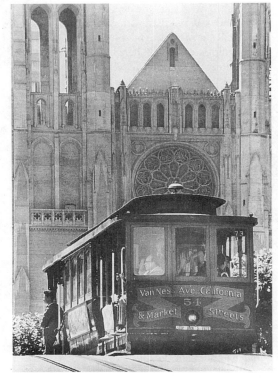

Located atop Nob Hill, this majestic French Gothic cathedral stands 265 feet tall and is the largest in the western U.S. It is graced with more than 60 opulent stained-glass windows, and its gilded bronze entrance doors are exact replicas of Lorenzo Ghiberti's Doors of Paradise at the Baptistry in Florence, Italy. Concerts using the cathedral's renowned 7,400-pipe organ are often scheduled, sometimes accompanied by the 44-bell carillon. The cathedral's reverberant acoustics and architecturally magnificent interior make these memorable experiences. The **Labyrinth**, a unique tool for walking meditation, is available both inside the cathedral and outside on a new plaza.

Annual **Cathedral Choir Christmas Concerts** feature the Grace

Cathedral Choir of Men and Boys singing both traditional and new carols. They are wondrous, inspirational events. A Festival of Lessons and a Midnight Mass are traditional on Christmas Eve, and a celebratory New Year's Eve event is also scheduled each year. And every few years the cathedral is the unusual, yet appropriate, setting for a screening of the original 1923 silent film classic *The Hunchback of Notre Dame* with live accompaniment by the organ.

Haight-Ashbury *Haight St. between Stanyan St. & Masonic St.*

It's almost possible to step back in time to the Summer of Love here. A few locals still don bell-bottoms, tie-dyed shirts, and love beads, and some of those items are still for sale in some shops. Not gentrified, the area is still a little rough around the edges, and Haight Street is now lined with an assortment of colorful boutiques and inexpensive restaurants and coffeehouses.

Visiting here also permits the chance to see some of the area's magnificent Victorian houses, including the most famous ones at 710 Ashbury, where The Grateful Dead once lived, and the mansion at 2400 Fulton, where the Jefferson Airplane lived. Janis Joplin once lived with Country Joe McDonald in apartment three at 112 Page Street, Big Brother & the Holding Company formed at 1090 Page Street, and the first free medical clinic in the U.S. still operates at 558 Clayton Street. On a more somber note, the notorious Manson "family" once lived at 636 Cole Street.

Historic Houses.

San Francisco is known for its abundance of beautiful turn-of-the-century Victorian houses. One of the pleasures of living here is visiting people who actually live in them. Visitors to the city interested in capturing a taste of that pleasure will enjoy stopping in at the two historic homes open to the public.

To see some of the city's "painted ladies," as the many colorfully painted Victorian homes are sometimes called, visit the area around **Alamo Square** at Hayes and Steiner streets. The 700 block of Steiner is packed with Queen Anne Victorians. Nicknamed "postcard row," it is often photographed commercially from the top of the park, with the skyline in the distance. Another good area is along the **Golden Gate Park Panhandle**, particularly on the Fell Street side, where well-maintained mansions are plentiful. (It is interesting to note that the Panhandle was originally the carriage entrance to the park and that it is home to some of the park's oldest trees—approximately 50 species.)

And, of course, everyone wants to see the house used in exterior scenes for *Mrs. Doubtfire*. Check it out in Pacific Heights at 2640 Steiner Street. Seeing the house from the outside will do. Interior scenes were filmed in a studio so there is no need to peek in windows.

• Haas-Lilienthal House *2007 Franklin St./Jackson St., 441-3004. House tour: W 12-4, last tour at 3; & Sun 1-4:30, last tour at 4. Adults $5, seniors & under 12 $3. Strollers not permitted. Walking tour: Sun at 12:30. Adults $5, seniors & under 12 $3.*

In 1886 architect Peter R. Schmidt built this 24-room, 7½-bath mansion of fir and redwood for Bertha and William Haas, a mercantile grocer. It cost $18,500. (Average homes then cost about $2,000.) The house survived the infamous 1906 earthquake relatively unscathed, with a small bulge in the plaster the only visible damage. It also escaped the fire that followed, though Mr. Haas's downtown offices were destroyed. Family members occupied the house until 1973, when it was donated to the Foundation for San Francisco's Architectural Heritage. Most of the furnishings, which include a lovely and extensive set of matching art noveau pieces in the main bedroom, are original to the house. Children often find the doll house in the second-floor nursery especially interesting.

On Sundays, a foundation-sponsored **walking tour** of the surrounding Pacific Heights neighborhood focuses on the exteriors of some of San Francisco's finest Victorian and Edwardian homes.

• **Octagon House** *2645 Gough St./Union St., 441-7512. Open 2nd & 4th Thur & 2nd Sun of month, 12-3; closed Jan. By donation.*

Built in 1861, when this architectural style was a fad throughout the country, this eight-sided house is now one of only two left in San Francisco. The National Society of The Colonial Dames of America in California has restored and furnished it and turned it into the only museum of Colonial and Federal decorative arts on the West Coast. Items on display date from 1700 to 1830 and are labeled with background information. Of special interest is a display featuring the signatures of 54 of the original 56 signers of the Declaration of Independence. The house's well-groomed garden and adjacent **Allyne Park** are both perfect for a stroll.

Mission San Francisco de Asis *16th St./Dolores St., in the Mission, 621-8203. Daily 9-4. Adults $2, 5-12 $1.*

Popularly known as Mission Dolores, this small mission is sixth in the California chain of 21. The mission chapel, completed in 1791, is the oldest intact building in the city. Its cool adobe interior offers pleasant respite from the occasional hot San Francisco day. The entire complex was restored from 1990 through 1995. Of special interest is the chapel ceiling, which is painted in Ohlone tribal patterns and colors originally produced by vegetable dyes. Also, the picturesque enclosed cemetery garden has been entirely re-landscaped to period correctness. All the plants now found here were once used in some way by the resident Native Americans. A tiny museum completes the complex.

Presidio of San Francisco *Visitor Center: on Montgomery St., Bldg. 102, 561-4323. Daily 10-5. Free.*

Used as a military garrison by Spain, Mexico, and the U.S., the Presidio was established by

Spain in 1776, taken over by Mexico in 1822, and then taken over by the U.S. as an Army post in 1846. It played a critical role in providing refuge for the 1906 earthquake victims. The Presidio is undergoing continuous major changes as it transforms from being an Army post into being a recreational area. Currently it has 11 miles of hiking trails and 14 miles of biking routes. Contact the Visitor Center for information on guided walks and bicycle tours. For information on the Presidio Museum, see page 65.

MUSEUMS

– Art Museums –

Ansel Adams Center for Photography *250 Fourth St./Howard St., South of Market, 495-7000, fax 495-8517. Tu-Sun 11-5, to 8 on 1st Thur of month. Adults $4, seniors & 12-17 $2.*

Dedicated to presenting photography as the model of today's visual culture, this museum has five galleries. One is dedicated to the work of Ansel Adams.

California Palace of the Legion of Honor *34th Ave./Clement St., in **Lincoln Park**, in the Richmond, 750-3600. Tu-Sun 9:30-5, to 8:45 on 1st Sat of month. Adults $7, 65+ $5, 12-17 $4.*

Situated on a scenic knoll overlooking the Golden Gate Bridge, this is the only museum in the country exhibiting primarily French art. Rodin's earliest casting of his sculpture, "The Thinker," greets visitors as they approach the entrance to this impressive neoclassical marble structure—a replica of the Hotel de Salm in Paris, where Napoleon established his new Order of the Legion of Honor in the 18th century. A recent expansion and reorganization has this museum holding the city's collection of European and ancient art. The museum was given to the city of San Francisco on Armistice Day in 1924 and is dedicated to the memory of California men who died in World War I.

The entrance to the **Holocaust Memorial** is on the north side of the parking circle. A semi-circular stairway leads down to an area where the cast bronze, white-painted pieces created by sculptor George Segal are displayed.

A scenic drive can be enjoyed by leaving the museum via Lincoln Avenue, on the north side of the museum. Follow it to its exit on Lombard. This route has several vista points of the Golden Gate Bridge and passes by Baker Beach, goes through the elegant Sea Cliff residential area, and continues into the Presidio.

Cartoon Art Museum *814 Mission St./4th St., South of Market, CAR-TOON. W-F 11-5, Sat 10-5, Sun 1-5. Adults $4, 62+ & students $3, 6-12 $2; free 1st W of month.*

Presenting both a permanent collection and changing special exhibits, this museum show-cases important developments in cartoon history from the early 18th century to the present. One of only two such museums in the country, its aim is "to preserve this unique art form and to enrich the public's knowledge of its cultural and aesthetic value." Free cartooning workshops on Saturday afternoons are included with admission.

Center for the Arts Yerba Buena Gardens *701 Mission St./Third St., South of Market, 978-2700, tickets 978-ARTS. Gallery: Tu-Sun 11-6, 1st Thur of month to 8. Adults $4, seniors & under 17 $2, free 6-8pm on 1st Thur of month.*

Art shows and live entertainment emphasizing the diverse artists and communities of the region are presented here. The center is located in Yerba Buena Gardens, a new development that holds an outdoor stage, two cafes, a butterfly garden, a redwood grove, public sculptures, a waterfall, and a multi-language memorial to Dr. Martin Luther King, Jr.

The Mexican Museum *In Fort Mason Center, Bldg. D, Laguna St./Marina Blvd., 441-0404. W-F 12-5, Sat & Sun 11-5. Adults $3, 11-16 $2; free 1st W of month, 12-7.*

Founded in 1975, this is the first museum in the U.S. devoted to Mexican and Mexican-American art. Exhibits change regularly. When space permits, items from the permanent pre-Columbian collection are displayed.

M. H. de Young Memorial Museum *In Golden Gate Park, 750-3600. W-Sun 9:30-5. Adults $6, 12-17 $3; free 1st W of month.*

A significant collection of American paintings is displayed here on colorful walls. It includes sculpture and decorative arts from colonial times into the mid-20th century as well as the country's best collection of American trompe l'oeil paintings from the turn of the century. The permanent collection of art from Africa, Oceania, Mesoamerica, and Central and South America features outstanding works from ancient to modern times; many are not seen elsewhere.

For three days every March the museum galleries are stunningly decorated with fresh flowers. For **Bouquets to Art,** members of Bay Area flower clubs and professional florists design arrangements inspired by museum paintings. Some mimic the paintings, other pick up the colors or feeling. Overall they enliven the galleries

The cafeteria-style **Cafe de Young** *(752-0116. L W-Sun; $. No reservations. No cards.)* serves simple foods prepared eloquently. The kitchen makes most items from scratch using fresh ingredients, and the menu offers a selection of salads and sandwiches along with a daily soup and pasta salad special. Diners can sit in a warm area inside, where tables are decorated with fresh flowers, or outside at umbrella-shaded tables surrounding a garden fountain.

Adjoining the de Young, the **Asian Art Museum** *(379-8801)* displays the best Asian collection in the U.S. It is the largest museum in the western world devoted exclusively to Asian art, and it also holds the largest collection of Indian sculpture outside India. This museum is scheduled to move to a Civic Center location in the year 2000.

Museo ItaloAmericano *In Fort Mason Center, Bldg. C, Laguna St./Marina Blvd., 673-2200, fax 673-2292. W-Sun 12-5. Adults $2, seniors & 12-18 $1; free 1st W of month.*

Dedicated to displaying the works of Italian and Italian-American artists, this museum's small exhibit space is stark and quiet.

San Francisco Museum of Modern Art

151 Third St./Howard St., South of Market, 357-4000, fax 357-4158. Thur-Tu 11-6, Thur to 9. Adults $7, 62+ & students 13+ with ID $3.50; reduced admission Thur 6-9: adults $3.50, students $1.75; free 1st Tu of month.

Re-situated now in a striking new building, this museum was the first in the West devoted entirely to 20th-century art. Its collection includes abstract art, photography, and the work of acclaimed contemporary artists. The museum gift shop holds an exceptional array of merchandise, and **Caffe Museo** offers a menu of scrumptious meals and light snacks.

– Floating Museums –

The collection of historic ships berthed along the San Francisco waterfront is the largest (by weight) in the world.

San Francisco Maritime National Historical Park.

• **Maritime Museum** *On Beach St./at foot of Polk St., across from Ghirardelli Square, 556-3002. Daily 10-5; guided tours daily at 12. Free.*

The architecturally interesting art deco building housing this museum was built by the Work Project Administration (WPA) in 1939. Appropriately, it resembles a ship, though it was originally meant to be used as a nightclub and aquatic activities center. The main floor displays parts of old ships, elaborately carved and painted figureheads, and exquisitely detailed ship models. The second floor is home to more models as well as to artifacts, paintings, photos, and maps. The museum hosts an annual **Festival of the Sea** *(929-0202 ext.22. Free.)* in September featuring sea music concerts, demonstrations of sailor arts, lectures, films, and sea poetry readings.

• **Hyde Street Pier** *2905 Hyde St./Jefferson St., 556-3002. Daily 9:30-5; in summer 10-6. Adults $3, seniors & 12-17 $1, family $7; free first Tu of month.*

The vessels moored on this scenic pier represent the time period from the turn of the century through World War II—a period of rapid growth for San Francisco begun by the 1849 Gold Rush. During this time the city was an important shipping center.

• *Balclutha.* A Cape Horn sailing ship built in Scotland in 1886, this 301-foot steel-hulled merchant ship carried whiskey, wool, and rice, but mainly coal, to San Francisco. On her return sailing to Europe she carried grain from California. Typical of Victorian British merchant ships, she is described colorfully by the men who sailed her as a "blue water, square-rigged, lime juice windbag." She is the last of the Cape Horn fleet and ended her sailing career as an Alaskan salmon ship. Renovated by donated labor and goods, she was opened to the public in 1955. Anchors and other maritime artifacts are displayed in the hold below her main deck, where interpretive exhibits also depict life on board.

• *Eureka.* Originally named the *Ukiah,* this double-ended, wooden-hulled ferry was built in Tiburon in 1890 to carry railroad cars and passengers across the bay. In 1922 she was rebuilt to carry automobiles and passengers and renamed the *Eureka.* Later she served as a commuter ferry (the largest in the world) between San Francisco and Sausalito, and yet later as a ferry for train passengers arriving in San Francisco from Oakland. She held 2,300 people plus 120 automobiles. Her four-story "walking beam" steam engine is the only such engine still afloat in the U.S. A model demonstrates its operation, and a ranger-guided tour through the engine room is sometimes available. Two decks are open to the public. The lower deck houses a display of antique cars, and the main deck features original benches and a historical photo display.

• **C.A. Thayer**. A fleet of 900 ships once carried lumber from the north coast forests to California ports. Only two of these ships still exist. One is the *C.A. Thayer*—a three-mast lumber schooner built in Fairhaven (near Eureka) in 1895. She made her last voyage in 1950 as a fishing ship. She was the very last commercial sailing ship in use on the West Coast. Visitors can descend into her dank wooden hold to see the crew's bunk room and then ascend to the captain's lushly furnished, oak-paneled cabin—complete with a gilded canary cage. A 25-minute film of her last voyage is shown several times each day, and guided tours are available. A fascinating way to experience this ship is at one of the **chantey sings** *(556-1871. 3rd Sat of month, 8pm-12; children's program 3-5pm. Reservations required. Free.)* sponsored by the National Park Service and held in her cozy hold. Participants should dress warmly and bring something to sit on as well as a chantey or two to share. A little something to wet the whistle wouldn't hurt either.

More ships moored at the pier are not open for boarding. The *Alma*, a scow schooner built in 1891 at Hunters Point, is a specialized cargo carrier and the last of her kind still afloat. The *Eppleton Hall*, built in England in 1914 and used in the canals there to tow coal ships, is the only ship in the collection not directly associated with West Coast maritime history. The *Hercules* is an ocean-going tugboat built in 1907. And the *Wapama*, the last surviving example of a steam schooner, is currently being restored in Sausalito.

Non-floating displays at the pier include a turn-of-the-century ark (or houseboat), a restored donkey engine that is sometimes operated for visitors, and the reconstructed sales office of the Tubbs Cordage Company.

S.S. Jeremiah O'Brien *Berthed at Pier 32, on The Embarcadero south of the Bay Bridge anchorage, 441-3101. M-F 9-3, Sat & Sun 9-4. Adults $5, seniors $3, 10-18 $2, under 10 $1.*

This massive 441-foot vessel is the last unaltered Liberty Ship from World War II still in operating condition. Between 1941 and 1945, in an all-out effort to replace the cargo ships being sunk in huge numbers by enemy submarines, 2,751 Liberty Ships were built to transport troops and supplies. At that time shipyards operated around the clock. Each ship was assembled from pre-fabricated sections and took only between six and eight weeks to build. Shockingly large, the *O'Brien* was built in South Portland, Maine in 1943. She was in operation for 33 years and sailed from England to Normandy during the D-Day invasion. In 1978 she was declared a National Monument. Since then dedicated volunteers, many of whom served on similar ships, have been working to restore her to her original glory. Visitors have access to almost every part of the ship, including sleeping quarters, captain's quarters, wheel house, and guns as well as the catwalks in the eerie three-story engine room. The triple expansion steam engine is operated nine weekends each year. The public can purchase tickets for the annual **Seamen's Memorial Cruise** each May, and the **Bay Cruise** each October during Fleet Week.

USS Pampanito *At Pier 45, foot of Taylor St., 929-0202. Daily 9-6. Adults $5, 6-12 $3.*

This 312-foot-long World War II submarine was built in Portsmouth New Hampshire in 1943. She is credited with the September 12, 1944 sinking of a 10,500-ton Japanese transport and 5,100-ton tanker as well as the destruction of a third ship in the South China Sea. She also rescued a group of British and Australian POWs. The self-guided tour is enhanced via an electronic wand that is activated at stations throughout the submarine. While walking through the cramped belly of the sub, a narrative by Captain Edward Beach, author of *Run Silent, Run Deep*, helps listeners imagine what it must have been like for men to be cooped up in this small space for days at a time.

Open Ships.

For information about visiting ships that are open for viewing, call the Port of San Francisco at 274-0400.

– Science Museums –

California Academy of Sciences *In Golden Gate Park, 750-7145, fax 750-7346. Daily 10-5; in summer 9-6. Adults $7, 65+ & 12-17, $4, 6-11 $1.50; free 1st W of month. Planetarium: Adults $2.50, under 18 $1.25. Laserium: 750-7138. Thur-Sun. Adults $5-$8, 6-12 $5. Laserium not recommended for children under 6.*

Founded in 1853 following the Gold Rush, this is the oldest scientific institution in the West and one of the ten largest natural history museums in the world. And this impressive museum complex grows better all the time. Visitors can experience a simulated 4.0 and 5.7 earthquake, watch time march on via a Foucault pendulum, and view a 1,350-pound quartz cluster in the impressive Gem & Mineral Hall. The permanent Far Side of Science Gallery exhibits original *Far Side* cartoons by Gary Larson. More exhibits include bird and animal dioramas, most notably the Wild California hall featuring life-size elephant seals and a 14,000-gallon aquarium, the African Water Hole featuring authentic animal sounds synchronized to a dawn-to-dusk lighting cycle, and Life Through Time, which focuses on evolution and takes visitors  on a dinosaur-studded 3.5 billion-year journey through life on Earth.

A classic European-style aquarium, the **Steinhart Aquarium** exhibits hundreds of fish tanks as well as a popular Blackfooted Penguin Environment *(feedings at 11:30 & 4)*, a tropical shark habitat, and The Swamp—featuring a waterfall and home to alligators, turtles, and snakes. Said to have the most diverse collection of species in the world, the aquarium also displays the largest living tropical coral reef in the country. The California Tidepool permits handling live sea animals such as sea stars and urchins, and the donut-shaped 100,000-gallon Fish Roundabout tank puts the viewers on the inside and the fish on the outside.

The largest planetarium in Northern California, **Morrison Planetarium** has a popular Star Talk program that provides information about what can be viewed in the current night sky. **The Christmas Star** has been presented annually in December since the planetarium opened in 1952. Viewers are taken back in time to view the night sky as it is believed to have appeared to the Wise Men in Nazareth almost 2,000 years ago. Evening **Laserium** shows project pulsating images on the planetarium ceiling. (The term "laserium" is a combination of the words "laser" and "planetarium.") A lightshow is coordinated to a music track by a live "laserist." The schedule offers rock and pop shows, and the sound level is plenty loud. Tickets can be purchased in advance ((510) 762-BASS) and at the academy's front entrance a half-hour before show time.

Exploratorium *3601 Lyon St., in the Marina, 561-0360, fax 561-0307. Tu-Sun 10-5, W to 9:30; in summer daily 10-6, W to 9:30. Adults $9, 65+ $7, 6-17 $5, 3-5 $2.50; free 1st W of month.*

Located inside the **Palace of Fine Arts,** which was designed by architect Bernard Maybeck in 1915 as part of the Panama-Pacific Exposition (an early World's Fair celebrating the opening of the Panama Canal) and is said to be the world's largest artificial ruin, this cavernous museum makes scientific and natural phenomena understandable through a collection of over 650 hands-on exhibits. It has been described by a former editor of *Scientific American* as the best sci-

ence museum in the world. Visitors can experience a dizzying ride on a Momentum Machine, step through a miniature tornado, and encase themselves in bubbles. To the shrieking delight of youngsters, a walk-in Shadow Box allows reverse images to remain on a wall. Teenage "Explainers" wearing easy-to-see orange vests wander the premises ready to help. Reservations should be made several weeks in advance to experience the **Tactile Dome** *(561-0362. Tickets $12, includes museum admission.)*, a geodesic dome with 13 chambers through which visitors can walk, crawl, slide, climb, and tumble in complete darkness with only their sense of touch to guide them. This experience is not recommended for children under age 7. It is pleasant to picnic outside by the picturesque reflecting pond populated with ducks and even a few swans.

The **Wave Organ,** a project sponsored by the Exploratorium, is located across Marina Boulevard at the eastern tip of the breakwater forming the Marina Yacht Harbor. This unusual musical instrument was designed by artist Peter Richards in collaboration with stonemason George Gonzales. Consisting of more than 20 pipes extending down through the breakwater into the bay, the organ provides a constant symphony of natural music. Listeners can relax in a small granite and marble amphitheater and enjoy views of the San Francisco skyline. The organ plays most effectively at high tide.

– Miscellaneous Museums –

Cable Car Museum *1201 Mason St./Washington St., 474-1887. Daily 10-5; in summer to 6. Free.*
Located two blocks from the heart of Chinatown, this interesting museum is inside the lovely brick cable car barn and powerhouse dating from the 1880s. Here visitors can view the huge, noisy flywheels controlling the underground cables that move the cable cars along at 9½-miles per hour. Three retired cable cars—including one from the original 1873 fleet—and assorted artifacts are on display, and an informative film with vintage photographs explains how the cable cars actually work. To complete the experience, catch a cable car across the street and take a ride downtown or to Fisherman's Wharf.

California Historical Society Museum *678 Mission St./3rd St., South of Market, 357-1848. Tu-Sat 1-5. Adults $3, 65+ & students $1, under 6 free.*
Recently moved from its former home in Pacific Heights, this small museum has set up shop within the former Hundley Hardware Building. Founded in 1871, the society's collection of artifacts documents California's history from the 16th century through the present. That adds up to over 500,000 photographs and 150,000 manuscripts, as well as thousands of books, maps, paintings, and emphera (the official word for odds and ends).

Guiness Museum of World Records *235 Jefferson St./Taylor St., at Fisherman's Wharf, 771-9890. Sun-Thur 11-10, F & Sat 10am-midnight. Adults $6.50, 62+ & 13-17 $5.50, 5-12 $3.50.*
The superlatives are all here: the smallest bicycle, the tiniest book, the biggest electric guitar, and much, much more.

Museum of the City of San Francisco *Beach St./Leavenworth St., in The Cannery, 3rd floor, 928-0289. W-Sun 10-4. Free.*
Particularly fascinating exhibits here relate to the 1906 earthquake. A meticulously restored 13th-century Moorish mosaic ceiling of hand-carved wood acquired from Hearst's collection is displayed, and an annex displays a collection of vintage movie projectors (the San Francisco area was the original home of the motion picture industry).

North Beach Museum *1435 Stockton St./Columbus, on 2nd fl. of EurekaBank, 391-6210. M-Thur 9-4, F 9-6. Free.*
Nostalgic photographs from this area's past are displayed along with an assortment of interesting artifacts.

Presidio Museum *At Funston Ave./Lincoln Blvd., 561-4331. W-Sun 10-4:30. Free.*
Housed in the oldest structure on the post, this small museum was the original post hospital. It documents the story of the Spanish, Mexican, and American armies. Outside, the front lawn is punctuated with obsolete cannons and artillery. Inside, a warren of rooms hold displays of artifacts and an extensive collection of historic photos covering the Spanish period through Vietnam. Children particularly enjoy the large collection of uniforms and the huge dioramas showing the Spanish Presidio as it appeared at various times—in the 1790s, in the 1906 earthquake and fire, and during the 1915 Panama Pacific International Exposition. Two restored shacks used for temporary housing after the '06 quake are on view behind the museum. (Approximately 17,000 such shacks were erected all over the city after the earthquake.)

Randall Museum *190 Museum Way/Roosevelt Way, near 14th St., 554-9600. Tu-Sat 10-5. Free.*
Located below Buena Vista Heights, this small museum has an indoor Animal Room inhabited by uncaged but tethered hawks and owls and other small, accessible animals. Most are

recovering from injuries inflicted in the wild. A highlight is the Petting Corral, where children can pet domesticated animals such as rabbits, chickens, and ducks. Exhibits are few but include an operating seismograph as well as dinosaur and fossil displays. Nature walks, movies, and children's science and arts and crafts classes are scheduled regularly.

On the second and fourth Saturday afternoon of each month, the Golden Gate Model Railroaders show off their **model railroad** *(12:30-5. Free.)*.

Ripley's Believe It or Not! Museum *175 Jefferson St./Taylor St., on Fisherman's Wharf, 771-6188, fax 771-1246. Sun-Thur 10-10, F & Sat to 12; in summer Sun-Thur 9am-11pm, F & Sat 10am-midnight. Adults $8.50, 60+ & 13-17 $7, 5-12 $5.25.*

Among the 250-plus exhibits from Ripley's personal collection of oddities are a cable car made from 300,000 match sticks and an authentic shrunken torso from Ecuador that was once owned by Ernest Hemingway. All this, and 2,000 more curiosities. It's unbelievable!

San Francisco Craft & Folk Art Museum *Fort Mason Center, Bldg. A, Laguna St./Marina Blvd., 775-0990, fax 775-1861. Tu-Sun 11-5. Adults $1, 62+ & 12-17 50c; free 1st W 11-7.*

Serving as a showcase for high quality contemporary crafts and folk art, this museum changes exhibits every two months.

San Francisco Fire Department Museum *655 Presidio Ave./Pine St., 563-4630. Thur-Sun 1-4. Free.*

A fascinating collection of antique fire apparatus is found in this small museum. It includes engines from the hand-drawn, horse-drawn, and motorized eras of fire-fighting. Of special interest is an ornate hand-pulled engine dating from 1849, which is said to be San Francisco's, and California's, first fire engine. In addition, old photographs, memorabilia, and artifacts combine to tell the story of fire-fighting in San Francisco, beginning in 1849 with the volunteer department and emphasizing the 1906 earthquake and fire. Visitors are welcome to stop in next door to visit fire station #10 and see what the modern rigs are looking like.

Tattoo Art Museum *841 Columbus Ave./Lombard St., in North Beach, 775-4991. M-Thur 12-9, F & Sat 12-10, Sun 12-8. Free.*

Located next to the studio of renowned tattooist Lyle Tuttle, this is the world's first tattoo museum. Photos and paintings trace the history of tattooing, and artifacts on display include everything from ancient bone tattooing needles to modern electric versions. To leave with a permanent souvenir, call ahead for an appointment.

Treasure Island Museum *410 Palm Ave., Bldg. One, on Treasure Island, 395-5067, fax 395-4450. M-F 10-3:30, Sat & Sun 10-4:30. Adults $3, under 12 free.*

Situated within an art deco building, this museum's permanent exhibits chronicle the history of the Navy, Marine Corps, and Coast Guard in the Pacific. A "Jewels in the Bay" exhibit covers California's last World's Fair (the Golden Gate International Exposition of 1939-40), America's first trans-Pacific commercial airplanes (the China Clipper flying boats of 1935-46), the histories of both Treasure Island and Yerba Buena Island, and the construction of both the Golden Gate and Bay bridges. Additionally, a magnificent view of San Francisco is available just outside the museum.

Wax Museum *145 Jefferson St./Taylor St., (800) 439-4305, 885-4834, fax 771-9248. Daily 9-11; in summer to midnight. Adults $11.95, 60+ $8.95, 13-17 $9.95, 6-12 $6.95.*

Several hundred wax celebrities are situated among an assortment of backgrounds. The Chamber of Horrors intrigues older children, as Fairyland does younger ones.

This block-long complex holds two more attractions, entry for which requires buying a more expensive combo ticket. The **Haunted Gold Mine** ejects visitors into a monster of a gift shop at the end, and the macabre, graphic, and bloody **Medieval Dungeon** is filled with scenes of torture devices.

Wells Fargo History Museum *420 Montgomery St./California St., in the Financial District, 396-2619. M-F 9-5. Free.*

In homage to the Old West, this two-story museum displays an authentic stagecoach, samples of various kinds of gold found in the state, a telegraph exhibit, and, of course, a re-creation of an old banking office. All this plus gold panning equipment and historical photos, too. The oldest bank in the West—Wells Fargo—is the sponsor, and the museum rests on the site of the bank's first office.

OUTDOORS/PARKS

Angel Island State Park *San Francisco departures from Pier 43½ at Fisherman's Wharf, (800) 229-2784, 546-2896. Adults $10, 5-11 $5.50. Tiburon departures from Main St., 435-2131. Adults $6, 5-17 $4. East Bay departures from Jack London Square, (510) 522-3300. Adults $12, 62+ & 13-18 $8, 5-12 $5. Schedules vary but usually operate daily in summer, weekends only rest of year. State Park information: 435-5390. Visitors Center: Sat & Sun 11-3:30. Free.*

Half the fun of a trip to Angel Island is the scenic ferry ride over. Visitors disembark at Ayala Cove. Picnic tables and barbecue facilities are nearby, as is a pleasant little beach for sunbathing. Packing along a picnic to enjoy in some remote spot is highly recommended, but the island does have a cafe. Approximately 12 miles of well-marked trails and paved roads allow hikers to completely circle the 740-acre island—the largest island in the bay. Some lead to old military ruins that are reminders of the island's past as a holding camp for quarantined immigrants (the island was once called the "Ellis Island of the West"), as a prisoner-of-war processing facility, and as a missile defense base. A 3.2-mile loop trail leads from the cove to the top of 781-foot-high Mount Livermore, where a picnic area and a 360-degree view awaits. A park map is available at the Visitors Center, and a variety of guided tours are available. Except for Park Service vehicles, cars are not permitted on the island. Tram service is usually available during the summer, and bikes can be brought over on the ferry or rented on the island. Camping in primitive environmental campsites can be arranged.

Beaches.

San Francisco is not the place to come to go to the beach. Los Angeles is where *that* California is. Still, the city does have a few good spots to soak up some rays, weather willing. The water, however, is usually either too cold or too dangerous for swimming.

• **Aquatic Park** *Foot of Polk St., at Fisherman's Wharf, 556-2904. Always open. Free.*

Located in the people-congested area across the street from Ghirardelli Square, this is a good spot for children to wade and there are great views of the bay.

• **Baker Beach** *Off Lincoln Blvd./25th Ave., 556-0560. Daily sunrise-sunset. Free.*

The surf here is unsafe and the temperature is often chilly. Still, there are usually plenty of people sunning and strolling, and the views of the Golden Gate Bridge are spectacular. Battery Chamberlin is located adjacent. Demonstrations of the world's last remaining 95,000-pound, 6-inch "disappearing gun" are conducted by rangers on weekends, and environmental programs are sometimes offered.

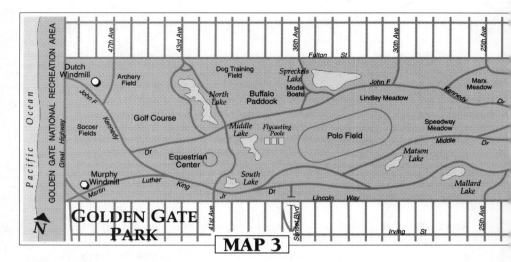

Golden Gate Park — MAP 3

- **China Beach** *End of Seacliff Ave./28th Ave., 239-2366. Daily dawn-dusk. Free.*
  Located in an exclusive residential area, this secluded cove is surprising to come upon. Visitors park on a bluff, then walk down steep stairs to the sheltered, sandy beach. The surf is gentle, so swimming and wading are possible, and changing rooms and restrooms are available in summer.

Fort Funston *South end of Great Highway/Skyline Blvd., 239-2366. Sunrise-sunset. Visitor Center: Daily 12-4. Free.*
A short, paved loop trail offers stunning coastal views. However, the reason most people come here is to watch the hang-gliders do their thing. An observation platform on a bluff above the ocean provides a bird's-eye view.

Golden Gate National Recreation Area (GGNRA) *556-0560.*
Dedicated to deceased Congressman Phillip Burton, who contributed greatly to establishing this park, the GGNRA is the world's largest national park in an urban setting and is one of the most heavily visited national parks in the U.S. Located in three California counties—San Francisco, Marin, and San Mateo—its total area is over 114 square miles, or 2½ times the size of San Francisco. These Bay Area sites are part of the GGNRA: Aquatic Park, Alcatraz, Baker Beach, China Beach, the Cliff House, Crissy Field, East Fort Baker, Fort Funston, Fort Mason, Fort Point, Gerbode Valley, Lands End, Marin Headlands, Muir Woods, Ocean Beach, Olema Valley, The Presidio, Stinson Beach, Sutro Heights Park, Sweeney Ridge, Tennessee Valley, and Tomales Bay. Also within the boundaries but not administered by the GGNRA: Angel Island State Park, Audubon Canyon Ranch, Mount Tamalpais State Park, Samuel P. Taylor State Park, and various ranches in the Tomales Bay-Lagunitas Creek area.

Golden Gate Park.
One of the world's great metropolitan parks, Golden Gate Park encompasses 1,017 acres. It is nearly 200 acres larger than Manhattan's Central Park, after which is was originally patterned. Once just sand dunes, it is now the largest man-made park in the world.
Each August, **Comedy Celebration Day** *(938-0151. Free.)* is held somewhere in the park. Bring a blanket, a picnic, and a smile. Laughs are provided by local professional comedians, who

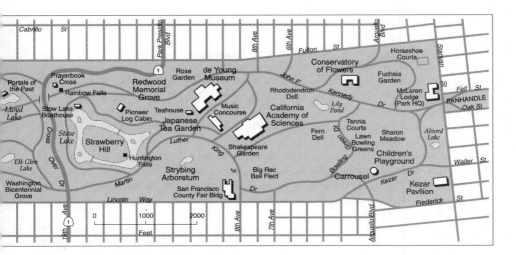

in the past have ranged from upstarts—who just naturally seem to try harder—to such established luminaries as Robin Williams, Bob Goldthwait, and Father Guido Sarducci. Content is promised to be appropriate for the entire family. In September, **Free Shakespeare in the Park** *(666-2222)* schedules performances here and in other Bay Area locations.

- **Biking/Skating.**

On Sundays, John F. Kennedy Drive is closed to automobiles. Car traffic is replaced with heavy bike, skate, and pedestrian traffic. Skate and bike rentals are available at shops along Stanyan Street. Skates are also usually available from trucks parked along Fulton Street.

- **Buffalo Paddock** *At west end of Kennedy Dr., west of 36th Ave. across from Anglers Lodge.*

Foreign visitors seem particularly impressed with viewing this small herd of authentic buffalo.

- **California Academy of Sciences.** See page 63.

- **Children's Playground** *On Bowling Green Dr., between King Dr. & Kennedy Dr., east of California Academy of Sciences. Daily 10-5.*

Constructed in 1887, this was the very first public playground in a U.S. park. Today it is filled with creative modern play structures.

Located adjacent, an antique **Carrousel** *(W-Sun 10-4:30; to 6 in summer. Adults $1, children 25¢.)* makes its rounds within a protective hippodrome enclosure. Built in 1914 by Herschel-Spillman, it has 62 beautifully painted hand-carved animals and its original Gebruder band organ.

- **Conservatory of Flowers** *Closed indefinitely due to severe storm damage in 1995.*

Built in Ireland in 1878 and modeled after the Palm House in London's Kew Gardens, this impressive example of Victorian architecture was shipped around Cape Horn in pieces in 1879. This tropical greenhouse is the oldest remaining building in the park and is thought to be the oldest conservatory in the U.S. It consists of a central dome flanked by two wings. The conservatory's oldest and largest plant—a 35-foot-tall Philodendron speciosum—is located in the central dome. Other noteworthy specimens include primitive cycads (from the dinosaur era), a collection of 2,800 rare cool-growing orchids that exist almost nowhere else, and two ponds—one filled with tropical water lilies and the other planted with ferns in classic Victorian style. Outside, 17- by 30-foot flower beds form floral messages. They are tilted at a 45-degree angle so that they can be seen from the street. This old European gardening technique, known as "carpet bedding," is costly and time-consuming and now almost extinct.

• **Golden Gate Park Stables** *John F. Kennedy Dr./36th Ave., at west end of park, 668-7360, fax 255-1789. Daily 8-6. $20-$25/person; riders must be 8 or older. Reservations required.*

Guided one-hour trail rides through the park are available, and on weekends trail rides to the beach are an option. Classes and private lessons are offered, and short pony rides are available for children 1 and older.

• **Japanese Tea Garden and Teahouse** *Next to deYoung Museum, 666-7200. Daily 9-6:30, Mar-Sept; 8:30-6:30 or dusk, Oct-Feb. Garden: Adults $2.50, 65+ & 6-12 $1; free 1st W of month. Tea: $2.50/person. No reservations. No cards.*

This garden is enjoyable to stroll through at any time of day, any time of year, and in almost any kind of weather. Visitors can climb up the steep arch of the "wishing bridge" (actually a drum bridge), make a wish, and drop a coin in the pond below. Steep steps lead to a miniature red pagoda, and a dragon hedge undulates nearby. A spectacular display occurs annually during the last week of March, when the **cherry blossoms** are in bloom.

Everyone seems to enjoy stopping for refreshment at the inviting open-air teahouse, where tea and oriental cookies are served by waitresses clad in traditional Japanese kimonos. It is quite pleasant and relaxing to observe nature while leisurely sipping jasmine or green tea and munching on exotic cookies. An interesting note: Makoto Hagiwara, who designed the garden in 1893 for the Mid-Winter Exposition, is credited with introducing the fortune cookie to America here in 1914.

• **M.H. deYoung Memorial Museum.** See page 60.

• **Shakespeare Garden** *Behind California Academy of Sciences.*

This formal, manicured garden is planted with the 150 varieties of flowers mentioned in William's plays. An attractive wrought-iron archway marks the entrance, where a brick pathway bordered by crabapple trees leads into the garden. Benches and grassy expanses invite lingering.

• **Stow Lake Boathouse** *752-0347. Daily 9-4; in summer to 5. Paddle boats, row boats, & electric boats $9.50-$14.50/hr. No cards.*

A boat on Stow Lake, which is the largest of the park's 11 lakes, provides both an unusual and memorable picnic spot. After pushing off in a row boat, it's pleasant to find a cove where there isn't much water movement and then get down to the business of eating a picnic meal. Be warned: When bread is tossed to the ducks and seagulls, they can fairly sink a boat with enthusiasm. Though the water is shallow and it isn't possible to get very far from shore, cushions in the boats double as life preservers. Life vests are also available upon request at no additional charge. Because boats are often wet inside, consider bringing along a blanket to sit on.

• **Strybing Arboretum** *Entrance adjoins San Francisco County Fair Bldg., 661-1316. M-F 8-4:30, Sat & Sun 10-5; tours daily at 1:30, on Sat & Sun also at 10:30. Free.*

Known for its magnolia and rhododendron collections, this lovely garden displays over 7,500 different plant species over its 70 acres. Many are unique to this climate, and most are labeled. Of special note are the Japanese-style Moon-viewing Garden, the Arthur Menzies Garden of California Native Plants, the redwood forest, the small fragrance garden, the Biblical Garden, the New World Cloud Forest, and the new Primitive Plant Garden.

A variety of annual events take place in the adjacent **San Francisco County Fair Building**. The **Mother's Day Rose Show** allows the opportunity to see a splendid variety of climbing, miniature, and old garden roses. Cuttings perfect for presenting to Mom are for sale, with proceeds benefiting the San Francisco Rose Society. It is the largest such show in Northern California. Sponsored by the San Francisco Mycological Society, the December **Fungus Fair** allows the opportunity for backyard mushrooms to be identified by experts. Wild fungi, including a number of poisonous varieties, are also displayed.

• **Walking Tours** *221-1311. Sat & Sun May-Oct. Free.*

All of these walks are led by volunteers and require no reservations. Except for the Japanese Tea Garden tour, which lasts 45 minutes, all tours run from 1½ to 2 hours.

• The **Japanese Garden Tour** covers the history and design of the garden. *Sun, M, W, & Sat at 2. Pay admission and meet inside main gate.*

• The **Lloyd Lake Tour** explores Portals of the Past, Rainbow Falls, Prayerbook Cross, and other park secrets. *3rd Sun of month at 2. Meet at park map in front of Lloyd Lake.*

• On **McLaren's Walk**, participants see some little-known spots such as the horseshoe courts and Fuchsia Garden. They stroll through the Rhododendron and Fern Dells and visit Children's Playground. *1st, 3rd, & 5th Sun of month at 1. Meet at park map in front of Japanese Tea Garden.*

• Participants on the **Strawberry Hill Tour** enjoy a spectacular view of the Golden Gate Bridge and San Francisco from atop the hill. They see Huntington Falls, explore the Pioneer Log Cabin, and visit the Redwood Memorial Grove and the Rose Garden. *Sat at 11. Meet at park map in front of Japanese Tea Garden.*

• The **Windmill Tour** takes in Spreckels Lake, the restored windmill, and the Buffalo Paddock. *1st Sun of month at 1. Meet at park map in front of windmill.*

Mountain Lake Park *Entrance at Lake St./Funston Ave.*

Well-hidden from the street, this park is an unexpected delight to come upon. Facilities include a lakeside path, a basketball court, tennis courts, a parcourse that begins at 9th Avenue, and a large, well-equipped playground off 12th Avenue. There are even ducks to feed. It is interesting to note that spring-fed Mountain Lake supplied all of the city's water between 1852 and 1870.

San Francisco Zoo *1 Zoo Rd./45th Ave., 753-7080. Daily 10-5. Adults $7, 65+ & 12-15 $3.50, 3-11 $1.50; free 1st W of month.*

A ride on the **Zebra Zephyr** tram *(Adults $2.50, 65+ & under 16 $1.50.)* gives a quick 20-minute introduction to the layout of this scenic zoo. Of special note are the half-acre Gorilla World, which is one of the world's largest gorilla habitats, and the Primate Discovery Center, with its 15 species of primates and unusual nocturnal primates exhibit. The zoo's collection of extremely endangered snow leopards is one of the most successful breeding groups in the world. The lions and tigers are particularly interesting to visit when they are fed each afternoon from 2 to 3—except on Monday, when they fast. New exhibits include a Wart Hogs enclosure, complete with mud wallows and burrowing areas, and Australian Walkabout—a two-acre multi-species enclosure holding marsupials and Australian bird species.

A separate **Children's Zoo** *(Daily 11-4. Adults $1, under 4 free.)* has a petting area with sheep and goats. An **Insect Zoo** populated with the likes of 6- to 8-inch-long walking sticks and giant Costa Rican wood cockroaches is also located here. It also has a functioning honeybee hive and 35 more arthropod species. An adjacent butterfly garden is filled with native plants labeled with the type of butterfly they attract. Just outside the Children's Zoo is a large playground and an antique **carousel** *($1/person)* built in 1921 by the William Dentzel Carving Company. The perfect souvenir is a plastic Zoo Storybox Key *($2)*, which children can insert in boxes throughout the zoo to hear interesting information about the animals in four languages: English (narrated by actor and local resident Danny Glover), Cantonese, Spanish, and Tagalog.

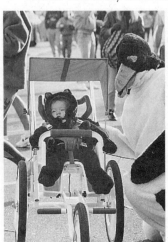

A three-mile family-oriented **Zoo Run** is held each January. The course winds through the zoo, allowing participants to swing by the Primate Discovery Center, lope past the giraffes, and strut alongside Penguin Island. A more challenging seven-mile run is also scheduled. A popular **Valentine's Day Sex Tour** is scheduled in February. And each year in July, members of the Zoological Society *($55/year/family)* are invited to **Night Tour.** Entertainment, demonstrations, behind-the-scenes tours, and admission are all free, and a picnic dinner is available for a small charge. Support the zoo and find out just what happens at the zoo after dark.

Sutro Heights Park *On 48th Ave., between Geary Blvd. & Anza St., 556-8642.*

Formerly the estate of Adolph Sutro, this magnificent park has expansive views of the southern coastline. It is perfect for a picnic, but hold on to little kids, as drop-offs can be sudden and dangerous.

PERFORMING ARTS

Moving pictures got their start in 1878 when Leland Stanford placed a $20,000 bet. He hired photographer Eadweard Muybridge to prove that the four hooves of a running horse are off the ground at the same time. The still photos were mounted on a carousel and spun so that the horse appeared to be moving. In 1880, Stanford won $20,000 and the first moving picture debuted at the exhibition hall of the San Francisco Art Association.

In preparation for a visit to San Francisco, or in remembrance of a trip past, the following movies are fun to watch. All were shot on location in San Francisco: **Birdman of Alcatraz** *(1962; Burt Lancaster; NR),* **The Birds** *(1963; Rod Taylor, Jessica Tandy, Suzanne Pleshett; PG13),* **Bullitt** *(1968; Steve McQueen; NR),* **Dark Passage** *(1947; Humphrey Bogart, Lauren Bacall; NR),* **Dirty Harry** *(1971; Clint Eastwood; R),* **Foul Play** *(1978; Goldie Hawn, Chevy Chase; PG),* **48 Hours** *(1982; Nick Nolte, Eddie Murphy; R),* **The Graduate** *(1967; Anne Bancroft, Dustin Hoffman, Katharine Ross; PG),* **Guess Who's Coming to Dinner?** *(1967; Spencer Tracy, Sidney Poitier, Katherine Hepburn; NR),* **Invasion of the Body Snatchers** *(1978; Donald Sutherland, Leonard Nimoy; PG),* **Jagged Edge** *(1986; Glen Close, Jeff Bridges; R),* **The Maltese Falcon** *(1941; Humphrey Bogart, Mary Astor; NR),* **Mrs. Doubtfire** *(1993; Robin Williams, Sally Field; PG13),* **Pacific Heights** *(1990; Melanie Griffith, Matthew Modine, Michael Keaton; R),* **Pal Joey** *(1957; Rita Hayworth, Frank Sinatra; NR),* **Play It Again, Sam** *(1972; Woody Allen; PG),* **The Presidio** *(1988; Sean Connery, Mark Harmon; R),* **San Francisco** *(1936; Clark Gable, Jeanette MacDonald; NR),* **Sister Act** *(1993; Whoopi Goldberg; PG),* **Star Trek IV—The Voyage Home** *(1989; Leonard Nimoy, William Shatner; PG),* **The Towering Inferno** *(1974; Steve McQueen, Faye Dunaway, William Holden; PG),* **True Believer** *(1989; James Woods, Robert Downey Jr.; R),* **Vertigo** *(1958; James Stewart, Kim Novak; PG),* **A View to a Kill** *(1985; Roger Moore, Grace Jones; PG),* **What's Up, Doc?** *(1972; Barbra Streisand, Ryan O'Neal; G),* **Woman in Red** *(1984; Gene Wilder; PG-13).*

Beach Blanket Babylon *678 Green St./Powell St., in Club Fugazi, in North Beach, 421-4222. W & Thur at 8, F & Sat at 7 & 10, Sun at 3 & 7. Tickets $18-$45.*

Begun back in 1974 as an underground production, this fast-moving and humorous musical revue is known for its colorful, creative costumes and huge headdresses. It is the longest running musical revue in the country. The show changes periodically but always brings pleasure. Sunday matinees are aimed at families and are the only performances open to minors (under age 21). No alcohol is served then. Parents should keep in mind that there is no profanity or violence, but sexual puns are abundant. For the past 15 years all performances have sold out, so reserve tickets early and arrive when the doors open to choose a table.

Mime Troupe *At neighborhood parks throughout Bay Area, 285-1717. July 4-Labor Day. Free.*

Since 1964, this Tony Award-winning troupe has been presenting sometimes caustic, always entertaining commentary on current events, political leaders, and the state of our world. The Troupe's original productions combine music, satire, and comedy. In spite of the description, children and families attend in large numbers and generally enjoy the spectacle.

TIX Bay Area/Half-Price Tickets *251 Stockton St., on Union Square, 433-7827. Tu-Thur 11-6, F & Sat 11-7.*

Day-of-performance half-price tickets are available for many music, dance, and theater events. They must be paid for with cash or traveler's checks, and no information is available by phone. Sunday and Monday events are available on Saturday. Proceeds are donated to local arts groups. Full price tickets for a vast array of performances are also available; phone information and ticket purchase using MasterCard or Visa is available. TIX by Mail permits purchasing half-price tickets through a quarterly catalog. For a copy, write to: TIX by Mail, 657 Mission Street #402, San Francisco, California 94105.

Young Performers Theatre *Fort Mason, Bldg. C, Laguna St./Marina Blvd., 346-5550, fax 346-4991. Sat at 1, Sun at 1 & 3:30. Adults $7, 1-12 $5.*

A combination of professional adult performers and young actors in training, this company uses imaginative stage settings and costumes. The fast-moving productions are usually short as well, making them a good introduction to theater for children ages 4 through 10. Past productions have included *Charlie and the Chocolate Factory, Wind in the Willows,* and *The Secret Garden.*

SHOPPING

The Cannery *Beach St./Leavenworth St./Hyde St./Jefferson St., 771-3112, fax 771-2424. Shops open M-Sat 10-6, Sun 11-6; in summer to 8:30 Thur-Sat.*

This charming red brick shopping complex was constructed in 1907 and was once the world's largest fruit and vegetable cannery. It now holds 30 shops and galleries, 9 restaurants and cafes, a comedy club, the Museum of the City of San Francisco (see page 65), and other diversions. Free entertainment by **street performers** is often scheduled under century-old olive trees in the inviting Courtyard.

Shops include the **Basic Brown Bear Factory** *(2nd floor, (800) 554-1910, 626-0781, fax 861-2660),* which purveys handmade bears of all kinds—from your basic brown to your quite elaborate creamy-colored Beary Godmother with pink satin wings and a magic wand. Prices are close to wholesale, and customers can stuff their own bear using a World War II-era machine that once pumped up life preservers. This is one of the few stuffed animal factories still manufacturing within the U.S., and the bears are not sold anywhere else. Free drop-in tours are available at the main factory *(444 DeHaro St. Daily at 1.).*

• **Restaurants.**

• **Jacks Cannery Bar** *1st floor, 931-6400. L & D daily; $. No reservations. AE, V.* Fresh seafood appetizers, salads, and sandwiches are on the menu here, and 110 beers are on tap. The bar is also noteworthy for its oak-paneled long hall, hand-carved fireplace, ornate ceiling, and Jacobean staircase—all of which were originally part of several English manor homes built in the 1600s and 1700s.

• **Quiet Storm** *3rd floor, 771-2929. L F-Sun, D daily; $-$$. 1 highchair, boosters. Reservations advised. AE, MC, V.* California cuisine with an Asian influence is served here in a room with a magnificent bay view. Live entertainment is scheduled most evenings.

Cost Plus Imports *2552 Taylor St./North Point St., near Fisherman's Wharf, 928-6200. Daily 9-9.*

The original store in a chain that now numbers 53, this gigantic importer has long been a favorite shopping stop for visitors. Back in the '60s, it was where everyone stocked up on "hippie" supplies: batik bedspreads, incense, candles. Current imports from around the world include inexpensive jewelry, kitchenware, furniture, baskets, and toys.

Embarcadero Center *Battery St./Sacramento St./Drumm St./Clay St., (800) 733-6318, 772-0500, fax 982-1780. Shops open M-F 10-7, Sat 10-5, Sun 12-5; restaurants open later. Validated parking; free on Sun.*

This enormous seven-block complex of high-rise buildings holds 140 shops and restaurants on its lower floors, as well as countless offices on the upper floors plus the huge Hyatt Regency hotel. A movie theater complex keeps things busy late into the night. **Justin Herman Plaza** is home to the **Vaillancourt Fountain**, nicknamed "#10 on the Richter" and described by an art critic as "something deposited by a dog with square intestines." A brochure mapping out a self-guided Sculpture Tour to the center's treasure-trove of art is available.

Factory Outlets.
• **Esprit Outlet** *499 Illinois St./16th St., 957-2550, fax 957-2556. M-F 10-8, Sat 10-7, Sun 11-5.*

Esprit's popular line of clothing for kids and teens (mainly females) originates in San Francisco. Their outlet is a great spot to pick up a stylish souvenir t-shirt or sweatshirt. During sales, bargain hunters have been known to wait over an hour just to get in.

• **Factory Outlet Heaven**, as I refer to this area, is located around 3rd and Brannan streets. Just follow the herds into the various outlet stores offering all manner of bargains. Hours run roughly Monday through Saturday from 10 to 4. Of special interest to females is the **Gunne Sax Outlet** *(35 Stanford St./Brannan St., 495-3326. M-Sat 9:30-5, Sun 11-5.).* This clothes manufacturer is known for its lush party, prom, and wedding dresses designed by Scott and Jessica McClintock.

Ghirardelli Square *900 North Point St./Larkin St., 775-5500. Daily 10-6; to 9 in summer.*

Built in 1900 as a chocolate factory and converted into a festival marketplace in 1964, this beautiful brick complex is said to have been the nation's first quaint, upscale shopping center. Now it is a National Historic Landmark and home to 48 shops and 10 restaurants. **Street performers** are scheduled on the courtyard stage each weekend (daily in summer).

• **Restaurants.** See also "Where to Eat" section.

  • **Ghirardelli Chocolate Manufactory** *771-9338. Sun-Thur 10am-11pm, F & Sat to 12; $. Highchairs. No reservations. MC, V.* A small working chocolate factory that uses original equipment from the early 1900s still operates in the back of this classic ice cream parlour. All of the chocolate sauces and syrups are made here, as are some of the candies sold in the shop. After reading the mouth-watering menu, which can be kept as a souvenir, each ice cream-lover takes a seat and awaits the fulfillment of their ice cream fantasy. Special concoctions include The Alcatraz Rock (a rocky road and vanilla ice cream island set in a bay of whipped cream and armored with a shell of Ghirardelli chocolate, nut rocks, and a cherry) and The Earthquake Sundae, which serves four or more people (eight flavors of ice cream with eight different toppings; cracks are filled with bananas and whipped cream and scattered with almonds, chocolate bits, and cherries). Hot fudge sundaes, sodas, and milkshakes are also available. Ghirardelli chocolate goodies, including a five-pound chocolate bar, are sold in a small adjoining shop.

  • **Gaylord India Restaurant** *771-8822. L & D daily, SunBr; $$. Reservations advised. AE, MC, V.* With its posh decor of oriental carpets, potted palms, and Chippendale-style chairs, plus its killer bay view, this restaurant wouldn't really need to have good food, too. But fortunately it does. Tandoori meats, freshly baked breads, excellent curries, and many vegetarian items are on the menu.

Japan Center *Three square blocks bounded by Post St., Geary St., Laguna St., and Fillmore St., 922-6776. Open daily; hours vary but shops generally open daily 10-5, restaurants to 9. Some businesses validate for center's fee lots.*

This five-acre cultural center houses shops, restaurants, art galleries, traditional Japanese baths, a Japanese-style market, a movie theater complex, and a hotel. Designed like an indoor mall, it has a series of passageways that permit getting from one building to another without crossing streets. A five-tiered, 100-foot-tall Peace Pagoda that was a gift from Japan is illuminated at night, and an eternal flame, brought from the Sumiyoshi Shrine in Osaka, burns above a reflecting pool.

A **Cherry Blossom Festival** *(563-2313. Free.)* is scheduled each April. This elaborate Japanese-style celebration of spring usually includes traditional dancing and martial arts demonstrations, taiko drum and koto performances, a bonsai exhibit, and tea ceremonies. A Japanese food bazaar operates continuously, and the festival culminates with a colorful Japanese-style parade. The **Nihonmachi Street Fair** *(free)* is held on the first weekend in August. In addition to a food bazaar it features contemporary ethnic bands and performing arts.

• **Restaurants** are scattered throughout the complex. Each opens exotic avenues of food exploration.

• **Benihana of Tokyo** *563-4844. L & D daily; $$. Highchairs. Reservations advised. AE, MC, V.* Diners here are seated at a community table with a large grill imbedded in the middle. Once the table is filled with diners, the chef dramatically begins to prepare each order as everyone watches. Though there are none, karate yells from the chefs wouldn't seem out of place. The chefs are adept performers with their knives, and the show is spectacular.

• **Benkyo-Do Co.** *922-1244. M-Sat 8-5.* This tiny shop has been selling Japanese pastries, candies, and rice crackers since 1906.

• **Isobune** *563-1030. L & D daily; $. Boosters. No reservations. MC, V.* At this small sushi bar, items are carried around the counter on little floating boats. Customers remove what looks interesting.

• **Mifune** *922-0337. L & D daily; $. Boosters, booths, child portions. No reservations. AE, MC, V.* Specializing in serving two types of easily digested and low-calorie homemade noodles (udon—fat, white flour noodles, and soba—thin, brown buckwheat noodles), this is a branch of a well-established chain of similar restaurants in Japan. Before walking through the noren (slit curtain), take a look at the plastic food displays in the exterior windows. Topping choices for either noodle type include chicken, beef, and shrimp tempura as well as more exotic raw egg, sweet herring, and seaweed. Sesame spice salt is on each table for pepping up the basically bland dishes. The child's Bullet Train plate is served in a ceramic replica of the famous Japanese train and consists of cold noodles with shrimp and vegetable tempura.

• **Sanppo** *1702 Post St./Buchanan St., 346-3486. L & D Tu-Sun; $$. Highchairs, boosters, child plate. No reservations. No cards.* Located across the street from the center, this cozy, country-style restaurant always has a line at the door—a sure tip-off that something is worth waiting for. Among the interesting appetizers are gomaae spinach (uncooked and sprinkled with sesame seeds), harusame salad (sweet potato noodles mixed with lettuce, onion, and a creamy dressing), and gyoza, which are similar to Chinese pot stickers. Entrees include a light tempura, fresh deep-fried oysters, and nasu hasamiyaki (grilled slices of ginger-marinated beef and eggplant). A large selection of noodle dishes is also available.

Pier 39 *The Embarcadero/Beach St., 705-5500. Most shops open 10:30-8:30; in summer from 8:30am. Parking lot adjoins; $5/hr., less with validation.*

Following just behind Disney World and Disneyland in bringing in the most visitors annually, this popular spot offers a myriad of diversions. Street performers entertain (the annual **International Street Performers Festival** is held here each June). Italian bumper cars and a vast video arcade are inside the **Funtasia** entertainment center at the pier entrance, as is **San Francisco—The Movie** *(956-3456. Adults $7.50, 55+ $6, 1-12 $4.50.)*—an enjoyable 30-minute motion picture by Academy Award-winning Keith Merrill that shows off some of the city's best locations. Nearby, **Music Tracks** *(981-1777. $11.95.)* permits the opportunity to sing a favorite oldie to background accompaniment and then take home the resulting tape; "I Left My Heart in San Francisco" is quite popular. At the far end of the pier is a contemporary two-tiered Venetian **carousel** *($2/person)* and **Turbo Ride** *(392-TURBO. Adults $6, 1-12 $4.)*—a simulated thrill ride that synchronizes hydraulically powered seats to the action on a giant movie screen. **Sea lions** have taken up permanent residence on the west side of the pier and can be seen there basking, barking, and belching on their floating docks. The newest attraction here is **UnderWater World** *((888) SEA-DIVE. adults $12.95, 62+ $9.95, 2-11 $6.50.)*, which uses moving sidewalks to transport visitors under the bay through transparent acrylic tunnels for a diver's-eye view of the fishes, sharks, and other sea life residing there; a 40-minute tape provides an informative narration.

Among the 110 shops is one that specializes in mounted butterflies, another in chocolate, and another in puppets. More specialize in hats, cat-related items, and items for the left-handed person. **The City Store** sells San Francisco-related memorabilia, including street signs, coffee mugs, and even antique parking meters.

• Restaurants.

Most of the full-service restaurants have seafood menus, but Italian, Chinese, and Swiss cuisines are also represented. Restaurant menu boards are found in various spots around the pier, giving visitors a chance to analyze offerings and prices. Fast-food is represented with fish & chips, hamburgers, pizza, hot pretzels, and more.

• **Neptune's Palace** *434-2260. L & D daily; $$$. Highchairs, boosters. Reservations advised. AE, MC, V.* Situated at the end of the pier, this airy spot stands out with its magnificent bay view of Alcatraz and tasty a la carte seafood menu. Its companion facility, the adjacent, more casual **Bay View Cafe**, offers a simple menu of soups, salads, and sandwiches as well as fresh seafood, plus it has a great view of the sea lions.

• **Eagle Cafe** *433-3689. B & L daily; $. Boosters. No reservations. No cards.* Situated at the entrance to the pier, this casual spot dates from 1920, when it was located across the street. The menu offers hearty breakfasts and a standout meatloaf sandwich at lunch, and strong drinks are always available at the antique bar.

Union Street.

This trendy area is filled with upscale shops and restaurants (see "Where to Eat" section), many inside old Victorian and Edwardian buildings. Flower stands add a seasonal burst of color on the four blocks running between Fillmore and Octavia streets, which has the heaviest concentration of shops, but boutiques continue on in both directions and down side streets. This area is referred to as Cow Hollow, in reference to the fact that it was once the city's dairy community.

For the annual **Union Street Fair** *(June. 346-4446. Free.)*, the street is usually closed off from Gough to Steiner. It begins with a Saturday morning Waiter Race in which competing waiters must open a bottle of wine, pour two glasses, and carry them on their tray intact to the top Green Street and back again. Music, food, and craftspeople round out the fun.

Union Square and Surrounds.

World-class shopping is found on the streets surrounding this large grassy square, which was originally a sand dune.

• **Britex Fabrics** *146 Geary St./Stockton St., 392-2910. M-Sat 9:30-6, Thur to 8.*

Even people who can't thread a needle enjoy browsing the four floors of magnificent fabrics and notions in this unique San Francisco store. It is the largest fabric store in the West.

• **Crocker Galleria** *50 Post St./Kearny St., 393-1505, fax 392-5429. M-F 10-6, Sat 10-5.*

This "covered street" links Post and Sutter streets. Sixty stores and two restaurants on three floors are situated under its spectacular arched skylight. The design was influenced by Milan's famous Galleria Vittorio Emmanuelle.

Located in the center, **Faz Restaurant & Bar** *(161 Sutter St., 362-0404, fax 362-5865. L M-F, D M-Sat; $-$$. Highchairs. Reservations advised. AE, MC, V.)* offers relaxing dining in a quietly elegant room. Among the tempting items on the Middle Eastern menu are house specialties such as dolmas (stuffed grape leaves), hummus, and tabouleh. Soups, salads, sandwiches, pizzas, and more substantial entrees, such as kabobs and seafood items, are also on the menu. Desserts include baklavah, a fig tart, a saffron brownie, and pistachio custard.

• **Department stores** include **Macy's**, **Neiman Marcus**, and **Saks Fifth Avenue**.

• **FAO Schwarz** *48 Stockton St./O'Farrell St., 394-8700. M-Sat 10-7, Sun 11-6.*

The city's largest toy store, this three-story wonderland is filled with elaborate toy displays and exclusive, unusual, and trend-setting merchandise. Shoppers are greeted at the door by a live toy solider, and just steps from the entrance is a whimsical two-story mechanical clock tower emitting charming music. A good selection of San Francisco-themed books and games is available.

• **Gump's** *135 Post St./Kearny St., 982-1616. M-Sat 10-6, Thur to 7.*

Opened in 1861, this is the oldest store in San Francisco. Known for its fine oriental imports, its legendary Jade Room holds one of the finest jade collections in the world. It carries the city's largest selection of fine china and crystal and also has an eye-popping collection of American crafts.

• **Maiden Lane** *Off Stockton St., between Post St. & Geary St.*

This charming street is closed off to cars during business hours and holds a variety of interesting shops.

• **Restaurants.** See also "Where to Eat" section.

   • **Cafe Akimbo** *116 Maiden Lane, 3rd fl./Stockton St., 433-2288, fax 433-2298. L & D M-Sat; $$. Reservations advised. AE, MC, V.* With walls accented cheerily with splashes of bright yellow and purple, this tiny dining room serves delicious entrees and salads.

   • **Rumpus** *1 Tillman Pl./Grant Ave., 421-2300. L & D daily; $$. Reservations advised. AE, MC, V.* Situated at the end of a chic downtown alley, this welcoming restaurant offers relaxation and tasty food to tired shoppers. Lunch is salads, sandwiches, and soups, while dinners are more substantial—perhaps an unusual risotto or a crisp-skinned pan-roasted chicken. Exceptional desserts have included a hot apple tart, a perfect creme brulee, and a dense lemon tart. Getting here is half of the fun. Being here is the other half.

• **San Francisco Shopping Centre** *865 Market St., 495-5656. M-Sat 9:30-8, Sun 11-6.*

Opened in 1988, this nine-story indoor shopping complex is one of the few vertical malls in the U.S. A must-see four-story spiral escalator—the only one in the U.S.—wends its way up through a sunlit atrium into the word's largest **Nordstrom**.

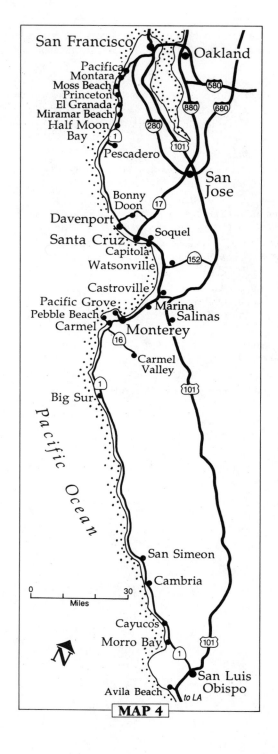

San Francisco
Oakland
Pacifica
Montara
Moss Beach
Princeton
El Granada
Miramar Beach
Half Moon
Bay
Pescadero

San
Jose

Bonny
Doon
Davenport
Santa Cruz
Soquel
Capitola
Watsonville

Castroville
Pacific Grove
Pebble Beach
Carmel
Marina
Salinas
Monterey

Carmel
Valley

Big Sur

Pacific Ocean

San Simeon

Cambria

Cayucos
Morro Bay

San Luis
Obispo
Avila Beach   to LA

0   30
Miles

N

MAP 4

Coast South

A LITTLE BACKGROUND

When the Bay Area is blazing with sunshine, this area can be disappointingly socked in with fog. And vice versa. The trip down Highway 1 from San Francisco features a breath-taking, cliff-hugging ride along the Pacific Ocean.

Pacifica

(Area Code 415)

WHERE TO STAY

Seabreeze Motel *100 Rockaway Beach Ave., 359-3903, fax 359-5624. 1 story; 20 rooms; 4 non-smoking rooms; $$. Continental breakfast; restaurant.*

This is the place for a quick, inexpensive escape. Rooms are simple, but the beach is only a few steps away and a merry steak and seafood restaurant, **Nick's** *(359-3900. B, L, & D daily; $$. Highchairs, boosters, booths, child portion. 100% non-smoking. Reservations advised. AE, MC, V.),* which is under the same ownership, is just next door.

WHERE TO EAT

Taco Bell *5200 Hwy. 1, 355-0591. L & D daily; $. Highchairs, child portions. No reservations. No cards.*

Located inside an attractive redwood building, this fast-food restaurant's exceptional beachfront location makes it worthy of a stop-in. Free entertainment is provided by always-present surfers in the ocean just outside.

Montara

(Area Code 415)

WHERE TO STAY

Point Montara Lighthouse Hostel *On 16th St., off Hwy. 1, 728-7177. 45 beds; rooms for families & couples.*

This restored 1875 lighthouse is now the cliffside setting for a picturesque retreat. Lodging is in a modern duplex that was formerly the lightkeeper's quarters. Facilities include two kitchens, a laundry, a volleyball court, a private beach, an outdoor hot tub (fee), and bicycle rentals. A continental breakfast is available at additional charge. See also page 391.

Moss Beach

(Area Code 415)

WHERE TO EAT

Dan's Place *Etheldore St./Virginia Ave., 728-3343. D daily; $-$$. Highchairs, boosters. Reservations advised on weekends. MC, V.*

After passing through the bar, diners enter a large, casual room with tables covered in red and white checked cloths and two walls of big windows looking out over the ocean. The clientele is basically townspeople who have patronized the restaurant for years. They come for the bargain family-style dinners that include a relish plate, soup or salad, pasta, entree (fish plus a daily special), bread and butter, and coffee. An extensive a la carte menu offers seafood, fresh steamed clams in season, steaks, fried chicken, and veal and pasta dishes—all served with relishes, a choice of vegetable or pasta, and bread and butter. Children are welcome to share or split an order.

WHAT TO DO

James Fitzgerald Marine Reserve *At the end of California Ave., 728-3584. Daily sunrise to sunset. Free.*

Excellent tidepooling can be enjoyed here. Usually some pools are accessible, with the occasional sea star or hermit crab caught by the tide. And because visitors are not permitted to remove anything, the sand is rich with shells and interesting natural debris. To see a large variety of specimens, visit when the tide is out. Naturalist-led walks are usually scheduled then on weekends. Call for times. Though the parking area can be deceptively warm and calm, the area by the ocean is usually windy and cold. Take wraps. Picnic tables are available near the parking lot.

Princeton-by-the-Sea

(Area Code 415)

WHERE TO STAY

Pillar Point Inn *380 Capistrano Rd., (800) 400-8281, 728-7377, fax 728-8345. 2 stories; 11 rooms; 100% non-smoking; $$$-$$$+. Unsuitable for children under 12. All VCRs & gas fireplaces. Afternoon snack, full breakfast.*

Facing a picturesque small boat harbor, this contemporary inn features a Cape Cod-style of architecture. Some of the spacious rooms have private steam baths; all sport cloud-like feather beds and harbor views. A complimentary video library is also available. Several good seafood restaurants and the busy harbor itself are just across the street.

WHERE TO EAT

Barbara's Fishtrap *281 Capistrano Rd./Hwy. 1, 728-7049, fax 728-2519. L & D daily; $-$$. Highchairs, boosters, child portions. No reservations. No cards.*

A view of the harbor and a casual atmosphere make this tiny roadside diner a pleasant stop for a quick meal. In addition to a rustic interior room, there is a glassed-in deck with heat lamps. Though there is sometimes a short wait to be seated, service is quick, encouraging a fast turnover. Lunch is served until 5 and includes New England-style clam chowder, bouillabaisse, fish & chips, and calamari as well as steak and a hamburger. The dinner menu additionally offers scallops, prawns, and steak—all served with a choice of soup or salad, French bread, French fries or baked potato, and a vegetable. The house specialty is rockfish fresh off the harbor fishing boats; it is available either broiled or dipped in batter and deep-fried tempura-style.

The Shore Bird *390 Capistrano Rd., 728-5541, fax 728-3057. L & D daily, Sunday Br; $$. Highchairs, boosters, child menu. No reservations. AE, MC, V.*

Situated inside an attractive Cape Cod-style structure built on the site where a speakeasy once stood, this refined restaurant features many tables with harbor views. The specialties are generous portions of fresh local fish, much of which is brought in by boats visible just across the street, and a salad-bar-to-your-table that permits composing a salad at table. All chowders, dressings, and desserts are made in-house, and steaks, ribs, and pastas are also available. A cozy bar area invites a before or after dinner drink, and, adding a romantic touch, every woman is given a long-stemmed rose upon leaving dinner and brunch.

WHAT TO DO

Whale-watching expeditions are scheduled January through April on Saturdays, Sundays, and some Fridays. Sponsored by non-profit **Oceanic Society Expeditions** *((800) 326-7491, 474-3385; $29-$32/person)*, each boat trip has a professional naturalist on board to educate participants about the whales and interpret their behavior. Children must be at least 5, and reservations are necessary. See also page 49.

El Granada
(Area Code 415)

WHERE TO EAT

Village Green *89 Portola Ave., 726-3690. B, L, & tea to 3 Thur-Tu; closed mid-Aug to mid-Sept; $. Highchairs, booster seats. 100% non-smoking. No reservations. MC, V.*

A touch of England is purveyed in this tiny, cozy, and cheery spot. Tables are covered with floral cloths, and the ocean can be glimpsed through lace-framed windows. Tea items are available all day. Cream tea includes two scones, jam, and wonderful sweet clotted cream. The tea plate consists of assorted finger sandwiches, savories, and sweets. Of course both are served with a pot of tea (or coffee) covered with a perky cozy, and each table has its own jar of tart homemade lemon curd. B&B accommodations are also available.

Miramar Beach
(Area Code 415)

WHERE TO STAY

Cypress Inn *407 Mirada Rd., (800) 83-BEACH, 726-6002, fax 726-1138. 3 stories; 12 rooms; 100% non-smoking; $$$+. Children free. Some TVs, all fireplaces. Afternoon snack, full breakfast; room service by arrangement.*

Located on a quiet frontage road across the street from the ocean, this impressive inn is decorated with bright accents of Mexican folk art. Each room in the main inn faces the ocean, so guests can always hear the soothing sound of the ocean in the background; each also has a private balcony, ocean view, and fireplace. Many guests enjoy just sitting in their room and watching the brown pelicans dive for fish. To experience a bit of heaven, reserve the third-floor Las Nubes room. Its name meaning literally "the clouds," this penthouse room has a luxurious tiled bathroom with an over-size whirlpool tub, plus a bank of windows overlooking the ocean. Occupants want to stay forever. Four rooms are located in a newly added beach house behind the main inn. The afternoon snack includes tea and exquisite hors d'oeuvres.

WHERE TO EAT

Miramar Beach Inn *131 Mirada Rd., (800) 454-VIEW, 726-9053, fax 726-5060. L M-Sat, D daily, SunBr; $$-$$$. Highchairs, boosters, booths, child menu. 100% non-smoking. Reservations advised. MC, V.*

Situated across the street from the ocean in a somewhat isolated spot, this casual restaurant offers expansive views and is especially nice at lunch and at Sunday brunch. The lunch menu has salads, hot sandwiches, hamburgers, omelettes, and homemade chowder with garlic bread. The pricier dinners include seafood, steak, and pasta and come with salad, fresh vegetables, and rice pilaf. After dining, visit the beach behind the rocky breakfront in front of the restaurant to take a walk, build a sand castle, or maybe observe a flock of brown pelicans bobbing on the surf and diving for food

WHAT TO DO

Bach Dancing and Dynamite Society *307 Mirada Rd., 726-4143, fax 712-0506. Sun at 3; closed Jan, Sept, & Dec. Adults $15, under 17 free.*

Live jazz and classical music are performed at this beach house. The door opens at 3 p.m., and the music begins at 4:30. Arrive early as there are no advance reservations. A buffet, with a wine and juice bar, is available, and minors are welcome. Call for schedule.

Half Moon Bay

(Area Code 415)

VISITOR INFORMATION

Half Moon Bay Coastside Chamber of Commerce *520 Kelly Ave., Half Moon Bay 94019, 726-8380, fax 726-8389.*

Coastside Harvest Trails *765 Main St., Half Moon Bay 94019, 726-4485.*

For a free map to the area's farms, send a self-addressed, stamped legal-size envelope.

GETTING THERE

Located approximately 25 miles south of San Francisco.

ANNUAL EVENTS

Chamarita *May or June. 726-2729.*

Held here for over 100 years, this Portuguese festival takes place seven weekends after Easter and includes a barbecue, parade, and carnival.

Half Moon Bay Art and Pumpkin Festival *October. 726-9652. Free.*

Children are invited to wear costumes and participate in the Great Pumpkin Parade.

Rounding out the fun are pumpkin-carving and pie-eating contests, arts and crafts booths, a variety of pumpkin foods, and assorted on-going entertainment. Pumpkin patches, brightly colored with their seasonal loot, are open nearby for picking.

WHERE TO STAY

Half Moon Bay Lodge *2400 S. Cabrillo Hwy., (800) 368-2468, 726-9000, fax 726-7951. 2 stories; 81 rooms; 60 non-smoking rooms; $$$-$$$+. Children under 12 free. Some wood-burning fireplaces. Heated pool, hot tub, fitness room.*

Located at the quiet southern end of town, this modern hacienda-style lodge motel overlooks the fourth fairway of the **Half Moon Bay Golf Links**, which was designed by Arnold Palmer and rated first in the Bay Area. An oversize hot tub is within a semi-enclosed room.

San Benito House *356 Main St., 726-3425. 2 stories; 12 rooms; 100% non-smoking; $-$$$. Unsuitable for children under 10. No TVs; some shared baths. Sauna. Continental breakfast; restaurant.*

Upstairs, guest rooms feature vividly colored solid walls, high ceilings, and bathrooms with old-fashioned claw-foot tubs. Guests can stroll in the formal English garden and, perhaps, indulge in some competition on the croquet lawn.

Downstairs, the charmingly decorated **restaurant** *(D Thur-Sun, SunBr; $$-$$$. Highchairs, boosters, child menu. 100% non-smoking. Reservations advised. AE, MC, V.)* invites romantic dining. The chef makes use of fresh local produce and seafood in preparing Mediterranean-style cuisine and is accomplished in producing delicious soups and French pastries. Reservations should be made when booking a room, as this cozy dining room is very popular with locals. A **deli** *(daily 11-3)* dispenses quick, inexpensive meals, and a lively Western-style **saloon** *(daily from 4pm)* is the perfect spot for a nightcap.

WHAT TO DO

Obester Winery *12341 San Mateo Rd. (Hwy. 92), 2 mi. E of town, 726-WINE, fax 726-7074. Tasting daily 10-5.*

Call for the "Bottle Your Own" schedule—when customers bring in their own bottles to be filled directly from the barrel. Usually a non-alcoholic grape juice varietal, such as Gewurztraminer or Pinot Noir, is served to kids while their parents taste the real thing.

Picnic. Put one together by visiting old-fashioned **Cunha's Country Store** *(Main St./Kelly Ave., 726-4071.)*, which has been in the same building for over 50 years, and the **Half Moon Bay Bakery** *(514 Main St., 726-4841.)*, which is still using its original brick ovens and is known for its French bread and Portuguese sweet bread. The bakery also makes its own donuts, and sandwiches are available to go.

While picking up supplies, allow some time for poking around in some of the shops on Main Street. Don't miss **Feed & Fuel** *(331 Main St., 726-4814.)*, an old-time farm supply store that sells farm, pet, and garden supplies to locals and has plenty of chicks, ducklings, bunnies, and other small farm animals to pet and purchase.

The area's spectacular beaches are popular picnic destinations summer through fall— when the weather tends to be warm and clear. **Dunes Beach**, which is part of **Half Moon Bay State Beach**, is a personal favorite.

Pescadero

(Area Code 415)

GETTING THERE

Located 50 miles south of San Francisco.

WHERE TO STAY

Pigeon Point Lighthouse Hostel *210 Pigeon Point Rd., 879-0633. 52 beds; rooms for families & couples.*

Named after the first big ship that crashed on the rocks here, this scenic lighthouse, built in 1871, is the second tallest freestanding lighthouse in the U.S. Visitors are housed in adjacent bungalows, and a hot tub is available in the evenings. See also page 391.

Public **lighthouse tours** are available *(879-0633. Sun 10-3, also 1st & 3rd Sat of month.)*, and excellent tidepools are located just to the north.

WHERE TO EAT

Duarte's Tavern *202 Stage Rd., 879-0464. B, L, & D daily; $-$$. Highchairs, boosters, booths. Reservations advised for D. AE, MC, V.*

Diners have been coming here since 1894 to enjoy drinks in the old-time bar and a home-cooked meal in the cozy, casual coffee shop. (The name is pronounced "Do-arts.") Breakfast, served until 1 p.m. on weekdays, features giant buttermilk pancakes and outstanding omelettes —especially the sautéed garlic and artichoke and the linguica (spicy Portuguese sausage) versions—as well as more usual items. At lunch or dinner try the delicious creamy artichoke heart or green chile soups, giant boiled artichokes with garlic mayo dip, fried oysters, homemade pie, and fresh applesauce. Grilled fresh fish is available at dinner, and a popular fixed-price cioppino feed is scheduled each Friday, Saturday, and Sunday night by reservation. (Artichoke items are made with artichokes picked fresh in nearby fields.)

Do take a walk through this tiny agricultural town. Of special note are the colorful fields of straw flowers, the old-fashioned general store, and a 130-year-old church. For a lovely ride through the back country, take the quiet, winding road that begins in front of the restaurant (State Road) and follow it seven miles north to San Gregorio, where the **Peterson and Alsford General Store,** an old-fashioned country emporium, provides an interesting stop for picnic supplies, and nearby **San Gregorio State Beach**, which often has sun when none is to be found elsewhere along this stretch of coast, provides a picturesque spot to enjoy it.

WHAT TO DO

Año Nuevo State Reserve *New Year's Creek Rd., 879-2025. Tours Dec-Apr; reservations required & can be made up to 8 weeks in advance at (800) 444-7275. $4/person + $5/vehicle.*

Huge elephant seals return to this beach each year to mate and bear their young. It is the only elephant seal rookery on the U.S. mainland. Docent-guided tours, lasting 2½ hours and covering three miles, take visitors close enough to observe the seals basking in the sun or sleep-

ing. Usually that is the extent of the activity seen, but occasionally one of the weighty bulls (some weigh almost 8,000 pounds!) roars into battle with a challenging male. When picking a tour date note that the males arrive in December (when most of the battles occur), the females arrive in January, and the babies start being born in late January. Mating usually occurs in February, when the population is at its peak. Then the adult seals, and tourists, begin to leave, making March and April—when the weaned pups are still around—a somewhat quieter time to visit. An even quieter time is the rest of the year, when advance tickets aren't necessary. Call ahead for schedule. Note that no food service is available at the reserve, and no drinking water is available along the tour trail.

Depending on the season, pick-your-own olallieberries (June and July), pumpkins (October), kiwi fruit (November), or Christmas trees are waiting across the street at 476-acre, usually sunny **Coastways Ranch** *(640 Cabrillo Hwy. (Hwy. 1), 879-0414. June-July daily 9-5, Oct-Dec 10-4; closed Jan-May & Aug-Sept.).* This ranch has been farmed by the Hudson family since 1917. Call ahead for current information on crops, and bring along garden gloves to protect hands. Picnic facilities and snacks are available.

Pescadero State Beach *New Year's Creek Rd., 879-2170.*

Sand dunes at the north end invite sliding, a creek invites wading, and tidepools invite exploring. The **Pescadero Marsh Natural Preserve**, a 210-acre refuge for waterfowl and wildlife that teems with migrating birds and native plants, adjoins. Marked trails are available for hiking, and docent-led nature walks are scheduled on weekends. Tidepool explorations are also scheduled when the tides are right. Call for current schedule.

Davenport

(Area Code 408)

WHERE TO STAY

Davenport Bed & Breakfast Inn *31 Davenport Ave./Hwy. 1, 9 mi. N of Santa Cruz, (800) 870-1817, 425-1818, fax 423-1160. 2 stories; 12 rooms; 100% non-smoking; $$-$$$. No TVs. M-F $7/person credit for breakfast in restaurant, Sat & Sun full breakfast; restaurant.*

Some of the eclectically decorated, colorful rooms here have skylights and ocean views. All guests are greeted with a complimentary drink in the restaurant bar.

WHERE TO EAT

Davenport Cash Store and Restaurant *(800) 870-1817, 426-4122, fax 423-1160. B, L, & D daily. High-chairs, boosters. 100% non-smoking. MC, V.*

Rebuilt on the site of an old-time cash store that was destroyed by fire in the 1950s, this spot's eclectic menu includes Mexican items, a hamburger, vegetarian dishes, and a variety of fresh house-made bread and pastries—all served in a comfortable, large open space. The cash store features yet more eclecticism, with everything from Italian soaps to African hats for sale.

WHAT TO DO

Bonny Doon Vineyard *10 Pine Flat Rd., Bonny Doon, 8 mi. north of Santa Cruz, then 5 mi. up the hill, 425-4518, 425-3856. Tasting W-M 12-5; tours by appt.*

The pleasant side trip taken to reach this winery follows a meandering country road to the tiny mountain town of Bonny Doon. Picnic facilities are provided in a redwood grove complete with a gurgling creek. Winery specialties include exotic French and Italian varietals and a Muscat Canelli. A rich raspberry-flavored Framboise dessert wine makes delicious sipping. Do try one of the unusual, brandy-like fruit eaux de vie.

Davenport Jail Museum *on Hwy. 1, 2 Davenport Ave./Ocean Ave., 425-7278. Sat & Sun 10-2. Free.*

Due to the generally peaceful nature of the area's residents, this two-cell jail, built in 1914, was used only once. In 1987 it was transformed into a small museum with exhibits on the history of Santa Cruz county's north coast.

Rancho del Oso Nature and History Center *3600 Hwy. 1, 16 mi. north of Santa Cruz, 427-2288. Sat & Sun 12-4. Free.*

Located on Waddell Creek and part of **Big Basin Redwoods State Park**, this bucolic spot has a marked nature trail leading through one of the few remaining native Monterey pine forests; a guided nature walk is scheduled every Sunday at 1. Former president Herbert Hoover's brother Theodore settled this valley in 1914 and his family home is now the museum. After viewing vintage photos and checking out the old logging artifacts and wildlife exhibit, consider a picnic either in the sheltered courtyard or on the deck overlooking the preserve.

Just across the street, **Waddell Beach** is a popular spot for wind-surfing and hang-gliding.

Santa Cruz
(Area Code 408)

A LITTLE BACKGROUND

Close enough to San Francisco to visit just for the day, Santa Cruz has long been a popular summer destination. Weather is reliably clear and sunny, and the beach features fine sand and a gentle surf. In fact, it is a Very Southern California-style beach town. The beach people add to the simile with zinc on their noses, surfboards hanging out of their cars, and The Beach Boys blaring from their tapedecks. Why, even the police officers wear shorts!

The 1989 Loma Prieta earthquake wreaked havoc here. The damage was severe along the popular Pacific Garden Mall, which is slowly being rebuilt.

VISITOR INFORMATION

Santa Cruz County Conference & Visitors Council *701 Front St., Santa Cruz 95060, (800) 833-3494, 425-1234, fax 425-1260.*

GETTING THERE

Located approximately 80 miles south of San Francisco. Take Highway 101 or Highway 280 to Highway 17, or Highway 1 all the way.

ANNUAL EVENTS

West Coast Antique Fly-In & Airshow *May. In Watsonville; 496-9559, 262-1287. Free-$10.*

Always held on Memorial Day Weekend, this is one of the largest antique fly-in and air shows on the West Coast. It features an assortment of antique and classic planes, including some from World Wars I and II and some home-built models.

Roses of Yesterday and Today *May & June. In Watsonville, 803 Browns Valley Rd. (call for directions); 724-3537, fax 724-1408. Daily 9-3. Free; catalog $3.*

Tucked into a redwood canyon, this demonstration garden for a mail-order nursery is an extraordinary sight when its approximately 450 varieties of old-fashioned roses bloom in unison. Picnic tables are available.

Cabrillo Music Festival *August. 426-6966, fax 426-6968. Free-$25.*

This is said to be one of the country's best small music festivals. The program includes a variety of contemporary orchestral works, including world premieres, and some events are scheduled at Mission San Juan Bautista.

WHERE TO STAY

Babbling Brook Inn *1025 Laurel St., (800) 866-1131, 427-2437, fax 427-2457. 12 rooms; 100% non-smoking; $$-$$$+; 2-night min. on Sat. Unsuitable for children under 13. Some wood-burning & gas fireplaces. Afternoon & evening snack, full breakfast; limited room service.*

Shaded by tall redwoods, this secluded hillside inn was built as a log cabin in 1909. Rooms have been added through the years. Now this rambling inn is the oldest and largest B&B in the area and is on the National Register of Historic Places. Most of the rooms are named after impressionist painters, and decorated in the artist's favorite themes and colors. And the inn delivers what its name promises: a babbling brook runs through the property, and there are even a few cascading waterfalls. The acre of beautifully landscaped grounds surrounding the inn also features paths, a covered footbridge, an 18th-century water wheel, and a lacy wrought-iron gazebo.

Casa Blanca Inn *101 Main St., (800) 644-1570, 423-1570, fax 423-0235. 2 stories; 33 rooms; $$-$$$+. Some kitchens; wood-burning & gas fireplaces. Restaurant, limited room service (child items).*

Located across the street from the beach and Boardwalk, this converted 1918 mansion features spacious, pleasantly decorated rooms. More rooms, boasting terraces and a country-style decor, are available in a newer 1950s annex.

Seafood dinners and Sunday brunch are served in the **Casablanca** restaurant *(426-9063; D daily, SunBr; $$-$$$. Highchairs, boosters, child portions. Reservations advised. AE, MC, V.)*, which features the largest wine cellar in the county.

Chateau Victorian *118 First St., 458-9458. 2 stories; 7 rooms; 100% non-smoking; $$$. Unsuitable for* *children under 18. No TVs; all wood-burning fireplaces. Afternoon snack, continental breakfast.*

Built around the turn of the century, this B&B is only a block from the beach and Boardwalk. Attention to detail is displayed throughout. A favorite room is the L-shaped Lighthouse Room on the second floor. The inn's largest room, it is furnished with a large armoire, a queen-sized brass bed, and two very comfortable oversize rolled-arm chairs that are positioned on either side of the fireplace.

Dream Inn *175 W. Cliff Dr., (800) 662-3838, 426-4330, fax 427-2025. 10 stories; 163 rooms; 120 non-smoking rooms; $$$-$$$+. Children under 12 free. All VCRs; some kitchens. Heated pool, child wading pool, hot tub, sauna. 2 restaurants, room service (child items).*

This hotel is located right on the beach, within easy walking distance of the Boardwalk, and each room has a private balcony or patio overlooking the beach and ocean. The pool and hot tub are one story up from the sand and enjoy the same view.

The **Compass Grille and Bar** has a fantastic beach and ocean view, and its windows are usually open to the sounds of waves breaking on the shore. A **scotch tasting** *($15)* of six single-malt varieties, all more than ten years old, can be experienced at the bar.

Ocean Echo Motel & Cottages *401 Johans Beach Dr., 462-4192. 15 units; $$; 2-night min. in summer. Some kitchens.*

Located a few miles south of the Boardwalk, these attractive rooms and cottages are on a private beach.

Santa Cruz Hostel *423-8304.*

This cottage complex is close to downtown and the beach. See also page 391.

Sea & Sand Inn *201 W. Cliff Dr., 427-3400, same fax. 2 stories; 20 rooms; some non-smoking rooms; $$-$$$+; 2-night min. on Sat. Children under 12 free. Afternoon snack, continental breakfast.*

Perched on a cliff high above the beach, all rooms have views of the ocean and Boardwalk. The soothing sound of the surf breaking on the shore below is continuous, and an extensive grassy area in front of the rooms is bordered with colorful plants and flowers and furnished with tables and chairs, inviting repose. Though there is no direct beach access, it is just a short walk to the beach and Boardwalk.

Motel Row. Many motels are located in the area surrounding the Boardwalk, including some inexpensive ones dating from the 1930s. Rooms are usually available at the last minute.

WHERE TO STAY NEARBY

Pajaro Dunes *2661 Beach Rd., Watsonville, (800) 678-8808, 722-9201, fax 728-7444. 1-3 stories; 125 units; 15 non-smoking units; $$$+; 2-night min. on weekends. All VCRs, kitchens, & wood-burning fireplaces. 19 tennis courts.*

Situated in the shoreline dunes, this private compound consists of condominiums, town-houses, and homes. Hiking and biking trails, jogging paths, and volleyball and basketball courts round out the recreational facilities. Bike rentals are also available.

WHERE TO EAT

The Crow's Nest *2218 E. Cliff Dr., 476-4560. L & D daily; $$. Highchairs, boosters, child portions. Reservations advised in summer. AE, MC, V.*

Fresh local seafood is the specialty here, but steaks, salads, and an enchilada are also on the menu. Children get a color-in menu and a prize from the treasure chest. Diners can be seated outdoors, protected by a glass windbreaker, and enjoy ocean views or watch the yachts come and go from the Santa Cruz Yacht Harbor. A cocktail lounge upstairs offers live entertainment and dancing.

El Palomar *1336 Pacific Ave., 425-7575, fax 423-3037. L & D daily, SunBr; $-$$. Highchairs, boosters, booths, child menu. 100% non-smoking. No reservations. AE, MC, V.*

Housed in the cool, attractively remodeled back room of a 1930s hotel, with high ceilings and colorful wall murals, this restaurant serves well-prepared, authentic Michoacan-style Mexican food. Tortillas are made by hand each day, and there is a large selection of Mexican beers. Unusual menu items include pozole (pork and hominy stew), carne asada (barbecued beef), and occasionally menudo (tripe soup). The fresh seafood specials are also usually quite appealing. Children might especially enjoy the sopes (little tortillas shaped like boats and filled with chicken, guacamole, or tasty ground beef).

Gabriella Cafe *910 Cedar St., 457-1677, fax 423-3919. L & D daily, Sat & SunBr. Highchairs. 100% non-smoking. Reservations advised. AE, MC, V.*

In an intimate space, with fresh flowers and candles adorning the tables and angel images throughout, this romantic, European-style hideaway produces delightful northern Italian fare. For starters, a roasted garlic-rosemary spread is one of several available to enhance the complimentary house-baked focaccia. Among several salads made with local organic produce are a house salad with edible flowers and a panzanella (bread salad). Main courses include eight-inch pizzeta, several kinds of pasta and a risotto, and fish or meat dishes such as chicken Diavola—a flavorfully marinated chicken breast grilled under a brick and served with a side of soft polenta and a sauteed vegetable. House-made desserts include a raspberry jam bread pudding and a rich tiramisu.

Hobee's *740 Front St., 458-1212. B & L daily, D W-Sun. Highchairs, boosters, child menu. 100% non-smoking. No reservations. AE, MC, V.*

The secret to success here is tasty, wholesome food prepared with plenty of vegetables and tofu and served in a cheerful atmosphere in comfortable surroundings. The breakfast menu, which is available all day, offers a selection of omelettes and scrambles as well as items such as whole wheat pancakes, cinnamon-orange swirl French toast, and granola. Lunch and dinner bring on a salad bar, homemade soups, and a variety of sandwiches and hamburgers.

India Joze Restaurant *1001 Center St., 427-3554, fax 427-0230. L M-Sat, D daily, SunBr; $$. Highchairs, boosters, child menu. 100% non-smoking. Reservations advised. MC, V.*

A variety of Asian cuisines, plus many vegetarian and vegan dishes, appear on this restaurant's exciting, exotic menu. The pleasant dining area is light and airy, and a large patio exudes a tropical atmosphere. The kitchen is well-known for its splendid desserts, which can also be enjoyed sans meal in an informal dining area. Each August the menu reflects the fact that the restaurant is the home of the **International Calamari Festival.** (Co-owners Beth Regardz and Joseph Schultz are co-authors of *The Calamari Cookbook*.) Before or after a meal here, browsing is pleasant in the adjoining **Santa Cruz Art Center** shops.

Santa Cruz Brewing Co. & Front Street Pub *516 Front St., 429-8838, fax 429-8915. L & D daily; $. Boosters, child menu. 100% non-smoking. Reservations advised. AE, MC, V.*

Located downtown, this cheerful spot claims to be "the first brewery on California's central coast since Prohibition." It dispenses made-on-the-premises brews: an European-style Lighthouse Lager, a Lighthouse Amber, and a dark Pacific Porter. A root beer made from an old-time

recipe is also available. Like the brews, the pub food is made fresh on the premises and includes steaks, oyster shots (spicy oysters in a shot glass), beer bread (made from the spent grains of beer-making), and fish & chips (battered deep-fried halibut). All this, plus an assortment of sandwiches and "munchies."

WHAT TO DO

Beach & Boardwalk *400 Beach St., 423-5590. From 11am, daily June-Sept, weekends Oct-May; call for closing time. Admission to Boardwalk free; individual rides $1.50-$3, all-day ride ticket $17.95; miniature golf $4.75-$5.75.*

Fortunately, this is one beach boardwalk that has not degenerated over the years. Built in 1907, it was spiffed up a few years ago with a cheerful painting. Now the only boardwalk left on the West Coast and the oldest amusement park in California, it offers a variety of arcade games, fast-food stands (don't miss the salt water taffy and caramel apples at **Marini's**), and souvenir shops—plus 20 major rides and 7 kiddie rides. The half-mile-long concrete walkway parallels a clean, gorgeous beach. Thrill rides include the **Giant Dipper**, a rickety wooden roller coaster built in 1924 and rated by *The New York Times* as one of the ten best in the country, and Logger's Revenge, a refreshing water flume ride. An old-fashioned **merry-go-round**, built in New Jersey by Charles Looff in 1911 and the largest of the four remaining classic carousels in Northern California, features 70 hand-carved horses (all with authentic horsehair tails) and 2 chariots as well as its rare, original 1894 342-pipe Ruth Und Sohn band organ and a brass (now steel) ring toss—one of the few left in the world. Both the roller coaster and the carousel are now National Historic Landmarks, and the Boardwalk itself is a California Historic Landmark. All this and indoor miniature golf, too!

History Museum of Santa Cruz County *705 Front St., 425-7278. Tu-Sun 11-4, Thur to 8. Adults $4, under 12 free.*

The permanent collection exhibited here focuses on the social history of Santa Cruz county.

Joseph M. Long Marine Laboratory *West end of Delaware Ave., 459-4308. Tu-Sun 1-4. Adults $2.*

This marine research station for U.C. Santa Cruz features both a small aquarium of local sea life and a touching pool stocked with hermit crabs, sea stars, and sea anemones. Outside, the skeleton of an 86-foot-long blue whale makes an impressive display. (The whale washed ashore up the coast on Pescadero Beach in 1979.) Guided tours are usually available and include viewing the tanks where sea lions are housed for study. Research is conducted here on a variety of topics, including marine mammal behavior, fish diseases, and coral genetics.

Lighthouse Point *On West Cliff Dr.*
• **Santa Cruz Surfing Museum** *429-3429, fax 469-4371. W-M 12-4; closed W Dec-Mar. By donation.*

This unique museum is housed within the small brick **Mark Abbott Memorial Lighthouse.**
• **Seal Rock**, home to a herd of sea lions, is visible off shore.
• **Steamer Lane.** Surfers can be viewed in action from here.

The Mystery Spot *465 Mystery Spot Rd., 3 mi. north of town (call for directions), 423-8897, fax 429-6653. Daily 9-5; in summer to 8:30. Adults $4, 5-11 $2.*

Located in a grove of redwoods, this small, quiet, cool spot measures only about 150 feet in diameter. Visitors are given a guided tour during which gravitational forces appear to be defied, and everyone leaves with a souvenir bumper sticker. (Finding it can be a bit of a mystery, too.)

Natural Bridges State Beach *2531 West Cliff Dr., at north end, 423-4609. Daily 8am-sunset. $6/vehicle.*

Enjoy a picnic in the sun on the sandy beach, or in the shade at sturdy tables. All but one of the mudstone arches, after which the beach is named, have collapsed, but there are still plenty of tidepools to explore. Swimming in the ocean is recommended only when a lifeguard is on duty, but sometimes a lagoon forms where small children can wade safely.

From October through February large numbers of **monarch butterflies** make their winter home here. A short nature trail leads to good viewing points where they can be observed hanging in clusters on mature eucalyptus trees. Guided walks are also often scheduled. During monarch season, a Visitors Center *(Daily 10-4)* displays informative exhibits.

Pacific Avenue/Downtown Santa Cruz *Pacific Ave. between Water St. & Cathcart St.*

These five landscaped blocks comprise downtown Santa Cruz. Once the park-like setting was home to a variety of boutiques, art galleries, and restaurants operating from within restored historic buildings. But the 1989 Loma Prieta earthquake turned the area into a disaster zone of destruction. Now things are hopping again, especially in the evening. **Bookshop Santa Cruz** *(1520 Pacific Ave., 423-0900. Daily 9-11.),* which had temporarily relocated inside a canvas tent, is now in a grand new building. Adjacent **Georgiana's Cafe** *(1522 Pacific Ave., 427-9900. Daily B, L, & D; $.)* offers quick and delicious dining options. At lunch, sandwiches are served on delicious breads, and a tempting assortment of pastries and coffees always awaits. Tables are available in the cozy indoors, as well as outside just off the sidewalk.

Santa Cruz City Museum of Natural History *1305 E. Cliff Dr., 429-3773, fax 469-4371. Tu-Sun 10-5. Adults $2, 13-18 $1.*

Located across the street from wonderful **Seabright Beach,** this museum displays the county's natural treasures. Exhibits include Native American relics, fossils, local wildlife specimens, an operating beehive, and a "touch tank" of live sea animals. Earthquake information is also provided.

Santa Cruz Mission State Historic Park *144 School St., 425-5849, fax 429-1840. Thur-Sun 10-4; call for tour times. Adults $2, 6-18 $1, family $5.*

A restored adobe building here is all that remains of the original mission complex. Originally part of a larger structure, this building is now the only remaining example of Indian mission housing in California. Among the exhibits now contained in its rooms is an example of living quarters for Native American families. Just off the adobe, a large Victorian garden gone wild, with several tall redwoods and a giant avocado tree that is one of the oldest in the state, invites a leisurely picnic. Living History Day, when docents in period dress oversee a variety of crafts activities, occurs each month; call for schedule.

A block away, **Mission Santa Cruz** *(126 High St., 426-5686. Tu-Sat 10-4, Sun 10-2; call to verify schedule. By donation.),* which was built in 1794, is 12th in the chain of missions. Destroyed in an earthquake in 1857, the mission was rebuilt in 1931 as this half-size replica. It now houses a small museum displaying original statues, candlesticks, and paintings, as well as ornate vestments and a baptismal font.

Santa Cruz Municipal Wharf *Near the Boardwalk, 429-3628. Daily 5am-2am.*

It is possible to either walk or drive to the end of this half-mile-long pier. Fishermen angle from the side, and seafood restaurants, snack stands, and picnic tables are scattered along its length. Seals can be fed through fishing holes at the end of the pier, and deep-sea fishing trips originate at concessions located here.

University of California, Santa Cruz Campus *1156 High St., 459-0111. Free parking Sat & Sun, M-F $3.*

Located high in the hills above town, the buildings of this spectacularly beautiful campus are hidden among a forest of old-growth redwoods. Gorgeous views of the Monterey Bay are enjoyed from many locations. Pick up a map at the Public Information Office *(459-2495)* and take a self-guided walking tour. **Guided tours** *(459-4008. M-F at 9:30, 12:30, & 3. Reservations required. Free.)* are also available, and free shuttle buses loop the campus daily. The **Arboretum** *(427-2998. Daily 9-5.)* has an extensive collection of plants from Australia and New Zealand and of South African protea. **Whole Earth** *(In Redwood Tower building, 426-8255. B & L daily, D M-F; $. No reservations. No cards.)* is a cafeteria-style natural foods restaurant with seating on a spacious deck under the redwoods. **Bay Tree Bookstore** *(459-4544. M-F 8:30-5:30, Sat 10-4.)* dispenses student books and supplies as well as the now-famous "U C Santa Cruz Banana Slugs" t-shirt worn by John Travolta in *Pulp Fiction.*

Wilder Ranch State Historic Park *1401 Old Coast Rd., off Hwy. 1, 2 mi. north of town, 426-0505. W-Sun 10-4; tours on Sat & Sun 11-4. $6/vehicle.*

The perfect spot to spend a lazy day in the country, this 4,000-acre turn-of-the-century ranch complex invites visitors to bring along a picnic. Formerly a dairy, it was built in an arroyo, or valley, that protects it from whipping coastal winds, and is reached via a short walk down from the parking lot. Visitors can inspect the owner's large Queen Anne Victorian home, an even older adobe, a bunk house, several barns, a chicken coop, and miscellaneous other structures. Domesticated animals bring life to the old buildings: horses, cows, goats, chickens, and guinea hens. Docents add to the atmosphere by dressing in old-fashioned garb. The Old Cove Landing Trail provides a four-mile nature walk. If all goes well, pond turtles, cormorants, and harbor seals might be sighted, and a fern grotto is also on the itinerary. A self-guiding brochure is available at the trailhead.

Capitola
(Area Code 408)

A LITTLE BACKGROUND

Dating back to 1861, this historic seaside resort was the state's first. Now it is an artsy-craftsy beach town. The lovely mile-long beach is sheltered between two bluffs and offers both swimming in calm ocean waters and wading in the fresh water of Soquel Creek. Be cautious, however, as sometimes that creek water isn't so fresh.

Fronting the beach, **The Esplanade** is lined with coffeehouses and restaurants serving everything from hamburgers to lobster. Many have outdoor patios overlooking the beach.

Because it is such a popular spot, in summer free shuttle buses are in service to take visitors from parking lots on Bay Avenue to the beach. Some shuttle bikes are also available for loan.

VISITOR INFORMATION

Capitola Chamber of Commerce *621-B Capitola Ave., Capitola 95010, (800) 474-6522, 475-6522, fax 475-6530.*

GETTING THERE

Located approximately 5 miles south of Santa Cruz.

ANNUAL EVENTS

Begonia Festival *September. 476-3566. Free.*

Begun years ago as a way to make use of the beautiful blooms discarded by local begonia growers interested only in the bulbs, this popular festival includes a sand castle contest, fishing derby, and nautical parade of flower-covered floats down Soquel Creek. Throughout the festival, the town's merchants and homeowners put on their own shows with begonia displays and decorations. (The only other begonia festival in the world is held in Ballarat, Australia.)

Capitola Venetian Hotel

WHERE TO STAY

Capitola Inn *822 Bay Ave., 462-3004, same fax. 2 stories; 56 rooms; 32 non-smoking rooms; $$-$$$+. Children under 6 free. Some kitchens & gas fireplaces. Heated pool. Small dogs welcome.*

At this tasteful, modern lodging facility each room has a private patio.

Capitola Venetian Hotel *1500 Wharf Rd., (800) 332-2780, 476-6471. 2 stories; 20 units; 8 non-smoking units; $-$$$; 2-night min. on weekends. All kitchens; some fireplaces.*

This mini-village of charming stucco apartments is located right on the beach. Some units have balconies and ocean views; the most spectacular has a panoramic ocean view and a fireplace in the bedroom. Built in the 1920s, this was California's first condominium complex.

Harbor Lights Motel *5000 Cliff Dr., 476-0505. 10 rooms; $$-$$$. Children under 5 free. Some kitchens; 1 fireplace.*

This ordinary motel boasts an extraordinary location just across from the beach. Some rooms have views of Monterey Bay, the village, and the beach.

WHERE TO EAT

Margaritaville *221 Esplanade, 476-2263. B, L, & D daily, SunBr.*

For description, see page 183.

Mimi's Ice Cream Cart.

In summer, be on the lookout for pretty Mimi pedaling her ice cream bike while peddling cold ice cream to hot and hungry tourists. It's been awhile since Mimi has been spotted. Hopefully she's still around and hasn't become just another wispy legend.

Shadowbrook *1750 Wharf Rd., 475-1511, 475-7664. D daily, SunBr; $$-$$$. Highchairs, boosters, child menu. 100% non-smoking. Reservations advised. AE, MC, V.*

Located on the banks of Soquel Creek, the heart of this popular restaurant is a log cabin originally built as a summer home in the 1920s. Diners descend to the restaurant either by riding a bright red, self-operated tram down a flower-laden hill from the street above, or by strolling down a winding step-path. Most tables offer views of the creek, often with the added entertainment of ducks and geese cavorting on the water. The menu features prime rib and fresh fish as well as a variety of specials. A house specialty is scampi prepared with succulent giant prawns. Dinners include a choice of either Caesar salad or a creamy artichoke soup, a fresh vegetable, and freshly baked sourdough bread. A jukebox provides music for dancing each evening in the bar, and live entertainment is scheduled on weekends. Though children are truly welcome, this restaurant exudes a romantic atmosphere.

WHAT TO DO

Antonelli Brothers Begonia Gardens *2545 Capitola Rd., Santa Cruz, 475-5222. Daily 9-5. Free.*

Acres of indoor plants, ferns, and beautiful begonia baskets can be viewed and purchased here. Peak of bloom is August and September, but a good show can also be enjoyed June through October. Picnic tables are available in the Hanging Begonia Room.

Bargetto Winery *3535 N. Main St., Soquel, 475-2258, fax 475-2664. Tasting & tours daily 9-5.*

This small family winery is known both for fruit wines, including olallieberry and apricot (a personal favorite), and excellent homemade wine vinegars. It also produces an unusual and authentic Mead (honey wine). Bring a picnic to enjoy on the rustic outdoor patio overlooking gurgling Soquel Creek.

Monterey Peninsula

A LITTLE BACKGROUND

Popular for years because of its proximity to San Francisco, this area (Monterey, Pacific Grove, Carmel, and Carmel Valley) is well-established as a vacation destination. A vast variety of overnight accommodations and restaurants is available. Once the off-season was the entire winter. Now, due to the area's immense popularity, there is no off-season and reservations are essential for both lodging and the more popular restaurants.

Recently established, the **Monterey Bay National Marine Sanctuary** is the nation's eleventh and largest protected marine area. It covers more than 300 miles—from the Farallon Islands near San Francisco in the north to Cambria in the south. Protected resources include the nation's most expansive kelp forests, one of North America's largest underwater canyons, and a deep ocean environment that is the closest to shore in the continental U.S. The Monterey Bay Aquarium acts as the sanctuary's interpretive center.

GETTING THERE

Located approximately 40 miles south of Santa Cruz.

STOPS ALONG THE WAY

Giant Artichoke Restaurant *11261 Merritt St., off Hwy. 1, Castroville, (408) 633-3204. B, L, & D daily; $. Highchairs, boosters. No reservations. MC, V.*

Located in "the artichoke capital of the world," where three-quarters of the nation's artichokes are grown, this novelty restaurant makes a good rest stop. To find it, just look for the giant artichoke. Artichoke specialties include French-fried artichokes with mayonnaise dip, artichoke soup, artichoke salad, artichoke quiche, and artichoke cake. Other more standard short-order items are also on the menu.

Monterey

(Area Code 408)

VISITOR INFORMATION

Monterey Peninsula Visitors & Convention Bureau *P.O. Box 1770 (380 Alvarado St.), Monterey 93942-1770, 649-1770, fax 648-5373.*

ANNUAL EVENTS

Adobe House Tour *July. 372-2608.*

This is a very popular self-guided walking tour of historic adobe homes and buildings.

Monterey Scottish Festival and Highland Games *August. At Monterey Fairgrounds; 375-8608, fax 899-7907. Adults $10, 65+ & 7-16 $8.50.*

Celebrating everything Scottish, this event is described as being much like a Celtic three-ring circus. One ring features piping (as in bagpipes) and drumming contests, with massive pipe bands competing against each other. Another ring features unusual athletic events such as the Caber Toss (in which a huge pole is tossed end-over-end for accuracy) and Putting the Stone (in which a heavy stone is tossed). And another presents the Highland Dancing Championships, which today is participated in predominantly by females. Events, including several sheepdog demonstrations, run continuously.

Monterey Historic Automobile Races *August.* **Grand Prix** *September. Both at Laguna Seca Racetrack in Salinas; (800) 327-SECA, 648-5111.*

Originally held in Pebble Beach, the Historic Automobile Races demonstrate the abilities of a broad range of vintage sports and racing cars. At the Grand Prix, Indy cars take the stage for three days featuring the world's best drivers.

Castroville Artichoke Festival *September. In Castroville; 633-CHOK. Adults $4, 6-12 $2.*

This is one of the state's oldest agricultural festivals. It was at this festival in 1947 that Marilyn Monroe was crowned the very first California Artichoke Queen.

Monterey Jazz Festival *September. At Monterey Fairgrounds; (800) 307-3378, 373-3366, fax 373-0244. Tickets $115-$165, under 2 free.*

The oldest continuously presented jazz festival in the country, this well-known event offers three days of non-stop entertainment. Tickets usually sell out by the end of July.

Christmas in the Adobes *647-6226.* **La Posada** *646-3866. Both in December.*

Adobes are decorated for the season and lighted with luminaria and candles, and a candlelight parade re-enacts Mary and Joseph's search for a room in Bethlehem.

WHERE TO STAY

Casa Munras Garden Hotel *700 Munras Ave, (800) 222-2446 CA, (800) 222-2558 US, 375-2411, fax 375-1365. 2 stories; 152 rooms; 81 non-smoking rooms; $$-$$$+. Children under 12 free. Some gas fireplaces. Heated pool. Restaurant.*

One of the first residences built outside the walls of the old Presidio in 1824, the original Casa was built of individual adobe bricks made by hand from native materials. Some of the dining room and porch of the original house remain. The house was converted into a hotel in 1941. Today its grounds are spacious, attractive, and peaceful, and all rooms are furnished with brass beds.

Hotel Pacific *300 Pacific St., (800) 554-5542, 373-5700, fax 373-6921. 3 stories; 105 rooms; 84 non-smoking rooms; $$$+; 2-night min. on weekends. Children under 12 free. All VCRs & gas fireplaces. 2 hot tubs. Afternoon snack, continental breakfast; limited room service.*

Situated near the Wharf, this newish lodging features adobe-style architecture and attractive gardens with fountains. It melds the amenities of a hotel with the convenience of a motel. All rooms are spacious suites equipped with down comforters and pillows as well as featherbeds, and nightly turndown service is provided.

Hyatt Regency Monterey *One Old Golf Course Rd., (800) 228-9000, 372-1234, fax 375-3960. 3-4 stories; 575 rooms; 300 non-smoking rooms; $$$-$$$+. Children under 18 free. 2 heated pools, 2 hot tubs, fitness room, parcourse, 6 tennis courts ($5/person/hr.; 2 with night lights, $10/person/hr.). Restaurant, room service (child items).*

Located on the outskirts of town, this quiet, luxurious resort is adjacent to the scenic **Old**

Del Monte Golf Course—the oldest golf course west of the Mississippi. **Knuckles Historical Sports Bar** has 14 TVs tuned to sports action in a casual, peanut-shells-on-the-floor atmosphere. Camp Hyatt, an organized activity program for children, operates during holiday periods.

Monterey Bay Inn *242 Cannery Row, (800) 424-6242, 373-6242, fax 373-7603. 4 stories; 47 rooms; 100% non-smoking; $$$-$$$+; 2-night min. on weekends. Children under 12 free. All VCRs. 2 hot tubs, sauna, fitness room. Evening snack, continental breakfast delivered to room; limited room service.*

Located a short walk from the aquarium, all rooms in this waterfront lodging feature private balconies, sleeper sofas, and plush robes. Most rooms also offer spectacular bay views, and all guests have access to the rooftop hot tub and its breathtaking view of the bay.

Monterey Marriott Hotel *350 Calle Principal, (800) 228-9290, 649-4234, fax 372-2968. 10 stories; 341 rooms; 60 non-smoking rooms; $$-$$$+. Children under 18 free. Heated pool, hot tub, fitness room. 2 restaurants, room service (child items). Dogs welcome. Parking $10.*

Located near the Wharf, this attractively designed hotel is built on the former site of the grand old Hotel San Carlos. At ten stories, it is the tallest building in town, and rooms are quiet and tastefully appointed. A sports bar presents live music in the evening, and a rooftop restaurant offers panoramic views of Monterey Bay.

Monterey Plaza *400 Cannery Row, (800) 334-3999, 646-1700, fax 646-0285. 285 rooms; $$$+; 2-night min. on weekends. Children under 18 free. Restaurant, room service. Parking $8.*

Built partially over the bay, this luxury hotel provides guests with terry robes and comfortably appointed rooms, some of which have great bay views.

Dinner at a bayside window table in the **Duck Club** *(B, L, & D daily; $$-$$$. Highchairs. 100% non-smoking. AE, MC, V. Validated valet parking.)* is a delight. For starters try the crab-laden crab cakes or delicious traditional Caesar salad. Entrees include several house-made pastas, a selection of fresh seafood, and, of course, duck: crisp-roasted with Valencia orange sauce or wood-roasted with green peppercorn mustard sauce. Dessert choices include a chocolate layer cake, a large selection of house-made ice creams, and a plate of four house-made cookies.

West Wind Lodge *1046 Munras Ave., (800) 821-0805, 373-1337, fax 372-2451. 2 stories; 52 rooms; 26 non-smoking rooms; $$-$$$+. Children under 10 free. Some VCRs, kitchens, & gas fireplaces. Indoor heated pool & hot tub, sauna. Continental breakfast.*

Though the architecture of this motel is unpresumptious, its facilities are noteworthy.

Motel Row.

Modern motel accommodations abound along Munras Avenue.

WHERE TO EAT

Abalonetti Seafood Trattoria *57 Fisherman's Wharf, 373-1851, fax 373-2058. L & D daily; $-$$. Highchairs, boosters, child portions. Reservations advised. AE, MC.*

This small, unpretentious restaurant is named for a famous dish in which the squid is pounded until tender, breaded, and then sautéed in butter. Over half the menu is devoted to versions of the house specialty—calamari (squid). Other seafood and Italian dishes, as well as pizza, are also available, and the dining room has a good view of Monterey Bay.

Clock Garden Restaurant *565 Abrego St., 375-6100. L M-F, D daily, Sat & SunBr; $$. Boosters, child portions. Reservations advised for D. AE, MC, V.*

Diners have a choice of sitting either inside this historic adobe, among a collection of antique clocks, or outside in a lovely courtyard garden. Weekend brunch in the garden with a frothy Ramos fizz is highly recommended. Reservations are not taken then or for lunch, when hamburgers and house-made soups join the menu, so be there when they open or expect a wait. The dinner menu features prime rib, barbecued ribs, and fresh seafood, and the kitchen is well-known for its Greek lemon soup.

Consuelo's *361 Lighthouse Ave., 372-8111. L & D daily, SunBr; $$. Highchairs, boosters, child portions. Reservations advised. AE, MC, V.*

Though it might be located more appropriately inside one of the area's historic adobes, this Mexican restaurant operates within an elegant Victorian mansion dating from 1886. Rooms in the house have been turned into semi-private dining areas, and the menu offers typical Mexican fare as well as a few more unusual items. A personal favorite is the flauta—a chewy flour tortilla filled with shredded beef, rolled, and then deep-fried and topped with a very good guacamole. Among the children's items are a soft quesadilla (sort of a Mexican grilled cheese sandwich) and a hamburger. Meals begin with two complimentary appetizers—a mixture of spicy carrots and peppers, and a giant crisp flour tortilla topped with melted cheese and served elegantly on a pedestal tray. Desserts include a piña colada and a Kahlua cheesecake as well as a more traditional flan. Olé!

Fresh Cream *99 Pacific St., 100-C Heritage Harbor, 375-9798, fax 375-2283. D daily; $$$. 100% non-smoking. Reservations advised. AE, MC, V.*

Situated on the second story of a building across from the Wharf, this classy, serene restaurant offers a great harbor view along with excellent classical French cuisine. Appetizers include a delicious dungeness crab cake with corn salsa and red bell pepper sauce, and house-made lobster raviolis with a rich lobster butter sauce and a sprinkling of both black and gold caviars. Among the entrees, which include fresh local fish and veal, is a flawless rack of lamb Dijonnaise and a succulent roast duck with black currant sauce. The spectacular desserts include a Grand Marnier soufflé and an incredible edible chocolate box holding a mocha milk shake.

Mike's Seafood Restaurant *25 Fisherman's Wharf, 372-6153. B, L, & D daily; $-$$. Highchairs, boosters, child portions. Reservations advised at D. AE, MC, V.*

Arrive before sundown to take advantage of the excellent bay views afforded from the tables in this busy and popular seafood restaurant. Steaks, hamburgers, and chicken are also on the menu.

The Sardine Factory *701 Wave St., 373-3775. D daily; $$$. Highchairs, boosters, child menu. 100% non-smoking. Reservations advised. AE, MC, V.*

Once home to a canteen patronized by cannery workers, this building now houses an elegant, award-winning restaurant with five very different dining rooms and over 25,000 bottles of wine in its cellar. The kitchen is known for its fresh seafood and aged beef. Special items include fresh abalone, fresh Australian lobster tail, and aged beef. Appetizers include a highly acclaimed abalone cream bisque created for President Reagan's inaugural, as well as fresh clams, mussels, oysters, and dungeness crab in season.

Whaling Station Inn Restaurant *763 Wave St., 373-3778, fax 373-2460. D daily; $$$. Highchairs, boosters, child portions. Reservations advised. AE, MC, V.*

Situated inside a building that dates from 1929 and once housed a Chinese grocery store, this restaurant produces creative and delicious food. On one visit seafood selections included barbecued Monterey Bay prawns—the fresh, sweet, firm-fleshed kind that are so hard to find nowadays—and blackened fresh salmon. Entrees were served with a house salad consisting of Cajun-spiced walnuts resting on a bed of Belgian endive, spinach, and baby lettuce—all tossed with a sweet dressing fragrant with sesame oil. Steamed baby carrots and asparagus on a bed of purple cabbage accompanied the entrees, and a diamond of spicy polenta completed the plate. Grilled quail, rack of lamb, and prime steaks are among the non-seafood entrees. Desserts are made fresh in the kitchen each day, and an irresistible tray of them is presented at the end of each memorable repast.

Wharfside Restaurant *60 Fisherman's Wharf, 375-3956, fax 375-2967. L & D daily; $$. Highchairs, boosters, child portions. 100% non-smoking. Reservations advised. AE, MC, V.*

In the window downstairs it is possible to watch the various varieties of ravioli (meat and spinach, cheese, squid, salmon, shrimp, crab, lobster) being laboriously prepared. Dining takes place upstairs, where great views of the bay can be enjoyed. The menu is rounded out with other pastas and seafood, and there are plenty of reasonably-priced side orders that should please children.

WHAT TO DO

Cannery Row.

Once booming with sardine canneries, Cannery Row became a ghost town in 1945 when the sardines mysteriously disappeared from the area's ocean. Now this mile-long road houses restaurants, art galleries, shops, a **Bargetto Winery Tasting Room** *(#700, 373-4053. Tasting daily 10:30-6.)*, **Steinbeck's Spirit of Monterey Wax Museum** *(#700, 375-3770, fax 646-5309. Daily 10-9. Adults $5.95, children $3.95, under 6 free.)*, and the **Monterey Bay Aquarium** *(see page 103)*. **A Taste of Monterey** *(#700, 646-5446, fax 375-0835. Tasting daily 11-6; fee $3, applies to purchase)*, provides samplings from local wineries along with a 180-degree view of the bay and a theater presenting wine-related videos.

Reading John Steinbeck's *Cannery Row* gets visitors in the mood for visiting this historic street. Lee Chong's Heavenly Flower Grocery, mentioned in Steinbeck's novel, is now **Wing Chong Market**—a collection of shops *(#835)*, and La Ida's Cafe is now **Kalisa's** restaurant *(#851)*. Doc's lab *(#800)* is currently owned by the city.

Just a block north of the aquarium, the **American Tin Cannery Outlet Center** *(125 Ocean View Blvd., 372-1442. M-W & Sat 10-6, Thur & F 10-9, Sun 11-5.)* is worth a detour. Within its attractive industrial interior are some especially noteworthy outlets: Joan & David, Carole Little, Come Fly a Kite, Royal Doulton, and Corning-Revere. Also, **First Awakenings** *(#105, 372-1125. B & L daily; $. Highchairs, boosters, booths, child menu. No reservations. AE, MC, V.)*, with its pleasant outdoor patio and soothing live guitar music, is a good choice for breakfast items such as fresh fruit crepes and a variety of omelettes, as well as for salads and sandwiches.

Edgewater Packing Company *640 Wave St., 649-1899, fax 373-6268. Open daily, restaurant from 7:30am, merry-go-round & shops from 11, closes at 11pm Sun-Thur, at 1am F & Sat.*

This family entertainment center has a game room, with both antique pinball machines and modern video games, and a candy shop stocked with cotton candy, caramel apples, and popcorn. It also has what might be the world's fastest **merry-go-round**. Built by Herschell-Spillman in 1905, it has 36 horses and 2 chariots.

Oscar's Emporia *(B, L, & D daily; $. Highchairs, boosters, child menu. 100% non-smoking. No reservations. AE, MC, V.)* serves family-friendly food, and breakfast is available all day. Of special note are the specialty house-made ice cream concoctions and the substantial pie portions. The adjacent **Warehouse Restaurant** *(375-1921. L & D daily, SunBr; $-$$. Highchairs, boosters, child menu. 100%*

non-smoking. No reservations. AE, MC, V.) features seafood, fresh lobster, aged steaks, and Italian items such as ravioli, lasagna, fettucini, and spaghetti with various toppings. Also in this complex, **O'Kane's Irish Pub** *(375-7564. L & D daily; $-$$. Highchairs, boosters. No reservations. AE, MC, V.)* serves inexpensive pub grub, and food prices are cut in half from 10 p.m. to midnight when ordered with a drink.

Bay Bikes *(646-9090. Daily 9-7. $10+/2 hrs., $20/day.)* rents both 21-speed mountain bikes and multi-passenger Italian surrey bikes to ride on the spectacular waterfront **bike trail** that hugs the bay from Fisherman's Wharf to Lover's Point. Riders can also opt to take the 17 Mile Drive, drop the bike off at the Carmel branch of the shop, and take a taxi back. Children's bikes, child seats and trailers, rollerblades, and jogging strollers are also available. Safety equipment is included with rentals.

El Estero Park *Del Monte Ave./Camino El Estero/Fremont Blvd., 646-3866. Daily 10-dusk. Free.*

Hiking and bike trails and a lake filled with hungry ducks await. Paddle boats and canoes can be rented, and children may fish from boats. Located by the lake on Pearl Street, **Dennis the Menace Playground** features colorful play equipment designed by former area resident Hank Ketchum—creator of the *Dennis the Menace* comic strip. Notable are a hedge maze with a corkscrew slide in its center, a long suspension bridge, and an authentic Southern Pacific train engine to climb on. Picnic tables and a snack concession are available.

Fisherman's Wharf *373-0600, fax 373-2027. Shops daily 10-10. Parking $2/hr.*

Lined with restaurants and shops, the Wharf also offers some inexpensive entertainment. Sometimes an organ grinder greets visitors at the entrance, his friendly monkey anxious to take coins from children's hands. Sea lions hang out around the wharf pilings and sometimes put on a free show. The **Glass Bottom Belle** *(372-7150. Adults $6, children $2.)* offers 20-minute narrated harbor tours, and several businesses also offer deep-sea fishing expeditions.

Jacks Peak County Park *25020 Jacks Peak Park Dr., off Hwy. 68 to Salinas, 372-8551. Daily 11-7; in winter 9-5. $2-$3/vehicle.*

This 525-acre park has eight miles of trails and a variety of picnic areas. Follow the nature trail up to Jacks Peak for a great view of Monterey Bay, Carmel Bay, and the valley.

Maritime Museum of Monterey *5 Custom House Plaza, 375-2469, fax 655-3054. Daily 10-5. Adults $5, 65+ $4, 13-18 $3, 6-12 $2.*

Beginning with the history of the Spanish ships that anchored in the area four centuries ago, this new museum celebrates California's seafaring heritage. See ship models, bells, compasses, and related items, and learn about the area's naval history. Most impressive is the two-story-tall, 10,000-pound 1889 Fresnel lens once used at the Point Sur Lighthouse.

Monterey Bay Aquarium *886 Cannery Row, 648-4888. Daily 10-6; in summer 9-6. Adults $13.75, 65+ $11.75, 13-17 $4.75, 3-12 $6. Advance reservations: (800) 756-3737; $3/order.*

Built on the site of what was once the Row's largest sardine cannery, this spectacular $112 million facility is one of the nation's largest seawater aquariums. It is run by a non-profit organization with the mission of stimulating interest in, increasing knowledge about, and promoting stewardship of Monterey Bay through innovative exhibits, public education, and scientific research. Well-arranged and architecturally interesting, the aquarium provides a close-up view of the underwater habitats and creatures of Monterey Bay—an area known for its spectacular and varied marine life. Among the more than 100 galleries and exhibits is one that displays a three-story-high kelp forest and another that displays the area's playful sea otters. More than 350,000 fish, mammal, bird, invertebrate, and plant specimens are on display, and almost all are  native to Monterey Bay. Don't miss the special walk-through aviary of shorebirds or the bat ray petting pool. Children especially enjoy the Touch Pool, where they can handle a variety of sea stars and other tidepool life. The Outer Bay, which opened in March of 1996, features the world's largest acrylic window. This new area permits peeking into a simulated ocean, with sharks, ocean sunfish, green sea turtles, and schools of tuna swimming in a million gallons of water. Both a fast-food cafeteria and a pricier restaurant are available inside; picnic tables are provided outside. It is also possible to get a hand-stamp for re-entry and dine somewhere nearby.

Monterey Bay Kayaks *693 Del Monte Ave., (800) 649-5357, 373- KELP, fax 373-0119. Daily 9-6. $45/4-hr. tour.*

Observe sea lions and otters up close near Fisherman's Wharf and along Cannery Row. Tours, guided by marine biologists, include a half-hour of safety instruction, and no experience is necessary. Kayaks hold two people. Children must be at least 4½ feet tall. Smaller children can be accommodated in a triple kayak with two adults.

Monterey Peninsula Museum of Art *559 Pacific St., 372-7591, fax 372-5680. W-Sat 11-5, Sun 1-4. $3 donation.*

Located downtown, this museum exhibits regional art and photography. Important artists of the Monterey Peninsula, including Ansel Adams and Edward Weston, are well represented. The strong graphics collection includes works by Rembrandt, Manet, and Picasso.

An extension of the museum, the historic **La Mirada adobe** *(720 Via Mirada St., 372-3689.*

Thur-Sat 11-5, Sun 1-4. By donation.) is located several miles away. One of the first adobes built during the Mexican occupation of Monterey, it features antique furnishings, more works of art, and dramatic gardens with more than 75 varieties of roses and 300 varieties of rhododendrons.

Monterey State Historic Park *#20 Custom Plaza, 649-7118, 647-6236. Daily 10-4, in summer to 5; walking tour daily at 10:15, 12:30, & 2:30. Tickets $1-$5.*

Part of the California State Park system, this facility consists of both historical sites and preserved adobes. Guided tours are given of the very special **Stevenson House** (said to be haunted by a forlorn woman dressed in black), the **Cooper-Molera Adobe** (a two-acre complex with chickens, sheep, carriages, and a visitor center), the **Larkin House,** and the **Casa Soberanes**; call for schedule.

The First Theater *(Pacific St./Scott St., 375-4916. Call for performance schedule, reservations, & ticket prices.)* was once a saloon and boarding house for sailors. The first play was presented here in 1848, and the Troupers of the Gold Coast are still going strong. Nowadays the melodramatic shows and olios change periodically, but they are still presented in the tiny theater just like they were in the old days. All productions were written before 1900. Best seating for kids is on benches in the back.

The Path of History, a self-guided walking tour following gold tiles embedded in the sidewalk, leads past 44 historic buildings and gardens.

Operating from the **Pacific House**, **California Heritage Guides** *(#10 Custom House Plaza, 373-6454, fax 647-6236. M-Sat 10-4.)* provides guided walking tours through Monterey's historic area. Customized tours and tours to other areas are also available.

Rent-A-Roadster *229 Cannery Row, 647-1929, fax 647-1928. Daily 10-6. $29.95+/hr.*

Easy-to-drive, authentic reproductions of 1929 Model A Ford Roadsters can be rented for a drive down the coast or a tour of the 17-Mile Drive. Roadsters seat four—two in the front and two in the rumble seat—and a red 1930 deluxe Phaeton model seats five. It is worth the rental price just to honk the old-fashioned horn and watch reactions. A free souvenir photo is provided with every rental.

Western Hang Gliders *1 Reservation Rd./Hwy. 1, Marina, 384-2622. Daily 9-sunset. Reservations recommended.*

Located on the dunes at Marina State Beach, this hang-gliding school offers a three-hour beginning course with five flights for $89.

Pacific Grove
(Area Code 408)

A LITTLE BACKGROUND

Originally settled as a Chinese fishing village, Pacific Grove was established in 1875 as a Methodist Episcopal Church summer camp. Some modest summer cottages and distinctive Victorian-style homes remain today. Due to some of the ordinances put into effect in those early days, only recently was a liquor store opened within the town limits.

VISITOR INFORMATION

Pacific Grove Chamber of Commerce *P.O. Box 167 (584 Central Ave.), Pacific Grove 93950, (800) 656-6650, 373-3304, fax 373-3317.*

ANNUAL EVENTS

Victorian Home Tour *April. Children under 12 not permitted.*

Monarch Butterflies *October. Free.*

Each year hundreds of thousands of stunning orange and black monarch butterflies return to Pacific Grove to winter on the needles of favored local pine trees. They migrate all the way from western Canada and Alaska and stay until March, when they again fly north.

Somewhat of a mystery is how they find their way here each year since, with a lifespan of less than a year, no butterfly makes the trip twice. It is, in fact, the great grandchildren of the prior year's butterfly visitors that return. Somehow the monarchs program a genetic message into their progeny, which then return to these same trees the following fall and repeat the cycle.

Reacting to the weather somewhat as does a golden poppy, monarchs prefer to flutter about on sunny days between the hours of 10 a.m. and 4 p.m. In fact, they can't fly when temperatures drop below 55 degrees. So on cold and foggy days, which are quite common in this area, they huddle together with closed wings and are often overlooked as dull pieces of bark or dead leaves. On cold days observers must be careful where they step: Monarchs that have dropped to the ground to sip dew off the grass might be resting there, having found it too cold to fly back to their perch.

During early March the butterflies can be observed mating. Watch for females chasing males in a spiral flight. (Males are recognized by a characteristic black dot on their wings.) When a female finds a male she likes, they drop to the ground to mate. Literally standing on his head at one point, the male, while still mating, then lifts the female back to a perch in a tree, where they continue mating for almost an entire day!

Butterfly nets should be left at home. To discourage visitors from bothering these fragile creatures, Pacific Grove has made molesting a butterfly a misdemeanor crime carrying a $1,000 fine.

To celebrate the annual return of the butterflies, the town of Pacific Grove, also known as Butterfly Town U.S.A., has hosted a **Butterfly Parade** every October since 1938. Completely non-commercial, this delightful parade provides the low-key pleasure of viewing local grade school children marching down the street dressed as butterflies. Traditional bands and majorette corps from local schools also participate. Weather always cooperates: This parade has *never* been rained on.

For more information on the monarchs, contact non-profit Friends of the Monarchs *(P.O. Box 51683, Pacific Grove 93950-6683, 375-0982.).* Largely behind the successful purchase by the city of the area by Butterfly Grove Inn, the group continues to work on behalf of the butterflies. Guided tours are available from mid-October through mid-February. To get a child's packet of information on the monarch (stories, a coloring page, etc.), send a request and $1 for postage and handling.

WHERE TO STAY

Andril Fireplace Cottages *569 Asilomar Blvd., 375-0994, fax 655-2693. 16 units; $$-$$$; 1-week min. in* *summer. Children under 5 free. VCRs avail.; all kitchens & fireplaces. Hot tub. Pets welcome.*

These woodsy cottages make for very comfortable lodging, especially for longer stays. The pine-paneled cottages surround a tree-shaded courtyard furnished with picnic tables, and it is just a one-block walk to the ocean.

Asilomar Conference Center *800 Asilomar Blvd., 372-8016, fax 372-7227. 2 stories; 314 units; 100% non-smoking; $$. Children under 2 free. Some TVs, kitchens, & wood-burning fireplaces. Heated pool. Full breakfast; dining room.*

Founded as a YWCA camp in 1913 and boasting eight buildings designed by architect Julia Morgan, this 105-acre facility is now used mainly as a conference grounds. It is part of the California State Parks system. When underbooked, rentals are made available to the general public. Reservations cannot be made more than a month in advance; last-minute accommodations are often available. In Spanish the word "asilomar" means "retreat by the sea," and, indeed, the grounds are located in a quiet, scenic area just a short walk from the ocean. Both guests and non-guests are welcome to participate in inexpensive, family-style conference meals at 7:30, noon, and 6; reservations are not necessary, and highchairs and booster seats are available.

Beachcomber Inn *1996 Sunset Dr., (800) 634-4769, 373-4769. 26 rooms; 100% non-smoking; $$; 2-night min. on weekends. Heated pool, sauna. Continental breakfast; restaurant.*

Factors rendering this typical motel special include its oceanside location, a 90-degree pool, and free bikes and safety helmets for the use of guests.

The **Fishwife Restaurant** *(1996½ Sunset Dr., 375-7107. L & D W-M, SunBr; $-$$. Child portions. AE, MC, V.)* is located adjacent and justly popular with locals. A large variety of fresh seafood and pastas is featured.

Butterfly Grove Inn *1073 Lighthouse Ave., 373-4921, fax 373-4921. 28 rooms; $-$$$; 2-night min. on weekends. Some kitchens & fireplaces. Heated pool, hot tub. Small dogs welcome.*

This attractive complex offers a choice of either suites in a vintage house or regular motel rooms. Located on a quiet side street, it is adjacent to a 2.7-acre grove of Monterey Pine trees particularly favored by the monarchs. Though the threat of developing this area has loomed for several years, it was recently decided that the town of Pacific Grove will purchase the lot. The area will be protected as a butterfly habitat, and the public will continue to have access.

The Centrella *612 Central Ave., (800) 233-3372, 372-3372, fax 372-2036. 3 stories; 26 rooms; 100% non-smoking; $$-$$$+; 2-night min. on weekends. Children under 5 free. Some TVs & wood-burning & gas fireplaces. Afternoon snack, full breakfast.*

This restored turn-of-the-century Victorian has won awards for its interior decor. Rooms are furnished with antiques and feature Laura Ashley wallpapers and fabrics, and some bathrooms have claw-foot tubs. Suites on the third floor are particularly nice. Families with children under 12 are accommodated only in the more expensive cottage suites, each of which has a fireplace and private garden.

The Gosby House Inn *643 Lighthouse Ave., 375-1287. 22 rooms; $$-$$$. No TVs; some fireplaces; some shared baths. Afternoon tea, continental breakfast.*

Located in the heart of the town's shopping area, this Queen Anne Victorian features a charming rounded corner tower and many bay windows. Built in 1887 by a cobbler from Nova Scotia, it is now an historic landmark. Noteworthy features include particularly attractive wallpapers, a well-tended garden, and an assortment of stuffed bears and bunnies that welcome guests throughout the inn (all are available for purchase).

For a hopelessly romantic getaway, make dinner reservations at **Gernot's Victoria House Restaurant** *(649 Lighthouse Ave., 646-1477. D Tu-Sun; $$-$$$. Boosters, child portions. Reservations advised. AE, MC, V.).* Located just next door in another restored Victorian, this lovely dining room offers a continental menu with selections such as Austrian Wiener schnitzel and wild boar Bourguignonne.

Seven Gables Inn *555 Ocean View Blvd., 372-4341. 14 rooms; 100% non-smoking; $$-$$$+; 2-night min. on weekends. Unsuitable for children under 12. No TVs. Afternoon tea, full breakfast.*

Located across the street from the ocean, this elegant yellow Victorian mansion was built in 1886. Rooms and cottages all have ocean views and are decorated with fine European and American antiques.

Motel Row. Numerous motels are located at the west end of Lighthouse Avenue and along Asilomar Boulevard.

WHERE TO EAT

Bay Cafe *589 Lighthouse Ave., 375-4237. B & L daily, D Thur-Sun; $. Highchairs, boosters. MC, V.*

The all-American menu here includes plate-size pancakes, house-baked meats, and made-from-scratch mashed potatoes and gravy.

Just next door, the **Grove Pharmacy** *(375-4139)* is worth a visit for its collection of butterfly-related souvenirs.

Lighthouse Cafe *602 Lighthouse Ave., 372-7006. B & L daily; $. Highchairs, boosters. 100% non-smoking. AE, MC, V.*

This small, comfortable cafe specializes in fluffy omelettes, char-broiled chicken and hamburgers, and house-made soups, salads, and sandwiches.

Old Bath House *620 Ocean View Blvd., 375-5195, fax 375-5379. D daily; $$$. Highchairs, boosters. 100% non-smoking. Reservations advised. AE, MC, V.*

Every table in this elegant Victorian has a splendid view of Monterey Bay. Entrees include imaginative preparations of meats and fish, including house specialty Beef Bindel—filet mignon in puff pastry with foie gras and wild mushrooms. Divine desserts are made in the restaurant's own pastry kitchen.

Tinnery *631 Ocean View Blvd., 646-1040, 646-5913. B M-Sat, L & D daily, SunBr; $$. Highchairs, boosters, booths, child portions. AE, MC, V.*

Located at Lover's Point, this comfortable, casual restaurant offers outstanding views of the bay. Breakfast is particularly pleasant, with omelettes, egg dishes, and strawberry pancakes on the menu. The eclectic international dinner menu includes entrees such as tempura prawns, pasta primavera, and prime rib.

WHAT TO DO

Butterfly Viewing.

The densest clusters of monarchs occur in the pine grove located behind the Butterfly Grove Inn. Another good viewing spot is the west side of **George Washington Park**, along Melrose Street south of Pine Avenue.

Lover's Point *626 Ocean View Blvd.*

Located at the southern tip of Monterey Bay, this park holds a chunky granite statue honoring the monarch butterfly. It offers a pleasant beach for sunbathing and wading, and a grassy picnic area with barbecue pits.

Pacific Grove Museum of Natural History *165 Forest Ave., 648- 3119, fax 372-3256. Tu-Sun 10-5. Free.*

Opened in 1882, this museum is dedicated to telling the natural history of Monterey County through exhibits of marine and bird life, native plants, shells, and Native American artifacts. Butterfly-related exhibits include photographs and displays, as well as an informative ten-minute videotape. The life history of the monarch is portrayed in drawings, and during the summer larvae are often on view. Milkweed—the only plant on which the female monarch will lay her eggs—attracts butterflies to a native plant garden outside the museum.

Each year during the third weekend in April this tiny museum sponsors a **Wildflower Show.** As many as 600 varieties are displayed.

Point Piños Lighthouse *On Asilomar Blvd., about 2 blocks N of end of Lighthouse Ave., 648-3116, fax 372-3256. Thur, Sat & Sun 1-4. Free.*

Docents dressed in period costume give informal tours of this oldest continuously operating Pacific Coast lighthouse, built in 1855 out of granite quarried nearby. The area surrounding the lighthouse is a good spot to walk, picnic, and observe sea otters; note that Doc's Great Tide Pool, from Steinbeck's *Cannery Row,* is here.

Poor Man's 17-Mile Drive.

There is no charge for taking this scenic 4.2-mile drive that passes rugged seascapes and some impressive Victorian homes. Begin at Ocean View Boulevard and 3rd Street. At Point Piños, turn left on Sunset Drive. Tidepooling is good in several spots, and from April to August beautiful lavender ice plant cascades in full bloom over the rocky beach front.

Carmel-by-the-Sea
(Area Code 408)

A LITTLE BACKGROUND

A well-established getaway destination, Carmel is best known for its abundant shops, cozy lodgings, and picturesque white sand beach.

It is also known for the things that it doesn't have. No street signs, streetlights, electric or neon signs, jukeboxes, parking meters, or buildings over two stories high are allowed in town. No sidewalks, curbs, or house numbers are found in the residential sections. These absent items help Carmel keep its small-town feeling.

Do be careful. Eccentric laws in the town make it illegal to wear high-heeled shoes on the sidewalks, throw a ball in the park, play a musical instrument in a bar, or dig in the sand at the beach other than when making a sandcastle.

It seems that almost every weekend some special event is scheduled in the area, making available lodging perpetually scarce. It is important to make accommodation reservations far in advance, especially for the quainter lodgings. Consider taking advantage of the special rates often available for mid-week stays.

VISITOR INFORMATION

Carmel Business Association *P.O. Box 4444 (San Carlos/5th, above Hog's Breath Inn), Carmel 93921, (800) 550-4333, 624-2522, fax 624-1329.*

ANNUAL EVENTS

AT&T Pebble Beach National Pro-Am *January. In Pebble Beach; (800) 541-9091. $15-$25.*

This was formerly known as the Bing Crosby Golf Tournament.

Carmel Art Festival *May. 624-2522, fax 624-1329. Free.*

Among the events are special exhibits, art demonstrations in the galleries, and the kick-off to the town's annual Art Walk—when galleries stay open late on Friday nights and host special events.

Carmel Bach Festival *July & August. 624-2046, fax 624-2788. $10-$50.*

Held annually since 1935 (except for two years off during World War II), this Baroque music festival varies its highlights from year to year. Candlelight concerts are usually presented in the town's picturesque mission, and a special children's concert is always scheduled.

Concours d'Elegance *August. In Pebble Beach; 659-0663.*

Car buffs don their dressiest summer attire for a stroll over the spacious lawn at the Lodge at Pebble Beach, where this elegant affair is held. Classic vintage and antique automobiles are displayed.

WHERE TO STAY

Carmel River Inn *Hwy. 1 at bridge, (800) 882-8142, 624-1575, fax 624-0290. 2 stories; 43 units; $$-$$$; 2-night min. on weekends. Children under 12 free. Some kitchens & wood-burning fireplaces. Heated pool.*

Located on the outskirts of town on the banks of the Carmel River, this lodging facility stretches over ten acres. Guests have a choice of motel rooms or individual cottages, many of which have balconies or patios overlooking the river.

Cobblestone Inn *Junipero/8th, (800) 833-8836, 625-5222, fax 625-0478. 24 rooms; 100% non-smoking; $$-$$$+. Children under 2 free. All gas fireplaces. Afternoon snack, full breakfast.*

Located only two blocks from the main shopping street, this charming inn is filled with teddy bears awaiting guests in fanciful poses. Should one capture a heart, all are available for adoption by purchase. Spacious guest rooms are furnished with country-style pine furniture and iron-frame beds. Shutters provide privacy, and fireplaces constructed with large river rocks provide atmosphere and warmth. Refrigerators are stocked with complimentary cold drinks. In the morning all guests are greeted with a newspaper at their door, and breakfast can be enjoyed either outside on a sunny slate-and-brick-paved courtyard filled with English flowers blooming in stone containers, or inside with the bears. Two bicycles are available for guests to borrow.

Colonial Terrace Inn *San Antonio/13th, 624-2741. 2 stories; 25 rooms, 3 non-smoking rooms; $$-$$$+; 2-night min. on weekends. Some kitchens & gas fireplaces. Continental breakfast.*

In business since 1925, this crisply attractive lodging features landscaped gardens and is located in a quiet residential area just one block from the beach.

Cypress Inn *Lincoln/7th, (800) 443-7443, 624-3871. 2 stories; 33 rooms; 12 non-smoking rooms; $$-$$$+; 2-night min. on weekends. Some gas fireplaces. Evening snack, continental breakfast. Pets welcome ($17).*

Featuring a Moorish Mediterranean style of architecture, this inn was built in 1929. Owned by actress Doris Day along with several partners, it is located right in town. Each room is distinctively decorated and comfortable and a few have ocean views. All rooms are equipped with a decanter of cream sherry, a fruit basket, bottled drinking water, fresh flowers, and the daily paper. Ms. Day's well-known love for animals is reflected in her inn's most unusual amenity—a special pet bed available by reservation!

Green Lantern Inn *7th/Casanova, 624-4392, fax 624-9591. 2 stories; 19 rooms; 100% non-smoking; $$-$$$+. Children under 5 free. Some fireplaces. Continental breakfast.*

Operating as an inn since 1926, this pleasant group of rustic multi-unit cottages is located on a quiet side street just a few blocks from the village and two blocks from the beach.

Highlands Inn *On Hwy. 1, 4 mi. south of town, (800) 682-4811, 624-3801, fax 626-1574. 2 stories; 142 rooms; $$$+. Children under 18 free. All VCRs; some kitchens & wood-burning fireplaces. Heated pool, 3 hot tubs, fitness room. 2 restaurants, room service (child items). Small dogs welcome.*

Located in a fragrant pine forest in the scenic Carmel Highlands, up a hill just pass the town gas station with its old-time pump and two authentic red English phone booths, this inn was built on its spectacular cliffside setting in 1916. Through the years it has been the host to many famous guests, including the Beatles and two presidents—Kennedy and Ford. The inn was extensively remodeled in 1984 into luxurious contemporary-style accommodations. Rooms designed for privacy make it possible to just hole up and listen to the birds tweeting and the sounds of the not-too-distant surf. All have ocean views and are equipped with robes and even binoculars. Complimentary bikes are available for guests to use, and upon check-in children are given a special amenities bag filled with goodies.

A wonderful breakfast buffet and lunchtime hamburgers are on the menu at the casual, moderately priced **California Market.** Diners can enjoy an expansive view of the rugged coastline either inside or outside on a balcony. The celebrated **Pacific's Edge** restaurant also features a stunning view (plan to dine here during daylight hours). One dinner enjoyed here began with a perfectly prepared boiled artichoke appetizer served with sesame mayonnaise; a ginger-carrot soup; a colorfully presented entree of grilled swordfish on grilled Maui onions topped with a chunky sauce of calamata olives, oven-dried tomatoes, and parsley; and a classic crème brulee chosen from an array of elegant desserts.

The Homestead *Lincoln/8th, 624-4119. 2 stories; 12 rooms; 6 non-smoking rooms; $$; 2-night min. on weekends. Some kitchens & gas fireplaces.*

Painted a cheery rust red, this home-turned-inn provides a variety of interesting rooms. It features a lovely garden and is conveniently located on a quiet corner lot just a few blocks from the village.

The Inn at Spanish Bay *2700 17-Mile Drive, Pebble Beach, (800) 654-9300, 647-7500, fax 644-7955. 3 stories; 270 rooms; 100% non-smoking; $$$+. All VCRs & gas fireplaces. Heated pool, hot tub, sauna, fitness room, health spa, 8 tennis courts (fee; 2 with night lights), 18-hole golf course. 3 restaurants, room service.*

Nestled ocean-front beside a protected marine sanctuary, this luxury resort was designed to complement its spectacular surroundings. The decor blends in with the misty wash of natural colors seen outside, and most rooms have a patio or balcony. Guided camera and nature walks are scheduled, and bicycles, a shuttle to Carmel and Monterey destinations, and milk and cookies at bedtime can be arranged. A full time Nature Concierge is on the staff, as is a talented floral arranger, and the **Ansel Adams Gallery** *(M-F 10-6)* operates as one of the resort's shops. The Scottish-style **Links at Spanish Bay** golf course—which Jack Nicklaus considers "possibly the best in the world" and about which Tom Watson enthuses, "Spanish Bay is so much like Scotland, you can almost hear the bagpipes"— surrounds the resort.

Roys' at Pebble Beach *(647-7423, fax 644-7957. $$.)* offers spectacular ocean views across the dunes along with the celebrated Euro-Asian cuisine of Hawaii-based chef Roy Yamaguchi. Noteworthy on the lunch menu are tasty spring rolls in a chili plum sauce and a well-seasoned Thai chicken salad with minty dressing. Fresh local seafood and designer pizzas are also on the menu, as are gorgeous killer desserts.

Lamp Lighter Inn *Ocean Ave./Camino Real, 624-7372. 9 units; 100% non-smoking; $$-$$$+. Children under 1 free. Some kitchens; 1 wood-burning fireplace.*

Conveniently located between the village and the ocean, this enclave has both charming rooms and gingerbread-style cottages. It very well might fulfill guest's fairy tale fantasies. Several of the cozy, comfortable cottages accommodate families; one known as the "Hansel and Gretel" has a special sleeping loft for kids. Another, the "Blue Bird Room," has a cathedral ceiling of age-patinaed redwood and a picture window looking into a large oak tree. Children especially enjoy finding all 17 elves in the Elves Garden. Accommodations in an annex, located one block closer to the beach, are a little less expensive and a lot less interesting; however, several have ocean views.

La Playa Hotel *Camino Real/8th, (800) 582-8900, 624-6476, fax 624-7966. 3 stories; 80 units; $$$-$$$+. Children under 12 free. Some kitchens & fireplaces. Heated pool. Restaurant, room service.*

This luxury Mediterranean-style hotel is conveniently located just two blocks from the beach and four blocks from town. Taking up an entire square block, it is the largest hotel, as well as the only full-service resort hotel, in Carmel. The beds in the thick-walled rooms all have rustic carved headboards sporting the hotel's mermaid motif, and the beautifully maintained gardens are always abloom with colorful flowers. A group of charming, spacious cottages situated a block closer to the ocean are also available.

The casual **Terrace Grill** *(B, L, & D daily)* features an elaborate Sunday brunch with a buffet of fresh fruits and pastries, Belgian waffles, and made-to-order omelettes. Diners can also opt to order from a menu, and a perfect spicy Bloody Mary is available from the bar. The restaurant's namesake terrace has both ocean and garden views and is covered overhead and heated, so al fresco dining can be enjoyed regardless of the weather.

Lincoln Green Inn *Carmelo/15th, (800) 262-1262, 624-1880. 1 story; 4 units; $$$+; 2-night min. on weekends. Some kitchens; all gas fireplaces. Pets welcome.*

Located on the outskirts of town, just a few blocks from where the Carmel River flows into the ocean, this cluster of comfortable English housekeeping cottages features living rooms with cathedral-beamed ceilings and stone fireplaces.

The Lodge at Pebble Beach *17-Mile Drive, Pebble Beach, (800) 654-9300, 624-3811, fax 626-3725. 161 rooms; 4 non-smoking rooms; $$$+; 2-night min. on weekends. All fireplaces. Heated pool, children's wading pool, sauna, 14 tennis courts (fee). 3 restaurants, room service.*

Complete luxury and the best of sporting facilities await guests here. Golfers can enjoy playing some of the best courses in the country. Horse rentals and equestrian trails are nearby, as are jogging and hiking trails and a parcourse.

Non-guests are welcome to stop in and enjoy the spectacular ocean view over a drink or meal. Try the **Club XIX** at lunch, when diners can sit on a terrace overlooking both the 18th hole and the ocean while enjoying bistro fare.

Mission Ranch *26270 Dolores St./Rio Rd., (800) 538-8221, 624-6436, fax 626-4163. 31 rooms; 100% non-smoking; $$-$$$+; 2-night min. on weekends. Some gas fireplaces. Fitness room, 6 clay tennis courts ($10/day/room). Continental breakfast; restaurant.*

Owned by actor Clint Eastwood, who has invested a fistful of dollars in furnishings, this former dairy farm is located near the Carmel mission. It has operated as a lodging facility since 1937. Special accommodation choices include roomy cottages that work well for families, the 1857 Victorian-style Martin Family Farmhouse with B&B-style rooms, and the 1852 Bunkhouse cottage; more ordinary rooms are also available.

Normandy Inn *Ocean Ave./Monte Verde, (800) 343-3825, 624-3825, fax 624-4614. 2 stories; 48 units; 24 non-smoking units; $$-$$$; 2-night min. on weekends. Children under 12 free. Some kitchens & wood-burning fireplaces. Heated pool (unavail. Jan-Mar). Continental breakfast.*

Conveniently located on the town's main shopping street and just four blocks from the ocean, this inn features an attractive half-beamed Normandy style of architecture and several large cottages. The comfortably appointed rooms are decorated in French country style, and the pool is invitingly secluded.

Pine Inn *Ocean Ave./Monte Verde, (800) 228-3851, 624-3851, fax 624-3030. 3 stories; 49 rooms; 17 non-smoking rooms; $$-$$$+; 2-night min. on weekends. Children under 18 free. 1 gas fireplace. Restaurant, room service (child items).*

Decorated in an elegant Victorian style, this inn opened in 1889 and is the oldest in town. It is conveniently located in the center of town.

San Antonio House *San Antonio/7th, 624-4334. 3 stories; 4 rooms; 100% non-smoking; $$$-$$$+; 2-night min. on weekends. Unsuitable for children under 12. All gas fireplaces. Continental breakfast.*

This attractive guest house offers large rooms, a lovely garden, and a location in a quiet residential area just one block from the beach. One room has a private patio, another its own doll house, and a breakfast tray is brought to each room in the morning.

Sea View Inn *Camino Real/12th, 624-8778, fax 625-5901. 3 stories; 8 rooms; 100% non-smoking; $$-$$$; 2-night min. on weekends. Unsuitable for children under 12. No TVs; some shared baths. Afternoon & evening snack, continental breakfast.*

Located three blocks from the beach, this converted Victorian home offers pleasantly appointed rooms. The most requested room features a cozy canopy bed.

The Stonehouse Inn *8th/Monte Verde, (800) 748-6618, 624-4569. 2 stories; 6 rooms; 100% non-smoking; $$-$$$+. Unsuitable for children under 12. 1 TV; 1 wood-burning fireplace; some shared baths. Afternoon snack, full breakfast.*

Built by local Indians in 1906, this rustic stone country house is close to the village. The original owner often entertained well-known artists and writers, and the antique-furnished rooms are now named in honor of some of those guests.

Sundial Lodge *Monte Verde/7th, 624-8578. 2 stories; 19 rooms; 100% non-smoking; $$$-$$$+; 2 night min. on weekends. Unsuitable for children under 5. Some kitchens. Afternoon snack, continental breakfast; restaurant.*

Located just one block from the center of town, next to City Hall (known for awhile as "Clint's Place"), this charming hotel is built around a flower-filled brick courtyard. Tea and sherry are served to guests in the afternoon.

Vagabond House Inn *4th/Dolores, (800) 262-1262, 624-7738, fax 626-1243. 2 stories; 11 rooms; $$-$$$+; 2-night min. on weekends. Unsuitable for children under 12. Some kitchens & wood-burning & gas fireplaces. Continental breakfast. Pets welcome.*

This rustic English Tudor-style building features cozily furnished rooms that open off a quiet, flower-bedecked courtyard.

WHERE TO EAT

Candy Shops.
• **Cottage of Sweets** *Ocean Ave./Lincoln, 624-5170. M-Thur 10-7, F-Sun 10-9.*

Among the sweet surprises in this charming candy cottage are imported chocolates, diet candy, gourmet jelly beans, and taffy.

• **House of Hansel & Gretel** *6th/Lincoln, 624-3125. Daily 9:30-5.*

They still make ribbon candy by hand here. Honeycomb, chocolate-covered caramels, and assorted flavors of hard candies made with natural flavorings are also available.

Carmel Bakery *Ocean/Lincoln, 626-8885. Daily 6:30am-9:30pm.*

Caramel apples, Cookie Monster cupcakes, and both alligators and turtles made of marzipan bread are just a few of the delicacies available at this popular bakery. Also particularly good are the apricot log pastries, wild blueberry scones, and focaccia with spicy pepper topping. Pastries and drinks can be enjoyed on the premises or while walking the boutique-laden streets.

Clam Box Restaurant *Mission/5th, 624-8597. L & D Tu-Sun; $$. Closed most of Dec. Highchairs, boosters, child portions. No reservations. AE, MC, V.*

Customers wait as happily as clams in the constant line to get seated in this tiny, cozy restaurant. That's because they know they're going to enjoy themselves once they get a table. The menu is predominantly seafood, but a hamburger is also available. A cozy bar is down the garden path, behind the restaurant, and makes a cheery spot to wait.

Em Le's *Dolores/5th, 625-6780. B & L daily; $. Boosters. No cards.*

Football broadcaster John Madden is part-owner of this cozy, casual spot. Among the large variety of breakfast items are buttermilk waffles, in a choice of light or dark bake, and wild blueberry pancakes. The basic all-American cuisine includes fried chicken, meatloaf, mashed potatoes, and apple pie. Pleasant views of sidewalk traffic and counter seating add to the low-key Carmel charm.

The Fabulous Toots Lagoon *Dolores/7th, 625-1915. L & D daily; $-$$. Highchairs, boosters, child menu. Reservations advised. AE, MC, V.*

Roaringly popular with locals, this friendly spot is known for its ribs prepared with a choice of four sauces. Brick oven-baked pizza, house-made pasta, and fresh fish are also on the eclectic menu. For dessert, the offerings include mud and turtle pies. For something lighter, consider a Jell-O shooter made with tequila, sweet & sour, and green Jell-O. To eat, just loosen the edge with a toothpick and then chuck it down the hatch.

The General Store/Forge in the Forest *5th/Junipero, 624-2233, fax 624-3522. L & D daily, SunBr; $-$$. Highchairs, child menu. 100% non-smoking. Reservations advised. AE, MC, V.*

In a sort of warren of spaces that includes a heated outdoor patio, this popular spot serves an eclectic menu of fresh seafood, pasta, pizza, salads, Mexican and vegetarian items, and sandwiches, and it stays open late for night owls.

Hog's Breath Inn *San Carlos/5th, 625-1044. L M-Sat, D daily, SunBr; $$. Boosters, child portions. No reservations. AE, MC, V.*

Owned by actor, director, and former mayor of Carmel Clint Eastwood, this rustic, secluded spot exudes a casual, cozy atmosphere. Redwood burl tables and comfortable, colorful, and appropriate director's chairs are scattered outdoors under a gigantic, rambling old oak tree. A huge mural by G. H. Rothe—the world's foremost mezzotint artist, a town gallery owner, and Clint's neighbor—graces the courtyard. Guests are warmed by fireplaces and heaters when the temperature drops, and seating is also available inside. The brunch menu offers eggs Benedict, omelettes, and plain eggs served with house-made blueberry muffins and homefried potatoes. Lunch features salads, sandwiches, and a weighty Dirty Harry Burger on a good-for-you whole wheat bun—all served with a house-made soup. Dinner brings on seafood, steaks, and pasta.

Short on time? Stop in for a drink, preferably seated upon one of the comfortable swivel chairs in the dark den that is the bar. Hot drinks and simple drinks tend to be best, and complimentary hors d'oeuvres are served weekdays from 4 to 6 p.m.

Jack London's *San Carlos/5th, 624-2336. L & D daily, SunBr; $-$$. Boosters. V.*

Even locals come here to enjoy the excellent bar drinks and cozy bistro atmosphere. Kids are welcome and can order fancy non-alcoholic drinks. Menu specialties include individual-size pizzas, a variety of hamburgers, and deep-fried calamari. Fresh fish selections change daily. Rich, velvety pasta carbonara Milano and a New York steak round out the eclectic menu. Dinner entrees come with a generous house salad topped with ranch dressing.

La Boheme Restaurant *Dolores/7th, 624-7500, fax 624-6539. D daily; $$. Closed most of Dec. 1 booster, child portions. 100% non-smoking. No reservations. MC, V.*

Cozy and colorfully decorated, and featuring an overhanging indoor roof built by a retired French race car driver, this charming petite cafe is outrageously romantic. Just one three-course fixed-price dinner is served each evening, plus one vegetarian entree option. With no menu choices to fret over, diners are free to concentrate on each other. The French and Italian country-style dishes are served informal family-style. One dinner enjoyed here began with a large, crisp salad accented with olives and substantial slices of ham, salami, and cheese. Then came a perfectly seasoned cream of broccoli soup, followed by a main course of pork loin in a cream sauce flavored with juniper berries. Strawberries Romanoff cost additional and made a refreshing, light dessert. The soup and entree change each evening, so it is a good idea to call ahead for the night's menu.

Patisserie Boissiere *Mission/Ocean, 624-5008. B Sat & Sun, L daily, D W-Sun; $$. Reservations advised at D. AE, MC, V.*

The menu at this elegant little gem offers house-made soups as well as more substantial entrees. Though it would be hard to do so, don't overlook the pastries and desserts—lemon cheesecake, chocolate whiskey cake, zabaglione, and plenty more.

Piatti *6th/Junipero, 625-1766.* For description, see page 266.

Picnic Pick-Ups.

• **Mediterranean Market** *Ocean/Mission, 624-2022. Daily 9-6.*

This well-stocked delicatessen offers freshly marinated artichoke hearts, sandwich meats, cheeses, skinny French baguettes, exotic beers, wines, bottled waters, and soft drinks. Caviar is also available, as are picnic baskets to carry it all away in.

• **Wishart's Bakery** *Ocean/Mission, 624-3870. Daily 6:30am-9pm.*

This is a popular branch of the Carmel Bakery.

Rocky Point *On Hwy. 1, 12 mi. south of town, 624-2933. L & D daily; $$-$$$. Highchairs, boosters, child portions. Reservations advised. MC, V.*

Take a scenic drive down the coast toward Big Sur, stopping here to enjoy the spectacular view along with a multi-course charcoal-broiled steak or fresh seafood dinner. Sandwiches and hamburgers are on the lunch menu, making it a relative bargain.

Sans Souci Restaurant *Lincoln/5th, 624-6220. D Thur-Tu. Highchairs, boosters. 100% non-smoking. Reservations advised. AE, MC, V.*

Quiet, elegant dining and a relaxing ambiance greet diners at this oasis of civility. Each course is perfectly executed and presented with flair. One meal enjoyed here began with sautéed wild mushrooms and asparagus tips with a sherry cream sauce. Then came grilled apple sausage and duck confit with raspberries and goat cheese over Carmel Valley greens moistened with a creamy balsamic and date vinaigrette. The entree was a rich lobster fricassée in the flakiest of puff pastries. The dessert soufflè, for which the restaurant is well known, was flavored with aromatic passion fruit, however just about any flavor imaginable can be prepared. Servers are attentive and attired in tuxedos.

Tuck Box English Tea Room *Dolores/Ocean, 624-6365; fax 624-5079. B, L, & afternoon tea W-Sun; $. Boosters. 100% non-smoking. No reservations. No cards.*

Featuring fairy tale architecture and verily reeking of quaintness, this tiny dining room can be quite difficult to get seated in. If ever it is without a long line in front, go! Seating is also available on a tiny outdoor patio. The limited breakfast menu offers simply prepared eggs served with delightful fresh scones and a choice of either homemade olallieberry preserves or orange marmalade. At lunch sandwiches, salads, and omelettes are available along with Welsh rarebit and a daily entree special. Afternoon tea features scones, pies, delicious English trifle, and, of course, plenty of hot English tea.

Across the street, tiny **Picadilly Park** invites relaxing contemplation with its benches, flower garden, and goldfish pond.

Village Corner *Dolores/6th, 624-3588, fax 622-8855. B, L, & D daily; $-$$. Highchairs, boosters, booths, child menu. Reservations advised. AE, MC, V.*

The large patio here, which is heated year-round, provides the chance to relax and watch the rest of the town stroll by. The Mediterranean bistro menu offers bruschetta and deep-fried local calamari for appetizers. Entree choices include several interesting pastas, as well as a delicious Cajun-style blackened salmon and a dramatic paella for two. Local wines pair perfectly.

WHAT TO DO

Art Galleries.
• **Galerie Blue Dog** *6th/Lincoln, 626-4444, fax 626-4488. Daily 10-6.*

This gallery is devoted entirely to the pop art blue dog of Louisiana Cajun artist George Rodrigue.

• **Gibson Gallery of Animation** *San Carlos/7th, (800) 292-6758, 624-9296.*

All the Disney characters and plenty more are featured in Carmel's only animation gallery.

• **New Masters Gallery** *Dolores/Ocean, (800) 336-4014, 625-1511, fax 625-3731. Daily 10-5.*

The work of accomplished contemporary artists is shown here.

Bay Sports *Lincoln/5th, 25-BIKE. Daily 9-dusk.* For description, see Bay Bikes on page 102.

Beaches.
• **Carmel Beach** *At the foot of Ocean Ave., 626-2522.*

Known for its white powdery sand and spectacular sunsets, this world-famous beach is a choice spot for a refreshing walk, a picnic, or flying a kite. Swimming is unsafe.

The **Great Sand Castle Contest** *(624-1255)* is held here each September or October, depending on the tides. Contestants are encouraged to bribe judges with food and drink.

• **Carmel River State Beach** *At the end of Scenic Rd., 649-2836. Daily 9-dusk. Free.*

Very popular with families, this beach has a fresh-water lagoon and an adjoining bird sanctuary. Located behind Carmel Mission, it is where the Carmel River flows into Carmel Bay and offers beautiful views of Point Lobos. Picnic facilities are available.

Mission San Carlos Borromeo del Rio Carmelo *3080 Rio Rd., 1 mi. south of town off Hwy. 1, 624-3600. M-Sat 9:30-4:30, Sun 10:30-4:30; services on Sun. By donation.*

Father Junipero Serra, who established this mission in 1770, is buried here at the foot of the altar. A museum displays Native American artifacts, mission tools, and re-creations of both the original mission kitchen and California's first library. A courtyard garden, featuring a restful pond stocked with colorful koi, accents the cemetery where over 3,000 mission Indians are buried. A **fiesta** is held each year on the last Sunday in September.

Across the street, 37-acre **Mission Trail Park** *(624-3543. Daily dawn-dusk. Free.)* has several hiking trails. The broad Serra Trail is an easy uphill hike. Doolittle Trail goes further on for great views of the bay and a visit to the 1929 Tudor **Flanders Mansion**, where it is possible to tour the grounds and stroll through the **Lester Rowntree Arboretum**.

Pacific Repertory Theatre *Monte Verde/8th, in the Golden Bough Playhouse, 622-0700, fax 622-0703. Performances Tu-Sun eve., Sat & Sun matinees. Tickets $15-$20, 65+ $10-$15, children $8-$12, under 5 not admitted.*

In a structure reconstructed on the site of a playhouse that has burned to the ground twice in the past (each time after performances of *By Candlelight!*), this ambitious company presents varied fare in an intimate venue.

Pebble Beach Equestrian Center *Portola Rd./Alva Ln., Pebble Beach, 624-2756, fax 624-3999. Group rides daily at 10, 12, 2, & 3:30. $45/person. Riders must be 12 or older. Reservations required.*

Riders have a choice of English or Western saddles. Escorted rides follow the extensive bridle trails that wind through scenic Del Monte Forest, around the legendary **Spyglass Hill Golf Course**, down to the beach, and over the sand dunes. English riding lessons are available.

Point Lobos State Reserve *3 mi. south of town off Hwy. 1, 624-4909. Daily 9-dusk; interpretive center 12-5. $6/vehicle.*

Described as "the greatest meeting of land and water in the world," Point Lobos provides the opportunity to see the rustic, undeveloped beauty of the Monterey Peninsula. The flat-topped, gnarled-limbed Monterey cypress trees are native to just the four-mile stretch between here and Pebble Beach, and sea otters are often spotted in the 1,250-acre reserve's protected waters. Self-guiding trails are available, and guided ranger walks are scheduled daily in summer. A restored whaler's cabin, built in 1851 by a Chinese fisherman, now serves as an interpretive center. Artifacts and photographs tell about the area's history and one display highlights the location's various incarnations in movies. Dress warmly and bring along binoculars, a camera, and maybe a picnic, too.

17-Mile Drive *At Pebble Beach exit off Hwy. 1, between Carmel and Monterey, 649-8500. Daily sunrise-sunset. $6.50/vehicle.*

The scenery along this world-famous drive is a combination of showplace homes, prestigious golf courses, and raw seascapes. Sights include the **Restless Sea**, where several ocean crosscurrents meet; **Seal and Bird Rock**, where herds of sea lions and flocks of shoreline birds congregate; the **Pebble Beach Golf Course**, one of three used during the annual AT&T National Pro-Am tournament; and the landmark **Lone Cypress** clinging to its jagged, barren rock base. Picnic facilities and short trails are found in several spots.

Sea otter

Consider splurging on lunch or dinner at one of the ocean-view restaurants (one is a reasonably-priced coffee shop) at the elegant Inn at Spanish Bay (see page 110) or Lodge at Pebble Beach (see page 111). The gate fee is reimbursed when the meal check is paid.

Shopping Complexes.

• **The Barnyard** *Hwy. 1/Carmel Valley Rd., 624-8886. Daily 10-5:30, restaurants 8am-10pm.*

This unusual complex is filled with shops worthy of a browse. Don't miss **Succulent Gardens** *(624-0426)* with its rare and unusual varieties of flowering cacti and succulents. **Thunderbird Bookshop & Cafe** *(624-1803, fax 624-0549. L daily, D Tu-Sun; $-$$. Highchairs, boosters, child portions. MC, V.)*, a combination bookstore/restaurant, features dining among world-famous authors. Sandwiches and hamburgers are available at lunch, full meals at dinner, coffee-and during the off hours.

• **Carmel Plaza** *Ocean/Junipero, 624-0137, fax 624-5286. M-F 10-5:30, Sun 12-5.*

The upscale collection of noteworthy shops here surrounds a courtyard filled with flowers and is worth a browse. **Come Fly a Kite** *(624-3422. Daily 10-5.)* is where to pick up a kite. Then head for the beach—the perfect spot to launch it.

Special Shops.

• **Dansk II** *Ocean/San Carlos, 625-1600. Daily 9-6.*

Bargain prices are to be had on discontinued items and seconds from this expensive line of kitchen accessories.

• **The Mischievous Rabbit** *Lincoln/Ocean, 624-6854. M-Sat 10-5, Sun 12-5.*

This tiny shop specializes in delightful Beatrix Potter-illustrated items.

• **The Secret Garden** *Dolores/5th, 625-1131.*

Tucked down a tiny pathway, this peaceful shop purveys a charming collection of garden accents.

Tor House *26304 Ocean View Ave., 624-1813, 624-1840. Tours F & Sat on the hour 10-3. Adults $5, students $1.50-$3.50; children must be 12 or older. Reservations required.*

Poet Robinson Jeffers built this medieval-style house and tower retreat out of huge granite rocks hauled up from the beach below. He did much of the work himself and was of the opinion that the manual labor cleared his mind and that, as he put it, his "fingers had the art to make stone love stone." All of his major works and most of his poetry were written while he lived with his wife and twin sons on this craggy knoll overlooking Carmel Bay.

Carmel Valley
(Area Code 408)

A LITTLE BACKGROUND

Reliably sunny and peaceful, Carmel Valley is often overlooked by visitors to the Monterey Peninsula. That's a shame, because it is a wonderful place to relax, and it's only a few miles from Carmel. Lodgings, restaurants, and shops dot Highway 16/Carmel Valley Road along its 15-mile stretch east into the hub of town.

VISITOR INFORMATION

Carmel Valley Chamber of Commerce *P.O. Box 288 (71 W. Carmel Valley Rd.), Carmel Valley 93924, (800) 543-8343, 659-4000, fax 659-8415.*

WHERE TO STAY

Carmel Valley Inn *Carmel Valley Rd., 10 mi. from Hwy. 1, (800) 541-3113, 659-3131, fax 659-0137. 44 rooms; 5 non-smoking rooms; $$-$$$. Children under 18 free. Heated pool, hot tub; 7 clay tennis courts (no fee). Restaurant, room service. Pets welcome.*

Surrounded by lush green foothills, the unpretentious rooms here open onto large grassy expanses that invite children to romp. No amenities basket or cable TV await guests, but coffee is available in the lobby each morning. Cars are parked away from the rooms, and there are no bellhops—meaning it is very quiet and money is to be saved on tipping. Facilities include an enclosed whirlpool hot tub available by reservation, a horseshoe pit, and a naturally-stocked frog pond.

Carmel Valley Ranch Resort *One Old Ranch Rd., 6 mi. from Hwy. 1, (800) 4-CARMEL, 625-9500, fax 624-2858. 1 story; 100 suites; 50 non-smoking rooms; $$$+; 2-night min. on weekends. Children under 17 free. Some VCRs; all wood-burning fireplaces. 2 heated pools, hot tub, sauna, fitness room, 12 tennis courts ($15/hr.; 2 clay), 18-hole golf course. 2 restaurants, room service (child items).*

Built in an elegant ranch-style architecture featuring local stone and oak, this luxurious resort is situated on 1,700 scenic acres surrounded by rolling hills. It is the only resort on the Monterey Peninsula with a guarded gate. Each suite features cathedral ceilings and has a large private deck, two TVs, and three two-line phones. Some suites have decks with private outdoor hot tubs. A children's playground is available, and a special children's program operates in the summer. Horseback riding is available on-site.

The Oaks restaurant *(B, L, & D daily, SunBr. Highchairs. 100% non-smoking. Reservations advised. AE, MC, V.)* sports a stunning view of the valley.

John Gardiner's Tennis Ranch *114 Carmel Valley Rd., 11 mi. from Hwy. 1, (800) 453-6225, 659-2207, fax 659-2492. 1 story; 14 rooms; $$$+; 5-day rate ($1,650-$1,750/person) includes lodging, meals, & tennis instruction. Closed Dec-Mar. Unsuitable for children under 18. Some wood-burning fireplaces. 2 pools (1 heated), hot tub, sauna, 14 tennis courts.*

Begun by John Gardiner in 1957, this legendary tennis retreat has been visited by three presidents (Nixon, Ford, and Reagan). The five-day clinics run Sunday through Friday and include approximately 25 hours of instruction; shorter programs are also available. And with 14 courts and only 14 guest rooms, there is never any waiting. When guests aren't on the courts, they're usually either relaxing on the private patio of their luxurious cottage, or admiring the extensive flower gardens, or satisfying their worked-up appetites with a sumptuous meal. Low-cal diets haven't been discovered here yet. Meals include items such as "angel fluff" pancakes for breakfast, soufflés for lunch, and beef Wellington or fresh fish with popovers for dinner.

Quail Lodge Resort & Golf Club *8205 Valley Greens Dr., 3 mi. from Hwy. 1, (800) 538-9516, 624-1581, fax 624-3726. 2 stories; 100 units; 55 non-smoking units; $$$+. Children under 12 free. Some gas fireplaces. 2 pools (1 heated), hot tub, 4 tennis courts ($10/person/day), 18-hole golf course. Restaurant, room service. Pets welcome.*

These lakeside cottages are situated on 850 acres of golf fairways, meadows, and lakes that were once the site of the Carmel Valley Dairy. Guests can use hiking trails and visit 11 lakes that are also wildlife sanctuaries. Attracting a classy crowd, the resort's parking lot has been witnessed holding a DeLorean and several Ferraris at the same time.

The dressy **Covey Restaurant** *(D daily. Highchairs, boosters, booths. 100% non-smoking. Reservations advised. AE, MC, V.)* overlooks a lake and offers refined European cuisine with a California touch.

Tassajara Zen Mountain Center *39171 Tassajara Rd. Reservations: (415) 431-3771 (M-F 9-12:30 & 1:30-4). 29 units; 100% non-smoking; $$$+; rate includes 3 vegetarian meals; 2-night min. on weekends. Closed Sept-Apr. Number of children permitted is controlled. No TVs; some fireplaces; some shared baths. Hot springs pool, steam rooms. Day use: 659-2229. $8-$12/person. Reservations essential.*

Owned by the Zen Center of San Francisco, this traditional Zen Buddhist monastery is located deep in the Ventana Wilderness in the Los Padres National Forest and is home to 50 monks. Getting there requires a 14-mile drive down a steep dirt road (a four-wheel-drive or stick-shift is strongly advised), but overnight guests have the option of arranging a ride in on a four-wheel-drive "stage." The famous hot mineral springs are semi-enclosed in a Japanese-style bathhouse. Men's and women's baths and steam rooms are separated, and swimsuits are optional. More activities include hiking, river wading, and picnicking. Guests stay in simple wooden or stone cabins with no electricity. Lighting is provided by kerosene lamps. And this isn't a place to sleep in. Bells go off at 5:30 a.m. to announce meditation time for any guests who would like to participate. Getting a reservation can be difficult. It is best to call early. For overnight stays, reservations open in mid-February. For day visits, reservations open on April 25. Day guests must bring their own towels and food.

WHERE TO EAT

The Iron Kettle *In White Oak Plaza, in Carmel Valley Village, 12 mi. from Hwy. 1, 659-5472. B, L, & afternoon tea Tu-Sun; $. Highchairs, boosters. No cards.*

Operating inside the Old Milk House, an historical landmark built in 1890 that was once an overnight stop for passengers on the Salinas-Tassajara stage, this homey and cute restaurant also offers patio seating. At breakfast it's homemade granola, oatmeal, scones, and egg dishes; at lunch it's simple sandwiches. Afternoon tea is served until 4 and features olallieberry and blueberry scones with homemade jam.

Katy and Harry's Wagon Wheel *In Valley Hills Shopping Center, Hwy. 16/Valley Greens Dr., 3 mi. from Hwy. 1, 624-8878. B & L daily; $. No reservations. No cards.*

Extremely popular with locals, this spot is usually packed. Tables are tiny, but portions are generous. Breakfast seems to be the busiest meal and is served until the 2 p.m. closing time. The menu then includes omelettes, eggs Benedict, oatmeal, assorted styles of pancakes (don't miss the owner's favorite—raspberry), and fresh-squeezed orange juice. A late breakfast permits chowing-down more than enough grub to satisfy a tummy until dinner. The hamburgers, French fries, and homemade beans are also reputed to be very good.

WHAT TO DO

Bernardus Winery 5 W. Carmel Valley Rd., 13 mi. from Hwy. 1, 659-1900, fax 659-1676. Tasting W-Sun 11-5.

The father of owner Ben (Bernardus) Pon is the designer of the Volkswagen bus and was the person who first exported the beetle to the U.S. Ben himself has been a professional race driver for Porsche and represented Holland in skeet shooting at the 1972 Olympics. With such an accomplished background, it isn't surprising that he would make a success of his upstart winery, which makes wines in the old French Bordeaux and Burgundian styles and is known for its Chardonnay and Sauvignon Blanc.

Chateau Julien Winery 8940 Carmel Valley Rd., 5 mi. from Hwy. 1, 624-2600, fax 624-6138. Tasting M-F 8:30-5, Sat & Sun 11-5; tours daily at 10:30 & 2:30.

Styled after an actual chateau located on the French-Swiss border, this castle-like structure has no formal tasting bar. Tasters just gather informally around a large table in the middle of the high-ceilinged room. While their parents are enjoying an informal tasting of Chardonnays and Merlots—the two varietals this winery is noted for—children can partake of juice and crackers. A garden patio invites picnicking.

Garland Ranch Regional Park Off Carmel Valley Rd., 8.6 mi. from Hwy. 1, 659-4488, fax 659-5902. Daily sunrise-sunset. Free.

Running along the banks of the Carmel River, this park boasts more than 5,000 acres. Self-guided hiking trails lead up into the mountains; the 1.4-mile Lupine Loop Trail provides an easy nature walk. This park is home to the very spot in the Carmel River where the boys in Steinbeck's *Cannery Row* caught frogs. Though frog collecting is not permitted, relaxing is. A Visitors Center provides orientation and maps.

Big Sur
(Area Code 408)

A LITTLE BACKGROUND

Big Sur is such a special place that many people who have been here don't feel generous about sharing it. However, facilities are so limited that it's hard to imagine the area getting overrun with tourists. Except, perhaps, in the thick of summer, when the weather is best.

The town of Big Sur seems to have no center. It stretches along Highway 1 for six miles, offering a string of amenities. Then, as one continues driving south, the highway begins a 90-mile stretch of some of the most spectacular scenery in the U.S.

Note that the river's bottom here is rocky. Bring along waterproof shoes for wading.

VISITOR INFORMATION

Big Sur Chamber of Commerce P.O. Box 87, Big Sur 93920, 667-2100.

Monterey Peninsula Visitors & Convention Bureau. See page 97.

GETTING THERE

Located approximately 25 miles south of the Monterey Peninsula.

WHERE TO STAY

Big Sur Lodge *Off Hwy. 1, 667-2171. 1 story; 61 rooms; $$-$$$+; 2-night min. on weekends. No TVs; some kitchens & fireplaces. Heated pool. Restaurant (May-Sept only).*

Located in Pfeiffer-Big Sur State Park, this complex has many two bedroom motel units. They are distributed throughout spacious, grassy grounds where deer are often seen grazing, and those close to the pleasant pool area seem most desirable. Guests have access to the state park's facilities. A casual, moderately-priced coffee shop serves meals all day in season.

Esalen Institute *Off Hwy. 1, 667-3000. Pool, hot tubs.*

Located on a breathtaking crest above the ocean, this legendary educational facility offers lodging and dining in conjunction with its workshops. Space is open to the general public when the facility is underbooked. Then a bed space runs $70 to $125 per person per day and includes three meals. Special family rates are available. Call for reservations no earlier than five days before date of desired visit. Some will want to be forewarned, others informed, that nude bathing is de rigueur in the hot tubs and swimming pool. (Hot tubs are open to non-guests from 1 to 3 a.m. by reservation. Call 667-3047. The fee is $10 per person.) Self-exploration workshops include massage, Rolfing, vision improvement, etc. Call for a copy of the workshop catalogue.

New Camaldoli Hermitage *Off Hwy. 1, 20 mi. south of town, 667-2456, 667-2341. 9 rooms; $45/person. Includes 3 simple vegetarian meals.*

Solitary, silent, non-directed retreats, in the Catholic tradition of the Benedictine order, are offered here and open to people of all faiths. Founded in 1958 by three Benedictine monks from Camaldoli, Italy, this quiet 800-acre wildlife and wilderness preserve allows guests to meditate, read, rest, and pray. Chapel services are available for those who wish to participate, and each modest room has an ocean view.

A **gift shop** *(Daily 8:30-11 & 1:15-5)* sells brandy-dipped fruitcake and date-nut cake made by the resident Camaldolese monks, as well as pottery and religious items.

Ripplewood Resort *On Hwy. 1, 667-2242. 1 story; 16 cabins; 100% non-smoking; $$. Children under 12 free. No TVs; 13 kitchens; 8 wood-burning fireplaces. Restaurant.*

Rustic, pleasantly decorated redwood cabins are located both above and below the highway. The ones below are in a dense, dark grove of redwoods just a stone's throw from the Big Sur River. A cafe serves breakfast and lunch.

Ventana-Big Sur Country Inn Resort *On Hwy. 1, (800) 628-6500, 667-2331, fax 667-2419. 2 stories; 59 rooms; 40 non-smoking rooms; $$$+; 2-night min. on weekends. Unsuitable for children under 18. All VCRs; 53 wood-burning fireplaces. 2 heated pools, hot tub, sauna, health spa, fitness room. Afternoon snack, continental breakfast; restaurant.*

The striking, clean-lined, and award-winning architecture of this serene resort seems to fit in perfectly with its spectacular, secluded location in the hills 1,200 feet above the ocean. It is a choice spot for a restive, revitalizing, and hedonistic retreat. Rooms—some of which have private hot tubs—are distributed among 12 buildings, and all have either a private balcony or patio and either a ocean or mountain view. Bathhouses containing Japanese hot baths and sun decks are located adjacent to the pools; clothing is optional in this area.

The **restaurant** *(L & D daily. Highchairs, boosters.)*, known for its accomplished California-style cuisine, has seating both in a cedar-paneled dining room with mountain and ocean views and out on a large terrace with a panoramic ocean view.

WHERE TO EAT

Deetjen's Big Sur Inn *On Hwy. 1, 667-2378. B & D daily; $-$$$. Highchairs, boosters, child portions. Reservations advised for D. MC, V.*

For aesthetic pleasure it's hard to beat lingering over a hearty breakfast at this Norwegian-style inn—especially when it's raining outside and the table is situated in front of the fireplace. The mellow, rustic, and informal setting of this inn provides a complementary background to the fresh, simple, and wholesome foods produced by its kitchen. Dinner by candlelight is more expensive and sedate, and children don't fit in as well then.

Rustic, casual **lodging** *(2 stories; 20 rooms; $$-$$$. Some wood-burning fireplaces & stoves; some shared baths.)* is available in units located amid a forest of redwoods and firs. Rooms are usually booked up far in advance.

Nepenthe *On Hwy. 1, 667-2345, 667-2394. L & D daily; $$. Highchairs. 100% non-smoking inside. No reservations. AE, MC, V.*

Located at the top of a cliff 808 feet above the ocean and offering a breathtaking view of the coastline, this famous restaurant was designed by a student of Frank Lloyd Wright. It is an elaboration of a cabin that was originally built by Orson Welles as a retreat for him and Rita Hayworth. When the weather is mild, lunchers can dine outside on a casual terrace. The menu features simple foods such as steak, fresh seafood, roasted chicken, house-made soup, and a very good hamburger. It is also possible to stop in at the bar for just a drink. Overall this restaurant seems to be living up to the promise of its name, which refers to a mythical Egyptian drug that induced forgetfulness and the surcease of sorrow.

Cafe Kevah *(667-2344. Closed Jan & Feb.)*, located downstairs, serves moderately-priced brunch and lunch items on a patio featuring the same striking view. On a warm afternoon it is an especially choice spot to enjoy a refreshing cold drink and tasty pastry.

The classy **Phoenix** gift shop provides pleasant browsing before or after dining.

WHAT TO DO

Big Sur is so non-commercial that there is little to list in this section. Visitors can look forward to relaxing, swimming in the river, picnicking on the beach, or taking a hike through the woods. Look out for poison oak, and bring along a good book.

Andrew Molera State Park *On Hwy. 1, 667-2315. $4/vehicle.*

Located near the photogenic **Bixby Bridge**, this beach park has plenty of hiking trails. Several are short and easy: The two-mile Bluffs Trail follows the ocean to a bluff; the one-mile Headlands trail leads to a scenic area above the mouth of Big Sur River; and the two-mile Bobcat Trail follows the Big Sur River through dense redwoods. Walk-in campsites are available.

Molera Trail Rides *(625-8664. Daily at 9, 1:30, and 4 hrs. before sunset. Closed Dec-Mar. $50/person; riders must be 7 or older. Reservations advised.)* offers four-hour rides to the beach.

Henry Miller Library On Hwy. 1, just south of Nepenthe restaurant, 667-2574, same fax. Tu-Sun 11-5.

Miller lived in Big Sur for 18 years. The former home of his good friend, Emil White, has been turned into a shrine honoring the late artist and author. It is filled with memorabilia, photos, and letters, and the bathroom features erotic tiles by Ephraim Doner. The library also serves as a community art center and book store, and picnicking on the redwood-sheltered lawn is encouraged. Special events are often scheduled on weekends.

Pfeiffer Beach.

Watch for unmarked Sycamore Canyon Road on the west side of Highway 1. This narrow road begins about 1.7 miles south of Fernwood Resort and winds for two lovely miles to a beach parking lot. The only easily accessible public beach in the area, it features striking rock formations and arches carved out by the rough surf. Visitors can wade in a stream that meanders through the sandy beach but should stay out of the turbulent ocean. If it all looks vaguely familiar, it might be because this is where Elizabeth Taylor and Richard Burton acted out some love scenes in *The Sandpiper.*

Pfeiffer-Big Sur State Park On Hwy. 1, 667-2315. Daily 10-10. $6/vehicle.

Activities at this 821-acre park include hiking (among the many trails is a half-mile nature trail), river swimming, and ranger-led nature walks and campfires, and an open meadow is perfect for playing baseball or throwing a Frisbee. Facilities include picnic tables, a restaurant, and a store. Campsites are available.

Point Sur State Historic Park Off Hwy. 1, 625-4419. W & Sat at 10 & 2, Sun at 10. Adults $5, 13-17 $3, 5-12 $2. No strollers.

The **Point Sur Lightstation**, which is the center of this park, was built in 1889. It is now open for strenuous 2½-hour guided tours that include a half-mile hike and a 300-foot climb. Tours are not recommended for small children. Because parking is limited, only the first 15 cars to arrive can be accommodated.

San Simeon and Cambria

(Area Code 805)

A LITTLE BACKGROUND

Located in the small town of San Simeon on the wind-blown coast south of Big Sur, the spectacular **Hearst Castle**™ is perched atop La Cuesta Encantada ("The Enchanted Hill"™). It was designed by architect Julia Morgan and is filled with art treasures and antiques gathered from all over the world. Though unfinished, the castle contains 38 bedrooms, 31 bathrooms, 14 sitting rooms, a kitchen, a movie theater, 2 libraries, a billiard room, a dining hall, and an assembly hall! Colorful vines and plants grace the lovely gardens, and wild zebras, aoudads (or tar goats), and sambar deer graze the hillsides—remnants of the private zoo that once included lions, monkeys, and a polar bear.

Before 1958 visitors could get no closer than was permitted by a coin-operated telescope located on the road below. Now maintained by the State of California Department of Parks and Recreation as an Historical Monument, the castle is open to the public. Five tours are available; all include a scenic bus ride up to the castle.

• **Tour 1** is suggested for a first visit and includes gardens, pools, a guest house, and the ground floor of the main house—Casa Grande.

• **Tour 2** covers the upper floors of the main house, including Mr. Hearst's private suite, the libraries, a guest duplex, the kitchen, and the pools.

• **Tour 3** covers the 36-room guest wing and includes the pools and a guest house.

• **Tour 4** stresses the gardens. It includes the elegant 19-room Casa del Mar guest house, the wine cellar, and the pools. This tour is given only April through October.

• The **Evening Tour** combines highlights of the daytime tours and additionally features volunteers in period dress, bringing the magnificent surroundings to life. This tour is given only in spring and fall on most Friday and Saturday evenings.

Reservations are recommended and can be made by calling (800) 444-4445. Tickets can also be purchased at the Visitor Center ticket office after 8 a.m. on the day of the tour. The charge for each of the four day tours is $14 for adults, $8 for children ages 6 through 12; the Evening Tour is $25 for adults, $13 for children.

Note: Children under 6 are free only if they sit on their parent's lap during the bus ride.

Tours require walking about ½ mile and climbing approximately 150 to 400 steps; comfortable shoes are advised. Strollers are not permitted. Tours take approximately two hours. Picnic tables and a snack bar are available near the Visitor Center.

VISITOR INFORMATION

San Simeon Chamber of Commerce *P.O. Box 1 (9511 Hearst Dr.), San Simeon 93452, (800) 342-5613, 927-3500, fax 927-8358.*

Cambria Chamber of Commerce *767 Main St., Cambria 93428, 927-3624, fax 927-9426.*

GETTING THERE

Located approximately 75 miles south of Big Sur.

For a more leisurely trip, try the train package offered by Key Holidays *(1141 Bont Ln., Walnut Creek, (800) 783-0783, (510) 945-8938), fax (510) 256-7597.).* Via rail is the way guests used to travel to the castle in its heyday. Invitations then always included train tickets. Today travelers can still relax and enjoy the scenery while Amtrak's Coast Starlight transports them to San Luis Obispo. From there, after seeing the local sights, they are transported by bus for a tour of the coast and on to Morro Bay for overnight accommodations. The next day participants are bused to the famed castle for a guided tour, then down scenic Highway l for a stop in the village of Cambria, and then back to San Luis Obispo for the train trip back. The package does not include meals. Rates vary, and special rates are available for children.

ANNUAL EVENTS

Christmas at the Castle *December. Adults $14, 6-12 $8.*

During the entire month the castle and guest houses are lighted and decorated in splendid fashion for the Christmas holidays—just as they were when Mr. Hearst lived there.

WHERE TO STAY

Bluebird Motel *1880 Main St., Cambria, (800) 552-5434, 927-4634, fax 927-5215. 2 stories; 37 rooms; $-$$$. Children under 6 free. 13 VCRs; 13 gas fireplaces.*

Situated by Santa Rosa Creek and within easy walking range of the village, this attractive motel surrounds a landmark mansion dating from 1880. Many rooms are creekside, with private balconies or patios, and some special family suites are available.

The Blue Whale Inn *6736 Moonstone Beach Dr., Cambria, 927-4647. 6 rooms; 100% non-smoking; 2-night min. on weekends. All gas fireplaces. Afternoon snack, full breakfast.*

Situated across the street from the ocean, this luxurious inn boasts ocean view mini-suites with canopy beds and private outdoor entrances. Guests have access to a communal sitting area with a panoramic ocean view, and breakfast is served in an adjacent room with a similar view.

Cambria Pines Lodge *2905 Burton Dr., Cambria, (800) 445-6868, 927-4200, fax 927-4016. 2 stories; 125 units; 22 non-smoking units; $$-$$$. Children under 3 free. Some wood-burning fireplaces. Indoor heated pool & hot tub, sauna. Full breakfast; restaurant. Dogs welcome.*

Located on a pine-covered hill above town, this is a spacious 25-acre facility with rustic cabins. The lodge was originally built in 1927 by an eccentric European baroness who wanted to live in opulent style near the Hearst Castle. Recently updated, the new Main Lodge now houses a moderately priced restaurant and the woodsy, casual Fireside Lounge, where live entertainment is scheduled every night in front of its large stone fireplace. Colorful peacocks run loose on the property, and a volleyball area is available to guests. A nature trail leads down into the village.

Cavalier Oceanfront Resort *9415 Hearst Dr., San Simeon, (800) 826-8168, 927-4688, fax 927-6472. 2 stories; 90 rooms; 22 non-smoking rooms; $$-$$$. Children under 1 free. All VCRs; 61 wood-burning fireplaces. 2 heated pools, hot tub, fitness room. 2 restaurants, room service. Pets welcome.*

The only ocean-front resort in San Simeon, this contemporary motel features over 900 feet of ocean frontage. Many rooms have ocean views; some also have private patios.

Fog Catcher Inn *6400 Moonstone Beach Dr., Cambria, (800) 425-4121, 927-1400. 2 stories; 60 rooms; 100% non-smoking; $$-$$$. All gas fireplaces. Heated pool, hot tub. Full breakfast.*

Situated across the street from the ocean, this pseudo English Tudor-style inn has special suites for families and for honeymooners. Many rooms have ocean views.

The J. Patrick House *2990 Burton Dr., Cambria, (800) 341-5258, 927-3812, fax 927-6759. 2 stories; 8 rooms; 100% non-smoking; $$$-$$$+; 2-night min. on weekends. No TVs; 7 wood-burning fireplaces, 1 wood-burning stove. Evening snack, continental breakfast.*

Situated in the woods above the East Village, this authentic log cabin holds one guest room; seven more are found in an adjacent Carriage House. All beds are covered with duvets and handmade quilts. A vegetarian breakfast is served in the sun room.

Pickford House *2555 MacLeod Way, Cambria, 927-8619. 2 stories; 8 rooms; 100% non-smoking; $$-$$$. 3 gas fireplaces. Afternoon snack, full breakfast.*

Though this inn was built in 1983, it is far from modern in feeling. All rooms have claw-foot bathtubs and bear the names and personalities of silent film stars. Notable among them is the Valentino Room, which is furnished with dark-wood antiques and has a great view. A late afternoon snack of fruit breads and wine is served at a massive inlaid mahogany bar dating from 1860, and breakfast features the traditional Danish pancake fritters known as aebleskivers.

White Water Inn *6790 Moonstone Beach Dr., Cambria, (800) 995-1715, 927-1066, fax 927-0921. 1 story; 17 rooms; 100% non-smoking; $$-$$$+; 2-night min. on weekends. All VCRs & gas fireplaces. Continental breakfast.*

Situated across the street from the ocean, this contemporary motel court offers two mini-suites with a private patio featuring an oceanview hot tub and six rooms with double whirlpool bathtubs. Breakfast is delivered to the room, and movies can be borrowed from the desk.

Motel Row.

Numerous motels are located along scenic Moonstone Beach Drive in Cambria.

WHERE TO EAT

The Brambles Dinner House *4005 Burton Dr., Cambria, 927-4716, fax 927-3761. D daily, SunBr; $$-$$$. Highchairs, boosters, booths, child portions. Reservations advised. AE, MC, V.*

Located inside a rambling 1874 English-style cottage with Victorian decor, this cozy dinner house has some very private booths and a special room for families. Known for its prime rib, traditional Yorkshire pudding, and fresh salmon barbecued over an oak wood pit, the kitchen also prepares an extensive selection of steaks, chicken items, and fresh seafood. Hinting at the owner's heritage, several Greek dishes appear on the menu: a tasty salad with Feta cheese, dolmathes (stuffed grape leaves), and saganaki (fried cheese). A hamburger is also on the menu, and a rich English trifle is among the desserts. Interesting paintings and china plates decorate the walls, and the entrance is crowded with a collection of clocks that are for sale.

Linn's Main Bin Restaurant *2277 Main St., Cambria, 927-0371. B , L, & D daily.*

For description, see Linn's S.L.O. Bin on page 178.

Robin's *4095 Burton Dr., Cambria, 927-5007, fax 927-2712. L M-Sat, D daily; $-$$. Highchairs, boosters, child portions. 100% non-smoking. Reservations advised. MC, V.*

Situated within a converted house, this pleasant spot uses homegrown herbs to prepare delicious renditions of ethnic and vegetarian dishes. The seafood bisque is a must, and curries are prepared to order. The menu includes a variety of salads, sandwiches, and pastas, as well as seafood and tofu dishes. A selection of house-made desserts rounds out the offerings. Patio seating is available.

Sebastian's General Store/Patio Cafe *422 San Simeon Rd., San Simeon, 927-4217. Store: daily 8:30-5:30. Cafe: B & L daily; $. Closed Nov-Mar. No reservations. No cards.*

Built in 1852 and moved to its present location in 1878, this store is now a State Historical Landmark. Inexpensive short-order items are served in the outdoor cafe. In winter watch for **monarch butterflies** congregating in the adjacent eucalyptus and cypress trees.

The Tea Cozy *4286 Bridge St., Cambria, 927-8765, same fax. Tea W-Sun 10-5. 100% non-smoking. No reservations. MC, V.*

In England it is customary to conclude a visit to one of the stately homes with a stop at a local tea room, and the English proprietors here are attempting to interest Americans in this tradition. Situated within a modest 1890s school teacher's house, this cozy tea room offers light meals and pastries along with a nice cup of tea (or coffee). The extensive Royal Tea is available only from 2 to 4 in the afternoon, but the smaller Cream Tea is served all day. Imported English foods and an interesting collection of antique china are also available for purchase.

WHAT TO DO

The Pewter Plough Playhouse *824 Main St., Cambria, 927-3877. Performances F & Sat. Tickets $10.*

Stage plays are scheduled year-round in this intimate theater.

The Soldier Factory *89 Main St., Cambria, 927-3804. Daily 10-5.*

An ideal souvenir stop, this shop offers everything from an inexpensive unpainted pewter animal to a dearly-priced and elaborately-painted Alice in Wonderland chess set. Assorted sizes and styles of pewter soldiers from various wars are also for sale, and the owner's private collection of toy soldiers is on display. The majority of items are designed, molded, and cast on the premises.

William Randolph Hearst Memorial State Beach *San Simeon. Daily 8am-sunset. $3/vehicle.*
In addition to providing a very nice swimming beach, this park has a 640-foot-long fishing pier. No license is required to fish from the pier.

Morro Bay
(Area Code 805)

A LITTLE BACKGROUND

Named El Morro in 1542 by explorer Juan Rodriguez Cabrillo, because it reminded him of a turbaned Moor, over time the rock's name evolved into Morro, which means "knoll" in Spanish. The huge volcanic rock, visible from just about everywhere in town, prompted others to refer to the area as the "Gibraltar of the Pacific." The rock stands 576 feet high and is now a State Monument. Peregrine falcons, said to be the fastest moving animal in the world and an endangered species, nest at the top.

Because the area's wide variety of landscapes offer a myriad of nesting sites for some of California's most interesting birds, bird watching is particularly good here.

Commercial fishing is this small, picturesque town's main industry. Albacore and abalone are the local specialties, and they frequently show up on restaurant menus.

Lodgings often fill up on weekends, so reservations should be made well in advance.

VISITOR INFORMATION

Morro Bay Chamber of Commerce *895 Napa #A-1, Morro Bay 93442, (800) 231-0592, 772-4467, fax 772-6038.*

GETTING THERE

Located approximately 30 miles south of San Simeon.

ANNUAL EVENTS

Morro Bay Harbor Festival *October. (800) 366-6043, 772-1155, fax 772-2107. Adults $5, 1-12 free.*

General merriment includes a sand sculpture spectacular, a Hawaiian shirt contest, and ship tours, plus live entertainment and plenty of seafood and wine tasting. Proceeds benefit community nonprofit organizations, which volunteer their time to the festival.

WHERE TO STAY

Blue Sail Inn *851 Market Ave., (800) 336-0707, 772-2766. 48 rooms; 10 non-smoking rooms; $$-$$$. Some fireplaces. Hot tub.*

This streamlined modern motel is centrally located, allowing guests to walk to restaurants. The hot tub area has a view of Morro Rock, as do most of the rooms.

Embarcadero Inn *456 Embarcadero, (800) 292-ROCK, 772-2700, fax 772-2700. 32 rooms; $$-$$$+. Children under 12 free. All VCRs; some gas fireplaces. 2 indoor hot tubs. Continental breakfast.*

Situated in a quiet spot at the south end of the busy Embarcadero strip, this attractive modern motel is constructed of weathered wood. All rooms have bay views and most have balconies. A library of videos is available at no charge to guests, and local calls are free.

The Inn at Morro Bay *60 State Park Rd., (800) 321-9566, 772-5651, fax 772-4779. 96 rooms; 48 non-smoking rooms; $$-$$$+. Children under 12 free. Some fireplaces. Heated pool. Restaurant, room service.*

Located at the southern end of town in Morro Bay State Park, this small resort is sheltered by a strand of old eucalyptus and provides a quiet, restful spot to spend the night. Choice rooms have gorgeous views of the estuary. An 18-hole public golf course is just across the street, and a heron rookery located in an adjacent grove of eucalyptus often treats guests to the raucous rantings of its occupants.

The **Paradise** restaurant offers diners a mesmerizing panoramic view of the estuary and sand spit, and the wildlife watching from here is very good. Depending on the time of year, herons can be observed carrying nesting materials and sea otters basking on their backs. Kayaks and sailboats come and go as well. A different theme menu is served each night. The three-course Sunday brunch is ordered from a menu that offers both a perfect eggs Benedict, served with a side of scalloped potatoes topped with wispy deep-fried potatoes, and a savory paella prepared with fresh local catch. Each entree includes a glass of champagne, fresh-squeezed orange juice, coffee, and access to a dessert bar laden with items such as giant chocolate-dipped strawberries and house-made ice cream with a variety of toppings.

WHERE TO EAT

Dorn's Original Breakers Cafe *801 Market Ave., 772-4415, fax 772-4695. B, L, & D daily; $$. Highchairs, boosters. Reservations advised. No cards.*

This casual restaurant features a great bay view and is especially pleasant at breakfast. The menu then offers a choice of hearty breakfasts, plus novelty items such as chocolate chip pancakes with chocolate syrup. The extensive dinner menu features fresh local fish and an award-winning Boston clam chowder.

The Great American Fish Company *1185 Embarcadero, 772-4407. L & D daily; $$. Highchairs, boosters, child portions. No reservations. MC, V.*

Located a short, scenic stroll from the center of town, this restaurant provides a comfortable, casual atmosphere and good views of the rock. The extensive menu includes mesquite-grilled fresh fish and shark, as well as deep-fried fresh local prawns and Monterey squid. A steak and hamburger are also available. Most dinners come with garlic bread, a vegetable, and a potato.

Hofbrau der Albatross *571 Embarcadero, 772-2411, fax 772-5001. L & D daily; $. Highchairs, boosters, child portions. 100% non-smoking. No reservations. AE, MC, V.*

Popular with locals and visitors alike, this casual spot features cafeteria-style service. The fish and chips are superb, and very good French dip sandwiches and hamburgers are also available. Seating is a choice of inside or outside at harbor-view tables. A cafe just opposite beckons for dessert.

Pacific Cafe *1150 Embarcadero, 772-2965. L & D daily; $-$$. 1 highchair, boosters. Reservations advised. MC, V.*

Situated across from the rock and featuring several heated outdoor tables, this casual restaurant has a strong repeat clientele of locals. Owned by chef Abba Imani, who proudly does all the cooking, it has extremely tight quarters and servers who provide excellent service. At dinner, the perfect starter is the house special of scampi fra Diavalo, which consists of seven perfect prawns in a tasty red sauce suitable for dunking with the soft, hot house bread. Entrees are selected from fresh offerings listed on a chalk board and sometimes include a salmon Lilliano—poached and wrapped around spinach and topped with a light red sauce—and snapper Griglia—grilled and topped with a light white wine sauce. Dessert choices might include marinated fresh strawberries, a fresh peach cobbler, or a house-made vanilla ice cream, and each meal ends with a complimentary liqueur. Lunch is a less expensive selection of salads, sandwiches, and hamburgers.

Rose's Landing *725 Embarcadero, 772-4441. L & D daily; $$-$$$. Highchairs, boosters, child menu. 100% non-smoking. Reservations advised. AE, MC, V.*

Good views can be enjoyed here in both the downstairs bar and the upstairs restaurant. Seafood dominates the dinner menu, but steaks and a few other items are also available. Complete dinners include either the house-specialty seafood chowder or a salad, either a baked potato or rice pilaf, steamed vegetables, hot garlic bread, and a relish tray. Lunch is a less expensive selection of salads, sandwiches, fish & chips, and burgers.

WHAT TO DO

Clam Digging.

Go for it! World-famous Pismo clams can be dug up on the beach just about anywhere.

Coleman Beach Park *Embarcadero Rd./Coleman Dr., east of Morro Rock.*

Children are sure to enjoy this idyllic playground in the sand.

Fishing.

The pier is a prime spot for fishing. Chartered fishing boats are also available.

Giant Chess Board *Embarcadero/Front, in Centennial Park, 772-6278.*

At the base of a 44-step stairway is one of the two largest chess boards in the U.S. (The other is in New York City's Central Park.) The redwood chess pieces stand 2- and 3-feet high and weigh from 18 to 30 pounds—making a game here physical as well as mental exercise. From noon to 5 p.m. each Saturday the Morro Bay Chess Club sponsors games on the giant 16- by 16-foot concrete board; the general public is welcome to challenge. Except for the hours mentioned, the board is available to the public weekdays from 8 to 5. Reservations must be made by filling out an application at the Recreation & Parks Department. Call for details.

Morro Bay Aquarium *595 Embarcadero, 772-7647. Daily from 9, closing time varies. Adults $1, 5-11 50¢.*

This teeny, tiny aquarium is a draw for the gift shop located in front. However, the price is right, and over 300 live marine specimens can be observed. All are said to be injured and distressed animals that can't be returned to the wild. Some preserved specimens are also displayed, and very noisy seals beg to be fed.

Morro Bay State Park *At south end of town, on State Park Rd., 772-2560.*
• **Bird Sanctuary.**

Following a trail through the marsh and hills allows for the possibility of catching glimpses of over 250 species of birds. This is said to be the third largest bird sanctuary in the world.
• **Heron and Cormorant Rookery** *At Fairbank Point, off State Park Rd.*

No one is allowed inside the rookery, which is one of the last where the Great Blue Heron can be found, but the herons can be viewed from an observation area.
• **Museum of Natural History** *772-2694. Daily 10-5. Adults $2, 6-12 $1.*

Situated at White Point on a scenic perch over the bay, this small museum presents lectures, slide shows, and movies about the wildlife and Native American history of the area. Large windows provide excellent views of the estuary, and a telescope permits up-close viewing of wildlife. Guided tours are sometimes available. In winter, guided walks are scheduled to see the **monarch butterflies** that congregate at Pismo State Beach; it is the largest overwintering colony of monarchs in the United States.

The Shell Shop *590 Embarcadero, 772-8014, fax 772-4137. Daily 9:30-7, to 5 in winter.*

The perfect souvenir stop, this shop has the largest selection of sea shells on the West Coast and offers them at bargain prices.

Tiger's Folly II Harbor Cruises *1205 Embarcadero, 772-2257. Daily June-Sept; Sat & Sun Oct-May; call for schedule. Adults $6, 5-12 $3.*

The one-hour harbor cruise aboard this sternwheeler requires no reservation, but the special Sunday champagne brunch cruise does.

WHAT TO DO NEARBY

Avila Beach *10 mi. south of town off Hwy. 101.*

This tiny, old-fashioned beach community is a great place to watch surfers and to swim in a generally mild surf.

Cayucos *6 mi. north of town on Hwy. 1.*

This quiet little beach town has a string of inexpensive motels. It also boasts both a fine beach with a gentle surf and a 400-foot fishing pier where equipment rentals are readily available.

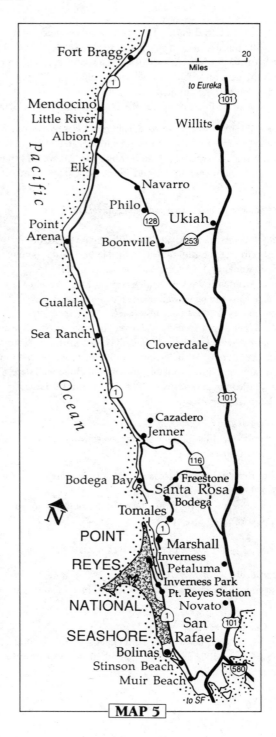

MAP 5

Coast North

A LITTLE BACKGROUND

Highway 1 north from San Francisco allows an escape into a quieter, less-populated area. The two-lane road winds through fragrant eucalyptus groves, then rustic countryside that is rife with wildflowers in spring. For long stretches it hugs oceanside cliffs. Note that on sunny summer days the road can become congested. Then, everyone wants to head to a beach and soak up some of the famous California sunshine that is so elusive in the northern part of the state.

A word of warning: The rocky cliffs and beaches along the coast are scenic and beautiful. In their awe, people sometimes forget that they are also dangerous. Though it is tempting to stand at the edge where the surf is pounding, people have been washed out to sea doing just that. Don't be one of them. Be careful. Stay on trails. Obey posted signs. And take special care not to let children run loose.

VISITOR INFORMATION

Redwood Empire Association *2801 Leavenworth St., 2nd floor, in The Cannery, San Francisco 94133-1117, (415) 543-8334, fax (415) 543-8337; Tu-Sat 10-6.*

Information on the coastal counties north of San Francisco can be obtained here.

GETTING THERE

From San Francisco, take Highway 101 to Highway 1 north.

Muir Beach
(Area Code 415)

A LITTLE BACKGROUND

It was in this area (the exact spot is still disputed) more than 400 years ago that Sir Francis Drake beached the *Golden Hinde*, formerly known as the *Pelican*, and claimed California for Queen Elizabeth I.

WHERE TO STAY AND EAT

The Pelican Inn *10 Pacific Way, 383-6000, fax 383-3424. 3 stories; 7 rooms; $$$-$$$+. No TVs. Full breakfast; restaurant.*

Sheltered by towering pines and alders, this authentic reconstruction of an actual 16th-century English Tudor inn was built in 1979. It offers snug rooms furnished with English antiques, canopied beds, and oriental carpets.

Elegant pub fare is served in the **restaurant** *(L & D Tu-Sun; $-$$. Highchairs, boosters, child portions. 100% non-smoking. No reservations. MC, V.)* at lunch, followed by continental meals in the evenings, and a simple tea service is always available. The lunch menu consists of house-made traditional English pub fare such as bangers and mash, cottage pie, and the ever-popular ploughman's plate. Dinner brings on prime rib, beef Wellington, and rack of lamb. British ales and beers complement the food, and a variety are on tap. Diners can be seated outside on an enclosed patio or inside in a rustic candle-lighted dining room furnished with several long communal tables and a number of more private individual ones. On cold, foggy days a fireplace warms the interior.

WHAT TO DO

Green Gulch Farm Zen Center *1601 Shoreline Hwy., just before town, 383-3134, fax 383-3128.*

Reached via a sharp downhill turnoff, this Zen retreat offers public meditation programs daily. On Sundays, a longer program includes a dharma talk. Visitors are also welcome then to take informal afternoon walks in the organic garden, which supplies the herbs and vegetables for Greens restaurant in San Francisco.

Overnight lodging is available in a peaceful Japanese-style **guest house** *(2 stories; 12 rooms; $$-$$$. 100% non-smoking. No TVs; all shared baths. Sauna. All meals included.)*, and guests may take their meals with the permanent residents. A separate apartment is available for families with children.

Mount Tamalpais State Park *801 Panoramic Hwy., 388-2070. Summit visitor center open Sat & Sun 10-5; guided hikes on Sat & Sun at 9:30am. $5/vehicle.*

From some locations, Mt. Tam, as the mountain is affectionately nicknamed, resembles the resting figure the local Native Americans called "The Sleeping Maiden," who was said to safeguard the area. This 6,233-acre park offers 50 miles of hiking trails, and the view from its 2,571-foot peak is spectacular. It is interesting to note that the mountain bike was first developed here for use on the park's hills. Campsites are available.

Since 1904, the 7.1-mile **Dipsea Race** has been run on the first Sunday of each June. Hordes of runners tromp the trail then from the center of Mill Valley to Stinson Beach. The **Mountain Play** *(June. 383-1100. $18, 3-18 $13.)* has been presented in the natural outdoor amphitheater atop the mountain annually since 1913. Plays have run the gamut from the obscure to Shakespeare to well-known Broadway musicals. In the old days people came on

burros, by stagecoach, or on the old Mount Tamalpais Scenic Railway, also known as the "Crookedest Railroad in the World" because it had 281 curves, including a five-fold switchback known as the Double Bow Knot, along its 8¼-mile route. Now many audience members ride the free shuttle buses up the mountain and, after the performance, hike four miles down to board a shuttle bus for the rest of the journey back to the parking area.

Muir Beach.

Reached by turning onto a leafy, blackberry-lined lane located just south of the Pelican Inn, this popular beach is unsafe for swimming. However, it is excellent for sunbathing and people-watching, and picnic tables are available.

Muir Beach Overlook.

Panoramic coastline views make this is great picnic spot. In winter, it is a good perch from which to watch the whale migration.

Muir Woods National Monument *Off Hwy. 1, on Panoramic Hwy., 388-2595. Daily 8-sunset. Free.*

Located just off Highway 1 and enveloping 560 acres, this magnificent, fragrant old-growth redwood forest has six miles of walking trails. Among them are an easy paved Main Trail with interpretive exhibits; seven more-challenging unpaved trails lead away from the crowds. Naturalist John Muir, for whom the forest was named, said of it, "This is the best tree lover's monument that could be found in all the forests of the world." The largest tree here measures 240 feet high by 16 feet wide. Because nearly two million people come here each year, only a visit early or late in the day (before 10 or after 4) provides the hope of some solitude; rainy days are also quiet. And no matter what time of year it is, visitors are advised to bring along warm wraps. The dense forest lets in very little sunlight, and the weather is usually damp, foggy, and cold. Discovery Packs, which are filled with tools that assist children in exploring nature, can be borrowed free from the Visitors Center. Picnicking is not permitted, but a snackbar dispenses simple foods.

Slide Ranch *2025 Shoreline Hwy., 381-6155, fax 381-5762. $10-$12/person. Reservations required.*

Perched dramatically on the ocean side of Highway 1 near Muir Beach, this ranch offers the city-slicker a chance to get back to the land . . . a chance to learn about a self-sustaining rural lifestyle through exposure to frontier arts . . . a chance to slow the pace. During Farm Day programs, adults and children age 6 and older learn together about things such as cheesemaking, composting, and papermaking. Though the program varies according to the season and the ages of participants, a typical day begins with smiling staff members greeting visitors in a fragrant grove of eucalyptus. A visit to the sheep and goat pen usually follows, giving children the chance to "pet a four-legged sweater" and milk a goat. More activities include collecting eggs, feeding chickens, carding and spinning sheep wool and rabbit fur, making bread and cheese, helping in the garden, and hiking along one of the coastal wildland trails.

Stinson Beach
(Area Code 415)

Note that there is no gas station in town. According to a local resident, "It disappeared one night and didn't come back."

WHERE TO STAY

Casa del Mar *37 Belvedere Ave., (800) 552-2124, 868-2124, fax 868-2305. 4 stories; 6 rooms; 100% non-smoking; $$$-$$$+; 2-night min. on weekends. Children under 6 free. No TVs; 1 wood-burning fireplace. Afternoon snack, full breakfast.*

Perched on a hill above town, this peachy-colored stucco, Mediterranean-style structure has three rooms with great views of the ocean and three with views of Mount Tamalpais—the inn's back yard. Its terraced garden was planted in the 1930s and was used as a teaching garden by the U.C. School of Landscape Architecture in the '70s. Now the owner tends to it and invites guests to pinch and prune, should the mood strike. The house itself was completely rebuilt. Wonderful breakfasts, sometimes prepared with ingredients from the garden, greet guests in the morning in a sunny dining area.

Steep Ravine Cabins *1 mi. south of town, (800) 444-7275, 388-2070. 10 cabins; $. No TVs; all wood-burning stoves.*

Perched on a rocky bluff overlooking the ocean, within Mount Tamalpais State Park, each of these primitive cabins dates from the 1930s and sleeps up to four people. Each has a small wood-burning stove, a picnic table and benches, sleeping platforms, and an outdoor barbecue. They do not have running water, electricity, or shower facilities. Primitive toilets, water faucets, and firewood are nearby. Guests must provide their own bedding, cooking equipment, and light source. Paths lead down to the beach, where six primitive campsites are also available.

WHERE TO EAT

Stinson Beach Grill *3465 Hwy. 1, 868-2002. L & D daily; $-$$. Highchairs, boosters. Reservations advised. AE, MC, V.*

Overlooking Highway 1, this informal grill has an eclectic menu offering everything from hamburgers to osso bucco. In between are a Greek salad, an impeccably fresh salmon with tomato-basil sauce, and a spicy blackened snapper. A large variety of complementary beers from micro-breweries are also available.

WHAT TO DO

Audubon Canyon Ranch's Bolinas Lagoon Preserve *4900 Hwy. 1, 3.5 mi. north of town, 868-9244. Sat, Sun, & holidays 10-4; mid-March through mid-July. By donation.*

Situated on picturesque Bolinas Lagoon just north of town, this 1,000-acre ranch is a non-profit project sponsored by the four Bay Area Audubon Societies. It is open only during the breeding season. Breeding pairs of Great Blue Herons (measuring four to five feet tall and with a wingspan of nearly six feet), snowy egrets, and Great Egrets nest noisily in the tall redwood trees located in the ranch's Schwarz Grove. Approximately 60 other bird species also make their home here, making this a bird watcher's paradise. Nests contain an average of two to five eggs, which incubate for about 28 days. Once hatched, baby birds, covered in fluffy down, waddle about their nests while waiting for their parents to return from gathering a meal of fish and crustaceans in nearby Bolinas Lagoon. (Baby egrets fly at seven weeks, herons at nine weeks.) A self-guiding nature trail, and several other scenic trails of varying length and challenge, lead to an overlook where telescopes are available and a ranch guide is on hand to interpret and assist. Visitors can rest on benches and observe these graceful birds as they court, establish a pecking order, build their nests, and begin rearing their young.

Exhibits in the Display Hall museum, a converted milking barn left from the days when the ranch was a dairy, give visitors more detailed information about the birds as well as about the geology and natural history of the area. Nearby, a stream-side, sod-roofed Bird Hide is designed so observers can see out, but birds can't see in. Its feeders attract a variety of unsuspecting birds, including many colorful humming-birds. A picnic area, from which the nesting site can be viewed, provides a scenic spot to relax and enjoy a leisurely lunch in peaceful surroundings.

Stinson Beach Park *868-0942. Free.*

This magnificent beach offers a little taste of the southern California beach scene. Conditions often permit swimming here, though the water is cold and lifeguards are on duty usually only in summer. Since the weather is often different from everywhere else in the Bay Area, it is wise to call and check conditions before setting out *(868-1922).*

Bolinas
(Area Code 415)

A LITTLE BACKGROUND

So shy of visitors is this tiny oceanside hamlet that residents spirit away directional signs as soon as they are posted. All visitors are hereby warned that reception in town can be chilly.

WHERE TO STAY

One Fifty-Five Pine *868-0263, fax 868-0201. 1 story; 2 cabins; 100% non-smoking; $$$; 2-night min. on weekends. Children under 1¹/₂ stay free. No TVs; all kitchens & wood-burning fireplaces. Full breakfast.*

It's impossible not to relax in one of these two knotty-pine cabins situated at the end of a rural dirt road. They were built by two brothers on three private, quiet acres just above Duxbury Reef—once considered a healing spot by the native Miwok Indians. One of the kitchens has multi-paned windows overlooking a huge rosemary bush that frames a grassy, brambly expanse to the ocean. This same cabin has an alcove with a cozy, narrow captain's bunk bed for kids and a bedroom with a skylight allowing the old folks to fall asleep under the stars. Guests are wise to bring along dinner. Breakfast items are provided so that guests can prepare what they like, when they like. It is just a short walk to the beach and tidepools.

WHERE TO EAT

Bolinas Bay Bakery & Cafe *20 Wharf Rd., 868-0211, fax 868-9408. B, L, & D daily; $. Highchairs, boosters, child portions. 100% non-smoking. No reservations. AE, MC, V.*

Situated at the end of a gravel pathway in a big old house, this pleasant spot offers an eclectic menu. Pastas, hamburgers, and pizza with both organic crust and organic tomato sauce are available. Bakery items are extensive and exceptional, and all are made with organic flour. The deli has plenty of salads, soups, and "other stuff" ready to go, and six beers and kombucha tea are on tap.

Point Reyes Area
(Area Code 415)

VISITOR INFORMATION

West Marin Chamber of Commerce *P.O. Box 1045 (11431 Hwy. 1), Point Reyes Station 94956, 663-9232, fax 663-8818.*

Reservations Services.
For information on the area's B&Bs call:
- **Inns of Marin** *(800) 887-2880, 663-2000.*
- **Inns of Point Reyes** *663-1420.*
- **Point Reyes Lodging** *(800) 539-1872, 663-1872, fax 663-8431.*
- **West Marin Network** *663-9543.*

WHERE TO STAY

Holly Tree Inn *3 Silverhills Rd., Point Reyes Station, (800) 286-HOLL, 663-1554, fax 663-8566. 2 stories; 4 rooms, 3 cottages; 100% non-smoking; $$$-$$$+; 2-night min. on weekends. No TVs; 2 kitchens; 2 wood-burning fireplaces, 2 wood-burning stoves. Afternoon snack, full breakfast.*

Tucked away in its very own valley just beneath the Inverness Ridge, this rustic B&B offers four attractively appointed rooms and a spacious cottage with a wood-burning stove, a stereo and tapes, and a claw-foot tub. A stream runs picturesquely through the property, and an informal playground with a wooden plank swing invites children to play. A rustic cottage, perched right on Tomales Bay and featuring a solarium with a hot tub, is also available.

Manka's Inverness Lodge *30 Callender Way/Argyle, Inverness, (800) 58-LODGE, 669-1034, fax 669-1598. 2 stories; 14 units; 100% non-smoking; $$-$$$+; 2 night min. on Sat. Children free in cabins. 4 TVs & VCRs; 4 kitchens; 4 wood-burning fireplaces, 1 gas fireplace, 1 wood-burning stove. Hot tub. Restaurant, limited room service (child items). Dogs welcome.*

This rustic 1917 arts and crafts-style hunting lodge was the first place in town with a phone; and it was a speakeasy in the 1940s. Both cozy lodge rooms and larger cabin units are available. Rooms 1 and 2 boast both a large weathered deck overlooking Tomales Bay and a claw-foot tub. Several rooms have a large four-poster bed made with whole logs: Guests climb a step stool, then sink into peaceful slumber upon its featherbed and under its fluffy down comforter.

Local game grilled in the fireplace is often on the dinner menu in the inn's intimate **dining room** *(D Thur-M. Highchairs, boosters.).* Breakfast is optional, inexpensive, and not to be missed. Served fireside in the lobby, one such gustatory extravaganza featured eggs scrambled with local goat cheese and hand-gathered mushrooms, a side of toasted herb bread, and both homemade rhubarb purée and blood orange marmalade.

Point Reyes Hostel *663-8811. 44 beds; family room avail. for those with children under 5.*

Nestled in a secluded valley, this former ranch house offers both a kitchen and outdoor barbecue for preparing meals. Two cozy common rooms with wood-burning stoves are also available to guests. See also page 391.

WHERE TO EAT

Knave of Hearts Bakery *12301 Sir Francis Drake Blvd., Inverness Park, 663-1236. Tu-Sun 8-5.*

Unexpectedly, this unpretentious, tiny spot is home to an outstanding European bakery/coffeehouse. The owner/husband makes almost everything himself and serves it up, too! Among the goodies are a moist, light chocolate genoise cake, a wonderful poppy seed-hazelnut torte, and kid-pleasing Danish pastries and large cookies. The owner/wife prepares the noteworthy breads and decorates the fruit tarts. A small counter overlooking picturesque farmland invites leisurely snacking and perhaps a browse of the Pulitzer Prize-winning local newspaper— *The Point Reyes Light.*

The Station House Cafe *11180 Hwy. 1, Point Reyes Station, 663-1515, 663-9443. B, L, & D daily; $-$$. Highchairs, boosters, booths, child menu. 100% non-smoking. Reservations advised on weekends. MC, V.*

Menu choices in this casual, popular spot include sandwiches, light and inexpensive entrees, and pricier daily specials that always feature fresh fish and local shellfish. Hamburgers are prepared with ground chuck from organically fed cattle raised at the local Niman-Schell ranch. Desserts include apple pie, devil's food cake, bread pudding, butterscotch pudding, and seasonal fruit pies. Truly all stages of hunger can be satisfied here at the same table. Additionally, service is fast and unpretentious.

WHAT TO DO

Johnson's Drakes Bay Oyster Company *17171 Sir Francis Drake Blvd., Inverness, 669-1149, fax 669-1262. Tu-Sun 8-4.*

A visit to this scenically situated enterprise allows viewing the various stages of the oyster-farming process. Oysters are available for purchase.

Llunch with a Llama. *Camelid Capers, 663-9371. Adults $45-$60, 6-12 $35-$50, under 6 free; bring-your-own picnic $25/$10; half-day trip with mini breakfast or lunch $30/person. Reservations required.*

These llama-chaperoned picnic hikes take place within Point Reyes National Seashore. The llamas carry in the picnic supplies and set the pace. Since they are definitely not in a hurry, the hike is leisurely. The picnic food—items such as salmon pâté, aram sandwiches, and purple Peruvian potato salad—is wonderful, and the guide-proprietor is considerate: He carries in on his own back the llamas' alfalfa lunch.

Point Reyes National Seashore *West of Olema, 663-1092. M-F 9-5, Sat & Sun 8-5. Free.*

Known for its beaches and hiking trails, this 65,000-acre refuge has plenty of other interesting things for visitors to do. Many activities are clustered around the Park Headquarters. A Visitor Center houses a working seismograph and a variety of nature displays. The **Morgan Horse Ranch** *(663-1763. Feeding daily at 8 & 4.),* where pack and trail animals for the national parks are trained, is adjacent. (The Morgan was the first American horse breed.) A short walk away a replica coast Miwok Indian village, **Kule Loklo,** has been re-created using the same types of tools and materials as the Native Americans themselves originally used.

Trails beginning near the headquarters include the self-guided Woodpecker Nature Trail, the .6-mile-long self-guided Earthquake Trail, which follows the San Andreas fault and passes a spot where the pacific plate moved 16 feet north in about 45 seconds during the 1906 earthquake, and the popular 4.1-mile Bear Valley Trail, which winds through meadows, fern grottos, and forests before ending at the ocean. The area has over 70 miles of equestrian trails, and guided trail rides, buggy rides, and hayrides are available at nearby **Five Brooks Stables** *(1000 Hwy. 1, Olema, 663-1570).* Also, mountain bikes are permitted on some trails, and walk-in backpacking campsites are available by reservation.

Further away from the headquarters is the 1870 **Point Reyes Lighthouse,** where winds have been recorded blowing at 133 miles per hour—the highest rate in the continental U.S. The bottom line is that it can get mighty windy, cold, and wet at this scenic spot. The lighthouse, reached by maneuvering 300 steps down the side of a steep, rocky cliff, is a popular spot in winter for viewing migrating gray whales. On weekends in January and February, shuttle buses are sometimes available.

Drake's Beach offers easy beach access and has a great little short-order cafe. The **Ken Patrick Visitor Center** *(669-1250. Sat & Sun 10-5.)* here has maritime history displays and a 250-gallon salt water aquarium. At the **Tule Elk Reserve** on Tomales Point, a herd of approximately 240 Tule elk can often be observed grazing. Nearby, **Historic Pierce Point Ranch** is open for a self-guided tour of its barn, bunkhouse, old and new dairy, and blacksmith shop.

The Point Reyes National Seashore Association offers seminars and classes in natural history, environmental education, photography, and art. Request a free catalog *(663-1200)*. One of the regular offerings is **A Walk with Mrs. Terwilliger.** This well-known Marin County naturalist prefaces her walks with a hands-on introduction to some of nature's casualties. Then the unusual, enthusiastic Mrs. T opens participant's eyes to the beauty of nature. A walk with her is "something special"—as she is fond of saying about nature's wonders—and something not soon forgotten. No childhood is complete without a nature walk led by her.

Tomales Bay Area

(Area Code 415)

WHERE TO EAT

Tony's Seafood *18863 Hwy. 1, Marshall, 663-1107. L & D F-Sun; $. Highchairs, boosters. No reservations. No cards.*

Many restaurants in this area offer oyster dishes made with the fresh local supply. Here, at tables with relaxing views of Tomales Bay, the specialty is oysters barbecued in the shell. Deep-fried oysters are also available, as is fresh fish and a hamburger. Beer, which seems to go especially well with oysters, is available from the bar.

WHAT TO DO

Tomales Bay State Park *669-1140. Daily 8-sunset. $5/vehicle.*

Access to the warm bay waters for swimming and wading is available at popular **Heart's Desire Beach**. The easy self-guided Indian Trail begins here and leads to a Miwok garden, where native plants used for food and medicine are labeled; it then climbs a slope that skirts the bay and ends at Indian Beach.

Bodega Bay

(Area Code 707)

VISITOR INFORMATION

Bodega Bay Area Chamber of Commerce *P.O. Box 146 (850 Hwy. 1), Bodega Bay 94923-0146, (800) 905-9050, 875-3422, same fax.*

ANNUAL EVENTS

Fisherman's Festival *April. 875-3422. Free.*

Held each year at the beginning of the commercial salmon season, this festival's highlights are a traditional parade of colorfully decorated commercial fishing boats and a Blessing of the Fleet, but bathtub races, stunt kite demonstrations, and a juried art show are also part of the fun. All proceeds benefit local non-profit organizations.

WHERE TO STAY

Bodega Bay Lodge *103 Hwy. 1, (800) 368-2468, 875-3525, fax 875-2827. 2 stories; 78 rooms; 18 non-smoking rooms; $$$-$$$+; 2 night min. Children under 12 free. All fireplaces. Solar-heated pool, hot tub, sauna, fitness room. Continental breakfast; restaurant.*

Situated at the southern end of town, overlooking the wetlands marsh and sand dunes of **Doran Park,** this rustically attractive modern motel features rooms with stunning ocean views. A wonderful whirlpool hot tub is sheltered from the elements by glass walls, but its ceiling is open to the possibility of a light mist or rain providing a cooling touch. Golfing can be arranged at an adjacent 18-hole course.

A convenient ocean-view **restaurant** *(D daily. Reservations required.)* serves elegant dinner fare prepared with the best local ingredients: fresh Tomales Bay oysters on the half shell, Petaluma escargot with Enfant Riant truffle butter, rack of Sonoma lamb with olive-basil Zinfandel glacé and minted Sebastopol apples. Delectable box lunches—packed with such goodies as marinated local fresh vegetables, herb-stuffed Petaluma game hens, and croissant sandwiches filled with Valley Ford lamb—are also available.

WHERE TO EAT

The Tides Wharf Restaurant *835 Hwy. 1, 875-3652, fax 875-3285. B, L, & D daily; $$. Highchairs, boosters, child portions. 100% non-smoking. Reservations advised. AE, MC, V.*

Always crowded, this popular spot offers a bargain breakfast and serves it until noon. Lunch and dinner menus, both nearly the same in content and cost, offer an extensive selection of seafood entrees. Fish is prepared rare, as is currently trendy, so those who prefer it flaky should specify that when ordering. A tasty tartar sauce is freshly made, and the dungeness crab cocktail, though made with frozen crab, is delicious. Complete dinners come with a starter of either a wonderful potato-rich New England clam chowder or a green salad with shrimp garnish, a vegetable, and sourdough bread. Less expensive seafood items such as fish & chips and deep-fried clam strips are available, as are fried chicken and steak for those who don't care for fish. In addition to fish & chips, the children's menu offers a hamburger, hot dog, and grilled cheese sandwich. (One kid was overheard here saying, "It's a really good hamburger for a *nice* restaurant.") Desserts, such as chocolate velvet and raspberry-almond tortes, and coffees are also available. Because most tables afford sweeping views of Bodega Bay, it is worthwhile scheduling a meal here before sunset.

Attractive contemporary rooms with ocean views are available across the street at **The Inn at the Tides** *(800 Hwy. 1, (800) 541-7788, 875-2751, fax 875-3285. 2 stories; 86 rooms; $$$-$$$+. Children under 12 free. VCRs to rent; 2 kitchens; 40 wood-burning fireplaces. Heated indoor-outdoor pool, hot tub, sauna. Continental breakfast; 2 restaurants, room service.).* At monthly Vintner's Dinners, five-course dinners are paired with wines from a guest winery whose representative is on hand to comment.

WHAT TO DO

Chanslor Guest Ranch *2660 Hwy. 1, 875-2721, fax 875-2785. Daily 8-8. Horses $20+/hr., ponies $8/15 min., petting zoo $1.50. Riders must be 8 or older. Reservations advised.*

Guided trail rides through the Wetlands Wildlife Preserve and beach rides across sand dunes are offered at this 700-acre working guest ranch. Pony rides for kids under 8 and hayrides for everyone are also available. A petting zoo lets kids get up close to a menagerie that includes donkeys, pigs, sheep, llamas, and pygmy goats. Several picnic tables and a barbecue area are provided for picnicking.

Lodging is available in several rustic houses *(1 story; 6 rooms; 100% non-smoking; $$-$$$. Unsuitable for children under 4; children under 12 free. All VCRs. Continental breakfast.).*

Osmosis Enzyme Bath & Massage *209 Bohemian Hwy., Freestone, 5 mi. east of town, 823-8231, fax 874-3702. Daily 9-9. Enzyme bath & blanket wrap $45, with massage $110. Unsuitable for children. Reservations required.*

Long popular in Japan, the enzyme bath available here is something like a mud bath—only lighter and more fragrant. It is said to improve circulation, break down body toxins, and relieve stress. The experience begins with a soothing cup of enzyme tea enjoyed in a tranquil tea garden. Then bathers, either nude or in a swimsuit, are submerged for 20 minutes in a hot mixture

of Hinoki cedar fiber, rice bran, and over 600 active plant enzymes that naturally generate heat. This is followed by a blanket wrap or massage. Private massages are given in outdoor Japanese pavilions nestled in a wooded area near Salmon Creek.

Sonoma Coast State Beach *875-3483, fax 875-3876. Daily 8-sunset. Free.*

Actually a series of beaches separated by rocky bluffs, this state beach extends for 18 miles from Bodega Head to Meyers Gulch just south of Fort Ross State Historic Park. It is accessible from more than a dozen points along Highway 1, and campsites are available.

• **Goat Rock Beach** *Off Hwy. 1, 4 mi. south of Jenner, 875-3483, 865-2391.*

Located where the Russian River flows into the ocean, this beach is popular with harbor seals. March is the beginning of pupping season, when Seal Watch volunteers are on hand to interpret and answer questions for viewers. See-ing the baby seals, many people are tempted to get closer, but visitors should stay at least 50 yards away. When pups are born they depend on the mother's milk for the first 48 hours. During that critical period the mother will often go out to feed, leaving newborn pups by themselves. If a mother finds humans around her pup when she returns, she will abandon it. Seals hang around this area in large numbers through July. Then the population thins out until the following March. Driftwood collecting is encouraged because pile-ups of wood debris are a potential fire hazard to the town. Note that swimming in the ocean is hazardous due to sleeper waves and riptides.

Jenner
(Area Code 707)

WHERE TO STAY

Fort Ross Lodge *20705 Hwy. 1, 12 mi. north of town, (800) 968-4537, 847-3333, fax 847-3330. 1 story; 22 units, 1 house; $$-$$$+. Children under 12 free. All VCRs; 18 wood-burning fireplaces. Hot tub, sauna.*

This collection of comfortable rustic-modern cabins is situated on a large, open, grassy bluff on the ocean side of the highway. Some units have ocean views; all have a small refrigera-tor, a coffee maker, a microwave oven, and a barbecue on a private patio. A beach access trail is available to guests.

Jenner Inn *10400 Hwy. 1, (800) 732-2377, 865-2377, fax 865-0829. 2 stories; 13 units; 100% non-smoking; $$-$$$+; 2-night min. on weekends. Children under 5 free. No TVs; 8 kitchens; 2 wood-burning fireplaces, 4 wood-burning stoves. Afternoon snack, continental breakfast; restaurant.*

Tucked into a curve in the highway at the point where the Russian River runs into the Pacific Ocean, this inn offers a choice of lodge rooms, cottages, and private homes. Three rooms in the River House get unobstructed views of the estuary and share a hot tub. A communal lounge is kept cozy by an antique wood-burning stove and offers guests a library filled with books and games.

Salt Point Lodge *23255 Hwy. 1, 17 mi. north of town, (800) 956-3437, 847-3234. 16 rooms; $$-$$$; 2-night min. on weekends. Some wood-burning stoves. Hot tub, sauna. Restaurant.*

Located across the street from the Pacific Ocean, this motel features a large expanse of lawn dotted with a giant slide and swing. Special family rooms have a queen bed and two twin bunk beds, and two rooms for two have an ocean view and a private deck and hot tub.

A small restaurant features an ocean view and serves breakfast, lunch, and dinner. The dinner menu is both ambitious and expensive, offering selections made with local oysters, fresh fish, chicken, and beef, plus a variety of tempting house-made desserts.

Timber Cove Inn *21780 Hwy. 1, 14 mi. north of town, 847-3231, fax 847-3704. 47 rooms; $$-$$$+; 2-night min. on Sat. Unsuitable for children. No TVs; some fireplaces. Restaurant.*

Perched on a rocky seaside cliff, this inn offers many rooms with magnificent ocean views and some with sunken tubs and private hot tubs. A tall Bufano sculpture, which acts as a landmark, juts above the lodge, and the lobby bar and restaurant feature a dramatic Japanese-modern style of architecture and expansive ocean views.

Timberhill Ranch *35755 Hauser Bridge Rd., Timber Cove-Cazadero, 19 mi. northeast of town, (800) 847-3470, 847-3258, fax 847-3342. 1 story; 15 cottages; 5 non-smoking cottages; $$$+; 2-night min. Unsuitable for children under 12. No TVs; all wood-burning fireplaces. Heated pool (unheated Nov-Feb), hot tub, fitness room, 2 tennis courts. Afternoon snack, continental breakfast; restaurant, room service.*

Modern cedar-log cottages, with private decks and luxurious amenities, offer a quiet retreat on this 80-acre working ranch. A leisurely six-course gourmet dinner in the dining room and a continental breakfast brought to the room are included in the room rate. Non-guests may visit for lunch or dinner by reservation.

WHAT TO DO

Fort Ross State Historic Park *19005 Hwy. 1, 11 mi. north of town, (707) 847-3286. Daily 10-4:30. $6/vehicle.*

Built by Russian and Alaskan hunters in 1812 as a trading outpost, this historic fort has been authentically restored by the state. The compound consists of two blockhouses equipped with cannons, a small Russian Orthodox chapel, a manacor's house, and a barracks. Picnic tables are available. Outside the gates, a picturesque bluff at the edge of the ocean offers a path leading down to the beach. An architecturally striking Visitors Center is located adjacent to the parking area.

Living History Day, which allow visitors to step back in time to the 1800s, is held annually on the last Saturday in July. Then, costumed staff and volunteers perform musket drills and fire cannons, craftspersons demonstrate their skills, and a blacksmith pounds at his forge.

Kruse Rhododendron State Reserve *On Kruse Ranch Rd., 22 mi. north of town, 847-3221. Daily sunrise-sunset. Free.*

Best known for its spring floral display *(Apr-May, depending on weather.)*, this 317-acre park has five miles of hiking trails that take visitors over picturesque bridges and through fern-filled canyons.

Salt Point State Park *25050 Hwy. 1, 20 mi. north of town, 847-3221. Daily sunrise-sunset. $5/vehicle.*

A popular spot with skin divers, this park is also choice for a walk along the beach. Stump Cove has an easy, short trail down to its scenic beach. Campsites are available.

The Sea Ranch

(Area Code 707)

WHERE TO STAY

Home Rentals. *Rams Head Realty & Rentals, 1000 Annapolis Rd., (800) 785-3455, 785-2427, fax 785-2429. 120 units; $$-$$$+; 2-night min. All kitchens; some fireplaces. Pets welcome in some homes.*

Stunningly beautiful wind-swept coastal scenery is the backdrop for the luxury vacation homes situated in this development. Each home is unique. For example, the spectacular ocean-front Monette House has three bedrooms and a very special hot tub in an enclosed room with sliding glass doors opening to the ocean. Rustic hike-in cabins are also available. Guests have access to two recreation centers and to hiking and jogging trails as well as a children's playground. A 9-hole golf course, designed in the Scottish manner by Robert Muir Graves, can be played at extra charge.

The Sea Ranch Lodge *60 Sea Walk Dr., (800) 732-7262, 785-2371, fax 785-2917. 2 stories; 20 rooms; 1 non-smoking room; $$$-$$$+; 2-night min. on weekends July-Oct. Children under 5 free. No TVs; 7 wood-burning fireplaces, 7 wood-burning stoves. 18-hole golf course (located 8 mi. away). Restaurant, room service.*

At this rustic modern facility, each room has an ocean view. Two rooms have private court-yards with hot tubs.

Gualala

(Area Code 707)

A LITTLE BACKGROUND

Named for an Indian word that is pronounced "wha-LA-la" and means "water coming down place," this town is located in a banana-belt of regularly warm weather. The area's many celebrity property owners include singer Kris Kristofferson and comedian Robin Williams.

VISITOR INFORMATION

Gualala Sea Ranch Coastal Chamber of Commerce *P.O. Box 338, Gualala 95445-0338, (800) 778-LALA.*

WHERE TO STAY

Gualala Hotel *On Hwy. 1, 884-3441, fax 884-3908. 19 rooms; $. Some shared baths. Breakfast.*

Built by the town's founders in 1903, when guests arrived from San Francisco by stage-coach, this historic inn was recently renovated. Rooms are decorated with period antiques, and five have private baths and ocean views.

Family-style dinners are served in the first-floor restaurant. In addition to an entree, dinners include a relish tray, soup, salad, pasta, vegetable, bread, and dessert. The atmospheric logging bar was once frequented by Jack London and is now popular with locals.

Mar Vista Cottages *35101 Hwy. 1, 5 mi. north of town, 884-3522. 1 story; 12 units; $$. No TVs; all kitchens; 2 wood-burning fireplaces, 1 wood-burning stove. Hot tub. Pets welcome.*

Most of these one- and two-bedroom cottages have ocean views; all are just a short walk from a sandy beach with a gentle surf.

The Old Milano Hotel *38300 Hwy. 1, 1 mi. north of town, 884-3256. 2 stories; 9 units; 100% non-smoking;*

$$-$$$+; 2-night min. on Sat. Unsuitable for children under 16. No TVs; 2 wood-burning stoves; some shared baths. Hot tub. Full breakfast; restaurant.

Built originally in 1905 as a railroad rest stop and pub, this elegantly refurbished cliffside Victorian hotel is now listed in the National Register of Historic Places. A garden cottage and a converted caboose—complete with upstairs brakeman's seats where occupants can enjoy watching the sun set—are available in addition to the hotel rooms. An expansive ocean view is enjoyed from the cliff-top hot tub.

Serenisea *36100 Hwy. 1, 3 mi. north of town, (800) 331-3836, 884-3836. 1-2 stories; 23 units; 4 non-smoking units; $$-$$$+; 2-night min. on weekends. Children under 1 free. Some TVs & VCRs; all kitchens; 10 wood-burning fireplaces, 13 wood-burning stoves. Pets welcome in some units.*

Most of these housekeeping cabins and vacation homes are spread over a scenic ocean bluff. Some have private hot tubs, and one has a private sauna. A trail leads down to the beach.

St. Orres *36601 Hwy. 1, 2 mi. north of town, 884-3303, fax 884-1543. 8 rooms, 11 cottages; $$-$$$+; 2-night min. on weekends. No TVs; 9 wood-burning fireplaces; some shared baths. Hot tub, sauna. Full breakfast; restaurant.*

This unusual inn is built of weathered wood in a Russian style of architecture featuring onion-domed turrets.

A fixed-price, three-course dinner is served in the striking three-story-tall dining room featuring large windows with ocean views *(D daily, SunBr; $30. 100% non-smoking. Reservations advised.).* Dishes often make use of locally foraged ingredients and wild game such as boar and venison.

Whale Watch *35100 Hwy. 1, 5 mi. north of town, (800) WHALE-42, 884-3667, fax 884-4815. 2 stories; 18 rooms; 100% non-smoking; $$$+; 2-night min. on weekends. No TVs; 5 kitchens; all wood-burning fireplaces. Sauna. Full breakfast; limited room service.*

Perched on an oceanside cliff, this dramatic contemporary-style lodging facility offers plenty of peace and quiet. Rooms are spread among five buildings; all have private decks and ocean views, and eight have two-person whirlpool bathtubs. The Bath Suite has a spiral staircase leading to a whirlpool bathtub for two that is positioned under a skylight and features an ocean view. The Crystal Sea offers a mesmerizing view of an ocean cove—from a couch, the bed, and another of those whirlpool tubs for two. In the morning, a delicious breakfast is brought to the room in a large willow basket tray. Guests can relax in the communal Whale Watch Room, with its cozy fireplace and panoramic view of the ocean; a telescope is provided for whale-watching. Guests also have access to a half-mile stretch of private beach.

Point Arena
(Area Code 707)

WHAT TO DO

Point Arena Lighthouse *At the end of Lighthouse Rd., 2 mi. off Hwy. 1, 882-2777. Daily 11-2:30; in summer M-F 11-3:30, Sat & Sun 10-3:30. Adults $2.50, under 12 50¢. House rentals: 3 units; $$; 2-night min. All VCRs; all kitchens & wood-burning stoves.*

Originally built in 1870, this lighthouse was destroyed in the '06 quake and then rebuilt. It was finally automated in 1976. Visitors can take a self-guided tour of the museum, which is filled with old photos and features a whale-watching room. Then it's a 145-step climb (equivalent to six stories) up the 115-foot light for a guided tour of the tower. Those who want to stay the night can book one of the bargain three-bedroom, two-bath lightkeeper's homes located adjacent.

Elk

(Area Code 707)

WHERE TO STAY

Harbor House *5600 Hwy. 1, 877-3203. 2 stories; 6 rooms, 4 cottages; 100% non-smoking; $$$-$$$+; 2-night min. on weekends. Unsuitable for children under 12. No TVs; 9 wood-burning fireplaces. Full dinner & breakfast included.*

Built entirely of redwood in 1917, this lovely inn has a path leading to a private beach where guests can sun, explore tidepools, and gather driftwood. Meals are served in a beautifully appointed dining room with a spectacular ocean view.

Mendocino

(Area Code 707)

A LITTLE BACKGROUND

Mendocino provides a rejuvenating, quiet escape from the hectic pace of city life. Now an Historical Monument, this tiny artists' colony is built in a pastel Cape Cod-style of architecture and exudes the feeling that it belongs to a time past. Visitors can really slow down their systems by parking their cars for the duration of a visit. It is easy to get anywhere in town via a short walk.

Visitors are advised that Mendocino has a limited water supply and should be careful not to waste water when in town. Also, there is a Volunteer Fire Department with an alarm that has been known to go off in the middle of the night. Resembling the scream of an air-raid siren, it can be quite startling—even when a person is aware of what it is.

The night life here is of the early-to-bed, early-to-rise variety. Consider this itinerary: dinner out, a stroll through town, a nightcap at the Mendocino Hotel or Sea Gull Inn, and then off to bed.

Make lodging reservations as far in advance as possible; in-town lodging is limited and popular.

VISITOR INFORMATION

Fort Bragg-Mendocino Coast Chamber of Commerce *P.O. Box 1141 (332 N. Main St.), Fort Bragg 95437, (800) 726-2780, 961-6300, fax 964-2056.*

GETTING THERE

Located approximately 150 miles north of San Francisco. Take Highway 101 to Highway 1, or Highway 101 to Highway 128 to Highway 1.

ANNUAL EVENTS

Mendocino Coast Whale Festival *March. In Mendocino and Fort Bragg; (800) 726-2780.*
In Mendocino, the fun includes a wine tasting, a seafood chowder tasting, and a wooden boat show. In Fort Bragg, it takes the form of a microbrewery beer tasting, a seafood chowder tasting, and a classic car show. The **Point Cabrillo Lightstation**, which is normally closed to the public, is open for tours, and whale-watching cruises are available.

Mendocino Music Festival *July. 937-2044. $12-$30.*
A variety of performances—including orchestra, chamber music, opera, and jazz—are presented in a small oceanside tent in Mendocino Headlands State Park. Master classes are scheduled, and free pre-concert lectures educate the audience about the music being performed.

WHERE TO STAY IN TOWN

Hill House of Mendocino *10701 Palette Dr., (800) 422-0554, 937-0554, fax 937-1123. 2 stories; 44 rooms; 22 non-smoking rooms; $$$-$$$+; 2-night min. on Sat. 4 wood-burning fireplaces. Continental breakfast; restaurant, room service.*
Located on a scenic hill above the village, this lodging facility was built in 1978. It has become famous as the setting for many of the early episodes of the TV series *Murder, She Wrote*, and the Bette Davis Suite is where the star lodged for six weeks while filming her final movie. Because of this Hollywood connection, it attracts many stars as patrons. Rooms are spacious and furnished comfortably with brass beds and lace curtains.

Joshua Grindle Inn *44800 Little Lake Rd., (800) GRINDLE, 937-4143. 2 stories; 10 rooms; 100% non-smoking; $$-$$$+; 2-night min. on weekends. Unsuitable for children. No TVs; 2 wood-burning fireplaces, 4 wood-burning stoves. Afternoon snack, full breakfast.*
Situated on two acres at the edge of town, the Victorian farmhouse that comprises this small inn was built in 1879 by the town banker. It has a New England country atmosphere, and Early American antiques furnish every room. Guest rooms are in the main house, a cottage, and a water tower.

MacCallum House Inn *45020 Albion St., (800) 609-0492, 937-0289. 3 stories; 19 rooms; 100% non-smoking; $$$-$$$+; 2-night min. on weekends. Children under 12 free. No TVs; 1 kitchen, 4 wood-burning fireplaces, 4 wood-burning stoves. Restaurant.*
Built in 1882 by William H. Kelley for his newlywed daughter, Daisy MacCallum, this converted Victorian home was one of the first B&Bs in the area. Though it no longer serves breakfast, its attractively decorated rooms are furnished with antiques, many of which belonged to the original owner. Accommodations are also available in newer structures adjacent to the house. The ten rooms in the house itself tend to be best suited to couples and parents with just one child.

In the evening, **MacCallum House Restaurant** *(937-5763. D daily. Closed Jan-mid-Feb. Boosters. 100% non-smoking. Reservations advised. MC, V.)*, an independent operation, serves elegant seafood and game entrees in the house's magnificent dining rooms. On cold nights, guests are warmed by crackling fires in two fireplaces built of smooth river stone. Light dinners and snacks are available across the hall in the cozy **Grey Whale Bar,** also operated by the restaurant. Interesting drinks include Daisy's Hot Apple Pie (a blend of apple cider, Tuaca, cinnamon, and whipped cream) and a non-alcoholic Velvet Rabbit (a frothy mix of cream, grenadine, and strawberries served elegantly in a brandy snifter).

Mendocino Hotel & Garden Suites *45080 Main St., (800) 548-0513, 937-0511, fax 937-0513. 2 stories; 51 rooms; 46 non-smoking rooms; $$-$$$+; 2-night min. on weekends. 25 TVs; some fireplaces; some shared baths. 2 restaurants, room service.*

Built in 1878, this hotel has been renovated in Victorian style. Its small rooms combine modern convenience with 19th-century elegance. Modern cottages, with luxurious suites featuring canopied beds and marble bathrooms, provide additional lodging behind the hotel. They are located amidst almost an acre of well-tended gardens.

A casual, greenhouse-like cafe serves both breakfast and lunch. Dinner is available in the more formal **restaurant** *($$$. Highchairs, boosters, child portions. 100% non-smoking. Reservations advised. AE, MC, V.)* furnished in old-fashioned oak. Fresh seafood and meat entrees are on the a la carte menu. Starters include a French onion soup and a very good Caesar salad, and the dessert tray always includes deep-dish olallieberry pie with homemade ice cream—the house specialty. The hotel's bar is a good spot to stop and enjoy a fancy drink among beautiful specimens of stained glass and oriental carpets.

Mendocino Village Inn *44860 Main St., (800) 882-7029, 937-0246. 3 stories; 13 rooms; 100% non-smoking; $$-$$$+; 2-night min. on weekends. Unsuitable for children under 10. No TVs; 5 wood-burning fireplaces, 5 wood-burning stoves; some shared baths. Afternoon snack, full breakfast.*

Built in 1882, this Queen Anne Victorian home is known as "the house of the doctors" because it was originally built by a doctor, and then bought in turn by three more doctors. All the cozy rooms are decorated with antiques and contemporary art. A suite is available in a converted two-story water tower with a private deck and ocean view.

Sea Gull Inn *44594 Albion St., 937-5204. 2 stories; 9 rooms; 100% non-smoking; $-$$$; 2-night min. on weekends. 1 TV. Continental breakfast; room service.*

Built in 1877 as a town house, this simple inn has a casual, friendly atmosphere. A mature garden, with giant fuchsias and a century-old rosemary bush, surrounds the inn. Breakfast includes hot beverages, orange juice, muffins, and raspberry scones.

Sears House Inn *44840 Main St., 937-4076. 4 rooms, 4 cottages; 100% non-smoking; $$-$$$; 2-night min. on weekends. No TVs; 5 kitchens; 2 wood-burning fireplaces, 3 wood-burning stoves; some shared baths. Pets welcome.*

Guests here have the choice of staying in an 1870 Victorian house, in a cottage, or in a converted water tower. Each room is stocked with a complimentary bottle of wine.

Whitegate Inn *499 Howard St., (800) 531-7282, 937-4892, fax 937-1131. 2 stories; 6 rooms, 1 cabin; 100% non-smoking; $$$-$$$+; 2-night min. on weekends. Children under 2 free. 5 wood-burning fireplaces, 2 wood-burning stoves. Evening snack, full breakfast.*

Built in 1880, this tasteful Victorian home is furnished with French and Victorian antiques. Live orchids grace every room, and lace-edged sheets and lofty down comforters adorn every bed. Some bathrooms feature claw-foot tubs. A lavish breakfast is served on antique china and sterling silver.

WHERE TO STAY NEARBY

Fensalden Inn *33810 Navarro Ridge Rd., Albion, 7 mi. south of town, (800) 959-3850, 937-4042. 2 stories; 8 rooms; 100% non-smoking; $$-$$$; 2-night min. on weekends May-Dec. Unsuitable for children under 7. 1 TV & VCR; 2 kitchens; 4 wood-burning fireplaces, 1 wood-burning stove. Evening snack, full breakfast.*

Originally a Wells Fargo stagecoach way station in the 1860s, this restful B&B sits atop 20 tree-lined acres of headlands meadow offering quiet respite. Among the rooms in the large main house is an upstairs two-room suite with a sweeping view of the cypress tree-lined pasture. Another two-story suite is built around an 1890s water tower, and a private bungalow with an unobstructed ocean view is situated at the head of the pasture. Antique furnishings are used throughout.

Heritage House *5200 Hwy. 1, Little River, 4 mi. south of town, (800) 235-5885, 937-5885, fax 937-0318. 66 units; $$$+. Closed Jan to mid-Feb. Children under 6 free. No TVs; 37 wood-burning fireplaces, 1 gas fireplace, 1 wood-burning stove. Afternoon snack, full dinner, & breakfast included; restaurant.*

Located on a craggy stretch of coast with magnificent ocean views, this inn offers a luxurious escape from city living. Rooms and cottages are scattered over 37 acres of well-tended gardens. Some are furnished with antiques; others are done in a contemporary style. Most have ocean views and decks. If it all looks familiar, it could be because it's been seen before in the movie *Same Time Next Year*, which was filmed here. The cabin the movie was filmed in has been divided into one called "Same Time" and another called "Next Year." Note that though some family amenities exist, children are generally discouraged.

Dinner is available in an elegant cliffside **restaurant** *(B & L M-F, D daily, Sat & SunBr. Highchairs, boosters. 100% non-smoking. Reservations advised for D. MC, V.).* Non-guests are welcome.

Little River Inn *7751 Hwy. 1, Little River, 2 mi. south of town, (888) INN-LOVE, 937-5942, fax 937-3944. 2 stories; 65 units; 50 non-smoking units; $$-$$$+; 2-night min. on weekends. Children under 12 free. All VCRs; 1 kitchen; 34 wood-burning fireplaces, 6 wood-burning stoves. 2 tennis courts (night lights $10/hr.), 9-hole golf course. Restaurant, room service (child items).*

Built in 1853 by an ancestor of the current owner, this gingerbread Victorian house became an inn in 1939 and now offers a choice of cozy attic rooms, cottages, and standard motel units. Most have ocean views. The beach and hiking trails of Van Damme State Park are adjacent, and the **restaurant** *(B & D daily. Highchairs, boosters.)* and oceanview bar are open to non-guests.

Mendocino Coast Reservations *1000 Main St., Mendocino, (800) 262-7801, 937-5033, fax 937-4236. 60 units; most non-smoking units; $$-$$$; 2-night min., 1-week in July & Aug. All kitchens; some fireplaces. Dogs welcome in some units.*

This vacation home rental service arranges lodging in studios, cabins, cottages, inns, and estate homes located on the Mendocino coast. Some units are oceanfront, some have ocean views, and some have private hot tubs.

Stanford Inn by the Sea *On Comptche-Ukiah Rd., Mendocino, (800) 331-8884, 937-5615, fax 937-0305. 3 stories; 29 rooms; 100% non-smoking; $$$+; 2-night min. on Sat. Children under 4 free. All VCRs; 3 kitchens; all wood-burning fireplaces. Indoor heated pool, hot tub, sauna. Afternoon snack, full breakfast. Pets welcome.*

Located on the outskirts of town, upon a bluff overlooking a scenic llama farm and duck pond, these modern luxury rooms are decorated with antiques, fresh flowers, and the work of local artists. Mountain bikes are available for guests to borrow at no charge.

WHERE TO EAT

Cafe Beaujolais *961 Ukiah St., 937-5614, fax 937-3656. D daily; $$. Closed Dec. Child portions. 100% non-smoking. Reservations advised. MC, V.*

Gone here are the days of great breakfasts and informal lunches. Now it is dinners only, using local meats, fish, and organic produce. Wonderful breads, including a dense Austrian sunflower bread and an unusual hazelnut, are baked on the premises in a wood-burning oven. A three course, fixed price *($20)* country menu is available Tuesday through Thursday. Should anyone get cravings for some of these goodies after returning home, a mail-order brochure is available. It offers especially delicious spicy gingersnaps and panfortes.

Mendocino Bakery *On Lansing St., 937-0836. Daily 8-7; $. 1 booster.*

The perfect spot for a light lunch, this super bakery dispenses tasty house-made soup and thick-crusted pizza warm from the oven. A hunk of the fragrant, moist gingerbread makes a memorable dessert, as do the chewy cinnamon twists and chocolate chip-oatmeal "cowboy" cookies. The bakery also dispenses an assortment of breads and breakfast pastries—all made without mixes or preservatives. Everything is exceptional.

Next door, the **Mendocino Chocolate Company** *(10483 Lansing St., (800) 722-1107, 937-1107. Daily 10-5:30.)* purveys delicious handmade candies. Samples are always available.

Mendocino Ice Cream Co. *45090 Main St., 937-5884. Daily 9-5; in summer daily 11-9; $. Booths.*

People wait in long lines to get the ¼-pound ice cream cones scooped up here. And, indeed, the award-winning ice cream is delicious—especially the Black Forest flavor made with rich chocolate ice cream infused with chocolate chips and cherry bits. The foot-long hot dogs are pretty good, too. Sodas and sandwiches round out the menu, and wooden booths are available for seating.

WHAT TO DO

Beachcombing.

Follow down to the beach the little path behind the church on Main Street. While there, make a **kelp horn** by cutting the bulb off the end of a long, thin piece of fresh bull kelp. Rinse out the tube in the ocean so that it is hollow. Then wrap it over one shoulder, and blow through the small end. The longer the tube, the greater the resonance.

Catch A Canoe & Bicycles, Too
On Comptche-Ukiah Rd., (800) 320-BIKE, 937-0273, fax 937-0305. Daily 9:30-5:30. $10+/hr.

Drifting down calm Big River affords the opportunity to picnic in the wilderness, swim in a secluded swimming hole, and observe a variety of wildlife. Canoe rentals include paddles and life jackets. Bicycle rentals are also available.

Ford House Museum and Visitor Center *735 Main St., 937-5397. Daily 11-4. $1 donation.*

Inside this historic 1854 home is an interpretive center focusing on the cultural and natural history of the area. During whale-watching season, a short orientation film is presented. Information on interpretive programs held at nearby **Mendocino Headlands State Park** can also be obtained here then. (From December through April, whales migrate close to shore and can sometimes easily be seen from the headlands "breaching," or jumping out of the water.) In good weather, a picnic at tables in the backyard offers a spectacular ocean view.

Kelley House Historical Museum *45007 Albion St., 937-5791. F-M 1-4; daily in summer. Adults $1.*

A gigantic cypress tree grows in the front yard of this home built by William H. Kelley (Daisy MacCallum's father) in 1861. The restored first floor displays a collection of photos from the 1800s, as well as changing exhibits of local artifacts and private collections.

Mendocino Art Center *45200 Little Lake St., 937-5818. Daily 10-4. Free.*

Three rooms display art here. Cookies and coffee are usually available in the lobby, and an inviting courtyard garden seems the perfect place to enjoy them. Activities related to fine arts and crafts are scheduled year-round, and the **Mendocino Theatre Company** presents performances March through December.

Russian Gulch State Park *On Hwy. 1, 2 mi. north of town, 937-5804, fax 937-2953. Daily dawn-dusk. $5/vehicle.*

A protected beach, a waterfall, and a blowhole are among the features at this rustic park. Picnic tables overlook an ocean cove, and campsites are available.

Van Damme State Park *8125 Hwy. 1, Little River, 2 mi. south of town, 937-5804. Daily dawn-dusk. $5/vehicle.*

Among the interesting features in this 2,069-acre park is a canyon filled with ferns and a ⅓-mile Bog Trail leading to a large area of skunk cabbage. Picnic facilities and campsites are available.

An unusual **Pygmy Forest,** where stunted trees grow in leached soil, is nearby. It has a short boardwalk trail; a brochure describing the various types of trees is available at the trailhead. To reach the forest, follow Little River Airport Road approximately three miles inland.

Wind & Weather *609 Albion St., (800) 922-9463, 937-0323, fax 964-1278. Daily 10-5.*

Located inside a converted water tower, this tiny specialty shop sells barometers, weather vanes, sundials, and other paraphernalia for measuring the weather. Don't miss it.

Fort Bragg
(Area Code 707)

GETTING THERE

Located approximately 15 miles north of Mendocino.

ANNUAL EVENTS

John Druecker Memorial Rhododendron Show *April. (800) 726-2780. Free.*

One of the largest such shows in the West, this is hosted by the Noyo Chapter of the American Rhododendron Society. An enormous exhibit includes everything from alpine dwarf species to huge trusses of hybrids.

World's Largest Salmon Barbecue *July. (800) 726-2780, 964-6535.*

In addition to feasting on king salmon, participants can look forward to music, dancing, a variety of educational salmon displays, and a fireworks show over the ocean. Proceeds benefit the non-profit Salmon Restoration Association and assist them in restocking Northern California salmon runs.

WHERE TO STAY

Colonial Inn *533 E. Fir St., 964-9979. 2 stories; 8 rooms; 100% non-smoking; $$. Closed part of Oct & part of spring. Children under 5 free. 5 TVs; 2 wood-burning fireplaces.*

Located in a quiet residential area, this massive 1912 wood-frame home was turned into a guest house in 1945. It features tastefully decorated rooms, one of which has an oversize fireplace. A public tennis court is just one block away.

DeHaven Valley Farm *39247 N. Hwy. 1, Westport, 10 mi. north of town, 961-1660, fax 961-1677. 2 stories; 8 units; 100% non-smoking; $$-$$$. Closed Jan. Children under 6 free. 1 wood-burning fireplace, 4 wood-burning stoves; some shared baths. Hot tub. Afternoon snack, full breakfast.*

Romance and family fun are both possible here. For romance, request the cozy Valley View room and enjoy its private bathroom, small corner fireplace, and view of the valley. The spacious Eagle's Nest, with its Franklin stove and expansive windows overlooking the valley, is another winner. With kids in tow, opt for one of the two cottages. One teenager who stayed here actually uttered, "Mom, you did right. This place is great!" A cozy communal living room in the traditional Victorian farmhouse is the gathering spot for afternoon refreshments. It holds a grand piano for self-entertainment and a TV with a large video library. Guests are welcome to play with the many resident cats and to walk the goats—although sometimes the goats seem to be walking the guests. Also, the tidepools of **Westport Union Landing Beach** await just across the highway, and a hilltop hot tub offers views of the valley and ocean. Delicious, intimate four-course dinners are available to guests by reservation.

The Grey Whale Inn *615 N. Main St., (800) 382-7244, 964-0640, fax 964-4408. 4 stories; 14 rooms; 100% non-smoking; $$-$$$+; 2-night min. on Sat. 6 TVs, 2 VCRs; 4 kitchens; 1 wood-burning fireplace, 2 gas fireplaces. Full breakfast.*

Originally built as a hospital, this stately redwood building was converted to an especially spacious inn in 1976. Some of the pleasantly decorated rooms have a private deck, some have good ocean views that permit viewing the whale migration, and one has a whirlpool bathtub for two. A large communal guest area is equipped with a TV, fireplace, pool table, and plenty of board games. The elaborate buffet breakfast sometimes includes a wonderful concoction of fresh bananas and blueberries mixed with a light cream cheese sauce. A relaxing stay here can be just what the doctor ordered.

Pine Beach Inn *16801 Hwy. 1, 4 mi. south of town, 964-5603. 51 rooms; 30 non-smoking rooms; $$-$$$. 2 tennis courts. Restaurant.*

This motel complex is located on 12 acres of private land. Facilities include a private beach and cove.

Motel Row.

Three traditional motels on the northern end of town offer good value and an extraordinary beachfront location.

- **Beachcomber Motel** *1111 N. Main St., (800) 400-SURF, 964-2402. $$-$$$+.*
- **Hi-Seas Beach Motel** *1201 N. Main St., (800) 990-7327, 964-5929. $$.*
- **Ocean View Lodging** *1141 N. Main St., 964-1951. $$.*

WHERE TO EAT

Cap'n Flint's *32250 N. Harbor Dr., 964-9447. L & D daily; $. Highchairs, boosters, child portions. 100% non-smoking. No reservations. No cards.*

Popular with locals, the menu here offers various kinds of fish & chips, clam chowder, and the house specialty—deep-fried shrimp won tons made with a tasty cream cheese filling. Hamburgers, hot dogs, sandwiches, and wine-based drinks are also available. Though the decor consists of well-worn, mismatched furniture, the view of picturesque Noyo Harbor is excellent.

Egghead Omelettes of Oz *326 N. Main St., 964-5005. B & L daily; $. Highchairs, boosters, booths, child portions. 100% non-smoking. No reservations. MC, V.*

Decorated with movie photos from *The Wizard of Oz* and related knickknacks, this cheerful, popular, and tiny diner serves 40-plus varieties of big omelettes. Regular breakfast items and an assortment of sandwiches are also available—all brought to diners via waitresses clad in ruby-red shoes. Families will appreciate the privacy afforded by enclosed booths.

The Restaurant *418 N. Main St., 964-9800. L Thur-F, D Thur-Tu, SunBr; $$. Highchairs, boosters, booths, child portions. 100% non-smoking. Reservations advised. MC, V.*

An ad for this restaurant reads, "If you like to eat, you'd probably like to eat at a place where people who like to eat, eat what they like—and like it!" It's an unusual ad—just like the restaurant, which, in completely unpretentious surroundings, serves good food at reasonable prices. The eclectic menu changes regularly, but the emphasis is on fresh local seafood and vegetarian items. A sample lunch menu offers a variety of sandwiches, plus a hamburger, Philly cheesesteak, chicken flauta, vegetable chili, and several salads and soups. Desserts are a chocolate shortcake with fresh berries and cream, a house-made ice cream, and a lemon tart. Dinner entrees the same night include Thai-style shrimp in green curry sauce, Denver lamb riblets with sweet & sour glaze, and chicken breast Amalfi topped with lemony arugula.

WHAT TO DO

Downtown Shopping.

A walk along Main and Laurel Streets allows a look at some of the town's most interesting shops. On North Main Street stop in at the **Mendocino Chocolate Company** at #542 *((800) 722-1107, 964-8800. Daily 10-5:30.)* for hand-dipped chocolates and truffles. Duck down Laurel Street to **Round Man's Smoke House** at #137 *((800) 545-2935, 964-5954, fax 964-5438.)* for smoked meat, fish, and cheese and an assortment of jerkeys. Across the street at #136, the informal **Laurel Deli & Desserts** *(964-7812. M-F 7-4, Sat 8-4.)* dishes up freshly made soups and sandwiches, as well as gigantic blackberry muffins and delicious pies. Back on Main Street stop in at #362, the **Northcoast Artists Gallery** *(964-8266. Daily 10-6.)*, where the works of local artists are displayed and available for sale. Just a bit further down at #330, **The Hot Pepper Jelly Company** *((800) 892-4823, 961-1422, fax 961-5462. Daily 10-5:30. Closed all of Jan.)* dispenses charming doily-topped jars of delicious pepper jelly as well as many other local food products.

The Fort Bragg Footlighters Gaslite Gaieties *248 Laurel St., 964-3806. W & Sat at 8pm; summer only. Tickets $7. Reservations advised.*

Gay Nineties music and nonsense highlight a program that appeals to all ages.

Georgia-Pacific Tree Nursery *90 W. Redwood Ave., 964-5651. Daily 9-4. Free.*

Visitors here get a view of four million seedling trees. A nature trail and picnic tables are available.

Guest House Museum *343 N. Main St., 961-2840, fax 961-2802. Tu-Sun 10-2. By donation.*

Get a sense of this area's history by viewing the old logging photos and artifacts on display inside this beautifully restored 1892 mansion constructed entirely of redwood. A steam donkey is among the displays in the manicured gardens.

Jughandle State Reserve *On Hwy. 1, 3 mi. south of town, 937-5804. Daily dawn-dusk. Free.*

A unique self-guided nature trail takes hikers through an **ecological staircase** consisting of five wave-cut terraces that demonstrate how plants and soils affect one another. During the five-mile, three-hour walk, the terrain changes from grass-covered headlands, to a pine and redwood forest, to a pygmy forest filled with full-grown trees measuring only one to two feet tall. Wear sturdy shoes, and bring water and a lunch.

Mendocino Coast Botanical Garden *18220 N. Hwy. 1, 2 mi. south of town, 964-4352, fax 964-3114. Daily 9-5; Oct-Mar 9-4. Adults $5, 60+ $4, 6-12 $1.*

Enjoy a self-guided tour through 47 acres of flowering plants. Known for its rhododendrons, fuchsias, and heathers, this garden also boasts a major collection of succulents, camellias, and old heritage roses. Picnic facilities are available.

Diners can sit on a sunny deck overlooking the gardens at **The Gardens Grill** *(18603 N. Hwy. 1, 964-7474. L M-F, D W-Sun, SunBr, in summer; hrs. change for rest of year; $-$$. Highchairs, boosters, child portions. Reservations advised. MC, V.).* Light lunches and dinners are offered. Sample items include an eggplant sandwich and a delicious torte of wild mushrooms and spinach. Grilled items are prepared over mesquite or apple wood.

Ricochet Ridge Ranch *24201 Hwy. 1, (888) TREK-RRR, 964-7669, fax 964-9669. Daily at 10, 12, 2, & 4. $28/hr.; riders must be 6 or older. Reservations required.*

Equestrian excursions vary from by-the-hour guided rides on the beach to week-long trips that make nightly stops at inns. They include treks on Fort Bragg's **Ten Mile Beach** and in Mendocino's majestic redwood forests. Catered trips, camping expeditions, and private tours can also be arranged.

Skunk Train/California Western Railroad
Foot of Laurel St., (800) 77-SKUNK, 964-6371, fax 964-6754. Daily; schedule varies. Round trip: adults $26, 5-11 $12, under 5 free if they don't occupy a seat. Reservations advised.

This train gets its name from the fact that the original logging trains emitted unpleasant odors from their gas engines. Loggers said they "could smell 'em before they could see 'em." Most of the Skunk Trains today are pulled by diesel engines. The train travels through dense redwood forest, through deep mountain tunnels, and over many bridges and trestles on its run between Fort Bragg and Willits, where there is a stopover for lunch. Stops are also made along the way to deliver mail. A half-day trip is also available.

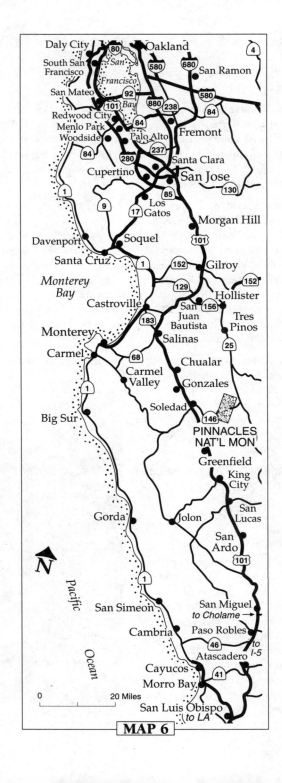

MAP 6

101 South

South San Francisco

(Area Code 415)

WHAT TO DO

Acres of Orchids *1450 El Camino Real/Hickey Blvd., 871-5655. Daily 9-6; tours at 10:30 & 1:30. Free.*

One of the largest orchid nurseries in the world, this family-owned business began small in the 1890s. Now it incorporates approximately 800,000 square feet of green houses. Reservations for the 45-minute tour are not necessary. Participants see a variety of orchids and learn how they are propagated and cared for. Plants are available for purchase, and assistance is given in choosing the best variety for any home environment.

San Mateo

(Area Code 415)

WHERE TO EAT

The Castaway *1631 Coyote Point Dr., 347-1027. L M-Sat, D daily, SunBr; $$. Highchairs, boosters, booths, child portions. Reservations advised. AE, MC, V.*

Tucked away in a picturesque spot abutting the bay, this attractive restaurant's entryway sports a lush, Polynesian flavor. Once inside, the atmosphere changes to a more local taste, with dramatic views of the water and the distant airport runway—with its attendant take-offs and landings—framed by mature eucalyptus and pine trees. An extensive Sunday brunch buffet offers eggs Benedict, quiche Lorraine, French toast, Belgian waffles, and made-to-order omelettes. In addition there is a cold seafood bar, a self-service ice cream station, and a carving station with roast beef, ham, and turkey. Complimentary champagne is included (kids get sparkling apple juice). Exotic bar drinks, such as mai tais and fruit daiquiris, are also available. Reduced brunch rates are available for diners seated between 9 and 10 a.m. Admission at the Coyote Point Park gate, through which diners must enter, is free when dining here.

Heidi Pies *1941 S. El Camino Real/20th Ave., 574-0505. B, L, & D daily; $. Highchairs, boosters, child menu. No reservations. AE, MC, V.*

The selection of freshly made pies is replenished constantly from this coffee shop's own kitchen. Pie choices include fruit (raisin and gooseberry in addition to more common varieties), meringue (black bottom, banana), and specialty (German chocolate, pecan, cream cheese). The house specialty is hot apple pie—plain, a la mode, with hot cinnamon sauce, with whipped cream, or with either Cheddar or American cheese. Short order items, including a hamburger and grilled cheese sandwich, comprise the rest of the menu. Weekdays between 2 and 4 p.m. coffee is only 55 cents when ordered with pie. Whole pies are available for take-out.

La Michoacana 251 S. B St., 348-9610. L & D daily; $. Highchairs, boosters. MC, V.

This tiny Mexican restaurant provides comfortable seating in its two-story dining area. All items are made fresh and are of exceptional taste, quality, and value, and a la carte and combination plates allow a satisfying meal whatever the stage of hunger. A small selection of Salvadorian dishes includes pupusas—handmade corn tortillas stuffed with delicious cheese and flavorful seasoned pork. Horchata, Mexican hot chocolate, and wine margaritas are among the drink choices, and flan is the single dessert.

Mei's Restaurant 71 East 3rd Ave., 347-2722, fax 347-8988.

For description, see King Yen on page 323. Both restaurants are under the same ownership, and the menu and decor are similar.

North Beach Pizza 240 E. 3rd Ave., 344-5000.

For description, see page 42.

The Pot Sticker 3708 S. El Camino Real/37th Ave., 349-0149. L & D daily; $$. Highchairs, boosters. Reservations advised. AE, MC, V.

The Chinese Mandarin-style cuisine served here is lightly spiced, has very little sauce, and is heavy on the vegetables. The menu has many expected items such as hot and sour soup, sizzling rice soup, Mongolian beef, and princess chicken, as well as more exotic items made with beef tripe and beef tendon, and, of course, pot stickers.

T.G.I. Friday's 3101 S. El Camino Real/Hillsdale Blvd., 570-4684. L & D daily, SunBr; $-$$. Highchairs, boosters, child menu. No reservations. AE, MC, V.

This comfortable fern bar produces tasty drinks from a massive bar dominating its center, and its vast menu offers everything from a French dip sandwich to a hamburger to a chimichanga to blackened filet mignon. The children's menu just might qualify as the world's most extensive. It doubles as a coloring book and offers everything kids love most and prepares it the way they like it—for example, the grilled cheese is made with American cheese and white bread. Furthering its family-friendly rep, kids are given a helium balloon as a parting gift.

WHAT TO DO

Coyote Point Recreation Area On Coyote Point Dr. Park: 573-2593. Daily sunrise to sunset. $4/vehicle. Museum: 342-7755. Tu-Sat 10-5, Sun 12-5. Adults $3, 62+ & 13-17 $2, 4-12 $1, free on 1st W of month.

This 670-acre park is equipped with a barbecue area, several playgrounds, inviting grassy areas, an 18-hole golf course, and a rifle range. It also has a swimming beach with bathhouse, and lifeguards are on duty in summer. As if all this isn't enough, it's also located on the descent route for the San Francisco International Airport, making it a wonderful place to just sit and watch planes landing.

Surrounded by an aromatic grove of eucalyptus trees, the architecturally impressive **Coyote Point Museum** was the first environmental museum in the U.S. It aims to educate visitors about local ecology and the environment. Live colonies of ants, termites, and bees can be viewed, and there are numerous hands-on and multi-media displays. An impressive outdoor

Wildlife Habitats area is adjacent with live native animals such as burrowing owls, a porcupine, and a banana slug. Exhibits include a walk-through aviary of native Bay Area birds and a colorful demonstration garden composed of plants that attract hummingbirds and butterflies. The new Nature's Marketplace shows how Native Americans used plants, shrubs, and trees in everyday life.

Redwood City
(Area Code 415)

WHERE TO STAY

Hotel Sofitel San Francisco Bay *223 Twin Dolphin Dr., (800) SOFITEL, 598-9000, fax 598-0459. 8 stories; 319 rooms; $$-$$$+. Pool, hot tub, sauna, health spa, fitness room, parcourse. 2 restaurants.*

Get a taste of France without leaving the Bay Area. This link in the sleek French hotel chain is situated among equally sleek hi-tech companies near the bay. Once inside the hotel, French touches include the charming accents of many employees, the provision of bath mitts instead of wash cloths, and the presentation of a freshly baked baguette from the hotel's bakery to take home at check-out. Pampering includes Nina Ricci bathroom amenities and evening turndown with a fresh rose and chocolate.

The **Sandra Caron Institut de Beaute** *(347-9666)*, which offers a full range of spa treatments, operates in an airy salon on the premises. Packages are sometimes available.

Elegant **Le Baccarat** serves classic French cuisine in posh surroundings. An a la carte menu with many expected French items is available, as is a five-course, fixed-price menu *($32)* that changes daily.

WHERE TO EAT

Pizza & Pipes *821 Winslow St./Broadway, 365-6543. L & D daily; $. Highchairs. Reservations accepted. AE, MC, V.*

When the huge Wurlitzer theater pipe organ here is being played *(Tu-Sun 6:30 pm-closing, Sat & Sun 12:30-4:30)*, all conversation is drowned out by lively renditions of songs such as "The Mickey Mouse Club Theme," "Chattanooga Choo Choo," and other all-time favorites. Kids love it. Some sing along, while others jump out of their seats to view through windows the movement of the pipes. This is definitely the place to go when children are cranky and ill-behaved. If they don't actually change their mood and have a good time, at least no one will hear them. Incidentally, the pizza is quite good.

Woodside
(Area Code 415)

GETTING THERE

Located on Highway 84 west, approximately 2 miles west of Highway 101.

WHAT TO DO

Filoli Estate *Canada Rd., 364-2880. Guided tours Tu-Thur by reservation; self-guided tours F & Sat; Feb-Nov. Adults $10, 2-12 $1, under 2 free.*

Under the protection of the National Trust for Historic Preservation, this 654-acre country kingdom features a 43-room modified Georgian mansion. Built in 1917 by architect Willis Polk, its ballroom is gilded with 200 pounds of gold extracted from the original owner's Empire Mine in Grass Valley. (The mansion is the setting for the 1978 film *Heaven Can Wait* and is seen as the exterior of the Carrington home shown at the beginning of TV's *Dynasty*.) Tours of the 17 landscaped acres of mature formal gardens include such delights as two herbal gardens, a garden designed to resemble a stained-glass window at Chartres cathedral in France, and a practical cutting garden. For information on the many special events held here, call 366-4640.

Menlo Park

(Area Code 415)

WHERE TO STAY

Stanford Park Hotel *100 El Camino, (800) 368-2468, 322-1234, fax 322-0975. 4 stories; 162 rooms. 28 fireplaces. Pool, hot tub, sauna, fitness room. Afternoon snack; restaurant, room service.*

Located just north of town, this hotel offers spacious rooms furnished with custom-made English yew wood furniture. Rooms also have an innovative computer-operated video system that allows guests to watch any of approximately 60 movies starting at any time around the clock.

WHERE TO EAT

Allied Arts Guild Restaurant *75 Arbor Rd., 324-2588. L M-Sat at 12, 12:30, 1, & 1:15; afternoon dessert & beverage M-F 1-2:30; $. Highchairs, boosters. 100% non-smoking. Reservations essential. No cards.*

Originally a tearoom, this restaurant was opened by the Palo Alto auxiliary of Children's Hospital at Stanford in 1932. In those days guild members prepared food in their homes and transported it to the premises for serving. Now a modern kitchen aids volunteers in preparing three-course luncheons that include a soup, hot entree with vegetable or salad, freshly-baked rolls, dessert, and choice of beverage. The menu is different each day, and all the recipes are for sale. In warm weather an attractive patio is opened for dining; request it when reserving. All profits and tips are used to help support Children's Hospital. Allow time to wander through the attractive Spanish colonial-style estate. Shops invite browsing, and the peaceful 3.5-acre gardens—designed after the Alhambra Gardens in Granada, Spain—invite a leisurely stroll.

Late for the Train *150 Middlefield Rd./Willow Rd., 321-6124. B & L M-F, D Tu-Sat, Sat & SunBr; $$. Highchairs, boosters. 100% non-smoking. Reservations advised. AE, MC, V.*

This formula-free restaurant has several different dining areas, including an outdoor patio that is particularly pleasant in warm weather, and an interesting collection of old-time sugar bowls and salt-and-pepper shakers decorate the tables. Meals are made to order with organic, additive-free ingredients whenever possible, and very little red meat is used. Brunch items include delicious eggs piperade (a two-egg omelette served with a fantastic scone and sides of both delicious fried potatoes and a mixture of lightly sautéed bell peppers, onions, and tomatoes), blintzes, whole grain pancakes, and an assortment of sandwiches, salads, and hot entrees. Lunch and dinner menus feature seafood, chicken, pasta, and vegetarian entrees.

WHAT TO DO

Sunset Magazine Garden *Willow Rd./Middlefield Rd., 321-3600. M-F 9-4:30. Free.*

Visitors are welcome to wander on their own through 7 acres of landscaped gardens surrounding an impressive 1.3-acre lawn.

Palo Alto
(Area Code 415)

WHERE TO STAY

Garden Court Hotel *520 Cowper St./University Ave., (800) 824-9028, 322-9000, fax 324-3609. 4 stories; 62 rooms; 35 non-smoking rooms; $$$+. Children under 12 free. All VCRs; 5 wood-burning fireplaces. Fitness room. Restaurant, room service (child items).*

Located just off the main street, this attractive hotel offers posh comfort. A central court-yard with fountains and flowers conveys a far-away-from-it-all feeling almost in the center of town.

On the ground floor directly beneath the hotel, **Il Fornaio Restaurant** *(853-3888. Reservations advised.)* serves up rustic pizzas in an elegant interior space and out on a sunny, peaceful courtyard.

Hidden Villa Ranch Hostel *26870 Moody Rd., Los Altos Hills, 949-8648, fax 948-4159. 35 beds; couple & family rooms. Closed June-Aug.*

Located on a 1,600-acre ranch in the foothills east of town, this facility was built in 1937 as the first hostel on the Pacific Coast. Guests sleep in rustic cabins. The property includes a work-ing farm, organic garden, and land preserve. See also page 391.

Holiday Inn *625 El Camino Real/University Ave., (800) 874-3516, (800) HOLIDAY, 328-2800, fax 327-7362. 4 stories; 343 rooms; 290 non-smoking rooms; $$-$$$+. Children under 18 free. 10 kitchens. Heated pool, fit-ness room. Restaurant, room service (child items). Pets welcome.*

Centrally located and offering the amenities typical of the chain, this comfortable lodging has an attractively landscaped garden area with a large koi pond.

WHERE TO EAT

Chef Chu's *1067 N. San Antonio Rd./El Camino Real, Los Altos, 948-2696. L & D daily; $$. Highchairs, boost-ers, booths. Reservations advised. AE, MC, V.*

Chef Chu watches closely over his large kitchen staff and sees to it that excellence prevails in this well-appointed restaurant. Impressive dishes include crisp fried won tons, tasty Szechwan beef, and a magnificent, sesame oil-fragrant hot and sour soup. Mu shu pork is served with unusual square pancakes for wrapping, and the beautifully presented lemon chicken consists of deep-fried whole chicken breasts, each glazed with lemon sauce and topped with a thin slice of lemon and a bright red maraschino cherry. Should there be a wait for seating, the reception area's large window provides interesting views of the busy kitchen.

Good Earth Restaurant *185 University Ave./Emerson St., 321-9449. B, L, & D daily; $-$$. Highchairs, boosters, booths, child menu. No reservations. AE, MC, V.*

An impressive selection of food that is both tasty and nutritious is on the menu in this comfortable spot. Breakfast items include hot cakes with molasses-honey syrup and a variety of muffins. Omelettes, served with ten-grain toast, are available all day. Salads, creative sandwiches (don't miss the popular and delicious cashew-chicken), several veggie burgers and pizzas, and an assortment of hot entrees and pastas flesh out the menu. Enticingly named fruit shakes and smoothies, made with non-fat yogurt and high protein powder, are also available.

Gordon Biersch Brewing Company *640 Emerson St., 323-7723.*

For description, see page 166.

Just Desserts *535 Bryant St./University Ave., 326-9992.*
For description, see page 38.

MacArthur Park *27 University Ave./near El Camino Real, 321-9990. L M-F, D daily, SunBr; $$-$$$. Reservations advised. AE, MC, V. Free valet parking.*
Situated just off the beaten path, this popular restaurant operates within a designated Historical Landmark. Designed for the U.S. War Department in 1918 by Julia Morgan, the architect of Hearst Castle, the building is now divided into several dining areas, including two indoor balconies and a grand barn-like room on the main floor. The kitchen is celebrated for its baby back ribs cooked in an oak wood smoker, dry-aged steaks, and California game. Dessert selections are made from a menu decorated with a mouth-watering color reproduction of Wayne Thiebaud's "Two Meringues." The original MacArthur Park is in San Francisco (see page 40).

Ming's *1700 Embarcadero Rd., (800) 355-6001, 856-7700, fax 855-9479. L & D daily; $-$$. Highchairs, boosters, booths, child menu. 100% non-smoking. Reservations advised. AE, MC, V.*
Located just off Highway 101, this sedate restaurant has existed in Palo Alto since the 1950s, when it opened on El Camino Real. Ming's beef—a somewhat sweet dish prepared with tender wok-charred beef, and a generic dish on many Chinese menus—was this restaurant's invention, as was its delicately flavored chicken salad. Made with shredded, deep-fried chicken, the salad is labor-intensive to make and in such heavy demand that one chef is employed to prepare just that. Another chef prepares fresh dim sum delicacies every morning; they are available from 11 a.m. to 5 p.m. Among them are steamed shark's fin dumplings, delicious fresh shrimp items, and an electric-bright mango pudding in strawberry sauce. Other noteworthy dishes include dramatic drunken prawns flambé and steamed fresh garlic lobster. A full vegetarian menu is also available.

Peninsula Fountain & Grille *566 Emerson Ave./Hamilton, 323-3131. B, L, & D daily; $. Highchairs, boosters, booths. No reservations. MC, V.*
Opened by the Peninsula Dairy in 1923, this popular spot was refurbished not too long ago and now, with red leatherette booths and an authentic soda fountain, looks even more old-fashioned than before. It is known for serving tasty simple food—oatmeal and buttermilk pancakes in the morning, a variety of sandwiches and hamburgers at lunch, and chicken pot pies and pork chops at dinner—at reasonable prices. Fountain items are made with ice cream from the nearby Peninsula Creamery.

Stars Palo Alto *265 Lytton Ave./Ramona, 321-4466. L & D daily; $$$. Reservations advised. AE, MC, V.*
Operating within a lovely Mission-style stucco building, this is a branch of the San Francisco restaurant. For description, see page 46.

WHAT TO DO

Barbie Hall of Fame *433 Waverley St./University Ave., 326-5841. Tu-Sat 1:30-4:30, also 10-12 on Sat. Adults $6, under 12 $4.*
Opened in 1984 on Barbie's 25th birthday, this unusual museum is packed with over 16,000 dolls and accessories. It is the largest Barbie collection open to the public and is 100 percent complete. Among its gems are the very first Barbie, all the Barbie wedding and ballerina dresses, and the female Barbie astronauts from 1965 and 1986.

Birthplace of Silicon Valley *367 Addison Ave./Waverley St.*

The product and the company that launched the high tech industry was developed in this garage by William Hewlett and David Packard. A monument beside the driveway tells the story.

The Elizabeth F. Gamble Garden Center *1431 Waverley St./Embarcadero, 329-1356, fax 329-1688. House: M-F 9-noon. Free. Garden: Daily dawn to dusk. Free.*

This Georgian revival house was once the home of Elizabeth F. Gamble, heiress to the Procter & Gamble fortune. Today it and the beautifully manicured classic Edwardian gardens— where an assortment of soothing fountains and scattered benches invite quiet reflection—are maintained by volunteers.

Palo Alto Duck Pond *At east end of Embarcadero Rd. Daily sunrise-sunset. Free.*

Located in a quiet, unpopulated area away from town, this is one of the Bay Area's best spots to feed ducks and birds. Usually it attracts a hefty number of hungry ducks and seagulls, sometimes even a few swans. In winter, plenty of unusual migrating birds are mixed in. A nearby small airport provides plane-watching fun.

Nearby, the **Lucy Evans Baylands Nature Interpretive Center** *(329-2506. Tu-Fr 2-5, Sat & Sun 1-5. Free.)* has exhibits that orient visitors to the area. Workshops, films, and slide shows are scheduled regularly. During daylight hours, visitors can walk out over the 120-acre salt marsh on an 800-foot-long raised wooden walkway. Naturalist-led walks are scheduled on weekends.

Palo Alto Junior Museum & Zoo *1451 Middlefield Rd./Embarcadero, 329-2111. Tu-Sat 10-5, Sun 1-4. Free.*

Opened in 1934, this was the first junior museum on the West Coast. Exhibits are of the hands-on variety and especially fun for young children. Special programs, movies, and workshops are scheduled regularly. An outdoor mini-zoo houses local animals such as raccoons, pelicans, ravens, and crows.

Stanford Shopping Center *On El Camino Real, just north of Stanford campus.*

This is the only shopping center in the world owned by a university. Among its 150 fashionable shops are a branch of the Wine Country's **Oakville Grocery** filled with esoteric foods; **Gleim Jewelers**, where the world's largest emerald is sometimes on display; a branch of Berkeley's **Monterey Market**; an open-air **Polo/Ralph Lauren Home Collection** shop; **Tribal Eye**, which offers African antiquities and handicrafts (the only branch is in Nairobi, Kenya); and **Bow Wow Meow**, a pet specialty store with catnip-filled cloth mice worth going out of the way for. **The Health Library**, operated by Stanford University Hospital as a community service, provides a library of medical information with helpful volunteer reference librarians. A variety of restaurants attract diners at all hours: a branch of **Max's Opera Cafe** (see page 40), a branch of **Piatti** (see page 266), and the unique **Bok Choy**.

The Stanford Theater *221 University Ave., 324-3700.*

This 1,200-seat movie palace has been meticulously restored to its 1925-era grandeur by former classics professor David Packard, Jr., son of the computer tycoon. Plush red mohair seats, elaborate ceiling paintings, and magnificent tile work in the lobby help take audiences back in time as they view pre-1950 Hollywood films. Silent films are often accompanied by an organist on the theater's Wurlitzer. Proceeds are used for film restoration.

Stanford University Campus *Facilities sometimes closed during academic breaks; call to confirm.*

Founded by Leland Stanford in 1885 on what had been his family's horse farm, California's premier private university is dedicated to the memory of Stanford's son, who died of typhoid fever at the age of 15. The **Quadrangle,** which is the oldest part of the campus, features buildings of Mission-style architecture. Hour-long **campus tours** *(723-2560. Daily at 11 & 3:15. Free.)* leave from the Visitor Information Booth at Memorial Auditorium. Tours of the two-mile-long **linear accelerator** are available by appointment *(926-2204).* East of the Quad, **Hoover Tower** *(723-2053. Daily 10-4:30. Adults $1, 65+ & under 13 50¢.),* Stanford's shorter version of the University of California's campanile, stands 285 feet tall—affording a panoramic view of the area from its observation platform, which is reached by an elevator. At the tower's base, a museum that is part of the **Hoover Institution on War, Revolution, and Peace** honors Stanford graduate and former president Herbert Hoover. Nearby, the **Thomas Welton Art Gallery** is home to revolving exhibitions of international and regional artists' works.

Built in 1892, the **Stanford University Museum of Art** *(723-4177. By donation.)* is the oldest museum west of the Mississippi and the first building to be built of structurally reinforced concrete. Having suffered severe damage in the 1989 earthquake, it is currently closed but scheduled to re-open in 1998. When open, the museum offers a collection of extraordinary jades, Asian and Egyptian treasures, Stanford family memorabilia, and California Native American exhibits (a noteworthy object in this latter collection is a canoe carved by Yurok Indians from a single redwood log). Its eclectic collection also holds the gold spike that marked the meeting of the two sections of the Transcontinental Railroad in 1869. The adjacent one-acre **Rodin Sculpture Garden** *(723-3469. Daily dawn-dusk; tours W, Sat, & Sun at 2.)* remains accessible. Together the museum and garden hold the world's second-largest collection of Rodin sculpture (the largest is in Paris).

The Winter Lodge *3009 Middlefield Rd./Oregon Expressway, 493-4566, fax 493-3294. Daily 3-5, call for other session times; Sept-Apr only. Admission $5, under 4 $1, skate rental $1.*

An outdoor ice skating rink in Palo Alto? Well, it's *not* on a frozen lake. Indeed, it's located in a nicely manicured residential section of town. But it *is* removed from traffic and surrounded by tall eucalyptus trees, and it's the *only* outdoor rink west of the Sierra. Designed for families and children, the rink measures about two-thirds the size of an average indoor rink, making it too small for competitive skating.

San Jose
(Area Code 408)

A LITTLE BACKGROUND

Currently touting itself as the "capital of Silicon Valley" (a title that seems valid considering that 24 of the area's largest computer companies have headquarters or divisions here), San Jose—the country's eleventh-largest city and California's third-largest and oldest, having been founded as a Spanish pueblo in 1777 (it also was the state capital from 1849 to 1851)—receives relatively little attention for its attractions. But that seems to be changing as the city concentrates on revitalizing its downtown area. Now visitors to the city center can enjoy its many cultural offerings as well as its reliably mild climate.

VISITOR INFORMATION

San Jose Convention & Visitors Bureau *333 W. San Carlos St. #1000, San Jose 95110-2720, (800) SAN-JOSE, 295-9600, fax 295-3937.*

GETTING THERE

Located approximately 50 miles south of San Francisco. Take Highway 101 all the way.

WHERE TO STAY

Embassy Suites Hotel *2885 Lakeside Dr., Santa Clara, (800) EMBASSY, 496-6400.*

For description, see page 346.

Fairmont Hotel *170 S. Market St., (800) 527-4727, 998-1900, fax 287-1648. 20 stories; 541 rooms; 180 non-smoking rooms; $$-$$$+. Children under 18 free. Some fireplaces. Heated pool (unavail. Nov-Apr), sauna, fitness room. 2 restaurants, room service.*

Built on the site of what was California's capitol building from 1849 to 1851, this luxury high-rise hotel is located within convenient walking distance of all the downtown attractions.

The Fountain Room, an old-fashioned soda fountain snazzed up with white tablecloths and floral china, offers elegant treats for kids of all ages.

Hotel De Anza *233 W. Santa Clara St., (800) 843-3700, 286-1000, fax 286-0500. 10 stories; 101 rooms; 85 non-smoking rooms. All VCRs. Fitness room. Evening snack; restaurant, room service. Parking $8.*

Referred to as the "Grand Lady of San Jose," this 1931 hotel is new again. Refurbished to its art deco grandeur, it exudes a cozy feeling, with attractively appointed, spacious rooms and well-designed tile bathrooms equipped with a phone and TV. Amenities include evening turn-down, complimentary shoe shine, terry cloth robes, and a "Raid the Pantry" nighttime snack buffet that permits bathrobe-clad guests to perch on the kitchen counter while gobbling up goodies such as chocolate chip cookies and salami cracker sandwiches. For a small additional fee, an extensive breakfast buffet can be enjoyed in a charming room, cleverly painted bright yellow to bring a cheery atmosphere into a windowless room.

Hotel Sainte Claire *302 S. Market St., (800) 824-6835, 295-2000, fax 977-0403. 6 stories; 170 rooms; $$-$$$+. Fitness room. Restaurant, room service. Parking $10.*

A national historic landmark dating from 1926, this meticulously restored downtown hotel was designed in a Spanish revival renaissance style by the same architects who did the Mark Hopkins in San Francisco. It boasts beautiful original hand-painted ceiling panels and an elegant public sitting lounge. Amenities in the attractively, sometimes whimsically decorated rooms, include featherbeds and cotton kimonos. In good weather, breakfast can be taken in an inner garden courtyard featuring vibrantly colored, hand-painted Spanish ceramic tiles.

A branch of the celebrated Tuscan-style **Il Fornaio** serves as the hotel restaurant.

The Pruneyard Inn *1995 S. Bascom Ave., Campbell, (800) 559-4344, 559-4300, fax 559-9919. 3 stories; 116 rooms; 58 non-smoking rooms; $$-$$$+. Children under 13 free. Some VCRs & fireplaces. Heated pool, hot tub, fitness room, parcourse. Full breakfast.*

One of only three hotels in the western U.S. that is located in a shopping center, this taste-fully decorated hotel is adjacent to the attractive **Pruneyard** shopping complex. In spite of the location, it manages to provide a secluded feeling. Turndown service is included.

Red Lion San Jose *2050 Gateway Pl., (800) RED-LION, 453-4000, fax 437-2898. 10 stories; 505 rooms; $$-$$$+. Children under 19 free. Heated pool, hot tub, sauna, fitness room. 2 restaurants.*

Popular with conventions, this comfortable hotel is well-appointed for the vacationer, too. A sumptuous Sunday brunch buffet is served in **Maxi's**.

WHERE TO EAT

Emiles *545 S. Second St., 289-1960, fax 998-1245. L on F, D Tu-Sat; $$$. Child portions. Reservations advised. AE, MC, V. Free valet parking.*

Owner-chef Emile Mooser grew up in the French part of Switzerland. He was trained in the wine country of Lausanne, above Lake Geneva, and now he produces a California-moderated synthesis of all that experience. In his long-lived, elegantly appointed downtown restaurant, the menu changes with the season. Sample appetizers include a vegetable ragoût with truffle oil, baked burgundy snails, and French onion soup. Entrees include several styles of fresh fish, rack of lamb, and a seasonal game—perhaps a tender, mild moose or wild boar flavored with a classic game sauce. Prompted by the chef's own need to cut butter from his diet, lighter dishes that avoid fats—cuisine minceur—are always available. Desserts are seductive, and the signature soufflé for two, flavored perhaps with cappuccino or Grand Marnier, is definitely to die for, excuse the expression. Adding to the overall tone of the experience, service is excellent, and chef Emile finds time to personally visit each table and chat amiably with diners.

Gordon Biersch Brewery Restaurant *33 E. San Fernando St., 294-6785. L & D daily; $-$$. Highchairs, boosters. Reservations advised. AE, MC, V.*

Located downtown, this upscale restaurant offers pleasant patio dining as well as seating in a spacious, airy dining room overlooking stainless steel brew tanks. The eclectic menu changes regularly and features salads, sandwiches, and individual pizzas as well as more serious entrees and desserts. In addition to three styles of house-made beer, the menu offers a selection of varietal wines and coffees, and the house bread is often a wonderful sourdough pumpernickel. Live jazz is sometimes scheduled outdoors on Sunday afternoons, and a variety of music is scheduled on Wednesday through Sunday evenings.

The Old Spaghetti Factory *51 N. San Pedro St., 288-7488. L M-F, D daily; $. Highchairs, boosters, child portions. MC, V.*

Oodles of noodle selections await spaghetti connoisseurs here. There is spaghetti with regular marinara sauce, with mushroom sauce, with white clam sauce, and with meat sauce. For those who can't make up their minds, there is spaghetti with a sampler of sauces. Meatballs, spinach tortellini, and baked chicken are also available. Complete dinners come with bread, salad, drink (coffee, tea, or milk), and spumoni ice cream. The restaurant is housed in what was once the warehouse for the *San Jose Mercury News* and features a variety of interesting spots to be seated: an antique barber's chair in the bar, within a restored streetcar, on a brass bed converted into a booth.

Pasand *3701 El Camino Real/Lawrence Expressway, Santa Clara, 241-5150. L & D daily.*

For description, see page 324.

Pizza & Pipes *3581 Homestead Rd./Lawrence Expressway, Santa Clara, 248-5680; L & D daily.*

For description, see page 159.

WHAT TO DO

Children's Discovery Museum *180 Woz Way, 298-5437, fax 298-6826. Tu-Sat 10-5, Sun 12-5. Adults $6, 55+ $5, 2-18 $4. Parking $2-$4.*

Children ages 3 through 13, for whom this museum was designed, are sure to be entertained. Located in **Guadalupe River Park,** the striking lavender-colored building housing what is the largest children's museum in the West was designed by Mexico City architect Ricardo Legorreta. Fortunately he included plenty of places for adults to sit and watch while their kids have a great time—doing everything from making a tortilla from scratch, to blowing gigantic bubbles, to climbing on a full-size fire engine. A snack bar serves inexpensive things that kids like to eat: hot dogs, hamburgers, peanut butter & jelly sandwiches. Steve Wozniak, of Apple Computer fame, sponsored the Jesse's Clubhouse exhibit named in honor of his son. Guess who the street the museum is located on, Woz Way, is named for?

The Gaslighter Theater *400 E. Campbell Ave., Campbell, 866-1408. F & Sat at 8. Adults $13.75, under 12 $10.*

A staff member says that this cozy theater is located "in lovely downtown Campbell—Santa Clara County's fastest growing ghost town." And, indeed, at night this seems to be the only show in town. After being greeted in the street and at the door by the exuberant cast, the whole family has fun inside hissing the villain and cheering the hero—while munching on, and throwing, complimentary popcorn. The two-part shows are not at all subtle, making them great for school-age children. Shows include both a melodrama (such as *Ignorance Isn't Bliss* or *No Mother to Guide Her*) and a vaudeville performance featuring dancing, singing, and comedy.

Kelley Park. *Parking $3.*
• **Happy Hollow Park and Zoo** *300 Senter Rd./Keyes Rd., 295-8383, fax 277-4470. Daily 10-5, Sun 11-6. Admission $4, 65+ $3.50, under 2 free; rental strollers $1.50.*

Children through age 10 love this mini-amusement park—the only combination park and zoo in the U.S. Spacious and shady, it offers a satisfying combination of kiddie rides and zoo animals. Several rides and use of a concrete maze and playground equipment are included with admission. Puppet shows are scheduled daily, and picnic tables are available. Zoo animals include Shetland ponies and a pygmy hippo, and there is a small seal pool and bird enclosure. For small change, children can hand-feed animals in a petting area. Note that mothers get in free here on Mother's Day, and fathers on Father's Day.
• **Kelley Park Express Train** *Irregular schedule. Round-trip $1.50.*

Boarded just outside the zoo, this choo-choo train makes stops at the following two park sites.
• **Japanese Friendship Garden** *277-4192. Daily 10-dusk. Free.*

Patterned after the Korakuen Garden in San Jose's sister city of Okayama, this 6½-acre garden includes four heart-shaped ponds populated with rare koi. Walk on the Moon Bridge for good luck; cross the Zigzag Bridge to get rid of evil spirits.
• **San Jose Historical Museum** *1600 Senter Rd., 287-2290. M-F 10-4:30, Sat & Sun 12-4:30. Adults $4, 65+ $3, 6-17 $2.*

This 25-acre, ever-growing complex contains over 25 relocated and reconstructed historic homes and business buildings. It depicts San Jose as it was in the 1890s. Begin a visit at the Pacific Hotel, where docent-led tours commence. Refreshments are available in **O'Brien's Ice Cream and Candy Store**—the first place to serve ice cream and sodas west of Detroit.

Lick Observatory *On Mount Hamilton Rd., approx. 23 mi. east of downtown, 274-5061. Daily 10-5; tours 1-4, on half-hour. Free.*

Situated 19 miles up a narrow, winding (347 curves), two-lane road at the top of 4,209-foot-high Mount Hamilton, this observatory—a division of U. C. Santa Cruz—overlooks San Jose and the Santa Clara Valley. Guided tours include seeing, but not looking through, the world's second-largest refractor telescope (120 inches), which has been in use for more than a century. Allow 90 minutes to reach the observatory and 2 hours to tour it. No food or gas is available in the area.

Mission Santa Clara de Asis *500 El Camino Real, on Santa Clara U. campus, Santa Clara, 554-4023, fax 554-4373. Daily 8-6. Free.*

Rebuilt in 1928, this is a replica of the eighth mission in the chain of California missions, which was founded in 1777 and destroyed by fire. (The original mission was built on a site beside the Guadalupe River.) Among the relics are three bells that were a gift from the king of Spain. Extensive gardens include thousands of roses—several of which are classified as antiques—and many varieties of trees and plants, including olive trees planted by Franciscan friars in 1822 and a giant 123-year-old Jacaranda tree; full bloom occurs April through May .

Municipal Rose Garden *On Naglee Ave., between Dana Ave. & Garden Dr., 287-0698. Daily 8-dusk. Free.*

Located two blocks from the Egyptian Museum, this garden boasts 5,000 plants and 186 varieties of roses. Surrounded by green lawns and tree-shaded picnic tables, the blooms are at their showy peak in May and June.

Paramount's Great America *On Great America Parkway, off Hwys. 101 & 237, Santa Clara, 988-1776. Call for schedule. Closed Nov- Feb. Age 7-54 $28.95, 55+ $19.95, 3-6 $15.95. Parking $5.*

There's no question about it. The thrill rides at Northern California's most elaborate theme park are spectacular, and the roller coasters are great shocking fun: the Vortex is the only stand-up roller coaster west of the Mississippi; the Demon features two 360-degree loops and a double helix; the Grizzly is based on the extinct Coney Island Wildcat and is the largest wooden

roller coaster in Northern California; and Top Gun takes suspended riders through some heart-stopping maneuvers. Then there are the Yankee Clipper and Logger's Run flume rides; the circa 1976 double-decker Carousel Columbia—the world's tallest and most expensive-to-build carousel, with modern fiberglass animals; the antique Ameri-Go-Round carousel with wooden animals—built by the Toboggan Company of Philadelphia in 1918 and originally housed at the Cincinnati Zoo; the Triple Wheel—the world's first triple-arm Ferris wheel; and the Drop Zone Stunt Tower—the tallest free-fall ride in the world. Smurf Woods and Fort Fun feature special rides and activities for children under 12. The world's largest indoor movie screen and three live shows round out the fun. Have a baby? Complimentary diapers and a mother's nursing station are available at the Pampers Baby Care Center in Fort Fun.

Raging Waters *2333 S. White Rd., (Capitol Expressway/Tully Rd.), 654-5450. Daily 10-6, June-Aug. Closed Sept-May. Admission $18.95, under 43" $14.95, after 3pm $12.95, 60+ $9.95. Parking $3.*

Located in **Lake Cunningham Regional Park**, this water-oriented amusement park claims to have the fastest waterslides this side of the Rockies. Sliders can reach speeds up to 25 miles per hour and can be dropped six stories into a catchpool below. In addition to the waterslides, there is an inner tube ride, a sled ride, a rope swing, and a myriad of other water activities. Among the amenities are 40 lifeguards, free changing rooms and showers, and inexpensive lockers. Where else can a family find such good, clean fun? Note that foods and beverages may not be brought into the park. Food service is available, and a public picnic area is provided just outside the main gate.

Rosicrucian Egyptian Museum *1342 Naglee Ave., 947-3636. Daily 9-5. Adults $6.75, 65+ $5, 7-15 $3.50. Strollers not permitted. Planetarium: Shows daily at 1 & 3. Adults $4, 65+ $3.50, 7-15 $3, under 7 free.*

This museum houses the largest exhibit of Egyptian, Babylonian, and Assyrian artifacts on the West Coast. Highlights of the collection include mummies, fine jewelry, and a full-size reproduction of a 4,000-year-old rock tomb—the only such tomb in the United States. Among the six human mummies is one that was recently found to have a nine-inch metal pin in his knee. This exciting discovery documents the first known attempt at knee surgery. Also in the collection are the mummies of several cats, some fish, a baboon, and the head of an ox. The surrounding 7.5-acre park is stunningly adorned with exotic trees and flowers and unusual Egyptian statuary. Picnicking is permitted. The **Rosicrucian Planetarium** is adjacent.

San Jose Flea Market *1590 Berryessa Rd., between Hwys. 680 & 101, 453-1110, fax 437-9011. W-Sun dawn-dusk. Free. Parking $1-$3.*

Said to be the largest in the world, this flea market features over 2000 vendors spread out over 120 acres. In addition, there are more than 35 snack stands and a ¼-mile-long produce section. A variety of free entertainment is also provided.

San Jose Museum of Art *110 S. Market St., 294-2787, fax 294-2977. Tu-Sun 10-5, Thur to 8. Adults $6, 6-17 $3; free 1st Thur of month. Strollers avail. for loan.*

Holding a collection of primarily contemporary American art, this unusual part-1892 Romanesque sandstone/part-1991 stark modern building is said to serve as a metaphor for contemporary art's ties to tradition.

The Tech Museum of Innovation *145 W. San Carlos St., 279-7150, fax 279-7167. Tu-Sat 10-5, Sun 12-5; daily in summer. Adults $6, 65+ & 6-18 $4.*

Formerly called "The Garage," this small interim museum was originally named in whimsical reference to the garages in which many Silicon Valley inventions had their humble beginnings—the most famous being the personal computer developed by Steve Jobs and Stephen Wozniak in their garage. The nickname was dropped in favor of something more befitting the major science and technology museum it will become when its new home is completed in late 1998. A whimsical audio-kinetic sculpture by George Rhoads is located just outside the entrance. Called "The Imaginative Chip," it is a Rube Goldberg-style object made with billiard balls moving through a maze of familiar objects and is meant to represent the movement of information in an integrated circuit chip. Inside, the museum focuses on current projects at local technology companies. Exhibits allow visitors to see how silicon chips are produced, to design a bike, and to meet Vanna the spelling robot. A guided tour is highly recommended. They are scheduled regularly and can also be requested on the spot. Volunteer "Explainers" are also on hand to answer questions, and video and newspaper clippings provide enlightening background information. Visitors can relax in the Info Lounge, where computers are hooked up to electronic information lines. A snack bar is also available.

Winchester Mystery House
525 S. Winchester Blvd., 247-2101. Tours daily 9:30-4, to 5:30 in summer. Adults $12.95, 65+ $9.50, 6-12 $6.50. Strollers not permitted.

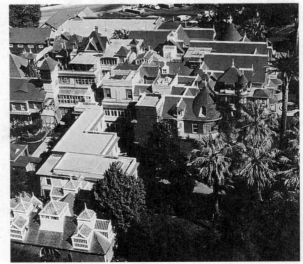

The story goes that Sarah Winchester, heir to the $20 million Winchester rifle fortune, believed that to make amends for a past wrong-doing she had to build additions to her circa 1884 Victorian mansion continuously, 24-hours-a-day. Her eccentric ideas resulted in some unusual features: asymmetrical rooms, narrow passageways, zigzag stairwells, and doors opening into empty shafts. The tour of this city landmark takes in 110 of the 160 rooms, climbs more than 200 steps, and covers almost a mile. The **Winchester Historical Firearms Museum**, which holds one of the largest collections of Winchester rifles on the West Coast, provides an interesting way to pass time while waiting for the tour to begin. Food service is available, and picnic tables are provided in a courtyard. A self-guided tour of the six acres of Victorian gardens, which are sprinkled liberally with fountains and statues, is included with admission. Spooky flashlight **Halloween Tours** are scheduled annually in October.

Wineries.

• **J. Lohr Winery** *1000 Lenzen Ave., 288-5057, fax 993-2276. Tasting 10-5 daily; tours Sat & Sun at 11 & 2.*

Operating on the site of a former beer brewery, this premium winery is tucked into a residential part of the city near Highway 880. All wine is made on the premises, but the grapes are grown on Lohr-owned vineyards scattered from Paso Robles to St. Helena.

• **Mirassou Winery** *3000 Aborn Rd., (E. Capitol Expressway exit off Hwy. 101), 274-4000, fax 270-5881. Tasting M-Sat 12-5, Sun 12-4; tours M-Sat at 1 & 3, Sun at 2.*

More of this area's Wine Country can be sampled by taking a freeway ride into the suburbs, where rows of grapevines announce this winery's entrance. At this location since 1937, it is now operated by the fifth generation of the same family, making Mirassou the country's oldest winemaking family (since 1854). A broad selection of premium wines can be sampled in a spacious tasting room. Special events are scheduled regularly and include cooking classes as well as Sunday brunches and sunset dinners featuring refined, elegant menus.

• **Ridge Vineyards** *17100 Monte Bello Rd., Cupertino, 867-3233, fax 867-2986. Tasting Sat & Sun 11-3; no tours.*

Started by three Stanford Research Institute engineers in 1959, this destination winery is positioned high on a limestone ridge way back in the Santa Cruz Mountains and is reached via a beautiful, curvy back roads route. On warm days tasting occurs outdoors and, with reservations, picnics can be enjoyed at vineyard-side tables with a magnificent view of the bay below. On cooler days tasting occurs inside a 100-year-old barn. Ridge has been called "the Chateau Latour of California," and the wines *are* good. So good, in fact, that a Zinfandel brought to Paris as a gift to a native was personally witnessed being sniffed by that native, who expressed surprise and then swallowed with absolute delight.

San Juan Bautista

(Area Code 408)

A LITTLE BACKGROUND

Once the largest city in central California, this town is now a sleepy remnant of that time. It's hard to believe that at one time seven stage lines operated out of the town and that there were numerous busy hotels and saloons. Now the town holds just a few Mexican restaurants, boutiques, and antique shops.

VISITOR INFORMATION

San Juan Bautista Chamber of Commerce *P.O. Box 1037 (402-A Third St.), San Juan Bautista 95045, 623-2454, fax 623-0674.*

GETTING THERE

Located approximately 45 miles south of San Jose. Take Highway 101 south, then Highway 156 east.

ANNUAL EVENTS

Early Days at San Juan Bautista *June. 623-4881. Adults $2, 6-12 $1.*

Visitors see re-enactments of 19th-century townspeople performing everyday tasks, such as tortilla-making and baking bread in a hornito oven, and the restored **Plaza Hotel**'s famous bar is opened for business.

La Virgen del Tepeyac *December. 623-2444.*

This early California folk opera is presented in the mission by El Teatro Campesino, a local acting company. Also scheduled are a candlelight tour of the mission and **La Posada**—a procession through the city streets in which Mary and Joseph are portrayed seeking shelter.

WHAT TO DO

Fremont Peak State Park *At end of San Juan Canyon Rd., 11 mi. from town, 623-4255, fax 623-4612; observatory 623-2465. Daily 8-sunset. $3/vehicle.*

A popular destination for picnickers and hikers, this park's summit is an easy 15-minute climb from the parking area. An observatory with a 30-inch reflecting telescope is open to the public twice each month; call for schedule. Campsites are available.

San Juan Bautista State Historic Park *19 Franklin St., 623-4881, fax 623-4612. Daily 10-4:30. Adults $2, 6-12 $1.*

This park's assortment of restored buildings allows visitors to see what life was like in this area in the early 1800s. The **Castro Adobe** sits on the plaza in a picturesque area perfect for picnicking.

Mission San Juan Bautista *(402 S. Second St., 623-4528. Daily 9:30-5. By donation.)* was founded in 1797 and is 15th in the chain of 21 California missions. Owned by the Catholic Church, it has the largest church of all the missions, and Thomas Doak, the first American settler in California, painted its bright red and blue reredos and altar. If everything looks familiar, it could be because this park was a major location in the Hitchcock movie *Vertigo*.

WHERE TO EAT

Jardines de San Juan *115 Third St., 623-4466. L & D daily; $. Highchairs, boosters. MC, V.*

What a wonderful fair-weather experience it is to sit outside under a sheltering umbrella on the brick courtyard here. Among the profusely flowering gardens, diners peruse the menu while sipping icy-cold margaritas and dipping tortilla chips in tasty salsa. Flautas consist of shredded beef rolled in a deep-fried tortilla and topped with guacamole. Tacos and enchiladas are also available. On weekends after 5 p.m. regional specialties join the menu. Red snapper Veracruz is available on Fridays, carne asada on Saturdays, and drunken chicken on Sundays. Limited amounts of these specialties are prepared, so diners must call to reserve their portion. Live music is scheduled on the outdoor stage each Saturday and Sunday from noon to 3:30.

San Juan Bakery *319 Third St., 623-4570. Daily 8-6.*

This old-fashioned bakery makes a wonderful sourdough French bread, a down-soft buttermilk bread, and an assortment of delicious pastries. The sugar cookies are particularly good and make a great car snack. Picnic supplies are also available.

Salinas
(Area Code 408)

A LITTLE BACKGROUND

Salinas is one of the biggest cities in the Salinas Valley. Known as "the salad bowl of the nation," this valley is where author John Steinbeck spent his formative years, and many of his novels are set here. In fact, the first working title for *East of Eden* was "Salinas Valley."

VISITOR INFORMATION

Salinas Valley Chamber of Commerce *P.O. Box 1170 (119 E. Alisal), Salinas 93902, 424-7611, fax 424-8639.*

GETTING THERE

Located approximately 20 miles south of San Juan Bautista via Highway 101. It is also possible to take Amtrak from Oakland or San Jose and return the same day. Call (800) 872-7245 for more information.

ANNUAL EVENTS

California Rodeo *July. (800) 771-8807, 757-2951. $7-$17.*

First presented in 1911, this outdoor rodeo is ranked fourth largest in the world. It is especially noted for its trick riders, clowns, and thoroughbred racing. Prize money totals over $200,000, attracting the best of the cowboys to the competitions.

Steinbeck Festival™ *August. 753-7401, fax 753-0574. $10.*

Each year one of Steinbeck's many novels is emphasized in this intellectual festival honoring the town's native son. Bus and walking tours, films, lectures, and panel discussions are all part of the festivities.

WHERE TO EAT

Cottage Cafe *737 Sanborn Pl., (Monterey Peninsula exit off Hwy. 101), 754-1968. B & L M-Sat; $. 1 highchair, boosters. MC, V.*

This tiny, friendly roadhouse produces a particularly good, crisp green salad, which makes sense since this area is known as the nation's salad bowl. Some seating is available in comfortable booths, and counter seating permits a fast in and out. Breakfast items are available all day, and hamburgers and a variety of sandwiches, including a great French dip, are on the menu.

First Awakenings *171 Main St., 784-1125.*

For description, see page 101.

The Steinbeck House *132 Central Ave., 424-2735. Seatings at 11:45 & 1:15 M-Sat; $. Closed 2 weeks in Dec. Highchairs, boosters, child menu. 100% non-smoking. Reservations advised. MC, V.*

In 1902 John Steinbeck was born in the front bedroom of this beautifully renovated 1897 Victorian house. In *East of Eden* he described it as ". . . an immaculate and friendly house, grand enough but not pretentious . . . inside its white

John Steinbeck and his sister Mary on Jill — the inspiration for The Red Pony

fence surrounded by its clipped lawn and roses . . ." Now a volunteer group owns the house and operates it as a gourmet luncheon restaurant. Serving seasonal produce grown in the Salinas Valley, the restaurant's menu changes daily and includes items such as spinach sausage en croute and green chile quiche. Lunch includes soup or salad and entree for $7.50; dessert and beverage are extra. Though the dining rooms are elegantly decorated, with Steinbeck memorabilia covering the walls, the atmosphere is casual. Comfortable travel attire is acceptable, and children are welcome. After lunch, a cellar gift shop invites browsing and perhaps selecting a souvenir book by Steinbeck.

From here it's just a short walk down the Victorian home-bedecked street to the **John Steinbeck Library** *(350 Lincoln St., 758-7311. M-W 10-9, Thur-Sat 10-6.)*—a public library founded in the author's honor.

Gonzales
(Area Code 408)

GETTING THERE
Located approximately 20 miles south of Salinas via Highway 101.

WHAT TO DO
The Monterey Vineyard *800 S. Alta St., 675-4000, fax 675-3019. Tasting daily 10-5; tours daily 11-3.*

This attractive modern winery displays changing art exhibits. Picnic tables, a pond populated with ducks and geese, and lush grassy areas offer a relaxing respite from freeway traffic.

Soledad
(Area Code 408)

WHAT TO DO
Mission Nuestra Señora de la Soledad *36641 Fort Romie Rd., off Paraiso Springs Rd., 3 mi. east of Hwy. 101, 678-2586. W-M 10-4. By donation.*

Named for the Spanish word for solitude, this mission was built in 1791 and is 13th in the chain of missions. It was abandoned in 1835 and crumbled into ruin. In 1935 volunteers rebuilt the chapel and living quarters.

Pinnacles National Monument *12 mi. southeast of town, 389-4485, fax 389-4489. Daily 9-5. $4/vehicle.*

Formed by ancient volcanic activity, this scenic area is home to craggy pinnacles and spires that are particularly surprising to come across because the area is otherwise so flat. Spring and fall are the best times to visit for hiking and camping, spring being particularly popular because of the stunning display of wildflowers. At other times, the temperature can be uncomfortable. A variety of raptors—prairie falcons, red-shouldered hawks, turkey vultures, and golden eagles—nest in the rocks and can sometimes be observed. The more developed east side of the park is reached by taking Highway 25 south, then Highway 146 west. There, a Visitor Center offers orientation, and a moderately difficult two-mile loop trail leads to the Bear Gulch Caves.

King City
(Area Code 408)

WHAT TO DO

Mission San Antonio de Padua *On Jolon Rd., 29 mi. southwest of Hwy. 1 via Jolon Rd., in Fort Hunter Liggett, 385-4478. M-Sat 10-4:30, Sun 11-5. By donation.*

Founded in 1771 by Father Serra, this is one of the largest restored and rebuilt missions. Original remains at the remote site include the well, grist mill, tannery, and parts of the aqueduct system. Known as the "Jewel of the Santa Lucias," it was the third mission. A museum exhibits Native American artifacts, and an annual **fiesta** is held the second weekend in June.

San Miguel
(Area Code 805)

GETTING THERE

Located approximately 65 miles south of Soledad via Highway 101.

WHAT TO DO

Mission San Miguel Arcangel *775 Mission St., 467-3256, fax 467-2448. Daily 9:30-4:30. By donation.*

Founded in 1797, this is the 16th in the chain of California's 21 missions. The present mission building was constructed in 1816. Though the outside architecture is simple, the delicate, unretouched neoclassical paintings inside, done by parish Indians under the direction of professional artist Esteban Munras, are especially noteworthy. The reredos feature marble pillars with intricate geometric patterns displaying a dazzling array of colors. Beehive ovens and olive presses are on view in the gardens, and shaded picnic tables are provided. A **fiesta** is held each September on the third Sunday.

Paso Robles
(Area Code 805)

VISITOR INFORMATION

Paso Robles Chamber of Commerce *1225 Park St., Paso Robles 93446, (800) 406-4040, 238-0506, fax 238-0527.*

GETTING THERE

Located approximately 5 miles south of San Miguel via Highway 101.

WHERE TO EAT

A&W Rootbeer Drive-In *2110 Spring St., 238-0360. Daily 10am-11pm; $. Child portions. No cards.*

An oasis off Highway 101, this A&W stand is right out of the '50s. A waitress appears when a car's headlights are turned on, and food is served on a tray that attaches to a partially rolled-down window. Choices are simple: hamburgers, hot dogs, French fries, onion rings, and cold root beer.

WHAT TO DO

James Dean Memorial *On Hwy. 46, Cholame (pronounced "show-LAMB"), 25 mi. east of town, 238-1390.*

Depending on a person's mood, this can be an interesting or bizarre side trip. This is where legendary actor James Dean crashed his racing-model Porsche roadster and died in 1955. A concrete and stainless steel obelisk shrine to Dean's memory stands just 900 yards from the actual death site. Constructed and maintained by a Japanese national who comes to pay homage twice a year, it is located in the parking lot of the **Jack Ranch Cafe.**

Wine Tasting.

This area's limestone soil is similar to that found in Provence in the south of France and produces flavorful grapes. The long, hot summers turn them into fodder for ripe, robust Merlots and Zinfandels.

A **scenic back roads tour** begins at the Vineyard Drive exit off 101 just north of Templeton. Take Vineyard Drive west for about eight miles through bucolic, oak-studded farm land, passing Peachy Canyon Road (which returns to the freeway). At Adelaida Road, turn right and continue for about two miles to **Adelaida Cellars** *(5805 Adelaida Rd., 239-8980, fax 239-4671. Tasting daily 10:30-4:30; fee.),* a scenically situated winery specializing in producing small quantities of low-tech premium wines fermented with natural yeast. Of special interest here is an expansive walnut orchard, the bountiful fruit of which is sold in the tasting room. Continue about ten miles east on Adelaida Road toward town, crossing 101, to **Eberle Winery** *(238-9607. Tasting 10-5 daily; in summer to 6.).* The winery's excellent reds can be tasted in a room filled with medals and awards from competitions, and picnic tables are provided on a sheltered patio. Tours of the cool caves are given sporadically.

For a free map to this area's many wineries, contact the **Paso Robles Vintners and Growers Association** *((800) 549-WINE, 239-VINE, fax 237-6439).*

Atascadero
(Area Code 805)

VISITOR INFORMATION

Atascadero Chamber of Commerce *6550 El Camino Real, Atascadero 93422, 466-2044.*

WHAT TO DO

The Charles Paddock Zoo *On Hwy. 41, 1 mi. west of 101, 461-5080. Daily 10-4; in summer to 5. Adults $2, 6-17 $1; free 1st Tu of month.*

Though small, this zoo takes good care of its diverse population. An adjacent park has shady picnic tables and a lake where paddle boats can be rented.

San Luis Obispo
(Area Code 805)

VISITOR INFORMATION

San Luis Obispo County Visitors & Conference Bureau *1037 Mill St., San Luis Obispo 93401, (800) 634-1414, 541-8000, fax 543-9498.*

GETTING THERE

Located approximately 30 miles south of Paso Robles via Highway 101. It is also possible to take Amtrak; call (800) 872-7245 for more information.

WHERE TO STAY

Embassy Suites Hotel *333 Madonna Rd., (800) EMBASSY, 549-0800, fax 543-5273. 196 suites; 98 non-smoking suites; $$$. Children under 12 free. Indoor heated pool & hot tub, fitness room. Full breakfast; restaurant, room service.*

This branch of the all-suites hotel chain is located adjacent to a large shopping mall with a series of fast-food outlets. For description, see page 346.

Garden Street Inn *1212 Garden St./Marsh St., 545-9802. 2 stories; 13 rooms; 100% non-smoking; $$-$$$+. Unsuitable for children under 16. Some fireplaces. Afternoon snack, full breakfast.*

This beautifully restored, enormous 1887 Italianate/Queen Anne-style mansion is just a block from downtown. Fragrant old citrus trees greet guests at the front gate, and a communal parlour area features an interesting browsing library.

Hostel *1292 Foothill Blvd., 544-4678, fax 544-3142. 20 beds; some private rooms.*

See also page 391.

Madonna Inn *100 Madonna Rd., (800) 543-9666, 543-3000, fax 543-1800. 3 stories; 109 rooms; 100% non-smoking; $$-$$$+. Children under 18 free. Some fireplaces. 2 restaurants.*

Begun in 1958 with just 12 rooms, this big pink motel now has 109 guest rooms. All are uniquely decorated, some more uniquely than others—like the Cave Man Room, with its stone walls, ceilings, and floors, plus a cascading waterfall shower; and the Barrel of Fun Room, in which all the furniture is made from barrels. A photo file at the check-in desk is available to help guests decide which room to book.

For those who are not spending the night, a snack in the flamboyant coffee shop or dinner in the more formal **Gold Rush Dining Room** *(B, L, & D daily. Highchairs, boosters, booths, child menu. 100% non-smoking. Reservations advised. MC, V.)*—where the menu is surf and turf-style and all the supporting courses are included—is a must. A bakery is open all day dispensing goodies such as French cream puffs, cinnamon pull-aparts, and an assortment of pies. And don't miss the restrooms—especially the men's room.

Motel Inn *2223 Monterey St., 543-4000.*

Opened on December 12, 1925, this is the world's very first motel. It is currently closed for a major renovation.

Quality Suites *1631 Monterey St., (800) 228-5151, 541-5001, fax 546-9475. 3 stories; 138 suites; 116 non-smoking suites; $$-$$$; 2-night min. on summer weekends. Children under 18 free. All VCRs. Heated pool, children's wading pool, hot tub. Evening snack, full breakfast.*

This chain is known for its spacious rooms and made-to-order buffet breakfasts. A complimentary evening cocktail hour is also provided, giving guests a chance to relax and mingle.

Motel Row.

A vast array of motels lines the north end of Monterey Street.

WHERE TO EAT

Benvenuti *450 Marsh St./Carmel, 541-5393. L M-F, D daily; $$. Reservations advised.*

Operating from within a transformed Victorian home, this refined, romantic restaurant offers an extensive menu of northern Italian dishes. Its namesake dish, fettucine Benvenuti, tops the pasta with a combination of prawns, scallops, and mushrooms in a tasty tomato sauce. The petto di pollo alla Diavola consists of a breaded chicken breast sautéed with brandy and Dijon mustard. More entrees include a pheasant with vodka sauce crowned with glazed white grapes, and ossobuco alla Milanese—braised veal shank with saffron risotto. Selections from the dessert tray include a house-made light tiramisu and, in season, perfect fresh red raspberries topped with Grand Marnier.

Farmers' Market *600 & 700 blocks of Higuera St., 541-0286, fax 781-2647. Thur 6-9pm. Free.*

Shoppers here can buy dinner fully prepared or pick up the fixings. This market is known for its delicious barbecued items, and live entertainment is provided free.

Hobee's *1443 Calle Joaquin, 549-9186. B, L, & D daily; $. Highchairs, boosters, booths, child menu. 100% non-smoking. No reservations. AE, MC, V.*

For description, see page 91.

Linn's S.L.O. Bin *1141 Chorro/Marsh St., 546-8444. B, L, & D daily, SunBr; $. Highchairs, boosters. No reservations. MC, V.*

Known for its expansive salad bar and large selection of desserts, this pleasant dining room has an unusual, varied menu that includes stuffed potatoes, pot pies, stir-frys, and sandwiches. An adjoining shop purveys the restaurant's own line of gourmet kitchen products.

Pepe Delgado's *1601 Monterey St., 544-6660. L & D Tu-Sun; $. Highchairs, boosters, booths, child portions. No reservations. MC, V.*

Comfortable booths and large, solid tables make this popular Mexican spot an especially good choice for families. The hacienda-style building features tile floors, velvet paintings, and papier-mâché parrots on perches hanging from the ceiling. Potent fruit margaritas and daiquiris come in small, medium, and large sizes and help diners get festive. A large variety of traditional Mexican items is on the menu, and many are available in small portions. Fajitas are particularly fun to order because they arrive sizzling on raised platters and are kept warm on the table by candles.

Rhythm Creekside Cafe *1040 Broad St., 541-4048, fax 461-1267. B, L, & D daily, Sat & SunBr & afternoon tea; $-$$. Highchairs, boosters. 100% non-smoking. Reservations advised. AE, MC, V.*

Featuring a small dining room, a balcony perched above San Luis Creek, and a patio down beside the creek, this enjoyable cafe is ideal at lunch, when a variety of interesting sandwiches, salads, and pastas are on the menu. On weekends, high tea is served from 2 to 4 p.m. in a courtyard under a lemon tree. Reservations are necessary then, and the menu features house-made scones, muffins, and desserts as well as salads and soups.

WHAT TO DO

California Polytechnic State University (Cal Poly) *On Grand Ave., 756-5734. Tours M, W, F at 10 & 2. Free.*

Tours of this attractive campus begin in the lobby of the Administration Building.

Gum Alley *Next to 733 Higuera St.*

For several decades gum-chewers have been depositing their product on these brick walls. Some have even taken the time to make designs. A vulgar, tacky eyesore to many, it is a cheap thrill for gum aficionados and most children. So don't get stuck here without a stick. Stock up on different colors of gum before arriving, and note that Double Bubble is reputed to stick best.

Hot Springs.

• **Avila Hot Springs** *250 Avila Beach Dr., (800) 332-2359, 595-2359. Daily 8am-10pm. Adults $7.50, 2-12 $5.*

Inner tubes can be rented *(50¢)* to use in a warm pool, and campsites are available.

• **Sycamore Mineral Springs** *1215 Avila Beach Dr., (800) 234-5831, 595-7302, fax 781-2598. 2 stories; 50 rooms; some non-smoking suites; $$-$$$+. Some kitchens & fireplaces. Heated pool, 23 hot tubs. Restaurant.*

Situated on a back road leading to the coast, this inn has outdoor mineral spring hot tubs that can be rented by the hour, and all rooms have private hot tubs. The springs' history dates to 1897, when two men drilling for oil were disappointed to find sulfur-based mineral water instead. First called the "oil wells," the springs became popular in the 1920s when W. C. Fields and others who stayed at the Hearst Castle stopped in.

Mission San Luis Obispo de Tolosa *782 Monterey St., 543-6850. Daily 9-4; in summer to 5. By donation.*

Founded in 1772, this is the fifth mission in the California chain. It was the first mission to introduce the red clay roof tile. The complex includes a museum and a fragrant rose garden. Its charming chapel has a simple façade with a belfry and vestibule—unique among the state's missions—and is still used for services. An adjacent plaza and park provide shady trees, large grassy areas, stream-hugging paths, and inviting open-air cafes.

The nearby **San Luis County Historical Museum** *(696 Monterey St., 543-0638. W-Sun 10-4. Free.)* is appropriately filled with historical exhibits that include a hurdy-gurdy and a school bell.

San Luis Obispo Children's Museum *1010 Nipomo St., 544-KIDS. Thur, F, & Sun 1-5; M & Sat 10-5; in summer M, Tu, Thur-Sat 10-5, Sun 1-5. Admission $4, under 2 free. Strollers not permitted.*

Located within a transformed transmission shop, this museum especially for kids holds numerous hands-on exhibits that entice them to explore and interact. They can become encased in a giant bubble, pilot a space shuttle to the moon, and anchor a newscast. Children under 16 must be accompanied by an adult.

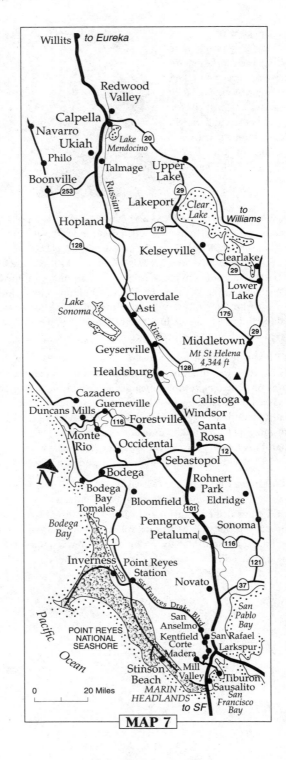

MAP 7

101
North

A LITTLE BACKGROUND

Across the Golden Gate Bridge from San Francisco, spectacularly scenic Marin County comprises a number of prosperous bedroom communities. It is home to numerous rock stars and celebrities, including *Star Wars* filmmaker George Lucas, who built his studios in the hilly back country.

Books and films have poked fun at the generally upscale residents, creating a stereotype of people with an easygoing, laid-back approach to life, seeking nothing more than to tickle each other with peacock feathers while soaking in a hot tub, and emphasizing their New Age flakiness. The reality is, of course, somewhere in between.

Consistently fair weather makes this area a popular destination with Bay Area residents, especially when other areas are covered by fog.

VISITOR INFORMATION

Marin County Convention & Visitors Bureau *Avenue of the Flags, San Rafael 94903, (415) 472-7470, fax (415) 499-3700.*

Marin Headlands
(Area Code 415)

A LITTLE BACKGROUND

Get oriented to this 12,000-acre park at the **Visitor Center** *(Alexander Ave. exit off Hwy. 101, 331-1540. Daily 9:30-4:30. Free.)* located inside Fort Barry's old chapel. Then take a soul-soothing walk along **Rodeo Beach**. When leaving, follow McCullough Road east to Conzelman Road, which leads past some of the old bunkers and gun batteries that attest to the area's military past. **Hawk Hill**, at Battery 129, is considered the best site on the West Coast to view birds of prey; over 25,000 hawks and other raptors migrate over this area each year. Farther on, several twists in the road offer magnificent views of the Golden Gate Bridge, and behind it, San Francisco. A picture taken here makes the subject look as if they are standing on the edge of the earth.

WHERE TO STAY

Hostel *331-2777. 103 beds; couples & family rooms. Tennis court.*

On the National Historic Register, this spacious, homey hostel retains its original charm. See also page 391.

WHAT TO DO

Bay Area Discovery Museum *557 E. Fort Baker, 487-4398, fax 332-9671. Tu-Thur 9-4, F-Sun 10-5; in summer Tu-Sun 10-5. Adults $7, 1-18 $6.*

This activity-oriented, hands-on museum is especially perfect for a rainy day outing. Themes include the bay environment, art, multimedia, and architecture. Among the related activities spread among seven buildings: constructing a model suspension bridge; crawling through the Underwater Sea Tunnel; building a personal enclosure in the Space Maze. The excitement is catching, and parents find themselves being pulled along from one activity to another by their eager children. Visitors can also explore the outdoor area immediately surrounding the museum, where a Model T can be played on. For those who are caught picnic-less, a cafe serves appropriate fare, and outdoor picnic tables afford a magnificent close-up view of the Golden Gate Bridge. Special programs, festivals, and workshops are scheduled regularly.

The Marine Mammal Center *289-7325. Daily 10-4. Free.*

Staffed by volunteers, this is one of the largest wild animal hospitals in the world. A variety of injured, sick, or orphaned marine mammals (seals, dolphins, porpoises, whales) are brought here to be nursed back to health. When ready, they are released back into their natural habitat. Docent-led tours are available on weekends, self-guided tours during the week.

Point Bonita Lighthouse *Trail to lighthouse open Sat & Sun 12:30-3:30; call for tour schedule.*

This lovely old light was the last on the Pacific Coast to be automated. The mostly dirt, ½-mile trail can be scary: It includes going through a tunnel and crossing a 120-foot suspension bridge. Full moon walks are sometimes scheduled.

Sausalito
(Area Code 415)

A LITTLE BACKGROUND

People come from everywhere to enjoy strolling Bridgeway, the main street of this warm and sunny town. A former fishing village, it is now a magnet for both artists and tourists and remains a pleasure for both. Restaurants and boutiques abound, and the view across the bay to Tiburon and San Francisco is superb.

In summer, a **shuttle** *(331-7262. Daily 11-5:30. Round trip $2.)* runs between the Ferry Terminal, the Bay Model, the Discovery Museum, and the Golden Gate Bridge.

VISITOR INFORMATION

Sausalito Chamber of Commerce *P.O. Box 566 (333 Caledonia St.), Sausalito 94966, 332-0505, fax 332-0323.*

GETTING THERE

Take the first exit off Highway 101 after crossing the Golden Gate Bridge. It is marked "Alexander Avenue." Another exit marked "Sausalito" is three miles farther north. Sausalito can also be reached from San Francisco via ferry.

ANNUAL EVENTS

Floating Homes Tour *August. 331-3999. Tickets $20.*

Approximately ten houseboats open their premises for tours during this exciting event at Waldo Point Harbor. A portion of the proceeds benefit the non-profit Sausalito Schools Foundation.

Sausalito Art Festival *September, on Labor Day weekend. 332-3555. Adults $10, 62+ & 6-12 $5.*

This juried exhibit of over 200 artists includes live music, international cuisine, and plenty of wine.

WHERE TO STAY

Casa Madrona Hotel *801 Bridgeway, (800) 567-9524, 332-0502, fax 332-2537. 36 units; $$$-$$$+; 2-night min. on weekends. Some kitchens & fireplaces. Hot tub. Evening snack, full breakfast. Parking $7.*

Nestled against a picturesque hill above Bridgeway, this hotel offers lodging in either a converted Victorian house in back, or in newer individually decorated rooms that are sprinkled down the hillside and feature water views. Arrangements can also be made to stay on a local houseboat. Breakfast is served to guests in the hotel's elegant restaurant.

Romantic **Mikayla** *(331-5888, fax 332-2537. D daily, SunBr; $$$. Highchairs, boosters, child portions. 100% non-smoking. Reservations advised. AE, MC, V. Valet parking $3.)* serves American cuisine in an elegant atmosphere with restive harbor views. The signature dish is charred New York steak with sauce Foyot.

WHERE TO EAT

Alta Mira Hotel *125 Bulkley Ave., 332-1350, fax 331-3862. B, L, & D daily. Closed Jan. Highchairs, boosters, child menu. Reservations advised. AE, MC, V. Valet parking $3.50.*

Situated in the hills above town, this refined spot serves traditional continental cuisines. Its terrace, which commands an excellent bay view, is a particularly choice spot to enjoy a leisurely breakfast, lunch, or Sunday brunch.

Guest rooms and cottages *(2 stories; 35 rooms; 4 non-smoking rooms; $$-$$$+. Closed Jan. 6 gas fireplaces. Restaurant, room service (child items).)*, many with bay views, are also available.

Margaritaville *1200 Bridgeway, 331-3226. L & D daily; $-$$. Highchairs, boosters, child portions. No reservations. AE, MC, V.*

Dining here can feel a bit like a tropical mini-vacation. Most inside tables have some view of the water, but the outside deck is the place to head for in warm weather. The bar takes up almost half the premises—a clue that this spot is popular with singles—and dispenses strong, tasty drinks, including fruit margaritas, fruit smoothies, and some unusual Caribbean concoctions. The decor exudes a tropical atmosphere, and the menu extends the feeling. The food is almost exclusively Mexican, but the music is Caribbean reggae. Huge portions are served on gigantic plates and platters, and although everything is well prepared and tasty, the sizzling fajita plates add extra excitement to any meal. Ingredients are fresh when possible, and there are many vegetarian selections as well as some more modest "platillos" for the lighter eater. On Kids Night *(W after 5)*, children under 12 eat free from a menu designed especially for them.

No Name Bar *757 Bridgeway, 332-1392. Daily 10am-2am.*

Famous for its low profile, this is where to stop and relax in the garden-like back room over a pitcher of Ramos fizzes. Live Dixieland jazz is performed every Sunday afternoon, and live jazz and blues are scheduled Wednesday through Saturday nights.

WHAT TO DO

Bay Model Visitor Center *2100 Bridgeway, 332-3870, 332-3871. Tu-Sat 9-4; in summer Tu-F 9-4, Sat & Sun 10-6. Free.*

Located on the outskirts of town, on the site of a shipyard that produced World War II Liberty Ships and tankers, this is a working hydraulic scale model of the Bay Area and Delta estuary systems. As big as two football fields, it was built to simulate bay water conditions for research. A computerized slide show and interpretive displays help make this complex scientific project understandable to the layman. The model operates irregularly; call for upcoming dates.

Heath Ceramics *400 Gate 5 Rd., 332-3732. Daily 10-5.*

Seconds of this classically simple contemporary ceramic dinnerware, which is used at both Chez Panisse in Berkeley and at nearby Lark Creek Inn in Larkspur, are sold here at reduced prices. Teapots and tiles are also produced—some using recycled glazes developed by the chemist-owner.

Sea Trek Ocean Kayaking Center *488-1000, fax 488-1707.*

Rent a kayak for just the day, or sign up for one lesson or a series. Special children's classes are available, and a customized Take the Kids Sea Kayaking program includes wet suits for the whole family

Village Fair *777 Bridgeway, 332-1902. Daily 10-6.*

This unusual indoor shopping center houses 35 shops and features a curvy, steep "Little Lombard" path to the upper floors.

Waldo Point *At north end of town.*

This private houseboat colony contains both the funky and exquisite. Visitors are not particularly welcomed by residents but are legally permitted to view the area if they respect posted no-trespassing signs. It is interesting to note that Otis Redding rented a houseboat on the main dock here in 1967. This dock is said to have been the inspiration for his well-known song titled "(Sittin' On) The Dock of the Bay."

Mill Valley
(Area Code 415)

A LITTLE BACKGROUND

Thought of by many as the quintessential Marin, this tiny, laid-back town originated as an enclave of vacation cabins built by San Franciscans eager to escape the city's notoriously cool summers. It rests in the shadow of Mount Tamalpais, the county's principal landmark. The unofficial center of town seems to be the **Depot Bookstore and Cafe** *(87 Throckmorton Ave.)*. Once the town's Northwestern Pacific Railroad depot, it offers both indoor and outdoor seating and a plethora of reading material. Mill Valley is also home to the original **Banana Republic** store— now a nationwide chain that sells comfortable travel clothing; its current location *(59*

Throckmorton Ave.) is not the original site. The town is also home to the modest original location of the **Smith & Hawken** garden-supply store *(35 Corte Madera Ave.).*

VISITOR INFORMATION

Mill Valley Chamber of Commerce *P.O. Box 5123 (85 Throckmorton Ave.), Mill Valley 94942, (800) 388-9701, 388-9700, fax 383-9469.*

GETTING THERE

Located approximately five miles north of Sausalito. Take exit off Highway 101 and follow signs to intersection of Miller and Throckmorton avenues.

ANNUAL EVENTS

Mill Valley Film Festival *October. 383-5346. Screenings $5-$7.50.*

Running for 11 days, this well-established festival offers screenings of both American independent cinema and foreign films, major film premiers, and tributes to top filmmakers and industry leaders. Seminars are scheduled for both aspiring filmmakers and the layman in search of enlightenment.

WHERE TO STAY

Mill Valley Inn *165 Throckmorton Ave., (800) 595-2100, 389-6608, fax 389-5051. 16 rooms, 2 cottages. 100% non-smoking; 2-night min. on weekends. Some fireplaces. Continental breakfast; room service.*

Conveniently situated downtown, this brand new, circa 1994 European-style pensione is tucked against a redwood-covered hill. Rooms are stylishly furnished with attractive handcrafted pieces from Northern California artists. Some have a balcony with views of the redwoods and Mt. Tamalpais, and two cottages offer privacy in a creekside forest setting. Breakfast in the morning is a buffet taken around the corner at Piazza D'Angelo; it includes an espresso bar and newspaper.

WHERE TO EAT

Avenue Grill *44 E. Blithedale Ave., 388-6003. D daily; $$. Highchairs, boosters, child portions. 100% non-smoking. Reservations advised. AE, MC, V.*

This noisy, yet cozy contemporary spot features an open dining room and is usually packed. The eclectic dinner menu offers everything from meatloaf to portobello mushrooms on polenta and is generally good. For dessert, a wonderful light crème brulee pairs beautifully with a coffee served in one of the restaurant's oversized cups. A large selection of unusual beers is available.

Buckeye Roadhouse *15 Shoreline Hwy., at Mill Valley/Stinson Beach exit off Hwy. 101, 331-2600, fax 331-6067. L & D daily, SunBr; $-$$. Highchairs, boosters, booths, child menu. 100% non-smoking. Reservations advised. MC, V.*

Situated inside a Bavarian-style chalet dating from 1937, but updated not too long ago to the tune of $1 million, this unfussy restaurant features generous portions of tasty American-style food at reasonable prices. The main dining room has high peaked ceilings, a large stone fireplace, and dark mahogany accents. Some tables have a pleasant view over the freeway to Strawberry Point. Mixed drinks are listed on the menu, among them a spicy, delicious Bloody Mary. Winners on the interesting lunch menu include a well-seasoned coleslaw, an ahi sandwich served with pesto mayo and crisp house-made potato chips, and great onion rings—sliced very thin and served with house-made ketchup. Several salads, a pizza, a hamburger, and beer sausages with garlic mashed potatoes are also on the menu. Dinner items are more pricey and include steaks and chops, fresh fish, and assorted game. If the dining room is crowded, an impromptu snack can be taken in the bar.

The Cantina *651 E. Blithedale Ave./Camino Alto, in Blithedale Plaza, 381-1070. L & D daily; $$. Highchairs, boosters, booths, child menu. Reservations advised. AE, MC, V.*

It is not unusual in Marin County to find a very good restaurant, such as this one, located in a shopping center. Popular at lunch, it becomes ridiculously crowded here at dinner, when waits can be long, but a variety of tangy margaritas and fresh fruit daiquiris can be ordered, with or without alcohol, to help pass the time. The predictable Mexican items and combination plates are on the large menu, as are a few more unusual ones—green enchiladas topped with a tart tomatillo sauce and outstanding deep-fried chimichangas topped with guacamole. Chicken mole, fajitas, sandwiches, hamburgers, and steaks are also available. The patio is choice for lunch on warm days; in the evening it is open for drinks only. Parents take note: On Monday through Wednesday evenings from 5:30 to 8:30, Fiesta Kids provides supervised babysitting on the premises for children ages 2 through 10. The cost is $2 per child, and quesadillas and soft drinks are included!

Jennie Low's Chinese Cuisine *38 Miller Ave., in Mill Creek Plaza, 388-8868. L M-Sat, D daily; $. Highchairs, boosters. Reservations advised. AE, MC, V.*

All items here are prepared without MSG. Co-owner, cooking teacher, and cookbook author Jennie Low has designed a menu making use of her own sauces, which are available bottled to take home. The menu stresses simple, home-style food that is easy on the spicing. Among the best dishes are velvety Snow White Chicken with snow peas and large mushrooms, and Hot Spicy Eggplant accented with earthy wood-ear mushrooms. Most of the noodle dishes are also very good, especially the noodle soup. The house tea is a fragrant lychee and black leaf blend that can also be purchased to take home. Because Low's favorite color is lavender, it is used on everything from the menu's type to the servers' uniform, and it is the color of everything she herself wears. And because her lucky number is eight, all menu prices end in eight. Working behind a large glass window, the busy chefs can be observed from the modern, clean-lined dining room.

In the same building, **Roots & Legends** *(381-5722)* purveys Chinese medicinal herbal preparations that promise to cure what ails you.

La Ginestra *127 Throckmorton Ave./Miller Ave., 388-0224, fax 388-2953. D Tu-Sun; $$. Closed 2 weeks in summer. Highchairs, boosters, booths, child portions. 100% non-smoking. No reservations. MC, V.*

Named for the Scottish broom flower that is native to both Mount Tamalpais and Sorrento, Italy, this popular, casual spot specializes in Neapolitan cuisine. The ample menu includes a large selection of pastas, pizzas, and veal dishes as well as a garden-fresh minestrone soup, a good cannelloni, and an excellent eggplant Parmesan. All are cooked to order and served with French bread and butter. Veal, chicken, and seafood entrees come with a choice of ravioli, spaghetti, French fries, or fresh vegetables. Fried or sautéed fresh squid is always on the menu along with gnocchi (potato dumplings) a la Napolentana, saltimbocca. and house-made spinach and cheese ravioli. Desserts include a rich house-made cannoli and tiramisu, and a frothy white wine zabaglione.

Piazza D'Angelo *22 Miller Ave., 388-2000. L & D daily; $-$$. Highchairs, boosters. 100% non-smoking. Reservations advised. AE, MC, V.*

Designed to resemble an Italian town square, this comfortable restaurant features a retractable skylight over its main dining room and two al fresco patios. Terra cotta floors, original modern art, and contemporary Italian music all help set the mood. Rotisserie-grilled meats are excellent, and the antipastos, pastas, risotti, and innovative pizzas baked in a wood-burning oven are also generally wonderful. The rich tiramisu dessert, served in an oversized stemmed glass, is ample for two.

Picnic Pick-Ups.
• **Mill Valley Market** *12 Corte Madera Dr./Throckmorton, 388-3222. M-Sat 7-7:30, Sun 9-7. MC, V.*

Family-owned since 1929, this small but well-stocked market sells everything required for a fabulous picnic. Extensive selections are available of honeys, mustards, green olives, vinegars, salad dressings, and jams, and a deli-bakery tucked in the back dispenses prepared salads and baked goods that include a great Danish and an exquisite oatmeal-prune muffin.

WHAT TO DO
Old Mill Park *Throckmorton Ave./Old Mill Rd., 383-1370.*

Holding the town's namesake sawmill, which dates from 1834, this park is sheltered by an old growth redwood grove and offers idyllic stream-side picnicking. A rustic sun-speckled playground area has picnic tables, some of which are situated inside a circle of giant redwoods.

Sweetwater *153 Throckmorton Ave., 388-2820.*

This locally legendary nightclub schedules intimate evening performances by an array of noteworthy rock and blues musicians. Bay Area residents Robert Cray and John Lee Hooker have been known to drop in to jam. Call for the current lineup and show times.

Tiburon
(Area Code 415)

A LITTLE BACKGROUND
Smaller and less well known than Sausalito, Tiburon's tiny Main Street is lined with boutiques, galleries, and restaurants.

VISITOR INFORMATION
Tiburon Peninsula Chamber of Commerce *96-B Main St., Tiburon 94920, 435-5633, fax 435-1132.*

GETTING THERE
Take the Tiburon Boulevard exit off Highway 101. Follow Tiburon Boulevard four miles east into town.

WHERE TO STAY
Tiburon Lodge *1651 Tiburon Blvd., (800) TIBURON, (800) 762-7770, 435-3133, fax 435-2451. 3 stories; 100 rooms; $$$-$$$+. Children under 12 free. Some VCRs; 3 kitchens. Heated pool. Full breakfast M-F only.*

The only overnight accommodation in town, this is just one block from Main Street. Some rooms have private whirlpool hot tubs, the most unusual of which is located in a black-tiled bathroom with piped-in music and underwater lights.

WHERE TO EAT
Guaymas *5 Main St., 435-6300. L & D daily, SunBr; $$. Highchairs, boosters. Reservations advised. AE, MC, V. Free validated parking M-F until 4 in Main Street Lot.*

Unusual, authentic regional Mexican fare is the specialty at this always-bustling spot. In pleasant surroundings of bleached-wood furnishings and adobe-style decor, diners enjoy sweeping views of San Francisco. On warm days, two outdoor decks are also available. Three styles of margaritas and a variety of Mexican beers are on the menu, and approximately 20 different tequilas can be ordered—with a complimentary sangrita chaser (a blend of tomato and orange juices spiked with chiles) if desired. All go well with the delicious complimentary house salsas and tortillas. In fact, a light meal can be made of just the appetizer platter. The imaginative menu here has no tacos, enchiladas, chiles rellenos, or refried beans. Instead, diners choose from a large selection of tantalizing seafood items and—the kitchen's forte—spit-roasted meats. Three kinds of tamales are served, each of which is delightful; fortunately, a sampler including one of each is an option. Even the desserts are intriguing: a creamy coconut custard flan, a spectacular deep-fried pouch filled with "drunken" bananas and rich vanilla bean ice cream, and delicate Mexican wedding cookies. Everything is made in-house from scratch, and it seems there isn't a loser on the menu.

Picnic Pick-Ups.
• **Let's Eat** *1 Blackfield Dr., in Cove Shopping Center, 383-FOOD, fax 388-3656. M-F 10-7, Sat 9-7, Sun 10-6. MC, V.*

Choose from a continuously changing menu of delicious salads—perhaps a wild rice with smoked cheese and grapes, or a flavorful Mexican chicken sprinkled generously with cilantro. Sandwiches are made to order, and a delicious "panhandle pastry" is sometimes available.
• **Sweet Things** *388-8583. M-F 7:30-7, Sat 8:30-6, Sun 9:30-6. MC, V.*

A few doors away, this spot specializes in great desserts that include a weighty carrot cake, a variety of interesting cookies, a Fallen Angel Torte, a Black Magic Cake, and a Fanny Annie cupcake consisting of devil's food with a cheesecake-like filling.

Sam's Anchor Cafe *27 Main St./Tiburon Blvd., 435-4527. L & D daily, Sat & SunBr; $-$$. Highchairs, boosters, child menu. No reservations. AE, MC, V.*

When the sun is shining, sitting outside on the deck here, watching the boats and seagulls, can be sublime. Dress is casual, and a typical weekend morning finds jet setters and celebrities dining happily right alongside everyday people. Singles make their connections here at brunch while parents relax with Sam's famous Ramos gin fizz. Cranky sounds from children don't travel far, but seem instead to magically vanish in the air. The brunch menu offers a variety of egg dishes, sandwiches, and salads, as well as a popular burger and fries. Unfortunately, the wait to get in can be long.

Sweden House Bakery *35 Main St./Ark Row, 435-9767. M-F 8-6, Sat & Sun 8-7; $. 1 highchair, boosters. MC, V.*

This cozy bakery is a good choice for a casual breakfast or lunch enjoyed either in the cozy interior or out on a small deck with a great view of the bay. For lunch, open-face sandwiches are made with a choice of either German six-grain or Swedish Limpa bread—a rye bread made with molasses and grated orange peel. Soups and salads are also available. It's also a great idea to just stop in and pick out a pastry from a tantalizing house-made selection that includes chocolate tortes, fruit tarts, raspberry shortbread, and chocolate chip cookies.

WHAT TO DO
Angel Island State Park.
For description, see page 67. A ferry leaves from a dock behind Main Street's restaurants.

Ark Row.

Located at the west end of Main Street, this series of shops operates from within land-bound houseboats, or arks, that are more than 100 years old. The **Windsor Vineyards** tasting room *(72 Main St.)* dispenses samplings of wines available only here; they also sell their wines with custom messages on the labels.

Blackie's Pasture *On Greenwood Beach Rd., off Paradise Dr.*

Blackie was a legendary local horse that grazed here from 1938 to 1966. He was beloved by children in the area, who would feed him goodies from their lunch bags on the way to school. His former pasture is paved over now and is a parking lot. Thankfully, his charming gravesite was spared and can be visited at the edge of the lot, and a metal statue in his likeness now stands there. A short walk away is **McKegney Green**, an expanse of grass overlooking the bay that just might be the perfect picnic spot. It is definitely perfect for kite-flying, and a bike trail runs the three miles from here into town.

China Cabin *52 Beach Rd./Tiburon Blvd., Belvedere, 435-1853. W & Sun 1-4; Apr-Oct only. Free.*

This exquisitely restored Victorian social saloon from the side-wheel steamer *SS China*, which provided transpacific mail and passenger service between 1866 and 1886, features 22-karat gold leaf trim, cut glass accents, walnut woodwork, and crystal and brass oil chandeliers.

National Audubon Society—California's Richardson Bay Audubon Center & Sanctuary *376 Greenwood Beach Rd./Tiburon Blvd., 388-2524. W-Sun 9-5. Adults $2, under 18 $1.*

The 11 acres of land and 900 acres of bay that comprise this wildlife sanctuary reflect grassland, coastal scrub, freshwater pond, and marsh habitats. A self-guided nature trail leads to a rocky beach and to a lookout spot with sweeping views of Richardson Bay and San Francisco. Except in summer, special programs are scheduled each Sunday.

Also on the property, the yellow 1876 **Lyford House** *(ext. 42. Sun 1-4; Nov-mid-Apr only.)* is the oldest Victorian home in Marin County. Once part of a dairy farm, it was barged to this location.

Old St. Hilary's Historic Preserve *Esperanza St./Mar West St., 435-1835. W & Sun 1-4; Apr-Oct only. Free.*

Two rare wildflowers grow in the fields surrounding this also-rare 1888 carpenter Gothic church. The Black Jewel and the Tiburon Paintbrush are found nowhere else in the world. When the spring wildflowers are blooming, this church displays these two and others from the 217 species protected here, and labels them for easy identification. An exhibit of wildflower photographs is also displayed.

Paradise Beach *On Paradise Dr., 1 mi. from town, 435-9212. Daily 7-sunset. $3-$5/vehicle.*

This sheltered 19-acre bay-front park has a large lawn area and barbecues. Fishing is permitted from a pier, and no license is required. The beach is small, quiet, and nice for wading. On warm days, the small parking lot fills early.

Larkspur

(Area Code 415)

GETTING THERE

Take the Paradise exit off Highway 101. Follow Tamalpais Drive west until it becomes Redwood.

WHERE TO EAT

Chai of Larkspur *25 Ward St., 945-7161, fax 945-7164. Tea M-Sun 12-6:30, F to 7:30. $12.50-$18.50. 100% non-smoking. Reservations advised. MC, V.*

Offering a tranquil respite from the bustle of everyday life, this tea shoppe and salon has a variety of tea services. Amid persimmon walls and chintz-covered chairs, tea-lovers sit and select perhaps a Mediterranean or Asian service, or maybe a traditional British high tea. Over 70 imported loose teas, tea accouterments, and tea-related gifts are also for sale.

The Lark Creek Inn *234 Magnolia Ave., 924-7766, fax 924-7117. L M-F, D daily, SunBr; $$-$$$. Highchairs, boosters, child menu. Reservations advised. AE, MC, V.*

Situated beneath a cluster of tall redwoods within an 1888 Victorian historical landmark, this destination restaurant is known for its seasonal farm-fresh American fare created by owner-chef Bradley Ogden. Seating is offered in the airy main dining room, in a smaller upstairs room, and on a brick patio—the spot of choice in warm weather. Produce, meats, poultry, fish, game, and other products are secured from local sources. One dinner enjoyed on the patio here, out under the stars on a night of perfect temperature, started with a salad of heirloom tomatoes and local goat cheese. It was followed by an oak-grilled salmon entree with a variety of baby vegetables, and the memorable house-made dessert conclusion was coconut cake with blackberry swirl ice cream. A branch is located in San Francisco; see One Market Restaurant on page 42.

Pasticceria Rulli *464-470 Magnolia Ave., 924-7478. Daily 7-7, F & Sat to 11; $. No cards.*

Offering what must be the most mouth-watering selection of sweets found this side of Salzburg, and displaying them in cases worthy of jewels, this treasure chest offers exquisite confections and Italian seasonal specialties. It is possible to select and indulge in-house, along with a coffee or other beverage, and an extensive hot panini (sandwich) menu is also available.

San Rafael
(Area Code 415)

VISITOR INFORMATION

San Rafael Chamber of Commerce *817 Mission Ave., San Rafael 94901, 454-4163, fax 454-7039.*

ANNUAL EVENTS

Marin County Fair *July. At Civic Center Fairgrounds; 499-6400. Adults $9, seniors & under 13 $7.*

Five days of fun include evening performances by big name entertainers and a low-level fireworks display. All entertainment and carnival rides are included in the admission fee.

WHERE TO STAY

Embassy Suites *101 McInnis Parkway, 499-9222.*

For description, see page 346.

WHERE TO EAT

Lundi *1143 4th St./B St., 456-7669. B & L daily; $. No reservations. No cards.*

Formerly known as Le Croissant, this tiny lunch counter continues to offer an interesting menu and to use fresh ingredients, making a visit here well worthwhile. The usual breakfast items are available along with crumbly-good corn muffins, made fresh in the kitchen, and a variety of coffees. Orange juice, grapefruit juice, and lemonade are fresh-squeezed and unsweetened. Lunch items include an excellent hamburger, frankfurter on a French baguette, and grilled Swiss on rye—all served with a side of French fries or potato salad. The wonderful jams, soups, and desserts—even the mayonnaise—are all made from scratch. Seating is at tiny tables or at a long counter with swiveling stools.

Mayflower Inne *1533 4th St./E. St., 456-1011. L Sun-F, D daily; $-$$. Highchairs, boosters, child portions. Reservations advised. MC, V.*

This place offers the chance to experience the cozy ambiance of an English pub without leaving the country. Waitresses have been known to greet customers with a cheery, "Hello, lovies" when presenting the menu. Among the traditional bland-but-hearty English items: steak and kidney pie, Cornish pasties (beef stew wrapped in a crescent pie pastry), bangers (English sausages), and fish & chips. Appetizers are a tad more interesting: a sausage roll (sausage baked in a pastry), a Scotch egg (a hard-boiled egg rolled in sausage meat and bread crumbs and then deep-fried). Drinks include assorted English ales and beers on tap, a non-alcoholic ginger beer, and, of course, tea. Dessert is a choice of fresh rhubarb pie, sherry trifle (a pudding), or chocolate cake. It is possible to relax in the English manner by indulging in a friendly game of darts or Ping Pong.

Pasand *802 B St., 456-6099. L & D daily.* For description, see page 324.

The Rice Table *1617 Fourth St./G St., 456-1808, same fax. D W-Sun; $$. Highchairs, boosters, booths. 100% non-smoking. Reservations advised. AE, MC, V.*

The Indonesian islands were once also known as the "Spice Islands," as that area is where many spices originate. During their domination of Indonesia, the Dutch served some of the best native dishes at huge feasts called "rijsttafel" or "rice table." A West Java version of this elaborate dinner is served in this cozy, nicely decorated room; a la carte items are also available. The rice table dinner *($16.95/person)* begins with shrimp chips and several dipping sauces, green pea vegetable soup, deep-fried lumpia (like Chinese spring rolls), a salad with lemon dressing, both white and saffron-yellow rice, pickled vegetables, and roasted coconut. Then come marinated pork, or chicken satay, shrimp sautéed in butter and tamarind, a mild chicken curry, beef sautéed in soy sauce and cloves, fried rice noodles, and a great dessert of fried bananas sprinkled lavishly with powdered sugar. Two other versions of the dinner—one with less dishes and one with more—and several less elaborate meals and special vegetarian meals are also available. Beer, which perfectly compliments the food, is available along with Indonesian-style coffee, tamarind juice, and several kinds of teas. Leftover food can be packaged to take home.

WHAT TO DO

China Camp State Park *Take Civic Center exit off Hwy. 101, follow N. San Pedro Rd., 456-0766. Daily 8-sunset. Free. Parking $2-$3.*

Once the largest fishing settlement along this shore, this fishing village was home to hundreds of Chinese fishermen in the late 1800s. Now visitors see the rustic, weathered remains of the pier and buildings. A Visitors Center displays period photographs and artifacts that document the shrimping and fishing that occurred until a 1911 ordinance outlawed the camp's primitive shrimp-trapping method. A charming small beach invites sunbathing and picnicking, and an old-time snack bar dispenses fast fare on weekends. In addition to the village, this 1,640-acre park has hiking trails through the hills, and campsites are available.

Guide Dogs for the Blind *350 Los Ranchitos Rd., 499-4000. Free.*

New guide dogs are presented to their visually-impaired partners here at a monthly gradu-ation ceremony. Tours of the kennels, campus, and dorms take place after the ceremony. It is possible to become a foster home to one of the dogs in transition, or to raise a puppy for this same service.

Marin County Civic Center *Civic Center exit off Hwy. 101.*

The last building designed by Frank Lloyd Wright before he died, this "bridge between two hills" is a national and state historic landmark. It also is where local resident George Lucas filmed his first big movie in 1971—*THX11380*—and it houses various city offices and a per-forming arts and convention center. Tours are available *(472-7470. W at 10:30 am.)*. A 14-acre lagoon is surrounded by a grassy area, perfect for picnicking and strolling.

Marin County Historical Society Museum *1125 B St., in **Boyd Park**, 454-8538. W-Sun 1-4. Free.*

Situated within a Victorian Gothic built in 1880, this museum is filled with area memora-bilia. It commemorates the life and travels of Louise Boyd, an Arctic explorer and the first woman to fly over the North Pole.

McNears Beach County Park *201 Cantera Way, 499-7816. Daily 8-8 in summer; call for off-season schedule. Admission $2 for walk-in, bike-in, or boat-in; $5-$7/vehicle.*

A former country club, this very popular spot is equipped with a heated swimming pool, concession stand, fishing pier, picnic area with barbecue pits and tables, and two tennis courts. A terrific sandy wading beach fronts San Pablo Bay.

Mission San Rafael Archangel *1104 5th Ave., 454-8141. Daily 11-4. Free.*

Founded in 1817, this was the 20th mission. It was replicated in 1949 on the approximate site of the original mission. Visitors can take a self-guided audio tape tour. A tiny adjoining museum displays original mission furniture and old photos of its reconstruction.

Wildcare: Terwilliger Nature Education and Wildlife Rehabilitation *76 Albert Park Ln./B. St., 453-1000, fax 456-0594. Daily 9-5. Free.*

Ill or orphaned animals are nursed back to health at this emergency veterinary hospital. When recovered, they are returned to their natural habitat. Visitors can view the animals, and a nature center has wildlife displays and hands-on exhibits. And this is where to sign up for "something special"—a nature discovery walk led by Mrs. Terwilliger herself. This organization also operates the Living with Wildlife Hotline, which provides tips on how to persuade various wild animals to take up residence elsewhere.

Novato

(Area Code 415)

VISITOR INFORMATION

Novato Chamber of Commerce *807 DeLong Ave., Novato 94945, 897-1164, fax 898-9097.*

ANNUAL EVENTS

Renaissance Pleasure Faire *August, September, & October. Off Hwy. 37 at Black Point Forest; (800) 52-FAIRE, 892-0937. Adults $17.50, seniors & 12-16 $14.50, 5-11 $7.50. Parking $5.* Regarded internationally as the most historically correct Renaissance-period event of its kind in the U.S., this faire is an authentic re-creation of an Elizabethan village as it would have appeared over 400 years ago during a harvest festival. More than 1,200 actors, musicians, jesters, jugglers, acrobats, dancers, puppeteers, and mimes dressed in Elizabethan costume are on hand to provide authentic period entertainment and mingle with visitors. Exotic food and drink, quality crafts, and appropriate diversions are purveyed throughout. Visitors are encouraged to dress in Renaissance costume. Indeed, this faire has been described as "the largest costume party in the world."

WHAT TO DO

Marin Museum of the American Indian *2200 Novato Blvd., in* **Miwok Park***, 897-4064. W-F 10-3, Sat & Sun 12-4; tour Sun at 1:30. By donation.*

Marin County's earliest residents, the Miwok Indians, are honored at this interactive museum. Exhibits and artifacts include tools, baskets, boats, and animal skins. Visitors can learn traditional Native American games, grind acorns with an authentic mortar, and visit a native plant garden.

Novato History Museum *815 DeLong Ave., 897-4320. W, Thur, Sat 8-4. Free.*

Built in 1850, the Victorian house this museum operates within is home to a collection of antique dolls, toy trains, and pioneer tools that reflect a history of the town.

Petaluma
(Area Code 707)

A LITTLE BACKGROUND

Located less than an hour's drive north of San Francisco, Petaluma offers an old-fashioned small town atmosphere. Perhaps this is why it was chosen as the filming location for both *American Graffiti* and *Peggy Sue Got Married.* In fact, director Francis Ford Coppola is quoted as saying, "You can find any decade you want somewhere in Petaluma."

Once known as the "World's Egg Basket," this area still produces plenty of eggs but is currently better known as a dairy center.

It's pleasant to spend a day here, just walking around the downtown area. Noteworthy among the numerous antique shops is the gigantic collective-run **Old Mill Antiques** located in **The Great Petaluma Mill** shopping complex. The residential area is also worth checking out for its large collection of Victorian homes.

VISITOR INFORMATION

Petaluma Visitor's Program *799 Baywood Dr. #1, Petaluma 94954, 769-0429, fax 762-4721.*

GETTING THERE

Located approximately 50 miles north of San Francisco. Take Highway 101 all the way.

ANNUAL EVENTS

Butter & Egg Days *April. 769-0429. Free.*

In the past the hometown parade that kicks off this celebration has been populated with giant papier-mâché cows, huge dairy trucks converted into floats, and flocks of children dressed as chickens. Other events have included the Cutest Little Chick in Town Contest (when the imaginative costumes of those marching chickens, limited to ages 1 through 8, are judged), an Egg Toss, and a Team Butter Churning Contest.

The **Petaluma Outdoor Antique Faire** *(763-7686)* takes place the next day on a street that is blocked off to traffic.

Ugly Dog Contest *June. 63-0931. Fair admission: adults $6.50, 7-12 $3, free for those who enter a dog.*

Just one of the many events scheduled at the annual **Sonoma-Marin Fair,** this good-spirited contest has three divisions: Pedigree Class, Mutt Class, and Ring of Champions.

Petaluma River Festival *August. 762-5331. By donation.*

Once home to the third busiest river in the state, this town celebrates its steamboat heyday with an old-fashioned pancake breakfast and boat rides galore. Usually the *Alma*, an 1891 scow schooner berthed at San Franciso's Hyde Street Pier, is on hand for tours and sea chantey sing-alongs led by park rangers.

Petaluma Summer Music Festival *August. 763-8920. $14-$20.*

This festival features diverse musical events that appeal to all ages. Many are scheduled in locations of historical interest.

World Wrist Wrestling Championships *October. 778-1430. $10.*

Begun in a local bar, this contest became a world's championship in 1962. Anyone who pays the $25 entry fee can vie for the titles of right-handed and left-handed heavyweight, middleweight, lightweight, featherweight, and bantamweight.

WHERE TO STAY

Cavanagh Inn *10 Keller St., 765-4657. 7 rooms; 100% non-smoking; $$. Some shared baths. Evening snack, full breakfast.*

The town's very first B&B, this large Victorian is just a few blocks from the historic downtown. It features gorgeous, rare heart redwood paneling. Guest rooms are located in both the main house and an adjacent cottage. Homemade cookies appear in each room at turndown, and breakfast is served in a beautifully appointed formal dining room.

Quality Inn *5100 Montero Way, (800) 221-2222, 664-1155, fax 664-8566. 2 stories; 110 rooms; 88 non-smoking rooms; $$-$$$+; 2-night min. May-Oct. Children under 19 free. Heated pool (unavail. Oct-Apr), hot tub, sauna. Continental breakfast. Dogs welcome.*

Located on the outskirts of town, this is a link in a chain known for its attractive Cape Cod-style of architecture and comfortable modern rooms. A generous buffet breakfast of hot drinks, pastries, cereals, and fresh fruit is served in the lobby.

WHERE TO EAT

McNear's Saloon & Dining House *23 Petaluma Blvd. N., 765-2121, fax 765-4671. L & D daily, Sat & SunBr; $-$$. Highchairs, boosters, booths, child menu. AE, MC, V.*

Located inside the historic 1886 McNear Building, this casual restaurant and sports bar serves an extensive eclectic menu. Diners can get great bar food, such as spicy buffalo wings and beer-batter mushrooms, as well as house-made soups, salads, sandwiches, hamburgers, barbe-cued chicken and ribs, pastas, and steaks. Happy Hour, from 5 to 6 p.m. daily, is a great time to visit for a drink and complimentary snacks. Kids have their own Happy Hour then, too, and get a free soft drink and game token with their dinner. On fair weather days, windows are opened wide in the front dining area near the sidewalk, allowing for pleasant people-watching. The attached **McNear's Mystic Theatre** presents live music on weekend evenings.

Sonoma Taco Shop *953 Lakeville St., in Gateway Shopping Ctr., 778-7921.*

For description, see page 197.

WHAT TO DO

Garden Valley Ranch *498 Pepper Rd., 3 mi. north of town (call for directions), 795-0919, fax 792-0349. W-Sun 10-4. Closed late Dec-mid-Jan. Adults $4, under 12 $2.*

This eight-acre ranch is the largest commercial grower of garden roses in the U.S. Among their well-known customers are the late Jacqueline Onassis (for daughter Caroline's wedding), Elizabeth Taylor, Whitney Huston, Barbra Streisand, and Martha Stewart. In one garden, over 4,000 rosebushes are cultivated for cuttings. In another, plants are grown for their perfume and some are used for potpourri. The best time for viewing is May through October, when the roses are in full bloom. The admission fee includes a self-guided tour brochure. When a private party is scheduled, the gardens are closed to the public, but the nursery and test garden remain open; call ahead to verify.

The Great Petaluma Desert *5010 Bodega Ave., 778-8278, fax 778-0931. F-Sun 10-5, in winter to 4. Free.*

Featuring one of the largest selections of rare and exotic cacti and succulents in the coun-try, this dramatic back roads nursery boasts nine greenhouses. Most of the stock is propagated on site. A few of the greenhouses are off-limits except to collectors who call ahead, but those that are accessible should satisfy most people. Among the most popular plants are tillandsia, also known as "air plants" because they require no soil.

Marin French Cheese Company *7500 Petaluma-Point Reyes Rd. (also known as Red Hill Rd.), (800) 292-6001, 762-6001, fax 762-0430. Sales room daily 9-5; tours daily 10-4, on the hour. Free.*

Located way out in the country, this cheese factory has been operated by the Thompson family since 1865. By now, they have perfected the art of making Camembert cheese. They also make good Brie, schloss, and breakfast cheeses. Tours take visitors through the factory and explain how these special cheeses are produced, and cheeses are sampled at the end. Picnic sup-plies are available in an adjoining store, where these house cheeses are on sale along with salami, French bread, sandwiches, crackers, soft drinks, juices, and ice cream. Two large grassy areas, one with a large pond, beckon for picnics. Some picnic tables are also available.

Petaluma Adobe State Historic Park *3325 Adobe Rd., 762-4871. Daily 10-5. Adults $2, 6-11 $1.*

The boundaries of General Vallejo's vast 66,000-acre land grant once stretched from the Petaluma River on the west, to San Pablo Bay on the south, to Sonoma on the east, to Cotati and Glen Ellen on the North. This rancho, which was part of the estate, has been restored to reflect life as it was here in 1840. The living quarters, a weaving shop, and a blacksmith's forge are seen on a self-guided tour. An assortment of animals, including sheep and goats, roam freely. Shaded picnic tables are located by Adobe Creek (fire regulations prohibit barbecuing).

Annual events include **Sheep Shearing** in April, **Living History Day** in May, and the **Old Adobe Fiesta**—with demonstrations of early California crafts and the chance for visitors to weave baskets and make hand-dipped candles—in August.

The Petaluma Queen *255 Weller St., (800) 750-7501, 762-2100, fax 769-5060. Cruise $15-$25, with meal $29-$49, children 3-11 half-price. L W-F, D W-Sun, Sat & SunBr. Reservations advised.*

Folks really have a great time rolling down the Petaluma River on this reproduction paddle wheeler. It's a good idea to be outside on the back deck when the riverboat is leaving and returning, because that is where the old-time calliope (pronounced ka-lie-a-pe) can be heard best (this is the only riverboat on the West Coast with a genuine riverboat calliope), while the paddle wheel can be viewed best from the bar on the second deck. All food is prepared on board. Lunchers get a choice of three entrees such as prime rib, shrimp salad, and chicken in pastry. At dinner, the choice is of four entrees, and weekend brunch is a buffet. Additionally, diners are treated to live piano music and the passing panorama of river scenery.

Santa Rosa

(Area Code 707)

VISITOR INFORMATION

Sonoma County Convention & Visitors Bureau *5000 Roberts Lake Rd. #A, Rohnert Park 94928, 586-8100, fax 586-8111.*

Sonoma County Farm Trails *P.O. Box 6032, Santa Rosa 95406, 996-2154.*

For a free map of area farms that sell directly to the consumer, send a stamped, self-addressed legal-size envelope. The map pinpoints the location of u-pick farms, as well as of farms that sell more unusual items such as fresh rabbits, pheasants, herbs, and mushrooms—even feather pillows and earthworms.

GETTING THERE

Located approximately 10 miles north of Petaluma via Highway 101.

ANNUAL EVENTS

Santa Rosa DixieJazz Festival *August. 539-3494, same fax. $15-$50.*

WHERE TO STAY

Doubletree Hotel Santa Rosa *3555 Round Barn Blvd., (800) 679-2242, 523-7555, fax 545-2807. 3 stories; 246 rooms; 170 non-smoking rooms; $$-$$$. Children under 18 free. Pool (heated in summer only), hot tub. Restaurant, room service (child items).*

Sprawled across one of the few hills in town, the facilities at this comfortable contemporary lodging include a 7.5-mile jogging trail. Guests also have access to golf and tennis facilities at a nearby country club.

Flamingo Resort Hotel & Fitness Center *2777 4th St./Hwy. 12, (800) 848-8300, 545-8530, fax 528-1404. 2 stories; 136 rooms; 100% non-smoking; $$-$$$+; 2-night min. on summer weekends. Children under 12 free. Heated pool, children's wading pool, hot tub, fitness center (fee), 5 tennis courts (fee). Restaurant, room service.*

When this spacious, unpretentious resort was originally built, it was out in the country. Now, due to urban sprawl, it is right in town. Providing all the comforts of a full-service resort, it also gives guests the convenience of a motel—parking just outside their room; not having to walk through a lobby—with the amenities of a hotel—a piano bar with live entertainment and dancing; express check-out. Facilities include a children's playground, shuffleboard, Ping Pong, and a lighted jogging path. The Olympic-size pool is heated year-round, and a state-of-the-art health club features sauna and steam rooms, basketball and volleyball courts, and massage service. Packages are available.

The Gables *4257 Petaluma Hill Rd., (800) GABLES-N, 585-7777, fax 584-5634. 2 stories; 7 rooms, 1 cottage; 100% non-smoking; $$$-$$$+; 2-night min. on Sat. Unsuitable for children under 12. No TVs; 1 kitchen; 2 wood-burning fireplaces, 2 gas fireplaces. Afternoon snack, full breakfast.*

Named for the 15 gables that crown this 1877 high Victorian Gothic revival house, featuring unusual key hole-shaped windows and 12-foot ceilings, this inn welcomes guests with spacious rooms furnished with antiques and claw-foot tubs. Among its unusual features are three Italian marble fireplaces that were shipped around the Horn and a steep mahogany spiral staircase. In the horse and buggy days, governors and legislators stopped their wagons here for country hospitality. More house history is found in the parlour, where historic photos of the house and a copy of a thesis on the house written by a Sonoma State professor are available for perusal and quilt pieces made by the original owner are displayed as wall decorations. The house is set on 3½ acres in a rural area reminiscent of the south of France; the original outhouse and a 150-year-old barn remain, and a bucolic deck invites sun worship. All this and one of Northern California's best inn breakfasts, too.

Hotel La Rose *308 Wilson St., (800) LAROSE-8, 579-3200, fax 579-3247. 4 stories; 49 rooms; 41 non-smoking rooms; $$$. Children under 13 free. Continental breakfast; restaurant, room service.*

Conveniently located in Railroad Square, this tasteful hotel was built in 1907 of cut stone quarried from the area now known as **Annadel State Park.** A National Historic Landmark, it combines turn-of-the-century charm with modern conveniences. Rooms are stylishly decorated and furnished with English country antiques and reproductions. Many rooms on the top floor feature pitched ceilings, and some have private balconies. A communal sun deck is available for relaxation.

Vintners Inn *4350 Barnes Rd., (800) 421-2584, 575-7350, fax 575-1426. 2 stories; 44 rooms; 100% non-smoking; $$$-$$$+; 2-night min. on Sat. Children under 5 free. 23 wood-burning fireplaces. Hot tub. Continental breakfast; restaurant, room service.*

This elegant country inn is surrounded by a 45-acre working vineyard. Located in three separate buildings, the rooms are all decorated with European antiques. The inn's restaurant is the highly acclaimed **John Ash & Co.** *(527-7687; $$$. Highchairs.).*

WHERE TO EAT

Santa Rosa is where John A. McDougall, author of The McDougall Plan for Super Health and Life-Long Weight Loss *and promoter of heart-healthy eating, makes his home. It is interesting to note his influence on this area. Most, if not all, of the restaurants have at least one heart-healthy item on the menu. Many have more. Surprisingly, even small fast-food spots such as the* **Sonoma Taco Shop** *(100 Brookwood St., in Creekside Ctr., 525-8585.), with its impressive 33 heart-healthy options, can be counted on to satisfy this need.*

Mixx *135 Fourth St., (800) 571-2283, 573-1344, fax 573-1344. L M-F, D daily; $$. Highchairs, boosters, booths, child menu. 100% non-smoking. Reservations advised. AE, MC, V.*

This restaurant is oversize in every way: seating, ceiling (20-feet high), wine glasses, food flavor. Sitting beneath the drooping lily light fixtures at one of the substantial tables feels great. Drinks can be ordered from a full bar, which as it happens is not just any bar. Built in the late 1800s in Italy, it was shipped around Cape Horn in 1904 and has been here ever since. In fact, the building has been either a bar or restaurant since that opening date. And then there is the food. Prepared by owner-chef Dan Berman and his wife Kathleen, who is the pastry chef, the eclectic menu designed to satisfy all stages of hunger is a delight. Appetizers include a spicy, complexly flavored puréed soup of guajillo chile, roasted tomato, and smoked chicken, and a perfect house salad of local greens accented colorfully with edible flowers. With preference given to ingredients available locally, the dinner menu features some relatively unusual items such as venison and free-range veal, this latter prepared memorably with a whole grain mustard sauce and garnish of garlicky, crisp Yukon gold potatoes. The restaurant is deservedly famous for its house-made ice creams and sorbets, and the crème brulee just might be the world's best.

Omelette Express *112 Fourth St., 525-1690. B & L daily; $. Highchairs, boosters, child items. 100% non-smoking. No reservations. AE, MC, V.*

Located in Railroad Square, this airy, popular cafe seats diners at old-fashioned oak tables on pressed-back chairs. All omelettes are available with egg whites only, and hamburgers, sandwiches, and a variety of salads are also on the menu.

Peter Rabbit's Chocolate Factory™ *2489 Guerneville Rd./Fulton Rd., (800) 4-R-CANDY, 575-7110, fax 579-5663. Tu-Sat 10-6.*

Located on the outskirts of town, in a building that belies the cute name, this candy store is worth seeking out. Visitors can usually observe some yummy or other being whipped up on huge marble slabs located adjacent to the retail area. Among the over 120 goodies produced are nut brittles, salt water taffy, and caramel corn that seems to get better with age. There are even chocolate-dipped prunes. Should addiction occur, everything is available by mail order.

Thursday Night Market *On Fourth St. & B St. Thur 5-8; May-Sept only. Free.*

At this festive event, local restaurants serve up inexpensive portions of barbecued turkey legs, sausage, kebobs, burgers, and oysters along with salads, calzone, chile, and burritos. Farmers are also on hand with fresh produce, arts and craftspeople display their wares, and plenty of street entertainers do their thing.

Willie Bird's Restaurant *1150 Santa Rosa Ave., 542-0861. B, L, & D daily; $-$$. Highchairs, boosters, child menu. 100% non-smoking. AE, MC, V.*

This casual, old-time restaurant celebrates Thanksgiving every day by serving their own tasty, natural brand of turkey in varied forms. Try the Willie Bird Special—the traditional turkey feast—or something more unusual, such as turkey scallopini or turkey sausage. Children's portions include a turkey hamburger and turkey hot dog. Plenty of non-turkey items are also available.

WHAT TO DO

CA Welcome Center *5000 Roberts Lake Rd., Rohnert Park, 3 mi. south of town, (800) 939-7666, 586-3795, fax 586-1383. Daily 9-5.*

Get oriented to this area's attractions and do some free wine tasting here. Local wines and foods are for sale, and special events are often scheduled.

Howarth Memorial Park *Summerfield Rd., access from Sonoma Ave. & Montgomery Dr., 543-3282. Rides: in summer Tu-Sun 11-4; in spring & fall Sat & Sun only. Closed Nov-Jan. 75¢-$1.*

There is something for everyone in this scenic park. Children especially enjoy the free playground, but, of course, also love the rides with an admission fee: miniature train ride, animal barn, pony rides, and merry-go-round. Paddle boat, rowboat, and sailboat rentals are available by **Lake Ralphine,** and hiking trails and tennis courts round out the facilities.

Luther Burbank Home & Gardens *Santa Rosa Ave./Sonoma Ave., 524-5445, fax 543-3030. Gardens: Daily 8-7; Nov-Mar to 5. Free. Museum & House Tours: W-Sun 10-4; closed Apr-Oct. Museum free; House Tours: adults $2, under 12 free.*

During his 50-year horticultural career, Luther Burbank developed over 800 new plants. This memorial garden displays many of his achievements, including a plumcot tree, the ornamental Shasta daisy, and a warren of spineless cacti. (He also developed the Santa Rosa plum and elephant garlic.) Burbank is buried here in an unmarked grave. Tours of his greenhouse and modified Greek revival-style home, which retains its original furnishings, last ½ hour. The adjacent **Carriage House Museum** offers annual exhibits related to Burbank's life and work.

Matanzas Creek Winery *6097 Bennett Valley Rd., 5 mi. east of Hwy. 101 (call for directions), (800) 590-6464, 528-6464, fax 571-0156. Tasting (fee $2) & tours daily 10-4:30.*

Located way off the beaten track, back in some rolling foothills far away from other enterprise, this winery farms several acres for lavender. In fact, it is the state's largest producer of lavender and grows both the Provence variety for cooking and the Grosso variety for scenting soaps and oils. Peak bloom is in June, and an assortment of products made with the bounty, including handmade soap and sachets, are sold in the gift shop. Additionally, the winery tasting room is surrounded by a beautifully maintained garden sprinkled with modern sculpture and several fountains, and two llamas are housed off the parking lot. A picnic area is available.

Railroad Square *Centered at Fourth St./Davis St., 578-8478.*

Now a national historic district, this area is thick with antique stores, restaurants, and specialty shops.

Redwood Empire Ice Arena *1667 W. Steele Lane, 546-7147. Open daily; call for schedule. Adults $5.50, under 12 $4.50, skate rental $2.*

Built in 1969, this ice skating rink has been called "the most beautiful ice arena in the world." Since it is owned by cartoonist Charles Schulz, the Alpine decor is unexpected. However, the fast-food coffee shop does have a few stained-glass windows depicting Snoopy.

Located adjacent, **Snoopy's Gallery and Gift Shop** *(546-3385. Daily 10-6.)* purveys the largest selection of "Peanuts" merchandise in the world. Cuddly Snoopys are available in sizes ranging from four inches to five feet. Copies of original "Peanuts" columns, matted and framed, are also available. Above the shop is a small museum containing Schulz's awards and some of his favorite drawings, as well as an assortment of other interesting items. Schulz has an office on the premises and is frequently sighted by skaters.

Each December the rink is converted into a theater for a special **Christmas Show,** when Snoopy always makes an appearance on ice skates. Some ice-side tables are available, and tickets sell out fast *(546-3385).*

Robert L. Ripley Memorial Museum *492 Sonoma Ave., 524-5233. W-Sun 10-4. Closed Nov-Mar. Adults $1.50, 7-18 75¢.*

Believe it or not, Robert Ripley was born, raised, and buried in Santa Rosa! Dedicated to his memory, this museum displays a wax reincarnation of Ripley as well as some of his original drawings and personal effects. A few oddities mentioned in his columns are also displayed, including stuffed Siamese twin calves and a 45-inch white rhinoceros horn that some suspicious types claim is actually wood. The museum is located inside the **Church of One Tree**, which was built in 1873 from the wood of a single redwood tree!

The beautifully landscaped gardens of **Julliard Park** are just outside. A self-guided tour of the park's unusual trees can be enjoyed with the help of a brochure available at the museum.

Sonoma County Museum *425 Seventh St., 579-1500, fax 579-4849. W-Sun 11-4. Adults $2, 65+ & 13-19 $1.*

Located inside the city's beautifully restored 1910 post office building, this museum exhibits material relating to the county's history.

Victorian Homes.

To view some lovely Victorian mansions, drive along MacDonald Avenue in the older part of town.

Guerneville and Russian River Area
(Area Code 707)

A LITTLE BACKGROUND

Once upon a time, in 1809, a party of Russians and Aleuts from the Russian-American Fur Company in Sitka landed at the mouth of what is now the Russian River. They named it "Slavianka," or "little beauty." In recognition of the Russian influence in the area, it was later referred to as the "Russian" River.

In the '20s and '30s the area became a summer resort favored by wealthy San Franciscans who traveled here by ferry and train. Then it faded in popularity and became a pleasant and uncrowded retreat. Today, slowly recovering from a state of decay, it is regaining its former popularity. The atmosphere is easy going, and it is acceptable to dine anywhere in casual clothing.

Guerneville, the hub of the Russian River resort area, is surrounded by many smaller towns. There are numerous public beaches, and many more are privately owned. There are also some unofficial nude beaches. Inquire in town about how to find, or avoid, them.

VISITOR INFORMATION

Russian River Region Visitors Bureau *P.O. Box 255 (14034 Armstrong Woods Rd.), Guerneville 95446, (800) 253-8800, 869-9212, fax 869-9215.*

Russian River Wine Road map *P.O. Box 46, Healdsburg 95448, (800) 723-6336, 433-6782.*

This free map provides details on wineries and lodgings stretching from Forestville to Cloverdale.

GETTING THERE

Located approximately 15 miles west of Santa Rosa. Take Highway 12 west to Highway 116. For a more scenic route take the River Road exit just north of Santa Rosa and follow it west.

ANNUAL EVENTS

Russian River Wine Road Barrel Tasting *March. 433-6782.*

Participants are permitted to get behind the scenes in wine-making and sample special wines that aren't normally available for tasting. Wineries provide tastes of wines still in the barrel, as well as some new vintages and old library treasures.

Apple Blossom Festival *April. In Sebastopol; 824-0501, fax 823-8439. Adults $5, 55+ $2, 6-12 $1.*

Scheduled each year to occur when the area's plentiful apple orchards are snowy white with blossoms, this festival includes a parade down Main Street and plenty of booths purveying apple-related crafts and foods.

Bohemian Grove *Last 2 weeks of July.*

Many of the world's most powerful political, military, and corporate leaders meet at this 2,700-acre private resort. The public is not invited.

Gravenstein Apple Fair *August. In Sebastopol; 996-2154, fax 996-2136. Adults $5, 5-12 $1.*

Held on and off since the turn of the century, this old-time country fair is staged amid the large, shady oak trees and rolling hills of **Ragle Ranch Park**. The fair specifically celebrates the flavorful, crisp, early-ripening Gravenstein apple, an old German variety dating from 1790 that is indigenous to the area and well-known for making the best juices and pies. In fact, this area is known as the world's Gravenstein capital. Fun at the fair is of the down-home variety, with opportunities to taste apples, observe bee-keepers in action, and pet a variety of farm animals. Apples and related foods and products are available for purchase directly from farmers. Proceeds fund the printing of the Sonoma County Farm Trails map.

Russian River Jazz Festival *September. In Guerneville; 869-3940. $28-$37, under 11 free.*

Music festivals don't get much more casual than this one. Audience members can actually float in the placid river on an inner tube while listening to a range of jazz. It's a good idea to pack an ice chest and picnic basket, but food and drink are available for sale. Note that no bottles or cans are permitted.

WHERE TO STAY

Applewood *13555 Hwy. 116, (800) 555-8509, 869-9093, fax 869-9170. 3 stories; 16 rooms; 100% non-smoking; $$$-$$$+; 2-night min. on weekends. Unsuitable for children under 21. 7 gas fireplaces. Heated pool (May-Oct only), hot tub. Full breakfast; restaurant.*

Built in 1922 as a private home, this mission revival-style mansion is now a county historical landmark. It is situated on six acres and features an idyllic pool area surrounded by mature vineyards and tall redwood trees. The hot tub is wonderful at night, especially when all the stars are out. Public tennis courts, located adjacent to the property, are reached via a short walk through a valley still populated with apple trees that once comprised an orchard. The inn's decor is tasteful and unfussy, and rooms are spacious and comfortable, with aesthetically pleasing touches such as down comforters, fragrant apple soap, and apple-green walls and towels. Some rooms have private patios or balconies overlooking the vineyards and peaceful pastures beyond. Breakfast is simple, yet special—perhaps a sectioned grapefruit topped with a perfect red maraschino cherry, followed by beautifully presented eggs Florentine prepared with tender baby spinach fresh from the inn's own garden. On warm days it can be enjoyed outdoors by the pool.

Enticing fixed-price four-course **dinners** *($30. Tu-Sat. Reservations essential. AE, MC, V.)* are prepared by the inn's creative owners and available to non-guests. There is only one seating. One menu enjoyed here began with Italian-style wild mushroom soup with vermouth, followed by hearts of romaine and butter lettuce dressed with a Parmesan-balsamic vinaigrette. The main course was succulent Tuscan roast chicken with potatoes and green beans. A dense

Drunken Chocolate Cake, served with a glass of port and followed by French roast coffee, completed the leisurely, very romantic meal. Local wineries are well represented on the wine list.

Creekside Inn & Resort *16180 Neeley Rd., (800) 776-6586, 869-3623, fax 869-1417. 2 stories; 16 units; 9 non-smoking units; $$-$$$; 2-night min. on weekends. Children under 2 free. 1 VCR; 10 kitchens; 7 wood-burning fireplaces; some shared baths. Unheated pool (unavail. Nov-Mar). Full breakfast (B&B rooms only).*

Located a short stroll from town, just across the historic town bridge, this quiet resort dates back to the '30s. Guests have a choice of lodgings. The main house operates as a B&B, with six rooms sharing two bathrooms. Nine modernized housekeeping cottages feature attractive half-timbered exteriors. One of the nicest is the Tree House, which derives its name from the fact that trees can be observed from every window. RV spaces are also available. Facilities include a large outdoor pool area with a barbecue, horseshoe pit, pool table, Ping Pong table, croquet lawn, and lending library. When rains are normal, Pocket Canyon Creek provides the soothing sound of running water as it meanders through the property.

Highland Dell Inn *21050 River Blvd., Monte Rio, (800) 767-1759, 865-1759, fax 865-4128. 3 stories; 8 rooms; 100% non-smoking; $$-$$$+; 2-night min. on Sat. Closed Jan. Unsuitable for children under 21. 3 VCRs; 1 wood-burning fireplace. Unheated pool (unavail. Nov-Apr). Full breakfast. Small dogs welcome.*

Perched in a quiet spot high above the banks of the Russian River, this inn dates back to 1906. It resembles an old Black Forest-style German hunting lodge, with antiques and historic photographs of local sites combined in an interesting decor. A lobby with soaring ceiling, enormous fireplace, and grand staircase greets guests, and a comfortably furnished sitting room with a wall of windows overlooking the river invites lingering over morning coffee or an afternoon liqueur. The cozy European feel continues with uneven floors, uniquely decorated yet unfussy rooms, and a cheery skylighted breakfast room. Rooms are furnished with comfortable mattresses and plenty of pillows, and some have claw-foot tubs populated with bright yellow rubber duckies. Breakfast often includes puffy German pancakes (sometimes called Dutch babies), a fabulous bacon, and excellent hash browns. With advance notice, cholesterol-free egg whites-only dishes and other special orders can be prepared. Two- to four-course dinners *($14-$27.50)* are sometimes available to guests. Surrounded by tall redwoods, a pool with a small waterfall is particularly inviting in summer.

Johnson's Beach & Resort *16241 First St., 869-2022. 20 rooms; $. Closed Nov-Apr. 7 kitchens.*

These old-time hotel rooms are adjacent to the river. Week-long rentals are discounted, and campsites are also available. Facilities include two rustic wooden swings, a large tire sandbox, pool and Ping Pong tables, and access to one of the best-equipped beaches in the area. A snack bar and both boat and beach paraphernalia rentals are available.

Ridenhour Ranch House Inn *12850 River Rd., (888) 877-4466, 887-1033, fax 869-2967. 2 stories; 8 rooms; 100% non-smoking; $$-$$$; 2-night min. on weekends. Children under 5 free. 5 TVs; 1 wood-burning fireplace, 1 wood-burning stove. Hot tub. Afternoon snack, full breakfast.*

Built of redwood in 1906, this canary-yellow ranch house was constructed by the first settlers in the area. Decorated with English and American antiques, the house has six guest rooms. Two more rooms are available in an adjacent cottage dating from 1934. Recreational facilities include a hot tub pleasantly situated beneath sheltering trees, a badminton area, and a croquet lawn. Across the highway, secluded beaches can be reached via a short walk down a lane lined with blackberry bushes. An expansive breakfast is prepared each morning in a restaurant-style kitchen by the Austrian owner-chef, who warns his guests, "If you don't eat well in the morning, you don't look well at the wineries." So he offers wonderful treats such as homemade Graven-stein applesauce and fruit preserves, gigantic croissants, a fruit smoothie with a touch of brandy from neighboring Korbel winery, a wonderfully light bread pudding, and some sort of egg dish—perhaps eggs Florentine—made with eggs collected from the ranch's own hens. Fresh cookies and sherry are always available in the living room, which is also well-equipped with games and reading matter. A highly recommended four-course dinner *($35)* is occasionally offered. It is available only to ranch guests, who must reserve their spot in advance.

Rio Villa Beach Resort *20292 Hwy. 116, Monte Rio, 865-1143, fax 865-0115. 2 stories; 12 rooms, 2 cabins; 10 non-smoking rooms; $$-$$$; 2-night min. on weekends May-Oct. Children under 2 free. 2 VCRs; 8 kitchens; 2 wood-burning fireplaces. Continental breakfast on weekends.*

Some of the rooms at this peaceful spot have private balconies with river views. Guests can relax on a large deck area surrounded by manicured grounds overlooking the river and enjoy a private beach.

Riverlane Resort *16320 First St., (800) 201-2324, 869-2323. 1 story; 12 cabins; $-$$; 2-night min. on weekends. Children under 3 free. All kitchens; 6 wood-burning fireplaces, 5 wood-burning stoves. Heated pool (unavail. Oct-Apr), hot tub.*

Located by the river, this pleasant enclave of cabins offers river access.

Village Inn *20822 River Blvd., Monte Rio, (800) 303-2303, 865-2304. 15 rooms; $-$$$; 2-night min. on weekends July-Sept. Some rooms suitable for children; children under 2 free. 13 TVs; 1 kitchen; some shared baths. Continental breakfast; restaurant, room service.*

Built as a summer home in 1906, this rustic structure was turned into a hotel in 1908 and has remained one ever since. A worthy claim to fame is that *Holiday Inn,* starring Bing Crosby, was filmed here. Lodging facilities vary from small sleeping rooms to suites with a riverfront deck. In summer the restaurant serves a popular Sunday brunch outdoors on a pleasant deck overlooking the river.

House Rentals.

Call the Visitors Bureau for the names of realty companies that rent private homes to vaca-tioners.

WHERE TO EAT

Burdons *15405 River Rd., 869-2615. D Thur-M; $$. Closed Jan. Boosters, child menu. 100% non-smoking. Reservations advised on weekends. AE, MC, V.*

The American-continental menu here features reliably well-prepared steaks, chops, and prime rib—the house specialty. Diners will also find pastas and fresh local fish on the menu, as well as a particularly tender rack of lamb featuring tiny chops garnished with green mint sauce and a side of creamy scalloped potatoes. All dinners come with house-made soup and a crisp tossed green or spinach salad. Dessert choices, which change daily, sometimes include a deli-cious strawberry shortcake made with tasty berries, a homemade biscuit, and the lightest whipped cream imaginable. Further enhancing the dining experience, the walls of the simple dining room are decorated with the chef's colorful, whimsical paintings.

Cazanoma Lodge *1000 Kidd Creek Rd., Cazadero, 3 mi. west of town, 632-5255, fax 632-5256. D (seasonal), SunBr; $$. Closed Dec-Feb. Highchairs, boosters, child portions. 100% non-smoking. Reservations advised. AE, MC, V.*

Nestled between two creeks in a protected valley, this 1926 lodge is reached via a one-mile-long dirt road. German specialties—barbecue spareribs, several schnitzels, a sausage platter with sauerkraut—are on the menu along with American fare. But the really unusual item here is **catch-your-own-trout**. That's right. Customers here have the option of catching it themselves from a well-stocked spring-fed trout pond—to make sure it's really *fresh*. For the unimpressed, the kitchen will do the job with a net. The dining room offers great views of the tranquil forest setting, and in warm weather a large deck under the redwoods is irresistible. Live music is usually scheduled on weekends.

Cabins and lodge rooms *(2 stories; 4 rooms, 2 cabins; 2 non-smoking rooms; $$-$$$; 2-night min. on Sat May-Sept. Children under 12 free. No TVs; 2 kitchens; 2 wood-burning fireplaces. Unheated pool (unavail. Oct-May). Evening snack, continental breakfast. Dogs welcome in cabins.)* are also available. Among the features on the 147 acres are a man-made waterfall, a swimming pool, and two miles of hiking trails.

Mom's Apple Pie *4550 Hwy. 116 N., Sebastopol, 823-8330. L & D daily; $. 1 highchair. MC, V.*

Located near the intersection of Highways 12 and 116, this little lunch counter is worth a stop for the tasty homemade soup and pie. Fried chicken and sandwiches are also available.

The Occidental Two *In Occidental.*

Both of these restaurants serve bountiful multi-course, family-style Italian dinners. They have highchairs, booster seats, and a reasonable plate charge for small children. Prices are moderate, and inexpensive ravioli and spaghetti dinners with fewer side dishes are also available. Reservations are suggested at prime dining times during the summer, and on weekends and holidays year-round. Both accept American Express, MasterCard, and Visa. People come to these restaurants to eat BIG. Picking a favorite can prove fattening.

• **Negri's**   *3700 Main St., 823-5301, fax 874-2158.*

Meals here start with a steaming bowl of minestrone soup, rounds of moist salami, and a hunk of crusty Italian bread. Then come more plates bearing pickled vegetables, marinated bean salad, creamy large-curd cottage cheese, and a salad tossed with Thousand Island dressing. When tummies begin to settle, the ravioli arrives—stuffed with spinach and topped with an excellent tomato-meat sauce. Then the entree arrives: a choice of crispy, moist fried chicken, saucy duck, or grilled porterhouse steak. (Seafood entrees are available on weeknights.) Entrees are served with a side of thick French fries and heavy zucchini pancakes. Then come the doggie bags. For those with room, apple fritters are available at additional charge.

• **Union Hotel**   *3731 Main St., 874-3555, fax 874-3662. L & D daily. 100% non-smoking.*

In operation since 1876, this restaurant seats 400 people in three enormous dining rooms and on an outdoor patio. Simplicity seems to be the key to its success. The entree choice is limited to roasted chicken, chicken cacciatora, duck, or steak. Side dishes include an antipasto plate of marinated kidney beans, cheese, and salami, plus minestrone soup, a delicious salad with light Thousand Island dressing, ravioli, zucchini fritters, potatoes, a fresh vegetable, and bread and butter. Dessert—apple fritters, spumoni ice cream, or apple pie—and coffee are extra.

River Inn Restaurant *16141 Main St., 869-0481. B, L, & D daily; $-$$. Closed Nov-Mar. Highchairs, boosters, booths, child portions. 100% non-smoking. No reservations. AE, MC, V.*

Extensive menu choices at breakfast include crisp waffles, thin Swedish pancakes, perfect French toast, omelettes, oatmeal, and fresh fruit. At lunch and dinner, just about everything imaginable is available. All this in a casual coffee shop atmosphere with many comfy booths.

Russian River Vineyards Restaurant *5700 Hwy. 116, Forestville, (800) TOPOLOS, 887-1562, fax 887-1399. L M-Sat, D daily, SunBr; closed M & Tu in winter; $$. Highchairs, boosters, child portions. 100% non-smoking. Reservations advised. AE, MC, V.*

In good weather, diners are seated outdoors in an attractive area shaded by grape arbors and umbrellas. In colder weather, tables are available inside the attractive converted farm house housing the restaurant. Greek dishes are the specialty, but extensive use is made of local ingredients, and a hamburger is on the lunch menu. A large selection of the winery's own vintages are available by the glass. This is the only family-owned and -operated winery-restaurant in the state.

A stop in at the adjacent tiny tasting room operated by the **Topolos at Russian River Vineyards** *(887-1575. Tasting daily 11-5:30; tours by appt.)* is recommended. Of special interest are the Zinfandels and the unusual, rich Alicante Bouschet. Children are served sparkling apple cider while their parents taste.

WHAT TO DO

Armstrong Redwoods State Reserve *17000 Armstrong Woods Rd., 869-2015. Daily 8am-1 hr. after sunset. $5/vehicle.*

A Visitors Center orients hikers to the trail system within this park. A free parking lot is located there, just outside the toll gate, and there is no admission fee for those who park their cars and walk in.

The **Armstrong Woods Pack Station** *(887-2939. Riders must be 10 or older or have guide's permission. Reservations required.)* offers trail rides *($35-$45)* and full-day lunch rides *($80-$90)*. One- and two-night pack trips *($300-$400)* are also available May through October.

Almost four miles further—at the end of a narrow, steep, winding road—**Austin Creek State Recreation Area** offers 20 miles of hiking trails, as well as rustic camping facilities and four hike-in campsites.

Duncans Mills *On Hwy. 116, 10 mi. west of Guerneville.*

Once a lumber village, this tiny town is now home to a collection of shops, a deli, a restaurant, a riverside campground with private beach, and a stable where horses can be rented.

J's Amusements *16101 Neeley Rd., 869-3102. Daily in summer; Sat & Sun, Sept & Mar-June. Closed in winter. $1.50-$3.75/ride.*

Various kiddie rides and entertainments await families in search of cheap thrills. Among them are a rickety mini-roller coaster, a tilt-a-whirl, a waterslide, and a 36-hole miniature golf course.

Kozlowski Farms *5566 Hwy. 116 N., Forestville, (800) 4-R-FARMS, 887-1587, fax 887-9650. Daily 9-5.*

This scenic farm is planted with 25 acres of apple trees and assorted berries. In season, the produce can be purchased in bulk. Homemade juices, berry vinegars, wine jellies, berry jams and fruit butters made without sugar, and much more are available year-round at the farm's barn outlet. A mail-order catalogue is also available.

Pet-A-Llama Ranch *5505 Lone Pine Rd., Sebastopol, 823-9395. Sat & Sun 10-4. Closed Jan-Mar. Adults $3, children $1, feed 50¢.*

Spread over 15 acres, this ranch is home to a herd of about 20 llamas. They love being petted and love it even more when someone purchases a cup of feed for them. Picnic tables are set up under trees adjacent to their pens. The farmhouse's garage doubles as a crafts shop, purveying items handmade with llama wool (shawls, blankets, hats). Sometimes fleece collected from a favorite llama is also available, and spinning wheels and drop spindles are displayed.

Swimming.

Anywhere along the banks of the Russian River is bound to be nice to lay a blanket. A prime spot is under the **Monte Rio bridge**, where parking and beach access are free. Another choice spot is **Johnson's Beach** (see page 202). Canoe and paddle boat rentals and snack stands are available at both. The riverbed and beaches are covered with pebbles, so waterproof shoes are advised.

A good game to play with children here is "Find the Siamese Twin Clam Shells." Be prepared with a special prize for the kid who finds the most intact pairs.

Wineries.

• **Korbel Champagne Cellars** *13250 River Rd., 887-2294, fax 869-2981. Tasting daily 10-4; tours daily 10-3, on the hour. Free rose garden tours Apr-Oct only, Tu-Sun at 11 & 3.*

The nation's oldest producer of methode champenoise champagne, this century-old winery also produces brandy and wine. Eight kinds of champagne can be tasted, and chilled splits, as well as minimal deli supplies, are available for impromptu picnics.

The grounds are landscaped with beautifully maintained flower gardens. An **Antique Rose Garden**, faithfully restored to its turn-of-the-century beauty, is filled with old-time flowers such as coral bells, primroses, and violets, as well as some more unusual plants. Among the more than 250 varieties of roses are rare specimens such as the original Burbank Tea, the Double Musk celebrated in Shakespeare's plays, and the True Ambassador, which was once thought to be extinct.

• **Mark West Estate Winery** *7010 Trenton-Healdsburg Rd., off River Rd., Forestville, 544-4813, fax 836-0147. Tasting daily 10-5:30; tours by appt.*

Located off the beaten path, back among some scenic vineyards and up on a little hill, this winery can be difficult to find. Do call ahead for directions. The winery is known for its use of only organic grapes and produces an unusual dry Gewurztraminer. Picnic tables are provided on a shaded lawn, and some deli items are available for purchase.

Just behind the tasting room, **California Carnivores** *(7020 Trenton-Healdsburg Rd., Forestville, 838-1630. Daily 10-4; call ahead in bad weather. Free.)* operates their unusual business out of a greenhouse. Over 500 varieties of insect-eating plants are raised, fed, and sold here. They include inexpensive Venus fly traps as well as more exotic varieties—one of which resembles the star of the movie *The Little Shop of Horrors.* According to the *New York Times* it is "a botanical museum." The *San Francisco Examiner* calls it an "arresting assemblage."

Healdsburg

(Area Code 707)

VISITOR INFORMATION

Healdsburg Area Chamber of Commerce *217 Healdsburg Ave., Healdsburg 95448, (800) 648-9922, 433-6935.*

GETTING THERE

Located 12 miles north of Santa Rosa.

ANNUAL EVENTS

World Croquet Championship Finals *May. In Windsor, 528-1181. Free, except day of the tournament when tickets cost approximately $175.*

Spectators are welcome to view the championships held at **Sonoma-Cutrer Vineyards** *(4401 Slusser Rd.; Tasting & tours by appt.)*, and picnics are de rigueur.

Pumpkin Festival *Last 3 weekends in October. At **Westside Farms** (7097 Westside Rd., 7 mi. south of town); 431-1432, fax 431-9433. $5/family.*

Visitors to this especially family-friendly event, held on a scenic old-time farm, enjoy hayrides and other down-home activities. A variety of farm animals are on hand, and a picnic area is provided. In addition to several varieties of pumpkins, both gourds and Indian corn are available for purchase. The farm is also open year-round by appointment.

WHERE TO STAY

Camellia Inn *211 North St., (800) 727-8182, 433-8182, fax 433-8130. 2 stories; 9 rooms; 100% non-smoking; $$-$$$; 2-night min. on Sat. Children under 2 free. No TVs; 4 gas fireplaces. Heated pool (unavail. Nov-Apr). Afternoon snack, full breakfast.*

Situated just two blocks from the town square, this 1869 Italianate Victorian townhouse offers a quiet retreat. The grounds surrounding the inn are planted with over 50 varieties of camellia, some of which were given to the original owner by Luther Burbank. In keeping with the theme, each room is named for a camellia variety. The tastefully furnished, high-ceilinged Royalty Room boasts an antique Scottish high bed with a ceiling-hung canopy and step stool. Originally the home's dining room, it also features an unusual ornate antique brass sink fitting. Several rooms have whirlpool bathtubs for two. An afternoon out by the oak-shaded, villa-style pool area is incredibly relaxing. Breakfast is served buffet-style in the dining room, where guests are seated at a large claw-foot mahogany table.

Dry Creek Inn *198 Dry Creek Rd., (800) 222-5784, 433-0300, fax 433-1129. 3 stories; 102 rooms; 85 non-smoking rooms; $$. Children under 12 free. Heated pool (unheated Nov-Mar), hot tub, fitness room. Continental breakfast; restaurant. Pets welcome ($10).*

Part of the Best Western chain, this is an attractive contemporary motel. All guests are greeted with a complimentary bottle of wine in their room.

Madrona Manor *1001 Westside Rd., (800) 258-4003, 433-4231, fax 433-0703. 3 stories; 21 rooms; 100% non-smoking; $$$-$$$+; 2-night min. Apr-Nov. Children under 12 stay free. No TVs; 13 wood-burning fireplaces, 4 gas fireplaces. Heated pool (unavail. Apr-Nov), hot tub. Full breakfast; restaurant. Dogs welcome in some rooms.*

Featuring an unusual mansard roof, this majestic mansion is situated off a sideroad that runs through rural vineyards. An imposing archway frames the long driveway leading up to the eight-acre estate. Built in 1881 as a country retreat, it is now a protected historic site operating as an inn. Five rooms feature furniture original to the house, and a public music room boasts a square rosewood piano. Amenities include thick terry cloth robes and plenty of freshly baked cookies.

For dinner, guests need just stroll to the elegant dining rooms known as **Restaurant at Madrona Manor** *(D daily. Highchairs, boosters, child portions. 100% non-smoking. Reservations advised. AE, MC, V.)*, where chef Todd Muir, formerly of Berkeley's Chez Panisse, prepares wonderfully complex dishes—often using produce from the estate's own gardens and orchards—for the fixed-price four-course dinner *($45, $65 with wine)*. One dinner enjoyed here featured a delicious soft shell crab tempura and a dessert sampler of peach shortcake, peach crisp, and peach ice cream that was peachy-keen. Featuring local Sonoma vintages, the wine list actually has a table of contents! Outside seating is available on a heated terrace.

WHERE TO EAT

Healdsburg Charcuterie *335 Healdsburg Ave., 431-7213. L M-Sat, D daily; $. No reservations. No cards.*

With a light, French influenced menu, this casual spot is perfect for a quick meal. Particularly tasty salads, which are often the item of choice in this generally warm area, include one with strips of blackened chicken breast served over a lightly dressed Caesar salad, and the Sebastopol—toasted walnuts, cubes of apple, golden raisins, and Gorgonzola over baby greens with poppy seed dressing. Sandwiches and pastas are also available at lunch, and at dinner more substantial entrees—such as baked chicken and rabbit fricassée—are added.

Picnic Pick-Ups.

• **Costeaux French Bakery & Cafe** *417 Healdsburg Ave., 433-1913, fax 433-1955. B & L daily; $. Highchairs, child portions. 100% non-smoking. No reservations. MC, V.*

Family owned and operated since 1923, this is a great spot to pick up picnic supplies or ribbon-tied box lunches. Huge sandwiches are prepared on a choice of light deli rolls or other house-made breads, plus there are wonderful house-made soups, deli salads, sandwiches, and pizzas. The awe-inspiring selection of desserts includes a caramel-macadamia nut tart, several cheesecakes, and an assortment of fresh fruit tarts and French pastries. Seating is either in the airy, high-ceiling interior or outside on a pleasant sidewalk patio. And don't miss seeing the bathroom, which is papered attractively with authentic wine labels.

• **Downtown Bakery & Creamery** *308-A Center St., 431-2719, fax 431-1579. M-F 6am-5:30, Sat & Sun 7-5:30.*

Co-owner Lindsey Shere did time in the kitchen at Berkeley's renowned Chez Panisse. She also wrote the best-selling cookbook *Chez Panisse Desserts*. So the exceptional breads, pastries, and ice creams produced in her kitchen here are not a complete surprise. When available, the focaccia, sticky buns, fruit turnovers, and fig newtons are not to be missed. And on warm Wine Country days, it is a refreshing pleasure to indulge in one of the shop's old-fashioned milk shakes or sundaes.

• **Dry Creek General Store** *3495 Dry Creek Rd., 433-4171, fax 433-0409. Daily 7-6, to 7 in summer.*

This old-fashioned general store/deli opened in 1881 and is now a state historical landmark. Claiming to be "the best deli by a dam site!," it is located by a dam site (the Warm Springs Dam) and it sure does dispense good picnic fare! Sandwiches are made to order, and there are plenty of house-made salads and garnishes.

• **Jimtown Store** *6706 Hwy. 128, 433-1212, fax 433-1252. M-Tu & Thur-F 6:30-3:30 (in summer to 5:30), Sat & Sun 8-5. Closed 2 weeks in Jan.*

Dating back to the late 1800s, this landmark general store specializes in preparing great picnics that can be enjoyed right on their patio or taken along to a winery. Among the eclectic gourmet sandwiches: Brie with olive salad, lamb with fig tapenade, roast turkey with balsamic onions. But ham and cheese, chicken salad, and peanut butter & jelly are also available. Picnic hampers are available for loan, complete with suggestions about where to find the perfect picnic spot. Antiques, folk art, and local products are also for sale.

WHAT TO DO

Healdsburg Veterans Memorial Beach *13839 Old Redwood Hwy., 433-1625. Daily 7am-8pm; June-Sept only. $3/vehicle.*

This is a choice spot to swim in the warm Russian River, which in summer has an average water temperature of 70 to 75 degrees. A lifeguard is on duty from 10, and canoe and inner tube rentals are available. Facilities include a diving board, children's wading area, a picnic area with barbecues, and a snack bar. Sunbathers have a choice of a large sandy beach or a shady lawn area.

Timber Crest Farms *4791 Dry Creek Rd., 433-8251, fax 433-8255. M-F 8-5, Sat 10-4.*

The high-quality dried fruits and dried tomatoes available here are made without sulfur, preservatives, or additives. The usual are available as well as the unusual—tropical starfruit, black Bing cherries, mission figs—and a bottled mixture of Dried Tomato Spice Medley is wonderful on crackers. Sometimes it is possible to observe the produce being harvested or prepared for packaging.

W.C. "Bob" Trowbridge Canoe Trips *20 Healdsburg Ave., (800) 640-1386, 433-7247, fax 433-6384. Check-in daily 8-12:30, Apr-Oct only. $39/canoe/day. Children must be 6 or older. Dinner: Adults $7.95, under 13 $5.95. Reservations necessary.*

The canoe fee for these unguided trips includes life jackets, paddles, and canoe transport. An after-canoeing barbecue takes place from 4 to 7 each weekend and includes steak or chicken, vegetable, baked beans, salad, garlic bread, and beverage. Trowbridge has five other rental sites along the river. A two-day trip is also available.

Windsor Waterworks & Slides *8225 Conde Lane, Windsor, 6 mi. south of town, 838-7760, fax 838-7690. M-F 11-7, Sat & Sun 10-7, June-Aug; 10-7 weekends only May & Sept. Closed Oct-Apr. Adults $11.95, 4-12 $10.95.*

In addition to several waterslides, this water-oriented facility holds a swimming pool, a wading pool, a volleyball court, a snack bar, and shaded picnic facilities.

WINERIES

Dry Creek Vineyard *3770 Lambert Bridge Rd., 3 mi. west of Hwy. 101, 433-1000. Tasting daily 10:30-4:30; no tours.*

Known for its Fume Blancs and Chenin Blancs, this winery has a cool, shady picnic area under a canopy of old pine and maple trees. A good time to visit is during the annual **Open House** *(Tickets $5)* held in June. That's the time to bring a picnic and celebrate the season with live music and wine tasting.

Foppiano Vineyards *12707 Old Redwood Hwy., 433-7272. Tasting daily 10-4:30; self-guided tour.*

Established in 1896, this family-owned winery offers a self-guided tour through the Chardonnay, Cabernet Sauvignon, and Petite Sirah vineyards. It takes about 30 minutes, and a free explanatory brochure is available in the tasting room.

Hop Kiln Winery *6050 Westside Rd., 433-6491, fax 433-8162. Tasting daily 10-5; no tours.*

This unique winery is reached by taking a quiet back road through miles of scenic vineyards. Wine tasting occurs inside a landmark 1905 hops-drying barn built by Italian stonemasons and once used to supply San Francisco breweries. Known for its big Zinfandels, the winery also produces unique Big Red and A Thousand Flowers blends. Two appealing picnic areas are available: One overlooks a duck pond and vineyards; the other is situated in the shade of a gigantic kadota fig tree planted in 1880.

Piper Sonoma *11447 Old Redwood Hwy., 433-8843. Tasting daily 10-5, Jan-Mar F-Sun only (fee $3-$5/glass); self-guided tours.*

Celebrated for its French-style champagnes, the lines of this ultra-modern winery are softened with attractive landscaping and a lily pond. A stop here allows killing the proverbial two birds with one stone. Park once, taste twice: The next winery is located just across the way.

Rodney Strong Vineyards *11455 Old Redwood Hwy., (800) 678-4763, 431-1533, fax 433-0939. Tasting daily 10-5; tours daily, call for schedule.*

Do sample the winery's Chardonnays and Cabernet Sauvignons. Picnic tables are available.

Simi Winery *16275 Healdsburg Ave., 433-6981, fax 433-6253. Tasting daily 10-4:30; tours at 11, 1, & 3.*

Opened in 1890, this friendly winery pours samples of reserve wines for a small fee. An inviting redwood-shaded picnic area is available.

Geyserville
(Area Code 707)

GETTING THERE

Located approximately 8 miles north of Healdsburg via Highway 101.

ANNUAL EVENTS

Fall Colors Festival *October. 857-3745.*

The whole town celebrates the end of the grape harvest with this festival.

WHERE TO STAY

The Hope-Merrill House *21253 Geyserville Ave., (800) 825-4BED, 857-3356, fax 857-3857. 2 stories; 12 rooms; 100% non-smoking; $$-$$$; 2-night min. on Sat. Children under 2 free. 1 TV; 1 wood-burning fireplace, 2 gas fireplaces. Heated pool (unavail. Oct-Apr). Full breakfast.*

This Eastlake Stick Victorian dates from 1870 and is exquisitely restored to that period with antique furnishings. It even has authentic Bradbury & Bradbury silk-screened wallpapers. In fact, the owner's restoration efforts won a first place award from the National Trust for Historic Preservation. When the temperature permits, a dip in the attractively situated pool beckons, and in the morning a full breakfast is served in the formal dining room. Should this lovely inn be booked, opt for the charming Queen Anne Victorian **Hope-Bosworth House** located across the street. Under the same ownership, these two houses share facilities. Guests at either house can reserve a gourmet picnic lunch for two *($30; includes basket)* featuring local foods.

A special two-part **Pick-and-Press package** is available for wannabe wine-makers. Participants check in at harvest time in September for a round of grape picking and pressing, plus, of course, some tasting and dining. They return in the spring for a bottling and labeling session, plus, of course, more tasting and dining, and then depart with two cases of their own wine sporting personalized labels. Call for details.

WHERE TO EAT

Chateau Souverain *400 Souverain Rd., Independence Lane exit off Hwy. 101, 433-3141. Closed first 2 weeks in Jan. Restaurant & cafe: L & D F-Sun; $-$$$. Highchairs, boosters. 100% non-smoking. Reservations advised. AE, MC, V. Winery: Tasting daily 10-5; no tours.*

In addition to offering tasting, this winery features a first-rate restaurant. Overlooking the scenic Alexander Valley, the restaurant presents a menu of refined cuisine designed to complement the all-Sonoma County wine list. The winery's own vintages are available by the glass. In good weather diners are seated outdoors. A more casual cafe serves a less expensive menu of salads, focaccia pizzas, and sandwiches. Live entertainment is scheduled on weekends.

WHAT TO DO

Lake Sonoma *3333 Skaggs Springs Rd., 433-9483.*

This scenic spot hosts all manner of water activities—fishing, boating, water-skiing, swimming. Everything from a canoe to a patio boat or houseboat can be rented from the **Lake Sonoma Resort** *(Stewarts Point Rd., 433-2200.).* A **Visitors Center** *(Thur-M 9:30-4, daily in summer. Free.)* displays the area's wildlife and provides a self-guided tour through the **Don Clausen Fish Hatchery.** When the salmon run here, usually from November through April, they can be observed using a man-made fish ladder.

Wineries.

• **Geyser Peak Winery** *22281 Chianti Rd., 1 mi. north of town at Canyon Rd. exit off Hwy. 101, (800) 255-WINE, 857-9400. Tasting daily 10-5; tours by appt.*

Shaded patio picnic tables here overlook Alexander Valley.

• **Lake Sonoma Winery** *9990 Dry Creek Rd., 431-1550. Tasting daily 10-5; tours by appt.*

Featuring a gorgeous view of the Dry Creek Valley, this winery is known for its Cabernet Sauvignons and Merlots and it was the first winery in the country to produce the rich Zinfandel-like Cinsault varietal. Tasters are welcome to picnic on a porch overlooking the vineyards, and on some weekends grills are fired up and waiting to barbecue.

• **Trentadue Winery** *19170 Geyserville Ave., 433-3104, fax 433-5825. Tasting daily 11-4:30; no tours.*

Don't miss a picnic here in the welcoming shade of a spacious grape arbor. Known for its spicy red Carignane and Sengoviese, this small family enterprise also sells some picnic supplies in its tasting room. Children get soft drinks, cookies, and candy to keep them happy while their parents taste.

Anderson Valley

(Area Code 707)

A LITTLE BACKGROUND

In Boonville, a town that has yet to install a stoplight, the townspeople speak an unusual 19th-century slang known as "Boontling." Here public telephones are labeled "Buckey Walter," quail are called—after the sound they make—"rookie-to."

VISITOR INFORMATION

Anderson Valley Chamber of Commerce *P.O. Box 275, Boonville 95415, 895-2379.*

GETTING THERE

Take Highway 128 north. This route includes an 11-mile corridor of redwoods known as the "tunnel to the sea."

ANNUAL EVENTS

California Wine Tasting Championships *July. In Philo; 895-2002, fax 895-2001. Free for spectators.*

Held at **Greenwood Ridge Vineyards**, this unique and festive event includes good food, live music, a chocolate-tasting contest, and novice, amateur, and professional wine-tasting competitions.

WHERE TO STAY

Highland Ranch *18941 Philo-Greenwood Rd., Philo, 895-3600, fax 895-3702. 1 story; 11 cabins; $$$+; 2-night min. Closed mid-Dec. Children under 6 free. No TVs; all wood-burning fireplaces. Unheated pool (unavail. Nov-May), 2 tennis courts. Full breakfast, lunch, & dinner included. Pets welcome.*

Guests at this secluded spot can enjoy the rural pleasures of fishing, swimming, and canoeing in three ponds, plus clay pigeon shooting, mountain biking, hiking, and horseback riding—all at no additional charge. Lodging is in modern redwood cabins.

Toll House Inn *15301 Hwy. 253, Boonville, 895-3630, fax 895-3632. 2 stories; 5 rooms; 100% non-smoking; $$$-$$$+. Closed Jan. Unsuitable for children under 12. 1 TV & VCR; 3 wood-burning fireplaces. Hot tub. Evening snack, full breakfast.*

Dating from 1912, this quiet B&B operates on a former sheep ranch.

Wellspring Renewal Center *8550 Rays Rd./Hwy. 138, Philo, 895-3893. 9 cabins; 100% non-smoking; $-$$. Children under 3 free. No TVs; 5 kitchens; 9 wood-burning stoves; some shared baths.*

Founded in 1979 as an interfaith center, this 50-acre facility located adjacent to Hendy Woods State Park offers programs focused on deepening spirituality and engendering creativity. Regularly scheduled programs include planting and harvesting weekends, meditation and healing retreats, an arts and crafts week, and storytelling workshops. A variety of lodging is available—lodge rooms, both rustic and improved cabins, and a campground at which guests can either pitch their own tent or rent a tepee or tent cabin. Prices vary from $8 to $28 per person per day, $3 to $10 for children ages 2 through 15. All guests are asked, but not required, to donate one hour of their time each day to a needed chore. Individuals, families, and groups are welcome.

WHERE TO EAT

Boont Berry Farm *13981 Hwy. 128, Boonville, 895-3576. M-F 9-6, Sat 10-6, Sun 12-6.*

This health food store has a cozy, old-fashioned atmosphere and is well-stocked with deli items, locally-grown organic produce, pastries, breads (including the town's famous Bruce Bread), and homemade ice cream. It is the perfect spot to pick up picnic supplies.

Boonville Hotel *14050 Hwy. 128, Boonville, 895-2210, same fax. D W-Mon; L F-Sun in summer. Closed 1st 2 weeks in Jan. Highchairs, boosters. 100% non-smoking. Reservations advised. MC, V.*

Owner-chef John Schmitt did his internship at his parent's former restaurant—the French Laundry in Yountville. Here he uses the local bounty for salads, soups, upscale pizza, and heartier main courses, as well as wonderful desserts, and he features local Anderson Valley wines.

Lodging *(2 stories; 8 rooms; 100% non-smoking; $$-$$$. Closed 1st 2 weeks in Jan. Children under 1 free. No TVs. Continental breakfast.)* is also available. Rooms are furnished with simple shaker furniture and with handmade furnishings made by local craftspeople.

Buckhorn Saloon *14081 Hwy. 128, Boonville, (800) 207-BEER, 895-BEER, fax 895-2353. L & D daily in summer; Oct-Mar, call for schedule. Highchairs, boosters, child portions. 100% non-smoking. No reservations. MC, V.*

This casual spot has an airy dining room overlooking the scenic countryside and an outdoor beer garden with horseshoe pits. Its inexpensive lunch menu features snack items—nachos, spicy chicken wings, sausages boiled in beer—as well as fish & chips and several kinds of hamburgers and deli sandwiches. At dinner, steaks and seafood are added. Breads are from the local Bruce Bread Bakery, and soups and desserts are house-made. Beers, brewed directly beneath the pub, include Poleeko Gold (light ale), High Rollers (wheat beer), Boont Amber (ale), Deependers Dark (porter), and Barney Flats (oatmeal stout). Fresh lemonade and an apple spritzer, made with local apple juice and sparkling mineral water, are also available. Brewery tours can sometimes be arranged on the spot by request.

WHAT TO DO

Anderson Valley Historical Museum *Hwy. 128/Anderson Valley Way, Boonville, 895-3207. F-Sun 1-4; from 11 in summer. Free.*

This old-fashioned, one-room red schoolhouse located just west of town is a worthwhile stop.

The Apple Farm *18501 Greenwood Rd., Philo, 895-2461, same fax. Fruit stand: Daily 9-5; later in summer & fall.*

Part of this enterprise is a 30-acre farm with 60 varieties of apples. The other part is a cooking school operated by the former proprietors of the highly acclaimed French Laundry in Yountville.

Picnic Spots.

• **Hendy Woods State Park** *On Greenwood Rd., off Hwy. 128, 937-5804. $5/vehicle.*

Situated along the Navarro River, this 805-acre park holds two groves of old-growth redwoods, a riverside picnic area with tables under a grove of sprawling walnuts, and a one-mile self-guided nature Loop Trail. Campsites are available.

• **Indian Creek City Park** *Located just east of Boonville.*

• **Masonite Corporation Demonstration Forest** *Located just past Navarro.*

Wineries.
• **Navarro Vineyards** *5601 Hwy. 128, Philo, (800) 537-9463, 895-3686, fax 895-3647. Tasting daily 10-5, in summer to 6; tours by appt.*

Known for its varied Gewurztraminers and varietal grape juices, which lucky children are offered tastes of, this winery is situated within a striking craftsman-style redwood building. Attractive picnic areas are provided on a deck overlooking the vineyard and under a trellis in the vineyard.

• **Obester Winery** *9200 Hwy. 128, Philo, (800) 310-2404, 895-3814, fax 895-3951. Tasting daily 10-5, in summer & fall to 6; no tours.*

Operated by the same people who own the winery in Half Moon Bay (see page 85), this branch is located in an old farmhouse with a spacious porch and picnic gazebo. Nonalcoholic grape juice—which is provided to children for "tasting" while their parents sample the harder stuff—and herbal wine vinegars are also produced.

• **Roederer Estate** *4501 Hwy. 128, Philo, 895-2288, fax 885-2120. Tasting daily 11-5 (fee $3; applies to purchase); tours by appt.*

Boasting state-of-the-art methode champenoise wine-making facilities, this winery has a tasting room with beautiful valley views.

Hopland
(Area Code 707)

VISITOR INFORMATION
Hopland Chamber of Commerce   *Box 677, Hopland 95449, 744-1171.*

GETTING THERE
Located approximately 25 miles north of Geyserville via Highway 101.

WHERE TO EAT
The Cheesecake Lady *13325 S. Hwy. 101, (800) CAKE-LADY, 744-1441, fax 744-1312. B & L daily; $. Child portions. 100% non-smoking. MC, V.*

This factory services restaurants and hotels throughout Northern California. Visitors are welcome to observe it in operation. In the cafe over 30 different desserts are available, along with premium Double Rainbow ice cream and drinks from an espresso bar. Cheesecakes can be shipped anywhere in the country through the mail order division.

The Hopland Brewery *13351 S. Hwy. 101, (800) 733-3871, 744-1015, fax 744-1910. L & D daily; $. Highchairs, child portions. Smoking in beer garden only. No reservations. MC, V.*

Opened in 1983, this microbrewery was the first brewpub in California since Prohibition. Ales are unpasteurized and unfiltered. Try a Blue Heron Ale (like English bitter) or a sweeter Red Tail Ale. Seating is either inside the 100-year-old brick pub room—featuring vintage stamped tin walls—or outside in a pleasant beer garden, where children can play in a large sandbox while adults sip suds in shade provided by hop vines. The simple, tasty pub food includes juicy hamburgers on whole wheat Boonville Bruce bread, house-made beer sausages, salads, and chips with salsa or guacamole. The **Mendocino Brewing Company brewhouse** is located out back. Tours are available with 24-hour notice.

Clear Lake

(Area Code 707)

A LITTLE BACKGROUND

Spring-fed Clear Lake is the largest fresh-water lake that is totally within California. (Lake Tahoe is partially in Nevada.) It measures 25 miles by 8 miles. The 70-mile drive around the perimeter takes 2½ to 3 hours.

From the 1870s into the early 1900s, this area was world-famous for its health spas and huge luxury resort hotels. Then, for various reasons, it fell into a state of disrepair and slowly lost its acclaim. Now it is basically a reasonably-priced family resort area.

Lake County's first traffic light was installed in 1982, and there are still no parking meters.

Clear Lake is situated on volcanic terrain, which gives it an unusual physical appearance and a profusion of hot springs. The Pomo Indians, who lived in this area many years ago, had a legend that predicted when there is no snow on 4,200-foot Mount Konocti in April, the volcano will erupt. Those who heed legends should check the April snowfall before making vacation plans.

VISITOR INFORMATION

Lake County Visitor Information Center *875 Lakeport Blvd., Lakeport 95453, (800) LAKESIDE, 263-9544, fax 263-9564.*

GETTING THERE

Located approximately 10 miles east of Hopland via Highway 175.

An alternate route follows Highway 29 north from St. Helena. This scenic route goes through the heart of the Wine Country. The rolling hills are strewn with blooming wild flowers during the spring, and with brilliantly colored foliage during the fall. Make the drive during daylight; this winding two-lane road is tedious and dangerous to drive at night, and, of course, the lovely scenery cannot be enjoyed then.

ANNUAL EVENTS

Summer Concert Series *June-August. In **Library Park** in Lakeport & **Austin Park** in Clearlake. Free.*

A little bit of everything is on the bill at this casual event. In the past the mostly-California bands have included Joe Louis Walker and Country Joe and the Fish.

WHERE TO STAY

Jules Resort *14195 Lakeshore Dr., Clearlake, 994-6491. 18 units; $; 1-week min. July & Aug. All kitchens; 1 fireplace. Heated pool (unavail. Nov-Mar), hot tub, sauna. Pets welcome.*

Lodging here is in pleasant old cabins. Facilities include a lakefront pool, private beach, fishing pier, and launching ramp. This place is so popular in the summer that it is necessary to book at least one year in advance!

The super **Jules Miniature Golf** course, which is not affiliated with the resort, is just across the street.

Konocti Harbor Resort & Spa *8727 Soda Bay Rd., Kelseyville, (800)862-4930, 279-4281. 250 rooms; $$-$$$. Children under 12 free. Some kitchens. 2 heated pools, 2 children's wading pools, health spa, 8 clay tennis courts (night lights). 2 restaurants.*

Nestled in the shadow of Mount Konocti on the rim of the lake, this beautifully landscaped resort enjoys a superb setting. Reminiscent of luxury resorts in Hawaii, it is a lot easier to reach and much less expensive. The list of facilities is extensive: pro tennis lessons, a children's playground, a recreation room, a jogging trail, a bar with live music in the evenings, a paddle wheel boat cruise, a miniature golf course, and a marina that rents fishing boats, water-skiing equipment, and pedal boats. Babysitting can usually be arranged, and tennis, spa, concert, and fishing packages are available. A spa fitness center offers an indoor pool and hot tub, a sauna and steam room, a gym, and a variety of pampering treatments.

The **restaurant** dining room has stunning lake views, offers an innovative American menu, and is comfortably equipped for children. The new **Classic Rock Cafe** offers fun and innovative meals in a rock museum setting.

A **Concert by the Lake** series, which has both dinner and cocktail seatings, brings in big names year-round. In good weather the shows are held in an outdoor amphitheater. Packages are available.

Skylark Shores Resort Motel *1120 N. Main St., Lakeport, (800) 675-6151, 263-6151, fax 263-7733. 45 rooms; 5 non-smoking rooms; $-$$$. Children under 1 free. Some kitchens. Heated pool (unavail. Oct- May).*

These modern motel units are located lakefront. The spacious, well-maintained grounds feature an expansive lawn, swings, and a wading area in the lake.

WHERE TO STAY NEARBY

Wilbur Hot Springs Health Sanctuary *3375 Wilbur Springs Rd., near intersection of Hwys. 16 & 20, 25 mi. east of lake, 22 mi. west of Williams, 473-2306. 3 stories; 20 rooms; 100% non-smoking; $$$; 2-night min. on weekends. Unsuitable for children under 3. No TVs; some shared baths. Pool, 4 hot tubs. Day use: $25/person. Reservations required.*

Soaking in one of the four tubs filled with hot sulfurous spring water and then plunging into the cool water of the outdoor pool are the main activities here. Clothing is optional in pool and tub areas only. The ambitious can take walks in the surrounding hills. Lodging is available in both private rooms and dormitory-style shared rooms that have no electric light in the evening. A parlor is equipped with a pool table and piano for entertainment, and guests can prepare their own meals in a large communal kitchen.

WHERE TO EAT

Konocti Klines' Oak Barrel *6445 Soda Bay Rd., Kelseyville, 279-0101. D W-Sun; $$. Highchairs, boosters, booths, child portions. 100% non-smoking. Reservations advised. MC, V.*

Reached by driving along a scenic rural road, this cozy, antique-furnished restaurant is a delightful surprise. The specialty of the house is fresh seafood, but steak and chicken are also available. A chalkboard menu announces a wide variety of entrees, each served with a delicious bowl of house-made soup and a salad of mixed lettuces. Fish & chips are an option for children, and local wine varietals can be ordered by the glass. For dessert, the house-made pear and walnut cake is not to be missed.

Park Place *50 Third St., Lakeport, 263-0444. L & D daily; $-$$. Highchairs, boosters, child portions. 100% non-smoking. Reservations advised. MC, V.*

Located lakefront and across the street from Library Park, this cafe offers incredible views from its outdoor rooftop dining area. For starters, don't miss the magnificent bruchetta—a baguette topped with pesto and sun-dried tomatoes and then grilled. The menu boasts a large selection of pastas, all made fresh daily. Several kinds of tortellinis and raviolis are available, as are fresh fish, steaks, and hamburgers.

WHAT TO DO

Fishing, hunting, swimming, boating, rock hunting, golfing, and water-skiing are the big activities here. Fishing is the biggest. The lake is reputed to be the best bass fishing spot in the West—maybe even the best in the entire country. The lake's nutrient-rich waters are credited with producing plenty of 10-pounders, and the lake record is a 17.52-pounder!

Lakefront public parks and beaches are located in Lakeport and Clearlake.

Anderson Marsh State Historic Park *On Hwy. 53 between Lower Lake & Clearlake, 994-0688. W-Sun 10-5. $2/vehicle.*

Acquired by the state in 1982, this 940-acre park contains an additional 470 acres of tule marsh. An 1855 ranch house is open to visitors, and tree-shaded picnic tables are provided.

A **Blackberry Festival**, featuring a variety of entertainment and homemade blackberry pie, is held annually on the second Saturday in August.

Clear Lake State Park *5300 Soda Bay Rd., Kelseyville, 3.5 mi. northeast of town, 279-2267. Daily sunrise-sunset. $5/vehicle.*

Located on the shores of the lake, this park offers swimming, fishing, a boat-launching ramp, picnic facilities, campsites, and miles of hiking trails—including the ¼-mile Indian Nature Trail and the 3-mile Dorn Nature Trail. A Visitor Center provides a slide show introduction to the area and a Touch Corner for children. Displays include local wildlife dioramas, a native fish aquarium, and exhibits on the area's Pomo Indian history.

Homestake Mining Company Tour *26775 Morgan Valley Rd., 15 mi. southeast of Lower Lake, (800) 525-3743, 263-9544. 1st & 3rd F & Sat of month at 10am; May-Oct only. Free. Reservations required. Strollers not permitted.*

Visitors to this modern gold mine are treated to a two-hour guided bus tour of the **McLaughlin Gold Mine**. Picnic facilities are available.

Lake County Museum *255 N. Main St., Lakeport, 263-4555. W-Sat 11-4.*

Formerly a courthouse, this brick building was built in 1871. It holds a renowned collection of Pomo Indian baskets, native plants, stone arrow heads and tools, and historic records.

Each year from mid-November through mid-January, this museum hosts a **Teddy Bear Exhibit**. Hundreds of bears—most of which are loaned to the museum by area residents—are displayed in festive scenes complemented by traditional music.

Lower Lake Historic Schoolhouse Museum *16435 Main St., Lower Lake, 995-3565. W-Sat 11-4.*

The restored Lower Lake Grammar School houses a reconstructed turn-of-the-century classroom. Museum exhibits include an extensive geological display, a scale model of the dam on Cache Creek, and collections from pioneer families.

Ukiah

(Area Code 707)

GETTING THERE

Located approximately 15 miles north of Hopland via Highway 101.

WHERE TO STAY

Orr Hot Springs *13201 Orr Springs Rd., 462-6277. 14 cottages, 3 rooms; 100% non-smoking; $$-$$$; 2-night min. on Sat. Children under 3 free. No TVs; 4 kitchens + communal kitchen; 2 wood-burning stoves; some shared baths. Unheated mineral water pool, natural hot springs pool, 4 private & 2 communal hot tubs, sauna.*

In the 1850s, when this mineral springs resort was built, patrons reached it via stagecoach. Now visitors reach it by driving a scenic, winding, two-lane road. A natural rock swimming pool built into the hillside is filled with cool mineral spring water, and several underground springs are tapped to fill four porcelain Victorian tubs in an 1863 bath house with body-temperature water. A gas-fired sauna features a stained-glass window and a clear skylight. Note that this is a clothing optional establishment. Guests sleep either in rooms or cottages built in the 1940s from locally milled redwood, or in a dormitory, and must bring their own food. Campsites and day-use rates are also available. **Montgomery Redwoods State Park**, which offers two loop trails for hiking, is just one mile down the road.

Vichy Springs Resort *2605 Vichy Springs Rd., 3 mi. east of Hwy. 101, 462-9515, fax 462-9516. 1 story; 12 rooms, 3 cottages; 100% non-smoking; $$$. Children under 1 free. No TVs; 3 kitchens; 3 gas fireplaces. Unheated pool & natural hot springs pool, hot tub, health spa. Full breakfast.*

Mark Twain taking the waters

Founded in 1854, this 700-acre resort has three cottages built then—two of which are the oldest still standing structures in Mendocino County—and a hotel built of redwood in the 1860s. It was named after the famous French springs discovered by Julius Caesar and is said to have the only naturally carbonated warm mineral baths in North America. In its heyday the resort attracted guests from San Francisco, who had to endure a day's journey to get here—by ferry across the bay, by train to Cloverdale, then by stagecoach to the resort. They came in search of curative powers attributed to the waters found here. Among the famous guests were writers Mark Twain, Jack London, and Robert Louis Stevenson, and presidents Ulysses S. Grant, Benjamin Harrison, and Teddy Roosevelt. The resort's 130-year-old concrete "champagne" tubs—filled with tingling 90-degree naturally carbonated water—are situated in a shady area overlooking a creek. Swimsuits are required. Guests can hike to a 40-foot-tall waterfall, mountain bike over dirt roads, and swim in a non-chlorinated Olympic-size pool. Picnic lunches can be arranged, and the resort's own bottled Vichy Springs Mineral Water is available. Non-guests are also welcome to use the facilities *($25/person).*

WHAT TO DO

Grace Hudson Museum and Sun House *431 S. Main St., 462-3370. W-Sat 10-4:30, Sun 12-4; tours of Sun House on the hour, 12-3. By donation: $2/person, $5/family.*

Named for the prominent painter who specialized in doing portraits of the area's Pomo Indians, this museum displays Native American games, musical instruments, and baskets as well as some of Ms. Hudson's personal paraphernalia. Her six-room home, the California craftsman-style Sun House, is adjacent to the museum. Built of redwood in 1911, it still holds most of its original furnishings. Picnic facilities are available in a park area within the 4½-acre complex.

Willits
(Area Code 707)

GETTING THERE

Located approximately 25 miles north of Ukiah via Highway 101.

WHERE TO STAY

Emandal Farm *16500 Hearst Rd., 16 mi. northeast of town, (800) 262-9597, 459-5439, fax 459-1808. Open for 1-week stays during Aug; weekends in spring and fall. Rates vary according to age & include 3 meals per day. All shared bathrooms.*

On weekend visits to this 1,000-acre working farm, guests arrive for Friday night dinner. Families are assigned a table for the weekend and then spend some blissful hours there chowing down superb home cooking prepared with the farm's own organically grown produce. Days are filled with leisurely activities—perhaps a short hike down to a sandy beach on the magnificent Eel River for a swim, or maybe a hike up the steep mountain behind the barn to Rainbow Lake. Some folks just doze in the hammocks outside each of the rustic one-room redwood cabins dating from 1916. Others get involved with the farm chores: milking the goats, collecting eggs, feeding the pigs. In the fall, the farm's very special jams, relishes, and baking mixes are available by mail order for the holidays.

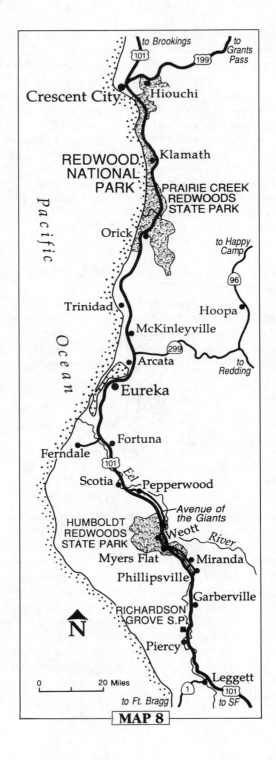

to Brookings
to Grants Pass
101
199
Crescent City
Hiouchi
REDWOOD NATIONAL PARK
Klamath
PRAIRIE CREEK REDWOODS STATE PARK
Orick
to Happy Camp
96
Pacific
Trinidad
Hoopa
McKinleyville
299
Ocean
Arcata
to Redding
Eureka
Fortuna
Ferndale
101
Scotia
Eel
Pepperwood
Avenue of the Giants
HUMBOLDT REDWOODS STATE PARK
Weott
River
Myers Flat
Miranda
Phillipsville
Garberville
N
RICHARDSON GROVE S.P.
Piercy
0   20 Miles
Leggett
to Ft. Bragg
1
101
to SF

MAP 8

The Avenue of the Giants
(Area Code 707)

A LITTLE BACKGROUND

Actually the old Highway 101, this spectacularly scenic drive begins at Phillipsville. Paralleling the freeway and the Eel River, this breathtaking route winds through grove after grove of huge redwoods. It continues for 32 miles to Pepperwood, where it rejoins the busier new Highway 101.

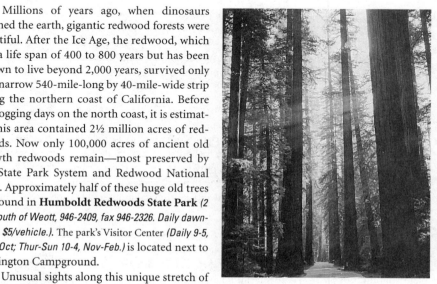

Millions of years ago, when dinosaurs roamed the earth, gigantic redwood forests were plentiful. After the Ice Age, the redwood, which has a life span of 400 to 800 years but has been known to live beyond 2,000 years, survived only in a narrow 540-mile-long by 40-mile-wide strip along the northern coast of California. Before the logging days on the north coast, it is estimated this area contained 2½ million acres of redwoods. Now only 100,000 acres of ancient old growth redwoods remain—most preserved by the State Park System and Redwood National Park. Approximately half of these huge old trees are found in **Humboldt Redwoods State Park** *(2 mi. south of Weott, 946-2409, fax 946-2326. Daily dawn-dusk. $5/vehicle.).* The park's Visitor Center *(Daily 9-5, Mar-Oct; Thur-Sun 10-4, Nov-Feb.)* is located next to Burlington Campground.

Unusual sights along this unique stretch of road are numerous. The 10,000-acre **Rockefeller Forest**—the world's largest grove of virgin redwoods—is near Weott. Also referred to as "the world's finest forest," it features hiking trails leading to the Flatiron Tree, the Giant Tree, and the 356-foot Tall Tree. Campsites are available. (**Richardson Grove State Park** *(8 mi. south of Garberville, 247-3318.)* also has campsites.) The **Children's Forest**, located across the south fork of the Eel River, is a 1,120-acre memorial to children, and **Williams Grove** features picturesque picnic and swimming sites on the river. In Myers Flat, the 275-foot-tall **Shrine Drive-Thru Tree** *(13078 Avenue of the Giants. $1.50, under 10 free.),* which is not part of the state park, has a circumference of approximately 64 feet and provides the opportunity to take an unusual picture in a natural fire cavity that has been widened to accommodate cars.

ANNUAL EVENTS

Reggae on the River *August. In Piercy; 923-3368.*

Held on the banks of the Eel River, this is considered one of the best reggae music festivals in the U.S.

WHERE TO STAY

Benbow Inn *445 Lake Benbow Dr., Garberville, (800) 355-3301, 923-2124, fax 923-2897. 3 stories; 55 rooms; 100% non-smoking; $$$-$$$+; 2-night min. on Sat. Closed Jan-Mar. 18 TVs & VCRs; 3 wood-burning fireplaces. Afternoon tea; restaurant.*

This magnificent English Tudor inn, which opened to the public in 1926, offers a variety of rooms—all of which are furnished with antiques. Some rooms have lake views and private patios; all rooms are equipped with a basket of mystery novels and a carafe of sherry. A majestic communal lounge with fireplace and library invites socializing, and game tables are always set with chess boards and jigsaw puzzles. Interesting art prints decorate the walls throughout. This spot enjoys perfect summer temperatures. Outside pleasures that make the most of it include colorful English gardens with grassy expanses, a small private beach and lake, a putting green, lawn games, and free bicycles. Off the property, a 9-hole golf course and heated swimming pool are within walking distance. A complimentary tea is served each afternoon at 3 p.m. (non-guests may partake for a small charge), and classic films are scheduled each evening. Special events are often scheduled, and holiday events and entertainment occur throughout December.

The elegant **restaurant** *(B, L, & D daily; $-$$$.)* serves an expansive menu, with both simple dishes and more sophisticated fare. In fair weather, a well-priced Sunday champagne brunch buffet is served outdoors on a large terrace overlooking the lake. Additionally, a cozy taproom bar dispenses good cheer and live entertainment on some evenings, and picnic baskets can be ordered by guests.

Hartsook Inn *900 Hwy. 101, 8 mi. south of Garberville, 247-3305, fax 247-3320. 62 units; $-$$. No TVs; 3 kitchens. Restaurant. Pets welcome.*

These cottages—some of which can accommodate up to 12 people—are sprinkled in a majestic 30-acre redwood setting adjoining Richardson Grove State Park. Some duplex units and motel rooms are also available. Guests can swim in the Eel River and have the use of a children's playground, lawn games, and a lounge with board games and a fireplace.

The **restaurant** *(D daily)* serves American and continental foods and is known for its house-made desserts.

Miranda Gardens Resort *6766 Avenue of the Giants, Miranda, 943-3011. 1 story; 16 units; $-$$$+. Some kitchens; 4 fireplaces. Heated pool (unavail. Nov-Apr), 2 tennis courts. Pets welcome.*

Lodging here is a choice of either motel rooms or cottages. A children's playground and plenty of outdoor games— croquet, shuffleboard, and horseshoes—are available.

WHAT TO DO

Confusion Hill *75001 N. Hwy. 101, Piercy, 925-6456. Daily 10-4; in summer 8-7. House: Adults $3, 6-12 $2. Train: Adults $3, 3-12 $2.*

At this spot water runs uphill, appearing to defy gravity, and a miniature train takes passengers on a ride through a tree tunnel to the crest of a hill in the redwoods.

Drive-Thru Tree Park *67402 Drive-Thru Tree Rd., Leggett, 925-6363. Daily 8-dusk. $3/car.*

Most average-size cars can squeeze through the hole in this 315-foot high, 21-foot diameter, 2,400-year-old giant redwood known as the Chandelier Tree. Bring a camera. Nature trails and lakeside picnic tables are also available.

Scotia

(Area Code 707)

A LITTLE BACKGROUND

Scotia is one of the last company-owned lumber towns in the United States. Owned by the Pacific Lumber Company, which has its headquarters here, the town was founded in 1869. Today it caters to workers with homes and facilities.

WHERE TO STAY

Scotia Inn *100 Mill St./Main St., 764-5683. 10 rooms; 100% non-smoking; $$-$$$+. Children free. 4 TVs. Continental breakfast; restaurant.*

The hotel that stood on this site in 1888 accommodated travelers waiting for the stage-coach south. The current hotel, built in 1923, greets guests with a magnificent lobby featuring walls of burnished redwood. Rooms are furnished with antiques, and bathrooms feature claw-foot tubs. A splurge on the Bridal Suite is worthwhile because of its impressive private Jacuzzi room. Dinner and Sunday brunch are served in grand style in the dining room.

WHAT TO DO

Demonstration Forest *On Hwy. 101, 5 mi. south of town. Daily 8-4; summer only. Free.*

To educate the public about modern forestry practices and permit seeing how a forest grows back after harvest, the Pacific Lumber Company offers self-guided tours through a part of its forest that was harvested in 1941. Picnic tables are available.

Pacific Lumber Company Mill Tour *125 Main St., 764-2222, fax 764-4396. M-F 7:30-2. Closed weeks of July 4th and Christmas. Free.*

Take a self-guided tour through the world's largest redwood lumber mill. Get a pass for the hour tour in the old Greek revival-style First National Bank building, which is now a logging museum.

Ferndale

(Area Code 707)

A LITTLE BACKGROUND

Composed of well-preserved and restored Victorian buildings, this village was founded in 1852. It remains largely unchanged since the 1890s and is now a State Historical Landmark. The principal industry here is dairy farming, but the town is also an artists' colony with plenty of galleries and antique shops. Shops of particular interest include the old-time **Ferndale Meat Company** at 376 Main Street, and the **Gazebo** at 475 Main, which sells all things Scandinavian. It is so civilized here, that the town bookstore leaves bargain used books out at night in its entryway; anyone who wants to purchase one can just slip a dollar through the mail slot. The scenic pioneer cemetery on a hill behind town is interesting to visit, and just south of town is **Cape Mendocino**—known as the Lost Coast because of its remoteness. Recently, the whole town starred in the 1994 film *Outbreak*.

VISITOR INFORMATION

Ferndale Chamber of Commerce *P.O. Box 325, Ferndale 95536, 786-4477, same fax.*

GETTING THERE

Located approximately 15 miles south of Eureka, and 5 miles west of Highway 101. The exit that leads through Fernbridge permits crossing the Eel River over an historic 1911 bridge that is the oldest reinforced concrete bridge in existence.

ANNUAL EVENTS

World Championship Great Arcata to Ferndale Cross Country Kinetic Sculpture Race *May; on Memorial Day Weekend. 725-3851.*

In this unusual competition, artistic people-powered sculptures race 38 miles over dunes and rivers from Arcata to Ferndale.

Fortuna Rodeo *July. In Fortuna; 725-6921.*

The oldest rodeo in the West, this event includes a chile cook-off, street games, a parade, a carnival, and more.

Humboldt County Fair and Horse Races *August. 786-9511, 725-1306.*

The oldest uninterrupted county fair in California, this event includes contests, carnival rides, sheep shearing, and more.

America's Tallest Living Christmas Tree *December. 786-4477.*

Heralding the Christmas spirit, this village annually rekindles its 125-foot Sitka spruce in a ceremony that has been a tradition since the 1930s.

Lighted Tractor Parade *December. (800) 346-3482, 444-2323.*

Area farmers decorate their antique and modern tractors, trailers, and wagons with Christmas lights and holiday scenes.

WHERE TO STAY

Gingerbread Mansion Inn *400 Berding St., (800) 952-4136, 786-4000, fax 786-4381. 3 stories; 10 rooms; 100% non-smoking; $$$-$$$+; 2-night min. on weekends. Unsuitable for children under 10. No TVs; 1 wood-burning fireplace, 4 gas fireplaces. Afternoon tea, full breakfast.*

Originally built in 1899 as a doctor's home, this carefully restored, cheery peach and yellow Queen Anne-Eastlake Victorian mansion boasts gables and turrets and elaborate gingerbread trim. Rooms are furnished with Victorian antiques, and each has its own charm: The Gingerbread Suite features antique "his" and "hers" claw-foot tubs perched toe to toe right in the bedroom, with framed art of bathing babies hanging on the wall above; several others have spectacular spacious bathrooms equipped with wood-burning fireplaces and twin claw-foot tubs placed side by side. Most recently, the third-floor attic has been converted into the opulent Empire Suite, with a dramatic 12-foot ceiling and marble floor. Guests are pampered with bathrobes and bubble bath, and break-

fast, served in the grand dining room, is enhanced by the use of the owner's collection of green cameo depression glass. A proper afternoon tea, with assorted sweets and savories, is served in the four guest parlors. All food is made on the premises—including the hand-dipped chocolates that announce bedtime. Guests can stroll or sit in the formal English garden and enjoy its unusual topiaries, two-story high camellia bushes, and variety of fuchsias; they can also sit on the second floor porch and watch the very limited street action.

WHERE TO EAT

Curley's Grill *460 Main St., 786-9696. L & D daily; $-$$. Highchairs, boosters. 100% non-smoking. Reservations advised. MC, V.*

Extremely popular with locals, this comfortable spot is known for generous servings of consistently good food at fair prices. The atmosphere is bright and cheery, and a collection of vintage salt and pepper shakes adds a touch of whimsy to each table. Highly touted dishes include a tortilla and onion cake and the house Caesar salad. Other sure things include the house-made soup of the day and the delicate fresh snapper sautéed with lemon and white wine. In addition to full dinners, a hamburger, a vegetarian burger, and several sandwiches and salads are also available. In good weather, a patio in back is particularly inviting.

WHAT TO DO

Ferndale Museum *515 Shaw Ave., 786-4466. W-Sat 11-4, Sun 1-4.*

Exhibits here include Victorian room settings, a cross-cut of a 1,237-year-old redwood, and a working seismograph. An annex displays farming, logging, and dairy equipment.

Historic Homes.
• **Fern Cottage** *786-4835, 786-4735. Call for hours. Adults $3, under 12 $2.*

This 19th-century settlement farmhouse is significant for its gracious, well-preserved architecture. The house's fabric and content have remained virtually unchanged for more than half a century.

• **Linden Hall** *786-4908. Call for hours; Mar-Dec only. Adults $3, under 12 $2.*

Built in 1901 by a prominent dairyman, this large, two-story Queen Anne Victorian features grand architectural details such as curly redwood moldings and parquet floors. The house contains many of its original furnishings as well as its original gas lighting fixtures and parlor wallpaper. A surrounding English country garden is being developed.

Loleta Cheese Factory *252 Loleta Dr., Loleta, (800) 995-0453, 733-5470. M-F 9-5, Sat 10-4; in summer also Sun 12-4.*

Known for their Monterey Jacks and smoked salmon Cheddar, this factory has big windows through which the cheese-making process can be observed. Cheeses are made from the rich milk of cows grazed on the grass and clover pastures of the Eel River Valley. Fourteen different kinds of cheeses can be tasted.

Eureka
(Area Code 707)

A LITTLE BACKGROUND

Ambitious logging activity has, over time, changed the scenery here quite a bit. The best of the remaining virgin redwoods are in this area's state parks, all of which were established in the 1920s.

Eureka is known as "the coolest city in the nation." The average temperature in July ranges from 52 to 60 degrees. In January it drops to between 41 and 53 degrees. In fact, the highest temperature ever recorded in Eureka was 87 degrees on October 26, 1993. The average annual rainfall is 39 inches, and fog can be heavy even in summer.

The winter off-season is an uncrowded (and cold) time to visit the north coast redwood

country around Humboldt Bay. Visitors then should pack warm clothing and kiss the sunshine good-bye as they prepare to enjoy the stunning beauty of this quiet, foggy area.

Eureka and nearby Arcata are both known for their well-preserved Victorian homes. Arcata, a smaller town and home to Humboldt State University, has an old-fashioned town square.

VISITOR INFORMATION

Eureka/Humboldt County Convention & Visitors Bureau *1034 Second St., Eureka 95501, (800) 346-3482, 443-5097, fax 443-5115.*

The Greater Eureka Chamber of Commerce *2112 Broadway, Eureka 95501, (800) 356-6381, 442-3738.*

GETTING THERE

Located approximately 130 miles north of Willits and approximately 280 miles north of San Francisco via Highway 101.

ANNUAL EVENTS

Independence Day Humboldt Bay 4th of July Festival *July. 444-8817.*

For this old-fashioned celebration, four city blocks are taken over by a street festival with live entertainment, train rides, and children's activities. It culminates with a fireworks extravaganza over Humboldt Bay.

A Coastal Christmas *December. (800) 346-3482.*

Call for a brochure describing seasonal activities.

Truckers Christmas Light Convoy *December. (800) 346-3482, 444-2323, 442-5744.*

Each year over 150 18-wheel big rigs—decorated with thousands of twinkling lights and loaded with "candy cane" logs—are seen truckin' on through town in a slow procession. A manger scene is carried by a crane, carolers sing from a hayhauler, and Santa's sled is pulled by cows.

WHERE TO STAY

Carter House *1033 3rd St./L St., (800) 404-1390, 444-8062, fax 444-8067. 4 stories; 6 rooms; 100% non-smoking; $$$+. Children under 12 free; unsuitable for toddlers. 1 TV & VCR; 1 fireplace. Afternoon & evening snack, full breakfast; room service.*

Looking like it has been here forever, this weather-darkened redwood home was actually built by innkeeper Mark Carter in 1982. It is a re-creation of the 1884 design of two San Francisco architects, one of whom designed Eureka's famous Carson Mansion. (The original house stood on the corner of Bush and Jones in San Francisco and was destroyed in the fire following the 1906 earthquake.) Rooms are all oversize and elegantly furnished. Evening wine and hors d'oeuvres are served in a pleasant parlor, and at bedtime cookies and cordials appear. Dinner is available in the dining room on weekends by reservation.

Across the street, the even newer **Hotel Carter** *(301 L St. 3 stories; 24 rooms; 100% non-smoking; $$$-$$$+. Children under 12 free. Some VCRs; 6 gas fireplaces. Afternoon & evening snack, full breakfast; restaurant, room service.)* provides casual, tasteful lodging amenable to families. Some large suites have showers built for two and in-room hot tubs large enough for a family of four, and a video library of almost 300 films is available to guests at no charge. An impressive wine shop operates off the lobby; a mail-order service is available in which two featured wines per month are sent to participants.

Just off the lobby of the Hotel Carter, **Restaurant 301** *(B & L daily. Highchairs, boosters, child portions. 100% non-smoking. Reservations advised. AE, MC, V.)* produces elegant meals that showcase the region's finest seasonal delicacies, including Kumamoto oysters and Pacific salmon. Designed to please both the eye and the palate, entrees are artistically arranged on oversize plates and garnished with such delights as fresh flowers and herb sprigs. Selections from a recent menu included flavorful squash cakes, chicken cacciatora with creamy polenta, and grilled pork loin with both house-made chutney and applesauce. A well-priced five-course, fixed price dinner is available, with optional selected wine pairings. In addition to an extensive, carefully chosen wine list, bar drinks are also available. Breakfast for the three inns is served here and includes a pastry buffet and hot entree.

Continuing the empire-building, **Bell Cottage** *(1023 3rd St. 1 story; 3 rooms. All VCRs; shared kitchen; 2 wood-burning fireplaces, 1 gas fireplace. Room service (child items)),* which is adjacent to the Carter House, has recently been added to the holdings.

Throughout all three inns, the owner's substantial collection of original local art can be viewed. Guests who are interested may visit the extensive herb and vegetable garden that supplies the restaurant. It is the most extensive inn kitchen garden on the West Coast.

"An Elegant Victorian Mansion" *1406 C St., 444-3144, 442-5594. 2 stories; 4 rooms; 100% non-smoking. Unsuitable for children. Some shared baths. Sauna. Afternoon snack, full breakfast.*

A National Historic Landmark, this spectacular 1888 Queen Anne-influenced Eastlake Victorian was originally built for the town mayor. It is located in a residential neighborhood overlooking Humboldt Bay. Opulently decorated with many of the innkeeper's family heirlooms, its public spaces include two parlors, a library, and a sitting room. Guests are entertained by such nostalgic pleasures as listening to the Victrola and watching silent movies. Each guest room is unique, but the Van Gogh Room is exceptional in that it displays an original watercolor by the artist as well as several original works by Dali. The afternoon snack here is old-time lemonade, or maybe an ice cream soda—*not* wine and cheese. The house is set on a tranquil, park-like estate complete with manicured Victorian flower gardens and a croquet lawn, and bicycles can be borrowed. Perfectly accenting the inn's splendor is the spirited innkeepers' enthusiasm for sharing information about anything that might intrigue a guest. Town tours from the rumble seat of a lovingly restored model T can be arranged, with the dramatic innkeeper dressed in charming era garb, complete with a straw hat. A visit here offers an unusual step back in time to a more gracious era; it is a sort of living history Victorian experience. A lavish, formal breakfast is enjoyed at an elegantly set table and includes the house coffee—a fragrant blend with hints of chocolate and hazelnut.

The Eureka Inn *518 7th St., (800) 862-4906, 442-6441, fax 442-0637. 4 stories; 105 rooms; 15 non-smoking rooms; $$-$$$. Children under 16 free. 1 kitchen; 1 wood-burning fireplace, 1 gas fireplace. Heated pool (unavail. Nov-Apr), hot tub, 2 saunas. 2 restaurants, room service. Dogs welcome.*

Built in English Tudor style in 1922 and now a National Historic Landmark, this stately hotel is within easy walking distance of Old Town attractions. An elaborate series of Christmas events is scheduled here each December.

Motel Row.

Last-minute accommodations can usually be found along both 4th Street and Broadway.

WHERE TO EAT

Humboldt County produces 90 percent of California's oysters. Most local restaurants feature them on their menus. Each June, the **Arcata Bay Oyster Festival** *celebrates the bounty.*

Lazio's Restaurant *327 2nd St., in Old Town, 443-9717, fax 443-9718. L & D daily, SunBr; $$. Highchairs, boosters, child menu. 100% non-smoking. Reservations advised. MC, V.*

Situated within a beautiful and historic building, this popular restaurant serves fresh local seafood as well as steaks and pasta.

Samoa Cookhouse *On Cookhouse Dr. (from Hwy. 101 take Samoa Bridge to end, turn left on Samoa Blvd., then take first left turn), 442-1659, fax 442-0864. B, L, & D daily; $. Highchairs, boosters, child prices. 100% non-smoking. No reservations. AE, MC, V.*

Originally built in the 1890s by the Georgia-Pacific Corporation to feed its loggers, this is the last surviving cookhouse in the West. There is no menu. Just sit down and food starts arriving. The hearty, delicious family-style meals are served at long tables in three large, noisy dining halls. Though the menu changes daily, a recent lunch consisted of marinated three-bean salad, long-simmered and flavorful vegetarian tomato Florentine soup, soft fresh baked bread with butter, assorted jams and honey, green salad with ranch dressing and croutons, rice pilaf, lemon-pepper chicken, saucy beans, peas, chocolate cake with chocolate pudding frosting and whipped cream topping, and coffee or tea. A fantastic value! Most dishes are prepared from scratch with fresh ingredients. The only items not included in the fixed price are milk and sodas.

After dining, visitors can wander through a logging mini-museum of artifacts and historic photos. To work off some calories or to work up an appetite, consider a walk along the area's driftwood-strewn beaches. To find them, follow any of the unmarked turnoffs from Samoa Boulevard.

Tomaso's Tomato Pies *216 E St., 445-0100. L M-Sat, D daily; $-$$. Highchairs, boosters, child menu. 100% non-smoking. No reservations. AE, MC, V.*

Menu items in this casual spot include a square Sicilian-style pizza with whole wheat crust, spinach pies, calzone, house-made soups, and hot pasta items. Portions run large, and delicious house-made breadsticks are served with all dinners. For dessert there are cakes, a variety of coffees, and hot chocolate made with real milk. A dumbwaiter, which delivers orders to the loft dining area, provides free entertainment.

WHAT TO DO

Arcata Marsh & Wildlife Sanctuary *On South G St., in Arcata, 826-2359. Interpretive center: Daily 1-5; guided tours Sat at 2.*

Home and temporary refuge to over 200 species of bird, this is a breeding area for ducks and other waterfowl and a feeding area for fish-eating birds such as osprey, herons, grebes, and egrets. At low tide, thousands of shore birds can be seen foraging on the mud flats of Humboldt Bay. Though birds are here year-round, the largest variety can be seen during the fall and spring migrations. Facilities include 4.5 miles of trails, observation blinds, an interpretive center, and a picnic area.

Blue Ox Millworks *Foot of X St., 3 blocks north of 4th St., (800) 248-4259, 444-3437, fax 444-0918. Tours M-Sat 9-5, Sun 11-4; closed Sun in winter. Adults $5, 6-12 $2.50.*

Dozens of antique woodworking machines can be viewed on this self-guided, one-hour tour. Many of the Victorian-era machines are currently used to reproduce gingerbread trim for Victorian homes. Of special interest are several "skid" buildings. Built on sleds, or "skids," these structures were once pulled through the snow to each new logging site.

Carson Mansion *143 M St./2nd.*

Built between 1884 and 1886, this is said to be the most photographed Victorian house in the world and is the "queen" of Victorian architecture. A mixture of several building styles—including Queen Anne, Italianate, and Stick-Eastlake—it took 100 men more than two years to build. Built during a depression, it was privately financed by pioneer lumber baron William Carson in order to avoid laying off his best men. It now houses a private club and can be viewed only from the exterior.

Clarke Memorial Museum *240 E St./3rd St., 443-1947. Tu-Sat 12-4. By donation.*

An important collection of local Indian baskets and ceremonial regalia is on display here along with an extensive collection of 19th-century regional artifacts and pioneer relics. The palatial 1912 building is also the background for displays of antique weapons and Victorian furniture and decorative arts.

Covered Bridges *Take Hwy. 101 south to Elk River Rd., then follow Elk River Rd. to either Bertas Rd. (2 mi.) or Zanes Rd. (3 mi.).*

These two all-wood covered bridges were constructed of redwood in 1936. **Berta's Ranch bridge** is the most westerly covered bridge in the U.S. **Zane's Ranch bridge** is the second most westerly covered bridge in the U.S. Both are 52 feet long.

Fort Humboldt State Historic Park *3431 Fort Ave., 445-6567. Daily 9-5. Free.*

This was U.S. Grant's headquarters in 1854. The hospital, which dates to 1863, has been restored and is now used as a museum. Exhibits within the park include some locomotives, a restored logger's cabin, and displays of pioneer logging methods. An excellent view of Humboldt Bay makes this a nice spot for a picnic.

At the annual **Steam Donkey Days**, held in April, antique equipment is put into action. Steam donkeys are operated and logging techniques are demonstrated. Train rides are also part of the fun.

Dolbeer steam donkey

Humboldt Bay Harbor Cruise *Foot of C St., 445-1910, fax 445-0249. Daily at 1, 2:30, 4, & 5:30. Closed Nov & Jan-Feb. Adults $9.50, 60+ $8.50, 4-12 $6.50.*

The 75-minute cruise aboard the tiny *M/V Madaket*, which once ferried workers to the lumber mills across the bay in Samoa, allows a view of the bustling activity and native wildlife of the bay. Built in 1910 in Fairhaven, California, it is the oldest operating passenger vessel in the U.S. and has the smallest licensed bar in the state. A dinner cruise sails on Saturdays at 7:30, and a Sunday brunch cruise sails at 11; both have an additional charge.

Old Town *1st St./2nd St./3rd St. from C St. to G St., 443-5097.*

This waterfront area consists of restored commercial and residential Victorian buildings. Many restaurants, boutiques, and antique shops are now located here. The **Romano Gabriel Sculpture Garden**—a folk art garden constructed from vegetable crates by the late artist Romano Gabriel—can be viewed at 315 2nd Street.

Sequoia Park Zoo *3414 W St./Glatt St., 442-6552. Tu-Sun 10-5; May-Sept to 7. Free.*

The backdrop for this combination zoo/playground/picnic area is a 52-acre grove of second-growth redwoods. Hiking trails, gardens, and a duck pond are also within the zoo, and a petting zoo is open during the summer.

Trinidad
(Area Code 707)

VISITOR INFORMATION
Trinidad Chamber of Commerce *P.O. Box 356, Trinidad 95570, 677-0591.*

GETTING THERE
Located 23 miles north of Eureka via Highway 101.

WHERE TO STAY
Bishop Pine Lodge *1481 Patrick's Point Dr., 677-3314, fax 677-3444. 1 story; 12 cabins; 6 non-smoking cabins; $$. 10 kitchens; hot tub. Pets welcome.*

These cozy, secluded cabins are situated among redwoods. A playground, complete with a rustic tree house, is on the spacious, well-maintained grounds, and the helpful owner knows where to find both the Roosevelt elk and the best restaurants.

The Lost Whale Bed & Breakfast Inn *3452 Patrick's Point Dr., (800) 677-7859, 677-3425, fax 677-0284. 2 stories; 8 rooms; 100% non-smoking; $$-$$$; 2-night min. on weekends & every night in summer. Children under 3 free. No TVs. Hot tub. Afternoon tea, full breakfast.*

Located on four acres of coastal property, this Cape Cod-style inn features eight spacious suites; five have spectacular ocean views. Guests sometimes wake up to the sound of sea lions barking out on Turtle Rock, and migrating whales can sometimes be observed from the dining room or deck while eating breakfast. A scenic, wooded trail leads to the inn's private beach, and Patrick's Point State Park is just down the road. Children, who are especially well cared for here, can look forward to picking berries, fantasizing in a playhouse, frolicking on a playground, and feeding the inn's ducks and goats. Two of the suites have special sleeping lofts for children.

WHAT TO DO
This scenic fishing village has a lighthouse and a very nice beach.

Humboldt State University Marine Laboratory *Edwards St./Ewing St., 826-3671. M-F 9-5 & some weekends. Free.*

This research facility has a small aquarium exhibit and a "petting pool" that are open to the public. A 30-minute lab tour is available by reservation.

Patrick's Point State Park *4150 Patrick's Point Dr., 6 mi. north of town, 677-3570. $5/vehicle.*

Agate Beach is reached via a steep, winding trail with lots of stairs. The Octopus Trees Trail passes by Sitka spruces, whose odd roots cause them to resemble octopuses. This 632-acre park is also home to **Sumeg Village**—an authentically re-created Yurok Indian village—and a small museum. Campsites are available.

Klamath

(Area Code 707)

GETTING THERE

Located approximately 60 miles north of Eureka.

WHERE TO STAY

Redwood Hostel *14480 Hwy. 101, 7 mi. north of town, 12 mi. south of Crescent City, 482-8265, fax 482-4665. 30 beds; family rooms.*

This northernmost link in the California coast hostel chain is located within national park boundaries. Operating within the historic circa 1890s pioneer DeMartin House, it has a full kitchen and spectacular ocean views. See also page 391.

Requa Inn *451 Requa Rd., 482-8205, fax 482-0844. 2 stories; 10 rooms; 100% non-smoking; $$. Closed Jan. Children free. No TVs. Full breakfast; restaurant.*

Comfortable, pleasantly decorated rooms are available in this restored historic hotel dating from 1885, and a surf & turf menu is served in the dining room. Fishermen particularly favor the location at the scenic mouth of the Klamath River in the center of Redwood National Park.

WHAT TO DO

Klamath River Jet Boat Tours *On Hwy. 101 S., (800) 887-JETS, 482-7775. May-Oct only; departure times and prices vary.*

This invigorating journey begins at the Klamath estuary called "Rekwoi"—the Native American word for where fresh water meets the Pacific Ocean. From there, the boat turns upriver for a closer look at the area's natural wildlife. With flat bottoms and no rudder or propeller, jet boats provide a smooth and safe, yet fast and exciting ride. Some trips include a barbecue dinner.

Prairie Creek Redwoods State Park *On Hwy. 101, 6 mi. north of Orick, 488-2171. Daily 9:30-5. $5/vehicle.*

The eight-mile unpaved gravel road to Gold Bluffs Beach and **Fern Canyon**—where a short and easy trail awaits—passes through a beautiful forest into an area of fern-covered cliffs. This 14,000-acre park tends to be foggy and cold and is a refuge for one of the few remaining herds of native **Roosevelt elk**. Campsites are available.

Redwood National Park *Visitor Centers in Orick, Crescent City, and Hiouchi, 464-6101, fax 464-1812. Daily 9-5; in summer 8-6. $5/vehicle.*

This magnificent national park encompasses 105,000 acres. Ranger-led interpretive programs are scheduled daily June through August. During the summer, horses can be rented for rides on scenic equestrian trails and for overnight pack trips. Inquire at the Visitors Center about summer ranger-guided kayak float trips on the Klamath River and about borrowing Family Adventure Packs to use with children. Permits are required for visiting the **Tall Trees Grove**, which contains the **world's tallest tree** (367.8 feet) as well as the second, third, and fifth tallest trees. The permits are free and can be obtained from the Orick Visitor Center. The walk takes about four hours and covers 3.2 miles.

Trees of Mystery *15500 Hwy. 101, (800) 638-3389, 482-2251, fax 482-2005. Daily dawn-dusk. Adults $6.50, 61+ $5, 6-12 $4.*

As visitors approach this privately-owned grove of redwoods, they are greeted by a 50-foot-tall Paul Bunyan and a 32-foot-tall Babe. This is really fun for kids, and even those who do not pay admission to the park can pose for a picture on Paul's boot. The trail inside, which is steep in parts, passes through a tunnel made from a hollowed-out log and continues on past a well-maintained group of unusual trees. In a setting at times reminiscent of Disney meets Ripley's Believe It of Not!, visitors see the Candelabra Tree with new trees growing off its fallen trunk, the famous Cathedral Tree with nine trees growing from one root structure, and similar natural wonders. The world's largest private collection of Native American artifacts is displayed in the back of this attraction's gift shop in the **End of the Trail Indian Museum**. There is no charge for admission to the museum, and it can be viewed without entering the park. Two snack bars and picnic facilities are available.

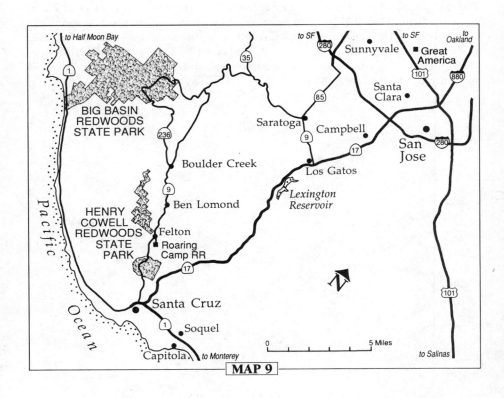

to Half Moon Bay

1

35

BIG BASIN
REDWOODS
STATE PARK

236

Boulder Creek

9

HENRY
COWELL
REDWOODS
STATE
PARK

Ben Lomond

Felton
Roaring
Camp RR

17

Santa Cruz

1

Soquel

Capitola

to Monterey

to SF

280

Sunnyvale

to SF

to
Oakland

Great
America

101

880

Santa
Clara

85

Saratoga

9

Campbell

17

San
Jose

280

Los Gatos

Lexington
Reservoir

Pacific

Ocean

101

5 Miles

0

to Salinas

MAP 9

Santa Cruz Mountains

Los Gatos and Saratoga

(Area code 408)

A LITTLE BACKGROUND

Tucked in the lush, green Santa Cruz mountains, Los Gatos is known for its many antique shops. Nearby Saratoga is an even smaller and quieter town.

VISITOR INFORMATION

Saratoga Chamber of Commerce *20460 Saratoga-Los Gatos Rd., Saratoga 95070, 867-0753, fax 867-5213.*

GETTING THERE

Located approximately 60 miles south of San Francisco. Take Highway 101 to Highway 17 to the Los Gatos exit.

WHERE TO STAY

Garden Inn of Los Gatos *46 E. Main St., Los Gatos, (800) 888-8248, 354-6446, fax 354-5911. 28 rooms; 20 non-smoking rooms; $$. Children under 10 free. Some kitchens. Heated pool (unavail. Nov-Apr). Continental breakfast.*

These rustic Spanish-style bungalows are in a quiet area just two blocks from Old Town. Complimentary use of a nearby health club is available to guests.

The Inn at Saratoga *20645 Fourth St., Saratoga, (800) 543-5020, 867-5020, fax 741-0981. 5 stories; 46 rooms; 20 non-smoking rooms; $$$-$$$+. Children under 18 free. Afternoon snack, continental breakfast.*

This recently built hotel combines an old-time Victorian feeling with modern luxurious amenities and a contemporary decor. Set in a quiet canyon behind busy Highway 9, its rooms all face a forest of old eucalyptus through which winds gurgling Saratoga Creek. Afternoon wine and appetizers are served inside in the cozy lobby and outdoors on a sylvan patio. Families will appreciate that **Wildwood Park**, with its ample playground, is just across the creek.

La Hacienda Inn *18840 Saratoga-Los Gatos Rd., Los Gatos, (800) 235-4570, 354-9230, fax 354-7590. 1 story; 21 rooms; $$-$$$. Children under 6 free. Some kitchens & wood-burning & gas fireplaces. Heated pool, hot tub, fitness room. Continental breakfast; restaurant, room service.*

Tucked away from the main highway, this pleasant inn features a large lawn area and cozy, redwood-trimmed rooms with private patios.

Los Gatos Lodge *50 Saratoga Ave., Los Gatos, (800) 231-8676, 354-3300, fax 354-5451. 2 stories; 123 rooms; 37 non-smoking rooms; $$$. Children under 12 free. Some kitchens & fireplaces. Heated pool, hot tub. Restaurant, room service. Dogs welcome.*

Located on attractive, spacious grounds, this contemporary motel provides a putting green and shuffleboard area.

Sanborn Park Hostel *15808 Sanborn Rd., Saratoga, 741-0166.*

This rustic arts and crafts-style building dates from 1908. It is constructed of logs and located in a secluded redwood grove in the area's foothills. The naturally fragrant, quiet spot has plenty of hiking trails, and a volleyball court and barbecue facilities are available to guests. See also page 391.

Just down the road at **Sanborn-Skyline County Park** are campsites, picnic tables, and the **Youth Science Institute**.

WHERE TO EAT

The Chart House *115 N. Santa Cruz Ave., Los Gatos, 354-1737, fax 395-4553. D daily; $$-$$$. Highchairs, boosters, child portions. Reservations advised. AE, MC, V.*

Located inside a stately old Victorian mansion, this restaurant features an a la carte menu of prime rib, steaks, and fresh seafood. Salads include house-made dressing, and both hot sourdough and squaw breads are available.

The Good Earth *206 N. Santa Cruz Ave., Los Gatos, 395-6868. B, L, & D daily; $-$$. Highchairs, boosters, booths, child menu. 100% non-smoking. No reservations. AE, MC, V.*

A good spot for a quick, light meal or snack, this restaurant's menu offers whole grain breads, fish and chicken specialties, and a large selection of vegetarian items. House-made soups, sandwiches, salads, hot entrees, omelettes, and fruit and yogurt shakes are also available. An extensive children's menu includes pancakes, noodles, a peanut butter & jelly sandwich, and several burgers.

Pedro's Cabo Grill *316 N. Santa Cruz Ave., Los Gatos, 354-7570, fax 395-8578. L & D daily; $$. Highchairs, boosters, booths, child portions. Reservations advised. AE, MC, V.*

This popular spot features an authentic Mexican decor and serves huge portions of delicious Mexican dishes. Especially tasty menu items include chimichangas (deep-fried flour tortillas filled with spicy shredded beef and topped with guacamole and sour cream) and quesadillas (large flour tortillas filled with Jack cheese and topped with guacamole and sour cream). If there is a wait, a cozy bar and pleasant outside patio invite sipping margaritas and munching tortilla chips and salsa.

WHAT TO DO

Garrod Farms Stables *22600 Mt. Eden Rd., Saratoga, 867-9527, fax 741-1169. W-M 8:30-4:30. Horses $20/hr., riders must be 9 or older; ponies $10/1/2-hr.*

Shetland ponies are available for children under 9 to ride; an adult must walk them with a lead rope. Horse trails roam over 200 acres.

The **Cooper-Garrod Vineyards** *(Tasting Sat & Sun 11-4:30.)* winery is also located here.

Hakone Japanese Gardens *21000 Big Basin Way, Saratoga, 741-4994. M-F 10-5, Sat & Sun 11-5. By donation. Parking $3-$5/vehicle.*

Now a city park, this garden was originally constructed by a private citizen to typify a mid-17th-century Zen garden. Now it is composed of four separate gardens: a Pond Garden, a Tea Garden, a Zen Garden, and a Bamboo Garden. Among its special features are a Japanese-style house built without nails or adhesives, a pond stocked with colorful koi, and an authentic Tea Ceremony room. It also boasts the largest collection of Japanese bamboo in the western world. Tea is served in the garden on summer weekends.

Los Gatos Museum *4 Tait St., Los Gatos, 354-2646. W-Sun 12- 4. By donation.*

Housed in a Spanish-style building dating from 1907, this small museum features exhibits on natural science and contemporary fine arts.

The tiny **Forbes Mill History Museum** *(75 Church St., 395-7375.)*, located in the remains of a flour mill dating from 1854, focuses on town history.

Montalvo Center for the Arts and Arboretum *15400 Montalvo Rd., Saratoga, 741-3421. Free. Arboretum: daily 9-5. Gallery: Thur-F 1-4, Sat & Sun 11-4. House tours: Thur & Sat at 10, Apr-Sept.*

Once the summer home of Senator James Phelan, this majestic 1912 Mediterranean-style estate is now the county center for fine arts. It also serves as a bird sanctuary. Self-guided nature trails wind through the 175-acres of gardens. Performing arts events, some especially for children, are presented April through September in a natural outdoor amphitheater and indoor Carriage House.

Parks.
• The 12-acre **Oak Meadow Park** *(Off Blossom Hill Rd., Los Gatos, 354-6809.)* has picnic facilities, baseball diamonds, hiking trails, a 1910 hand-carved English clockwise carousel *($1)*, a well-equipped playground with an authentic fire engine and airplane to climb on, and the **Billy Jones Wildcat Railroad** narrow-gauge steam locomotive *(395-7433. Daily in summer 10:30-4:30; rest of year Sat & Sun, 11-3. $1, under 3 free.)*.
• The 151-acre **Vasona Lake County Park** *(Off Blossom Hill Rd., Los Gatos, 358-3741, fax 358-3245. Daily 8-dusk. $3/vehicle.)* is dominated by a huge reservoir where visitors can fish and rent rowboats and paddle boats. Visitors can also use the barbecue facilities and playground and visit the **Youth Science Institute** *(296 Garden Hill Dr., 356-4945. M-F 9-4:30; in summer, also Sat 12-4:30. Free.)* and its exhibits on water ecology and conservation.

Saso Herb Gardens *14625 Fruitvale Ave., Saratoga, 867-0307. Sat 9-2:30. Closed Oct-Mar. Free.*

Taking advantage of the ideal climate for cultivating herbs, this nursery has one of the largest collections of organically grown culinary, medicinal, and ornamental herbs on the West Coast. Browse in its beautiful natural setting, or plan ahead to attend one of the workshops or free lecture tours.

Wineries.
• **Mariani Winery & Saratoga Vineyards** *23600 Congress Springs Rd./Hwy. 9, Saratoga, 741-2930, fax 867-4824. Tasting daily 11-5; tours by appt.*

Established in 1892, with original plantings dating from 1910 and 1920, this rustic tasting room is located at the end of a steep, woodsy back road. It is surrounded by tall redwoods and 14 acres of vineyards. Picnic tables are available.
• **Mirassou Champagne Cellars** *300 College Ave., Los Gatos, 395-3790, fax 395-5830. Tasting W-Sun 12- 5; tours at 1 & 3.*

High in the hills above town, this historic site was formerly occupied by the Novitiate Winery. All of the champagnes are field-pressed from night-harvested Monterey County grapes.

San Lorenzo Valley
(Area code 408)

A LITTLE BACKGROUND

Tucked into a dense redwood forest, the simple motels and cabins in this area are mostly relics left from a long ago heyday. Still, the abundance of tall trees, trails, and swimming holes, as well as reasonable prices, make the area a choice destination for bargain-hunting vacationers.

Traveling is best done in daylight. Though the back roads are lightly traveled, they are also curvy and slow. And, of course, the forest scenery is part of the reason for coming here.

VISITOR INFORMATION

San Lorenzo Valley Chamber of Commerce *P.O. Box 67 (6257 Highway 9), Felton 95018, 335-2764.*

GETTING THERE

Located approximately 70 miles south of San Francisco. Take Highway 280 to Highway 84 to Highway 35 to Highway 9.

WHERE TO STAY

Ben Lomond Hylton *9733 Hwy. 9, Ben Lomond, 336-2292, fax 336-5017. 1 story; 21 rooms, 1 cottage; 5 non-smoking rooms. $-$$$. 1 kitchen. Heated pool (unavail. Nov-Mar).*

Situated on the San Lorenzo River, these standard motel rooms are shaded by tall redwoods.

Fern River Resort *5250 Hwy. 9, Felton, 335-4412, fax 335-2418. 1 story; 13 cabins; 100% non-smoking; $-$$. Children under 3 free. 12 kitchens; 2 gas fireplaces.*

These modern cabins are located on the river across from Henry Cowell Redwoods State Park. The five-acre lot features a redwood-shaded outdoor recreation area with volleyball, tetherball, and Ping Pong, and guests have use of a private beach on the river.

Jaye's Timberlane Resort *8705 Hwy. 9, Ben Lomond, 336-5479. 10 cabins; $$-$$$; 2-night min. in summer. All kitchens; 2 fireplaces. Solar-heated pool (unavail. Oct-Apr).*

These renovated cabins are scattered on spacious grounds shaded by redwoods.

Merrybrook Lodge *13420 Big Basin Way, Boulder Creek, 338-6813. 1 story; 6 cabins, 2 rooms; $$; 2-night min. on weekends. 6 kitchens; 2 wood-burning fireplaces, 4 wood-burning stoves. Dogs sometimes welcome at additional charge.*

Tucked among towering redwoods, some of these units overlook Boulder Creek.

WHERE TO EAT

Scopazzi's Restaurant *13300 Big Basin Way, Boulder Creek, 338-4444. L & D W-Sun; $$. Highchairs, boosters, child menu. 100% non-smoking. Reservations advised. AE, MC, V.*

This spacious, rustic mountain lodge has operated as a restaurant since 1902. Known for Italian meals, its menu offers cannelloni, veal scaloppine, and chicken cacciatora along with fried prawns, pepper steak flambé, and quail en cocotte. Children should be pleased to see the options of a hamburger, a grilled cheese sandwich, and spaghetti.

Tyrolean Inn *9600 Hwy. 9, Ben Lomond, 336-5188, fax 336-2804. L & D W-Sun, SunBr; $$. Highchairs, boosters. Reservations advised. AE, MC, V.*

Appearing as something right out of Germany's Black Forest, this family-operated restaurant prepares exquisite Austrian-German cuisine. An interesting assortment of imported beers is available, including a refreshing Weiss Bier, which is cloudy with yeast and served in a tall glass over a wedge of lemon. Entrees include sauerbraten and schnitzels, and among the desserts are a house-made fresh apple strudel and Black Forest cake. With 24 hours notice the kitchen will prepare any venison, hare, or duck specialty dish desired. In good weather, lunch is available on a patio sheltered by mature redwoods. Dinner is served in a romantic, cozy dining room heated by two fireplaces.

Seven vintage **cottages** *($-$$; 2-night min. on summer weekends. 2 kitchens; 1 gas fireplace.),* with warmly patinaed redwood paneling, are also available.

WHAT TO DO

Ben Lomond Dam Park *9525 Mill St., Ben Lomond, 462-8318, fax 462-8330. Daily 1-6; summer only. $1.*

A sandy beach and swimming can be enjoyed at this dammed-up deep-water swimming hole. A playground and shaded picnic tables with barbecue facilities are also provided, and equipment rentals are available. Lifeguards are on duty.

Big Basin Redwoods State Park *21600 Big Basin Way, Boulder Creek, 338-8860, fax 338-8863. Daily 8-10. $5/vehicle.*

California's oldest state park, Big Basin has over 80 miles of hiking and nature trails. Self-guiding Redwood Trail leads to interesting redwoods such as the Animal Tree and the Chimney Tree. Another popular 10.3-mile trail leads to 70-foot-high Berry Creek Falls. A Nature Lodge features exhibits, and campfire programs are often scheduled. Campsites and 36 inexpensive tent cabins can be reserved; hike-in campsites are also available.

Felton Covered Bridge Park *Off Graham Hill Rd./Mt. Hermon Rd., Felton, 462-8333, fax 462-8330. Daily 8-sunset. Free.*

Built over the San Lorenzo River in 1892, this redwood bridge has been restored to its original condition and can be walked on. A State Historical Landmark, it measures 34 feet high and is the tallest bridge of its kind in the U.S. Facilities include picnic tables, barbecues, and a playground.

Hallcrest Vineyards *379 Felton Empire Rd., Felton, 335-4441. Tasting & tours daily 11-5:30.*

Situated atop a scenic hill, this winery boasts good views of both its half century-old vineyard and of Henry Cowell Redwoods State Park. All wines here are made from organically grown grapes, and their Organic Wine Works division is the only federally licensed organic wine processor in the United States; no sulfites are used, and they are approved for vegans. The Estate White Riesling, for which the winery is noted, and the non-alcoholic premium varietal grape juice, which children are also welcome to sample, are of particular interest. A picnic area features an expansive lawn and tables shaded by oak trees; some provisions are available for purchase during summer.

Henry Cowell Redwoods State Park *101 N. Big Tree Park Rd., off Hwy. 9, Felton, 335-4598. Daily 6-sunset. $5/vehicle.*

A number of trails lead through this park's redwood groves, including the easy, mile-long Redwood Circle Trail that visits the hollow General Fremont Tree within which it is said the general once camped. Trail guides can be secured at the Nature Center. Campsites are available.

Highlands County Park *8500 Hwy. 9, Ben Lomond, 462-8333. Daily dawn-dusk. $2/vehicle in summer; free rest of year. Pool: M-F 2-4, Sat & Sun 1:15-5:30; summer only. $1, under 3 free.*

The grounds of this old estate have been transformed into a park with pool, playground, two softball diamonds, three tennis courts, a volleyball court, and picnic tables. Nature trails lead to a sandy river beach.

Roaring Camp & Big Trees Narrow-Gauge Railroad *Graham Hill Rd., Felton, 335-4484. Call for schedule. Adults $13, 3-12 $9.50.*

This six-mile, hour-long steam train ride winds through virgin redwoods and crosses over a spectacular trestle. About the time passengers start feeling a little restless, the train makes a short stretch stop at Cathedral Grove—an impressive circle of tall, 800-year-old redwood trees said to have a 3,000-year-old root system! Another stop is made at Bear Mountain, where riders may disembark for a picnic or hike and then return on a later train. Remember to bring warm wraps. Though this area enjoys warm to hot weather in the summer, it can get chilly on the train ride.

Another train, the **Big Trees & Pacific Railway** *(Adults $15, 3-12 $11)*, makes two trips each day between Roaring Camp and the Santa Cruz Boardwalk. The round-trip excursion takes 2½ hours.

An outdoor chuck wagon barbecue operates near the depot *(Sat & Sun 12-3; May-Oct.)*, and the **Red Caboose Saloon** dispenses short order items. Be sure to save some tidbits for hungry ducks and geese in the lake.

Many special events are scheduled each year, including a **Civil War Encampment and Battles** in May and a chocolate **Easter egg hunt** for kids during spring vacation.

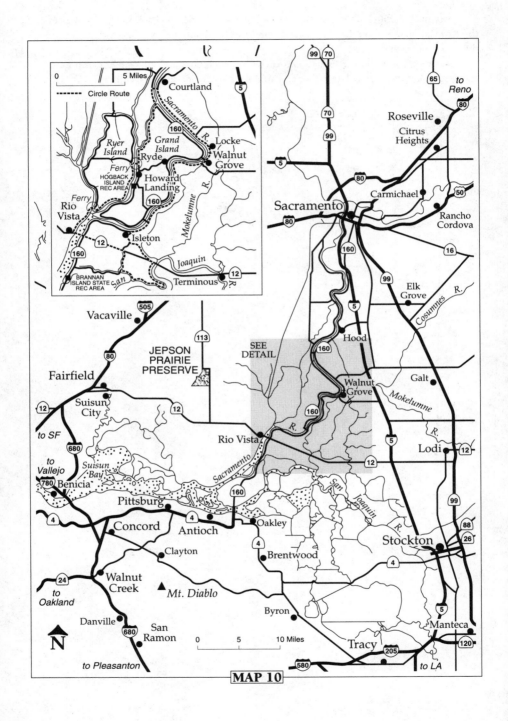

MAP 10

The Delta

A LITTLE BACKGROUND

Composed of flat land, crisscrossed by more than 700 miles of rivers and sloughs (pronounced "slews"), this area is filled with scenic roads running along raised levees. Bridges abound (there are at least 70), and many raise to accommodate large boats. Popular for a houseboat vacation (see page 387), this area is also pleasant for just a day trip. Pack a good detailed map, as the roads here are maze-like, and try to avoid driving at night, when the levee roads can be dangerous.

Trendy hasn't yet hit this area and probably never will. Food is basic, and wine is sometimes mistreated. However, people in the area enjoy a good time, and many eating establishments book live entertainment in the evening.

VISITOR INFORMATION

California Delta Chambers *14900 W. Highway 12, #D-27, Lodi 95242, (916) 777-5007.*

Hal Schell's Delta Map and Guide *(P.O. Box 9140, Stockton 95208, (209) 951-7821.)* is an indispensable aid. It is available in many Delta stores for $2.25. To secure one in advance, send $3.25 to the above address.

GETTING THERE

Located approximately 60 miles east of San Francisco. Take Highway 80 north to Highway 4 east, and continue following Highway 4 as it turns into Highway 160 (River Road) and crosses the gigantic arch that is the John A. Nejedly Bridge. Highway 160 continues north into Sacramento.

ANNUAL EVENTS

Pear Fair *July. In Courtland; (916) 775-1053.*

The Delta is the foremost pear growing area in the country. This annual celebration of the harvest features a parade, kiddie rides, and, of course, plenty of pear foods. Contests include pear bobbing, pear pie-eating, and pear peeling—in which the longest continuous peel after ten minutes wins. A competition to find the area's largest pear is also part of the fun.

The following towns are listed in the order in which they appear on the circle tour highlighted with broken lines on the map on page 242. It is possible to start the tour at any point. Following it takes drivers through the area's most scenic towns, across several different types of bridges, and on two car ferries.

Isleton
(Area Code 916)

A LITTLE BACKGROUND

Located at the geographic center of the Delta, this picturesque, isolated town is one of the larger in the area. Once a bustling port city with a population of more than 2,000, it is now home to only 840 people.

VISITOR INFORMATION

Isleton Chamber of Commerce *P.O. Box 758, Isleton 95641, 777-5880, fax 777-4330.*

ANNUAL EVENTS

Chinese New Year Festival *February. 777-5880.*
The town celebrates its Asian heritage with the Great March of China, lion dancers, an Asian gift bazaar, ancient cultural rites, oriental foods, and the Invitational Rickshaw Races.

Great Isleton Crawdad Festival *June; Father's Day weekend. 777-5880.*
Benefiting this small town's Children's Fund, this festival features live music and entertainment, activities such as a Crawdad Race and a Crawdad Petting Zoo, and plenty of cooked crawdads for eating.

WHERE TO EAT

Hotel Del Rio *209 2nd St., 777-6033. B, L, & D daily; $-$$. Child portions. Reservations advised. MC, V.*
The specialty of the house here is prime rib in three sizes: petite, regular, and double. Broasted chicken and deep-fried prawns round out the menu, and big plates of Cajun-style crawdads are sometimes available. All entrees include visits to the salad bar. Live music is scheduled in the bar on Saturday and Sunday nights. Inexpensive rooms, furnished attractively with antiques, are available upstairs.

Walnut Grove
(Area Code 916)

A LITTLE BACKGROUND

This town, which grew up on both sides of the river, is linked by the first cantilever bridge built west of the Mississippi. Most of the decaying east side of town, which holds the remnants of a Chinatown, is on the National Register of Historic Places. The west side is a well-maintained residential area.

VISITOR INFORMATION

Walnut Grove Area Chamber of Commerce *P.O. Box 100 (14133 Market St.), Walnut Grove, 95690, 776-2060.*

WHERE TO EAT

Giusti's *On Walnut Grove Rd., 4 mi. west of town, 776-1808. L & D daily, SunBr; $$. No cards.*

In a rustic landmark building standing at the junction of the North Fork of the Mokelumne River and Snodgrass Slough, this restaurant has been dishing up family-style Italian meals since 1896. The dining room overlooks the river.

Locke

(Area Code 916)

A LITTLE BACKGROUND

Said to be the only town in the country that was built entirely by and for Chinese immigrants, this tiny town dates back to 1915. Its narrow Main Street is lined with picturesque weathered wooden buildings, many of which are still inhabited. Aging Chinese residents are often seen sitting on benches on the wooden walkways, just watching. When leaving here, continue the circle tour as indicated or backtrack to Walnut Grove, cross the river, and continue south to Ryde.

WHERE TO EAT

Al's Place *On Main St., 776-1800. L & D daily; $. Highchairs, boosters. No cards.*

Once a speakeasy, this restaurant's unsavory looks might cause many people to pass it by. But once through the bar, which can be rowdy even at lunchtime, diners enter a windowless back room and can seat themselves at simple Formica picnic tables with benches. The only thing on the menu is a steak sandwich, served with a side of tasty grilled garlic bread. Jars of peanut butter and jam adorn each table and are meant to be used with the steak. Parents can sometimes strike a deal with a waitress to bring extra bread so their kids can make peanut butter & jelly sandwiches. At dinner, when the place gets more crowded, the steak goes up a bit in price and is served with soup, salad, pasta, and sourdough bread. When leaving, stop by the bar to find out how dollar bills get stuck to the two-story-high ceiling. It only costs $1 to find out.

WHAT TO DO

Dai Loy Museum *On Main St., 776-1684. Thur-Sun 11-4:15. Adults $1, children 50¢-75¢.*

Located within what was the town gambling hall from 1916 to 1951, this museum fills visitors in on the town's history as a Chinese outpost. Visitors can view the Central Gaming Hall, with its original furniture and gaming tables, and the low-ceilinged dealers' bedrooms located upstairs. Interesting era photographs hang on the walls throughout.

Ryde

(Area Code 916)

WHERE TO EAT

Grand Island Inn *14340 Hwy. 160, 3 mi. south of Walnut Grove, 776-1318, fax 776-1195. L Sat, D F & Sat, SunBr; $$. Reservations advised. MC, V.*

Built in 1926 and once owned by actor Lon Chaney, this colorful pink stucco, four-story hotel operated a basement speakeasy during Prohibition. It is claimed that Herbert Hoover, who was a Prohibitionist, announced his presidential candidacy in 1928 in this very hotel while standing, ironically, above a large stash of bootleg booze. Now beautifully restored, this art deco hotel once again serves elegant dinners in its dining room. Live music accompanies Saturday night dinner. Guest rooms are also available.

Across the island, the **Grand Island Mansion** *(775-1705)*, operated by the same owners, is open only on Sunday for an opulent brunch.

WHAT TO DO

Car Ferries. *Free.*

Catch the old-time diesel-powered, cable-guided **Howard's Landing Ferry**, also known as the *J-Mack,* off Grand Island Road. It holds about six cars, and waits are usually short. (Note that it closes down for lunch from 12 to 12:30.) Once on Ryer Island, take Ryer Road south to the **Ryer Island Ferry**, also known as *The Real McCoy.* After crossing, follow the road into Rio Vista.

The Real McCoy

Hogback Island Recreation Area
Grand Island Rd. $3/vehicle.

A grassy picnic area is bounded on one side by Steamboat Slough and on the other by a boat-launching lagoon. This isn't a good swimming area, but there are access spots that are good for getting feet wet.

Rio Vista

(Area Code 707)

VISITOR INFORMATION

Rio Vista Chamber of Commerce *75 Main St., Rio Vista 94571, 374-2700.*

WHERE TO EAT

Foster's Big Horn *143 Main St., 374-2511. L & D W-M; $-$$. Highchairs, boosters.*

Opened in 1931, this restaurant's walls are lined with more than 300 mounted big game heads—including a full-grown elephant that is the largest mammal trophy in any collection in the world, the largest mounted moose head in the world, and a rare giraffe head. Gathered by the late hunter William Foster, who shot most of the wild animals himself, it is the world's largest collection of big game trophies. An attractive bar in front leads to an open dining room with high ceilings and comfortable booths. Sandwiches and hamburgers are on the lunch menu, steak and seafood on the dinner menu.

The Point Restaurant *120 Marina Dr., in Delta Marina, 374-5400. L & D Tu-Sat, SunBr; $$. Highchairs, boosters, booths. AE, MC, V.*

Overlooking the Sacramento River at its widest point, this comfortable, well-maintained restaurant has many roomy booths. The lunch menu features house-made soups and sandwiches. At dinner, entrees include prime rib, scampi, and chicken Dijon. Photos illustrating Humphrey the Whale's well-publicized visit to the area are displayed in the entryway.

WHAT TO DO

Brannan Island State Recreation Area *17645 Hwy. 160, 3 mi. south of town, (916) 777-6671. $5/vehicle.*

Located on a knoll, this 350-acre park offers slough-side picnic and swimming areas. Campsites are available.

Victorian Homes *On Second St.*

Second Street is also known as **Millionaires' Row.**

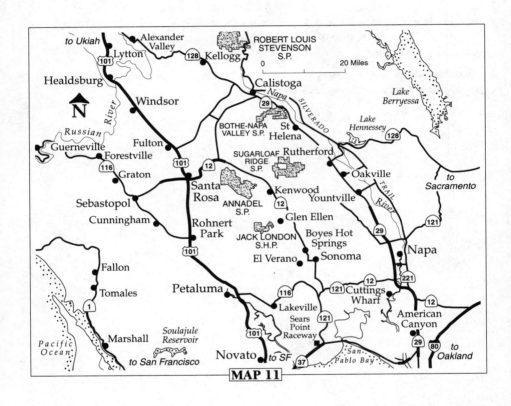

MAP 11

Wine Country

A LITTLE BACKGROUND

California's first wineries were appendages of the 21 Franciscan missions that were built a day's ride (by horseback) from each other in a chain reaching from San Diego to Sonoma. The wine was produced by the missions for sacramental use. Eventually the church gave up producing wine, and the art passed into the realm of private enterprise.

Presently Sonoma County and Napa County are literally erupting with new small family wineries. Wine-making is becoming a hobby with many city folks who have bought themselves modest vineyard retreats.

The most popular route for wine tasting in this area is along Highway 29 between Oakville and Calistoga. When visiting this stretch of highway, which is heavily concentrated with wineries, the problem is to remain selective in tasting. Experts suggest not planning to taste at more than four wineries in one day.

Young children can be difficult on a winery tour. Out of courtesy to the other tour participants (a noisy child interferes with the guide's presentation), parents might consider having a member of their party stay with the children while the others go on a tour. Or visit a winery with a self-guided tour. Most wineries allow tasting without taking a tour. It's a nice idea to bring along some plastic wine glasses and a bottle of grape juice so the children can "taste," too.

Many wineries have picnic areas. An ideal itinerary is to tour a winery, taste, and then purchase a bottle of wine to drink with a picnic lunch.

A wrinkle in the pleasure of wine tasting is that many wineries now charge for tasting. Sometimes the charge permits tasters to keep their glass as a souvenir, and sometimes the charge is applied to a wine purchase. Tasting fees tend to be imposed by smaller wineries with more expensive vintages, and their purpose seems to be to keep the less serious tasters away.

Some tasting rooms will provide vertical tastings, which portray the aging process of a varietal, and cross tastings, which show the different results that varied treatment of the same grapes can cause. To arrange a special tasting, call ahead.

ANNUAL EVENTS

Carols in the Caves *December. (707) 224-4222. $25.*

In spectacular settings, David Auerbach performs selections using rare and unusual instruments he has collected from around the world: the panpipes of South America, the Celtic harp of Ireland, the steel drums of Trinidad. Instruments and winery sites change each year. Mr. Auerbach also performs in winery caves during the summer and fall; call for schedule.

Sonoma
(Area Code 707)

VISITOR INFORMATION

Sonoma Valley Visitors Bureau *453 First St. East, Sonoma 95476, 996-1090, fax 996-9212.*

GETTING THERE

Located approximately 45 miles north of San Francisco. Take Highway 101 to Highway 37 to Highway 121 to Highway 12.

ANNUAL EVENTS

Valley of the Moon Vintage Festival *September. 996-2109.*

Begun in 1887 as a celebration of the harvest, this old-time event kicks off in the historic Barracks each year with an evening tasting of elite Sonoma Valley wines. Free daytime events include a Blessing of the Grapes, several parades, and a re-enactment of the Bear Flag Revolt. (During the revolt American soldiers seized the town from General Vallejo, taking down the Mexican flag and raising the bear flag—which later became California's state flag.) Messy grape stomping competitions, in which one person stomps and the other holds a bottle under the spicket, are also part of the fun.

WHERE TO STAY

El Dorado Hotel *405 First St. West, (800) 289-3031, 996-3030, fax 996-3148. 27 rooms; 100% non-smoking; $$-$$$. Heated pool. Continental breakfast; restaurant. Small dogs welcome.*

Built in 1843, this historic inn was recently gutted and remodeled with plenty of Mexican paver tiles and beveled glass. Each of the contemporary rooms contain handmade furnishings such as iron four-poster beds and large mirrors softened by rustic twig frames. A split of wine greets guests upon arrival.

On the first floor of the hotel, appealing **Piatti** ristorante *(996-2351. L & D daily; $$. Boosters, child portions. 100% non-smoking. Reservations advised. MC, V.)* has outside seating at heavy marble tables on a rustic tiled patio dominated by a majestic old fig tree. On cooler days, the large inside dining room is equally inviting. The menu of deliciously innovative Italian cuisine changes regularly, and there are always several daily specials and a risotto. A variety of unusual pizzas are baked in a wood-burning oven, and most of the pastas are made by hand in the kitchen. Piatti oil—a delicious dipping sauce for bread made with virgin olive oil, balsamic vinegar, salt, pepper, garlic, red pepper flakes, and chopped parsley—is served gratis upon request. Both local and imported Italian wine varietals are available by the glass, and trendy tiramisu is always on the dessert menu.

Sonoma Hotel *110 W. Spain St., (800) 468-6016, 996-2996, fax 996-7014. 3 stories; 17 rooms; $$-$$$; 2-night min. on weekends in season. Unsuitable for children under 12. No TVs; some shared baths. Continental breakfast; restaurant.*

Dating from the 1870s, when it was the town theater, this hotel is located on the town square. Rooms are furnished in carefully selected turn-of-the-century antiques, and private bathrooms feature claw-foot tubs. The friendly resident ghost—a Chinese man named Fred who dresses in coolie-style clothing—is said to roam the third floor and has been seen late at night sweeping the sidewalk outside.

Sonoma Mission Inn & Spa *18140 Hwy. 12, Boyes Hot Springs, 3 mi. north of town, (800) 862-4945, 938-*

9000, 996-5358. 3 stories; 170 rooms; 100% non-smoking; $$$-$$$+; 2-night min. on Sat. Children under 14 free. 32 wood-burning fireplaces. 2 heated mineral pools, 2 mineral hot tubs, sauna, health spa, fitness room, 2 tennis courts (fee; night lights). 2 restaurants, room service.

Built in 1927, this sedate luxury resort features pink adobe architecture. All rooms are cooled with both efficient, old-fashioned ceiling fans and modern air-conditioning. The most requested room is located in the turret; it is completely round and has a view of the pool and gardens. Though children are welcome, this is an adult-oriented resort: Children under 18 are not allowed in the well-equipped, full-service spa, but are permitted in one of the pools.

WHERE TO EAT

The Cafe at Sonoma Mission Inn *18140 Hwy. 12, Boyes Hot Springs, 3 mi. north of town, 938-9000. B, L, & D daily, Sat & SunBr; $-$$. Highchairs, boosters, booths, child menu. 100% non-smoking. Reservations advised. AE, MC, V.*

Operated by the Sonoma Mission Inn, this spacious, casual dining room offers seating at tables and in comfy booths. The restaurant is well-known for its extensive and delicious breakfast menu, which has everything from oatmeal with raisins and brown sugar to eggs Benedict. At lunch and dinner the menu features eclectic American foods such as sandwiches, soups and salads, wonderful hamburgers, and trendy pizzas.

During the week before Christmas, **Breakfast with Santa** is scheduled each morning, and Santa visits each table with gifts for children. Make reservations by calling 939-2410.

The Coffee Garden Cafe *415-421 First St. West, 996-6645. B, L, & D daily; $. Highchairs. No reservations. MC, V.*

Located on the Plaza within the 1830s Don Salvador Vallejo Adobe, this cafe offers salads, sandwiches, and coffees. Order in front, then sit in back in the casual patio garden planted with a large variety of native flora.

Feed Store Cafe & Bakery *529 First St. West, 938-2122. B & L daily; $. Highchairs, boosters, child menu. 100% non-smoking. Reservations advised. MC, V.*

Located in a former feed store on the town plaza, this restaurant makes use of fresh local produce, meats, and cheeses. Absolutely not to be missed at lunch are the big, beer-batter-dipped, deep-fried onion rings. They go magnificently with one of the sandwiches or hamburgers. A variety of salads made from local greens is available, and a different hearty house-made soup is offered every day. A rotating selection of desserts prepared by the restaurant's award-winning bakery includes fresh fruit pies, old-fashioned chocolate cake, lemon torte, and carrot cake. Before departing, stop at the bakery for take-home supplies.

The General's Daughter *400 W. Spain St., 938-4004, fax 938-4099. L M-Sat, D nightly, SunBr; $$. Highchairs, boosters, booths. 100% non-smoking. Reservations advised. MC, V.*

General Vallejo's third daughter, Natalia, built this Victorian in 1864 with her husband, Attilla Haraszthy, whose family grew grapes in the valley. Situated on over an acre of land just three blocks from the plaza, the house has been beautifully renovated, and its pastel walls are adorned with attractive farm-related paintings by Rod Knutson. Diners have a choice of several seating spaces, plus a patio area in good weather. And the food lives up to the surroundings. Starters include crisp buttermilk and cornmeal-coated onion rings with lemon-pepper aioli, and a flavorful salad of Sonoma County mixed greens with roasted goat cheese, sun dried tomatoes, and hazelnuts dressed lightly with a roasted garlic and balsamic vinaigrette. Main courses include light sandwiches—a particularly tasty curry lamb-Feta cheese on cracked wheat is served with a delicious potato salad—and a vegetarian mixed grill, as well as more substantial meat and fish items. Desserts are made on the premises by a full-time pastry chef and include an inexpensive sorbet and biscotti for the sated. Ending a meal with a cigar on the west porch is also an intriguing possibility.

Picnic Pick-Ups.

• **Lainie's Cuisine to Go** *678 W. Napa St., 996-5226. Tu-F 11-7, Sat 11-5; April-Oct Tu-F 11-7.*

Call ahead and have a picnic waiting for pick-up, or stop in at this tiny take-out and make on-the-spot selections. Perhaps an artichoke and rice salad or a jicama tabbouleh with mint dressing. Most definitely a foccacia round topped with caramelized onions and, of course, a cappuccino brownie. The menu changes weekly, but it seems that everything is delectable, making it worth the drive to the outskirts of town.

• **Sonoma Cheese Factory** *2 W. Spain St., (800) 535-2855, 996-1931, fax 996-1912. Daily 8:30-5:30.*

Located right on the plaza, this crowded shop stocks hundreds of cheeses (including their famous varieties of Sonoma Jack made from old family recipes), plus cold cuts, salads, and marvelous marinated artichoke hearts. Sandwiches are made to order. A few tables are available inside; more are outside on a shaded patio. The workings of the cheese factory can be observed through large windows in the back of the shop.

• **Sonoma French Bakery** *470 First St. East, 996-2691. M 7-1:30, Tu-F 7-5:30, Sat 7:30-6, Sun 7:30-4.*

This renowned bakery makes both sweet and sourdough French breads without yeast. They are so delicious people are willing to wait in a long line to purchase them. Flutes, rolls, croissants, gâteau Basque bread, French and Danish pastries, and cream puffs are just a few of the other delights available.

WHAT TO DO IN TOWN

Depot Park Museum *270 First St. West, 938-1762. W-Sun 1-4:30. Free.*

Operated by volunteers from the Sonoma Historical Society, this tiny museum is housed in the restored Northwestern Pacific Railroad Depot and features changing historical and railroad exhibits. Adjacent Depot Park has a playground and picnic area. A bicycle path, which follows the old railroad tracks, originates at Sebastiani Winery.

Sonoma Plaza.

This town square, the largest in the state and a National Historic Landmark, was designed by General Vallejo in 1834 for troop maneuvers. Basically an old-fashioned park, it is great for picnics and has a playground and a tiny duck pond. City Hall, which is located here, acted as the Tuscany County Courthouse on TV's *Falcon Crest.*

Sonoma State Historic Park *Located off Plaza along Spain St., 938-1519. Daily 10-5. Adults $2, 6-12 $1.*

This extensive park preserves structures dating from the early 1800s, when General Vallejo, founder of Sonoma, was Mexico's administrator of Northern California. The two-story, white-washed adobe **Barracks,** which once housed Vallejo's soldiers, now contains historical exhibits. Vallejo drilled his soldiers across the street in what is now the town square.

Next door and across the street from the Barracks is the re-created **Mission San Francisco Solano**. Founded in 1823 and the most northerly and last in the chain of California missions, this historic site has been through a lot. It was burned to the ground twice, was the victim of a Native American uprising, and was seriously damaged in the 1906 earthquake. Then it went through a period of being used as a saloon, as a winery, and even as a hennery. Currently it exhibits a permanent collection of watercolors depicting each of California's 21 missions. The paintings were done in 1903 by Chris Jorgensen, who traveled from mission to mission via horse and buggy. An impressive old prickly pear cactus forest graces the mission courtyard, and the chapel is said to host a ghost.

General Vallejo's Home, a Victorian Gothic with its original furnishings, is located one mile east. Shaded picnic tables and another giant prickly pear cactus garden are found here.

Sonoma Traintown Railroad *20264 Broadway, 938-3912. F-Sun 10-5; daily in summer. Adults $3.50; 55+ & 2-16 $2.50.*

A miniature steam train (a diesel engine is used on weekdays) winds through ten acres during the 20-minute ride here. It passes through forests and tunnels and crosses both a 70-foot double truss bridge and a 50-foot steel girder bridge. During a five-minute stop at a miniature 1800s mining town, where the train takes on water, riders enjoy the pleasures of a petting zoo inhabited by sheep, goats, birds, and miniature horses. An antique merry-go-round, snack bar, and picnic area are available at the station.

Toscano Hotel *20 E. Spain St., 938-0510. Tours F-Sun 1-4. By donation.*

This beautifully restored mining-era hotel was built in 1858.

Vasquez House *129 E. Spain St., in El Paseo de Sonoma, 938-0510. W-Sun 1:30-4:30.*

Built in 1856, this refurbished wood-frame house features a tearoom where visitors can relax over homemade pastries and a pot of tea.

WHAT TO DO NEARBY

Aeroschellville *23982 Arnold Dr., at airport off Hwy. 121, 2 mi. north of Sears Point Raceway, 938-2444. Daily 9-5:30. $70-$195. Reservations advised.*

A pilot here claims an aerobatic ride in an authentic 1940 Stearman biplane, once used to train World War II combat pilots, "tops any roller coaster ever built." Calmer scenic rides and glider rides are also available, and old and antique planes can be viewed at the airport.

Sears Point Raceway *At intersection of Hwys. 37 & 121, (800) 870-RACE, 938-8448, fax 938-8430. Closed Dec-Jan. Call for schedule & ticket prices; under 12 free.*

Facilities for car races here include a 2.52-mile course with 12 turns and a ¼-mile drag strip. Concession stands dispense fast food, and an assortment of grassy hillsides provide perfect picnic perches.

WINERIES

Buena Vista Winery *18000 Old Winery Rd., (800) 926-1266, 938-1266, fax 939-0916. Tasting daily 10:30-4:30; tour daily at 2, in summer also at 11am.*

Founded in 1857, this is California's oldest winery. Visitors park among the grapevines and take a short, pleasant walk in. After tasting wines in the welcoming old Press House (don't miss the nutty cream Sherry, which is available only at the winery), select a bottle for a picnic outside at one of the tables shaded by stately old eucalyptus trees growing on the banks of a tiny brook. If kids are along, purchase a chilled bottle of Gewurztraminer grape juice for them. A variety of picnic supplies are also available in the winery's shop.

Cline Cellars *24737 Arnold Dr. (Hwy. 121), 2 mi. south of town, 935-4310. Tasting & tours daily 10-6.*

Situated on the original site of Mission San Francisco de Solano, this winery is known for its Rhone-style wines. Grapes for the wines are grown on the family ranch in Oakley. Six thermal pools filled by underground mineral springs dot the property. Once warm, they have been cool since the last big earthquake, and some are now populated with fish and turtles. A picnic area bounded by rose bushes and three of the ponds is available behind the farmhouse tasting room.

Gloria Ferrer Champagne Caves *23555 Hwy. 121, 996-7256, fax 996-0720. Tasting daily 10:30-5:30 (fee $2.75-$5/glass); tours 11-4, on the hour.*

Located back from the highway atop a hill in a Catalan hacienda-style building, this tasting room provides views across the vineyards. In warm weather, tasters can enjoy a patio; in cooler weather, they can gaze at the view from inside, warmed by a large fireplace. The winery is part of Spain's Freixenet family, which has been making wine since the 12th century. The tour visits the man-made caves and provides insight into the making of sparkling wine.

Gundlach-Bundschu Winery *2000 Denmark St. (another entrance is on Thornsberry Rd.), 938-5277, fax 938-9460. Tasting daily 11-4:30; self-guided tours.*

Located in the back country, off a winding road about three miles from the plaza, this pioneer winery was established in 1858. Now the great-great grandson of German founder Jacob Gundlach's partner continues the tradition. Jim Bundschu and his merry wine-makers produce wines they like to drink themselves—wines with intense varietal character. White wines tend to be dry and flavorful, reds dark and complex. Unique to the winery, the Kleinberger varietal, which is a kind of Riesling, is produced by vines brought over in 1860 and is sold only at the winery. Picnic tables are perched on a small hill overlooking a pond and the vineyards. When leaving, be sure to take the alternate road out. Each route provides different scenery.

"If you can't say 'Gundlach-Bundschu Gewurztraminer,' you shouldn't be driving!"

Ravenswood *18701 Gehricke Rd., (800) NO-WIMPY, 938-1960, fax 938-9459. Tasting daily 10-4:30; tours by appt.*

A prime producer of Zinfandel, this winery has a special barbecue available on summer weekends. A picnic area overlooks the vineyards.

Sebastiani Vineyards *389 Fourth St. East, (800) 888-5532, 938-5532. Tasting daily 10-5; tours daily 10:30-4.*

This winery has been owned continuously by the same family since 1904—longer than any other in the country. It is best known for its Symphony and Pinot Noir Blanc, which are available only at the winery. While here, take time to view the world's largest collection of carved oak wine casks, and a display across the street featuring an extensive collection of Native American mortars and pestles. A pleasant picnic area is also available.

Viansa Winery *25200 Arnold Dr. (Hwy. 121), 2 mi. south of town, (800) 995-4740, 935-4700, fax 996-4632. Tasting & self-guided tours daily 10-5.*

Built on top of a hill commanding magnificent views of the area, this winery opened in 1990. Owned by Sam Sebastiani and his wife Vicki (and named by merging the first two letters of each of their first names), this beautifully crafted Tuscan-style winery building was inspired by a monastery near Farneta, Italy. Noteworthy wines include the Barbera Blanc, a light blush wine perfect for picnics and sold only at the winery, and, of course, the Cabernet Sauvignons. They can be tasted in the state-of-the-art tasting room that features a magnificent "wall of wines" behind the tasting bar.

The **Italian Marketplace** food hall is designed after the mercato in Lucca, Italy, and the extraordinary food offerings *almost* overshadow the wines. Using Vicki's recipes, the kitchen staff prepares wonderful things for picnics: country pâté, torta rustica, hot-sweet mustard, foccacia bread, panini (Italian sandwiches), a triple chocolate chunk cookie, tiramisu. More goodies include porcini mushroom tomato sauce (made with Viansa Cabernet Sauvignon) and spiced figs (made with Sonoma black mission figs and Viansa Cabernet Sauvignon using Vicki's grandmother's recipe). Some of the items make use of produce from the winery's adjacent vegetable garden. On nice days, picnics can be enjoyed at tables located outside on a knoll with a panoramic view of the Sonoma and Napa valleys. On cooler days, tables are available inside. The winery welcomes children and provides them with a complimentary souvenir balloon.

January through March are the prime months to view birds here at the **Viansa wetlands.** That is when the greatest numbers are in transit on their southward trek. Guided tours are given in the summer and fall *(Sat & Sun at 10:30 & 2).*

Glen Ellen and Kenwood

(Area Code 707)

A LITTLE BACKGROUND

Like the curve of a scimitar blade, the Valley of the Moon stretched before them, dotted with farm houses and varied by pasture-lands, hay-fields, and vineyards. The air shimmered with heat and altogether it was a lazy, basking day. Quail whistled to their young from thicketed hillside behind the house. Once, there was a warning chorus from the foraging hens and a wild rush for cover, as a hawk, high in the blue, cast its drifting shadow along the ground.

—Jack London, from *Burning Daylight*, published in 1910

Jack London, a man with an eye for landscapes, didn't coin the name "**Valley of the Moon.**" The valley stretching north from Sonoma was referred to as "Valle de la Luna" as early as 1841. But London, who lived on a ranch here when he wasn't on the road, popularized the term—and the place—in his novels.

Now, almost a hundred years later, there are still no high-rise buildings or shopping malls here. Instead visitors are treated to unimpeded views of tree-covered hills and vineyards that appear to stretch forever. It is the perfect antidote to the congestion of civilization.

GETTING THERE

Located approximately 10 miles north of Sonoma on Highway 12.

ANNUAL EVENTS
World Pillow Fighting Championship
July. In Kenwood; 833-2440. Free.

This very serious all-day competition takes place on a greased pipe positioned over a muddy morass into which losers, and sometimes winners, are buffeted.

WHERE TO STAY

Kenwood Inn & Spa *10400 Sonoma Hwy. 12, Kenwood, (800) 353-6966, 833-1293, fax 833-1247. 2 stories; 12 rooms; 100% non-smoking; $$$+; 2-night min. on Sat. Unsuitable for children under 21. No TVs; all wood-burning fireplaces. Unheated pool, hot tub, health spa. Full breakfast.*

Hugging a hillside covered with olive trees, this sensual, aesthetically pleasing Tuscan-style inn looks very much like an old Italian villa. Guests are greeted at the desk by an inviting arrangement of seasonal fruits. Painted in gray and ochre tones, the various buildings enclose a center courtyard, mixing attractively with the green of the garden and seasonally punctuated by orange globes hanging from persimmon trees and yellow orbs ripening on lemon bushes housed in terra-cotta pots. Fountains and archways are everywhere. Rooms are furnished with a combination of antiques and comfortable newer pieces, and the blissful beds feature both a feather bed and a lofty down comforter.

WHERE TO EAT

The Buckley Lodge *1717 Adobe Canyon Rd., Kenwood, 833-5562, fax 833-4945. L & D W-M, SunBr; $$-$$$. AE, MC, V.*

Situated off the main highway, in a rustic setting reached via a winding, woodsy canyon road, this restaurant is a delightful surprise to come upon. Operating in the past as a hunting lodge, a speakeasy, and a brothel, and then as The Golden Bear Restaurant from the early 1940s to 1993, the property has been extensively refurbished by its new owner. Inside tables feature comfortable chairs, glimpses of the surrounding woods, and visual access to interesting paintings by local artists. A bucolic patio beside Sonoma Creek is opened to dining in warm weather. Weekend brunch—when the menu offers items such as smoked salmon Benedict with dill Hollandaise served with a side of exotic purple Peruvian potatoes and onions, and French toast with fresh berries and orange-mint butter—is a particularly nice time to dine here. Dishes are beautifully presented, and any choice seems a good one. Wines are well-priced, and many are from local wineries and available by the glass.

After dining, continue up Adobe Canyon Road to **Sugarloaf Ridge State Park** *(833-5712. Daily dawn-dusk. $5/vehicle.)*, where 25 miles of wilderness trails, a horseback riding concession, and campsites await.

The Glen Ellen Inn *13670 Arnold Dr., Glen Ellen, 996-6409. L Tu-F, D Tu-Sun; $$. Boosters. 100% non-smoking. Reservations advised. MC, V.*

This modest, charming place is sort of a California-style roadhouse. Diners are seated in one of several small rooms, and in warm weather more tables are tucked into a sunken herb garden outside. From the teeny, tiny kitchen, owner and husband Christian Bertrand produces a non-stop parade of delicious fare. Dinner begins with a basket of scones fresh from the oven, often delivered to the table by co-owner and wife Karen, who sometimes waits tables all by herself. Items on the dinner menu have included an exquisitely light puff pastry pocket filled with mushrooms and sausage in a Brandy cream sauce, and a late harvest ravioli stuffed with the unexpected taste sensation of a mixture of pumpkin, walnuts, and sun-dried cranberries served on a bed of oven-glazed butternut squash. Save room for one of the killer desserts: perhaps a vertical chocolate mousse contained within a tall chocolate "basket," or maybe homemade vanilla ice cream topped with a marvelous caramel-toasted coconut sauce.

WHAT TO DO

Jack London State Historic Park *2400 London Ranch Rd., Glen Ellen, 938-5216. Daily 10-5, to 7 in summer; museum 10-5. $5/vehicle.*

Jack London, who wrote 191 short stories and 51 books, was once one of the highest paid authors in the country. This 830-acre park contains the ruins of his 26-room Wolf House (reached via a pleasant half-mile trail), his grave, and **The House of Happy Walls**—a museum built in his memory by his widow. Beauty Ranch includes the cottage he actually lived in and Pig Palace, a deluxe piggery designed by London. It was all given to the state by London's nephew.

Guided one- and two-hour horse rides, some with a picnic included, are available within the park. For information and reservations contact the **Sonoma Cattle Co.** *(996-8566, fax 938-8366. $30/hr., $40/2 hrs. Riders must be 8 or older.).*

To get in the mood for this trek, read a London classic such as *The Call of the Wild* or *Martin Eden.* Or on the way to the park stop at the wee **Jack London Bookstore** *(14300 Arnold Dr., 996-2888, fax 996-4107. W-M 10:30-5.),* which in addition to stocking rare and out-of-print books, with a specialty in those by Jack London, also has a good selection of mysteries. The proprietor can provide assistance in selecting a London title.

Morton's Warm Springs *1651 Warm Springs Rd., Kenwood, 833-5511, fax 833-1077. May-Sept only; call for schedule. Adults $3.50-$5, 2-11 $3-$4.*

Long ago these mineral springs were used by Native Americans to heal their sick. Nowadays they are used for recreational purposes. Two large pools and one toddler wading pool are filled each day with fresh mineral water averaging 86 to 88 degrees. Lifeguards are on duty. Facilities include picnic tables and barbecue pits shaded by large oak and bay trees, a snackbar, a large grassy area for sunbathing, a softball field, horseshoe pits, a basketball court, and two volleyball courts. A teenage rec room is equipped with a juke box, Ping Pong tables, and pinball machines, and dressing rooms and lockers are also available. There are a few rules: no cutoffs in the pools; no glass allowed.

WINERIES

Benziger Family Winery *1883 London Ranch Rd., Glen Ellen, 935-4046. Tasting daily 10-4:30; tram tours daily at 11 & 2.*

Just up the hill from the little crook in the road that is Glen Ellen, this family-operated winery provides a free 30-minute tram tour through the vineyards and hands-on experience with vines, grapes, and trellising techniques. The tour is followed by tasting a wide selection of wines. A shorter, self-guided walking tour is also available. In addition, there is a gallery displaying original art from which various of their wine labels are designed, a peacock cage, and extensive picnic facilities.

B.R. Cohn Winery 15140 Sonoma Hwy. 12, Glen Ellen, 938-4064, fax 938-4585. Tasting daily 10-4:30; no tours.

Originally part of a Spanish land grant and a dairy during the '40s and '50s, this 65-acre estate is now a winery owned by the manager of The Doobie Brothers. All of the old farm buildings have been converted into winery buildings, and Sonoma Valley's largest olive orchard—eight acres of Picolini olive trees that were planted over 125 years ago—is now farmed for premium extra-virgin olive oil bottled in tall, long-necked French bottles. The winery's distinctive, intense cabernets are credited to the area's unique microclimate. Several picnic areas are available, and music and theater performances are sometimes scheduled in a new amphitheater.

Chateau St. Jean Vineyards and Winery 8555 Sonoma Hwy. 12, Kenwood, (800) 543-7572, 833-4134, fax 833-4200. Tasting daily 10:30-4; self-guided tour.

This winery specializes in white varietals. The tasting room is inside a 1920s chateau, and the grassy, shaded picnic area has several fountains and fish ponds.

Kunde Estate Winery 10155 Sonoma Hwy. 12, Kenwood, 833-5501, fax 833-2204. Tasting daily 11-5; guided tours F-Sun, self-guided tours daily.

Tucked between expansive vineyards and the Surgarloaf foothills, this fourth-generation family-owned and -operated winery produces a spicy Zinfandel from gnarled vines growing in a 28-acre vineyard planted over 113 years ago. Tours are given of the half-mile-long aging caves, which are camouflaged by a hill planted with Chardonnay grapes. Children are given grape juice to drink while the adults taste wine, and a picnic area is situated by a fountain and pond under a shady grove of oak trees.

Smothers Winery 9575 Sonoma Hwy. 12, Kenwood, (800) 795-WINE, 833-1010, fax 833-2313. Tasting daily 10-4:30; no tours.

Many people stop here just to see if Tommy is around. (Dick is no longer involved with the winery.) Those after the label's cachet might be disappointed to learn that the wines are now labeled Remick Ridge. Children get grape juice and pretzels while their parents taste, and a small shaded area is equipped with picnic tables.

Napa
(Area Code 707)

BACKGROUND INFORMATION

Considered by most tourists to be the center of the wine country, this town is more accurately referred to as the "Gateway to the Wine Country." The center of its old town is of interest on its own merits, but the Wine Country's heaviest concentration of wineries is further north. Recently, a group of wineries has also begun to develop on the southern edge of town.

VISITOR INFORMATION

Napa Valley Conference and Visitors Bureau *1310 Napa Town Center, Napa 94559, 226-7459.*

Napa Valley Tourist Bureau *6488 Washington St., Yountville 94599, 944-1558.*

In addition to dispensing *The Napa Valley Guide ($10.95)*, this private enterprise operates a reservation service for lodging, restaurants, and activities.

GETTING THERE

Located approximately 60 miles north of San Francisco. Take Highway 101 to Highway 37 to Highway 121 to Highway 12 to Highway 29.

ANNUAL EVENTS

Napa Valley Wine Auction *June. Events held throughout the valley; 963-5246.*

Though tickets run $1,250 per couple, this four-day event usually sells out early. Its popularity might be explained by the fact that many wine-makers open their homes and wineries to unique public events in the interest of helping raise money for local health centers. For example, one year the Rutherford Hill Winery hosted a refined candlelight dinner in their hillside caves, while Stag's Leap Wine Cellars hosted a festive Greek dinner and dancing extravaganza in their courtyard. A Friday night Vintner Dinner and Saturday afternoon auction take place at the lush Meadowood Resort.

WHERE TO STAY

The Hennessey House Bed & Breakfast Inn *1727 Main St., 226-3774, fax 226-2975. 2 stories; 10 rooms; 100% non-smoking; $$-$$$+; 2-night min. on Sat. 1 TV & VCR; some wood-burning & gas fireplaces. Sauna. Full breakfast.*

Listed in the national Register of Historic Places, this 1889 Eastlake Queen Anne Victorian's exterior is painted stylishly in five different colors. Six rooms are in the main residence, four more in a carriage house. Some have oversize whirlpool tubs or claw-foot tubs, others have featherbeds. Breakfast is served in what is claimed to be Napa County's finest 19th-century hand-painted, stamped tin ceiling. It is, indeed, magnificent. Complimentary sherry is provided in each room, and a wine and cheese hour is hosted on weekends.

Inn at Napa Valley *1075 California Blvd., (800) 433-4600, 253-9540, fax 253-9202. 205 suites; 123 non-smoking units; $$$-$$$+. Children under 12 free. All kitchens. Indoor heated pool, hot tub, sauna. Evening drinks, full breakfast; restaurant (fall only), room service (child items).*

Part of the Crown Sterling Suites chain, this facility offers suites equipped with a bedroom, a front room with hide-a-bed, a kitchenette, and two TVs. Breakfast is the all-you-can-eat variety with eggs cooked to order, bacon, sausage, pancakes, fried potatoes, toast, fresh fruit, muffins, cereals, and beverages. It can be enjoyed either in a pleasant indoor atrium or outside by a pond inhabited by ducks and both black and white swans.

WHERE TO EAT

Alexis Baking Company *1517 Third St., 258-1827. B & L daily, D M-F; $. Highchairs, boosters.*

This combination bakery-cafe is a must-stop for breads and pastries to take home. But most people wind up having a casual meal, too. A vast array of delicious, freshly made foods are available to choose from. Breakfast offerings include Dutch babies and hot cinnamon rolls. Lunch is a selection of pastas, sandwiches, soups, and salads, and dinner includes fussy appetizers such as baked goat cheese coated with pistachios and served with sweet potato fries, plus fresh fish and pizza.

P.J.'s Cafe *1001 Second St., 224-0607, fax 224-0228. B F-Sun, L & D daily; $. Highchairs, boosters, booths. 100% non-smoking. Reservations advised. AE, MC, V.*

Located on Alexandria Square in one of Napa's historic buildings, this comfortable spot dishes up big portions of simple foods. The menu offers sandwiches, pastas, pizzas, salads, and soups—all made from scratch and served with fresh-baked oatmeal and cheese breads. Special requests are accommodated.

WHAT TO DO

Napa Valley Wine Train *1275 McKinstry St., (800) 427-4124, 253-2111. Daily; call for schedule. Closed 1st week in Jan. Reservations required.*

This leisurely three-hour, 36-mile excursion takes passengers through the heart of the Wine Country. Unfortunately, there are no stops to visit wineries. However, the train consists of opulently restored vintage lounge cars and a 1916 Pullman converted into a kitchen complete with a stainless steel galley and a window-wall allowing chefs to be viewed in action. At additional charge, passengers are served Saturday or Sunday brunch *($56.50)*, lunch *($63)*, or dinner *($69.50)* on board. Wine is extra, but the tip is included. Diners are seated in richly appointed dining cars outfitted with the refined pleasures of damask linen, bone china, and silver flatware. Almost everything is prepared right on the train using fresh ingredients, and the menu offers several choices in each category. One lunch enjoyed aboard included a tasty baby lettuce salad with Cambozola cheese and a hazelnut-sherry vinaigrette, filet mignon with Cabernet-Roquefort sauce, and a creamy tiramisu served in an oversize cappuccino cup. A deli car *($25; children under 13 half-price M-Thur.)* that is perfect for families with young children offers an inexpensive a la carte menu. Special events such as murder mystery dinners are sometimes scheduled.

WINERIES

Carneros Alambic Distillery *1250 Cuttings Wharf Road, 253-9055, fax 253-0116. Sensory evaluation (fee $2; permits 10% discount on retail merchandise, excluding spirits) & tours daily 10:30-4:30; in summer 10-5.*

Situated off Highway 121 amid a peaceful expanse of vineyards, this producer of rare and expensive traditional French-style Alambic brandy is the first facility of its kind in the U.S. It houses the largest stock of aging alambic brandies in the country. Since its French owners are Remy Martin Cognac, it makes sense that the distillery resembles those found in the brandy-making regions of France. Though federal law prohibits brandy tasting, visitors are permitted to enjoy a comprehensive "aroma evaluation" after a tour.

Chateau Potelle Winery *3875 Mt. Veeder Rd., 3.5 mi. from Oakville (take the Oakville Grade west, turn left on Mt. Veeder Road), 255-9440, fax 255-9444. Tasting Thur-M 12-5 (call to verify); no tours.*

Reached via a scenic back country road, this small winery features a picnic area with tables overlooking the vineyards.

Codorniu Napa *1345 Henry Rd. (call for directions), 224-1668, fax 224-1672. Tasting (fee $4) & tours M-Thur 10-5, F-Sun 10-3.*

Situated off Highway 121, this spectacular Spanish-owned winery can be difficult to find but is well worth the effort. Its stunning minimalist architecture has it set right into a grassy hill—providing a sod roof that helps insulate wines stored beneath. Visitors reach the tasting room by walking up a pyramid-like staircase on either side of a cascading man-made waterfall. Stunning panoramic views can be enjoyed at the top. In the spirit of the Codorniu family's creation of the first methode champenoise sparkling wine in Spain in 1872, the winery is creating a distinctly California sparkling wine here. After sampling in the spacious tasting room or outside on the inviting deck, a mini-museum of wine-related artifacts awaits leisurely perusal.

Domaine Carneros *1240 Duhig Rd., 6 mi. southwest of town, 257-0101, fax 257-3020. Tasting daily 10:30-6 (fee $4-$6); tours M-F at 11, 1, & 3, Sat & Sun hourly 11-3.*

Situated off Highway 121, this imposing classic French chateau sits atop a hill surrounded by vineyards. The chateau is inspired by the Chateau de la Marquetterie, a historic 18th-century residence in Champagne, France owned by the winery's principal founder. After climbing a *lot* of steps, visitors reach the elegant tasting salon and garden terrace. Here information is dispensed about the methode champenoise procedure that produces the champagnes of French founder Taittinger, as well as their local sparking wines made in the same tradition. Flavored mineral water is provided to children while their parents taste.

The Hess Collection Winery *4411 Redwood Rd., 255-1144, fax 253-1682. Tasting daily 10-4 (fee $2.50); self-guided tours. Gallery admission free.*

Located on the slopes of Mt. Veeder, off a road that winds first through the suburbs and then through scenic woods, this unusual winery is owned by Swiss entrepreneur Donald Hess. Here he grows grapes in rocky soil on steep, terraced hillsides and turns them into premium wines. Built in 1903, the winery was once the original Napa Valley home for the Christian Brothers. Extensively remodeled, it features the original stone walls and a stunning 13,000-square-foot art gallery. The gallery's eclectic collection holds 130 contemporary paintings and sculptures, including works by Robert Motherwell and Frank Stella, as well as an absolutely stunning portrait by Swiss artist Franz Gertsch titled "Johanna II." At various points in the galleries, portholes look into rooms where steel fermentation tanks and bottling machines are located. Visitors can also view a 12-minute narrated slide presentation of the wine-making operations. The winery is known for its Chardonnay and Cabernet Sauvignon, and its Mt. Veeder Estate Merlot is available for purchase only at the winery. Valser mineral water from Switzerland is provided to children accompanying their tasting parents.

The Silverado Trail

(Area Code 707)

A LITTLE BACKGROUND

Stretching approximately 30 miles from Napa to Calistoga, this scenic route offers a quieter, less-crowded wine tasting experience.

WHERE TO STAY

Meadowood Resort & Hotel *900 Meadowood Lane, St. Helena, (800) 458-8080, 963-3646, fax 963-3532. 82 units; $$$+; 2-night min. on weekends. Children under 12 free. Some kitchens & fireplaces. 2 heated pools, health spa, 7 tennis courts (fee). 2 restaurants, room service.*

This luxury resort allows guests an escape from reality. A variety of cabins—all with skylights and old-fashioned porches—are scattered throughout the property, providing plenty of privacy, and it can be arranged for room service to deliver a breakfast basket to the door. Facilities on the 156 acres of lush, wooded grounds include a 9-hole golf course, a children's playground (one of the two pools is also dedicated to children), two regulation English croquet lawns, and three miles of hiking trails. The health spa has an exercise room, a whirlpool hot tub, a heated lap pool, massage and treatment facilities (one treatment is a Chardonnay facial), and bike rentals. The resort also operates a **Wine School.** A package that includes classes, winery tours, meals, and lodging is available.

For twelve nights in December, the resort hosts **The Twelve Days of Christmas.** Celebrity chefs from around the country prepare sumptuous menus at nearby Merryvale Vineyards. Guests are seated at one very long candelabra-lit table in the winery's magnificent two-story Cask Room, the stone walls of which are lined with century-old 2,000-gallon wooden wine barrels. Special packages that include lodging and dinner are available.

Silverado Country Club and Resort *1600 Atlas Peak Rd., Napa, (800) 532-0500, 257-0200, fax 257-5400. 260 units; 25 non-smoking units; $$$-$$$+. Children under 14 free. All kitchens; some fireplaces. 1 heated pool, 8 unheated pools, hot tub, sauna, 23 tennis courts (fee; 3 with night lights), 2 golf courses; 3 restaurants, room service (child items).*

Once part of General Vallejo's Rancho Yajome, this 1200-acre resort is now the largest tennis complex in Northern California. Its heart is a gracious 1875 mansion, where guests are greeted and registered and within which are the resort's two restaurants. Though all accommodations are in individually-owned condominiums, the location, architectural style, and decor of each vary. Some units are available on the grounds adjacent to the mansion. Staying in one of these allows an easy walk to most of the facilities. Larger condos, some opening right onto the golf course, are further away and require a drive of one or two miles. Facilities include jogging trails, bicycle rentals, and two golf courses designed by Robert Trent Jones, Jr.

WHAT TO DO

Lake Berryessa *In Napa, take Hwy. 128 east, 966-2111, fax 966-0409. Daily.*

This man-made lake is over 25 miles long, 3 miles wide, and has 165 miles of shoreline. Boats and water-skis can be rented, and the swimming and fishing are excellent. Camping and lodging facilities are available.

WINERIES

Mumm Napa Valley Winery *8445 Silverado Trail, Rutherford, (800) MUM-NAPA, 942-3434, fax 942-3470. Tasting 10-5, in summer 10:30-6 (fee $3.50+); tours daily 11-3, in summer to 4.*

In good weather tasters can sample Brut Prestige, Blanc de Noirs, and Winery Lake Cuvee while sitting under umbrellas on a patio with a magnificent view of the valley's vineyards. A permanent exhibit of Ansel Adams photographs tells *The Story of a Winery,* and changing exhibits of fine art photography can be viewed in the winery's art galleries.

Nichelini Winery *2950 Sage Canyon Rd. (Hwy. 128), 11 mi. east of Rutherford, (800) WE-TASTE, 963-0717, fax 963-3262. Tasting & tours Sat & Sun 10-5; in summer to 6; weekdays by appt.*

Established in 1890, this historic, out-of-the-way winery is in a gorgeous location well off the main drag, down a rural side road leading to Lake Berryessa. Pack a picnic to enjoy at tables sheltered by old, old trees. Operated now by four of founder Anton Nichelini's grandchildren, it is the oldest continuously owned family winery in Napa Valley. The winery produces great Zinfandels using vines planted long, long ago by the elder Nichelini.

Pine Ridge Winery *5901 Silverado Trail, Napa, (800) 575-9777, 252-9777, fax 253-1493. Tasting daily 11-5 (fee $3); tours by appt. at 10:15, 1, & 3.*

The tiny tasting room here is a pleasant place to sample the premium Cabernets produced by this winery's Stags Leap District grapes. Tasters can also stroll through a Demonstration Vineyard. A picnic area is situated under a young grove of tall pines, and two board swings await the kiddies.

Rutherford Hill Winery *200 Rutherford Hill Dr., Rutherford, (800) 726-5226, 963-1871, fax 963-4231. Tasting daily 10-4:30 (fee $3; keep tasting glass); tours daily at 11:30, 1:30, & 3:30, also at 12:30 & 2:30 on Sat & Sun.*

Visitors pass through massive 15-foot-tall doors as they enter the tasting room here. The tour includes seeing the most extensive wine-aging cave system in the U.S. A sylvan hillside picnic area, with spacious tables sheltered by old oaks and a pleasant view of the valley, beckons across the street from the tasting room.

Yountville and Oakville

(Area Code 707)

VISITOR INFORMATION

Yountville Chamber of Commerce *P.O. Box 2064 (6516 Yount St.), Yountville 94599, (800) 4-YOUNT-VILLE, 944-0904, fax 944-4465.*

ANNUAL EVENTS

Robert Mondavi Summer Festival *July & August. In Oakville; (800) MONDAVI, 26-1395.*

Ah, the pleasure of sitting on the grass, surrounded by vineyards and rolling foothills, while listening to great jazz. The entertainers (who in the past have included Ella Fitzgerald, Al Hirt, and the Preservation Hall Jazz Band—on the *same bill!*) probably enjoy the dusk concerts as much as their audience. After an intermission featuring wine and cheese tasting, the concerts conclude under the stars. Picnics are encouraged, and catered repasts are available by advance reservation. Ticket-holders may begin selecting seats at 4:30. The winery's retail shop remains open until 7, when the concerts begin.

This winery also hosts a **Great Chefs at the Robert Mondavi Winery** series each year. Both one-day and weekend-long formats are scheduled. The $750 and up fee includes meals and cooking classes, plus demonstrations by world-famous chefs.

WHERE TO STAY

Bordeaux House *6600 Washington St., Yountville, (800) 677-6370, 944-2855, same fax. 2 stories; 7 rooms; 100% non-smoking; $$-$$$. Some wood-burning fireplaces. Continental breakfast.*

This ultra-modern inn features a curved red-brick exterior and lush French- and English-style gardens.

Burgundy House *6711 Washington St., Yountville, 944-0889. 2 stories; 6 rooms; 100% non-smoking; $$-$$$; 2-night min. on weekends. Unsuitable for children under 12. No TVs; 1 wood-burning fireplace. Full breakfast.*

Built in 1890 as a brandy distillery, this stone structure was constructed of local field stone and river rock. It has walls that are 22 inches thick. The rustic construction of the interior is complemented by rooms decorated with antique pine and oak furniture, and windows covered with lace. An inspired breakfast is served—depending on the weather—in either the downstairs lobby or the backyard rose garden.

Maison Fleurie *6529 Yount St., Yountville, (800) 788-0369, 944-2056, fax 944-9342. 3 stories; 13 rooms; 100% non-smoking; $$$-$$$+. Children under 2 free. Some gas fireplaces. Heated pool (unheated Nov-Apr), hot tub. Afternoon snack, full breakfast.*

Formerly known as the Magnolia Hotel, this rustic, vine-covered main building was built in the center of town as a hotel in 1873. Rooms, some of which are located in two adjacent buildings, are decorated in French country style. Amenities include oversize pool towels, free use of mountain bikes, evening turndown, and a morning newspaper. Upon request, breakfast is delivered to the room.

Napa Valley Lodge *2230 Madison St., Yountville, (800) 368-2468, 944-2468, fax 944-9362. 2 stories; 55 rooms; 28 non-smoking rooms; $$$-$$$+. Some fireplaces. Heated pool, hot tub, sauna, fitness room. Continental breakfast.*

Located on the outskirts of town, this Spanish-style motel is across the street from a park and playground. Each room has a private patio or balcony.

Napa Valley Railway Inn *6503 Washington St., Yountville, 944-2000. $$-$$$+; 2-night min. on weekends. Children under 7 free. No TVs.*

Railroad enthusiasts are sure to enjoy a night in a brass bed at this unusual lodging facility. Three cabooses and six rail cars—authentic turn-of-the-century specimens sitting on the original town tracks—have been whimsically converted into comfortable suites complete with private bath, sitting area, and skylight. Guests are greeted with a chilled bottle of wine.

Vintage Inn *6541 Washington St., Yountville, (800) 351-1133, 944-1112, fax 944-1617. 2 stories; 80 rooms; 60 non-smoking rooms; $$$+; 2-night min. on Sat, Mar-Nov. Children under 1 free. All wood-burning fireplaces. Heated pool, hot tub, 2 tennis courts. Afternoon snack, continental breakfast. Pets welcome.*

This attractive modern lodging facility is centrally located next to Vintage 1870. In summer, bicycles are available for guests to rent.

WHERE TO EAT

The Diner *6476 Washington St., Yountville, 944-2626. B, L, & D Tu-Sun; $. Closed last 2 weeks in Dec. Highchairs, boosters, child portions. 100% non-smoking. No reservations. No cards.*

This unpretentious, chef-owned spot offers counter seating as well as tables and booths. California-ized Mexican specialties enhance the cafe menu, and all items are made with quality ingredients. Breakfast choices include the house specialty of crispy cornmeal pancakes served with smoky links, as well as German potato pancakes, house-made sausage patties, and old-fashioned oatmeal. At lunch it's hamburgers, sandwiches, and soda fountain treats, among them an unusual buttermilk shake said to taste like liquid cheesecake. Dinners include sophisticated specials and, in season, a dessert cobbler made with fresh apricots and blackberries and topped with a scoop of vanilla ice cream.

The French Laundry *6640 Washington St., Yountville, 944-2380. L F-Sun, D Tu-Sun, in summer D daily; $$$. Closed part of Jan. 100% non-smoking. Reservations essential. AE, MC, V.*

Indeed once a French laundry, this rustic old stone building now holds one of the Wine Country's most popular culinary gems. Owner-chef Thomas Keller offers diners either a five-course or seven-course "chef tasting" menu. An additional five-course vegetarian menu is also available. The kitchen specializes in freshly prepared, innovative, labor-intensive dishes. A first course with a sense of humor is the "tongue and cheek," a mold of tender meats topped with baby leeks and a tad of horseradish cream. Main courses have included roasted monkfish with minced vegetables flavored with lemon verbena, long-roasted breast of veal, and a vegetarian provençale cannelloni. The cheese course might be grilled goat cheese with wilted endive and candied beets or a roasted Anjou pear with blue cheese and walnuts. Great desserts include a tart tatin made with peaches and topped with sour cream ice cream, and "coffee and dough-nuts"—a cappuccino semifreddo and a cinnamon sugar doughnut. Several complimentary surprise sweets end the meal, and the check appears tabulated on a laundry tag. The noteworthy wine list concentrates on Napa Valley vintages that are, amazingly, marked up just a few dollars.

Mustards *7399 Hwy. 29, Yountville, 944-2424, fax 944-0828. L & D daily; $$. Boosters. Reservations advised. MC, V.*

The best place to be seated at this popular bar and grill, where tables are set with crisp white napery, is the cool, screened porch. The atmosphere is casual and chic and the menu imaginative. Selections include soups, salads, and sandwiches (a winning grilled ahi tuna with basil mayonnaise and a good hamburger) as well as entrees such as barbecued baby backribs, mesquite-grilled Sonoma rabbit, and marinated skirt steak. Fresh fish specials are also available. The thin, light onion rings are superb, and house-made ketchup can be ordered to go with them. Garlic lovers will be pleased with a roasted head to spread on the complimentary baguette. Varietal wines are available by the glass. Rich desserts—among them a good bread pudding—and specialty coffees invite lingering.

The **Cosentino Winery** *(7415 St. Helena Hwy. (Hwy. 29), 944-1220, fax 944-1254. Tasting daily 10-5 (fee $2; applies to purchase & keep tasting glass); self-guided tour.)* is located just next door. Built in 1990, this winery is known for producing the country's first designated Meritage wine. Referred to as The Poet, this wine is composed of a marvelous blend of Cabernet Sauvignon, Cabernet Franc, and Merlot. It is pleasant to reserve a picnic lunch from Mustards to enjoy at the winery's bocce ball court-side tables.

Piatti *6480 Washington St., Yountville, 944-2070, 944-9317. L & D daily; $$. Highchairs, boosters, booths, child portions. 100% non-smoking. Reservations advised. AE, MC, V.*

This is the original location in what has become a chain. The sheltered patio here is as inviting on a warm day as the expansive interior is on a cool one. The kitchen prepares grilled fresh fish, rotisserie meats, house-made pastas, and a great pizza. For more description, see page 250.

Picnic Pick-Ups.

• **Oakville Grocery Co.** *7856 Hwy. 29, Oakville, 944-8802, fax 944-1844. Daily 10-6.*

Everything needed to put together a fantastic gourmet picnic can be found here. Select from a large variety of mustards, vinegars, jams, fresh fruits, imported beers, and natural juices, as well as cheeses, sandwiches, salads, sausages, and other deli items, plus a large assortment of enticing desserts. If the choice seems overwhelming, call 48 hours in advance to order a pre-packed picnic box.

• **Pometta's Deli** *7787 Hwy. 29, on Oakville Grade, Oakville, 944-2365, fax 944-1513. M-Sat 9-5, Sun 10-4.*

Located just off busy Highway 29, this down-home-style deli has been operating here since 1952. Known for its wine-marinated barbecued chicken, it also offers made-to-order sandwiches, house-made salads and soups, and cold soft drinks. Informal indoor and outdoor seating is available.

Stars Oakville Cafe *7848 St. Helena Hwy. (Hwy. 29), Oakville, 944-8905, fax 944-0469. L W-Sun, D daily. Reservations advised. AE, MC, V.*

This is a more casual version of celebrity chef Jeremiah Tower's Stars restaurant in San Francisco. Seating is tight in the rustic dining room, but a sheltered patio expands the space. The limited cafe menu offers items such as a warm frisee salad with duck confit, house-made soup, and rabbit or squab baked in a wood-burning oven. Usually a seafood item is also available. Desserts are noteworthy and might include a Meyer lemon pot de creme, a pear crisp with crème fraîche, or a Basque cake stuffed with pastry cream. The wine list emphasizes Napa Valley bottlings.

WHAT TO DO

Hot Air Balloon Rides.

Tour the Napa Valley via hot air balloon. Trips average one hour in the air; altitude and distance depend on which way the wind blows.

• **Adventures Aloft of Napa Valley** *6525 Washington St., Yountville, in Vintage 1870, (800) 944-4408, 944-4408, fax 944-4406. Adults $175, 13-18 $150, 6-12 $125. Reservations required.*

This is the Wine Country's oldest balloon company, with the most experienced pilot team available. The flight includes pre-flight coffee and pastry and a post-flight sit-down breakfast enhanced with a local sparkling wine.

• **Napa Valley Balloons** *6975 Washington St., Yountville, (800) 253-2224, 944-0228, fax 944-0219. Adults $165, 5-9 $85.*

This business offers a similar experience, plus an enamel lapel balloon pin and a photo of the launch or landing.

Vintage 1870 *6525 Washington St., Yountville, 944-2451, fax 944-2453. Daily 10-5:30.*

This lovely old brick building, a former winery, now houses a number of interesting specialty shops and restaurants. Antique wine glasses can be purchased at the **Golden Eagle Bazaar.** The **Yountville Pastry Shop**, an European-style bakery, offers breads, fancy pastries, and tiny quiches as well as coffee. **Cooks' Corner Deli** has picnic supplies, **Gerhards Sausage Kitchen** a variety of fresh sausages made without nitrates (which can be packed on ice to travel), and **The Chocolate Tree** ice cream concoctions and delicious homemade candies. The 15-minute **Napa Valley Show**, which follows the seasons in the vineyards with slides and music, is offered daily in the Keith Rosenthal Theatre. Hot air balloons can often be viewed from the children's play area outside.

WINERIES

Domaine Chandon *One California Dr., Yountville, 944-2280. Daily May-Oct; W- Sun Nov-Apr. Tasting 11-6 (fee); tours 11-5:30.*

This attractive French-owned winery specializes in sparkling wines produced by the traditional methode champenoise. It is reached by crossing a wooden bridge spanning a scenic duck pond surrounded by beautifully landscaped grounds. Built with stones gathered on the site, its arched roofs and doorways were inspired by the caves of Champagne, France. For tasting, visitors are seated at tiny tables covered with French floral cloths in the **Vins Le Salon**. Sparkling wine can be purchased by the glass, and a variety of sparkling wine cocktails are also available. Complimentary bread and cheese are provided to help keep things steady. Children are allowed in the salon and can order mineral water or orange juice.

The spacious, elegant dining room in the **restaurant** (*944-2892, fax 944-1123. L daily May-Oct, W-Sun Nov-Apr; D W-Sun; $$$. 100% non-smoking. Reservations advised. AE, MC, V.)* is lovely, but in good weather the terrace is the premier spot to be seated. Chef Philippe Jeanty, who has been with the restaurant since it opened, prepares an innovative California-style menu that reflects his French Champagne heritage. Dishes are designed especially to complement the winery's sparkling wines. Specialties include cream of tomato soup in puff pastry, house-smoked salmon carpaccio, and venison tournedos wrapped in pancetta. The dessert selection is exciting and extensive. In addition to the winery's own sparkling wines, available by the glass, the wine list includes still varietals from neighboring vintners. Men are requested to wear jackets at dinner.

Vichon Winery *1595 Oakville Grade, Oakville, (800) VICHON-1, 944-2811, fax 944-9224. Tasting daily 10-4:30; tours Sat & Sun at 11 & 3, also by appt. M-F at 10:30 & 2.*

After driving about a mile up this scenic side road off busy Highway 29, visitors are greeted by an informal tasting room and shaded picnic tables with a magnificent vineyard view. A bocce ball court is also available to customers. A catered picnic and tour that includes a visit to the Robert Mondavi Winery is available May thorough October (*$25. Reservations required.).*

St. Helena

(Area Code 707)

VISITOR INFORMATION

Note that St. Helena Highway, Main Street, and Highway 29 are all the same road.

St. Helena Chamber of Commerce *P.O. Box 124 (1080 Main St.), St. Helena 94574, (800) 799-6456, 963-4456, fax 963-5396.*

GETTING THERE

Located approximately 15 miles north of Yountville via Highway 29.

WHERE TO STAY

Ambrose Bierce House *1515 Main St., 963-3003. 2 stories; 3 rooms; 100% non-smoking; $$-$$$; 2-night min. on Sat. Unsuitable for children under 12. No TVs. Continental breakfast.*

Named after the witty author who wrote *The Devil's Dictionary* and who was portrayed by Gregory Peck in the movie *The Old Gringo,* this 1872 house was once Ambrose Bierce's home. One pleasantly decorated room is named after Eadweard Muybridge, who is known as the "father of the motion picture." It holds two interesting artifacts—an 1897 Eastman Kodak No. 2 Hawk-eye camera and a Smith and Wesson No. 2 that is just like the one Muybridge used in 1874 to shoot his wife's lover. Located at the northern end of town, the inn is within convenient walking distance of shopping and dining.

El Bonita Motel *195 Main St., (800) 541-3284, 963-3216, fax 963-8838. 3 stories; 42 rooms; 7 non-smoking rooms; $-$$$; 2-night min. on weekends. Some kitchens. Heated pool, hot tub, sauna. Some pets welcome.*

Featuring an art deco decor, this motel has a shaded, grassy pool area and offers an alternative to classy, cutesy, and expensive Wine Country lodgings.

Harvest Inn *One Main St., (800) 950-8466, 963-WINE, fax 963-4402. 2 stories; 54 rooms; $$-$$$+; 2-night min. on weekends. Some fireplaces. 2 heated pools, 2 hot tubs. Continental breakfast. Small pets welcome.*

Situated on a 21-acre working vineyard, this contemporary English Tudor-style inn has beautifully landscaped grounds and rooms furnished with antiques. Bicycles are available to rent.

La Fleur *1475 Inglewood Ave., 963-0233, same fax. 2 stories; 7 rooms; 100% non-smoking; $$$; 2-night min. on weekends. Unsuitable for children under 12. No TVs; some wood-burning fireplaces. Full breakfast.*

Set back from the main highway, this charming 1882 Queen Anne Victorian B&B is *real quiet.* A large rose garden invites relaxing, and some of the spacious rooms feature claw-foot tubs. Breakfast is served in a cheery solarium with vineyard views, and sometimes guests are able to see hot air balloons floating above the vines.

It's just a short stroll through the flower garden to the tiny **Villa Helena Winery** *(1455 Inglewood Ave., 963-4334, fax 963-4748. Tasting & tours by appt.)* located next door. Call ahead to alert the owner, a former metallurgical engineer from Los Angeles, so that he can be in his office to assist with tasting his Charbono, dessert wines, and unusual Viognier white varietal. He also provides what he calls "the shortest tour in the Napa Valley."

Villa St. Helena *2727 Sulphur Springs Ave., 963-2514, fax 963-2614. 2 stories; 3 rooms; $$$-$$$+; 2-night min. on Sat. Unsuitable for children under 12. No TVs; some wood-burning fireplaces. Pool. Continental breakfast.*

Movie stars reputedly know how to live: in style, in comfort, in seclusion. This Mediterranean-style inn, situated on a 20-acre country estate, offers all of these things. Perhaps that is why it is easy to believe the rumors bandied about regarding past guests: BIG names from Hollywood's heyday. After passing through a closed, privacy-preserving gate, guests follow a scenic, winding back country road, arriving at the estate's arched garages. Once inside the villa, it is a surprisingly long walk, over expanses of shining Mexican terra cotta tile that appear to go on forever, to the three spacious bedchambers. A complimentary bottle of Sauvignon Blanc awaits to refresh weary travelers. This roomy retreat is unpretentiously furnished in eclectic period furniture and features a comfortable library in the west wing, a very large breakfast room/solarium and living room in the center area, and a formal dining room in the east wing. The three wings surround a grassy center courtyard, which abuts a landscaped hillside and boasts a large, inviting pool. The front yard provides panoramic views of the Napa Valley and Mt. St. Helena in the distance. Nights here are very, very quiet.

The Wine Country Inn *1152 Lodi Ln., 963-7077. 3 stories; 24 rooms; 100% non-smoking; $$-$$$+; 2-night min. on some rooms. Unsuitable for children under 13. No TVs; some fireplaces. Heated pool, hot tub. Evening snack, full breakfast.*

Built in the style of a New England inn, without a lot of fuss and frill, this attractive, quiet lodging is located back from the main highway on top of a small country hill. Rooms are decorated with floral wallpapers and tasteful antiques, and many have views of the surrounding vineyards and hills. An evening wine tasting features different wineries, sometimes with the wine-maker in attendance, and the filling breakfast, served on attractive handmade crockery, includes house-made granola and breads.

WHERE TO EAT

Brava Terrace *3010 N. St. Helena Hwy., 963- 9300, fax 963-9581. L & D daily; $$. Closed W in winter & 2 weeks in Jan. Highchairs, boosters, child portions. 100% non-smoking. Reservations advised. AE, MC, V.*

On warm afternoons and evenings the casual deck seating here, amid trees and a gurgling creek, is highly desirable, but two attractive indoor rooms are also most welcoming. A great hamburger shares the menu along with a cassoulet (made with green lentils imported from Puy, France) and both a pasta and risotto du jour. Desserts include a chocolate chip crème brulee and an old-fashioned apple-raisin pie with vanilla-chocolate chip ice cream. Coffees and dessert wines are also available.

Gillwoods *1313 Main St., 963-1788. B & L daily, D Thur-Sun; $. Highchairs, boosters. 100% non-smoking. Reservations advised for D. AE, MC, V.*

This comfortable downtown cafe is known for its breakfasts. All kinds of egg dishes and an assortment of three-egg omelettes are on the menu, as is preservative-free Mother Lode bacon and toasted home-baked bread. And then there's corned-beef hash, buttermilk pancakes, French toast, hot cereals, and granola. Beginning at 11 a.m., salads and sandwiches are also available, and for dinner it's large portions of American-style home cooking.

Picnic Pick-Ups.

• **The Model Bakery** *1357 Main St., 963-8192. Tu-Sat 7-6, Sun 8-4.*

Among the great breads baked in 1920s-era brick-and-sand ovens here are pain de vin (whole wheat sourdough), sour rye, crusty sourdough, and both sweet baguettes and rounds. Then there are croissants stuffed with either ham and cheese or spinach and Feta cheese, panini, and mini pizzas. Chocolate chocolate chip cookies, oatmeal-raisin cookies, and biscotti make pleasing desserts, and coffee and espresso drinks are also available. Seating is provided for on-the-spot indulgence.

• **Napa Valley Olive Oil Manufacturing Co.** *835 McCorkle Ave., between Charter Oak & Allison, 963-4173, fax 963-4301. Daily 8-5.*

Everything needed for a picnic is available here: cheese, sausage, olives, bread sticks, focaccia, biscotti. This Old World-style Italian deli also offers a variety of pastas, sauces, and dried mushrooms, plus its own cold-pressed olive oil and homemade red wine vinegar—all placed helter-skelter in barrels and on make-shift tables. It's really quite unusual. A picnic area is provided outside.

Terra *1345 Railroad Ave., 963-8931. D W-M; $$$. Closed 1st 2 weeks of Jan. 100% non-smoking. Reservations advised. MC, V.*

Fronted by planter boxes filled with gorgeous flowers, this trendy spot has a stone-walled, cave-like interior and offers a cool respite from the area's often warm weather. The eclectic menu selections offered by owner-chef Hiro Sone, formerly of Spago in Los Angeles, combine the styles of France, northern Italy, and the Pacific Rim. They are unusual and flavorful and change periodically: radicchio salad tossed with a balsamic vinaigrette and lots of Parmesan; broiled sake-marinated sea bass with shrimp dumplings in shiso broth; grilled salmon with red Thai curry sauce and basmati rice; chocolate truffle cake with espresso ice cream.

Tra Vigne *1050 Charter Oak Ave., 963-4444, fax 963-4444. L & D daily; $$. Highchairs, boosters, booths, child portions. 100% non-smoking. Reservations advised. MC, V.*

Situated in a rustic stone building, with a stunning high-ceilinged room furnished with both comfortable tables and booths, this justly popular restaurant specializes in northern Italian cuisine. Outside seating under mulberry trees, which twinkle with lights at night, is quite desirable on warm days and evenings. (The stone patio was once part of the now defunct St. Helena Winery.) A round of crusty bread and some olive oil for dipping are provided to enjoy while perusing the menu. Interesting house-made pastas and pizzas share the menu with fresh fish, meats, and poultry, and it seems that there is nothing that is not delicious. The antipasti items and daily specials are often intriguing, and the desserts include such goodies as fresh fruit gelato and biscotti with sweet wine. Wine varietals are available by the glass and include both local and Italian selections.

Take-out sandwiches and salads are available in the adjoining **Cantinetta** *(963-8888)*, where informal outdoor seating is also an option. The restaurant's own olive oils—infused variously with garlic, rosemary, mint, chives, or porcini mushroom—can also be purchased here.

Stop in next door at **Merryvale Vineyards** *(1000 Main St., (800) 326-6069, 963-2225, fax 963-1949. Tasting daily 10-5:30 ($3 fee); tours by appt.)*, which has made its home in the former Sunny St. Helena Winery—the first winery built in the Napa Valley after the repeal of Prohibition. Merryvale hosts a **wine component tasting seminar** *(Sat. at 10am. $10. Reservations required)*.

The Wine Spectator Greystone Restaurant *2555 Main St., 967-1010. L & D W-M.*

Operating within a magnificent 1889 landmark building constructed of locally quarried volcanic stone, which was formerly The Christian Brothers winery, **The Culinary Institute of America at Greystone** is the only center in the world dedicated exclusively to continuing education and career development for professionals in the food, wine, and hospitality fields. A visit to the restaurant affords the opportunity to enjoy Mediterranean tapas, mezze, and antipasti and to see **Brother Timothy's corkscrew collection**, which consists of over 1,800 corkscrews from around the world.

WHAT TO DO

Bale Grist Mill State Historic Park *3369 Hwy. 29, 3 mi. north of town, 942-4575. Daily 10-5. Adults $2, children $1, under 6 free.*

Reached via a shaded, paved stream-side path, this grist mill ground grain for farmers from the 1840s through the turn of the century. The damp site and slow-turning millstones were reputedly responsible for the exceptional cornmeal produced here. Now interpretive displays are located inside the gable-roofed granary, and the 36-foot diameter water wheel has been restored to full operation. Corn and wheat are ground at 1 and 3 p.m. on weekends and are available for purchase. Picnic tables are provided in several shaded areas.

The Silverado Museum *1490 Library Lane, 963-3757, fax 963-0917. Tu-Sun 12-4. Free.*

This museum contains over 8,500 pieces of Robert Louis Stevenson memorabilia. There are paintings, sculptures, and manuscripts as well as his childhood set of lead soldiers. Consider a family read-in of *A Child's Garden of Verses* or *Treasure Island* before or after this visit. The modern stucco library building, situated on the edge of a scenic vineyard, also contains the **Napa Valley Wine Library**.

WINERIES

Beaulieu Vineyard *1960 St. Helena Hwy., Rutherford, (800) 264-6918, 967-5200, fax 963-5920. Tasting & tours daily 10-5.*

Founded in 1900 by Frenchman Georges deLatour, this winery is known for its Cabernet Sauvignons and Chardonnays. A $10 fee is charged for a special tasting of four or five library or reserve wines.

Beringer Vineyards *2000 Main St., just north of town, 963-4812, fax 963-8129. Tours daily 9:30-4, every half-hr.; tasting follows.*

Established in 1876, this winery's Visitor Center is located in a beautiful oak-paneled, stained-glass-laden reproduction of a 19th-century German Tudor mansion known as the Rhine House. Its tour is considered to be one of the most historically informative. The winery is noted for its Chardonnays and Cabernet Sauvignons, and its best vintages can be tasted in the Founder's Room for a $2 to $3 per sample tasting fee. Unfortunately, picnicking is not permitted on the beautifully landscaped grounds.

Freemark Abbey *3022 St. Helena Hwy. N., 2 mi. north of town, 963-9694, fax 963-0554. Tasting daily 10-4:30 (fee $5; applies to wine purchase or keep tasting glass); tour at 2.*

The large, lodge-like tasting room here has oriental carpets covering its hardwood floor. Comfortable furniture arranged around a fireplace invites leisurely sampling. The winery is noted for its Chardonnays and Cabernet Sauvignons. A picnic area is provided to purchasers of wine.

Next door, **Hurd Beeswax Candles** *(3020 St. Helena Hwy. N., (800) 977-7211, 963-7211, fax 963-4358. Daily 10-5.)* operates in an old stone building constructed in 1896. The factory area is open to view, and an active beehive, hidden behind two wooden window covers, can be observed.

Niebaum-Coppola Estate Winery *1991 St. Helena Hwy., Rutherford, (800) RUBICON, 963-9099, fax 963-9084. Tasting daily 10-5 (fee $5; applies to purchase); tours by appt.*

Founded in 1879 by a Finnish sea captain who made his fortune in the Alaskan shipping trade, this is one of the oldest wineries in the Napa Valley. Until recently known as Inglenook Vineyards, it was sold to film director Francis Ford Coppola who has owned a home on part of the property since the 1970s. A Tucker automobile is parked in the tasting room and the director's Oscars are displayed, but best of all his wines are now available for tasting. A terrace provides space for picnicking. The **Centennial Museum** documents the winery's history.

Prager Winery and Port Works *1281 Lewelling Lane, St. Helena, (800) 969-PORT, 963-PORT, fax 963-7679.*

Located down a country lane, the valley's premier port purveyor offers a rustic, informal tasting room for sampling the wares.

St. Supery Winery and Wine Discovery Center *8440 St. Helena Hwy., Rutherford, (800) 942-0809, 963-4507, fax 963-4526. Tasting & tours daily 9:30-4:30; in summer to 6 (fee $2.50, includes lifetime tasting pass).*

The guided tour includes a traipse through the property's Queen Anne Victorian **Atkinson House**. A self-guided tour of the vineyard demonstration garden is also available. Children get a coloring book and crayons to occupy them while parents taste.

V. Sattui Winery *1111 White Lane, (800) 799-2337, 963-7774, fax 963-4324. Tasting & self-guided tour daily 9-5; in summer to 6.*

Established in the North Beach area of San Francisco in 1885, this winery was shut down during Prohibition, then re-established in St. Helena in 1976. Family-owned for four generations, the current wine-maker is the great-grandson of founder Vittorio Sattui. V. Sattui wines are sold only at the winery. The Johannisberg Rieslings and Cabernet Sauvignons that they are best known for can be tasted in the stone winery building featuring three-foot-thick walls and chiseled archways. Picnic supplies are available in a deli well-stocked with house-made salads and with what is claimed to be the largest selection of international cheeses on the West Coast. Plenty of oak-shaded picnic tables are provided on a two-acre picnic grounds.

Calistoga
(Area Code 707)

A LITTLE BACKGROUND

Calistoga sits on top of a hot underground river. Originally called "Indian Hot Springs," the town's current name was devised from a combination of California and Saratoga—a spa area in New York that was the inspiration for an early 25-cottage spa development by town founder Sam Brannan, California's first millionaire. More of the town's history is to be discovered in *The Silverado Squatters* by Robert Louis Stevenson.

Calistoga is enjoying a renaissance as a popular weekend and summer retreat. Its many unpretentious spas are geared to helping visitors relax, unwind, and get healthy in pools filled from hot springs. Most offer services such as mud baths, steam baths, and massages, and many make their mineral pools available for day use for a small fee.

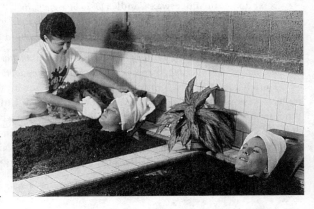

While here, don't miss taking a mud bath, one of life's great experiences. The mud is prepared using a mixture of volcanic ash (collected from nearby Mount St. Helena), peat moss, and naturally heated mineral water. After a period of nude immersion, the bather takes a mineral bath and a steam bath, and then, swaddled in dry blankets, rests and cools. Ahhh. (Note that pregnant women, people with high blood pressure or heart conditions, and children under 14 are cautioned against taking mud baths.)

VISITOR INFORMATION

Calistoga Chamber of Commerce *1458 Lincoln Ave. #9, Calistoga 94515, 942-6333, fax 942-9287.*

GETTING THERE

Located approximately 10 miles north of St. Helena via Highway 29.

WHERE TO STAY

Brannan Cottage Inn *109 Wapoo Ave., 942-4200. 1 story; 6 rooms; 100% non-smoking; $$-$$$+2-night min. on weekends. Unsuitable for children under 12. 1 TV. Full breakfast.*

Located a pleasant two-block walk from town, this Greek revival Victorian cottage was built by Sam Brannan in 1860. It is listed on the National Register of Historic Places. A large palm tree planted by Brannan, and mentioned by Robert Louis Stevenson in *The Silverado Squatters*, still grows in the garden. Rooms are named after flowers and most open onto a quiet courtyard, where breakfast is served in warm weather.

Calistoga Spa Hot Springs *1006 Washington St., 942-6269. 2 stories; 57 units; 100% non-smoking; $$-$$$; 2-night min. on weekends. Children under 1 free. All kitchens. 3 hot spring pools, hot tub, fitness room.*

This conveniently located, unpretentious, and particularly family-friendly spa offers motel rooms that open onto the pool area. Four outdoor mineral water pools are available: a 100-degree soaking pool, an 83-degree lap pool, a 93-degree children's wading pool, and a 104-degree covered Jacuzzi. Non-guests can also use the pools *(8:30am-9pm. $10/person.).* Mud baths, mineral baths, steam baths, and massage are available.

Dr. Wilkinson's Hot Springs *1507 Lincoln Ave., 942-4102. 2 stories; 42 rooms; 36 non-smoking rooms; $$-$$$; 2-night min. on weekends. Children under 2 free. Some kitchens. 1 indoor heated pool, 2 outdoor heated pools, hot tub, health spa, steam room.*

Operated by the Wilkinson family, this pleasant spa features an indoor 104-degree mineral pool with a view of the nearby foothills, a cooler 92-degree outdoor mineral pool, and a refreshing 82-degree outdoor swimming pool. Pools are not open to non-guests. Mud baths, mineral baths, steam baths, and massage are available, and a separate facial salon offers an assortment of treatments. Lodging is in motel units. The **Hideaway Cottages** and **The Victorian House**, which are unsuitable for children, are also available nearby.

Indian Springs Spa & Resort *1712 Lincoln Ave., 942-4913, fax 942-4919. 1 story; 17 units; 50% non-smoking; $$$-$$$+. Children under 2 free. All kitchens; some gas fireplaces. Heated mineral water pool, health spa, 1 clay tennis court.*

Built on the site of the town's first spa (which was built in 1860 by Sam Brannan), this resort is where Robert Louis Stevenson vacationed in 1880 and is said to have written part of *The Silverado Squatters*. It is the state's oldest continuously operating pool and spa facility. The spa dates back to 1910 and includes a Mission-style Olympic-size swimming pool filled with 90-to 102-degree geyser mineral water; it is open to non-guests for day use *(adults $10-$20, children $7-$10)* and is especially popular with children. And this is the only spa in town offering relaxing all ash mud baths. Accommodations are 1940s housekeeping bungalows that were refurbished in 1988. Croquet is also available to guests.

Mountain Home Ranch *3400 Mountain Home Ranch Rd., 6 mi. from town, 942-6616, fax 942-9091. 3 stories; 14 units; $$-$$$+. Closed Dec & Jan. Children under 1 free. No TVs; some kitchens & wood-burning fireplaces & stoves. 2 unheated pools (summer only), 1 tennis court. Continental breakfast (Sept-June only); restaurant (Sept-June only). Pets welcome.*

Guests at this informal rural spot stay in their choice of modern cabins with either a private deck or porch, lodge rooms, or rustic cabins (summer only). Summer activities include swimming, hiking, and fishing. Rates are higher in summer and include both breakfast and dinner.

Mount View Hotel *1457 Lincoln Ave., (800) 816-6877, 942-6877, fax 942-6904. 2 stories; 33 rooms; 100% non-smoking; $$-$$$+; 2-night min. on Sat. Unsuitable for children under 16. Some VCRs. Heated pool, hot tub, health spa. Restaurant.*

This beautifully restored grand hotel, built in 1918 and furnished with an eclectic mix of contemporary and antique pieces, is a National Historic Landmark. Nine theme suites are furnished in period pieces, including two in art deco style, and three private cottages have their own decks and hot tubs. An upscale European-style spa offers a variety of treatments; packages are available.

Operated by celebrity chef Jan Birnbaum, **Catahoula Restaurant** *(942-BARK. L & D W-Mon. Closed Jan. Reservations advised.)* offers an imaginative menu of Southern-style American cuisine as well as spectacular desserts. The menu focuses on items from the wood-burning brick oven, braised dishes, and freshly baked sourdough breads. **The Saloon** serves lunch daily and hosts a popular Sunday Blues Brunch. Special events centered around food and wine are scheduled regularly.

The Pink Mansion *1415 Foothill Blvd., (800) 238-PINK, 942-0558, same fax. 5 rooms; $$$-$$$+. Some fireplaces. Indoor pool & hot tub. Full breakfast.*

Nestled into a hillside on the outskirts of town, this restored 1875 mansion is painted a pleasant shade of pink. A large front porch equipped with a couch swing invites leisurely contemplation of the surroundings, and the indoor pool and hot tub have a relaxing view of a redwood grove behind the house. Several rooms have claw-foot tubs, and the Angel Room is bedecked with former owner Aunt Alma's angel collection. A lavish breakfast is served in the elegant dining room.

WHERE TO EAT

All Seasons Cafe & Wine Shop *1400 Lincoln Ave., 942-9111, fax 942-9420. L & D Thur-Tu, Sat & SunBr; $$-$$$. Highchairs, boosters. 100% non-smoking. Reservations advised. MC, V.*

Dress is very casual in this narrow dining room, and children are welcome and accommodated. One dinner enjoyed here began with great house-made bread and a flawless warm spinach salad prepared with pancetta, house-smoked chicken, and Feta cheese. It was followed by a perfectly roasted chicken accompanied by wonderful roasted potatoes, whole cloves of garlic, artichokes, and olives. Dessert was a memorable fresh cherry cobbler with house-made vanilla ice cream—served on a plate strewn artistically with flower petals.

Calistoga Inn *1250 Lincoln Ave., 942-4101, fax 942-4919. B, L, & D daily; $$-$$$. Highchairs, boosters. Reservations advised. MC, V.*

The specialty here is simply-prepared seafood, and the menu changes daily. Consider grilled catfish with tomatoes and garlic, grilled thresher shark with red bell pepper sauce, or ceviche of barracuda. Duck, veal, steak, and pastas are often on the menu, as are irresistible desserts such as Santa Rosa plum sorbet or raspberries with chocolate crème fâiche. In warm weather diners are seated outside on a patio overlooking the Napa Valley River. An informal brewpub operating in the bar area offers five house brews—one of them a Pilsner-style lager (the house specialty)—and inexpensive pub food such as house-made potato chips, a variety of salads, a good hamburger, and jerk chicken.

Modest, inexpensive lodging with shared baths is available upstairs. Several sets of adjoining rooms are suitable for families.

Cinnabar Cafe *1440 Lincoln Ave., 942-6989. B, L, & D daily; $-$$. Highchairs, boosters, booths, child portions. 100% non-smoking. Reservations advised. AE, MC, V.*

Attractive and unpretentious, this spot serves reasonably priced, honest food. Breakfast is the expected items plus 19 kinds of three-egg omelettes, sautéed fresh boned trout, buttermilk or buckwheat pancakes, and house-made granola. Lunch includes made-from-scratch soups and breads and a large variety of sandwiches and hamburgers. Dinner is a pricier selection of fresh fish and prime rib.

WHAT TO DO

American Balloon Adventures 2420 Kathy Way, (800) 333-4359, 942-6546. Adults $165, under 12 $100. Reservations required.

Because the winds will almost certainly carry it over the scenic vineyards, the northern end of the valley is said to be the best area to take off in a hot air balloon. These one-hour flights lift off between 5:30 and 7 a.m. and include breakfast at a local restaurant.

Bothe-Napa Valley State Park 3801 St. Helena Hwy. N., 942-4575. Daily 8-sunset. $5/vehicle. Pool: Summer only. Adults $3, under 18 $1.

Swimming in the naturally heated pool is a favorite activity at this lovely park, but picnicking and hiking are also popular. Campsites are available.

Calistoga Gliders 1546 Lincoln Ave., 942-5000. Daily 9-6; to 7:30 May-Oct. $79/1 person, $110/2. Reservations advised on weekends.

The 20-minute glider ride/sightseeing trip covers approximately ten miles. Longer flights are also available.

Old Faithful Geyser of California 1299 Tubbs Lane, 942-6463, fax 942-6898. Daily 9-5; in summer to 6. Adults $5, 65+ $4, 6-12 $2.

Located in the crater of an extinct volcano, this idyllic site is home to one of only three geysers in the world that erupt regularly and merit the name Old Faithful. (The other two are in Yellowstone National Park in Wyoming and on North Island in New Zealand.) This one erupts approximately every 40 minutes and shoots 350-degree water 60 feet into the air. The show lasts from three to four minutes. Plenty of picnic tables and a snack bar are available.

Petrified Forest 4100 Petrified Forest Rd., 4 mi. west of town, 942-6667. Daily 10-5; in summer to 6. Adults $3, 55+ $2, 4-11 $1.

A self-guided ¼-mile path leads through this unusual forest. Open to the public since 1870, it contains petrified redwood trees that are over three million years old and as long as 126 feet. Facilities include a small museum and picnic tables.

Sharpsteen Museum and Sam Brannan Cottage 1311 Washington St., 942-5911. Daily 12-4; in summer 10-4. Free.

Created by Ben Sharpsteen, a Walt Disney Studio animator and Oscar-winning producer, this exceptionally well-designed museum displays an elaborate and extensive diorama of Calistoga as it appeared in 1865—when Sam Brannan opened the town's first spa and began its reputation as a restorative resort area. The beautifully furnished cottage exemplifies the style in which wealthy San Franciscans lived when they vacationed here in the late 1800s. A working model of the Napa Valley Railroad is also displayed.

Smith's Mount St. Helena Trout Farm 18401 Ida Clayton Rd., 14 mi. from town (call for directions), 987-3651, fax 987-0105. Sat & Sun 10-6, Feb-Oct. Closed Nov-Jan. $1-$5.

All ages can enjoy fishing on this lake. Poles and bait are free. The charge for fish caught is determined by size, and cleaning and packaging are included.

WINERIES

Chateau Montelena Winery *1429 Tubbs Lane (call for directions), 942-5105, fax 942-4221. Tasting daily 10-4 (fee $5; applies to purchase of $20+); tours at 11 & 2, reservations required.*

This winery, which is noted for its Chardonnays and Cabernet Sauvignons, can be difficult to find. Reservations are needed for the unusual island picnic area in Jade Lake where two islets, reached via footbridge, hold miniature picnic pavilions. The lake features a berthed Chinese junk and is populated with ducks, swans, and geese.

Clos Pegase *1060 Dunaweal Lane, (800) 366-8583, 942-4981, fax 942-4993. Tasting daily 10:30-5 (fee $2.50); tours at 11 & 2.*

Because of its stark stucco architecture, this winery opened in 1987 amid much controversy. There were those who liked it and those who didn't. (It is interesting to note that its post-modern design was the winner in a contest sponsored by the San Francisco Museum of Modern Art.) Surrounded by young vineyards, with tall, thin cypress trees lining an outdoor walkway and modern sculpture dotting the landscape, it has a surreal quality. Named after Pegasus, the winged horse of Greek mythology that gave birth to wine and art, the winery appropriately displays a collection of fine art within its caves. Among the treasure-trove are ancient vineyard tools and rare free-blown wine bottles, carafes, and glasses dating from the 3rd century B.C. to the present. Picnic tables are available.

Sterling Vineyards

Sterling Vineyards *1111 Dunaweal Lane, (800) 726-6136, 942-3344, fax 942-3445. Tasting & self-guided tour daily 10:30-4:30. Gondola ride: Adults $6, under 18 $3.*

Accessible via a four-minute gondola ride, this winery was built to resemble a Greek monastery. It features a stunning and unusual white stucco, cubist style of architecture. Spectacular views of the Napa Valley are provided throughout the self-guided winery tour. For tasting, visitors are seated at tables either in a spacious interior room or on an outdoor terrace, and children are given a complimentary juice drink. A picnic terrace with a magnificent view is also available.

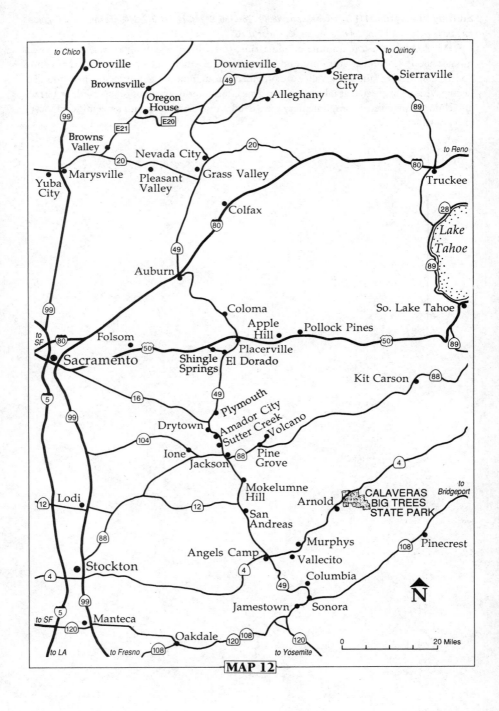

MAP 12

Highway 49–Gold Rush Country

The Mother Lode, as this area is sometimes referred to, stretches along the entire route of Highway 49, south from Mariposa and north through Nevada City, ending in Downieville. (On the other hand the Mother Lode *vein*, which runs from Northern California to South America, surfaces in the area between Jamestown and Auburn.)

The main Gold Rush towns can all be visited by driving along Highway 49. But many scenic side roads, leading to tiny hamlets with intriguing names such as Fiddletown and Rescue, invite exploration.

This area provides history, adventure, and scenic beauty. Not yet heavily promoted and packaged, it also provides many low-key and inexpensive vacation joys for the hype-weary traveler. A thorough visit could take weeks, but a satisfying visit takes only a few days. For a weekend visit, don't attempt to drive the entire route. Visit one portion and then go back another time to see the rest.

Because the area is steeped in history, consider doing some reading for more background information. Two classic books about the area that are also good for reading out loud are *The Celebrated Jumping Frog of Calaveras County* by Samuel L. Clemens (Mark Twain) and *The Luck of Roaring Camp* by Bret Harte.

Currently there is said to be another gold rush on. Many nervous people are staking claims, so caution is advised when doing any unguided panning or prospecting.

GETTING THERE

Located approximately 135 miles east of San Francisco. Take Highway 80 to Highway 580 to Highway 205 to Highway 120 to Highway 49.

Jamestown
(Area Code 209)

A LITTLE BACKGROUND

Filled with architecturally interesting old buildings, this historical boom town's economy is now fueled by myriad antique shops.

WHERE TO STAY

Jamestown Hotel *18153 Main St., (800) 205-4901, 984-3902, fax 984-4149. 2 stories; 8 rooms; 100% non-smoking; $$. Unsuitable for children under 7. No TVs. Continental breakfast; restaurant.*

Built in the 1850s, this hotel is furnished with Victorian antiques and has many spacious suites with sitting rooms.

A nicely appointed **restaurant** dining room *(L&D daily. Highchairs, boosters, child portions.)* serves an eclectic menu of prime rib, seafood, chicken, veal, pasta and hamburgers. An attractive adjacent saloon specializes in fancy drinks, California wines, and tasty appetizers.

The National Hotel *77 Main St., (800) 894-3446, 984-3446, fax 984-5620. 2 stories; 11 rooms; 100% non-smoking; $$. Unsuitable for children under 10. TVs upon request; some shared baths. Full breakfast; restaurant, room service. Pets welcome.*

A sense of history awaits at this really *old* hotel. Built in 1859, it has been in continuous operation ever since. In fact, it is one of the ten oldest continuously operating hotels in the state and is now an official historical landmark. Until 1978 rooms were rented to men only and went for $4 a night. Indoor plumbing was added in 1981! Much of the antique furniture is original to the hotel, and that which isn't is right in tune with the era. Overall, everything is far more luxurious now than anything those gold miners ever experienced.

The hotel's **restaurant** *(L & D daily, SunBr. Highchairs, boosters, child menu. 100% non-smoking. Reservations advised. AE, MC, V.)* is an especially inviting spot for dinner after the drive in. On warm evenings diners are seated outside on a pleasant patio. Strong points of the menu include fresh fish with creative sauces, a wine list with the largest selection of Gold Country wines available anywhere, and exceptional desserts. Located just off the parlor, an old-time saloon, featuring its original redwood long bar with brass rail and also an 1881 cash register, is the perfect spot for a nightcap.

WHERE TO EAT

Country Kitchen Cafe *18231 Main St., 984-3326. B & L daily; $. Highchairs, boosters, child portions. AE, MC, V.*

Located in a structure that dates from 1865 and is one of the oldest wooden commercial buildings remaining in town, this cafe offers simple food in pleasant surroundings. House-made soups, pastries, and pies are particularly good. Kids will probably be happy to find that both a hot dog and a peanut butter & jelly sandwich are on the menu. Ice cream treats are also available, and a candy counter dispenses a variety of sweets. A gift shop operating upstairs is worth a visit.

Smoke Cafe *18191 Main St., 984-3733. L Sat & Sun, D Tu-Sun; $-$$. Highchairs, boosters, child portions. No reservations. MC, V.*

Located within a modern Santa Fe-style building with soft stucco edges and lots of tile, this popular upscale spot specializes in Mexican cuisine and has pollo de mole poblano and chile verde on its menu. A hamburger is also available.

WHAT TO DO

Gold Prospecting Expeditions *18170 Main St., (800) 596-0009, 984-GOLD, fax 984-0711. Trips daily 10-5. 1-hr. trip $20/person, $35/family.*

Operating out of the town's old livery stable, this business organizes prospecting trips appropriate for children as well as adults. All equipment is supplied. Participants get down and dirty in a stream, where they are taught the basics. It is claimed gold has been found on every trip lasting two hours or more, and the rule is "finders, keepers." Trips by river raft or helicopter can also be arranged. Children can pan for free in a trough located in front of the shop.

Railtown 1897 State Historic Park, *on Fifth Ave., 984-3953, fax 984-4936. Train: Sat & Sun at 11, 12, 1, & 3; May-Aug only. Adults $6, 6-12 $3. Round-house tours: Daily 10-4. Adults $2, 6-12 $1.*

Be sure to allow time to watch the hubbub that surrounds preparing the train for departure. The depot is always full of excitement as the huge steam trains roll in and out, sounding
their screaming whistles and belching a mix of fire, smoke, and steam. The **Mother Lode
Cannonball**, an historic steam train, takes passengers on a 40-minute, six-mile round trip to
Woods Creek Siding. Several other special trips are sometimes available. A tour is given of the
old six-stall **roundhouse** turntable and machine shop, where the trains are still serviced. If it all
looks familiar, that could be because many TV shows and movies have been filmed here. The list
includes *Bonanza, Little House on the Prairie, The Virginian, High Noon,* and *Pale Rider.*

Sonora
(Area Code 209)

A LITTLE BACKGROUND

Once known as the "Queen of the Southern Mines," when it was the richest and wildest town in
the southern Mother Lode, this town still bustles and is a popular stopover spot for skiers and
other travelers on their way to vacation cabins and recreation. Because it is a crossroads, it has
been built up more than most Gold Rush towns and is far from quiet. But off the main thor-
oughfares a taste of the old Sonora of Victorian homes and quiet streets is still to be found. It is
interesting to note that in Spanish "tuolumne" means "stone houses."

VISITOR INFORMATION

Tuolumne County Visitors Bureau *P.O. Box 4020 (55 W. Stockton St.), Sonora 95370, (800) 446-1333,
533-4400, fax 533-0956.*

ANNUAL EVENTS

Wild West Film Fest *September. (800) 446-1333.*

This event celebrates the area's long history as a filming site for western movies—over 400
films have been made here since 1919. During the day, vintage western films are shown continuously, and an assortment of genre celebrities are available for autographs. The highlight is a
professional rodeo on Saturday night, with traditional rodeo clowns and several contests children can participate in before starting time

WHERE TO STAY

Gunn House Motel *286 S. Washington St., (800) 606-GUNN, 532-3421. 2 stories; 20 rooms; some non-
smoking rooms; $-$$. Solar-heated pool. Continental breakfast; restaurant. Pets welcome.*

Built in 1850, this adobe house was once the residence of Dr. Lewis C. Gunn. Then it served for awhile as the offices for the *Sonora Herald*—the area's first newspaper. Rooms are restored and furnished with antiques. The cozy office is staffed with helpful personnel, and a pool-side cocktail lounge is available to guests.

Hostel *11800 Columbia College Dr., on the Columbia College campus, 533-2339. 36 beds; family & couples rooms.*
　　See also page 391.

WHERE TO EAT

Good Heavens *49 N. Washington St., 532-FOOD. L Tu-Sun, SunBr; $$. 1 highchair. Reservations advised. MC, V.*
　　Within a restored historic brick building, this cozy, fussy little spot serves freshly made, delicious items. The lunch menu features made-from-scratch soups, inventive sandwiches and salads, and house-made desserts. The exceptional homemade jams can be purchased to go.

WHAT TO DO

Autumn Colors Drive.
　　Take Highway 108 about 30 to 35 miles east of town for a dazzling display of fall leaf colors. Populated with aspen, this entire area is usually vibrant with color after the first frost, which generally happens in early October. Beginning in late October, colorful leaves can be seen right in town.

Mark Twain's Cabin *Off Hwy. 49, midway between town & Angels Camp.*
　　Built on **Jackass Hill**, this replica of Twain's cabin is constructed around the original chimney. It can be viewed from the outside only. Twain lived here in 1864 and '65, when he wrote *The Celebrated Jumping Frog of Calaveras County* and *Roughing It*.

Tuolumne County Museum and History Center *158 W. Bradford Ave., 532-1317. Sun-F 10-4, Sat 10-3:30. Free.*
　　Located inside a jail built in 1866, this museum displays Gold Rush-era relics that include pioneer firearms and gold samples. Picnic tables are available.

Columbia State Historic Park
(Area Code 209)

A LITTLE BACKGROUND

In her prime, with over 6,000 people calling her home, Columbia was one of the largest mining towns in the southern Mother Lode. Her nickname, "Gem of the Southern Mines," was reference to the $87 million-plus in gold mined here (a figure calculated when gold was $35 an ounce).

　　Since 1945 this reconstructed Gold Rush town has been a state historic park. It is open daily from 9 to 5, and admission is free. Streets are blocked off to all but foot traffic and an occasional stagecoach. A museum introduces visitors to the town's history, and more exhibits are scattered among the many restored historic buildings.

　　In fact, the whole town is basically a living museum. Private concessionaires operate modern versions of businesses that would have been found here in the 1800s. Cold mugs of beer and old-fashioned root beer-like sarsaparilla are poured in the town saloon. A blacksmith ekes out a living practicing his craft in a ramshackle shed, and a candy kitchen uses 100-year-old recipes and antique equipment to turn out such old-time favorites as horehound, rocky road, and almond bark. Customers in the photography studio don Gold Rush-era clothing for portraits taken with vintage camera equipment, but developed with quick modern processes. Visitors can even tour a still-operating gold mine and learn to pan for gold in a salted sluice.

If it all looks familiar, note that *High Noon* and episodes of *Little House on the Prairie* were filmed here.

VISITOR INFORMATION

Columbia State Historic Park *P.O. Box 367, Columbia 95310, 532-4301.*

ANNUAL EVENTS

Victorian Easter Parade and Egg Hunt *March or April; on Easter Sunday.*

Fireman's Muster *May.*

A Miners Christmas *December; first 2 weekends.*

WHERE TO STAY

City Hotel *Main St., (800) 532-1479, 532-1479, fax 532-7027. 2 stories; 10 rooms; 100% non-smoking; $$. Children under 4 free. No TVs; all shared baths. Full breakfast; restaurant, limited room service.*

This 1856 hotel provides overnight lodging in keeping with the town's flavor. The restored rooms are furnished with Victorian antiques from the collection of the California State Parks Department. Eager-to-please students from the Columbia College Hospitality Management program dress in period clothing and supplement the full-time staff by performing such esoteric duties as fluffing pillows and, in the beautifully appointed restaurant downstairs, de-crumbing tables. Guests are encouraged to congregate in the parlor in the evening for Sherry, conversation, and games. To make the trek down the hall to the bath more civilized, guests are loaned a wicker basket packed with shower cap, slippers, robe, soap, and shampoo.

The hotel **restaurant** *(D Tu-Sat, SunBr; $$. Highchairs, boosters, child portions. 100% non-smoking. Reservations advised. AE, MC, V.)* prepares elegant regional cuisine, and fixed-price, seasonal four-course dinners *($26-$31)* are available. The cozy **What Cheer Saloon**, which retains its original cherry-wood bar that was shipped around the horn from New England, adjoins.

Columbia Gem Motel *22131 Parrotts Ferry Rd., 1 mi. from park, 532-4508. 1 story; 11 units; $-$$. Pets welcome.*

Typical motel-room decor greets guests inside tiny cabins scattered in an attractive pine tree setting.

Fallon Hotel *Washington St., (800) 532-1479, 532-1470, fax 532-7027. 2 stories; 14 rooms; 100% non-smoking; $$. Closed M-W Oct-May. Children under 4 free. No TVs; many shared bathrooms. Continental breakfast.*

This historic hotel, dating from 1857, has undergone a $4 million renovation and is now beautifully restored to its Victorian grandeur. Many of the furnishings are original to the hotel. Several large second-floor rooms with balconies are perfect for families. The hotel is operated in similar style as the City Hotel and is under the same management. An **ice cream parlor** operates on the main floor, and packages that include lodging, dinner, and a theater performance are available.

WHAT TO DO

Columbia Stage Line and Stable *532-0663. Daily 10:30-4:30, mid-May-Aug; Sat & Sun rest of year. Stage: Adults $4.50-$5.50, 65+ & under 13 $4-$5, under 5 free when held on adult's lap. Stable: pony rides $5, horse or pony trail rides $8-$50.*

Ride in an authentic stagecoach and experience the ride many gold seekers did years ago. Or take a trail ride into the back woods through limestone canyons. Gentle ponies are available for small children.

Fallon House Theatre *532-4644. Reservations advised.*

Located in the rear of the Fallon Hotel, this historic theater has been in operation since the 1880s. The second-longest continually operating playhouse in California, it stages first-run and classic dramas and musicals and employs both professional and student talent. The semi-professional repertory company does eight major productions each year.

Gold Mine Winery *22265 Parrots Ferry Rd., 532-3089, 1/4-mile south of park. Tasting daily 11-7; tours Sat & Sun at 2.*

Sample an apple-tasting May wine flavored in the German tradition with sweet woodruff. Or, during the fall holidays, try the fragrant Spiced Jubilee mulled wine.

Murphys
(Area Code 209)

A LITTLE BACKGROUND

A map to the town's buildings and sights is available from merchants and at the check-in desk in Murphys Hotel.

ANNUAL EVENTS

Music from Bear Valley *July. In Bear Valley; 753-2574.*

Held high in the Sierra in a circus-style red-and-white-striped tent, this festival presents a musical smorgasbord.

WHERE TO STAY

Dunbar House, 1880 *271 Jones St., (800) 692-6006, 728-2897, fax 728-1451. 2 stories; 4 rooms; 100% non-smoking; $$$-$$$+; 2-night min. on weekends. Unsuitable for children under 10. All VCRs & wood-burning stoves. Hot tub. Afternoon snack, full breakfast.*

This restored Italianate-style home was the filming location for the TV series *Seven Brides for Seven Brothers.* Rooms are decorated with antiques, lace, and down comforters. Guests are greeted each afternoon by an appetizer buffet, and a complimentary bottle of local wine awaits in each room's private refrigerator. Buggy rides through town can be arranged.

Murphys Historic Hotel *457 Main St., (800) 532-7684, 728-3444, fax 728-1590. 3 stories; 29 rooms; 13 non-smoking rooms; $$; 2-night min. on some weekends May-Sept. Children under 12 free. 20 TVs; some shared baths. Continental breakfast; restaurant.*

Built in 1856 and now a National Historical Monument, this very old hotel provided lodging for such Gold Rush-era luminaries as U.S. Grant, J.P. Morgan, Mark Twain, Horatio Alger, and Black Bart—each of whom has a room he actually stayed in named after him. Modern motel rooms, with no legends attached, are available adjacent to the hotel. Though the hotel rooms are immeasurably more interesting, they have one big drawback: The noisy hotel bar, reputed to be the best in the Mother Lode, is kept jumping until the wee hours by townspeople and travelers alike. Those who want to sleep should opt for a less interesting, but quiet, motel room. Special skier packages are available in winter.

The hotel **restaurant** *(B, L, & D daily; $-$$. Highchairs, boosters, child menu. 100% non-smoking. Reservations advised. AE, MC, V.)* is popular with locals. Menu choices consist of hearty, made-from-scratch American country and continental fare, and portions tend to be large.

WHERE TO EAT

The Peppermint Stick *454 Main St., 728-3570. M-Sat 10-10, Sun 12-9, June-Aug; shorter hours rest of year; $. Highchairs, boosters, child portions. 100% non-smoking. No reservations. No cards.*

When it was built in 1893, this building served the town as an ice house. Now it is a cheerful ice cream parlor serving old-fashioned sodas and cleverly named sundaes. Sandwiches, soups, and candies are also available, and everything can be packed to go.

WHAT TO DO

Black Bart Players *580 S. Algiers, 728-8842. Weekends in Apr, Aug-Sept, & Nov only; 8pm. Tickets $7.50. Reservations advised.*

This little theater group performs musicals, melodramas, mysteries, comedies, and classics.

Calaveras Big Trees State Park *1170 E. Hwy. 4, Arnold, 15 mi. east of town, 795-2334. Daily dawn-dusk. $5/vehicle.*

This ancient forest houses the mammoth, and now rare, giant sequoia variety of redwood. The Big Trees Nature Trail is a choice trek for families with young chil-

dren. Other trails are also available, as are campsites and picnic and barbecue facilities. In warm weather, the Beaver Creek Picnic Area has a good wading area for children. (Picnic provisions can be picked up in Arnold, where there are delis, markets, and restaurants.) A cross-country ski trail is available in winter, and a horseback-riding concession operates in summer.

Mercer Caverns *1665 Sheepranch Rd., off Hwy. 4, 1 mi. north of town, 728-2101. Daily 9-4:30, June-Sept; rest of year Sat & Sun 11-3:30. Adults $5, 5-11 $2.50. Strollers not permitted.*

Discovered over 100 years ago in 1885, this well-lighted 55-degree limestone cavern takes about a half-hour to tour. It is said to be the longest continually operating commercial cavern in the state.

Moaning Cavern *5350 Moaning Cave Rd., west of town in Vallecito, 736-2740. Daily 10-5; June-Aug 9-6. Adults $6.75, 65+ $6.50, 6-12 $3.50. Strollers not permitted.*

The 45-minute tour ascends a 100-foot-high spiral staircase into the largest public cavern chamber in California. It is said to be big enough to hold the Statue of Liberty! The cavern was originally discovered by Native Americans, many of whom are thought to have fallen to their death here. In fact, the oldest human remains in the U.S. were found here. A more expensive three-hour **rappel tour** allows a 180-foot rope descent into the cave; reservations are necessary. Campsites are available.

Old Timers Museum *Main St., across street from Murphys Hotel, 728-1160. F-Sun 11-4; in winter Sat & Sun only. Free.*

Dating from 1856, this is the oldest stone building in town. It is interesting to note that the stones were fitted together without mortar. The building now houses Gold Rush-era memorabilia.

Wineries.

• **Milliaire Winery** *276 Main St., 728-1658. Tasting & tours F-M 11-5.*

Operating out of a converted carriage house-gas station, this tiny winery is known for its intense, full-bodied wines. It also produces three delicious dessert wines: a late harvest Zinfandel, a Zinfandel Port, and Semillon.

• **Stevenot Winery** *2690 San Domingo Rd., 1 mi. past Mercer Caverns, 728-3436. Tasting daily 10-5; tours by appt.*

Located in a canyon on the site of the first swimming pool in Calaveras County, this relatively big (40,000 cases annually), relatively old winery (circa 1978) is housed in a series of old buildings. The cool, rustic Alaska House tasting room has a sod roof and split-log walls. Picnic tables are sheltered under a grape arbor and have a view of the surrounding vineyards.

Angels Camp
(Area Code 209)

VISITOR INFORMATION

Calaveras Lodging and Visitors Association *P.O. Box 637 (1211 S. Main St.), Angels Camp 95222, (800) 225-3764, 736-0049, fax 736-9124.*

ANNUAL EVENTS

Jumping Frog Jubilee *May; third weekend. 736-2561. $5-$9.*

Visitors are invited to bring their own frog to enter in this historic contest, but rental frogs are available on site. In 1986 Rosie the Ribiter set the current world's record by landing, after three leaps, 21 feet 5¾ inches from the starting pad. She earned her jockey $1,500. The prize money is usually won by frog jockeys who are serious about the sport and bring 50 to 60 frogs. So far, a rental frog has never won. The **Calaveras County Fair** is part of the fun and features carnival rides, livestock exhibits, a rodeo, a destruction derby, headliner entertainers, and fireworks.

WHERE TO EAT

There is only one recommended restaurant for this town. Could this have something to do with Mark Twain's description of some coffee ("day-before-yesterday dishwater") and soup ("hellfire") suffered long ago at the Hotel Angels?

Picnic Pick-Up.

• The Pickle Barrel *1225 S. Main St., 736-4704. M-Thur 8-4, F-Sun 8-8.*

This friendly Italian deli will pack picnic supplies to go, and provides tables for those who decide to stay. Reservations are suggested for dinner, which features prime rib and a variety of pastas.

Informal picnic areas can be found by the river. Scenic **Utica Park** has picnic tables and a children's play area.

WHAT TO DO

Angels Camp Museum *753 S. Main St., 736-2963. Daily 10-3, Apr-Nov; W-Sun rest of year. Adults $1, 6-12 25¢.*

A repository of Gold Rush memorabilia, this museum displays a blacksmith shop, an extensive rock collection, and a carriage barn filled with vintage wagons and buggies.

San Andreas
(Area Code 209)

VISITOR INFORMATION

Calaveras County Chamber of Commerce *P.O. Box 115 (3 N. Main St.), San Andreas 95249, 754-4009, fax 754-4107.*

It is interesting to note that in Spanish "calaveras" means "skulls."

WHERE TO STAY

Black Bart Inn and Motel *35 Main St., 754-3808. 40 rooms; 8 non-smoking rooms; $; some shared baths. Pool (unavail. in winter). Restaurant.*

This lodging facility is named after the infamous highwayman, Black Bart, whose career ended in this town. He robbed 29 stagecoaches between 1875 and 1883, always using an unloaded gun. Rooms are available in both the old hotel and a more modern motel located adjacent.

WHAT TO DO

Calaveras County Historical Museum *30 N. Main St., 754-6579. Daily 10-4. Adults 50¢, 6-13 25¢.*

Items on display upstairs in this restored 1867 courthouse include Miwok Indian and Gold Rush artifacts. Among the nicely organized exhibits is a full-size display of a Gold Rush-era general store. The jail cell Black Bart once occupied is downstairs in a rustic courtyard planted with native California plants and trees.

California Caverns at Cave City *9565 Cave City Rd., off Mountain Ranch Rd., 10 mi. east of town, 736-2708. Daily 10-5, June-Oct; call for fall & spring schedule; closed in winter. Adults $7.50, 65+ $7, 6-12 $4. Strollers not permitted.*

This cavern was first opened to the public in 1850. The nearly level Trail of Lights tour, which takes 80 minutes, follows the footsteps of John Muir, Mark Twain, and Bret Harte. Another more strenuous **spelunking tour** *($75)* through the unlighted portion of the cavern is available by reservation only. It "involves climbing rocks and a 60-foot ladder, squeezing through small passages, crossing 200-foot-deep lakes on rafts, and viewing breathtaking formations unequaled in any other cavern in the West." Reservations are necessary, and participants must be at least 12 years old, in good health, and not pregnant.

Mokelumne Hill

(Area Code 209)

WHERE TO STAY

Hotel Leger *8304 Main St., 286-1401, fax 286-2105. 2 stories; 13 rooms; 100% non-smoking; $$. 3 wood-burning fireplaces; some shared baths. Unheated pool. Restaurant.*

Once considered among the most luxurious of Gold Rush hotels, this 1879 lodging still provides comfortable rooms. Many have sitting areas, and all are furnished with tasteful period pieces. "Leger" is now pronounced here "legger," although a while back French owners pronounced it "la-JAY."

A **restaurant** *(D Thur-Sat, SunBr)* and the old-time **Frontier Saloon** are located on the ground floor. Sometimes plays are scheduled in the **Court House Theatre**.

Jackson

(Area Code 209)

VISITOR INFORMATION

Amador County Chamber of Commerce *P.O. Box 596 (125 Peek St.), Jackson 95642, (800) 649-4988, 223-0350, fax 223-4425.*

It is interesting to note that in Spanish "amador" means "lover of gold."

ANNUAL EVENTS

Italian Picnic and Parade *June; first weekend. In Plymouth, at Italian Picnic Grounds at Amador County Fair Grounds; 267-0206. Free.*

Since 1882 the public has been invited to this festive event sponsored by the Italian Benevolent Society of Amador County. The fun includes kiddie rides, dancing, a parade down Highway 49 in Sutter Creek, and an all-you-can-eat barbecue *($12.50. Reservations essential.)*.

WHERE TO STAY

Country Squire Motel *1105 N. Main St., 223-1657. 1 story; 12 rooms; 8 non-smoking rooms; $-$$. Children under 1 free. Continental breakfast. Dogs welcome.*

Located out in the country adjacent to the old Kennedy Gold Mine site, this comfortable motel housed one of the last private gambling casinos in California. (The casino was closed in 1952.) Some of the units are restored and some are motel-modern. Gold panning can be practiced in the backyard "crick," and ducks, goats, and sheep roam freely on farmland across the way. Plenty of grass beckons children to romp.

National Hotel *2 Water St., 223-0500. 4 stories; 30 rooms; 2 non-smoking rooms; $-$$; Sat night must include D & SunBr reservations in restaurant.*

This hotel claims to be the oldest in continuous operation (since 1862) in California. Room decor is modest, as are the prices. Prior guests have included every California governor since 1862, two Presidents (Garfield and Hoover), and John Wayne.

The cozy **Louisiana House** restaurant *(D F-Sun, SunBr; $$. Highchairs, boosters, child portions. Reservations advised. AE, MC, V.)* operates in the cellar.

WHERE TO STAY NEARBY

The Heirloom *214 Shakeley Lane, Ione, 12 mi. from town, 274-4468. 2 stories; 6 rooms; 100% non-smoking; $$; 2-night min. on some Sat. Unsuitable for children under 12. No TVs; 2 wood-burning stoves; some shared baths. Afternoon snack, full breakfast.*

Being located in a town once known as Bed Bug could be a bit of a disadvantage for some lodgings. This B&B is so charming, however, that this history is easily overlooked. Resembling a colonial mansion and situated on 1½ acres of grassy, tree-rich grounds, this 1863 red brick Greek revival house is situated down a country lane right on Sutter Creek. Two rooms are in an adjacent sod-roof adobe cottage. A full French country-style breakfast is served on Limoges china either in the fireplace-warmed dining room or, in good weather, in the garden; the breakfast can also be enjoyed privately on guest room balconies.

Roaring Camp Mining Co. *In Pine Grove, 296-4100. 20 cabins; $340/week/couple for a prospector cabin, $125/extra person, $82.50/child under 18. Closed Oct-Apr. Shared modern bath house. Restaurant.*

Guests leave their cars behind and make the one-hour trip into the remote canyon here via truck. They stay in this former mining camp in rustic prospector cabins without electricity, and they must bring all their own gear and food. Recreation consists of swimming, fishing, and panning for gold in the Mokelumne River, as well as hiking and perhaps collecting rocks. Guests may keep up to one ounce of found gold; anything over one ounce per cabin must be split with Roaring Camp. A saloon, short order restaurant, and general store are available when guests get tired of roughing it. Weekly stays run Sunday to Sunday. For stays of less than a week, call the Monday before the anticipated date of arrival. Shorter four-hour day tours are also available. On Saturday evenings a group of diners is trucked in for a riverside steak cookout; weekly guests are invited to join this event at no charge.

WHAT TO DO

Amador County Museum *225 Church St., 223-6386. W-Sun 10-4. By donation. Scale models operate Sat & Sun on the hr.; $1, under 8 free.*

Located within an 1859 red brick house, this museum displays scale models of the Kennedy Mine tailing wheels and head frame and of the North Star Mine stamp mill. A brightly painted wooden train engine, which was once used as a prop on TV's *Petticoat Junction,* is permanently parked in front.

Kennedy Mine Tailing Wheels Park *On Jackson Gate Rd., 1 mi. north of town. Daily dawn to dusk. Free.*

Unique to the Gold Country, four huge 58-foot-diameter wheels—built in 1912 to lift waste gravel, or "tailings," into flumes so that they could be carried to a holding area—can be viewed by taking a short walk on well-marked trails on either side of the road. Two of the wheels have already collapsed. Better hurry to see this site before time takes its toll on the other two. The abandoned Kennedy Mine can also be seen from the site. Picnic tables are available.

Wine Tasting.

Many wineries are located in this area, with a heavy concentration occurring around the nearby town of Plymouth. Contact the Chamber of Commerce for a free map-brochure.

Sutter Creek

(Area Code 209)

A LITTLE BACKGROUND

Seven gold mines were once located on this quiet Main Street. Now it is lined with modern gold mines—antique shops.

WHERE TO STAY

Sutter Creek Inn *75 Main St., 267-5606, fax 267-9287. 2 stories; 17 rooms; 100% non-smoking; $$-$$$+; 2-night min. on Sat. Children under 4 free. 2 TVs; 10 wood-burning fireplaces. Afternoon snack, full breakfast.*

Opened as an inn in 1966, this 1859 Greek revival structure was one of the first B&Bs west of the Mississippi. Rooms are available in the house as well as in an adjacent carriage house. As guests arrive each day, homemade lemonade and cookies are served in the garden. In the morning coffee is served by the fireplace, and then at 9 a.m. sharp a full sit-down breakfast is served family-style at long trestle tables in the dining room and kitchen. For those who have been longing to spend the night in a bed suspended from the ceiling by chains, this inn fulfills that and other yearnings. (The guests really *swing* here.) Some visitors have even seen a friendly ghost, although it has been 26 years since the last sighting. Croquet and hammocks beckon from the gardens, and handwriting analysis and both foot and body massage are available by appointment at an additional fee.

WHERE TO EAT

Bellotti Inn *53 Main St., 267-5211. L & D W-M; $$. Closed 2nd week in July & Christmas week. Highchairs, boosters, child portions. 100% non-smoking. Reservations advised. MC, V.*

Located inside an historic building, this well-established saloon and restaurant serves bountiful Italian family-style dinners with veal, chicken, and steak entrees. A la carte items and a hamburger are also on the menu.

Inexpensive **hotel rooms** *(3 stories; 8 rooms; 100% non-smoking; $. No TVs; some shared baths.)* are also available.

Volcano

(Area Code 209)

A LITTLE BACKGROUND

The scenic, rural drive here from Sutter Creek is ill-marked, poorly paved, and best maneuvered during daylight. And experience indicates that directions and information obtained around these parts are often vague or misleading, leaving plenty of room for error. A good map can be worth its weight in gold.

Because this tiny town is built in a depression on top of limestone caves, it is green year-round. Sleepy and quiet now, during the Gold Rush it was a boom town well-known for its boisterous dance halls and saloons. It also opened the state's first public library.

ANNUAL EVENTS

Daffodil Hill *Mid-March until bloom is over in April. 18310 Rams Horn Grade, off Shake Ridge Rd., 3 mi. north of town, 296-7048. By donation.*

Originally planted in the 1850s by a Dutch settler, then added to and maintained by Grandma McLaughlin, this six-acre garden boasts more than 300 varieties of bulbs. There are many, many daffodils, with a few tulips and hyacinths mixed in, too. More bulbs are planted every year by McLaughlin's grandchildren and great-grandchildren. Currently over 400,000 bloom together each spring, making for a spectacular display. Peacocks, chickens, and sheep wander the grounds, and there is a picnic area with tables. It is a pleasant surprise that this seasonal extravaganza of bloom is so non-commercial.

WHERE TO STAY

St. George Hotel *16104 Volcano-Pine Grove Rd., 296-4458, same fax. 3 stories; 20 rooms; 100% non-smoking; $$, on Sat $$$ but includes D & B. Closed Jan-Feb. No TVs; some shared baths. Full breakfast; restaurant.*

This solidly constructed hotel offers a choice of rooms in either the main hotel, built in 1862, or in an annex built almost a hundred years later in 1961. For safety reasons families with children under 12 must stay in the newer and charmless, albeit comfortable, annex located around the corner, their consolation being a private bathroom. In the hotel, a cozy memorabilia-crammed bar and a parlor area with fireplace and games invite relaxing.

The hotel **restaurant** *(D W-Sat, B Sat & Sun; $-$$. Highchairs, boosters, child portions. 100% non-smoking. Reservations required. AE, MC, V.)* serves a special prime rib dinner on Saturday and a chicken dinner on Sunday.

WHERE TO EAT

The Jug and Rose *3 Main St., 296-4696. B & L Sat & Sun; $. 1 highchair, child portions. Reservations advised. No cards.*

Famous for all-you-can-eat sourdough pancake breakfasts, this charming spot has been in business since 1855. In the Gold Rush days it was located in a different spot and known as The Stone Jug Saloon. A prior owner had the ruins of the saloon moved to its present site stone by stone. Sourdough pancakes are served with a topping choice of warm spice syrup, strawberries and sour cream, or boysenberry. (The pancakes have been served only since 1958, when Sourdough Jack visited from Alaska with his crock of sourdough.) Lunch brings homemade soups and sandwiches to the menu. Tea-time goodies and exotic sundaes lure afternoon customers. How about a Sierra Split (three flavors of ice cream, wild blackberry topping, and banana) or Candy-Jar Delight (peppermint and chocolate ice creams topped with chocolate and marshmallow sauces). A Sprize Sundae is made especially for kids, and The Plain Jane is available for scardy cats. All items are served with fresh flower garnishes. For kids there is a scaled-down version of the old-fashioned ice cream parlor-style tables and chairs and a basket full of toys.

WHAT TO DO

Indian Grinding Rock State Historic Park *14881 Pine Grove-Volcano Rd., Pine Grove, southwest of town, 296-7488. M-F 11-3, Sat & Sun 10-4. $5/vehicle.*

The largest of the grinding rocks—a huge flat bedrock limestone measuring 175 feet by 82 feet—has over 1,185 mortar holes and approximately 363 petroglyphs (rock carvings). All were made by Native Americans who ground their acorns and other seeds here with pestles. A reconstructed **Miwok Village** contains a ceremonial roundhouse, a covered hand-game area, several cedar bark houses, and an Indian game field. Additional facilities include a self-guided nature trail and a regional museum that orients visitors with a video show and interpretive displays. Picnic facilities and campsites are available. A **"Big Time" Miwok Celebration** is scheduled each September.

"Old Abe" Volcano Blues Cannon.

Located in the center of town in a protected shelter, this cannon helped win the Civil War—without firing a shot! Cast of bronze and brass in Boston in 1837 and weighing 737 pounds, it somehow reached San Francisco and was smuggled to Volcano in 1863. It was used by the town to control renegades who were drawn here in search of quick wealth. For the complete story, ask around town.

Sing Kee's Store.

Built in 1857 and formerly a general store, this building is now a gift shop.

Soldiers' Gulch.

Rocky terrain, a gurgling stream, and scenic stone ruins, which include the façades of several ancient buildings, provide a picturesque backdrop against which to enjoy a picnic or just a few moments of quiet contemplation.

Volcano Pioneers Community Theatre Group *223-4663. F & Sat at 8 & occasionally Sun. Closed Nov-Mar. Tickets $10. Reservations required.*

The first little theater group to form in California was the Volcano Thespian Society in 1854. Performances are held in the intimate 50-seat **Cobblestone Theater**, and children are welcome.

Amador City
(Area Code 209)

A LITTLE BACKGROUND

With a population of 202, this is said to be the smallest incorporated city in the state.

WHERE TO STAY

Mine House Inn *14125 Hwy. 49, (800) MINE-HSE, 267-5900. 2 stories; 8 rooms; 100% non-smoking; $$-$$$; 2 night min. on Sat. Children under 2 free. No TVs; 2 gas fireplaces. Unheated pool (unavail. Oct-Apr). Continental breakfast.*

Built in 1881 as the headquarters for the Keystone Mine, this attractive restored brick building now houses guest rooms furnished with Gold Rush-era antiques. Each room is named for its original function: the Mill Grinding Room, the Vault Room, the Retort Room. In the morning, guests just push a buzzer and breakfast is delivered to the door. One Easter, long ago, a family that was staying here arranged for an Easter basket to arrive in this same mysterious manner. The kid still hasn't figured out how the parents pulled off that one!

WHERE TO EAT

Buffalo Chips Emporium *14179 Hwy. 49, 267-0570. B & L W- Sun; $. 1 highchair, 1 booster seat. No cards.*

Some folks just buy a simple cone here and then sit outside on one of the weathered benches to leisurely watch the busy world drive by. Others prefer to sit inside what was once the town's Wells Fargo Bank and indulge in a fancy fountain item.

Drytown

A LITTLE BACKGROUND

Once home to 27 saloons, Drytown is now known for its equally abundant antique shops.

WHAT TO DO

Piper Playhouse *On Hwy. 49, (800) 825-2974. Sat at 8 + some matinees. Closed Oct-Apr. Tickets $13.50-$15. Reservations required.*

The Claypipers have been performing raucous melodramas here for over 30 years. However, since a fire in 1988 burned to the ground the old Joaquin Murietta Dance Hall, which dated from the 1930s and used to occupy the site, the troupe now performs in a newer building. The less expensive tickets are in the balcony, and children who sit on a lap don't need a ticket.

Shingle Springs
(Area Code 916)

WHERE TO EAT

Sam's Town *3333 Coach Lane, Cameron Park exit off Hwy. 50, 677-2273. B, L, & D daily; $-$$. Highchairs, boosters. AE, MC, V.*

The floors of this funky combination restaurant/honky-tonk piano bar/general store/memorabilia museum/game arcade are littered with peanut shells discarded by happy revelers. Food runs the gamut from a hamburger and soda to prime rib and champagne. Outside decorations include a covered wagon and a cannon.

El Dorado
(Area Code 916)

WHERE TO EAT

Poor Red's *6221 Main St., 622-2901. L M-F, D daily; $. Highchairs, boosters, child portions. No reservations. AE, MC, V.*

Judging just from the outside, which looks to be an unsavory bar, this former Wells Fargo stage stop might easily be passed by. But then weary travelers would miss the experience of dining on exquisite ham, ribs, chicken, and steak—all cooked over an open oak wood pit and served in generous portions. Because this restaurant is very popular and also very small, weekend dinner waits can run over an hour. Some patrons pass that time downing Gold Cadillacs at the old-time horseshoe bar. (It is interesting to note that Poor Red's is the largest user of Galliano in North America, Galliano being the main ingredient in those Gold Cadillacs.) Some pass it studying the mural behind the bar that depicts the town as it appeared in the late 1800s. Others pass it feeding the jukebox, and yet others beat the wait by ordering take-out.

Placerville
(Area Code 916)

A LITTLE BACKGROUND

Placerville, which in Spanish means "the golden one," was once known as Hangtown because hangings here were so common. This is where the Hangtown Fry (eggs, bacon, and oysters) originated. Railroad magnate Mark Hopkins, meat-packer Philip Armour, and automobile-maker John Studebaker all got their financial starts here as well.

VISITOR INFORMATION

El Dorado County Chamber of Commerce *542 Main St., Placerville 95667, (800) 457-6279, 621-5885, fax 642-1624.*

ANNUAL EVENTS

Apple Hill *September-December. Daily 9-6. 644-7692.*

Located on a mountain ridge east of town, the route for the Apple Hill tour follows an historic path originally blazed out in 1857 by Pony Express riders. In the fall, 42 apple ranches along this route sell 22 varieties of tree-fresh apples at bargain prices. And they're *crunchy*, because they're *fresh*! An impressive selection of homemade apple goodies can also be purchased: fresh-pressed apple cider, hard cider, apple wine, spicy apple butter, caramel apples, apple jelly, dried apples, apple cake, apple sundaes, apple syrup, and, of course, apple pie. Many of the farms have picnic facilities, and some have snack bars. A few also have hiking trails, fishing ponds, pony rides, train rides, and live jazz, and three wineries are also located here. Several apple varieties are available into December. For a free map, send a legal-size stamped, self-addressed envelope with $1 postage to: The Apple Hill Growers, P.O. Box 494, Camino 95709.

Nine Christmas tree farms open the day after Thanksgiving. Cherry season begins on Father's Day weekend, when the **West Coast Cherry Pit-Spitting Championships** are held.

WHAT TO DO

El Dorado County Historical Museum *100 Placerville Dr., 2 mi. west of town in El Dorado County Fairgrounds, 621-5865. W-Sat 10-4; also Sun 12-4, Mar-Oct. By donation.*

Historic exhibits in this "great hall" include a Wells Fargo stagecoach and a wheelbarrow made by John Studebaker in the days before he manufactured cars.

Gold Bug Mine *Off Bedford Ave., 1 mi. north of town, 642-5232, fax 642-5236. Daily 10-4 in summer; Sept-Apr, Sat & Sun only. Adults $2, 5-16 $1, cassette tour $1.*

Visitors here can take self-guided tours through a cool ¼-mile-long lighted mine shaft, see a working model of a stamp mill inside an authentic stamp mill building, picnic at creek-side tables, and hike in rugged 61-acre **Gold Bug Park**. This is the only mine in the Mother Lode that is on public property.

Wineries.

• **Boeger Winery** *1709 Carson Rd., Schnell School Rd. exit off Hwy. 50, (800) 655-2634, 622-8094, fax 622-8112. Tasting daily 10-5; tours by appt.*

The stone cellar tasting room here is part of the original winery that operated from the 1860s through the 1920s. During Prohibition the winery became a pear farm. Then, in the early 1970s, it once again became a winery. Shaded stream-side picnic tables beckon, and a sandbox awaits children.

• **Sierra Vista Winery** *4560 Cabernet Way, (800) WINE-916, 622-7221. Tasting M-F 10-4, Sat & Sun 10-5; tours by appt.*

Enjoy a magnificent view of the entire Crystal Range of the Sierra Nevada while picnicking at this pleasant winery.

Coloma
(Area Code 916)

A LITTLE BACKGROUND

This is where James Marshall discovered gold in 1848. The entire town is now a National Historic Landmark.

ANNUAL EVENTS

U.S. National Gold Panning Championships *October. 622-3470.*

Gold prospectors from around the world seek their fortunes at the state historic park. A '49er tent city, an authentic wagon train encampment, and a gold rush market are part of the fun.

WHAT TO DO

Marshall Gold Discovery State Historic Park *On Hwy. 49, 622-3470, fax 622-3472. Park: Daily 8-sunset. $5/vehicle. Museum: Daily 10-5 in summer; shorter hours rest of year. Free.*

This lovely 265-acre park encompasses 70 percent of the town. It contains a reconstruction of the original **Sutter's Mill** (where the Gold Rush began) as well as picnic facilities, nature trails, and Gold Rush-era buildings and artifacts. An exact replica of the piece of gold Marshall found is on display in the museum (the original is at the Smithsonian in Washington, D.C.). The mill is sometimes operated; call for schedule. Picnic facilities are available. The **James W. Marshall Monument** is located on a hill overlooking the town. Marshall's grave is here, and a statue honoring him depicts him pointing to the spot where he discovered gold.

Whitewater Connection *See page 389.*
The office and base camp for this white water rafting outfit is located adjacent to the state park. Participants on American River trips are permitted to camp out at the outfitter's riverside facility. Half- and full-day trips are offered daily from mid-April through September; longer trips are also available.

Auburn
(Area Code 916)

VISITOR INFORMATION

Placer County Visitors Information Center *13460 Lincoln Way, Auburn 95603, (800) 427-6463, 885-5616.*
It is interesting to note that in Spanish "placer" means "surface mining".

WHERE TO STAY

Motel Row.
Many motels are located at the top of the hill on Lincoln Way and across the freeway on Bowman Road.

WHERE TO EAT

Cafe Delicias *1591 Lincoln Way, 885-2050. L & D daily; $. Highchairs, boosters, booths, child portions. AE, MC, V.*
Located in one of the town's oldest buildings, this casual Mexican restaurant serves especially good flautas and homemade tamales.

Ikeda's *13500 Lincoln Way, ¼ mile east of Auburn Ravine-Foresthill exit off Hwy. 80, 885-4243. Daily 10-7; to 9 in summer & on weekends; $. Highchairs. No cards.*
Since the 1950s, this casual snack bar has been serving travel-weary diners fast-food fare: hamburgers, corn dogs, burritos, deep-fried whole mushrooms, fruit pie, fresh fruit salad, frozen yogurt, ten flavors of hot chocolate, and thick fresh fruit milkshakes. An adjacent produce market sells some tempting car snacks, among them giant cashews and pistachios, both of which are grown in the area.

WHAT TO DO

Gold Country Museum *Museum: 1273 High St., in Gold Country Fairgrounds, 889-4134. Tu-Sun 10-4. House: 291 Auburn-Folsom Rd., 889-4156. Tu-F 11-3, Sat & Sun 12-4. Adults $1, 65+ & 6-16 50¢.*
Located within a building constructed of logs and stones, this old-time museum emphasizes mining exhibits. Visitors can walk through a 48-foot mine shaft and view a working model of a stamp mill. Local Maidu Indian artifacts and an extensive doll collection are also on display.
Docent-led tours are available of the nearby Greek revival-style **Bernhard House**, a restored Victorian farmhouse built in 1851 and furnished with Victorian antiques.

Grass Valley
(Area Code 916)

A LITTLE BACKGROUND

It was here, in what was once the richest gold mining region in the state, that gold mining became a well-organized industry. Many advanced mining techniques were developed and first used here.

VISITOR INFORMATION

Grass Valley/Nevada County Chamber of Commerce *248 Mill St., Grass Valley 95945, (800) 655-4667, 273-4667, fax 272-5440.*

Because of its location inside a replica of the historic home once occupied by scandalous Gold Rush personality Lola Montez, this office is worth visiting in person.

ANNUAL EVENTS

Bluegrass Festival *June. 296-3772.*

Cornish Christmas Celebration *December. 272-8315.*

Experience an old-time Christmas at this event celebrating the traditions of the Cornish miners who settled this Gold Rush town. Visitors can dance in the downtown streets, which are closed to traffic, and ride in a horse-drawn carriage.

WHERE TO STAY

Holbrooke Hotel *212 W. Main St., (800) 933-7077, 273-1353, fax 273-0434. 2 stories; 38 rooms; 12 non-smoking rooms; $$-$$$. Some gas fireplaces. Continental breakfast; restaurant.*

Established in 1851, this meticulously restored Victorian grand hotel has hosted four presidents (Grant, Garfield, Cleveland, and Harrison), stagecoach robber Black Bart, and author Mark Twain. Current guests can step back in time in beautifully appointed rooms featuring brass beds and the original claw-foot tubs. Most rooms hold only two people, but in a few larger rooms a child can be accommodated with a rollaway bed. A century-old wrought-iron elevator cage lifts guests from floor to floor. This lodging facility, which consists of both the hotel and the 1874 **Purcell House** behind it, is conveniently located in the center of town.

Both the **Golden Gate Saloon**, which is said to be the oldest continuously operating saloon in the Gold Country and which features an ornate bar that was shipped around the Horn, and an elegant **restaurant** *(L & D daily, SunBr)* with full family amenities operate on the main floor.

Sivananda Ashram Yoga Farm *14651 Ballantree Lane, 272-9322, fax 477-6054. 8 rooms; 100% non-smoking; $$. Children half price. No TVs; all shared bathrooms. Meals included.*

The bell rings here at 5:30 each morning to awaken guests. Attendance at scheduled meditation and yoga classes is mandatory. In between guests dine on vegetarian meals and have plenty of free time to enjoy the natural surroundings of the 80-acre farm. Lodging consists of both dormitories and single and double rooms, and during the summer guests may bring their own tents.

WHERE TO EAT

Mrs. Dubblebee's Pasties *251 S. Auburn St., 272-7700. M-F 9-6, Sat & Sun 10-5:30; $. No cards.*

Located inside a pristine white Victorian home, this unusual eatery specializes in pasties. (In fact, the original owner of this shop, William Brooks, invented the pasty-making machine now used throughout the world.) These meat and potato turnovers were once popular lunch fare among the area's Cornish miners, who carried them down into the mines in their pockets. At lunchtime, they reheated their pasties on a shovel held over candles secured in their hard hats. Fruit turnovers and drinks are also available. How about a hasty tasty pasty picnic? (Actually, "pasty" rhymes with "nasty.")

More pasties are available at **Marshall's Pasties** *(203 Mill St., 272-2844.)*, where they are made by hand, and at **King Richard's** *(217 Colfax Ave., 273-0286.)*, where they are made using the Brooks machine—which can sometimes be observed in operation.

Tofanelli's *302 W. Main St., 272-1468. B, L, & D daily; $. Highchairs, boosters, child portions. 100% non-smoking. MC, V.*

Every kind of breakfast item imaginable is on this menu, including design-your-own-omelettes, whole wheat pancakes and waffles, and a large variety of teas. Salads, sandwiches, and several kinds of hamburgers—including a tofuburger and a veggieburger—join the menu at lunch. All this and an attractive brick and oak decor, too.

WHAT TO DO

Bridgeport Covered Bridge *Take Hwy. 20 west 10 mi. to Pleasant Valley Rd., turn right (north) and follow south fork of Yuba River 9 mi. to Bridgeport; 432-2546.*

Built over the south fork of the Yuba River in 1862 and in use until 1971, this is the longest (256 feet) single-span wood-covered bridge in the world. It is now a State Historical Landmark. Not currently maintained and in shaky condition, it should be walked across with caution. A scenic picnic area is situated on the riverbank, and there are several hiking trails. Those who have witnessed it claim the wildflower display here in March is spectacular.

Empire Mine State Historic Park *10791 E. Empire St., 273-8522. Daily 10-5; guided tour at 1; call to verify hours. Adults $2, 6-12 $1.*

Once the largest and richest hard rock mine in the state, the Empire Mine was operated for over a century—from 1850 to 1956. Though it still holds millions of dollars worth of gold, the ore is too expensive to extract and the mine is now a 784-acre state park. Of special interest are the stone **Bourn Mansion** *(Hours vary; guided tour on weekends.)*, which was designed and built by Willis Polk in 1897 in the style of an English country lodge, and the 13-acre formal gardens—featuring an antique rose garden and several reflecting pools—that surround it. The mining area illustrates many facets of the business and allows visitors to look down a lighted mine shaft. There are also approximately 22 miles of self-guided back-country hiking trails. Picnicking is permitted only on the outskirts of the parking lot.

Grass Valley Museum *410 S. Church St./Chapel St., 272-4407 or 272-4725. Tu-F 10-3; also Sat & Sun June-Oct. By donation.*

Built in 1863 as Mount Saint Mary's Convent and Orphanage, this was the state's first orphanage for non-Indian children. The building now displays Gold Rush memorabilia and furnishings, as well as a fully equipped doctor's office, classroom, parlor, and music room from that era.

North Star Mining Museum *Allison Ranch Rd./south end of Mill St., 273-4255. Daily 10-4. Closed Nov-Apr. By donation.*

Once the power house for the North Star Mine, this rustic stone building houses a collection of old photographs, mining dioramas and models, and a 30-foot-diameter, 10-ton Pelton water wheel dating from 1896—the largest such wheel every constructed. It also displays the largest operational Cornish pump in the country. A grassy picnic area is located across adjacent Wolf Creek.

Oregon House. *Located 35 mi. west of town. Take Hwy. 20 west to Browns Valley, then Hwy. E21 north to Oregon House, and follow E20 east.*

• **Collins Lake Recreation Area** *On Collins Lake Rd., 692-1600. 5:30am-10pm Mar-Aug; shorter hrs. rest of year. $5/vehicle, boat rentals $5-$12.50/hr.*

Popular with fishermen, this 1,000-acre lake also has lakefront campsites and RV hook-ups.

• **Renaissance Vineyard & Winery** *12585 Rices Crossing Rd., (800) 655-3277, 692-2222, fax 692-2497. Tasting & tours by appt. (optional $5 donation).*

The drive through the scenic Sierra Nevada foothills required to reach this isolated valley would be worthwhile even if this special winery weren't waiting at the end. Operated by the Fellowship of Friends, a non-denominational religious group, the winery is situated on a scenic hillside terraced with grapevines.

Renaissance Bistro *(692-2938. L W-Sun; $. 1 highchair, 1 booster, 1 booth, child portions. 100% non-smoking. Reservations advised. MC, V.),* which is also on the property, serves a seasonally changing menu of entrees designed to pair well with Renaissance wines. When the weather is warm, deck seating is available, and on hotter days the air-conditioned interior of the dining room brings welcome relief.

Nevada City

(Area Code 916)

A LITTLE BACKGROUND

Said to be the best privately preserved and restored small city in the state, this picturesque mining town is also said to contain residential and commercial buildings representative of all the major 19th-century architectural styles. Scenically situated on seven hills, the town boasts a particularly fine assortment of lovely gingerbread-style Victorian homes, and the entire downtown district is on the National Register of Historic Places. It is interesting to note that in Spanish "nevada" means "snow-covered."

VISITOR INFORMATION

Nevada City Chamber of Commerce *132 Main St., Nevada City 95959, (800) 655-NJOY, 265-2692.*

ANNUAL EVENTS

International Teddy Bear Convention *April. 265-5804, fax 265-0197. Adults $5, under 12 $1.50, bears free.*

Bears from all over the world come out of hibernation for this warm, fuzzy event. Bearaphernalia and bear necessities and luxuries abound, and all kinds of bears are available for adoption. A tour of the charming bear-stuffed **Teddy Bear Castle** at 431 Broad Street is part of the fun.

4th of July Parade *July.*

Held in Nevada City on even years and in Grass Valley on odd, this old-fashioned celebration begins with a parade, followed by diversions—food stalls, competitions, entertainment—at the fairgrounds. As might be expected, it culminates in a fireworks extravaganza.

Constitution Day Parade *September.*

The signing of the U.S. Constitution is honored with marching bands, drill teams, floats, fire engines, and horsemen. Pre-parade activities include a re-enactment of the signing and a demonstration of colonial dancing.

Fall Colors *Mid-October through mid-November.*

Victorian Christmas *December; on the 3 W eves. & usually all day on the Sun before Christmas.*

WHERE TO STAY IN TOWN

Grandmere's Inn *449 Broad St., 265-4660. 3 stories; 7 rooms; 100% non-smoking; $$$-$$$+; 2-night min. on weekends. Children under 12 free. No TVs. Afternoon snack, full breakfast.*

This 1856 colonial revival home was built by Aaron Sargent, who wrote the 19th constitutional amendment granting women the vote. (The author of the 15th amendment, which freed former slaves, also lived in Nevada City.) On the National Register of Historic Places, it is beautifully decorated in French country style with antique pine furnishings and gorgeous floral fabrics. It is conveniently located at the **Top of Broad Street**—one of the town's earliest residential areas.

National Hotel *211 Broad St., 265-4551, fax 265-2445. 3 stories; 42 rooms; 100% non-smoking rooms; $$-$$$. Children under 12 free. 2 kitchens; 1 gas fireplace; some shared baths. Unheated pool. Restaurant, room service.*

Located on the town's main street, this claims to be the oldest continuously operating hotel west of the Rockies—maybe even west of the Mississippi. Among the luminaries who have been guests here are both Herbert Hoover, who stayed here when he was a mining engineer for the Empire Mine, and Mark Twain. Built in 1856, it is a State Historical Landmark and features high ceilings, cozy floral wallpapers, and old-time furniture. Families of four can be accommodated in two separate rooms with a bath between.

The plush, old-fashioned **Victorian Dining Room** *(B, L, & D daily, SunBr; $-$$. Highchairs, boosters, child portions. 100% non-smoking. Reservations advised. AE, MC, V.)* features a steak and lobster dinner menu.

Northern Queen Inn *400 Railroad Ave., 265-5824, fax 265-3720. 2 stories; 86 units; 10 non-smoking units; $$. Some kitchens & wood-burning stoves. Heated pool, hot tub. Restaurant.*

Located on the outskirts of town beside Gold Run Creek, this pleasant lodging complex has modern motel rooms, cottages, and two-story chalets. Also part of the complex is a small collection of full-size trains that includes a 1920s railbus, a 1910 wood-burning locomotive, and another engine that had roles in several classic western movies.

Piety Hill Inn *523 Sacramento St., (800) 443-2245, 265-2245. 1 story; 9 cottages; 100% non-smoking; $$-$$$; 2-night min. on weekends. Children under 3 free. 1 kitchen; 1 wood-burning stove. Hot tub. Full breakfast.*

This 1930s auto court motel has one- and two-room cottages with antique furnishings.

Red Castle Inn *109 Prospect, (800) 761-4766, 265-5135. 7 rooms; 100% non-smoking; $$-$$$; 2-night min. on Sat, Apr-Dec. Unsuitable for children under 10. No TVs; some wood-burning stoves. Full breakfast.*

Situated on a hilltop above town, this beautifully restored and plushly furnished Gothic revival mansion was built in 1860. Said to be one of only two of this style left on the West Coast, it features gingerbread and icicle trim and has old-fashioned double brick walls. Some guests have reportedly seen the spirit of Laura Jean, who was once a governess here.

WHERE TO STAY NEARBY

Herrington's Sierra Pines *On Hwy. 49, 60 mi. north of town, in Sierra City, 862-1151. 1 story; 21 units; $-$$; 2-night min. on Sat. Closed Dec-Mar. 3 kitchens; 3 wood-burning fireplaces. Restaurant. Pets welcome.*

Located on the north fork of the Yuba River, this lodging facility features duplex units and one cabin. The **restaurant** *(B & D daily. Highchairs, boosters.)* is known for its baked goods and rainbow trout, which are caught fresh each morning from the property's own trout pond.

Kenton Mine Lodge *On Foots Crossing Rd., 40 mi. north of town in a quiet canyon at the end of a 3-mi. dirt road, in Alleghany, 287-3212. $$. No TVs; 3 kitchens; all wood-burning stoves; some shared baths. Sauna.*

One of the most favored areas of the current gold rush is the area surrounding the tiny Sierra town of Alleghany. City-slickers are advised to be careful around here, though, as many miners camp on top of their claims, and some have been known to get mean when confronted with trespassers. To assure safety and warmth while trying one's luck at panning for gold, consider spending time at this remote, semi-refurbished mining camp dating from the 1930s. Though vivid imaginations have been known to run wild here (several guests have commented that the winding forest road in from Nevada City is not unlike the one seen at the beginning of the horror movie *The Shining*), once the freaked-out city traveler relaxes and acclimates to the unaccustomed peace and tranquility, apprehensions dissolve. Guests sleep in either weathered cabins or B&B-style rooms. Gold-panning equipment can be borrowed for use in gurgling Kanaka Creek, which runs through the property, and a stamp mill and abandoned gold mine dating from the late 1800s provide interesting exploring. A modestly priced breakfast and lunch is served family-style at long tables in the Cookhouse; a full bar is also operated. Campsites are available.

Packer Lake Lodge *3901 Packer Lake Rd., 60 mi. north of town, in Sierra City, 862-1221. 14 cabins; $$. Closed Nov-Apr. Children under 2 free. No TVs; 8 kitchens; 6 wood-burning stoves; some shared baths. Restaurant. Dogs welcome.*

Located at the end of a road in a remote corner of the Sierra Nevada, this rustic resort has eight housekeeping cabins with sun decks overlooking Packer Lake. Housekeeping cabins are rented by the week and include use of a rowboat. (No motorboats are permitted on the lake.) Six sleeping cabins are also available by the night.

Salmon Lake Lodge *On Gold Lake Rd., 10 mi. from Sierra City, (415) 681-7985 (reservations number is in San Francisco). 14 cabins; $$-$$$; 1-week min. June-Oct. Closed Nov-Apr. No TVs; some kitchens; 14 wood-burning fireplaces, 14 wood-burning stoves; some shared baths. Dogs welcome.*

Located in the glaciated high country of Sierra County, this remote resort has been in continuous operation for almost a century. Guests park their cars at the east end of Salmon Lake and are transported by a staff-operated barge across the lake. There they sleep in one of the cabins or tent-cabins and are provided free access to an assortment of boats. Some cabins are fully equipped, but guests in tent-cabins must provide their own bedding, kitchen utensils, and supplies. The experience is like luxurious camping. To ease cooking chores, guests are invited twice each week to a catered barbecue (additional fee) held on an island in the center of the lake.

Sierra Shangri-La *On Hwy. 49, 45 mi. north of town, in Downieville, 289-3455. 1 story; 11 units; 100% non-smoking; $$-$$$; 1-week min. cabins in summer. Closed Jan-Mar. Children under 2 free. No TVs; 8 kitchens; 1 wood-burning fireplace, 6 wood-burning stoves.*

There is little to do here except commune with nature. Guests can relax, do some fishing and hiking, and enjoy the sight and sound of the Yuba River rushing past their cabin door. Some units are perched right over the river, allowing guests to fish from their deck in the spring. Three B&B units are also available.

WHERE TO EAT

The Country Rose Cafe *300 Commercial St., 265-6252. L & D daily, SunBr; $-$$. Boosters, booths, child portions. 100% non-smoking. Reservations advised. AE, MC, V.*

An inviting country French menu is served in a charming inside area, with wooden booths and rose print tablecloths, and in a bucolic outdoor area with a creek running through it. Delicious house-made soup and sandwiches, French hot chocolate, and a great lemon chiffon pie are just a few of the menu gems.

Friar Tuck's *111 N. Pine St., 265-9093. D daily; $$. Highchairs, boosters, child portions. Reservations advised. AE, MC, V.*

Operating in a building dating back to 1857, this cozy restaurant has many dining rooms and is furnished with large, comfortable wooden booths. The extensive menu offers a variety of casual fondue items—including a chocolate dessert version—as well as grilled fresh fish, rack of lamb, roast duck, ribs, and steak. The wine list runs the gamut from inexpensive local labels to expensive rare vintages; varietals are available by the glass. Non-drinkers and children can get high on a Princess Leia or Darth Vader—updated versions of the old-time Shirley Temple and Roy Rodgers. Relaxing live guitar music is piped throughout, and an authentic 19th-century pub bar from Liverpool, England adds to the atmosphere.

Mexican Inn *401 Commercial St., 265-6138. L & D W-Sun; $. Closed Jan. Highchairs, boosters, booths, child menu. No reservations. AE, MC, V.*

Operating within a converted cottage tucked away on a back street, this is a branch of a long-popular restaurant in Grass Valley. In warm weather, the sheltered outdoor patio, with its gurgling fountain, is particularly inviting. All the traditional Mexican favorites are deliciously prepared, and wine cocktails and house-made desserts are available.

WHAT TO DO IN TOWN

Firehouse Museum #1 *214 Main St., 265-5468. Daily 11-4; closed W Nov-Mar. By donation.*

Located inside a charming 1861 Victorian firehouse, this museum is said to be haunted. Among the intriguing pioneer memorabilia on display are a Chinese altar, snowshoes made for a horse, and a noteworthy collection of Maidu Indian baskets.

Nevada City Winery *321 Spring St., (800) 203-WINE, 265-WINE, fax 265-6860. Tasting Sun-Thur 12-5, F-Sat 11-5:30; tour on Sat at 3.*

Housed now in an old foundry building where gold mining tools were once cast, this winery is located only two blocks from where it originated a century ago. It is known for its Cabernets, Merlots, and Zinfandels.

Nevada Theatre *401 Broad St., 265-6161. Thur-Sun. Films $6. Live performances: Adults $11-$17, children half-price.*

Opened in September of 1865 and lectured in by both Mark Twain and Jack London, this is the oldest theater building in California. It has been refurbished to appear as it did when it first opened. The inside is very small and all seats are close to the stage, making it an excellent spot to expose children to a live performance. The audience is usually filled with locals, and they bring their children when the production is appropriate. Movies are often scheduled on Sunday evenings.

WHAT TO DO NEARBY

Independence Trail *Off Hwy. 49, 6 mi. north of town, 272-3823. Free.*

Basically level and easy for both wheelchairs and baby strollers to navigate, this 2½-mile nature trail was built in 1856 as the Excelsior Canal. It was used to run water through the mountains for hydraulic gold mining. Another section of the trail permits hikers to cross flumes suspended over deep crevices and a waterfall. The area features an outstanding display of wildflowers in April and May.

Malakoff Diggins State Historic Park *23579 N. Bloomfield Rd., off Hwy. 49, 17 mi. northeast of town, 265-2740, same fax. $5/vehicle. Museum: Daily 10-4, May-Sept; rest of year Sat & Sun only.*

Inhabited by over 1,500 people in the 1870s, when it was the largest hydraulic gold mining operation in the world, **North Bloomfield** is now a ghost town. Several buildings have been restored, but there are no commercial stores. The park museum, a former dance hall, has an interpretive display on hydraulic mining, and visitors can hike on numerous trails and fish in a small lake. Picnic facilities are available. Three primitive cabins, three walk-in campsites, and thirty regular campsites are available. Note that the drive from Nevada City takes just under an hour, and a portion of the road is unpaved. Travelers with large RVs or trailers should enter the park via the Tyler-Foote route, located 11 miles north of Nevada City on Highway 49.

Oregon Creek Swimming Hole *On Hwy. 49, 18 mi. north of town.*

Located in the middle fork of the Yuba River, this popular spot has sandy beaches, both deep swimming and shallow wading spots, and picnic facilities. A **Tahoe National Forest** campground is also located here.

Sierra County Historical Park and Museum *100 Kentucky Mine Rd., Sierra City, on Hwy. 49, 60 mi. north of town, 862-1310. W-Sun 10-5, June-Sept; Sat & Sun only in Oct. Closed Nov-May. Adults $4, 13-16 $2. Museum only $1, under 13 free.*

A 45-minute guided tour through the reconstructed 1850s **Kentucky Mine Stamp Mill** located here permits viewing the original machinery, which is still intact and operable. The museum operates inside a reconstructed wood-frame hotel dating from the mid-19th century. Picnic tables and barbecue facilities are situated under a canopy of oak trees.

A **Kentucky Mine Concert Series** of eclectic material is held on Friday evenings in July and August in an amphitheater within the complex.

Sierra Hot Springs *1 Campbell Hot Springs Rd., Sierraville, off Hwy. 89, 80 mi. north of town, 994-3773, fax 994-3479. Baths open 24-hours daily. Day-use: Adults $6, under 6 free.*

Swimsuits are optional in the indoor and outdoor hot springs at this secluded spa, which has been open since the 1850s. An organic vegetarian restaurant serves brunch and dinner on weekends.

Rooms can be rented in the newly renovated 1909 **Globe Hotel**, as well as in a rustic lodge. The inexpensive rates include unlimited use of the springs.

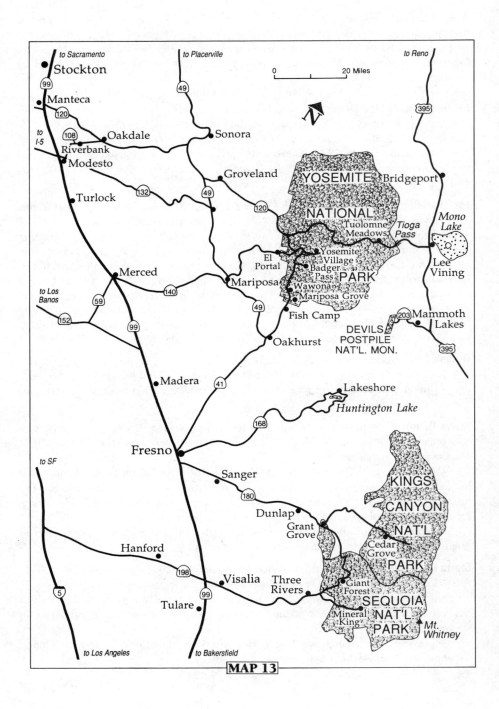

MAP 13

The High Sierra

Yosemite National Park

(Area Code 209)

A LITTLE BACKGROUND

Yosemite Park is a place of rest. A refuge ... in which one gains the advantage of both solitude and society ... none can escape its charms. Its natural beauty cleanses and warms like fire, and you will be willing to stay forever ... —John Muir

Yosemite is worth returning to in every season. Doing so permits enjoying the spectacular beauty of the park's dramatic seasonal changes. Most visitors see this grand national park in the summer, when it is at its busiest, with congested roads and accommodations filled to capacity. All this makes it hard to focus on what was the original draw—the scenic, natural beauty of the High Sierra. To catch a glimpse of the Yosemite described by Muir, it is essential to visit in the off-season: in fall when the colorful foliage change is spectacular; in winter when snow blankets the valley floor; in spring when the falls are at their fullest.

Yosemite's high country was designated a national park in 1890. The valley, which was under state supervision, was added to the national park in 1906. (It is amazing to realize that the valley comprises just one percent of the park's terrain.) Among the park's scenic wonders are **El Capitan**—the largest piece of exposed granite in the world—and **Yosemite Falls**—the highest waterfall in North America.

Bear in mind that falls and rivers can be dangerous as well as beautiful. Be carefully, especially when hiking with children.

A $5 admission fee, which is good for seven days, is collected at all park entrances. When they pay, visitors are given a copy of the *Yosemite Guide* activities newsletter and a park map.

VISITOR INFORMATION

National Park Service *Yosemite National Park 95389, 372-0265.*

GETTING THERE

Located approximately 240 miles east of San Francisco. Take Highway 80 to Highway 580 to Highway 205 to Highway 120. To minimize the need for chains in winter, take low-elevation Highway 140 in from Merced.

ANNUAL EVENTS

Chefs' Holidays *January & February. At The Ahwahnee.*

Guest chefs give cooking presentations and prepare gala banquets.

Vintners' Holidays *November & December. At The Ahwahnee.*

Two days of free wine seminars hosted by esteemed wine-makers culminate in a sumptuous feast in The Ahwahnee Dining Room. Courses are especially designed to complement wines sampled in the seminars.

Bracebridge Dinner *December 22, 24, & 25. At The Ahwahnee. $215/person, 8-12 $184, not appropriate for under 8.*

Since 1927 the fare at this three-hour mock-medieval feast has been seven courses of elegant Christmas dishes. Pageantry, carols, and jesters entertain diners between courses. Attending this memorable dinner is a pleasure not many get to enjoy. Participants must apply for reservations a full year in advance. Still, applications are so numerous that guests must be chosen by lottery.

STOPS ALONG THE WAY

Attractions are listed in the order encountered driving in from the Bay Area.

Oakwood Lake Resort *874 E. Woodward Rd., Manteca, (800) 626-LAKE, 239-2500, fax 239-2060. Daily 10-7 in summer; May & Sept weekends only 10-5. All-day pass: Over 4' tall $18.95, 42"-48" $9.95, under 42" free. Parking $2.*

This is North America's biggest waterslide park, with over one mile of fiberglass waterslides. It holds the state's tallest speed slide—the eight-story-high V-MAX—and biggest children's activity pool, as well as the Rapids Ride, which is maneuvered on an inner tube. Most slides have over 300 feet of enclosed tunnel and several 360-degree turns. Resort facilities include a fishing lake, a playground, and acres of shady barbecue and picnic areas. Bungee-jumping, batting cages, and go-carts, are available at an additional fee. Special rates for half-day visits and picnic use are available, and campsites are available year-round.

Hershey's Visitors Center *120 S. Sierra Ave.,*
Oakdale, 848-8126, fax 847-2622. Tours M-F 8:30-3.
Free. Strollers not permitted.

A good way to prepare for a visit to this
factory, which supplies 13 western states with
Hershey's chocolates, is by reading the children's book, or seeing the movie, titled *Charlie
and the Chocolate Factory.* Tour participants
sign-in at the Visitors Center and then ride a
shuttle bus to the factory. Upon entering the
factory, the lucious chocolate aromas become
intense, and when viewing the multiple 10,000-
gallon vats of liquid chocolate being stirred by
heavy granite rollers, it's easy to become quite
stirred oneself. And though it can't be heard
on the tour, it's fun to know that the candy

machines make a puckering noise as they deposit chocolate kisses on a moving conveyor belt—
thus the name "kiss." Workers in this noisy, warm, and fragrant factory look happy. *Real* happy.
Maybe that's because they get to eat as much chocolate as they want for *free.* At the end of the
45-minute tour, each participant receives a sweet treat and the opportunity to purchase official
Hershey's souvenirs.

A **Chocolate Festival** is held annually in May. It features chocolate tastings and a Hershey's
kiss-eating contest. Yum!

Fast-food heaven seems to be in Oakdale. Numerous cafes and produce stands are also
located along Highway 120.

Knight's Ferry Covered Bridge *2 mi. east of Oakdale, 881-3517, fax 881-3203. Visitor center M-F 8-4:30;
in summer also Sat & Sun 10-2. Free.*

Built in 1863 and measuring 330 feet long, this bridge is the longest and oldest covered
bridge west of the Mississippi. It is closed to cars now, but pedestrian traffic is still permitted. A
park on the highway side of the Stanislaus River provides picnicking and fishing spots. On the
other side of the river is a rustic Gold Rush-era town with a general store, several restaurants,
and another park.

Unguided raft, canoe, and kayak rentals can be arranged through **River Journey** *((800) 292-
2938, 847-4671, fax 847-1300).*

Groveland.

This rustic mountain town is home to the **Iron Door Saloon**, which was built in 1853 and
claims to be the oldest saloon in the state. In summer, the inexpensive **Groveland Motel** *(962-
7865. $-$$$.)* gives pooped parents the option of renting a cabin for themselves and an adjacent
carpeted tepee for the kids; mobile home units are also available.

WHERE TO STAY

Reservations are essential. Call 252-4848 for information or to make reservations at any park
lodging facility. It is especially difficult to obtain accommodations in the summer and on holi-
day weekends. Rates for two range from $40 to $237. A bargain Midweek Ski Package is available
in the winter.

PARK LODGING: IN THE VALLEY

The Ahwahnee *127 units; 45 non-smoking units; $$$+. Some fireplaces. Pool. Afternoon tea; restaurant, room service. Free valet parking.*

Built in 1927 of granite blocks and concrete beams, this sedate luxury hotel is a National Historic Landmark. It is decorated with priceless Native American baskets and oriental rugs, and interesting historic photos and artwork hang on the walls. The grand Great Lounge, with a walk-in fireplace at either end, is delightful to sit in. Some cottages are available.

Campgrounds *$; most Apr-Oct only; several open year-round.*

For reservations, call (800) 365-2267.

Curry Village *628 units; 20 non-smoking units; $-$$. No TVs; some shared baths. Pool. Restaurant.*

Accommodations and facilities are similar to Yosemite Lodge, but inexpensive tent-cabins, which are located along the Merced River and sleep up to six people, are also available.

Yosemite Lodge *495 units; 89 non-smoking units; $-$$. No TVs; some shared baths. Pool. 3 restaurants.*

Accommodations vary from primitive cabins without plumbing to comfortable modern hotel rooms.

PARK LODGING: ELSEWHERE

High Sierra Camps *56 units; $$; Sept-June only. Unsuitable for children under 7. No TVs; communal bath house. Dining tent.*

Five camps provide dormitory-style tent accommodations and two meals. Guests provide their own linens. Reservations are assigned by lottery. Applications are accepted October 15 through November 30, and the drawing is held in mid-December.

Tuolumne Meadows Lodge *69 units; $. No TVs; communal bath house. Dining tent.*

This all tent-cabin facility is located at the park's eastern entrance.

Wawona Hotel *On Hwy. 41, 30 mi. from valley. 104 rooms; 30 non-smoking rooms; $$; open Apr-Nov & Christmas vacation; weekends only Jan-Easter. No TVs; some shared baths. Unheated pool, 1 tennis court, 9-hole golf course. Restaurant.*

Built in 1879, this Victorian hotel is located six miles from the park's southern entrance, near the Mariposa Grove of Big Trees. A National Historic Landmark, it is said to be the oldest resort hotel in the state. Most rooms accommodate only two people; a few in the annex, added in 1918, accommodate three. Facilities include a "swimming tank" built in 1917.

A special **Christmas program** is scheduled each year. Details vary from year to year, but in 1991 it included a stagecoach ride across the covered bridge to the Pioneer History Center, where all the cabins were decorated for the holidays. Santa arrived in a horse-drawn wagon dating from the 1800s, and a special Christmas Eve and New Year's Eve dinner was served. Call for current details.

White Wolf Lodge *28 units; $. No TVs; shared bath house. Dining tent.*

Located at Tioga Pass, 31 miles from the valley, this complex consists of tent-cabins and a few cabins with private baths. Breakfast and dinner are available.

LODGING UNAFFILIATED WITH THE PARK

The Redwoods Guest Cottages *In Wawona, 6 mi. inside park's south entrance, 375-6666, fax 375-6400. 126 units; 5 non-smoking units; $$; 2-night min., 3-night min. in July & Aug. Children under 4 free. Some TVs & VCRs; all kitchens; some wood-burning fireplaces. Pets welcome in some units.*

These rustic, modern homes and cottages are furnished with linens and kitchenware.

Tenaya Lodge at Yosemite *1122 Hwy. 41, Fish Camp, 2 mi. outside park's south entrance, (800) 635-5807, 683-6555. 4 stories; 242 rooms; 150 non-smoking rooms; $$$-$$$+. Children under 18 free. 1 indoor heated pool & hot tub, 1 outdoor heated pool & hot tub, 2 saunas, 2 steam rooms, fitness room. 2 restaurants, room service.*

Built in 1990, this plush lodging facility is a cross between the park's Yosemite Lodge and The Ahwahnee hotel. A majestic public reception area features three-story-tall beamed ceilings, and all of the comfortable rooms have forest views. Complimentary guided nature walks are scheduled most mornings, weather permitting. In winter, ski and snowshoe rentals are available at the hotel, and guests can strike out on a scenic cross-country ski trail through adjacent **Yosemite National Forest**. In summer, campfire programs, wagon rides, and rentals of 21-speed mountain bikes are added to the agenda. **Camp Tenaya**, a children's program, operates from 9 to 4 weekends and holidays fall through spring, daily in summer. It offers an evening program from 6 to 10. A $25 to $35 fee is charged for each session.

WHERE TO EAT

PARK DINING

All of these valley facilities are open daily and equipped with highchairs and boosters. All take MasterCard and Visa.

The Ahwahnee Dining Room *372-1489. B, L, & D; $-$$$. Child portions. Reservations essential for D.*

The best time to dine in the rustic splendor of this magnificent dining room is during daylight hours. Only then can the spectacular views of the valley offered by the 50-foot-tall, floor-to-trestle-beamed ceiling leaded-glass windows be fully enjoyed. Dinner is expensive, and men are expected to wear a sport or suit jacket and women to dress accordingly. Guests of the hotel get first choice at reservations, so non-guests should be prepared for either an early or late seating. Children fit in best at breakfast or lunch.

Cafeterias *Curry Village and Yosemite Lodge. B, L, & D; $.*

Meals here are quick and informal.

Four Seasons Restaurant *Yosemite Lodge. B & D; $-$$. Child portions.*

The dinner menu offers American fare—steak, fried chicken, fish, and hamburgers.

Mountain Room Broiler *Yosemite Lodge. D; $$-$$$. Child portions.*

The walls in this stunning room are papered with striking black and white photo murals of mountain climbers, and floor-to-ceiling windows look out on Yosemite Falls. The menu features broiled fresh fish and aged beef as well as smoked trout, sautéed button mushrooms, and warm cheese bread.

Get rid of the kinks developed on the long ride in at the adjacent **Mountain Room Bar**.

Picnic Pick-Ups.

Box lunches can be reserved from hotel kitchens the evening before they are needed. Supplies can also be picked up at **Degnan's Deli** in the Village.

Wawona Hotel Dining Room *375-1425. B, L, & D, SunBr. Child portions. Reservations advised for D.*

A visit for the inexpensive Sunday brunch is highly recommended. Served in the hotel's wonderful vintage dining room, where huge multi-paned windows provide views of the surrounding pines, it consists of simple, satisfying fare. Breakfast or lunch during the rest of the week is also pleasant.

DINING OUTSIDE THE PARK

Erna's Elderberry House *48688 Victoria Lane, Oakhurst, 15 mi. outside park's south entrance, 683-6800, fax 683-0800. L W-F, D W-M, SunBr; in summer, D also on Tu; $$$. Closed 1st 3 weeks of Jan. Highchairs, child portions. Reservations essential. AE, MC, V.*

Hillside dining "in the classic tradition of old Europe" is promised here. The staff prepares a different six-course, fixed-price *($58)* meal every night. One meal enjoyed here in the elegantly appointed front room began with a flute of elderberry-flavored champagne. It continued with a scallop and sorrel timbale artistically positioned on a nest of pasta, followed by corn and cilantro soup, and then fresh pears poached in Riesling. The main course was alder wood-smoked chicken sausages served with wild rice and a colorful array of vegetables. A simple, elegant salad followed. Dessert, which is served outside on a candle-lighted garden terrace, was a duo of Chocolate Decadence in fresh mint sauce and puff pastry filled with caramelized apples and creamed gourmand. Three wines selected to complement each dinner are offered by the glass.

Elegant lodging is available in the property's castle-like **Chateau du Sureau** *(683-6860, fax 683-0800. 2 stories; 9 rooms; 100% non-smoking; $$$+; 2-night min. on weekends. Unsuitable for children under 7. TVs & VCRs by request; 9 wood-burning fireplaces. Unheated pool. Afternoon snack, full breakfast; restaurant, room service.)*, which features an outdoor chess court and serene walking paths. ("Sureau" is the French word for "elderberry.")

WHAT TO DO

PARK ACTIVITIES

The Ansel Adams Gallery *In the Village, 372-4413.*
Special edition photographs by this well-known photographer can be purchased here.

Bicycle Rentals *Yosemite Lodge: 372-1208. Daily 9-5. Curry Village: 372-8319. Daily 8-8; Apr-Oct only. $5.25/hr., $20/day.*
All rental bikes are old-fashioned one-speeds. A map to the eight miles of bike paths is provided, and helmets are available at no charge. Child carriers are not available.

Big Trees Tram Tour *On Hwy. 41, 35 mi. from valley. Tours 9-4; May-Oct only. Adults $7.50, seniors $6.75, children $4.*
Approximately 500 giant sequoias are located in this 250-acre grove. Some measure 15 to 25 feet in diameter, and some are over 2,000 years old. Open-air trams take visitors on guided tours of a six-mile scenic loop. In winter, this is a choice spot for cross-country skiing.

Bus Tours *372-1240. Valley floor $8.50-$16, grand tour $21.50-$42.*

Float Trip.
Scenic and calm is the area on the Merced River between Pines Campground and Centinnel Bridge. Raft rentals are available in June and July.

Glacier Point *1-hr. drive from valley. Bus tour $5-$10 one-way, $10.25-$19.50 round-trip.*
From this spot gazers enjoy a 270-degree view of the high country and a bird's-eye view of the valley 3,214 feet below. Several trails lead down to the valley. Consider arriving in the morning (get a one-way ticket on the **Glacier Point Hiker's Bus**) and spending the rest of the day hiking back down.

Hiking.
Participate in a ranger-guided walk or take any of the many self-guided trails. Maps can be purchased in the park stores. The most popular trail in the park is said to be the Mist Trail to Vernal Fall; it features breathtaking vistas and a close up view of the 317-foot-tall waterfall.

Indian Cultural Museum *Next to the Village Visitor Center. W-Sun 9-12 & 1-4.*

Visitors learn about the Awaneechee Indians through artifacts, cultural demonstrations, and recorded chants. A reconstructed village located behind the museum features a self-guided trail that points out plants used by the Native American residents for food, clothing, and shelter.

Junior Ranger Program.

This program is available June through August for children ages 8 through 12. Consult the *Yosemite Guide* for details.

Movies.

Scenic movies and slide shows are scheduled some evenings. Check the *Yosemite Guide* for times and locations.

Mono Lake Paiute Indians circa 1901

Pioneer Yosemite History Center *On Hwy. 41, in Wawona, 25 mi. from valley. Daily dawn-dusk.*

This village of restored historic pioneer buildings is reached by walking across an authentic **covered bridge**. Originally located in different areas around the park, the structures were moved here in the 1950s and '60s. In summer, history comes to life with demonstrations of soap making, yarn spinning, rail splitting, and other pioneer crafts. Horse-drawn carriage rides are sometimes available.

Rock Climbing Lessons *Curry Village: 372-8344. Daily, year-round. Tuolumne Meadows: 372-8435. Summer only. $65-$80.*

Learn rock climbing at the **Yosemite Mountaineering School**, one of the finest in the world. Beginners are taught safety essentials for dealing with the area's granite rock and can expect to climb as high as 80 feet in the first lesson. Oddly, snow and ice climbing are offered only in the summer. Participants must be at least age 14.

Valley Stables *372-8348. Guided 2-hr. horse rides at 8, 10, & 1; $35/person. Half-day mule rides/$45, all-day/$67.*

Said to have the largest public riding stock in the world, this concession can arrange for custom pack and fishing trips.

Winter Activities. See page 381 and 384.

ACTIVITIES OUTSIDE THE PARK
The first three destinations are reached via the Tioga Pass.

Bodie State Historic Park *8 mi. south of Bridgeport, (619) 647-6445. Daily 8-dusk; tour of stamp mill on Sat & Sun at 11 & 2, summer only. $5/vehicle.*

Located at the end of a 13-mile sideroad off of Highway 395, the last 3 miles of which are unpaved, this 486-acre park is the largest unrestored ghost town in the West. In 1879, when 10,000 people lived here, there were 2 churches, 4 newspapers, and 65 saloons. It was said to be quite rowdy. A little girl who moved here in its heyday wrote in her diary, "Good, by God! We're going to Bodie." This passage has also been interpreted as "Good-bye God! We're going to Bodie." Due to fires in 1892 and 1932, only about five percent of the town structure remains. No food services or picnic facilities are available.

Devil's Postpile National Monument *(619) 934-2289. Daily 7:30-5:30.*

This 60-foot-high formation is constructed of polygonal basaltic columns formed long ago by quickly cooling lava. Visitors can take a pleasant one-mile walk through the monument; another short hike leads to 101-foot-high Rainbow Falls. The road is closed to private vehicles. In summer, a **shuttle bus** *((619) 924-5500. $7, 5-12 $4.)* is available from the Mammoth Mountain area.

Mono Lake *Off Hwy. 395, (619) 647-3000, (619) 647-3044. Nature Center: Daily 9-8; guided nature walks daily in summer at 10 & 1, rest of year Sat & Sun at 1. Call for directions.*

John Muir described this desolate area as, "A country of wonderful contrasts, hot deserts bounded by snow-laden mountains, cinder and ashes scattered on glacier-polished pavement, frost and fire working together in the making of beauty." Mark Twain called it the "Dead Sea of the West." An ancient Ice Age lake, estimated to be at least one million years old, Mono Lake features an unusual terrain of pinnacles and spires formed by mineral deposits. It is filled with water that contains more than 2½ times the salt found in ocean water. Perhaps this is what attracts the 50,000-plus seagulls that flock in during April, stay into August, and then head back to the coast. Situated at over 7,000 feet above sea level, it is one of the largest lakes in the state. Campsites are available. Fall is the ideal time for a visit. For restaurant and lodging information, call (619) 647-6629. Note that the Tioga Pass is closed in winter.

• **Mono Basin Visitor Center** *Just outside of Lee Vining, (619) 647-3044. Daily in summer; informative talks at 11 & 2.*

Overlooking the lake, this new facility has interpretive displays that provide insight into the area. Nature study outings and hikes are scheduled daily in July and August.

• **Mono Lake Committee Visitor Center** *On Hwy. 395/Third St., Lee Vining, (619) 647-6595. Daily 9-9.*

Visitors can view a brief slide show about the lake, and a free hour-long sunset walk is offered daily at 6 p.m. Naturalist-led canoe tours are offered on summer weekends; there is a small charge for use of equipment.

Yosemite Mountain Sugar Pine Railroad *56001 Hwy. 41, Fish Camp, 4 mi. south of park's southern entrance, 1-hr. drive from valley, 683-7273. Call for schedule. Train: $9.75, 3-12 $4.75. Jenny rail cars: $6.50, 3-12 $3.50.*

A reconstruction of the Madera Sugar Pine Co. Railroad that made its last run in 1931, this narrow-gauge steam train takes passengers on a 45-minute, four-mile scenic excursion through the **Sierra National Forest**. Passengers, sitting in open-air touring cars upon logs that have been carved out to form long benches, are given live narration on the area's history. They may stop over at the midway point to picnic or hike. Moonlight rides, which include a steak barbecue and campfire program, are scheduled on Saturday nights in summer. Smaller Jenny rail cars, powered by Model A engines, take passengers on shorter 30-minute rides along the same route when the train is not operating. A picnic area and snack shop are available.

Sequoia and Kings Canyon National Parks
(Area Code 209)

A LITTLE BACKGROUND

Though located just south of Yosemite National Park, these two scenic national parks are often overlooked. It's a shame because they, too, offer spectacular scenery and are much less crowded.

Sequoia National Park was established in 1890. It was California's first national park, and it is the country's second oldest national park. (Yellowstone is the oldest.) Kings Canyon National Park was established in 1940. Combined, they encompass 864,383 acres.

The main attraction at these parks is the enormous sequoia trees, with their vibrant cinnamon-colored bark. The trees can be viewed in both Sequoia Park's **Giant Forest** and Kings Canyon's **Grant Grove**. The largest is the **General Sherman Tree** in Sequoia National Park. It towers 275 feet high, measures 36½ feet in diameter, and is between 2,300 and 2,700 years old. This makes it higher than Niagara Falls, as wide as a city street, and already middle-aged when Christ was born! It is said to be the largest living thing on the planet.

Mt. Whitney is also located in Sequoia Park and, at 14,494 feet, is the highest point in the United States outside of Alaska. From the east side of the Sierra, it is a one- to three-day hike to its peak; from the west side it is a seven- to nine-day hike.

Admission to the parks is $5 per vehicle.

General Grant Tree

VISITOR INFORMATION

Sequoia and Kings Canyon National Parks *Three Rivers 93271, 565-3134.*

GETTING THERE

Located approximately 250 miles southeast of San Francisco. Take Highway 80 to Highway 580 to Highway 99 south, to either Highway 180 east or Highway 198 east.

ANNUAL EVENTS

Caravan to Nation's Christmas Tree *December. 875-4575.*

Since 1926, the 267-foot-tall **General Grant Tree** in Kings Canyon National Park has been the site of a special Christmas service. In honor of its official status as the Nation's Christmas Tree, a wreath is placed at its base each year by members of the National Park Service. A car caravan leaves from the tiny town of Sanger, and seats are also available by reservation on a chartered bus.

WHERE TO STAY

Montecito-Sequoia Lodge. See pages 382 and 387.

Park Lodging *561-3314. 304 units; 40 non-smoking units; $$-$$$. Children under 12 free. No TVs; some fire-places & wood-burning stoves; some shared baths. Restaurant.*

At Sequoia, lodging includes both spartan and deluxe cabins as well as motel rooms. Kings Canyon has similar facilities, but they are generally less luxurious and there are fewer of them.

Arrangements can be made to backpack 11 miles into the High Sierra tent-cabin camp at Bearpaw. Dinner and breakfast are included, and reservations are necessary.

Campsites are available on a first-come, first-served basis. In the summer, reservations are accepted for Lodgepole Campground.

For more information, request a park brochure that explains the various options in detail.

WHAT TO DO

Caves.

• **Boyden Cavern** *In Sequoia National Forest, just outside Kings Canyon, 736-2708. Tours daily 10-5, June-Sept. Closed Oct-May. Adults $6, 6-12 $3. Strollers not permitted.*

This cave is located in spectacular 8,000-foot-deep Kings River Canyon—the deepest canyon in the United States. The guided tours take about 45 minutes.

• **Crystal Cave** *In Sequoia. Schedule varies; May-Sept only. Adults $4, 6-11 $2.*

This 48-degree marble cavern is reached via a steep ¼-mile trail. The guided tour takes about an hour.

Fishing.

The most popular spots are along Kings River and at the forks of the Kaweah River. A California fishing license is required. Ask about fishing regulations at park visitor centers.

Horse Rentals *In Cedar Grove, Wolverton, Grant Grove, & Mineral King.*

Trails.

Over 900 miles of hiking trails are in these parks.

Unusual Trees.

Many of these trees are encountered on the drive along the 46-mile **General's Highway** connecting the two national parks. Some require either a short walk to reach or a drive down a side road. From December through May, this highway is occasionally closed by snow.

• **Auto Log.** Cars can be driven onto this fallen sequoia for a photograph.

• **Senate Group and House Group of Sequoias.** These are among the most symmetrically formed and nearly perfect of the sequoias. They are reached via the Congress Trail, an easy walk that begins at the General Sherman Tree.

• **Tunnel Log.** Cars can be driven through this tunnel carved through a tree that fell across the road in 1937.

Visitor Centers *At Lodgepole & Grant Grove. Daily in summer 8-6; rest of year 9-5. Free.*

See exhibits on the area's wildlife as well as displays on Native Americans and sequoias. Inquire here about the schedule of nature walks and evening campfire programs.

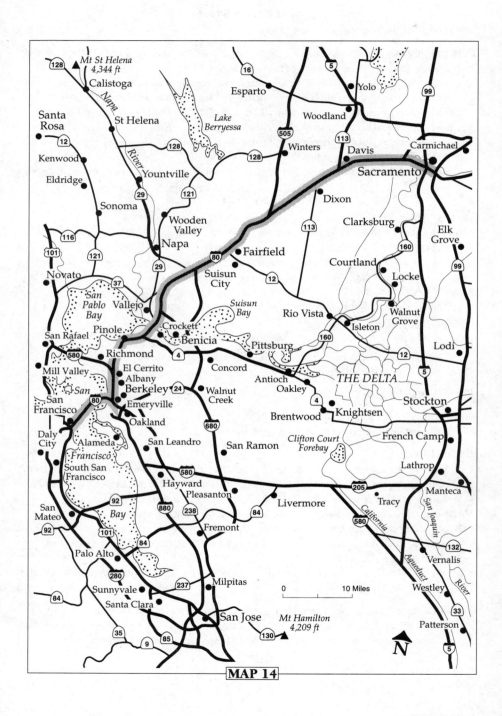

MAP 14

Berkeley

(Area Code 510)

A LITTLE BACKGROUND

The always fascinating community of Berkeley is a study in contrasts. Visitors arrive with a variety of expectations. Some seek the intellectual climate associated with a community built around the University of California, the state's most prestigious public university. Others expect to see weird people and hippie communes. Those who know their food come seeking the acclaimed restaurants, and those who know one of the town's nicknames, Berserkeley, expect to see a bit of that. Then there is the well-known ultra-liberal political climate, in which someone who would be thought a liberal elsewhere is here considered to be a conservative, which explains another nickname—the People's Republic of Berkeley. In reality, Berkeley is all these things, and, making any stereotype impossible, it is also the place where the word "yuppie" was coined.

VISITOR INFORMATION

Berkeley Convention & Visitors Bureau *1834 University Ave., Berkeley 94703-1516, (800) 847-4823, 549-7040, fax 644-2052.*

GETTING THERE

Take the Bay Bridge and follow the signs to I-80 north. The main Berkeley exit is University Avenue.

ANNUAL EVENTS

Live Oak Park Fair *June. 986-9337. Free.*

Among the festivities are juried arts and crafts booths, live entertainment, and multiethnic foods. The park itself—with its huge shade trees, rolling lawns, and meandering creek—is inviting to visit anytime.

Open Studios *June. 763-4361. Free.*

For this combination gallery exhibit and self-guided tour of artists' workplaces throughout the East Bay, more than 400 artists open the doors to their studios, workshops, lofts, and homes so that they can meet with the public. Many works are for sale.

Solano Avenue Stroll *September. 527-5358. Free.*

This mile-long block party is the oldest and largest free street festival in the East Bay. It is possible for strollers to eat their way from one end to the other.

WHERE TO STAY

Bancroft Hotel *2680 Bancroft Way/College Ave., (800) 549-1002, 549-1000, fax 549-1070. 3 stories; 22 rooms; 100% non-smoking; $$-$$$. Children under 12 free. Continental breakfast. Parking $6.*

Located directly across from the campus, this 1928 landmark arts and crafts-style hotel, designed by Walter T. Steilberg, an associate of Julia Morgan, offers peaceful, airy rooms with sweeping views of San Francisco Bay and the Berkeley hills. Many also have large balconies or decks

Berkeley City Club *2315 Durant Ave./Dana St., 848-7800, fax 848-5900. 6 stories; 40 rooms; 100% non-smoking; $$-$$$. No TVs. Indoor heated pool, fitness room. Continental breakfast; restaurant (for guests only).*

Founded in 1927 and opened in 1930 as the Berkeley Women's City Club, this magnificent building, an historical landmark, was designed by Julia Morgan—the well-known architect who designed Hearst Castle. It is beautifully appointed with oriental rugs and tasteful vintage furniture that enhance the Old World beauty of the lead-paned windows and aged redwood trim. Rooms are comfortably furnished, and some have good views of either the San Francisco Bay or the campus and hills. A bar is available for guests only, and a beauty salon and massage service operate on site.

Claremont Resort & Spa *41 Tunnel Rd., at Ashby Ave./Domingo Ave., (800) 551-7266, 843-3000, fax 843-6239. 6 stories; 239 rooms; 155 non-smoking rooms; $$$+. Children under 18 free. 2 heated pools, hot tub, 4 saunas, 2 steam rooms, health spa, fitness room, 10 tennis courts ($5/hr.; 6 with night lights). Restaurant, room service (child items). Valet parking $8.*

Built originally by a Kansas farmer who struck it rich and wanted to fulfill his wife's dream of living in a home resembling an English castle, the first incarnation of this hotel burned to the ground in 1901. The current Victorian hotel, built in 1915, once charmed architect Frank Lloyd Wright into describing it as ". . . one of the few hotels in the world with warmth, character and charm." The hotel now provides all the amenities of a resort in an urban setting. The lobby and hallways are decorated with a collection of contemporary art, and wine tastings and food samplings occur there on Saturday afternoons. A full-service European-style spa offers a variety of revitalizing treatments and packages.

The elegant **Pavilion Room** *($$$. Highchairs, boosters, reduced child price. Reservations advised. AE, MC, V. 2-hr. parking validation.)* provides a good bay view. Sunday brunch here is an extravagant buffet of salads, fresh fruit, seafood, and meats. A design-your-own-omelette station and a dessert table laden with fine cakes, chocolate eclairs, chocolate fondue, and several flavors of mousse are also available. Of special interest at lunch and dinner is the low-fat spa cuisine, which can be satisfyingly tasty. The **Terrace Bar** is the first in the state in a major hotel to become 100 percent smoke-free. In addition to more common drinks, healthy "smart drinks"—made with amino acids and other natural ingredients and bearing names that include Berry Brain Blaster and Cosmic Coconut—can be ordered.

The French Hotel *1538 Shattuck Ave./Cedar St., 548-9930, same fax. 3 stories; 18 rooms; 12 non-smoking rooms; $$-$$$. Cafe, room service.*

In this European-modern hotel situated just across the street from Chez Panisse, all rooms have a private patio. Just off the lobby, the hotel's coffee house has sidewalk tables that are popular in good weather.

Gramma's Rose Garden Inn *2740 Telegraph Ave./Ward St., 549-2145, fax 549-1085. 3 stories; 39 rooms; 100% non-smoking; $$-$$$+. Children under 4 free. 1 kitchen; 14 wood-burning fireplaces, 7 gas fireplaces. Evening snack, full breakfast; restaurant. Pets welcome.*

Situated seven blocks from the university, this charming lodging complex includes two landmark Tudor-style mansions, a carriage house, and a garden house with attractively decorated, comfortable guest rooms—some with views of San Francisco. The houses open onto a central garden oasis filled with fountains, patios, and hundreds of rose bushes, and the cookie jar is always full for snacking.

The **Greenhouse Restaurant** *(D Tu-Sat, SunBr; $$. Highchairs. Reservations advised. AE, MC, V.)* operates off the lobby in the main house. Its charming, intimate dining room features trompe l'oeil garden paintings as well as real garden views through old greenhouse windows. One dinner enjoyed here began with a tasty endive and pear salad accented with candied pecans and goat cheese. A pan-roasted chicken breast with provençale herbs on a calypso bean cassoulet was the main course, and the desserts were scary-rich.

Hotel Durant *2600 Durant Ave./Bowditch St., (800) 2-DURANT, 845-8981, fax 486-8336. 6 stories; 140 rooms; 75 non-smoking rooms; $$$. Children under 12 free. Continental breakfast; restaurant, room service. Parking $5.*

Particularly popular with parents in town to visit their children at the university, this atmospheric hotel's hallways are decorated with historic photographs of the campus. It is located just one block from the university, and some of the attractively appointed rooms feature campanile views.

Henry's Publick House & Grille has a cozy, comfortable pub atmosphere. Food is well-prepared and includes a very good hamburger, fresh fish items, and a variety of inexpensive sandwiches and salads.

WHERE TO EAT

Berkeley was the first city in the state to introduce legislation regulating smoking in public places. It was also the first city to require non-smoking sections in restaurants. Now all restaurants here are 100% non-smoking, except in bar areas, and smoking in workplaces is also prohibited.

Ajanta *1888 Solano Ave./The Alameda, 526-4373, fax 526-3885. L & D daily; $$. Highchairs, boosters. Reservations advised. AE, MC, V.*

With its ever-changing menu of creative, complex regional Indian dishes, this simple restaurant is always a delight. Complete dinners are well-priced, but ordering a la carte doesn't cost much more and offers the opportunity to try some unusual items. Presentation is part of the pleasure. One dinner here began with papadam, a crisp lentil wafer served gratis to all diners. The appetizer was alu tikki—deep-fried potato and pea patties. Then came chewy nan bread and mango chutney, plus house-made whole carrot relish and lime pickles. The entree was served with an attractively arranged dinner plate bearing three scoops of saffron-laced rice that were anchored in the middle by a mound of spinach purée. Dessert was a light mango mousse. Entrees include various curries, tandoori meats (including their signature lamb rib chops) and fish, and a good selection of vegetarian and vegan dishes; all can be ordered in any degree of spiciness.

Berkeley Thai House *2511 Channing Way/Telegraph Ave., 843-7352. L & D daily; $. Highchairs, boosters. Reservations advised at D. MC, V.*

In good weather, a table on the wooden deck here is a choice spot to relax with a cooling, sweet Thai iced tea. On nippier days, or in the evening, the cozy inside dining room, which is decorated with Indonesian artifacts, is an option. Specials are chalked on a board by the entrance and are usually a good bet. Most dishes are simply seasoned. Favorites include spicy-hot basil chicken; full-flavored cashew nut chicken; moo-prik-khing—a superb stir-fry dish with pork and fresh green beans in a spicy sauce; panang neur—beef and sweet basil in a spicy red curry sauce with a coconut milk base; and pad thai—a sweet orange-colored noodle dish accented with ground peanuts, bean sprouts, bean cake, and a few tiny shrimp.

Bette's Oceanview Diner *1807 4th St./Hearst Ave., 644-3230. B & L daily; $. Boosters, booths. No reservations. MC, V.*

In this casual, noisy diner, with its 1950s truck stop decor and menu of traditional American food, it's fun to sit on a counter stool and watch the cooks hustle. More entertainment is provided by the jukebox and its eclectic mix of everything from '50s classics to reggae. Breakfast choices are available all day and include spicy scrambled eggs, steak and eggs, omelettes, griddle cakes with real maple syrup, French toast, and some combination plates—The New York (smoked salmon, bagel, cream cheese, red onion, and tomato) and The Philadelphia (scrapple, poached eggs, toast, and grilled tomato). Blintzes are sometimes also available. Lunch is a satisfying assortment of well-prepared classic sandwiches, house-made soups, and homey items such as meatloaf, grilled bockwurst, and potato pancakes. Thick old-fashioned milkshakes are available, too, but oddly no hamburger or fries. By the way. About that ocean view. There is none. Oceanview is the name of the neighborhood in which the restaurant is located.

Next door, **Bette's To Go** *(548-9494. M-Sat 6:30-5, Sun 8-4.)* has take-out pastries, sandwiches, salads, pizza by the slice, and other goodies.

Brennan's *720 University Ave./4th St., 841-0960. L & D daily; $. 1 highchair, boosters. No reservations. MC, V.*

Reminiscent of a shamrock, with its dark green exterior and bright green interior, the hall-like dining room of this Berkeley institution is dominated by a enormous rectangular bar. Always crowded and boisterous, it has a variety of beers on tap and is furnished with simple Formica tables. The hofbrau-style food is basically meat and potatoes, and each night has its special. Hot sandwiches are served with made-from-scratch mashed potatoes smothered in gravy, and side dishes include a tasty stuffing, macaroni salad, potato salad, and coleslaw.

Cactus Taqueria *1881 Solano Ave./The Alameda, 528-1881. L & D daily; $. Highchairs, boosters. No reservations. No cards.*

Mexican fast food at its best is served cafeteria-style at this popular taqueria. Burritos are custom made, with a choice of several kinds of tortillas (chile- or tomato-red, spinach-green, plain), black or pinto beans, and a large variety of well-seasoned fillings. Tacos and tamales are also available. Tortillas are lard-free, meats are from Nieman-Schell, and tortilla chips are fried in safflower oil. House-made drinks include several fruit agua frescas and horchata (a sweet rice drink), and two kinds of addictive salsa are on each table—a tangy green tomatillo and a smoky mole. Seating is at colorfully-stained natural wood tables, and an indoor water fountain provides a restive background sound.

Cafe de la Paz *1600 Shattuck Ave./Cedar St., upstairs in Cedar Center, 843-0662, fax 843-0669. D daily; $$. Highchairs, boosters. Reservations advised. AE, MC, V.*

Wildly popular with locals, this exciting spot serves authentic interpretations of traditional and contemporary Latin American cuisine. Specialties include cachapas de Jojoto from Venezuela (corn pancakes topped with a sweet pepper sauce), tamal de pollo from Guatemala (corn masa with chicken mole and a spicy chile sauce), and carne asada fajitas con salsa barbacoa (beef topped with a spicy-smoky-sweet sauce). The welcoming dining room, with its large windows and soothing water fountain, add to the experience.

Cafe Panini *2115 Allston Way/Shattuck Ave., in Trumpetvine Court, 849-0405. M-F 9-4; $. No reservations. No cards.*

Popular with university students and staff, this tiny spot produces divine gourmet sandwiches. Diners place their orders at the counter, pay, and then select a seat either in the brick-walled interior or out in the sunny courtyard—the supreme choice on a sunny day. Sandwiches are made with magnificent sourdough baguettes, produced locally by Semifreddi Bakery, and topped with an enticing choice of combinations. A personal favorite is the mushroom-sun-dried tomato-pesto with melted mozzarella. As at Chez Panisse—where the owner was once a waitress and then a wine buyer—all ingredients are fresh. Tuna is not from a can. Meats are cooked in house. Mayonnaise is made from scratch. Herbs are fresh. A soup, a pasta salad, and some great house-made desserts are also available.

Caffe Giovanni *2420 Shattuck Ave./Channing Way, 843-6678. L & D daily, Sat & SunBr; $$. Highchairs, boosters, child portions. Reservations advised. AE, MC, V.*

In business since 1961, this ever-popular Italian restaurant offers a variety of calzones, pizzas, and pastas, plus salads, sandwiches, a tasty house-made minestrone soup, and fresh fish items. Favorite entrees include a great veal scaloppini Marsala smothered with mushrooms and a ricotta-filled ravioli Mama Savaria. Dolci usually include a cannoli and zabaglione.

Cha-Am *543 Shattuck Ave./Cedar St., 848-9664. L M-Sat, D daily; $. Highchairs, boosters. Reservations advised. AE, MC, V.*

The current leader in the informal ranking of the city's best Thai restaurants, this gem features a festive atmosphere, an attentive staff, and a kitchen that produces complex flavors and interesting combinations. Among the winners on its exciting menu are: laap-gai (a chopped chicken salad tossed with fresh mint and coriander), pad-makua-yao (chicken sautéed with basil, chile, and eggplant), and pad-ped-gung (prawns sauteed with sweet curry sauce, fresh Thai herbs, and green beans).

Chez Panisse *1517 Shattuck Ave./Cedar St. L & D M-Sat; $$-$$$. Boosters, booths. Cafe: L reservations, or D reservations for before 6 or after 9, accepted on the same day; 548-5049. Downstairs: Reservations essential; can be made up to 1 month in advance; 548-5525. AE, MC, V.*

Opened in 1971 by U.C. graduate Alice Waters as a hangout for her friends, this restaurant features definitive California cuisine prepared with the freshest ingredients and serves a different fixed-price menu *(M $35, Tu-Thur $55, F & Sat $65)* each night in its legendary downstairs dining room. A less expensive upstairs cafe serves a seasonal menu of simple items such as baked goat cheese salad or Spanish-style grilled chicken with lentils. A 15 percent service charge is automatically added to the bill; it is divided by the entire staff. The area surrounding this restaurant is known as the "Gourmet Ghetto." Allow time to explore.

China Station *700 University Ave./4th St., 548-7880. L & D daily; $$. Highchairs, boosters. Reservations advised. AE, MC, V.*

Located inside the former Berkeley Southern Pacific railroad depot, this popular Chinese restaurant specializes in Cantonese and Szechwan seafood. Excellent choices include wonderfully seasoned and very messy crab in black bean sauce (a seasonal dish), spicy-hot Szechwan prawns, and deep-fried rock cod filets in sweet and sour sauce. Live Maine lobster is also available. Non-seafood items that are particularly good include lemon chicken (crispy-skinned chicken breasts topped with lemon rounds and surrounded with bright red maraschino cherries), minced squab in lettuce cups, fat and juicy pot stickers, and noodle dishes—especially chow fun. For dessert, don't miss the unusual and delicious fried milk puffs. These creamy, light, deep-fried milk-flour balls are sprinkled with powdered sugar and served hot. Exotic mixed drinks and a variety of beers and wines are available from a large bar. Service here is attentive, and attention is paid to details. And to the delight of young and old alike, trains still rumble by periodically on the outside tracks.

Edy's *2201 Shattuck Ave./Allston Way, 843-3096. B, L, & D daily; $. Highchairs, boosters, booths. Reservations accepted. MC, V.*

Opened in 1932, this downtown ice cream parlor retains its original wooden booths, carved in Germany in the 1930s. Dreyer's ice cream is used exclusively, and classic hot fudge and caramel sundaes are topped with sauces made fresh from Old World recipes. Sodas, freezes, and fancy cakes are also on the menu, as are a large selection of breakfast and lunch items that are available throughout the day.

FatApple's *1346 Martin Luther King Jr. Way/Rose St., 526-2260. B, L, & D daily; $-$$. Highchairs, boosters. No reservations. No cards.*

This popular restaurant's forte is good food made from scratch using basic ingredients: The lean ground chuck used for hamburgers is ground on the premises; soup is made fresh; blue cheese salad dressing is made with the real stuff; robust Peet's coffee is freshly ground and served with heavy whipping cream. The famous hamburger is served on a toasted house-made wheat or white bun, and just-right milk shakes are served in the metal mixer canister. For dessert, it's impossible to go wrong with a slice of the puffy apple pie the restaurant is named for, but the chocolate velvet and lemon meringue are also delicious. Breakfast features fresh-squeezed orange juice, crisp waffles served with 100 percent pure Vermont maple syrup, and freshly baked pastries.

Ginger Island *1820 4th St./Hearst Ave., 644-0444. L & D daily; $$. Highchairs, boosters. Reservations advised. AE, MC, V.*

Operating in the inviting contemporary space where celebrity chef Mark Miller first dished out his Southwestern Cuisine (he's gone on to the Coyote Cafe in Santa Fe and Red Sage in Washington, D.C.), this exciting restaurant now serves up American cuisine with an Asian flair. The appetizer won tons are sensuously soft, moist pockets exploding with flavor, and the grilled lamb brochette entree served with couscous and fiery hot harrisa is long-remembered. More enticements are found in the hamburger served with potato, yam, and taro fries, and the curry noodles with shrimp and peanuts. Every meal should end with the wonderful gingery ginger cake served with freshly house-made caramel sauce. Drinks include a potent Singapore Sling served in a tall glass, iced lichee tea, and a made-to-order house ginger ale.

Just Desserts *1823 Solano Ave./Colusa Ave., 527-7344; and 2925 College Ave./Ashby Ave., 841-1600.*

For description, see page 38.

King Tsin *1699-1701 Solano Ave./Tulare Ave., 525-9890. L & D daily; $$. Highchairs, boosters. Reservations advised. MC, V.*

The first Mandarin Chinese restaurant in town, this popular spot serves a consistently well-executed menu. No MSG is used in preparing the tasty items that include hot and sour soup, spiced prawns (coated with batter, deep-fried, and served in a spicy-sweet sauce), Mongolian beef (smothered in green onions and served on a bed of crisp rice noodles), vegetarian green beans, and dramatic sizzling meat and fish plates. Mixed drinks can be ordered from the full bar.

King Yen *2995 College Ave./Ashby Ave., 845-1286. L & D daily; $-$$. Highchairs, boosters. No reservations. MC, V.*

Three brothers are the exclusive cooks here, which translates into no bad nights when the main cook is off. Among the best items are tasty Szechwan beef (batter-dipped meat is deep-fried, then stir-fried with a spicy-sweet sauce) and delicately seasoned mu shu pork. Good vegetarian items include crispy spring rolls, dry-braised long green beans, and bean curd with black bean sauce; chow mein and hot and sour soup also can be requested without meat. Both white and brown rice are available, and exotic beggar's chicken and Peking duck can be ordered in advance. MSG is not used in the kitchen. The high-ceilinged main dining room, with its generous flower arrangements and potted plants, is as delightful as the food.

Kirin *1767 Solano Ave./Ensenada Ave., 524-1677. L & D daily.*

For description, see page 39.

Larry Blake's *2367 Telegraph Ave./Durant Ave., 848-0886. L & D daily; $-$$. Highchairs, boosters, booths. Reservations accepted. AE, MC, V.*

A campus hangout since 1940, this restaurant is well-known for its hamburgers and steaks. Weekdays, lunch is served both downstairs, in the funky rathskeller with its sawdust-covered floor and old wooden booths, and upstairs, where excellent views of the sidewalk parade outside are to be had. Live music is scheduled most evenings, and a cover is charged.

La Val's *1834 Euclid Ave./Hearst Ave., 843-5617. L & D daily; $. Highchairs, boosters, booths. No reservations. AE, MC, V.*

Located on the quieter north side of the U.C. campus, this long-popular student hangout has good pizza, pastas, and brew—all at great prices. The very casual seating inside is sometimes enhanced with overhead TVs broadcasting sporting events, and a courtyard beer garden with picnic tables is inviting on warm afternoons. Older children can spend waiting time playing video games; younger ones can ride in a miniature moving car. Live music and plays are scheduled downstairs in the **Subterranean**. Food can also be ordered there, and children are welcome. There is a cover charge.

The Med (iterraneum Cafe) *475 Telegraph Ave., 549-1128. M-F 7am-midnight, Sat & Sun from 7:30am; $. No reservations. No cards.*

With a casual atmosphere and untidy decor, this coffeehouse is now an institution. It seems to have been serving students forever. Don't miss their Berliner coffee—a sort of coffee ice cream float—and the fabulous moist chocolate layer cake with rum custard filling.

O Chame Restaurant & Tea Room *1830 4th St./Hearst Ave., 841-8783. L & D M-Sat; $$. 1 highchair. Reservations advised. AE, MC, V.*

Reminiscent of Chez Panisse in its simplicity and use of the freshest ingredients, this soothing and tranquil spot has a refined menu that changes weekly. Among the offerings are some whimsical presentations—a "tower" salad composed of stacked slices of daikon radish, smoked salmon, and mango—as well as more traditional presentations—soup prepared with king salmon, mustard greens, fresh shitake mushrooms, and soba noodles. A variety of sakes, including the Hakusan brand produced domestically in the Wine Country, and an extensive list of teas are also available. Dessert can be simple but exquisite: fresh sweet cherries served chilling amid ice cubes. Beautiful bento box lunches are available to go.

Pasand *2286 Shattuck Ave./Bancroft Way, 549-2559. L & D daily; $-$$. Highchairs, boosters, booths. Reservations accepted. AE, MC, V.*

Authentic South-Indian Madras cuisine is served here in casual, comfortable surroundings. Live Indian music is performed nightly from 6:30 to 9:30 by musicians seated on a stage in the main dining room. Menu choices include Biriani entrees, succulent chicken tikka kabab from a Tandoori oven, and an assortment of meat and vegetable curries. When the appetite is small, dosas are the way to go. The Masala dosa consists of a lentil flour crepe stuffed with delicious vegetable curry; it is served with sambar (a soup) and two tasty sauces.

Picante Cocina Mexicana *328 6th St./Gilman St., 525-3121. L & D daily, SunBr; $. Highchairs, boosters, booths. No reservations. No cards.*

Claiming to be the largest taqueria in the Bay Area, this casual spot is located in the town's low-rent district. Indeed, with two large indoor dining rooms and a pleasant outside area boasting a soothing wall fountain, there is plenty of seating. Menu choices include the expected burritos, tamales, tacos, quesadillas, and tostadas. Especially good fillings include the carnitas (slow-cooked pork), pollo asado (grilled chicken with fresh salsa), rajas (roasted Poblano chiles with sauteed onions and Mexican cheese), and chorizo y papas (spicy Mexican sausage and potatoes). Among the drinks are several aguas frescas (fresh fruit drinks), margaritas made with agave wine, and a large selection of Mexican beers.

Picnic Pick-Ups.

• **Andronico's Market** *1550 Shattuck Ave./Cedar St., 841-7942. Daily 7-11. MC, V.*

This upscale supermarket carries delicious take-out fare and locally made gourmet treats. It is located within what was once the consumer-owned Co-op supermarket that operated here from 1938 to 1988 and was the country's largest urban cooperative.

• **Food Stalls** *At the campus entrance, on Bancroft Way/Telegraph Ave. M-F 11-3, more or less; $. No cards.*

These informal stands offer simple fast foods such as donuts, soft pretzels, fresh juices and smoothies, falafel (a Middle Eastern vegetarian sandwich made with pocket bread), and other ethnic dishes. Nearby benches, steps, and grassy areas offer impromptu picnic possibilities. And since this famous intersection attracts all kinds of entertainers—jugglers, musicians, revivalists, you-name-it—the amazing floor show that surrounds is free.

• **Made to Order** *1576 Hopkins St./Monterey Ave., 524-7552. M-Sat 9:30-6. MC, V.*

Wonderful deli fare, including freshly prepared salads and sandwiches, is found here. Favorites include meat pies and the rarely-available Grandma's potatoes.

• **Monterey Market** *1550 Hopkins St./Monterey Ave., 526-6042. M-Sat 9-6. No cards.*

This low-key but much-heralded produce market caters to the sophisticated Berkeley palate with an amazing assortment of baby vegetables, unusual melons, and exotic wild mushrooms. The market also supplies the area's fine restaurants, and prices are unexpectedly low.

• **Noah's Bagels** *1883 Solano Ave./The Alameda, 525-4447, fax 525-4408. M-F 7-6:30, Sat 7-6, Sun 7-5. No cards.*

The very first Noah's store opened in nearby Emeryville. This branch was among the first in what has now become a large chain. Promising "a taste of old New York," this shop delivers a bagel that is described by the owner as "crusty outside, chewy inside, tasty and big." They come in many flavors, including "super onion" and "multi-grain," and a variety of freshly made "shmears," or cream cheese spreads, are the perfect topping. Bagel sandwiches are made to order, and plenty of supporting items and cold drinks are also available. Noah says, "Protect your bagels . . . put lox on them!"

• **Ultra Lucca** *2905 College Ave./Ashby Ave., 849-2701. M-F 10-7:30, Sat 10-7, Sun 10-6. MC, V.*

This spacious traditional Italian delicatessen offers the best local breads, a selection of house-made salads and pastas, and a plethora of imported and domestic cheeses and wines. Sandwiches are made to order, and an area is available for eating-in.

• **Whole Foods Market** *Telegraph Ave./Ashby Ave., 649-1333. Daily 9am-10pm. MC, V.*

This Texas-based natural foods retailer purveys an amazing selection of good-for-you foods, and its busy bakery and deli-coffee bar offer the makings for a great picnic. Seating is also available in comfortable booths inside and at sheltered tables outside. Special child-sized shopping carts are fun for children.

Plearn *2050 University Ave./Shattuck Ave., 841-2148. L & D M-Sat; $-$$. 1 highchair, boosters. No reservations. MC, V.*

Very popular, and with a "Thai-tech" decor, this restaurant's best dishes include: yum-nua (a yummy mixture of beef slices seasoned with onion, ground chiles, fragrant fresh mint, and lime juice), him-ma-pan (chicken with cashew nuts and chiles), and pat-prik-king (pork with chiles and string beans). For a pittance more, an entree is served with both rice and an iceberg lettuce salad topped with an exotic bright yellow, tangy-sweet dressing. For dessert, a crispy deep-fried banana topped with a light coconut sauce can be pleasant.

Rick & Ann's *2922 Domingo Ave./Ashby Ave., 649-8538. B, L, & D Tu-Sun; $. Highchairs, boosters, child portions. No reservations. MC, V.*

The extensive breakfast menu at this cozy neighborhood restaurant is served until 2:30 p.m. and features both the usual and the more unusual—gingerbread waffles, hash prepared with beets, lacy corn cakes, French toast made with challah dipped in orange-cardamom batter. The superb homefries are made from fresh potatoes fried until they are *done* and served topped with sour cream and chopped green onions. At lunch, hamburgers, salads, and a variety of sandwiches are added to the menu. Diners can actually hear the bacon sizzling in the open kitchen. Banquettes along the wall, Shaker-style chairs, and tables with hammered metal tops lend a solid feeling. Kids get a coloring place mat and a basket of crayons to keep them occupied.

Skates *100 Seawall Dr., at foot of University Ave., 549-1900. L & D daily, SunBr; $$. Highchairs, boosters, booths, child portions. Reservations advised. AE, MC, V.*

With thick carpeting and ceiling fans, the dining room here offers seating in both oversize booths and at tables. Window tables take best advantage of the stunning three-bridge view. Brunch items include an omelette and frittata, French toast, a shellfish Benedict with lemon-dill scones, and special macadamia nut-banana sourdough pancakes. The extensive lunch menu offers deep-fried Cajun shrimp in coconut beer batter, a hamburger on focaccia bun, and a variety of soups, salads, and pastas. The dinner menu brings on more fresh fish items. The traditional desserts include a hot fudge sundae, a burnt cream custard, and, in season, a giant strawberry shortcake.

Spenger's Fish Grotto *1919 4th St./University Ave., 845-7771. B, L, & D daily; $$. Highchairs, boosters, child menu. No reservations. MC, V.*

Begun in 1890 as a country store, Spenger's then became a fish market and after Prohibition evolved into a bar and restaurant. Now, with a seating capacity of 400, it easily qualifies as one of Berkeley's most popular restaurants and has the biggest free parking lot in town. Two bars, one with a gigantic TV screen, offer respite should there be a wait. Once seated in one of the cozy rooms, diners choose from a large selection of seafood as well as steak, frog legs, and a hamburger. A well-stocked fish market adjoins.

Taiwan *2071 University Ave./Shattuck Ave., 845-1456. B Sat & Sun, L & D daily; $. Highchairs, boosters. No reservations. AE, MC, V.*

Native Taiwanese specialties are among the representative dishes from most of the Chinese provinces that are served here. Portions are generous. Favorites include spinach with garlic, dry-braised green beans, General Tsao's chicken, spicy fish-flavored chicken, beef a la Shangtung (deep-fried pieces of battered beef in a tasty sauce), showy sizzling beef and chicken platters, Mongolian beef, and spicy prawns. More exotic items include Taiwan pickle cabbage with pork tripe soup, boneless duck web, and numerous squid dishes. Beggar's chicken and Peking duck are available when ordered one day in advance. On weekends, a Chinese breakfast is served. The fortune cookies here are unusually prophetic. The strip inside mine once read, "You would make an excellent critic."

Thai Thai *1045 San Pablo Ave./Marin Ave., Albany, 526-SIAM. L M-F, D daily; $. Highchairs, boosters. Reservations accepted. MC, V.*

Located off the beaten trendy path, this culinary gem is well-worth an excursion. Seating is in either the front dining room—a simulated thatched-hut—or in the back room—where shoes are removed before being seated on floor cushions at low-to-the-ground tables. Tasty cocktails such as Singapore slings and mai tais can be ordered from a full-service bar and marry well with the spicy cuisine. Especially tasty items include tom yum kar gai (spicy-sour chicken soup with mushrooms and coconut milk), pra rama rong song (beef in a peanut sauce over spinach and other vegetables), and vegetarian curry (mixed vegetables in a hot curry sauce). Specials are always available, too.

Walker's Restaurant and Pie Shop *1491 Solano Ave./Curtis St., Albany, 525-4647. B & L Tu-Sat, D Tu-Sun; $$. Highchairs, boosters, child portions. No reservations. MC, V.*

Most everyone in these parts has been here at some point for one of the famous down-home-style meals. Complete dinners are just that. They include house-made soup, either a green salad or a gelatin salad, popovers, an entree with fresh vegetable and either baked or scalloped potato, and a slice of their famous flaky-crusted pie. Entrees include fish, fried chicken, ham, New York steak, prime rib, and daily specials. Lunch is a similar menu, but includes lighter options such as sandwiches and hamburgers. Pies are available for take-out; it is wise to reserve a favorite a day in advance.

WHAT TO DO

Adventure Playground *160 University Ave., next to Cal Sailing Club, 644-8623. Sat & Sun 11-4; in summer M-F 9-5, Sat & Sun 11-5. Free.*

The story goes that after World War II an European designer built a series of modern playgrounds. But the children continued, indeed preferred to play in the bombed-out buildings and to construct their own play equipment from the plentiful rubble and debris. Taking that cue, he designed the first Adventure Playground. This U.S. version offers a storage shed full of tools and scrap wood that children can use to build forts and clubhouses and other things, and then leave them up or tear them down when they are done. The playground also has a tire swing, a climbing net, and a fast-moving trolley hanging from a pulley. Outside the fence is a par course and a large grassy area with a more traditional tiny-tot play area.

Across the street, **Shorebird Nature Center** *(644-8623)* has a 100-gallon aquarium. Special family programs are often scheduled, as are marina tours and walks.

Nearby, at the end of University Avenue by the bay, is a bow-and-arrow-wielding sculpture by artist Fred Fierstein. The artist is said to have plopped it there himself in 1985 when he got tired of waiting for Berkeley politicians to decide to do it for him. He had offered "The Guardian" to the city at no cost, but after long deliberation it was rejected as too aggressive. (And the animal appears to urinate when it rains). Berkeley residents then voted to keep it there, but their decision might not be final. See it now.

Audubon Cellars Winery *600 Addison St./2nd St., 540-5384. Tasting & tours M-F by appt.*

A winery in Berkeley? Yes, that's right. But don't expect to see vineyards. This winery buys its grapes from growers in the Sonoma and Napa valleys.

Berkeley Iceland *2727 Milvia St./Derby St., 843-8800. Daily; schedule varies. Adults $5.50, under 18 $4.50-$5.50, skate rental $2.*

With a rink measuring 100 by 200 feet, this ranks as one of the three largest ice skating rinks in the country.

Berkeley Rose Garden *On Euclid Ave./Buena Vista Way, 644-6530. Daily sunrise-sunset. Free.*

Planted at the turn of the century, this garden was originally conceived as a classical Green arboretum. It is a particular delight in late spring and summer, when the roses are in full bloom. Benches sheltered by arbors covered with climbing roses make for pleasant picnicking and provide gorgeous views of the bay and San Francisco. Tennis courts adjoin. The garden is a popular spot for weddings, and most evenings find a knot of people at the top watching the sun set. Across the street, **Codornices Park** is equipped with a playground, a basketball court, and a long, exciting, and potentially dangerous concrete slide.

Fourth Street *1800 block. Stores generally open M-Sat 10-6.*

Surprisingly, in a city of Berkeley's size and income level, there are no department stores or traditional shoping malls. Designed, built, and owned by a Berkeley developer/architectural firm, this trendy block features a 1920s industrial style of architecture. Buildings are kept at two stories, and the owner controls leasing of the entire block, hand-picking the unusual stores that tend to be home-oriented. This is a shopping mall done Berkeley-style.

- **Builders Booksource** *(#1817, 845-6874)* stocks books on architecture and design.
- **Elica's Paper***(#1801, 845-9530)* has an impressive selection of handmade Japanese papers.
- **The Gardener***(#1836, 548-4545)* specializes in elegant accessories for the garden.
- **Hear** *(#1809, 204-9595)* is a music store that permits listening before buying.
- **Lighting Studio** *(#1808, 843-3468)* displays the very best and latest in lighting fixtures.
- **Sur La Table** *(#1806, 849-2252)* purveys fine kitchen equipment at fair prices.

Judah L. Magnes Museum *2911 Russell St./College Ave., 549-6950. Sun-Thur 10-4; tours on W & Sun. By donation.*

The first Jewish museum established in the western U.S., this institution exhibits Jewish ceremonial and fine arts from communities around the world. It is housed in a converted 1908 mansion, the gardens for which were landscaped by John McLaren, designer of San Francisco's Golden Gate Park.

Kidshows *2640 College Ave./Derby St., 839-0886. Oct-May only. Tickets $7, under 1 free.*

This children's performance series for ages 3 through 10 presents programs in the beautiful redwood interior of the magnificent **Julia Morgan Theatre**. The intimate live theater programs are designed to inspire and move children, and parents usually enjoy them, too. An informal atmosphere allows for interaction between the audience and the performers, so adults feel none of the usual pressure to hush their children. Performances are also held in Oakland at the **Calvin Simmons Theatre** and in Walnut Creek at the **Dean Lesher Regional Center for the Arts**.

Takara Sake USA *708 Addison St./4th St., 540-8250. Tasting daily 12-6. Free.*

Visitors can sample several kinds of sake and plum wine in the spacious tasting room of this country's largest sake brewery. A raised tatami room invites removing shoes and relaxing for a bit. Upon request, an informative slide show tells about the history and making of sake.

Telegraph Avenue *4 blocks between Bancroft Way & Dwight Way, south of campus.*

Fondly referred to as "the Ave" or "Tele" by locals, this famous, or perhaps infamous, avenue is probably best known for its role as a gathering spot and point of confrontation during the 1960s Free Speech Movement. It has now slipped into a more peaceful state. On weekdays rushing students crowd the sidewalks, and on weekends shoppers crowd its many boutiques. A stroll here passes a street bazaar of crafts stalls selling souvenirs such as colorful tie-dyed t-shirts and peace symbol jewelry. Thoroughly modern chain stores are also well represented.

• **Annapurna***(#2416)* is a psychedelic "head shop" left over from the turbulent 1960s.

• **Bookstores** in the 2400 block include **Cody's**, which stocks new obscure tomes along with the latest best-sellers and holds Wednesday evening poetry readings, and **Moe's** and **Shakespeare & Co.** which sell unusual used editions.

Tilden Regional Park.

This beautiful, well-developed 2,058-acre park has 35 miles of hiking trails as well as numerous picnic spots, many with tables and barbecues.

• **Botanic Garden** *841-8732. Daily 8:30-5. Free.*

Located across from the carousel, this ten-acre garden was begun in 1940. It offers the opportunity for a leisurely, quiet walk. Over 3,000 drought-resistant species and subspecies are displayed, and native plants are also featured.

• **Environmental Education Center** *525-2233. Tu-Sun 10-5. Free.*

This is a good place to get oriented and obtain current information about park attractions. Exhibits stress local natural history. Educational programs and naturalist-guided walks, many designed especially for families and children, are scheduled regularly.

• **Golf Course** *848-7373. Daily sunrise-sunset. M-F $21, Sat & Sun $30; special twilight rates .*

This scenic 18-hole course is open to the public.

• **Lake Anza** *848-3385. Daily 11-6, May-Oct. Adults $2.50, 62+ & 1-15 $1.50.*

This low-key swimming area has lifeguards on duty, and a snack bar is available. The area is open in off-season at no charge but without lifeguards.

• **Little Farm** *Daily 8:30-4:30. Free.*

This brightly painted, well-maintained farm is home to cows, donkeys, sheep, ducks, chickens, goats, rabbits, pigs, and assorted other barnyard animals.

• **Merry-Go-Round** *524-6773. Sat & Sun 10-5; in summer daily 11-5. $1.*

One of only four remaining classic carousels in Northern California, this antique gem is located in the center of the park. Built in 1914 by the Herschel-Spillman firm in New York, it spent time at Urbita Springs Park in San Bernardino, at Ocean Beach in San Diego, and at Griffith Park in Los Angeles before it settled here. It was restored in 1978. In addition to horses, it sports an assortment of colorful animals, including a stork, a dragon, and a frog. Its large band organ, which operates like a player piano, is regarded as one of the finest examples of its kind.

- **Pony Rides** *527-0421. Sat & Sun 11-5, spring & fall, weather permitting; Tu-Sun in summer. $2.*

Children age 2 and older are strapped securely into a saddle with a back support and given an exciting ride in the pony wheel. Children 5 and older can ride horses on the fast track in a larger ring.

- **Tilden Steam Train (Redwood Valley Railway)** *Grizzly Peak Blvd./ Lomas Cantadas, 548-6100. Sat & Sun 11-4:45, weather permitting; in summer daily 11-6. $1.50.*

This 15-inch gauge, 5-inch scale narrow gauge, oil-burning miniature steam train (whew!) follows a scenic route that includes one tunnel and two trestles. The ride covers 1¼ mile and lasts 12 minutes.

U.C. Theatre *2036 University Ave./Shattuck Ave., 843-6267. Adults $4-$6.50, seniors & under 13 $4.*

Berkeley's last single-screen cinema, this gargantuan 1,250-seat 1917-vintage theater shows something new (really something *old*) every day on its giant 40-foot-wide by 27-foot-high screen. It holds the record for the longest running film at a U.S. theater: The *Rocky Horror Picture Show* has been showing here every Saturday night at midnight since 1978. And it is almost worth the price of admission just to see the campy "no-smoking" spot starring director John Waters that usually shows before every film. Also noteworthy are the snackbar items: fresh popcorn topped with real butter, made-from-scratch herbal ice tea, biscotti from Bette's Bake Shop, and bulk trail mix!

University of California *Telegraph Ave./Bancroft Way, 642-6000.*

The foremost attraction here is, of course, higher learning. Known for academic excellence, U.C. Berkeley boasts a faculty distinguished by eight Nobel Prize winners. Many noteworthy facilities on the 1,232-acre campus are open to the public.

- **Annual Cal Day Open House** *In April. Free.*

Most of the university departments sponsor exhibits and events.

- **Berkeley Art Museum** *2626 Bancroft Way/College Ave., 2nd entrance at 2621 Durant Ave., 642-0808, fax 642-4889. W-Sun 11-5, Thur to 9. Adults $6, 12-18 $4; free Thur 11-12 & 5-9.*

Many visitors think that this building is itself as interesting and unusual as its contents. Built in a cubist style of architecture, this striking museum is reminiscent of New York's Guggenheim—except that it is angular instead of circular. The permanent collection stresses modern and Asian art and includes a large collection of paintings by Modernist Hans Hofmann.

In the basement, the casual cafeteria-style **Cafe Grace** *(2625 Durant Ave., 548-4366. L daily; $. 1 highchair. No reservations. No cards.)* dispenses high quality, delicious California-style deli fare as well as coffees and pastries. Seating is in an attractive interior space with large windows looking out into the museum's sculpture garden. Diners can also opt to enjoy their repast al fresco in a sunny courtyard.

Also in the basement, the **Pacific Film Archive** *(642-1412. Adults $5.50, 65+ & under 12 $3.50.)* is known internationally for its film exhibitions and scholarship. It is one of five world-class pub-

lic archival film collections in the U.S. It has the largest collection of Japanese titles outside of Japan and one of the world's largest collections of silent and early films from the former Soviet Union and pre-1960 Eastern Europe, plus hundreds of experimental movies by West Coast filmmakers. Daily public programs are filled with gems for film buffs. The theater is clean, the sound system excellent, and the audience well-mannered. No snacks are available. A charming **Teddy Bear Film Festival and Parade** is held annually in November on the weekend after Thanksgiving. Children are invited to bring their teddies and join in an informal parade that precedes the screening. To avoid unbearable disappointment, purchase tickets in advance.

• **Botanical Garden** *On Centennial Dr., 642-3343. Daily 9-4:45; tours Sat & Sun at 1:30. Free.*

Located behind the campus in lush Stawberry Canyon, this "library of living plants" covers over 30 acres and contains over 12,000 different types of plants. The plants are organized into 16 collections according to geographic origin, taxonomic affinity, and economic value. Of special interest are the herb garden, rhododendron dell, redwood grove, California native plants area, old rose garden, and Chinese medicinal herb garden stocked with over 90 rare plants. Children particularly enjoy the greenhouse filled with carnivorous plants and the lily pond stocked with colorful koi. Grassy areas perfect for picnicking are scattered throughout this peaceful spot.

• **Campanile** *In center of campus, 642-3666. Elevator: M-Sat 10-3:30, Sun 10-1:30. 50¢.*

Modeled after the slightly taller campanile in St. Marks Square in Venice, this campus landmark stands 307 feet tall—the equivalent of 30 stories. When classes are in session, ten-minute mini-concerts are hand-played on its 61-bell carillon three times each week day at 7:50 a.m., noon, and 6 p.m. On Saturdays it plays at noon and 6 p.m., and on Sundays a 45-

minute recital is performed at 2—the perfect time to enjoy a picnic on the surrounding lawns. An elevator takes visitors up 200 feet to an observation platform, where a 360-degree view of the area can be enjoyed.

• **Campus Tour** *Visitors center in University Hall, room 101, 2200 University Ave./Oxford St., 642-5215. M-F at 10 & 1; call first re. tour on Sat at 10. Free.*

This guided tour is a good way to get an overview of the campus. A self-guiding tour brochure is also available here.

• **Lawrence Hall of Science** *On Centennial Dr., below Grizzly Peak Blvd., 642-5132. Daily 10-5. Adults $6, 62+ & 7-18 $4, 3-6 $2.*

Located high in the hills behind the campus, this participatory museum was established by the university in 1958 as a memorial to Ernest Orlando Lawrence. Lawrence developed the cyclotron and was the university's first Nobel laureate. Of special interest to school-age children, this button-pusher's paradise holds educational games, an Earthquake Information Center, a seismograph, and a mini-planetarium. On weekends, a Biology Lab permits experimenting with mazes and learning about a variety of small animals.

The short-order **Galaxy Sandwich Shop** provides a magnificent panoramic view of the bay and San Francisco. A computer here is keyed to the menu, allowing tabulation of the nutritional value of food choices.

• **Museum of Paleontology** *Near Oxford St./University Ave., 1101 Valley Life Sciences Bldg., 642-1821, fax 642-1822. M-F 8-5, Sat & Sun 1-4. Free.*

Initiated in the 1860s, the collection of fossils here is one of the largest and oldest in North America. Among the displays are a complete Tyrannosaurus rex skeleton, the largest Triceratops skull ever found, a frozen mammoth, ancient bacteria, and the skeleton of a sabre tooth tiger—California's state fossil.

In the same building, the **Museum of Vertebrate Zoology** *(Room 3101; 642-3059, fax 643-8238.)* holds one of the largest and most important collections of vertebrates in the world.

• **Phoebe Apperson Hearst Museum of Anthropology** *At Bancroft Way/College Ave., 103 Kroeber Hall, 643-7648. W-Sun 10-4:30, Thur to 9; in summer, W-Sun 10-4. Adults $2, seniors $1, 3-16 50¢; free on Thur.*

Part of the campus since 1901, this museum stores the largest anthropological research collection (over 4 million artifacts) in the western U.S.

DNA Model at Lawrence Hall of Science

Crockett

(Area Code 510)

WHERE TO EAT

Nantucket Fish Company *Foot of Port St., 787-2233. L & D daily; $$. Highchairs, boosters, child portions. Reservations advised. AE, MC, V.*

Situated at the end of a twisting road under the Carquinez Bridge, on the other side of the tracks, this popular restaurant specializes in serving New England-style fresh fish items. Most are available either charcoal-broiled or pan-fried. Shell fish is lightly breaded and deep-fried Cape Cod-style; it is also available in casseroles with Newburg or Mornay sauce. Shellfish cioppino is either old-fashioned style (in the shell) or lazy man's style (out of the shell). Lobster and steak comprise the higher-priced end of the menu. All dinners are served with a choice of either creamy white clam chowder or a salad topped with shrimp, Parmesan cheese-topped French bread, a fresh vegetable prepared with flair, and a choice of either French fries or seasoned rice. Cheesecake in several unusual flavors is available for dessert. The restaurant itself is unpretentious, and all tables have a view of the water. If there is a wait to be seated, drinks and seafood appetizers can be ordered from the bar and enjoyed either indoors or out on the pier.

Crockett is the major center for sugar production on the West Coast. Driving back to the freeway, the large red brick building seen to the east is the circa 1906 C & H Sugar refinery.

Vallejo

(Area Code 707)

VISITOR INFORMATION

Vallejo Convention & Visitors Bureau *495 Mare Island Way #C, Vallejo 94590, (800) 4-VALLEJO, 642-3653, fax 644-2206.*

This bureau also offers information on Benicia.

GETTING THERE

Located 30 miles northeast of San Francisco.

WHAT TO DO

Marine World Africa USA *Marine World Parkway/Hwy. 37, 643-ORCA. W-Sun 9:30-5; in summer daily 9:30-6. Adults $26.95, 60+ $22.95, 4-12 $18.95. Parking $3. Darling dolphin-shaped stroller rentals available.*

The exciting animal shows here feature killer whales, dolphins, sea lions, elephants, chimpanzees, tigers, and exotic birds. Then there is the spectacular Water Ski & Boat Show put on by handsome and beautiful daredevil humans. Visitors can walk through animal habitat areas to see the African animals and to ride an Asian elephant or Dromedary camel *($2)*. Also in this section is the Prairie Crawl—a maze of tunnels with dome pop-outs right in the prairie dogs' enclosure—and the Gentle Jungle petting area. Butterfly World is the only walk-through free-flight

butterfly habitat in the western U.S., and a walk-in Lorikeet Aviary provides up-close observation of these brightly colored birds and the opportunity to feed them. Among the newest attractions are Walkabout! An Australian Adventure and Walrus Experience. Younger children enjoy the Whale-of-a-Time-World playground, with its punching bag forest and giant climbing net, and diaper-changing facilities and water faucets are in all the restroom— yes, even the *men's!* Consider taking the ferry from San Francisco—the Blue & Gold Fleet *((415) 705-5555)* departs from Pier 39—or BART *((415) 992-2278; runs M-Sat.).*

Benicia

(Area Code 707)

A LITTLE BACKGROUND

Founded in 1847 by General Vallejo and named for his bride, this low-key town was the state capital for a short time in 1853. Situated on the Carquinez Strait, about 30 miles northeast of San Francisco, it was also a very busy port. Now it is known for its many **antique shops** (located along First Street) and the **Benicia Glass Studios** consortium of glass-blowing factories (located on H Street). Note that many of the shops are closed on Mondays and Tuesdays.

VISITOR INFORMATION

Benicia Chamber of Commerce *601 First St., (800) 559-7377, 745-2120, fax 745-2275.*

GETTING THERE

Located seven miles east of Vallejo via I-780.

WHERE TO STAY

Union Hotel *401 First St., (800) 544-2278, 746-0100, fax 746-6458. 3 stories; 21 rooms; $$-$$$. Unsuitable for children under 12. 1 VCR. Continental breakfast; restaurant.*

Located right on the main street, in the part of town reflecting the ambiance of a quieter era, this 1882 Victorian hotel offers 12 individually decorated rooms. For example, the Victoriana Room is decorated with rich, dark floral wallpaper and furnished with an assortment of antiques, among them a substantial armoire. A nine-room annex, the **Union Gardens**, is located down the street.

For dinner, hotel guests just catch the elevator down to the attractive **restaurant** *(L & D daily, Sat & SunBr. Highchairs, boosters, child portions. 100% non-smoking. Reservations advised. AE, MC, V.).* One meal here began with an unusual and delicious papaya and avocado salad with hazelnut vinaigrette dressing. The main course was grilled ahi with a sweet and tangy pineapple-cilantro sauce, and dessert was a block of ice cream-like hazelnut parfait swimming in a dark chocolate sauce swirled with white chocolate sauce. Then it's just a few steps over to the cozy **lounge** for a relaxing after-dinner drink. Featuring an impressive 110-year-old mahogany bar and faux tin walls, it is a showcase for live jazz.

WHAT TO DO

Benicia Capitol State Historic Park *115 W. G St., 745-3385. Daily 10-5; house tours Sat & Sun 12-3:30. Adults $2, 6-13 $1.*

Historic information and artifacts await visitors inside this restored two-story, red brick Greek revival building that once served as the state capitol. It is furnished with period pieces. Also in the park, the 1858 Victorian **Fischer-Hanlon House**—a renovated Gold Rush hotel— holds an impressive collection of period furniture.

Fairfield

(Area Code 707)

WHAT TO DO

Anheuser-Busch Tours *3101 Busch Dr., 429-7595. Tu-Sat 9-4, on the hour. Free.*

The tour here starts with a short video explaining how a Bud is made. Then visitors don plastic safety glasses and head out to see the beer bottled and capped—or canned—and boxed. Back in the Hospitality Room everyone gets free samples. Snacks and soft drinks are also provided.

Herman Goelitz Candy Company *2400 N. Watney Way, in Solano Business Park, 428-2838. Tours: M-F 9-3. Free. Store: M-Sat 9-5.*

Family-run since 1898, this company is credited with inventing candy corn in 1900 and the famous, and flavorful, Jelly Belly® jelly bean in 1976. After taking the half-hour tour, everyone gets a souvenir bag of the company's jelly beans. When available, the gift shop sells Belly Flops— sometimes called rejects—at bargain prices.

Western Railway Museum *5848 Hwy. 12, Suisun City, between Fairfield & Rio Vista (exit Hwy. 80 at Hwy. 12, then drive east), 374-2978. Sat & Sun 11-5; W-Sun in July & Aug. Adults $6, 5-17 $3.*

Located between two sheep pastures in the middle of a flat, arid no-man's land, this very special museum displays and actually operates its collection of historic electric streetcars and

steam train engines. Among the dozen or so operating electric cars are both an articulated car (hinged so it can go around corners) that ran on the Bay Bridge from 1939 to 1958 and a bright red car from the Peninsular Railway. Several cars operate each weekend and run along a 1.5-mile stretch of track with overhead electric trolley wires. Cars are operated by the same volunteers who spent countless hours lovingly restoring them. Stationary cars, waiting for repairs, can be viewed in several large barns. An oasis-like picnic and play area is available to visitors, and a bookstore with a past (check out the plaque above the bench in front) offers a large collection of railroad books and paraphernalia. All fees collected are used to restore and maintain the streetcars. (It costs between $25,000 and $50,000 to restore a car and, because the labor is volunteer, it can take as long as ten years!)

The museum also operates special trains over the Sacramento Northern Railway for the **Spring Wild Flower Excursion**, which runs from the museum to Jepson Prairie Reserve, usually on weekends in March through May. **Ghost Trains** run at Halloween, **Santa Claus Specials** during December.

Sacramento
(Area Code 916)

A LITTLE BACKGROUND

It is fiery summer always, and you can gather roses, and eat strawberries and ice-cream, and wear white linen clothes, and pant and perspire at eight or nine o'clock in the morning.
—Mark Twain

Sacramento has been the state capital since 1854. Most of its major historic attractions are concentrated in the downtown area.

VISITOR INFORMATION

Sacramento Convention & Visitors Bureau *1421 K St., Sacramento 95814, 264-7777, fax 264-7788.*

GETTING THERE

Located approximately 90 miles northeast of San Francisco via Highway I-80.

By Cruise Ship.

Clipper *((800) 325-0010, (314) 727-2929)* offers a six-day, five-night cruise.

By Train.

Amtrak *((800) 872-7245)* trains leave for Sacramento daily from San Jose, San Francisco (via bus connection to Oakland), and Oakland. Special family fares are available. Overnight train-hotel packages can be reserved through **Amtrak Vacations** *((800) 440-8202)*. Call for fare and schedule information and to make reservations.

Scenic Route by Car.

Take Highway 160 through the Delta (see page 243).

ANNUAL EVENTS

Camellia Festival *March. 442-8166.*

Sacramento claims to be the camellia capital of the world. Floral exhibits, a parade, and a queen contest celebrate this gorgeous flower.

Sacramento Jazz Jubilee *May; on Memorial Day weekend. 372-5277. Tickets $10-$70.*

This is the world's largest traditional jazz festival.

California State Fair *August. 263-3000. Adults $7, 62+ $5, 5-12 $4; parking $4.*

There's something for everyone at the oldest state fair in the West, which is also the largest agricultural fair in the U.S. Pleasures include monorail and carnival rides, thoroughbred racing, educational exhibits, and live entertainment. Special for children are a petting farm, pony rides, and a nursery where baby animals are born each day.

Waterworld USA Family Waterpark *(1600 Exposition Blvd., 924-0556. Daily 10:30-6; June-Aug only. Over 4' tall $14.99, under 4' $9.99, under age 3 free.)* operates adjacent to the fair site. It features the largest wave pool in Northern California, the highest waterslides in the West, and an assortment of other attractions.

WHERE TO STAY

Motels abound. Call a favorite chain for reservations, or contact the Convention & Visitors Bureau for a list of lodgings.

Abigail's Bed & Breakfast *2120 G St./22nd St., (800) 858-1568, 441-5007, fax 441-0621. 3 stories; 5 rooms; 100% non-smoking; $$$-$$$+. Unsuitable for children. Hot tub. Afternoon snack, full breakfast.*

Located on one of the city's wide residential streets, this turn-of-the-century colonial revival mansion boasts cozy rooms with delicious wallpapers and charming antiques. Some bathrooms are equipped with antique claw-foot tubs and old-time brass shower heads. Homemade cookies, hot cider, and cold lemonade are always available, and an elegant breakfast is served in the formal dining room.

Delta King *1000 Front St., in Old Sacramento, (800) 825-KING, 444-KING, fax 444-5314. 5 stories; 44 rooms; 100% non-smoking; $$$. Children under 6 free. Continental breakfast; restaurant. Parking $6.*

Launched in 1927, this flat-bottomed riverboat plied the waters between Sacramento and San Francisco in the late 1920s and '30s. After having spent 15 months partially submerged in the San Francisco Bay, she was treated to years of restoration work costing $9.5 million. Now appropriately moored dockside in Old Sacramento, her rooms are furnished with brass beds and wicker accent pieces. All have private bathrooms with an old-fashioned pedestal sink and pull-chain, tall-tank toilet. A few even have claw-foot tubs. The most special room—The Captain's Quarters—is the vessel's wheelhouse and features a private second-story observation deck.

An elegant dinner with a river view can be enjoyed by guests and non-guests alike in the **Pilothouse Restaurant** *(L M-Sat, D daily, SunBr. Highchairs, boosters, child menu. 100% non-smoking. Reservations advised. AE, MC, V.)*, located on the Promenade Deck. Entrees include luxury items such as prawns, steak, and rack of lamb. A well-executed Caesar salad is dramatically prepared table-side and not to be missed. An enticing dessert tray is also available. Live music performed on a grand piano is provided most evenings in a cozy lounge-style bar adjoining the restaurant. On Friday and Saturday nights the **Paddlewheel Saloon**, a lively bar that overlooks the boat's 17-ton paddle wheel, presents an interactive murder mystery dinner show. Live performances are also scheduled on weekends in an intimate theater down on the Cargo Deck. Intermissions are long, allowing plenty of time to visit the lobby bar. Dinner/theater and overnight packages are sometimes available.

Hostel *900 H St., 443-1691, fax 443-4763. 70 beds; couples rooms.*

Operating within an 1885 Victorian mansion, this jewel is centrally located and convenient to major attractions. See also page 391.

Radisson Hotel *500 Leisure Lane, (800) 333-3333, 922-2020, fax 649-9463. 2 stories; 309 rooms; $$-$$$+. Children under 18 free. Heated pool, hot tub, fitness room, parcourse. Restaurant.*

Located on the outskirts of downtown, this low-rise hotel complex is run much like a vacation resort. Rooms are spacious and comfortable, and some overlook a natural spring-fed lake and koi pond. On weekends throughout the summer, jazz and orchestra performances are scheduled in the property's own amphitheater and are free to guests. Bicycle rentals are available for rides along the scenic Jedediah Smith bike trail, which runs along the American River Parkway adjacent to the hotel. (The 35-mile trail runs along the river from Old Sacramento to Folsom. The hotel is about five miles from the Old Sacramento end.) A courtesy shuttle takes guests to the impressive indoor **Arden Fair Shopping Mall** located nearby.

Sterling Hotel *1300 H St./13th St., (800) 365-7660, 448-1300, fax 455-6102. 3 stories; 16 rooms; 100% non-smoking; $$-$$$+. Continental breakfast M-Sat, SunBr; restaurant.*

This converted Victorian mansion is located just three blocks from the capitol. It claims to be the only hotel in the country with private, oversize Jacuzzis in each all-marble bathroom. Room 303, which is furnished with a posh Oriental carpet and has a balcony overlooking the front yard's magnolia trees, is especially nice. The hotel's highly rated greenhouse-style restaurant, **Chanterelle**, serves continental food.

WHERE TO EAT

Buffalo Bob's Ice Cream Saloon *110 K St., in Old Sacramento, 442-1105. Daily 10-6; $. Highchairs, boosters. No cards.*

A variety of sandwiches and hot dogs are available here, as is old-time sarsaparilla to wash it all down with. Ice cream concoctions dominate the menu and include exotic sundaes such as Fool's Gold (butter brickle ice cream topped with butterscotch and marshmallow, whipped cream, almonds, and a cherry) and Sierra Nevada (peaks of vanilla ice cream capped with hot fudge, whipped cream, almonds, and a cherry).

Fanny Ann's Saloon *1023 2nd St., in Old Sacramento, 441-0505. L & D daily; $. No reservations. AE, MC, V.*

This narrow, four-level restaurant has a raucous ambiance and funky decor that provide the makings for instant fun. Children and adults alike enjoy the casual atmosphere and American-style fare: good half-pound hamburgers, assorted styles of nine-inch hot dogs, curly French fries, and large bowls of homemade soup. A variety of sandwiches and salads are also available. After orders are placed with the cook at the window in back, diners can relax with a game of pinball or get a downright cheap drink at the old bar. When one mother inquired whether there were booster seats, the cheerful hostess replied, "I'll hold the kids on my lap."

Fat City Bar & Grill *1001 Front St., in Old Sacramento, 446-6768. L & D daily; $$. Child menu. 100% non-smoking. AE, MC, V.*

Located within a high-ceiling brick warehouse dating from 1849, this popular spot features Tiffany-style lamps, stained-glass windows, and Victorian-style furnishings. Unusual drinks can be enjoyed at the old mahogany bar. Dining tables overlook sidewalk traffic. The menu offers appetizer items such as Southern fried chicken strips and French onion soup, as well a variety of pasta dishes and specialty hamburgers. Old-fashioned desserts such as strawberry shortcake and hot fudge sundaes wind things up.

Fox & Goose Public House *1001 R St./10th St., 443-8825. B & L daily, D M-F; $. Highchairs, boosters, booths, child menu. 100% non-smoking. No reservations. MC, V.*

Located within a 1913 building that was once the Fuller Paint and Glass Company, this English-style pub features high ceilings, rustic unfinished floors, multi-paned windows, and roomy booths. Breakfast doesn't get any better. The menu then offers British-style grilled tomato, bangers, and crumpets, as well as American standards and a large variety of omelettes. Many items are made on the premises—including granola, scones, muffins, and thoroughly cooked homefries—and free-range chicken eggs are available. Lunch items include Cornish pasties, Welsh rarebit, English tea sandwiches, and a classic ploughman's lunch, plus desserts of burnt-cream custard and layered trifle. Live music is scheduled in the evenings, when pub grub is served until 9:30. Over 15 English and Irish beers are on tap, and a good selection of California wines is available.

Jammin' Salmon *1801 Garden Hwy., 929-6232. L M-Sat, D daily, SunBr; $-$$. 1 highchair, 1 booster. Reservations advised. AE, MC, V.*

A table on the peaceful deck here overlooking the placid Sacramento River is a great warm-weather idea. The lunch menu offers a variety of salads and sandwiches, as well as some more substantial fish entrees. Dinner is more pricey.

Down-river, the funkier, rowdier **Virgin Sturgeon** *(1577 Garden Hwy., 921-2694. B Sat & Sun, L & D daily; $-$$. Boosters, child portions. No reservations. MC, V.)*, reached via a ramp through a converted truck rig, is popular with politicians and "river rats" (people with boats). It is known for serving great Cuban black beans and rice, steamed clams, barbecued pork ribs, and mushroom cheeseburgers. Situated atop a barge, it has outdoor deck seating as well as cozy interior seating.

Several other wildly popular restaurants can also be found in this area.

WHAT TO DO

American River Parkway *366-2072, fax 855-5932. Daily dawn-dusk. $4/vehicle.*

This is basically 23 miles of water fun. Call for a free map and more information about facilities.

• **Bike Trail.**

The paved Jedediah Smith National Recreation Trail runs for 23 miles along the American River.

• **Fishing.**

The best month for salmon and steelhead is October. Favorite spots are the Nimbus Basin below the dam and Sailor Bar. A state license in required.

• **Nature Walks.**

The **Effie Yeaw Nature Center** *(6700 Tarshes Dr., in **Ancil Hoffman County Park**, Carmichael, 489-4918, fax 489-4983. Daily 10-5. Free. Parking $4.)* features displays and hands-on exhibits of the area's natural and cultural history. A Maidu Indian Demonstration Area and a 77-acre Nature Area with three self-guided nature trails are also part of the center.

• **Raft Trips.**

Trips begin in the **Upper Sunrise Recreation Area**, located north of the Sunrise Boulevard exit off Highway 50. In summer several companies rent rafts and provide shuttle bus return.

Bridges.

Located near Old Sacramento, the **Tower Bridge** sometimes can be observed going up. To the right of it, the **I Street Bridge** is one of the few remaining pedestal bridges in the country; sometimes it can be observed turning.

California State Capitol Building *10th St./L St., 324-0333. Tours daily 9-4. Free.*

In 1981 the Capitol was renovated to the tune of $68 million. It is said to have been the largest restoration project in the history of the country. The main reason for the project was to make the building earthquake safe. Restored now to its turn-of-the-century decor, it is quite a showcase. Free tour tickets can be picked up in the basement a half-hour before each tour. A small museum with a ten-minute orientation film entertains visitors while they wait.

A short-order cafeteria operates in the basement for meals and snacks, and the full-service **Capitol Cafe** operates weekdays on the sixth floor.

Tours of the surrounding park, which is home to over 300 varieties of trees and flowers from all over the world and to one of the largest camellia groves in the world, are scheduled daily in summer at 10:30 a.m. The circular **California Vietnam Veteran's Memorial** is located by the rose garden at the park's east end *(15th St./Capitol Ave.)*. The 22 shiny black granite panels of this privately funded monument are engraved with the 5,822 names of California's dead and missing.

Crocker Art Museum *216 O St./3rd St., 264-5423, fax 264-7372. Tu-Sun 10-5, Thur to 9. Adults $4.50, 7-17 $2.*

Located within a magnificent Italianate building dating from 1874, this is the oldest public art museum west of the Mississippi. Collection highlights include Master drawings, 19th-century American and European paintings, and contemporary Northern California art in all media. Family activities are scheduled every weekend, and lectures, films, and Sunday afternoon concerts are often scheduled. Picnic tables are available across the street in lovely **Crocker Park**.

Governor's Mansion State Historic Park *1526 H St./16th St., 323-3047. Tours daily 10-4, on the hour. Adults $2, 6-12 $1.*

Built in 1877, this 30-room Victorian mansion was bought by the state in 1903 for $32,500. During the next 64 years it was home to 13 governors and their families. It remains just as it was when vacated by its last tenant—Governor Reagan. Now serving the public as an interesting museum, it displays 15 rooms of furnishings and personal items left behind by each family. Visitors see Governor George Pardee's 1902 Steinway piano, Earl Warren's hand-tied Persian carpets, and Hiram Johnson's plum velvet sofa and chairs. Among the interesting artifacts are marble fireplaces from Italy and gold-framed mirrors from France. The official State of California china, selected by the wife of Goodwin Knight in the late 1950s, is also on display.

Music Circus *1419 H St., adjacent to the Sacramento Convention Center, 557-1999. Daily in July & Aug. Tickets $19-$35, children half-price at some performances.*

Said to be the only tent theater west of the Mississippi, this 2,500-seat facility presents summer stock musicals suitable for the entire family.

Old Sacramento.

Situated along the Sacramento River, Old Sacramento was the kickoff point for the gold fields during the Gold Rush. It was the western terminus for both the Pony Express and the country's first long distance telegraph, and the country's first transcontinental railroad started here. Said to be the largest historic preservation project in the West, Old Sacramento is a 28-acre living museum of the Old West. Vintage buildings, wooden sidewalks, and cobblestone streets recall the period from 1850 to 1880. Restaurants, shops, and historic exhibits combine to make it both an entertaining and educational spot to visit. Guided tours of the area *(324-0040)*, begin at the California State Railroad Museum on selected Saturdays. Information on self-guided tours can be obtained at the **Visitor Information Center** *(On corner of 2nd St./K St., 442-7644. Daily 9-5.)*. Horse-drawn vehicles can be hired for rides from Old Sacramento to the Capitol.

• **California State Railroad Museum** *111 I St./2nd St., 445-7387. Daily 10-5. Adults $5, 6-12 $2; ticket good on same day for admission to Central Pacific Passenger Depot.*

This gigantic three-story building holds the largest interpretive railroad museum in North America. Inside, 21 beautifully restored, full-size railroad locomotives and cars representing the

1860s through the 1960s are on display. Among them are an apartment-size, lushly furnished Georgia Northern private car, complete with stained-glass windows, and a Canadian Pullman rigged to feel as if it is actually moving. A film, a 30-projector multi-image slide show, and assorted interpretive displays tell the history of American railroading. Docent-led tours are often available, and well-trained, railroad-loving volunteers, wearing historically authentic railroad workers' garb, are always on hand to answer questions. Upstairs, great views of the trains below are available from an oversize catwalk. A large collection of toy trains—including a 1957 pastel pink Lionel train designed especially for little girls—is also displayed.

Nearby, the **Central Pacific Passenger Depot** *(930 Front St.)* displays nine more locomotives and cars. Visiting this reconstructed train depot provides the opportunity to step back in time to 1876—an era when riding the train was the chic way to travel. An audio tour wand that picks up recorded descriptions of displays is provided. On scheduled weekends, the **Sacramento Southern Railroad excursion steam train** leaves from the depot and takes passengers for rides to **Miller Park**.

• **Discovery Museum** *101 I St., 264-7057, fax 264-5100. W-F 12-5, Sat & Sun 10-5; in summer Tu-Sun 10-5. Adults $3.50, 6-17 $2.*

This three-story brick building is a replica of Sacramento's first public building. The museum inside houses an extensive collection of gold specimens (worth $1 million), old photos, and historic farm equipment. The 113-foot free-standing fiberglass flagpole in front is said to be the tallest in the entire country. The Discovery Learning Center, with the area's only planetarium, is nearby *(3615 Auburn Blvd., 277-6181)*.

• **Eagle Theatre** *925 Front St., 446-6761. F & Sat at 8pm. Tickets $10.*

A reconstruction of California's first theater building, which was built in 1849, the Eagle now presents Gold Rush-era plays and musicals. Children's programs are also sometimes scheduled. Call for current production information and for schedule of free tours.

• **Schoolhouse** *Front St./L St., 483-8818. M-F 9:30-4, Sat & Sun 12-4.*

Now a museum, this one-room schoolhouse has a play yard with old-fashioned board swings kids can use.

Sutter's Fort State Historic Park *2701 L St., 445-4422. Daily 10-5. Adults $2, 6-12 $1; in summer: adults $5, 6-12 $2.*

A reconstruction of the settlement founded in 1839 by Captain John A. Sutter, this is the oldest restored fort in the West. Exhibits include carpenter, cooper, and blacksmith shops as well as prison and living quarters. An audio tour is included with admission. The admission fee is higher in summer because interpreters demonstrate crafts and daily life of the 1840s.

The **California State Indian Museum** *(2618 K St., 324-0971. Daily 10-5. Adults $2, 6-12 $1.)*, established in 1940, is located adjacent. The bark clothing samples are of special interest, as is the permanent basket collection featuring colorful Pomo feather baskets. Films are presented throughout the day. Picnicking is particularly pleasant beside a duck pond across from the museum.

Towe Ford Museum of Automotive History *2200 Front St., 442-6802, fax 442-2646. Daily 10-6. Adults $5, 65+ $4.50, 15-18 $2.50, 5-14 $1.*

Opened in 1987, this cavernous museum displays 180 antique cars. With every year and model of Ford from 1903 to 1953 on exhibit, it is the most complete antique Ford collection in the world. In addition to the cars, the museum has a Mighty Wurlitzer Theater Pipe Organ with 1,200 pipes. Free mini-concerts are presented on Sunday afternoons in the spring and fall. A shuttle bus from Old Sacramento operates daily in summer and on weekends during the rest of the year. If driving, call for directions; this museum is difficult to find.

Victorian Houses.

Elaborate Victorian homes are found between 7th and 16th streets, from E to I streets. Don't miss the Heilbron house at 740 O Street and the Stanford house at 800 N Street.

William Land Park *On Freeport Blvd. between 13th Ave. & Sutterville Rd.*

This 236-acre park has a supervised playground, children's wading pool, 9-hole golf course, and fishing pond for children under 16. It also incorporates:

• **Fairytale Town** *1501 Sutterville Rd., 264-5233. Daily 10-5; in summer 9-4. Adults $2.75-$3, 3-12 $2.25-$2.50.*
   Nursery rhymes and fairy tales come to life in this 2½-acre amusement park.

• **Funderland** *1550 17th Ave., 456-0115, fax 383-7735. Daily 10-6, June-Aug; rest of year F-Sun only. Closed Dec & Jan. 85¢-$1/ride.*
   In operation since 1948, this amusement park for young children delights with nine family rides. Pony rides are available adjacent.

• **Sacramento Zoo** *Land Park Dr./Sutterville Rd., 264-5885, fax 264-5887. Daily 10-4; in summer 9-4. Adults $4-$4.50, 3-12 $2.50-$3. Stroller rental avail.*

This modest but spacious 15-acre zoo is home to over 120 species of exotic animals. It holds just enough exhibits to keep visitors busy for a pleasant few hours. A snack bar dispenses a limited, but appropriate and satisfying, menu: hot dogs, sodas, cookies, etc.

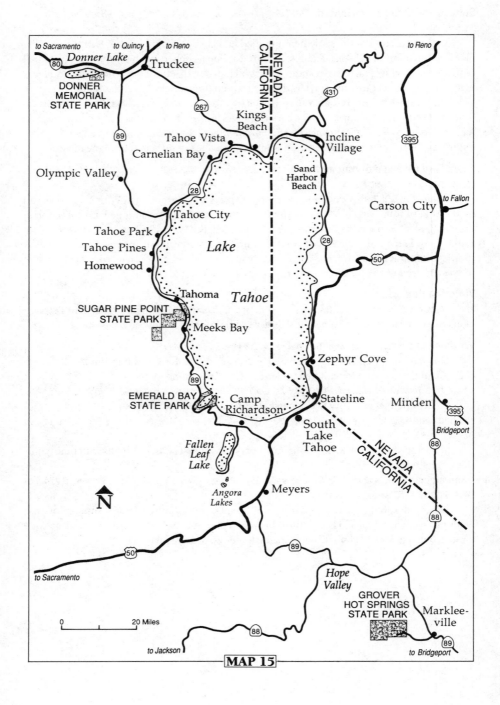

MAP 15

Lake Tahoe

South Lake Tahoe
(Area Code 916)

A LITTLE BACKGROUND

. . . At last the Lake burst upon us—a noble sheet of blue water lifted six thousand three hundred feet above the level of the sea, and walled in by a rim of snowclad mountain peaks that towered aloft full three thousand feet higher still!

It was a vast oval. As it lay there with the shadows of the great mountains brilliantly photographed upon its surface, I thought it must surely be the fairest picture the whole earth affords . . .

—Mark Twain

Lake Tahoe lies two-thirds in California and one-third in Nevada. It is the largest (192 square miles surface) and deepest (1,645 feet) Alpine lake in North America and the second largest in the world. At 6,227 feet above sea level, its crystal clear, deep-blue summer waters provide a striking contrast with the extensive green forests and majestic mountains encircling it.

Once a remote area, Tahoe is now a popular and well-equipped vacation destination offering a wide range of recreational activities along with its spectacular scenery. Swimming, hiking, boating, tennis, golf, bicycling, horseback riding, river rafting, camping, fishing, water-skiing, and backpacking are among the summer outdoor activities to be enjoyed. In winter, the skiing is excellent.

On the Nevada side, gambling is another big attraction. Most lodgings provide transportation to the casinos and have discount casino coupons for their guests. In addition, the casinos offer on-demand pick-up shuttle service from most lodgings.

Children may go into a casino with adults but are not allowed to "loiter" (not even babies in backpacks!) or play the slot machines. Fortunately, childcare is relatively easy to find in this area. Many lodging facilities maintain a list of local sitters, and childcare centers that take drop-ins are listed in the Yellow Pages. Also, the Lake Tahoe Visitors Authority provides a free listing of day care providers.

In addition to having more slot machines than any other casino at Lake Tahoe, Harrah's has an unsupervised **video arcade** for children under 48-inches tall. It operates year-round from 9 a.m. to midnight; admission is $3 for the first hour, $1 for each 15 minutes thereafter. A large indoor playground is also provided, but parents must stay with their children. Sure beats sitting on the curb reading comic books like some people did when they were kids. For further information call (800) 648-3773. Harvey's operates a daily Kid's Camp. Rates are $50 per child per day, which includes lunch and a t-shirt, and $30 per child per evening session. For further information call (800) 553-1022.

VISITOR INFORMATION

Lake Tahoe Visitors Authority *1156 Ski Run Blvd., South Lake Tahoe 96150, (800) AT-TAHOE (lodging reservations referral service), 577-3550 (entertainment and special events information; road and weather conditions), 544-5050, fax 544-2386.*

GETTING THERE

Located approximately 200 miles north of San Francisco. Take Highway 80 to Highway 50 to the lake.

ANNUAL EVENTS

Lights on the Lake *July 4.*

This spectacular show is the largest display of fireworks west of the Mississippi. Each shell is choreographed and computer synchronized to a soundtrack.

Autumn Colors *October.*

The area around Kirkwood Ski Resort (see page 375) is home to groves of aspen. Hope Valley, north of Kirkwood on Highway 89, is particularly colorful.

STOPS ALONG THE WAY

I-80 North. See pages 317 through 341.

Folsom *Off Hwy. 50, 25 mi. east of Sacramento.*

This small town provides an easy stop. Restored Gold Rush-era homes and buildings—many inhabited by antique shops—line historic Sutter Street.

• **Folsom Chamber of Commerce** *200 Wool St., 985-2698.*

Information about the town is available at the chamber's office inside the town's old train depot.

• **Folsom City Zoo** *Natoma/Stafford, 985-7347. Tu-Sun 10-4. Adults $2, 5-12 $1.*

This tiny zoo exhibits native non-releasable North American animals, a few exotics, and the largest captive wolf pack in Northern California.

• **Folsom Dam** *7794 Folsom Dam Rd., 989-7275, fax 989-7208. Tours M-Sat 10-1. Free.*

Built between 1948 and 1956, this impressive dam measures 340 feet high and 1,400 feet long.

• **Folsom Lake State Recreation Area** *7806 Folsom-Auburn Rd., 988-0205. Daily 6am-10pm; Oct-Mar 7-7. $6/vehicle.*

Overnight camping is permitted in this 18,000-acre park.

• **Lake Forest Cafe** *13409 Folsom Blvd., 985-6780. B & L W-Sun; $. Highchairs, boosters, child portions. 100% non-smoking. AE, MC, V.*

Among the breakfast items to be enjoyed here are 41 kinds of omelettes, a variety of Jewish specialties, and freshly baked giant cinnamon rolls.

Sam's Town. See page 293.

Poor Red's. See page 293.

Placerville. See page 294.

WHERE TO STAY

LAKEFRONT

Inn By the Lake *3300 Lake Tahoe Blvd. (Hwy. 50), (800) 877-1466, 542-0330, fax 541-6596. 3 stories; 100 rooms; 34 non-smoking rooms; $$-$$$+. Children under 12 free in existing beds. 7 kitchens; 1 wood-burning fireplace. Heated pool, hot tub, sauna. Continental breakfast.*

Located in a grove of pine trees across the street from the lake, this attractive contemporary hotel offers comfortable, quiet rooms and a free shuttle to the casinos and ski areas.

Royal Valhalla Motor Lodge *4104 Lakeshore Blvd., (800) 999-4104, 544-2233, fax 544-1436. 2 stories; 80 units; $$-$$$. Some kitchens. Heated pool (unavail. Nov-Apr), hot tub. Continental breakfast.*

Pick from one-, two-, or three-bedroom units, many of which have lake views. Guests have use of a private beach.

Tahoe Beach & Ski Club *3601 Lake Tahoe Blvd. (Hwy. 50), 541-6220, fax 541-6187. 3 stories; 128 rooms; some non-smoking rooms; $$$-$$$+. All kitchens. Heated pool (unavail. Oct-Apr), 2 hot tubs, 2 saunas.*

Located one mile from the casinos, this lakeside hotel provides a convenient shuttle. Added amenities include 400 feet of private beach and a **Marie Callenders** restaurant located just next door.

Timber Cove Lodge *3411 Lake Tahoe Blvd. (Hwy. 50), (800) 528-1234, 541-6722, fax 541-7959. 3 stories; 262 rooms; 130 non-smoking rooms; $$; 2-night min. on Sat July-Sept. Children under 12 free. Heated pool, hot tub. Restaurant, room service.*

This well-situated motel has a private beach, marina, and pier, and many of the rooms have lake views.

CASINOS

The major casinos offer large numbers of luxury hotel rooms.
- **Caesars** *(800) 648-3353.*
- **Harrah's** *(800) 648-3773.*
- **Harvey's** *(800) 648-3361.*
- **Horizon** *(800) 648-3322.*

CONDOS AND HOMES

Accommodation Station *(800) 344-9364, 542-5850, fax 542-4863. 85+ units; 10 non-smoking units; $$-$$$+; 2-night min. Most VCRs; all kitchens & fireplaces.*

Privately-owned condominiums, cabins, and houses can be rented through this agency. Rate is determined by the number of bedrooms and type of accommodation.

Lake Tahoe Accommodations *((800) 544-3234, 544-3234)* is a similar service.

Lakeland Village *3535 Lake Tahoe Blvd. (Hwy. 50), (800) 822-5969, 544-1685, fax 544-0193. 3 stories; 212 rooms; $$-$$$+; 2-night min. on weekends. Children under 18 free. Some VCRs; all kitchens; 110 wood-burning fireplaces, 91 gas fireplaces, 11 wood-burning stoves. 2 heated pools, children's wading pool (unavail. Oct-May), 2 hot tubs, sauna, 2 tennis courts ($9/hr.).*

Though located beside a bustling highway, this condominium complex manages to retain a secluded, restive feeling. Some units are lakefront; all are within a short walk. Amenities include a private beach, a children's playground, a horseshoe pit, and watercraft rentals. During the Christmas holidays, sleigh rides are available through the resort's 19 wooded acres.

OTHER

The Christiana Inn *3819 Saddle Rd., 544-7337, fax 544-5342. 2 stories; 6 rooms; 100% non-smoking; $$-$$$+; 2-night min. on weekends. Closed in May. Children under 12 free. 4 wood-burning fireplaces. Continental breakfast; restaurant.*

Built in 1965, this charming Tyrolean-style inn sits high above the lake near the slopes of Heavenly Valley. Each suite is uniquely decorated—several have private saunas—and the inn is furnished with antiques throughout. A decanter of warming brandy awaits guests in each room, and breakfast is delivered to the room in the morning.

The inn's elegant **restaurant** *(D daily. Boosters, booths, child portions. 100% non-smoking. Reservations advised. MC, V.)* serves American Continental cuisine—beef Wellington, rack of lamb, cherries jubilee, baked Alaska—at tables lighted by a fireplace. Known for its extensive wine cellar, it is also open to non-guests.

Embassy Suites Resort *4130 Lake Tahoe Blvd. (Hwy. 50), (800) EMBASSY, 544-5400. 9 stories; 400 units; 325 non-smoking units; $$$-$$$+. Children under 12 free. All VCRs. Indoor heated pool, hot tub, sauna, steam room, fitness room. Evening cocktails, full breakfast; 3 restaurants, room service.*

The first new hotel built in the Tahoe Basin since restrictions were imposed, this link in the popular Embassy Suites chain features a nightclub, a fitness center, and a seven-story-tall indoor atrium with waterfalls. Winter amenities include on-site ski rental, repair, and storage, plus next-day lift ticket sales and a complimentary shuttle to the Heavenly Valley ski area. And, as an ad for the hotel declares, ". . . you don't have to gamble to get a free breakfast and free drinks": An all-you-can-eat breakfast and evening cocktails are complimentary to guests. But for those who do want to gamble, Harrah's is right next door.

Tahoe Seasons Resort *3901 Saddle Rd., (800) 540-4874, 541-6700, fax 541-0653. 8 stories; 180 units; $$$. Children free. All VCRs; 150 gas fireplaces. Heated pool, hot tub, 2 tennis courts (no fee). Restaurant, room service (child items).*

Each unit here is a spacious suite equipped with a microwave and refrigerator as well as an oversize whirlpool bathtub big enough for two. A shuttle is provided to the casinos. And since it is located just across the street from the Heavenly Valley ski area, skiers who stay here can just walk there in the morning. No chains. No parking hassles. And if someone in the party doesn't want to ski, it's possible to get a room with a view of the slopes so they can stay cozy in front of a fireplace and just watch. The resort also provides on-site ski rentals and both chain installation and removal services.

Motel Row.

Highway 50 into town is littered with more motels than is to be believed. However, this might be changing. South Lake Tahoe's redevelopment plan, which focuses on upgrading rather than expanding, dictates that for every new hotel room built, 1.31 old rooms must be removed.

FURTHER AWAY

Sorensen's Resort. See page 375.

Zephyr Cove Resort *760 Hwy. 50, Zephyr Cove, Nevada, 4 mi. north of Stateline, (702) 588-6644, fax (702) 588-5021. 2 stories; 31 units; 6 non-smoking units; $$. 15 kitchens; 8 wood-burning fireplaces. Restaurant.*

Located in a lovely forested area by the lake, these rustic cabins and lodge rooms provide a convenient yet out-of-the-way spot to stay. Facilities include a beach, a marina with boat rentals, a stables, and an arcade. Campsites are also available. Do reserve early; cabins are usually booked-up a year in advance!

WHERE TO EAT

Cantina Bar & Grill *765 Emerald Bay Rd., ¹/₄ mi. north of the Y, 544-1233, fax 544-0823. L & D daily; $-$$. Highchairs, boosters, booths, child menu. No reservations. MC, V.*

There is almost always a wait to be seated in this festive and popular spot, but that's no reason to stay away. Waiting time can be passed sitting in the bar with a pitcher of margaritas (tasty niña coladas for kids) and some nachos. The menu has changed a lot over the years, but it just keeps getting better. Delicious choices include carnitas (roast pork), a large variety of giant burritos, and fresh fish.

Casinos.

For some of the best and least expensive food in this area, try the casino restaurants and buffets. Among the best are:

• **Bill's Casino**.

When the lines at the casino restaurants are just too long, the **McDonald's** here can be a sanity saver. It is the first McDonald's ever built in a casino and has a separate entrance for families. In Bill's, be sure to take a free pull on **Billy Jean**—the world's largest free-pull slot machine.

• **Caesars Cafe Roma** *(800) 648-3353, (702) 588-3515. B, L, & D daily; $. Highchairs, boosters, child portions. No reservations. AE, MC, V.*

This coffee shop is open round-the-clock.

• **Harrah's Forest Buffet** *(800) 648-3773, (702) 588-6611. B & L M-Sat, D daily, SunBr; $-$$. Highchairs, boosters, child portions. No reservations. AE, MC, V.*

Located on the 18th floor, this classy restaurant provides spectacular lake and mountain views, plus outstanding food at a reasonable price. Harrah's **North Beach Deli** is the place to get a picnic lunch packed to go in a Harrah's fanny pack.

In addition to bargain dining, the casinos also offer fine dining. The elegant **Summit** restaurant *((800) 648-3773. D daily; $$$. Reservations advised. AE, MC, V.)*, on the 16th and 17th floors of Harrah's, offers heady views and refined cuisine. Located in what was originally the Star Suite, where the rich and famous headliners were once put up, it offers a new menu every day. Items are beautifully presented, and service is impeccable. One meal enjoyed here began with crispy-crusted mini baguettes and sweet butter shaped like roses. An appetizer of chilled gulf shrimp was arranged in a red seafood sauce swirled with horseradish hearts, and a salad of baby lettuces was arranged in a scooped-out tomato so that it resembled a bouquet. The entree was a perfect rack of lamb with an anise crust and a side of mashed potatoes sprinkled with truffles, followed by a dessert Frangelico soufflé with a hazelnut-praline crème fraîche.

• **Harvey's Carriage House** *(800) 553-1022, (800) 648-3361, (702) 588-2411. B, L, & D daily; $-$$. Highchairs, boosters, child portions. No reservations. AE, MC, V.*

Open round-the-clock, this restaurant is known for its delicious fried chicken dinners. Harvey's also holds **Classic Burgers**—a '50s-style malt shop—and the largest **video arcade** at the lake.

The Fresh Ketch Lakeside Restaurant *2433 Venice Dr. E., 541-5683. L & D daily; $$. Highchairs, boosters, child portions. Reservations advised. AE, MC, V.*

Located at the Tahoe Keys Marina, the lake's only protected inland marina, this restaurant offers water views and fresh seafood. In addition to a daily special, the menu also has scampi, calamari steak topped with anchovy butter, cioppino, king crab legs, and live Maine lobster.

Plenty of non-fish items are also offered, including steaks and hamburgers. Among the interesting desserts are both Key lime and hula pies.

Heidi's Restaurant *3485 Lake Tahoe Blvd. (Hwy. 50), 544-8113, fax 544-4118. B & L daily; $. Highchairs, boosters, booths, child menu. 100% non-smoking. No reservations. MC, V.*

Breakfast is served all day long in this cozy, casual restaurant. The menu includes pancakes, French toast, crepes, Belgian waffles, and omelettes, as well as just about any other breakfast item imaginable, and orange juice is fresh-squeezed. At lunch, a variety of sandwiches, hamburgers, and salads are added to the menu.

Monument Peak Restaurant *Top of Ski Run Blvd., Wildwood/Saddle Dr., (702) 586-7000. L & D daily; call for winter D schedule; $-$$. Closed Oct, Nov, & May. Highchairs, boosters, child portions. 100% non-smoking. Reservations advised. AE, MC, V. Tram: adults $10.50, under 12 $6.*

A bright red aerial tram lifts diners 2,000 feet above Lake Tahoe to enjoy magnificent views while dining. Call for the current menu and for details on the tram/dinner package.

The moderately strenuous two-mile Tahoe Vista Trail begins here and offers a panoramic view of the lake. Guided 1½-hour hikes are scheduled at 11 a.m. and 1 p.m. daily; meet on the restaurant's sun deck.

WHAT TO DO

Amusement Centers.

These spots are open daily in summer and as the weather permits in winter.

• **Magic Carpet Golf** *2455 Lake Tahoe Blvd. (Hwy. 50), 541-3787.*

This is the kind of colorful miniature course that has giant plaster dinosaurs and a new theme at each hole. Choose from either 19- or 28-hole rounds.

• **Tahoe Amusement Park** *2401 Lake Tahoe Blvd. (Hwy. 50), 541-1300.*

Facilities include a variety of kiddie rides, a giant slide, and go-carts.

Angora Lakes Trail *On Spring Creek Rd., off Hwy. 89.*

Take the road to Fallen Leaf Lake, which passes a waterfall, and then turn left at the sign to Angora Lakes. It is an easy ½-mile hike from the end of the road to the lakes, where quiet picnic and swimming spots can be found.

Beaches and Biking.

The **Pope-Baldwin Recreation Area** *(On Hwy. 89, between the Y & Emerald Bay, 573-2674. Daily 8-6; closed in winter. $3/vehicle.)* is lined with good beaches. This same stretch of highway has several bike rental facilities and a nice bike trail.

Boat Rentals.

Various kinds of boats are available at **Ski Run Marina** *(544-0200)*, **Tahoe Keys Marina** *(541-2155)*, and **Timber Cove Marina** *(544-2942)*. Water-skiing and wind-surfing lessons and rentals also are available at Ski Run Marina.

Boat Tours.

• **M.S. Dixie** *760 Hwy. 50, Zephyr Cove, Nevada, 4 mi. south of Stateline, (702) 588-3508. Call for schedule. Closed Oct-Mar. Adults $14, seniors $12, 3-11 $5. Reservations advised.*

Actually used on the Mississippi River as a cotton barge in the 1920s, this paddle wheel steamer cruises to Emerald Bay. She boasts a glass-bottom viewing window. Dinner cruises, with live music for dancing, and breakfast/brunch cruises are also available at an additional charge.

• **Tahoe Queen** *At foot of Ski Run Blvd., (800) 23-TAHOE, 541-3364. Call for schedule. Adults $14, under 12 $5. Reservations required.*

This big paddle wheeler offers two-hour cruises to Emerald Bay. The boat has a large window in its floor for underwater viewing. Call for information on the sunset dinner/dance cruise and the winter ski shuttle to the North Shore.

• **Woodwind** *760 Hwy. 50, Zephyr Cove, Nevada, (702) 588-3000. Call for schedule. Closed Nov-Mar. Adults $16, 2-12 $8. Reservations advised.*

Only 30 passengers fit on this 41-foot trimaran with glass-bottom viewing window. A sunset champagne cruise is also available at additional charge.

Camp Richardson Corral and Pack Station *On Hwy. 89 North, Camp Richardson, 541-3113. Daily; June-Sept only. Guided rides $20/hr. Riders must be 6 or older. Reservations necessary.*

Operated by the same family since 1934, this stables has breakfast rides *($28)*, dinner rides *($35)*, and wagon rides *($10, under 3 free)*. Fishing trips, overnight pack trips, and spot pack trips can be arranged, and sleigh rides are available December through March when there is enough snow.

Casino Shows.

Big name entertainment is always booked into these showrooms. Call ahead for reservations to the early or late cocktail shows. Seats are assigned. Children 6 and older are usually admitted, but it depends on the show's content.

• **Caesars Circus Maximus** *(800) 648-3353, (702) 588-3515.*

• **Harrah's South Shore Room** *(800) 648-3773.*

• **Harvey's Emerald Theater** *(800) 553-1022, (702) 588-2411. 100% non-smoking.*

Holding just 288 seats, this is said to be the only mini-showroom in the world. There are no bad seats.

• **Horizon's Grande Lake Theatre** *(800) 322-7723, (702) 588-6211.*

Drive Around the Lake.

A leisurely drive around the 72-mile perimeter of Lake Tahoe takes about three hours. Allow all day, though, as there are many tempting places to stop for picnicking, swimming, and exploring.

Grover Hot Springs State Park *3415 Hot Springs Rd., Markleeville, 35 mi. southeast of SLT, 4 mi. east of Markleeville, 694-2248. Daily 9-9 in summer; rest of year M-F 2-9, Sat & Sun 9-9. Adults $4, under 18 $2. Parking $5.*

Beautifully situated in a valley meadow ringed by pine-covered slopes, this state park features a three-foot deep, 104-degree mineral pool filled by six nonsulfurous springs and a 70- to 80-degree fresh-water pool. The pools are well-maintained, and lifeguards are on duty. Because the number of bathers permitted is limited, there is sometimes a wait, and swimsuits are always required. Short hiking trails, picnic facilities, and campsites are also available. In winter this is a popular après-ski destination.

Lake Tahoe Historical Society Museum *3058 Lake Tahoe Blvd., 541-5458. Daily 11-4 in summer; rest of year Sat & Sun 12-4. Adults $1, 65+ 75¢, 5-14 50¢.*

The history of Lake Tahoe's south shore is chronicled here.

Lake Tahoe Visitor Center *On Hwy. 89, north of Camp Richardson, 573-2674. Daily 8-5:30. Closed Nov-May. Free.*

Campfire programs and guided nature tours are scheduled regularly, and there are several self-guided trails. Mountain stream life can be viewed from an underwater perspective in the **Taylor Creek Stream Profile Chamber**. Visit in October to see the annual run of the Kokanee salmon and to take part in the annual **Kokanee Salmon Festival**.

Tahoe Trout Farm *1023 Blue Lake Ave., off Hwy. 50, 541-1491. Daily 10-7; June-Aug only. Charged by size of fish caught.*

Though there is, of course, no challenge to catching trout here, there are some compelling reasons to give it a try. No license in required, bait and tackle are furnished free, and there is no limit. Anglers are virtually guaranteed to go home with tasty dinner fare. Even young children, who frustrate easily, will probably succeed in catching a fish. (Do bear in mind that some children are appalled at just the *idea* of catching a fish—let alone actually *eating* it).

Tallac Historic Site *Off Hwy. 89, 3 mi. north of Hwy. 50, 541-5227, fax 573-2693. Museum: Daily 10-4 in summer; grounds open rest of year. Free.*

Three early 20th-century summer estates and 23 cottages are situated on this 74-acre site. Special cultural and historical programs are sometimes scheduled, and picnic tables and barbecues are available.

A **Great Gatsby Festival** is held here each August. Celebrating the area's partying past, this festival brings history to life with era arts and crafts demonstrations plus some old-fashioned fun and games.

Vikingsholm Castle *On Hwy. 89, Tahoma, 525-7277. Tours daily 10-4; June-Aug only. Adults $2, 6-17 $1. Strollers not permitted on tour.*

   Butterflies, waterfalls, and wildflowers are enjoyed on the steep, dry one-mile trail that descends to this magnificent 39-room, sod-roof Swedish home built in 1928. Constructed completely by hand using native materials, it was completed in one summer. It is part of **Emerald Bay State Park**. Picnic tables are available, and swimming is permitted in an area with a sandy beach.

Winter Activities. See page 375

North Lake Tahoe
(Area Code 916)

VISITOR INFORMATION

North Lake Tahoe Chamber of Commerce *P.O. Box 1757 (245 North Lake Blvd.), Tahoe City 96145, 581-6900, fax 581-6904.*

Tahoe North Visitors & Convention Bureau *P.O. Box 5578 (950 N. Lake Blvd.), Tahoe City 96145, (800) TAHOE-4-U (reservations service), 581-8724, fax 581-4081.*

Incline Village Crystal Bay Visitors & Convention Bureau *969 Tahoe Blvd., Incline Village, Nevada 89451-9500, (800) GO-TAHOE, (702) 832-1606, fax (702) 832-1605.*

GETTING THERE

Located approximately 210 miles north of San Francisco. Take Highway 80 to Truckee, then Highway 267 south to the lake.

   The Chicago-bound Amtrak train leaves Oakland on Mondays, Wednesdays, Fridays, and Saturdays at 9 a.m. and arrives in Truckee at 3 p.m. For fare and schedule information and to make reservations, call (800) 872-7245.

ANNUAL EVENTS

Music at Sand Harbor *July. At Sand Harbor State Park in Nevada; 583-7625. Tickets $20-$25.*

   Imagine sitting in a natural sand-bowl amphitheater overlooking beautiful Lake Tahoe while enjoying great, live contemporary music. Then try adding a sprinkling of stars, both celestial and earthly. That's "Tunes in the Dunes"— the nickname given by locals to this event.

Concours d'Elegance *August. In Carnelian Bay; (800) TAHOE-4-U. Adults $16, 62+ $13, 6-16 $8.*

   The Tahoe Yacht Club organizes this extravaganza of boats.

Lake Tahoe Shakespeare Festival *August. At Sand Harbor State Park in Nevada; (800) 74-SHOWS, 832-1606. Tickets $12-$20.*

   Description as above. "Bard on the Beach," another nickname bestowed by fond locals, is the biggest event of the summer at the lake. Bring a picnic, a blanket, and some low-leg beach chairs.

STOPS ALONG THE WAY

I-80 North. See pages 317 through 341.

Auburn. See page 296.

Grass Valley. See page 296.

Nevada City. See page 299.

Truckee *Located 40 mi. from lake via Hwy. 267.*

Much of the original architecture in this old mining town is preserved. Many shops and restaurants on the main street operate within interesting, sometimes beautifully restored, historic buildings. The town's yellow Victorian Southern Pacific Depot dates from 1896 and is now the Amtrak and Greyhound station as well as the Visitors Center.

• **Truckee Donner Chamber of Commerce** *12036 Donner Pass Rd., Truckee 96161, 587-2757, fax 587-2439.*

• **Truckee-Donner Visitor Information Center** *10065 Donner Pass Rd., on Commercial Row, Truckee 96160, (800) 548-8388, 587-2757.*

This service assists with lodging reservations.

• **The Truckee Hotel** *10007 Bridge St., (800) 659-6921, 587-4444, fax 587-1599. 4 stories; 36 rooms; 100% non-smoking; $$-$$$. Children under 4 free. 3 TVs; some shared baths. Afternoon tea on weekends, continental breakfast.*

Originally built as a stage coach stop in 1868, this beautifully renovated Victorian offers stylish period lodging.

• **Squeeze In** *10060 Commercial Row, 587-9814. B & L daily; $. Highchairs, boosters. 100% non-smoking. No reservations. No cards.*

At breakfast in this long, narrow cafe, diners have a choice of 57 kinds of omelettes. A variety of other breakfast dishes and sandwiches are also on the menu.

WHERE TO STAY

CONDOS ON THE LAKE

Rates in condos vary tremendously depending on number of people, length of stay, and time of year. Most are equipped with kitchens and TVs.

Brockway Springs *101 Chipmunk St., Kings Beach, 546-4201, fax 546-4202. 78 units. All VCRs; most wood-burning fireplaces. Heated pool, children's wading pool, sauna, 2 tennis courts (no fee).*

Most units here have stone fireplaces and balconies overlooking the lake. The resort features ½ mile of private lakefront.

Chinquapin *3600 North Lake Blvd., Tahoe City, (800) 732-6721, 583-6991, fax 583-0937. 172 units. All TVs, kitchens, & fireplaces. Heated pool (June-Sept only), sauna, 7 tennis courts.*

The one- to four-bedroom units here feature vaulted, beamed ceilings, natural rock fireplaces, and lake views. Some of these units also have private saunas, and all are equipped with washers and dryers. Additional resort amenities include three private beaches, boating facilities, a fishing pier, and a one-mile paved beachfront path.

Coeur du Lac *136 Juanita Dr., Incline Village, Nevada, (800) 869-8308, (702) 831-3318, fax (702) 831-8668. Heated pool (June-Aug only), indoor hot tub, sauna.*

Located one block from the lake, this attractive complex also has a recreation center.

CONDOS FURTHER OUT

Carnelian Woods *5005 North Lake Blvd., Carnelian Bay, 546-5547, fax 583-8540. ¹/₄ mi. from lake. 30 rental units. Recreation center with heated pool (June-Sept only), 2 hot tubs, 2 saunas, 3 tennis courts, 1-mile parcourse.*

Further amenities here include sports facilities and bicycle rentals. In winter, a two-mile cross-country ski course and snow play area are available.

Granlibakken *End of Granlibakken Rd., Tahoe City, (800) 543-3221, 583-4242. 1 mi. from lake. 160 rooms. Children under 2 free. Some kitchens & fireplaces. Heated pool & children's wading pool (May-Sept only), hot tub, sauna; parcourse & 6 tennis courts (May-Sept only). Full breakfast.*

Situated in a 74-acre forested valley, this resort also has a jogging trail. In winter it maintains a ski and snow play area. See also page 376.

Kingswood Village *1001 Commonwealth Dr., off Hwy. 267, Kings Beach, 546-2501 (call collect for reservations). ³/₄ mi. from lake. 60 rental units. Heated pool (June-Aug only), hot tub, sauna, 3 tennis courts.*

Amenities here include access to a private lakefront beach club.

Northstar-at-Tahoe *Northstar Dr., off Hwy. 267, Truckee, (800) GO-NORTH, 526-1010. 6 mi. from the lake. 250 units; 125 non-smoking units. All VCRs; most kitchens & wood-burning fireplaces. 2 heated pools, 3 hot tubs, 2 saunas, fitness center, parcourse, 10 clay tennis courts (no fee), 18-hole golf course. 5 restaurants.*

In addition to the condos, hotel rooms and homes are also available for rental. A complimentary shuttle bus makes it unnecessary to use a car within the complex. Facilities include a teen center and, at an additional fee, a supervised summer children's recreation program for ages 2 through 10 and horseback riding. Tahoe's largest mountain bike park is here, with 100 miles of trails. A climbing wall and orienteering courses are also available. See also page 376.

Squaw Valley Lodge *201 Squaw Peak Rd., Olympic Valley, (800) 922-9970, 583-5500, fax 583-0326. 3 stories; 178 rooms; 40 non-smoking rooms. All kitchens, 24 gas fireplaces. Heated pool (June-Sept only), 3 indoor hot tubs, 2 outdoor hot tubs, sauna, steam room, health spa, fitness room, 2 tennis courts (no fee).*

Claiming to be "just 84 steps from the Squaw Valley tram," this resort is convenient for both skiers and non-skiers. Staying here allows skiers to avoid a congested early morning commute to Squaw's parking lot. When ready to ski, it is possible to just walk, or even ski, over to the lifts. For non-skiers, a room facing the slopes allows complete warmth and comfort while watching the rest of the group whiz by. It is interesting to note that the pool here is treated with gentle-on-the-eyes bromine instead of chlorine.

LAKEFRONT MOTELS

The Dunes Resort *6780 North Lake Blvd., Tahoe Vista, 546-2196. 9 units; $-$$$. Some kitchens &, fireplaces.*

Both motel rooms and pleasant housekeeping cottages are available, and weekly rates are discounted. Facilities include a large grassy area and a private beach with barbecue pit and volleyball net.

Lakeside Chalets *5240 North Lake Blvd., Carnelian Bay, (800) 2-WINDSUrf, 546-5857. 5 cabins; $$-$$$; 2-night min. on weekends. Children under 2 free. All kitchens & fireplaces. Dogs welcome.*

Facilities for these cozy, woodsy cabins—all of which have lake views—include a pier and sun deck. A wind-surfing school operates on the premises in the summer, and equipment rentals are available.

The Mourelatos' Lakeshore Resort *6834 North Lake Blvd., Tahoe Vista, (800) 2RELAX-U, 546-9500. 33 units; $$-$$$. Children under 1 free. Some kitchens.*

These woodsy housekeeping cottages and newly renovated motel rooms are situated in a pine forest that opens onto a private beach on the lake. A children's playground is provided.

Villa Vista Resort *6750 North Lake Blvd., Tahoe Vista, 546-1550, fax 546-4100; $$; 2-night min. in cottages. Children under 1 free. Some kitchens & fireplaces. Solar-heated pool (June-Aug only).*

Both motel rooms and cottages are available. Facilities include a sandy beach and a deck overlooking the lake.

OTHER

Hyatt Regency Lake Tahoe Casino *On Lakeshore/Country Club Dr., Incline Village, Nevada, (800) 233-1234, (702) 832-1234, fax (702) 831-7508. 11 stories; 482 units; 217 non-smoking rooms; $$$-$$$+. Children under 18 free. Some fireplaces. Heated pool, indoor hot tub, fitness room, 2 tennis courts. 3 restaurants, room service (child items).*

Guests here have a choice between a room in an 11-story high-rise, in a 3-story annex, or in a lakeside cottage, and Lady Luck can be tested 24 hours a day in the 13,000-square-foot casino. Of special note is the resort's magnificent private beach, complete with beach boys who set up lounge chairs and umbrellas wherever desired. In summer, guests can relax with the water lapping at the shore just beneath their toes. When thirsty, a server can be beckoned by raising a little red flag on the lounge chair, causing one to ponder, "Can it get better than this?" Jet skis and paddle boats can be rented at an adjacent marina. At night, an oceanfront fire pit furnished with comfortable chairs and a hammock invites lingering under the tall pines. During ski season, free shuttle service is provided to nearby ski resorts, and both ski rentals and discounted lift tickets are available on the premises. Packages come and go. When making reservations, inquire about current specials.

Camp Hyatt, a program for children ages 3 to 12, operates on weekends year-round, daily during summer and holidays. There is a fee to participate during the day, but the evening program is always free. And the inexpensive room service menu for kids is unbelievable: applesauce, corn-on-the-cob, gooey chocolate cake, and hot chocolate with marshmallows!

The resort's imposing **Lone Eagle Grille** features an Old Tahoe-style atmosphere, with massive wood-beamed ceilings, gigantic fireplaces made of local rock, and large windows with lake views. Lunch is soups and salads, some pastas and pizzas, and plenty of tempting desserts. The dinner menu offers updated surf-and-turf and a good Caesar salad.

Resort at Squaw Creek *400 Squaw Creek Rd., Olympic Valley, (800) 327-3353, 583-6300, fax 581-5407. 9 stories; 402 rooms; $$$+; 2-night min. on weekends. Children under 16 free. 17 kitchens; 60 gas fireplaces. 2 heated pools, 1 children's wading pool, 4 hot tubs, sauna, health spa, fitness room, parcourse, 2 tennis courts ($12/hr.), 18-hole golf course. 5 restaurants, room service (child items).*

This sleek, black-toned high-rise hotel becomes almost invisible tucked up against a mountain. The majestic property is impressively landscaped, with a 250-foot man-made waterfall feeding a rushing stream that cascades over boulders. One of the pools has a twisting 120-foot-long waterslide, and the toddler pool includes a large sandy beach for extra diversion. Two-story windows in the substantial lobby provide a magnificent valley view. The Mountain Buddies children's program operates year-round for ages 4 through 13; reservations are required and there is an additional fee. Bicycles can be rented and ridden along a scenic route beside the Truckee River. In winter, ski-in/ski-out access is available to Squaw Valley, and both an ice skating pavilion and horse-drawn sleigh rides are available.

Motel Row.

Last-minute lodging can usually be found among the numerous motels and cabins lining the lake in Kings Beach and Tahoe Vista. Chances are best, of course, on weekdays and in the off-season.

WHERE TO EAT

Alexander's Bar & Grill *Olympic Valley, 583-2555. L & D daily; in summer D only. Boosters, child menu. Reservations advised for D; not taken for L. AE, MC, V. Tram: 583-6985. Daily 10-4; in summer 10-10. Adults $15, 65+ $5-$12, under 13 $5; after 5pm everyone $5; High Camp facilities additional.*

This restaurant is located on the slopes of the Squaw Valley ski area and is reached via a scenic **aerial tram ride**. Call the restaurant for dining details.

A lovely, though difficult, hike to Shirley Lake begins at the tram building. Hikers pass waterfalls and huge boulders as they follow Squaw Creek about 2½ miles to the lake.

At 8,200-foot elevation, the new **High Camp Bath & Tennis Club** is open year-round. Facilities include an Olympic-size outdoor ice skating rink, six tennis courts, a pool and hot tub, and a stables. Mountain biking, volleyball, and bungee jumping are also available.

Hacienda del Lago *760 North Lake Blvd., in Boatworks Shopping Center, Tahoe City, 583-0358. D daily; in summer L & D daily; $. Highchairs, boosters, child portions. No reservations. MC, V.*

It is definitely worth a wait to be seated here in the front room featuring a panoramic lake view. People tend to pass the wait drinking fruit margaritas in the bar. (Smoothies are popular with children.) Beware. Anesthetized by these potent, tangy drinks, it is quite easy to over-indulge on the large portions of tasty Mexican food. The menu includes a variety of burritos, chimechangas (deep-fried burritos), and enchiladas. A colossal taco salad consists of a crispy-fried flour tortilla bowl filled to the brim with salad goodies, and make-your-own tacos are available with pork, turkey, or beef stuffing. For those who know when to stop, there are a la carte portions. For those who don't, there is flan topped with whipped cream.

Lakehouse Pizza *120 Grove St., Tahoe City, 583-2222. L & D daily; $. Highchairs, boosters. No reservations. MC, V.*

This casual spot offers lakefront views and a choice of sitting either inside or outside on a deck. Menu choices include pizza, sandwiches, salads, hamburgers, and exceptionally good house-made potato chips.

Sunnyside Resort *1850 West Lake Blvd., Tahoe City, (800) 822-2-SKI, 583-7200. B M-Sat, L & D daily, SunBr; $-$$. Highchairs, boosters, child portions. Reservations advised. MC, V.*

In the past it has been hard to beat a summer meal enjoyed outside on the huge deck here—watching the sailboats on the lake or listening to live jazz on Sunday afternoons. This restaurant has a history of regularly changing its menu format and phone numbers, so call before visiting. Overnight lodging is also available.

Water Wheel *1115 West Lake Blvd., Tahoe City, 583-4404. D daily; $$. Closed M Mar-May & Sept-Nov. Boosters. Reservations advised. AE, MC, V.*

Diners here are treated to a view of the Truckee River and some of the tastiest Chinese Szechwan cuisine in Northern California. Hailing from Taipei, Taiwan, chef Nelson has a way with a wok and whips up old family recipes to delight his loyal customers. The portion of the menu devoted to spicy Szechwan dishes appears flawless. Highly recommended are the beef Szechwan (beef in a tangy, crunchy sauce of minced woodear, water chestnuts, and green onions), twice-cooked pork (a colorful arrangement of brilliant chartreuse cabbage, bright orange carrot rounds, and pork in a spicy hot sauce redolent of sesame oil and garlic), and Szechwan spicy pork (shredded pork with minced water chestnuts, mushrooms, garlic, and peppers in a flavorful sauce—served with little pancakes). Drinks mixed by Lily are almost as tasty as the food.

Wolfdale's Cuisine Unique *640 North Lake Blvd., Tahoe City, 583-5700. D W-M; daily in July & Aug; $$-$$$. Child portions. 100% non-smoking. Reservations advised. MC, V.*

The attractive circa 1880 house this restaurant is located within was floated over on a barge from the Nevada side of the lake at the turn of the century. It was converted into a restaurant in the 1960s. During the two seatings scheduled each evening, talented owner/chef Douglas Dale combines Italian and Japanese cooking techniques to produce exceptional fresh fish and meat entrees—all artistically arranged and served with house-baked herb bread. The appetizers and house-made desserts are also exceptional. Adding to the aesthetics of this dining experience, everything is served on handmade pottery especially designed to enhance the food.

WHAT TO DO

Best Beaches.
• **Commons Beach** *In Tahoe City; stairway across from 510 North Lake Blvd.; parking lot behind Tahoe City Fire Station.*

This family beach boasts a large grassy area and a lakefront playground.
• **Sand Harbor State Park** *In Nevada, 4 mi. south of Incline Village. $4/vehicle.*

This is a perfect beach. The sand is clean and fine, lifeguards are usually on duty, and there are plenty of parking spaces and picnic tables.
• **William Kent Beach** *South of Tahoe City. $2/vehicle.*

Parking is difficult, but this small, rocky beach is worth the hassle.

Bike Trails begin in Tahoe City and follow the shoreline and the Truckee River. Rentals are available in Tahoe City and at other locations along the lake.

Donner Memorial State Park *12593 Donner Pass Rd., off Hwy. 40, 2 mi. west of Truckee, 582-7892. Daily 8-dusk. Closed Oct-May. $5/vehicle. Museum: Daily 10-4; in summer to 5. Adults $2, 6-12 $1.*

Located on Donner Lake, this park is a monument to the tragic Donner Party stranded here by blizzards in 1846. Picnic facilities, lake swimming, hiking trails, nature programs, and campsites are available. The **Emigrant Trail Museum** features exhibits on the area's history.

Fishing Charters.

Get the names of captains and a fishing license at one of the local sporting goods shops. The captains usually supply bait and tackle.

Gatekeeper's Museum *130 West Lake Blvd., in* **William B. Layton Park***, Tahoe City, 583-1762, fax 583-8992. Daily 11-5, June-Aug; W-Sun in May & Sept. Closed Oct-Apr. Free.*

The structure this museum is located within—a replica of a 1910 lodgepole pine log cabin—was originally inhabited by a succession of keepers whose job it was to raise and lower the gates of the dam. Displays include Native American artifacts and Lake Tahoe memorabilia. A new annex holds the **Marion Steinbach Indian Basket Museum**, which displays 800 Native American baskets. The surrounding 3½-acre lakeside park is equipped with picnic tables and barbecue facilities.

Ponderosa Ranch *100 Ponderosa Ranch Rd., Incline Village, Nevada, (702) 831-0691. Daily 9:30-5. Closed Nov-Mar. Adults $8.50, 5-11 $5.50. Breakfast hayride $2/person, summer only.*

Created especially for filming scenes for the TV series *Bonanza*, this ranch is now open to the public for tours. Visitors get a bumpy ride from the parking lot up the hill to the ranch, and then a guided tour. After the tour, there is time to explore and visit both a petting farm and what is said to be the world's largest collection of antique farm equipment. Fast-grub is available, and the tin cups in which beer and soft drinks are served make great souvenirs. A bargain breakfast hayride begins at 8 a.m. and ends at 9:30 a.m.

Squaw Valley Stables *1525 Squaw Valley Rd., Olympic Valley, 583-RIDE, fax 583-6187. Daily 8:30-5; May-Sept only. Guided rides $18/hr.; riders must be 7 or older; ponies $6.*

The proprietor here says, "We have all kinds of horses . . . gentle horses for gentle people, spirited horses for spirited people, and for those who don't like to ride we have horses that don't like to be ridden." Pony rides in a large arena are available for children ages 2 through 7; parents must lead the pony.

Sugar Pine Point State Park *On west shore, Tahoma, 9 mi. south of Tahoe City, 525-7982, 525-7232 (winter). Daily 8-dusk. $5/vehicle. Mansion: Tours on the hour 11-4; July & Aug only.*

In this gorgeous, peaceful setting, the three-story 1902 Queen Anne **Ehrman Mansion** has 16 rooms open for public viewing. The **General Phipps Cabin**, built in 1872 of hand-split logs, is also on the property. A magnificent beach invites swimming and sunning. Picnic tables, hiking trails, and a 1930s tennis court are also available, and campsites are open year-round. In winter, cross-country skiing and ranger-led snowshoe walks join the agenda.

Truckee River Bridge *At junction of Hwys. 89 & 28 (the Y), Tahoe City.*

The only outlet from the lake, the dam below this bridge has gates that control the flow of water into the river. Spectators gather here to view and feed the giant rainbow trout that congregate beneath the bridge. (They like to eat bread and crackers.) The nickname "Fanny Bridge" comes from the sight that develops as people bend over the bridge railing to see the fish.

Truckin' on the Truckee/River Rafting *Begins at the Y in Tahoe City. Daily 9-3:30; June-Oct only. Rates vary. No children under 4.*

What better way to spend a sunny summer Alpine day than floating down the peaceful Truckee River a la Huckleberry Finn? All that's needed is a swimsuit, water-friendly shoes, and some suntan lotion. Packing along a picnic and some cold drinks is also a good idea, and a day-pack keeps hands free for paddling. White-water enthusiasts stay away. This trip is so civilized that there are even portable toilets strategically placed along the riverbank. The four-mile, three-hour trip ends at **River Ranch** *(on Hwy. 89, (800) 535-9900, 583-4264.)*, where the restaurant prepares an outdoor barbecue lunch on a huge deck overlooking the river; lodging is also available. Tahoe City concessionaires offer a package that includes raft, life jacket, paddles, and return ride. It is first-come, first-served, so get here before 11 a.m. to avoid crowds and to get an early-bird discount. (The drought of the early 1990s dried up the river and stopped the fun here for a while. Check with the Visitors Bureau for the current status of the river.)

A 3½-mile off-road bicycle trail runs along the river here from the River Ranch into Tahoe City.

Watson Cabin Living Museum *560 North Lake Blvd., Tahoe City, 583-8717, fax 583-8992. Daily 12-4; mid-June-Aug only. Free.*

Built in 1908 and 1909, this log cabin is the oldest building at the north end of the lake still on its original site.

Winter Activities. See page 376.

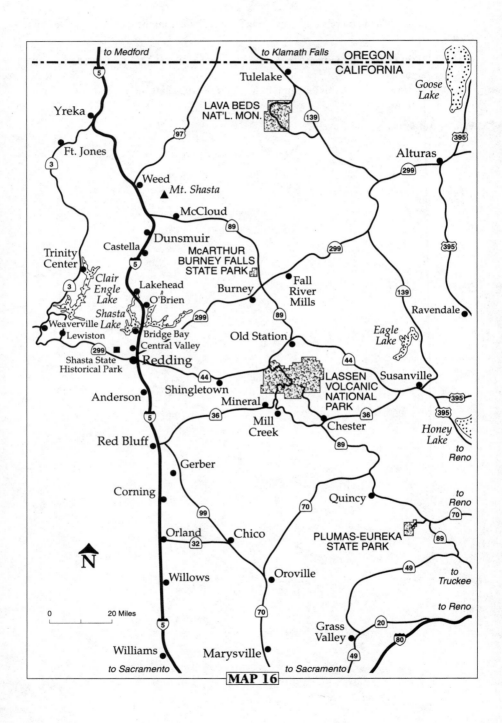

MAP 16

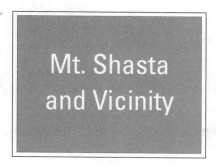

Mt. Shasta and Vicinity

A LITTLE BACKGROUND

This 12,162-foot-tall volcanic mountain features five glaciers. It can be climbed in summer and skied in winter. Poet Joaquin Miller, who considered Mount Shasta the most beautiful mountain in the West, described it as "lonely as God and white as a winter moon." New Agers rank it up there with Stonehenge and the Egyptian pyramids, apparently because of its unusual energy fields. Peculiar stories, involving UFOs and even Big Foot, abound in this area.

VISITOR INFORMATION

Shasta-Cascade Wonderland Association *14250 Holiday Rd., Redding 96003, (800) 326-6944, (916) 275-5555, fax (916) 275-9755.*

GETTING THERE

Located approximately 235 miles north of San Francisco. Take Highway I-80 north to Highway 5 north.

Lake Shasta Area

(Area Code 916)

VISITOR INFORMATION

Mt. Shasta Visitors Bureau *300 Pine St., Mt. Shasta 96067, (800) 926-4865, 926-4865.*

ANNUAL EVENTS

South Shasta Model Railroad *April & May; on Sundays. In Gerber, 12 mi. south of Red Bluff, 385-1389. Adults $4, 5-12 $3.*

This miniature ¼-inch O-gauge reproduction of the 100-mile Southern Pacific Railroad line from Gerber to Dunsmuir operates in a farmhouse basement. It includes 16 handmade steam locomotives, 100 cars, and over 900 feet of track. Visitors can also ride on a 2-foot gauge steam train and visit a museum of antique farm equipment.

WHERE TO STAY

Houseboats. See page 387.

Motel Row. Inexpensive motels are located at Bridge Bay and in the Lakehead area.

WHAT TO DO

Lake Shasta Caverns *In O'Brien, 15 mi. north of Redding, (800) 795-CAVE, 238-2341, fax 238-2386. Tours daily; call for schedule. Adults $14, 4-12 $7.*

Discovered in 1878, these caverns weren't opened for tours until 1964. The 2-hour tour begins with a 15-minute catamaran cruise across the McCloud arm of Lake Shasta. Then visitors board a bus for a scenic, winding ride up the steep mountainside to where the caverns are located. In this case, getting there really is half the fun. Nature trails, picnic facilities, and a snack bar are also available.

Shasta Dam *16349 Shasta Dam Blvd., Shasta Lake, 5 mi. off Hwy. 5, 275-4463. Daily 9-4; in summer, tours on the hour; call for winter schedule. Free.*

Built in 1945, this is the second largest dam in the U.S. and the highest center overflow dam in the world—three times higher than Niagara Falls! The guided tour includes a bus ride to the base of the dam, a film showing how dams are built, and a walk through a power plant and exhibit room.

Shasta State Historic Park *On Hwy. 299, 10 mi. west of I-5, Old Shasta, 243-8194. Free.* **Courthouse Museum:** *W-Sun 10-5. Adults $2, 6-12 $1. Includes same-day admission to Weaverville Joss House State Historic Park (see page 370).*

Prosperous and bustling during the Gold Rush, this gold mining ghost town is now an interesting museum of restored buildings and picturesque ruins located on either side of the highway. In the old courthouse, which is now a museum, a lovely eclectic collection of early California art is displayed Louvre-like—all crowded together. A collection of Modoc Indian baskets can also be viewed. The courtroom is completely restored, and down a steep stairway is the basement jail with its heavy-duty ironwork; just outside is the gallows. A large picnic area with tables and grassy expanses is adjacent, and across the highway the old bakery, though no longer operating, serves up some inexpensive baked goods and drinks.

Dunsmuir

(Area Code 916)

A LITTLE BACKGROUND

Surrounded by a million acres of forest and wilderness areas, this wildly scenic town is known as "The Home of the Best Water on Earth." And, indeed, pure spring water from glaciers on Mt. Shasta is delivered via lava tubes to every tap in town. With its sheltered, always-flowing public water fountain on the two-lane road through town, it is reminiscent of some of the small restorative towns seen in Germany's Black Forest area.

The town's history is the railroad. At the turn of the century, it was a division point on the railroad and a popular resort area, and in the 1920s things were really booming. Celebrities stopped here by the train-load, including Clark Gable and Babe Ruth, and the town's California Theatre was a movie palace. The phasing out of steam locomotives in the 1950s drastically hurt the area, and in 1961 Highway I-5 bypassed the town—a mixed blessing that allowed the town to retain its charm.

VISITOR INFORMATION

Dunsmuir Chamber of Commerce *P.O. Box 17, Dunsmuir 96025, (800) DUNSMUIR, 235-2177.*

WHERE TO STAY

Castle Stone Cottage Inn *In Castella, 6 mi. south of town, 235-0012; $$; 2-night min. All kitchens & wood-burning stoves.*

Arriving here brings to mind Goldilocks' arrival at the Three Bears' cabin: It feels as if someone lives here and will be back shortly. Built in the 1920s for the local railroad workers, these enchanting rural stone cottages have been lovingly renovated into incredibly cozy retreats furnished with fascinating bric-a-brac and equipped with fluffy beds and shelves of books. Front porch chairs face a charming garden, and the sounds of the Upper Sacramento River across the way—where trout fishing is reputed to be quite fine—provide soothing background. Occasionally a train rattles through the tranquil backyard—sometimes sounding a haunting whistle—near where an old ski-lift chair has been ingeniously converted into a tree swing for two. What a joy to discover that this charmed spot right out of a fairy tale is *real!*

Cave Spring Resort *4727 Dunsmuir Ave., 235-2721. 1 story; 25 units; $. All VCRs. Pool, hot tub, 1 tennis court. Restaurant.*

Situated on the outskirts of town, just above the river, this old-time mountain resort seems like something out of a time warp. It offers simple motel rooms, cabins, and RV accommodations, and facilities include a playground and bocce ball court on the spacious, cedar-sheltered grounds.

Nutglade Station *5827 Sacramento Ave., 235-0532, fax 235-4113. 6 rooms; $. Continental breakfast; restaurant.*

Situated in the town's historic district, this unusual old hotel is decorated with kitchy 1950s paint-by-the-numbers art and color-coordinated era furniture and fabrics. As nutty as it sounds, it works. According to the inn's brochure, rooms in the front allow tenants to "look down on the Dunsmuir turntable, see Amtrak pull in, and be lulled to sleep by the lumbering locomotives."

The downstairs **coffee shop** is well-known around town for its prize-winning cappuccino, grilled sandwiches, and selection of beers. An adjacent wood-paneled **bar** holds an antique snooker table and a vintage shuffleboard.

A few doors down, the **Brown Trout Gallery** *(5841 Sacramento Ave., (800) 916-ART, 235-0754. W-Sun.)* purveys some interesting crafts and art, but of special note is the stream running underneath that can be viewed and heard through a hole in the floor.

Railroad Park Resort *100 Railroad Park Rd., (800) 974-RAIL, 235-4440, fax 235-4470. 27 units; 4 non-smoking units; $$. 3 kitchens. Unheated pool, hot tub. Restaurant. Small pets welcome.*

Guests here can sleep in an authentic antique caboose or a deluxe box car unit. Each is furnished with antiques and equipped with a claw-foot tub, and special family units have bunk beds. Three cabins and some creek-side campsites are also available. The nearby Cascade Mountains and their granite Castle Crags Spires can be observed while frolicking in the pool, and a prime rib or seafood dinner can be enjoyed in a restaurant inside an authentic McCloud River Railroad car.

WHERE TO EAT

Cafe Maddalena *5801 Sacramento Ave., 235-2725, fax 235-0639. D Thur-Sun; $$. Closed Jan-Mar. Highchairs, boosters. MC, V.*

Located across the street from the old train station, this well-loved restaurant has a cozy interior of knotty-pine walls. The talented chef-owner hails from Sardinia and takes pride in whipping up authentic, well-executed Italian dishes that would be extraordinary to find anywhere, but seem especially so here, so far from a major city. Recent choices included house-made ravioli stuffed with ricotta and artichokes and topped with fresh tomato, and a superb pizza topped with a mixture of spinach, oyster mushrooms, garlic, eggplant, and mozzarella. Sometimes the chef even makes fresh mozzarella. Among the desserts are a tiramisu and an eggless bitter lemon flan.

The Old Rostel Pub & Cafe *5743 Sacramento Ave., 235-2028. Always open; $-$$.*

Established in 1892, this beau arts building is newly renovated and operating as a saloonrestaurant. The menu offers buckwheat pancakes and a variety of omelettes at breakfast, sandwiches and a hamburger at lunch, and steaks, chops, fish, and pasta at dinner. A large selection of micro-beers are on tap. **Hotel rooms** *((800) 235-2028)* are also available.

WHAT TO DO

Castle Crags State Park *Castle Creek Rd., Castella, 10 mi. south of town; 235-2684, fax 235-2684. Daily sunrise-sunset. $5/vehicle.*

Mile-high, snaggle-tooth granite peaks dominate this 6,000-acre park. Hiking trails, picnic areas, and swimming holes are available. For a smashing picnic spot with a view of the crags and Mt. Shasta, drive up the narrow one-lane road to Vista Point. The one-mile loop Indian Creek Nature Trail has gentle slopes and provides an easy leg-stretch. Campsites are available.

Hedge Creek Falls *On Dunsmuir Ave. at north end of town.*

The short, easy path leading here follows the Sacramento River. Once there, it is possible to walk behind the base of the falls. Picnicking is lovely here, and a table and gazebo are provided at the trail head. It is said that the notorious Black Bart once used the area for a hideout.

McCloud

(Area Code 916)

A LITTLE BACKGROUND

Set in the shadow of Mt. Shasta, this scenic mill town was owned by the McCloud Lumber Company from 1897 to 1965. It looks now much as it did then, when it was a company town. The streets here are wide, boardwalks front the business buildings, and there is little traffic but plenty of trees.

GETTING THERE

From Highway I-5, take Highway 89 ten miles into town.

WHERE TO STAY AND EAT

McCloud Guest House *606 W. Colombero Dr., (916) 964-3160. 5 rooms; $$. Continental breakfast, restaurant.*

Sitting on a hill above town amid six acres of gardens, this 1907 California craftsman-style house has a large veranda and is furnished with antiques, including an ornate pool table in the lounge. Its acclaimed dinner-only restaurant is open to the public.

McCloud Hotel *408 Main St., (800) 964-2823, 964-2822, fax 964-2844. 2 stories; 18 rooms; 100% non-smoking; $$-$$$. Afternoon tea, continental breakfast.*

A registered national landmark, this yellow hotel was built in 1916 on the same foundation as a prior hotel that burned down that same year. It once had 93 rooms and provided housing for mill workers and teachers, and its basement was the town library until the 1960s. Now meticulously restored, its old-fashioned lobby invites lingering over an old-time board game or book. The spacious rooms are individually decorated and furnished with rescued and restored pieces original to the hotel and area. Four suites feature canopy beds, whirlpool tubs for two, and a private balcony. Breakfast can be delivered to the room.

Across the yard, **The Dining Room** *(424 Main St., 964-2225. D W-Sun; $$. Highchairs, boosters, child portions.)* operates in the historic Dance Country building, which has housed restaurants since 1915. It serves classics such as prime rib, New York steak, and fettucini Alfredo along with more unusual items such as chicken strudel. Outside, an enormous porch and yard provide seating for **The North Yard: Barbecue & Brew**, a more casual, inexpensive extension of the restaurant that is also open for lunch and specializes in barbecue. Especially inviting for families, it has baskets of peanuts on the table to munch on and feed the resident jays, and a large grassy expanse invites children to romp while parents finish their meals.

WHAT TO DO

McCloud Railway Company *(800) 733-2141, 964-2142. Sat at 4:30. Adults $8, under 13 $5. Dinner train: Sat at 6; summer only. $70.*

On this hour-long excursion to Signal Butte, passengers are seated in open-air cars. Refurbished 1915 coach cars are used on the three-hour Sunset Dinner Train.

Lassen Volcanic National Park and Area

(Area Code 916)

A LITTLE BACKGROUND

Now a dormant volcano, imposing 10,457-foot Lassen Peak last erupted in 1915. It is thought to be the largest plug dome volcano in the world. The best time to visit is July through September, when the 35-mile road through the park is least likely to be closed by snow. Visitors can take several self-guided nature walks, and guided hikes and campfire talks are scheduled in the summer. Wooden catwalks supplement the trail through popular **Bumpass Hell**, an area featuring geological oddities such as boiling springs and mud pots, pyrite pools, and noisy fumaroles. The trail covers three miles and takes about three hours round-trip. The park also offers over 150 miles of back country trails, including a 17-mile section of the **Pacific Crest Trail**. A free park newsletter/map orients visitors and lists daily activities. Eight campgrounds are available on a first-come, first-served basis. For skiing information, see page 374. Park admission is $5 per vehicle.

VISITOR INFORMATION

Park Headquarters *P.O. Box 100 (38350 Hwy. 36), Mineral 96063-0100, 595-4444, fax 595-3262.*

Lassen County Chamber of Commerce *P.O. Box 338 (84 N. Lassen St.), Susanville 96130, 257-4323, fax 251-2561.*

GETTING THERE

Take Highway 36 east from Red Bluff or Highway 44 east from Redding.

WHERE TO STAY

Little lodging is found here, but many forest campsites are available on a first-come, first-served basis. Visitors should bear in mind that this area is remote and does not offer big-city facilities such as supermarkets.

Drakesbad Guest Ranch *At end of Warner Valley Rd., 18 mi. from Chester, 529-1512, fax 529-4511. 1 story; 19 units; $$$+. Closed Oct-May. Special children's rates; children under 2 free. No TVs. Natural hot springs pool. Includes 3 meals; restaurant. Dogs welcome.*

Located in a secluded, scenic mountain valley within the national park, this rustic resort was a hot springs spa in the mid-1800s. It has been a guest ranch since the turn of the century and is now the only guest ranch located within a national park. Most of the rustic cabins, bungalows, and lodge rooms have no electricity, so kerosene lanterns are used for light. The ranch is close to some of Lassen's thermal sights: one mile from the steaming fumaroles at **Boiling Springs Lake**, two miles from the bubbling sulfurous mud pots at the **Devil's Kitchen**. Guests can rent horses from the ranch stables and take guided rides into these areas. All this and a good trout-fishing stream, too! Day visitors should call ahead for horse or dining reservations. Overnight guests should book one year in advance.

Hat Creek Resort *On Hwy. 89 just north of Hwy. 44, Old Station, 11 mi. from north entrance to Lassen Park, 335-7121. 17 units; $-$$; 2-night min. in cabins. Some kitchens.*

These bargain motel units and old-time housekeeping cabins—the kind with linoleum floors and homemade curtains—are located beside rushing Hat Creek. Guests can fish in the creek, roast marshmallows over an open fire, and check out the stars at night.

WHERE TO STAY FURTHER AWAY

Spanish Springs Ranch *Ravendale, east of Lassen on Hwy. 395, 40 mi. north of Susanville, 80 mi. north of Reno, (800) 272-8282, RAVENDALE-30, fax 234-2041. $125/day, 13-17 $100, 3-12 $60, under 3 free. All meals included.*

Located in the remote northeast corner of the state, this 70,000-acre working cattle ranch offers a variety of vacation options as well as plenty of horseback riding. Guests can opt for the main lodge—where the luxurious amenities congregate—or for the less luxurious, and less expensive, bunkhouse. In spring and fall, five-day horse drives are scheduled, and weekly rates and special packages are also available.

Wild Horse and Burro Sanctuary *On Wilson Hill Rd., Shingletown, 5 mi. south of Hwy. 44, 21 mi. from Lassen, 474-5770, fax 474-5728. 5 units; 1 night/$235/person, 2 nights/$335/person; Apr-July 4 & Sept-Oct only. Unsuitable for children under 14. No TVs; shared bath house. All meals included.*

This protected preserve for wild mustangs and burros is the only wild horse sanctuary in the nation. Guests ride out of a base camp to observe the 300-plus population in their natural habitat. Meals are served by an open campfire, and overnight accommodations are in new, but rustic, cabins overlooking Vernal Lake. Prices include everything.

WHERE TO EAT

Uncle Runt's Place *On Hwy. 44, Old Station, 335-7177. L & D Tu-Sun, Apr-Jan; Thur-Sun rest of year; $. Highchairs, boosters, child portions. Reservations advised. No cards.*

Located right on Hat Creek, this cozy restaurant caters to locals and has a short-order menu of sandwiches, hamburgers, and dinner specials.

WHAT TO DO

McArthur-Burney Falls Memorial State Park *24898 Hwy. 89, Burney, 30 mi. north of Old Station, 335-2777. Daily 8-4; Apr-Sept to 10. $5/vehicle.*

A lovely one-mile nature trail winds past the soothing rush of the 129-foot waterfall here, allowing for closer inspection of the volcanic terrain for which this area is known. Paddle boats

can be rented at man-made **Lake Britton**, where facilities include picnic tables, a sandy beach, and a wading area for children. Swimming is allowed only in designated areas, as the lake has a steep drop-off. Campsites are available.

A boat is needed to reach isolated **Ahjumawi Lava Springs State Park**, which features one of the largest systems of freshwater springs in the world. Descendants of the Native American Ahjumawi tribe reside in the area. Call for maps and information.

Twelve miles away, the town of Burney offers modern motels and supermarkets.

Spattercone Crest Trail *1/2 mi. west of Old Station, across street from Hat Creek Campground. Free.*

This two-mile, self-interpretive trail winds past a number of volcanic spattercones, lava tubes, domes, and blowholes. It takes about two hours to walk and is most comfortably hiked in early morning or late afternoon.

Subway Cave *1 mi. north of Old Station, near junction of Hwys. 44 & 89, 335-2111. Free.*

Lava tubes were formed here about 2,000 years ago, when the surface of a lava flow cooled and hardened while the liquid lava beneath the hard crust flowed away. This cave, which is actually a lava tube, winds for 1,300 feet (about ¼ mile). Always a cool 46 degrees, it makes a good place to visit on a hot afternoon. However, it is completely unlighted inside, so visitors are advised to bring along a powerful lantern. Even "chickens" can enjoy the cave—by making a furtive entry and then picnicking in the lovely surrounding woods.

Lava Beds National Monument
(Area Code 916)

A LITTLE BACKGROUND

It doesn't hurt to be warned ahead of time that this national monument is located in the middle of nowhere. Perhaps you've heard the expression "out in the tules." This could be where it originated.

The monument has a campground, but the nearest motels and restaurant are far away in Tulelake. It's a good idea to pack-in picnic supplies as there is nowhere to buy food within many miles of the monument. The area also buzzes with insects, is a haven for rattlesnakes, and sometimes has plague warnings posted. Still, it is an unusual place that is well worth a visit.

The Visitors Center at the southern entrance offers a good orientation. Historically this area is known as the site of the 1872 Modoc War—the only major Indian war to be fought in California. Geologically the area is of interest because of its concentration of caves—approximately 300.

Park admission is $4 per vehicle.

VISITOR INFORMATION

Monument Headquarters *P.O. Box 867, Tulelake 96134, 667-2282.*

GETTING THERE

Continue north from Lassen Park to Highway 299. Then head north on Highway 139 through sparsely populated forest and farmland.

STOPS ALONG THE WAY

Fort Crook Museum *43030 Fort Crook Museum Rd., on Hwy. 299, Fall River Mills, 336-5110. Tu-Sun 12-4, May-Oct only. Free.*

Composed of a three-story main building and five outer buildings, this large museum complex displays six rooms of antique furniture, a collection of early farm implements and Native American artifacts, the old Fall River jail, a one-room school house from Pittville, and a pioneer log cabin.

WHAT TO DO

Caves.

Located in the parking lot of the **Visitors Center** *(9-6 in summer, 8-5 rest of year)*, Mushpot Cave has interpretive displays and is the only lighted cave here. A loop road provides access to most of the other 19 caves that are open without passes, including some with descriptive names such as Blue Grotto, Sunshine, and Natural Bridge. Catacombs must be crawled through. To explore other caves, it is required that visitors register at the Visitors Center . . . just in case. Lanterns are available to borrow.

Tule Lake and Lower Klamath Basin National Wildlife Refuges *4 mi. south of Oregon state line, 667-2231, fax 667-3299. Visitor Center: Daily 8-4. Free.*

The gravel road north out of the monument passes through the Tule Lake portion of this scenic area. These refuges are home to a variety of interesting birds that can easily be viewed from a car. In winter they have the densest concentration of bald eagles in the U.S. south of Alaska.

Trinity Alps

(Area Code 916)

A LITTLE BACKGROUND

Densely forested, this is wonderful camping country. There really isn't much to do here except relax and perhaps fish, boat, or hike.

VISITOR INFORMATION

Trinity County Chamber of Commerce *P.O. Box 517 (317 Main St.), Weaverville 96093, (800) 421-7259, 623-6101.*

WHERE TO STAY

Cedar Stock Resort and Marina *45810 Hwy. 3, Trinity Center, 15 mi. north of Weaverville, (800) 982-2279, 286-2225. 12 cabins; $$; 1-week min. in summer. Closed Nov-Feb. No TVs; all kitchens. Restaurant. Dogs welcome.*

This quiet spot offers lodging in a cabin in the woods or on a houseboat on **Clair Engle Lake**. Guests provide their own bedding and linens. The marina also rents boats and slips, and the bar and restaurant offer a terrific view of the lake.

Coffee Creek Ranch *Off Hwy. 3, Coffee Creek, 40 mi. north of Weaverville, (800) 624-4480, 266-3343, fax 266-3597. 1 story; 15 cabins; 100% non-smoking; $125-$150/person; 2-night min. in spring & fall, 3-night min. June-Aug. Special rates for children. No TVs; 1 wood-burning fireplace, 10 wood-burning stoves. Heated pool (unavail. Nov-Mar), children's wading pool, hot tub, fitness room. All meals included; restaurant.*

The private one- and two-bedroom cabins here are located in the woods. Activities include horse-drawn hayrides, movies, steak-frys, outdoor games, square and line dancing, archery, gun practice on a rifle range, panning for gold, and supervised activities for children 3 to 17. Horseback riding is included in the price in spring and fall; in summer, there is an additional charge. Cross-country skiing, sleigh rides, and dog sled rides are available in winter.

Trinity Alps Resort *1750 Trinity Alps Rd., Trinity Center, 12 mi. north of Weaverville, 286-2205, same fax. 43 cabins; $455-$865/cabin/week; 1-week min. June-Aug, 3-night min. May & Sept. Closed Oct-Apr. No TVs; all kitchens. 1 tennis court (no fee). Restaurant. Pets welcome.*

Arranged especially to please families, this 90-acre resort is composed of rustic 1920s brown-shingle cabins with sleeping verandas—all scattered along rushing Stuart Fork River. Guests provide their own linens or pay additional to rent them. Simple pleasures include crossing the river via a suspension bridge, hanging out at the general store, and enjoying dinner at the riverside **Bear's Breath Bar & Grill**. Scheduled activities include square dancing, bingo, and evening movies. Horseback riding is available at additional cost, and kids can ride their bikes endlessly.

WHAT TO DO

Jake Jackson Memorial Museum and Trinity County Historical Park *508 Main St., Weaverville, 623-5211. Daily 10-5, May-Oct; 12-4 Apr & Nov. Closed Dec-Mar. By donation.*

Trinity County's history is traced here through mining equipment, old bottles, and photographs. A reconstructed blacksmith shop and miner's cabin are also displayed. Outside, a creekside picnic area beckons. A full-size steam-powered stamp mill, located on the block just below the museum, is operated on holidays.

Weaverville Joss House State Historic Park *412 Main St., Weaverville, 623-5284. Tours on hour 10-4; call for days open. Adults $2, 6-13 $1. Includes same-day admission to Courthouse Museum at Shasta State Historic Park (see page 362).*

Located in a shaded area beside a creek, this Chinese Taoist temple is still used for worship. It provides cool respite on a hot summer day. Built in 1874 on the site of a previous temple that burned to the ground, it is the oldest continuously used Chinese temple in the state.

Yreka

(Area Code 916)

VISITOR INFORMATION

Siskiyou County Visitors Bureau *808 W. Lennox St., Yreka 96097, (800) 446-7475, 842-7857, fax 842-7666.*

Yreka Chamber of Commerce *117 W. Miner St., Yreka 96097-2999, (800) ON-YREKA, 842-1649.*

GETTING THERE

Located approximately 50 miles north of Mount Shasta, and halfway between Portland, Oregon and San Francisco.

WHAT TO DO

Siskiyou County Museum *910 S. Main St., 842-3836. Tu-Sat 9-5. Adults $1, 6-12 75¢.*

Local artifacts and history are emphasized. Of special interest is the occasional exhibits on local pioneer families, one of which was the Terwilligers. A 2¼-acre Outdoor Museum is located adjacent. Among its original and replica historic buildings are a schoolhouse, a Catholic church, a blacksmith shop, a miner's cabin, and an operating general store.

The Yreka Historic District *Along Miner St.*

More than 75 19th-century homes can be seen here, with most of them situated on the four blocks of Third Street located between Lennox and Miner. The Chamber of Commerce provides a descriptive tour brochure.

Yreka Western Railroad *300 E. Miner St., 842-4146. W-Sun at 10am, June-Aug; Sat & Sun in Sept & Oct. Closed Nov-May. Adults $9, 3-12 $4.50.*

A ride on the Blue Goose excursion train, pulled by a restored 1915 Baldwin steam locomotive that had a role in the movie *Stand by Me*, treats passengers to spectacular views of Mount Shasta. After the hour ride to Montague, there is an hour layover during which passengers can tour the historic town and enjoy a treat in an old-fashioned ice cream parlor. A 1,000-square-foot model railroad is displayed in the old depot, which now operates as a railroad museum.

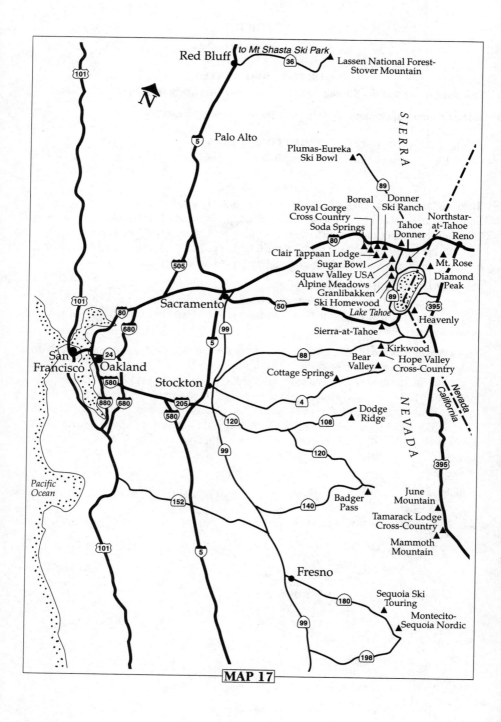

Red Bluff

to Mt Shasta Ski Park

Lassen National Forest-
Stover Mountain

Palo Alto

SIERRA

Plumas-Eureka
Ski Bowl

Royal Gorge
Cross Country
Soda Springs

Boreal

Donner
Ski Ranch

Tahoe
Donner

Northstar-
at-Tahoe

Reno

Clair Tappaan Lodge
Sugar Bowl
Squaw Valley USA
Alpine Meadows
Granlibakken
Ski Homewood

Mt. Rose

Diamond
Peak

Lake Tahoe

Heavenly

Sacramento

Sierra-at-Tahoe

Kirkwood
Hope Valley
Cross-Country

San
Francisco

Oakland

Stockton

Cottage Springs

Bear
Valley

NEVADA

Nevada
California

Dodge
Ridge

Pacific
Ocean

Badger
Pass

June
Mountain

Tamarack Lodge
Cross-Country

Mammoth
Mountain

Fresno

Sequoia Ski
Touring

Montecito-
Sequoia Nordic

MAP 17

Winter Snow Fun

Downhill Skiing

Downhill ski areas are plentiful in Northern California. The season runs from the first snow, usually in late November, through the spring thaw in April. Several resorts are known for staying open longer.

Lifts usually operate daily from 9 to 4. To avoid parking problems and long lines for lift tickets and rentals, arrive early. On-site equipment rentals are usually available and convenient. Note that lift tickets are often discounted mid-week.

The least crowded times at the resorts are the three weeks after Thanksgiving, the first two weeks in January, and late in the season. The two weeks around Christmas are ridiculous.

Those who know say it is worthwhile to buy ski equipment if someone skis more than ten days per season. Otherwise, it is financially beneficial to rent. Avoid buying children plastic skis; they break very easily.

Cross-country Skiing

Cross-country skiing becomes more popular each year. One reason for this surging popularity is the advantages it has over downhill skiing: no lift tickets to purchase; equipment is less expensive; is considered safer; can be enjoyed in groups; allows escape from crowds. However, the sport also has several disadvantages: requires more stamina; is less exhilarating.

Specialized cross-country centers offer equipment rentals, maintained trails, and warming huts. Trail maps are usually available at the center headquarters. Some centers also offer lodging, guided tours, and the option of downhill facilities.

Children age 4 and older are usually taught in classes with their parents, but some centers have special children's classes. Parents who have the strength can carry younger children in a backpack or pull them along in a "pulk."

It is a good idea for beginners to rent equipment and take a few lessons to learn safety guidelines and basic skiing techniques. Once the basics are learned, this sport can be practiced just about anywhere there is a foot of snow.

The state **Sno-Park** program makes it easier to park at popular trail heads. Parking areas are kept cleared of snow, and overnight RV camping is permitted at some locations. The permit costs $20 and is good from November 1 through May 30. One-day permits cost $3. For more information call (916) 324-1222.

Snow Play

Toboggans, saucers, inner tubes, and sleds are the equipment people use for snow play. For safety's sake, take note that sleds are lots of fun to use but extremely dangerous. Truck inner tubes are also dangerous because the rider is high off the ground with nothing to hold on to and no way to steer.

When people do not pay attention to safety rules, snow play can become dangerous. (I once had the wind knocked out of me by an antsy bear of a man who didn't wait for me and my young child to come to a stop before he pushed down the same hill in his saucer. After the collision he said, "Sorry. But you shouldn't have been there." I'm sure worse stories are waiting to be told.)

Some commercial snow play areas allow people to use their own equipment, but others require that people rent the concession's equipment.

Dress for cold, wet weather. Wear wool when possible, and pack a change of clothes. Protect feet with boots. When boots aren't available, an inexpensive improvisation is to wrap feet in newspapers, then in plastic bags, and then put on shoes. Also, cutting a few holes in a large plastic garbage bag allows it to serve as a raincoat. Always wear gloves to protect hands from sharp, packed snow.

The high-speed fun of **snowmobiling** is an exciting adventure. Many snowmobile concessions provide protective clothing and equipment. Though not inexpensive, especially for a family, it is an exhilarating, memorable experience.

Note: *In the following listings, difficulty of terrain at downhill ski resorts is specified in percentages: %B (beginner), %I (intermediate), %A (advanced).*

Way Up North
(Area Code 916)

Coffee Creek Ranch. See page 369.

Lassen National Forest—Stover Mountain *258-2141; 3 mi. southwest of Chester. Open Sat & Sun only. Downhill: 1 surface. 50%B, 50%I. Lifts $8. Cross-country: 39.5 mi. marked trails, some groomed. Free. Lodging nearby; packages available. Snow play area.*

California's "undiscovered National Park" is an excellent area for families and beginners. The scenery includes hot steam vents and mud pots, allowing for unusual and interesting cross-country ski touring. Snowshoe walks are sometimes scheduled. See also page 366.

Mt. Shasta Ski Park *104 Siskiyou Ave., Mt. Shasta, 926-8610, fax 926-8607, snow phone 926-8686; 10 mi. east of Mt. Shasta City. Downhill: 4 triples, 1 surface. 20%B, 60%I, 20%A. Lifts $27, 65+ $17, 1-6 $3. Children's ski school (4-7); lessons (8-12). Snowboard facilities. Cross-country: 17 mi. groomed trails. $10, 65+ $6, 8-12 $6. Lodging nearby, 926-3446, 926-3030.*

Night skiing is available at this low-key, family-oriented ski area.

Plumas-Eureka Ski Bowl *In Plumas-Eureka State Park, 836-2317; 25 mi. east of Quincy. Downhill only. F-Sun only. 2 poma lifts, 1 rope tow. 25%B, 50%I, 25%A. Lifts $17.*

South Lake Tahoe

Heavenly Ski Resort *South Lake Tahoe, (800) 2-HEAVEN, (702) 586-7000, fax (702) 541-2643, snow phone (916) 541-SKII. Downhill only. 1 tram, 3 quad, 8 triple, 7 double, 5 surface. 20%B, 45%I, 35%A. Lifts $46, 13-15 $31, 6-12 & 65+ $19. Children's ski school (4-12). Snowboard terrain park. Lodging nearby, (800) 2-HEAVEN; adjacent townhouses, (800) 822-5967; packages avail.*

Situated in two states, this is the largest, and one of the most scenic, ski areas in the country. Runs on the California side offer breathtaking views of Lake Tahoe. This resort has been rated as having the best intermediate skiing in California; it also has exhilarating expert slopes and offers both night and helicopter skiing.

Hope Valley Cross-Country Ski Center at Sorensen's Resort *14255 Hwy. 88, Hope Valley, (800) 423-9949, (916) 694-2203 & 694-2266; on Hwy. 88, 16 mi. south of Lake Tahoe. Cross-country only; 60 mi. marked trails. By donation. Children's ski school (5-12). Lodging on premises.*

Small and informal, this is a great place for families. Lodging is available in 29 housekeeping cabins. Some are newish log cabins equipped with kitchenettes and wood-burning fireplaces. Others are older and smaller. The resort is open year-round and is 100% non-smoking; a sauna and cafe are among the facilities. In the summer it offers both a family-oriented fly fishing school and history tours of the Emigrant Trail and Pony Express Trail.

Kirkwood Ski Resort *1501 Kirkwood Meadows Dr., Kirkwood, (800) 967-7500, (209) 258-6000, fax (209) 258-8899, snow phone (209) 258-3000; on Hwy. 88, 30 mi. south of South Lake Tahoe. Downhill: 7 triple, 3 double, 2 surface. 15%B, 50%I, 35%A. Lifts $41, 60+ $20, 13-24 $31, 6-12 $5. Childcare center (3-6); children's ski school (6-12). Snowboard terrain parks. Cross-country: (209) 258-7248; 48 mi. groomed trails. Trail fee $14, 60+ $10, 1-12 $5. Lodging on premises in condominiums, (800) 967-7500; packages avail.*

This very large, uncrowded family area is reputed to have the best natural snow, and food, in the Sierra. It is often snowing here when it is raining at other Tahoe ski areas. Horse-drawn sleigh rides are available, and the cross-country area offers inexpensive Family Days as well as guided overnight trips that include lodging and meals.

Sierra-at-Tahoe *1111 Sierra-at-Tahoe Rd., Twin Bridges, (916) 659-7453, snow phone (916) 659-7475, fax (916) 659-7453; on Hwy. 50, 12 mi. west of South Lake Tahoe. Downhill only. 3 quad, 1 triple, 5 double, 1 surface. 25%B, 50%I, 25%A. Lifts $39, 70+ $5, 13-19 $29, 6-12 $19. Childcare center (2-5); children's ski school (3-12). Snowboard terrain parks. Lodging nearby (800) AT-TAHOE.*

This ski area is reputed to be particularly popular with college students and families with teenagers. Free shuttles are available from South Lake Tahoe.

SNOW PLAY

Borges' Sleigh Rides *On Hwy. 50 next to Caesar's Tahoe casino, Stateline, (800) 762-RIDE, (702) 588-2953. Daily 10-dusk, weather permitting. Adults $10, 1-10 $5.*

Take a ride around a meadow in an old-fashioned "one-horse open sleigh."

Hansen's Resort *1360 Ski Run Blvd./Needle Peak Rd., 3 blocks from Heavenly ski area, South Lake Tahoe, (916) 544-3361. Daily 9-5. 1-hr. session $6/person.*

Facilities include a saucer hill and a packed toboggan run with banked turns. All equipment is furnished. Lodging is available.

Husky Express Dog Sled Tours *In Hope Valley, 25 mi. south of South Lake Tahoe, (702) 782-3047. Adults $50, under 12 $20. Reservations required.*

As the sled swooshes over the scenic trails through the trees on these enjoyable excursions, the frisky, well-tempered huskies seem to be having as much fun as the passengers. So does the "musher," who never utters the word "mush" but instead hollers "Hike!" or "Let's Go!" Two sleds are available, and each can carry two adults or a combination of kids and adults that doesn't exceed 375 pounds. Two-hour picnic tours are also available.

Snow Hikes. *Sierra State Parks, P.O. Box 266, Tahoma 96142, (916) 525-7232.*

Request a schedule of free ranger-led snowshoe and cross-country hikes in Lake Tahoe area state parks by sending a stamped, self-addressed legal size envelope to the above address. Hikes are scheduled October through April, depending on the snow level.

North Lake Tahoe
(Area Code 916)

Alpine Meadows *2600 Alpine Meadows Rd., Tahoe City, (800) 441-4423, 583-4232, fax 583-0963, snow phone (916) 581-8374; off Hwy. 89, 6 mi. north of Tahoe City. Downhill only. 2 quad, 2 triple, 7 double, 1 surface. 25%B, 40%I, 35%A. Lifts $45, 70+ free, 7-12 $18, 1-7 $6. Children's snow school (4-6); children's ski lessons (7-12). Snowboarding not permitted. Lodging nearby, (800) TAHOE-4-U; packages avail.*

Alpine is usually open through Memorial Day and some years is open into July, giving it the longest ski season at Lake Tahoe. Free one-hour guided tours that show skiers the main runs and how to avoid crowds are offered daily at 10 a.m. The **Tahoe Adaptive Ski School** *(581-4161)* for people with disabilities operates here, and the **Family Ski Challenge** is scheduled each March.

Granlibakken *Tahoe City, (800) 543-3221, 581-7333, fax 583-7641. 1 mi. south of Tahoe City. 2 surface. 50%B, 50%I. Lifts $15, 65+ & 1-12 $8; 50% discount to lodging guests. Children's ski school (5). Snow play area $4/person.*

This small ski area is protected from the wind and caters to beginners and families with small children. It is said to be the oldest ski resort at Tahoe and to have the least expensive lift ticket. See also page 353.

Northstar-at-Tahoe *Snow phone 562-1330, fax 562-2215; off Hwy. 267, 6 mi. south of Truckee. Downhill: 562-1010. 1 gondola, 4 quad, 2 triple, 2 double, 3 surface. 25%B, 50%I, 25%A. Lifts $43, 70+ $5, 60-69 $22, 5-12 $19, under 5 free. Childcare center (2-6); children's ski school (5-12); children's ski lessons (3+). Snowboard* *terrain parks. Cross-country: 562-2475; 40 mi. groomed trails. Trail fee $15, 5-12 $8, under 5 free. Lodging in modern condos on premises, (800) GO-NORTH; packages avail.*

This attractive ski area is said to be the least windy at Tahoe. Catering to families, it is good for beginners and excellent for intermediates. Lift ticket sales are limited to assure that the slopes don't get overcrowded, so arrive early. Organized activities are scheduled throughout the week, and free one-hour introductory tours, in which participants are shown the best runs and given a history of the area, are given daily at 10 a.m. Sleigh rides and snowmobile tours are available. See also page 353.

Ski Homewood *5145 W. Lake Blvd., 525-2992, fax 525-0417, snow phone 525-2900; on Hwy. 89, 6 mi. south of Tahoe City. Downhill only. 1 quad, 2 triple, 1 double, 4 surface. 15%B, 50%I, 35%A. Lifts $34, 60+ $12, 9-13 $11. Childcare center (2-5); children's ski school (6-12). Snowboard terrain park. Lodging nearby, (800) 822-5959.*

The slopes here are ideal for intermediates and provide panoramic views of Lake Tahoe. Ferry service from South Lake Tahoe is provided by the *Tahoe Queen*.

Squaw Valley USA *1960 Squaw Valley Rd., Olympic Valley, (800) 545-4350, 583-6985, fax 581-7106, snow phone 583-6955; off Hwy. 89, 5 mi. north of Tahoe City. Downhill: 1 tram, 1 gondola, 4 quad, 9 triple, 13 doubles, 5 surface. 25%B, 45%I, 30%A. Lifts $45, 65+ & 1-12 $5. Childcare (2-3); children's ski school (4-12). Snowboarding permitted. Cross-country: 10 mi. groomed trails. Trail fee: $12, 65+ & 1-13 $10. Lodging on premises; packages avail.*

Squaw Valley made its name in 1960 when it was home to the VIII Winter Olympic Games. Today it is a world-class ski area known internationally for its open slopes and predictably generous snowfall, which usually allows Squaw to stay open into May. Expert skiers consider it to be the best ski resort in the state because it has the steepest, most challenging slopes. Indeed, there are good slopes for every ability level. A special area for children ages 2 through 12 is equipped with three rope tows and one platter. Ice skating is available at the **Olympic Ice Pavilion** at High Camp, and three miles of night skiing is available mid-December through mid-March from 4 to 9 p.m. nightly.

SNOW PLAY

Carnelian Woods Condominiums. See page 353.

North Tahoe Regional Park Winter Activity Area *Tahoe Vista, 546-7248, fax 546-7116, snow phone 546-5043; off Hwy. 28 at end of National Ave. Parking $3.*

This 108-acre park has a snow play area for toboggans and saucers. Snowmobiles can be rented on weekends for use on a ¼-mile oval racing track and 2½ miles of trails. Cross-country trails *(8 mi., all groomed. Trail fee $3.)* and picnic tables round out the facilities.

Snowfest! *583-7625, fax 583-8145.*

Held for a week each year in March, this is the largest winter carnival in the West. In the past activities have included a fireworks display over the slopes at Squaw Valley followed by the awe-inspiring sight of scores of torch-bearing skiers making a twisting descent down Exhibition Run. Other popular events include The Great Ski Race (a 30-kilometer Nordic ski competition) and the Localman Triathlon (a competition in winter survival skills in which participants must stack firewood, shovel snow, and put on tire chains).

Sugar Pine Point State Park. See page 357.

Donner Summit

(Area Code 916)

Boreal *426-3666, snow phone same, fax 426-3173; Castle Peak exit off Hwy. I-80, 10 mi. west of Truckee. Downhill only. 2 quad, 2 triple, 5 double. 30%B, 55%I, 15%A. Lifts $34, 5-12 $10. Childcare center (2-12); children's ski school (4-12). Snowboard terrain park. Lodging on premises, 426-3668; packages avail.*

Known for being relatively inexpensive and convenient to the Bay Area, this resort has the Sierra's most extensive night skiing facilities. Slopes are especially good for beginners and low-intermediates, and skiers of all ability levels can ride on the same chairs together. The "Shared Parent" program allows two parents to buy just one ticket if they want to take turns skiing and babysitting their children.

Clair Tappaan Lodge *Norden, 426-3632; on Hwy. 40, 3 mi. east of Norden/Soda Springs exit off Hwy. I-80. Cross-country only. 7 mi. groomed trails. Trail fee: $5 donation.*

This area is said to be the snowiest in the continental U.S. Both the massive timbered lodge, which was built by volunteers in 1934, and the track system are owned and operated by the Sierra Club. A special package *($37+, members $33+, 4-12 $17)*, includes bunk bed lodging, three hearty meals served family-style, and use of the trails. As at hostels, everyone is expected to do a chore. Overnight trips to wilderness areas can be arranged.

Donner Ski Ranch *Norden, 426-3635, fax 426-9350, snow phone 321-SNOW; on Hwy. 40, 3 mi. from the Norden/Soda Springs exit off Hwy. I-80. Downhill only. 1 triple, 5 double. 25%B, 50%I, 25%A. Lifts $20, children $10. Snowboard terrain park. Lodging on premises; packages avail.*

Best for beginners and intermediates, this area offers no frills. Bargain rates are available mid-week.

Royal Gorge Cross Country Ski Resort *9411 Hillside Dr., Soda Springs, (800) 500-3871(outside No.Calif.), 426-3871, fax 426-9221, snow phone 426-3871; 1 mi. from Soda Springs/Norden exit off Hwy. 80, near Donner Pass. Cross-country only. 190 mi. groomed trails. Trail fee $19.50, 7-14 $8.50. Children's ski school (4-9 & 9-14). Lodging on premises; packages avail.*

Modeled after Scandinavian ski resorts, this was the first cross-country ski resort in California. The overnight **Wilderness Lodge** here is not accessible by road. Guests are brought in by snowcat-drawn sleigh (sorry, no reindeer or horses yet) and leave by skiing the two miles back out. Accommodations are rustic. In the old 1920s hunting lodge, everyone shares the same toilet areas. Bathing facilities—showers, a sauna, and an outdoor hot tub—are located in an adjacent building and are reached by a short trek through the snow. Sleeping facilities are tiny roomettes, each with either a double bed or a bunk bed and a cloth-covered doorway. Several three-bed rooms are available for families. The food, however, is remarkably civilized. A chef works full-time in the kitchen preparing attractive, tasty, and bountiful French repasts. Oh, yes. The skiing. Guests may cross-country ski whenever they wish, and the capable staff gives lessons each morning and guided tours each afternoon. Guided moonlight ski tours are scheduled after dinner. A two-night weekend *($299, 5-16 $225)* includes everything except equipment, which can be rented on the premises. Lower rates are available midweek.

Royal Gorge also operates a more accessible B&B, **Rainbow Lodge** *(426-3871)*, nearby.

The cross-country ski center is open to non-guests and features the largest cross-country track system in the U.S. Facilities include ten warming huts, four trail-side cafes, and four surface lifts. The Rainbow Interconnect Trail allows skiers to enjoy eight miles of scenic downhill cross-country skiing; shuttle buses return skiers to the trailhead. A special program is available for skiers with disabilities.

Soda Springs Ski Area *Soda Springs, 426-3666, fax 426-3173, snow phone same; at Soda Springs exit off Hwy. I-80, 4 mi. west of Donner Summit. Downhill only. 1 triple, 1 double. 30%B, 50%I, 20%A. Lifts $15, under 8 free. Children's ski school (4-12); children's lessons. Snowboarding permitted. Lodging nearby.*

Built on the former site of one of the first Sierra ski resorts, this relatively new ski area is among the closest to the Bay Area and is particularly well-designed for beginners. It is owned by the Boreal ski area and shares some facilities with it. All or part of the resort can be rented on weekdays.

Sugar Bowl Ski Resort *Norden, 426-3651, fax 426-3723, snow phone 426-3847; on Hwy. 40, 2 mi. east of Soda Springs exit off Hwy. I-80. Downhill only. 1 gondola, 3 quad, 5 double, 1 surface. 15%B, 40%I, 45%A. Lifts $40, 60+ $20, 5-12 $10. Childcare (3-6); children's ski school & lessons (6-12). Snowboard terrain park. Lodging on premises; packages avail.*

Exuding a 1930s Tyrolean charm, this ski resort is one of the Sierra's oldest and is said to have had the first chairlift in the state. It is further known for having short lift lines, good runs at all ability levels, and a lack of hotdoggers. Skiers park their cars carefully (to avoid tickets), and then ride a gondola or chairlift up to the resort.

Tahoe Donner *11603 Snowpeak, Truckee, fax 587-0685, snow phone 587-9494; off Hwy. I-80. Downhill: 587-9444. 1 quad, 1 double, 1 surface. 40%B, 60%I. Lifts $26, 70+ free, 56-69 & 7-12 $12. Children's ski school (3-6); children's ski lessons (7-12). Snowboard terrain park. Cross-country: 587-9484. 42 mi. groomed trails. Trail fee $15, 70+ free, 60-69 $13, 7-12 $9. Children's ski school (5-9). Lodging in modern condos & homes on premises, 587-6586 or 587-5411.*

Especially good for families, this small resort has a snow play area. The number of lift tickets sold each day is limited, assuring that it never gets too crowded. The cross-country ski center offers lighted night skiing and schedules special tours: Ski With Santa, Morning Nature Tour, Sauna Tour, Donner Trail Tour.

SNOW PLAY

Sierra Sweepstakes Sled Dog Races *Annually in January. Held at Truckee Tahoe Airport off Hwy. 267, 4 mi. south of Truckee, 587-3657, fax 587-8064.*

The largest such races in the West, this two-day event features teams of huskies, samoyeds, setters, and bloodhounds.

Western SkiSport Museum *At Boreal Ridge exit off Hwy. I-80, 426-3313, fax 426-3501. W-Sun 10-4. Free.*

See just how cumbersome that charming old-time ski equipment really was. Skis were used by pioneers to help open this mountain area. This museum chronicles the history of skis in the West from the gold camps to current times. Vintage ski films are shown upon request.

The old days

Nevada
(Area Code 702)

Diamond Peak *1210 Ski Way, Incline Village, (800) 00-TAHOE, 832-1177, fax 832-1281, snow phone 831-3211; off Hwy. 28. Downhill: 2 quad, 5 double. 18%B, 46%I, 36%A. Lifts $35, 70+ free, 60-69 & 6-12 $14. Childcare center & children's ski school (3-6); children's ski lessons (3-12). Snowboard terrain park. Lodging nearby, (800) GO-TAHOE. Cross-country: 20 mi. groomed trails. Trail fee: $13, 60-69 & 6-12 $8.*

Well-sheltered, this family-oriented resort is especially good on inclement days. It is the first and only ski resort to use the European-style easy-loading "Launch Pad" system—similar to a moving walkway—on both quad chairlifts. The cross-country center also has snowshoe facilities, and complimentary shuttle service is available to Incline Village.

Mt. Rose Ski Area *22222 Mt. Rose Hwy., Reno, (800) SKI-ROSE, 849-0704, fax 849-9080, snow phone 849-0706; on Hwy. 431, 11 mi. northeast of Incline Village. Downhill only. 3 triple, 2 quad. 30%B, 35%I, 35%A. Lifts $38, 60+ $19, 6-12 $14. Children's ski school (4-10); children's ski lessons (4+). Snowboard terrain park.*

At 9700-feet, this is the highest base elevation at Tahoe.

East
(Area Code 209)

Bear Valley Ski Area *Bear Valley, on Hwy. 4, 45 mi. east of Angels Camp. Downhill: 753-2301, fax 753-6421, snow phone 753-2308. 2 triple, 7 double, 2 surface. 30%B, 40%I, 30%A. Lifts $30, 13-17 $28, 7-12 $13, 65+ & under 7 free. Childcare center (2-6); children's ski school (4-8). Snowboard terrain park. Cross-country: (800) 794-3866, 753-2834 or 753-2327, fax 753-2669; 40 mi. groomed trails. Trail fee $15, 60+ & 1-9 free. Lodging in condos, homes, & lodge 3 mi. from ski area, 753-BEAR.*

Intermediate or better ability skiers staying in this secluded resort village can ski the three-mile Home Run trail back to the resort area at the end of the day. A bus takes skiers to and from the village area lodgings and the slopes. Bear is one of the biggest ski areas in the state and generally has short lift lines. However, that Ski Bare campaign must have caught people's attention: Now there are lines where once there were none. The resort is popular with families and especially good for beginners and intermediates.

The cross-country area has snowshoeing and an **ice skating rink** *(Dec-Feb only. $4, skate rental $3.)* on a natural frozen pond. Stays can be arranged at ski-in snowbound cabins.

Inexpensive modern rooms, with bathrooms down the hall, are available at nearby **Red Dog Lodge** *(753-2344).*

Cottage Springs *795-1401 or 795-1201; on Hwy. 4, 8 mi. east of Arnold. Downhill only. 1 double, 1 surface. 75%B, 25%I. Lifts $15, 1-10 $10. Lodging nearby. Snow play area; rental fee.*

This is a good area to learn to ski. Night skiing is available on Saturdays.

Dodge Ridge *Pinecrest, 965-3474, fax 965-4437, snow phone 965-4444; 32 mi. east of Sonora off Hwy. 108. Downhill only. 2 triple, 5 double, 4 surface. 20%B, 60%I, 20%A. Lifts $34, 62+ $10, 13-17 $28, 7-12 $16, under 6 free. Children's ski school (4-12). Snowboarding permitted. Lodging nearby, (800) 446-1333.*

This low-key, family-oriented ski area is known for short lift lines.

SNOW PLAY

Bear River Lake Resort *40800 Hwy. 88, Pioneer (on Bear River Reservoir), 295-4868; 42 mi. east of Jackson, 3 mi. off Hwy. 88. M-F 7-7, Sat & Sun to 11. Free. Parking $5/vehicle. Lodging on premises.*

Visitors may use their own equipment in this groomed snow play area. Snowcats, cross-country equipment, snowshoes, saucers, and tubes are available for rental, and back country cross-country trips can be arranged.

Long Barn Lodge Ice Rink *Long Barn, (800) 310-3533, 586-3533; 23 mi. east of Sonora off Hwy. 108. Call for schedule. Adults $4.50, under 13 $3.50, skate rental 50¢.*

Located behind a bar and restaurant built in 1925, this rink is covered but has two sides open to the outdoors.

South

Badger Pass *In Yosemite National Park (see p. 305); off Hwy. 41 on Glacier Point Rd., 23 mi. from the valley. Downhill: (209) 372-1446, snowphone (209) 372-1000, fax (209) 372-1362. 1 triple, 3 double, 1 surface. 35%B, 50%I, 15%A. Lifts $28, 65+ free, 4-12 $13. Childcare center (3-9); children's pre-ski school (4-6). Snowboarding permitted. Cross-country: (209) 372-8444; 21 mi. groomed trails. Trail use free with park admission. Lodging nearby; packages avail.*

Badger Pass opened in 1935, making it California's first, and oldest, organized ski area. A prime spot for beginners and intermediates and especially popular with families, it has a natural bowl with gentle slopes that provide shelter from wind. A free shuttle bus delivers valley guests to the slopes. Ask about the bargain Midweek Ski Package.

A **snow play area** is located several miles from the slopes. It is not always accessible, and there are no equipment rentals.

Yosemite's first ski lift
(Skier's stood skis upright in center of "upski," then sat down beside them to be
pulled up the hill via funicular cable.)

Cross-country skiing is arranged through **Yosemite Cross-Country School**—the oldest cross-country ski school on the West Coast. Survival courses, snow camping, and overnight tours that include lodging and meals are also available.

June Mountain *June Lake, (619) 648-7733, snow phone (619) 934-2224, fax (619) 648-7367; 4 mi. south of Hwy. 395, 58 mi. north of Bishop. Downhill only. 1 tram, 2 quad, 4 double. 35%B, 45%I, 20%A. Lifts $35, 13-18 $25, 65+ & 7-12, $18. Childcare center (newborn-6); children's ski school (3+). Snowboarding permitted. Lodging nearby; packages avail.*

This compact, uncrowded area is excellent for beginners and popular with families. Snowboard rentals and lessons are available.

For lodging try **June Lodge** *((714) 648-7713).* A former hunting lodge, it was once a popular retreat for Clark Gable, Humphrey Bogart, and other era movie stars.

Mammoth Mountain *1 Minaret Rd., Mammoth Lakes, (800) 832-7320, (619) 934-0745, fax (619) 934-0603, snow phone (619) 934-6166; 50 mi. north of Bishop. Downhill only. 2 gondolas, 6 quad, 7 triple, 14 double, 2 surface. 30%B, 40%I, 30%A. Lifts $43, 13-18 $33, 65+ & 7-12 $22. Childcare center (infant-12); children's ski school (4-12); children's ski lessons (7-12). Snowboarding permitted. Lodging on premises, (800) 367-6572, (619) 934-2581.*

One of the three largest ski areas in the country, Mammoth is located on a dormant volcano and has the highest elevation of any California ski area. It also is said to have some of the longest lift lines and one of the longest seasons—usually staying open through June and sometimes into July. A seven-hour drive from the Bay Area, it is understandably more popular with Southern Californians.

The **Hilton Creek Youth Hostel** *((619) 935-4989. 22 beds; some family rooms.)* is located about 20 miles away. The focus here is on cross-country skiing, and special packages are available. See also page 391.

Montecito-Sequoia Nordic Ski Resort *(800) 227-9900, (415) 967-8612, fax (415) 967-0540, snow phone (209) 565-3324; on Hwy. 180 between Kings Canyon & Sequoia National Parks. Cross-country only. 28 mi. groomed trails. Fee $12, children $7.50. Babysitting (2-4); children's lessons (5-10). Lodging on premises; packages avail.*

Skiers here enjoy breathtaking ski tours and snowshoe walks through groves of giant sequoias. Arrangements can be made for videotaping lessons, and parents can rent "pulkas" to pull their children along in. Because of its high altitude location at 7,500 feet, this resort usually retains its snow and stays open for skiing through spring.

Lodge guests have plenty to do besides skiing. In the lodge they feast on "California fresh" cuisine and have access to snacks around the clock. There are board games, Ping Pong, and plenty of movies for the VCR. Outside activities include snow sculpture, igloo building, and ski football. A session on the naturally frozen **ice skating rink** *((209) 565-3388. Daily. $6, skate rentals $2.50.)* is also a possibility, as is a soak in the outdoor hot tub overlooking the Great Western Divide. But just resting in front of the massive stone fireplace is also an option. See also page 387.

Sequoia Ski Touring Center *Sequoia National Park; Giant Forest, (209) 565-3435; Grant Grove, (209) 335-2314. Cross-country only. 110 mi. ungroomed trails. Trail use free with park admission. Children's lessons. Lodging nearby (see p. 314).*

The big attraction here is the scenic national park ski trails leading through groves of cinnamon-colored giant sequoias. Free hot drinks are provided, and moonlight tours and overnight tours are available. **Snow play areas** are located at Azalea campground and Big Stump picnic areas.

Ice skating rink at Curry Village, Yosemite

Tamarack Lodge Resort Cross-Country Ski Center *Mammoth Lakes, (800) 237-6879, (619) 934-2442, fax (619) 934-2281; on Twin Lakes, 2.5 mi. from Mammoth Lakes Village. Cross-country only. 30 mi. groomed trails. Trail fee $15, seniors & 11-17 $10. Children's ski lessons (6-11). Lodging on premises; packages avail.*

Lodging is a choice of either rooms in a rustic 1923 alpine lodge or housekeeping cabins, some of which have fireplaces or wood-burning stoves.

SNOW PLAY

Yosemite National Park *See page 305.*

Ice skate in the shadow of Glacier Point, with a spectacular view of Half Dome, at the scenic outdoor **ice skating rink** in Curry Village *((209) 372-8341. Call for schedule. Adults $5, under 13 $4.50, skate rentals $2.).* Skating pointers are free.

Free ranger-led **snowshoe walks** are also available at Badger Pass *((209) 372-4461. $1 snowshoe maintenance fee. Children must be age 10+.).* A good place to snowshoe without a guide is the Sequoia Forest Trail in Mariposa Grove.

Family Camps

Most adults remember the good old days when they were a kid and got to go away to summer camp. Most adults think those days are gone for good. Well, they're not. A vacation at a family camp can bring it all back!

Family camps provide a reasonably-priced, organized vacation experience. They are sponsored by city recreation departments, university alumni organizations, and private enterprise. The city and private camps are open to anyone, but some university camps require a campus affiliation.

And its isn't necessary to have children to attend. One year at one camp a couple was actually honeymooning! Elderly couples whose children have grown occasionally attend alone, and family reunions are sometimes held at a camp. Whole clubs and groups of friends have been known to book in at the same time.

Housing varies from primitive platform tents and cabins without electricity, plumbing, or bedding to comfortable campus dormitory apartments with daily maid service. Locations vary from the mountains to the sea. Predictably, costs also vary with the type of accommodations and facilities. Some camps allow stays of less than a week, but most require a week-long commitment. Children are usually charged at a lower rate according to their age.

Most family camps operate during the summer months only. Fees usually include meal preparation and clean-up, special programs for children, and recreation programs for everyone. Activities can include river or pool swimming, hikes, fishing, volleyball, table tennis, badminton, hayrides, tournaments, campfires, crafts programs, songfests, tennis, and horseback riding.

Each camp has its own special appeal, but all offer an informal atmosphere where guests can really unwind. Often over half the guests return the following year. Repeat guests and their camp friends tend to choose the same week each year.

For detailed rate information, itemization of facilities, session dates, and route directions, contact the camp reservation offices directly and request a free brochure. Reserve early to avoid disappointment.

CITY/GROUP CAMPS

Berkeley Tuolumne Family Camp *City of Berkeley Camps Office, Berkeley, (510) 644-6520, fax (510) 644-6015. Located on the south fork of the Tuolumne River near Yosemite National Park. Daily rates.*

Platform tents without electricity; provide own bedding; community bathrooms; family-style meals. Programs for toddlers-6, 6-12, & teens. Swimming instruction in river; cookout & breakfast hikes.

Camp Concord *Concord Department of Leisure Services, Concord, (510) 671-3273, fax (510) 671-3412. Located near Camp Richardson at South Lake Tahoe. Daily rates. Cabins with electricity; provide own bedding; community bathrooms; cafeteria-style meals. Special program for ages 3-6 & 7-16. Horseback riding & river rafting at additional fee.*

Camp Mather *San Francisco Recreation and Park Department, San Francisco, (415) 666-7073, fax (415) 668-3330. Located on the rim of the Tuolumne River gorge near Yosemite National Park. Daily rates. Cabins with electricity; provide own bedding; community bathrooms; cafeteria-style meals. Playground area; program for age 6 and older. Pool, lake swimming, tennis courts (no fee); horseback riding at additional fee.*

Camp Sacramento *Department of Parks and Recreation, Sacramento, (916) 277-6098. Located in the El Dorado National Forest 17 mi. south of Lake Tahoe. Daily rates. Cabins with electricity; provide own bedding; community bathrooms; cafeteria-style meals. Program for ages 2-16; babysitting avail. at additional fee.*

Camp Sierra *Associated Cooperatives Inc., Berkeley, (510) 595-0873. Located in a pine forest between Huntington & Shaver Lakes 65 mi. east of Fresno. Weekly rates. Cabins with electricity, lodge rooms, or bring own tent; provide own bedding; community bathrooms; family-style meals. Special activities for teens, playground and crafts program for younger children. Discussion groups.*

Feather River Camp *Office of Parks, Recreation, and Cultural Affairs, Oakland, (510) 238-3791, fax (510) 238-2224. Located in the Plumas National Forest north of Lake Tahoe near Quincy. Daily rates. Cabins & platform tents with electricity; provide own bedding; community bathrooms; family-style meals. Play area & activities for ages 2-6; program for age 6 and older. Theme weeks.*

Gualala Family Camp *Berkeley-Albany YMCA, Berkeley, (510) 848-6800, fax (510) 848-6835. Located 7 mi. inland from the coast near Gualala. 2-3 night weekend in July. Shared cabins with electricity & lodge rooms; community bathrooms; meals provided. Childcare for 1-6; programs for older children. Fitness classes, canoeing, swimming, arts & crafts, hiking, campfire programs.*

San Jose Family Camp *San Jose Conventions, Arts & Entertainment, San Jose, (408) 277-4666, fax (408) 277-3535. Located in Stanislaus National Forest 30 mi. from Yosemite National Park. Daily rates; tent cabins without electricity (electricity avail. at additional fee); provide own bedding; community bathrooms. Cafeteria-style (B & L) & family-style (D) meals. Play area, program for age 3 and older. Dammed-off river pool.*

Silver Lake Family Resort *Department of Parks and Recreation, Stockton, (209) 937-8371, fax (209) 937-8260; Located 40 mi. south of Lake Tahoe. Daily rates. Platform tents & cabins with electric lights; provide own bedding; community bathrooms; cafeteria-style meals. Program for toddlers & older children. Swimming in lake, horseback riding nearby.*

PRIVATE ENTERPRISE CAMPS

Coffee Creek Ranch. See page 369.

Emandal Farm. See page 219.

Greenhorn Creek Guest Ranch *(800) 334-6939, (916) 283-0930, fax (916) 283-4401. Located 70 mi. north of Lake Tahoe in Feather River country. Weekly rates; open Apr-Nov. Rustic cabins & lodge rooms with maid service; private bathrooms; family-style meals. Childcare for 4-6 during horseback rides. Heated pool, hot tub, horseback riding, hayrides, fishing pond, hiking; golf & tennis nearby.*

This is where to go to rough it in comfort and to enjoy a heavy schedule of horse-related activities. Daily and weekend rates can be secured on a space-available basis by calling two weeks in advance.

Montecito-Sequoia High Sierra Vacation Camp *(800) 227-9900, (415) 967-8612, fax (415) 967-0540. Located in Sequoia National Forest between Kings Canyon & Sequoia National Parks. Weekly rates. Lodge; bedding provided; private baths. Also rustic cabins; community bathrooms. Buffet meals. Parent/child program for babies 6mo.-23mo.; programs for age 2 and older. 2 tennis courts, lake swimming, pool, hot tub, sailing, canoeing, boating, archery, fishing, riflery; extra fee for water-skiing and horseback riding. See also page 382.*

UNIVERSITY CAMPS

Lair of the Golden Bear *Sponsored by California Alumni Association at University of California, Berkeley, (510) 642-0221, fax (510) 642-6252. Located in Stanislaus National Forest near Pinecrest. Weekly rates. Tent cabins with electricity; provide own bedding; community bathrooms; family-style meals. Organized activities for ages 2-18. Heated pool, 3 tennis courts, swimming and tennis lessons, complete athletic facilities.*

This is actually two separate camps—Camp Blue and Camp Gold—that operate side by side. Each has its own staff and facilities.

Houseboats

Living in a houseboat for a few days is an unusual way to get away from it all. It is possible to dive off the boat for a refreshing swim, fish for dinner while sunbathing, and dock in a sheltered, quiet cove for the night.

Houseboats are equipped with kitchens and flush toilets. Most rental agencies require that renters provide their own bedding, linens, and groceries. Almost everything else is on the floating hotel—including life jackets.

Rates vary quite dramatically depending on the time of year and how many people are in the party. Summer rentals are highest, and a group of six to ten people gets the best rates. In-season weekly rates range from $675 to $3,495—depending on the size and quality of the boat. Fuel is additional. Some rental facilities have enough boats to offer midweek specials and three-day weekends; some offer a Thanksgiving special that includes the turkey

and pumpkin pie. During the off-season, rates drop by approximately one-third, and some facilities will rent their boats for just a day. Contact rental facilities directly for current stock and rates.

CLAIR ENGLE LAKE
• **Cedar Stock Resort and Marina.** See page 369.

LAKE OROVILLE
• **Bidwell Marina** *(800) 637-1767, (916) 589-3152, fax (916) 589-4873.*
• **Lime Saddle Marina** *(800) 834-7517, (916) 877-2414.*
For more information on this area contact:
Oroville Chamber of Commerce *1789 Montgomery, Oroville 95965, (800) 655-GOLD, (916) 533-2542, fax (916) 538-2546.*

LAKE SHASTA
• **Bridge Bay Resort** and **Digger Bay Marina** *(800) 752-9669. Bridge Bay (916) 275-3021. Digger Bay (916) 275-3072, fax (714) 588-7400.*
• **Holiday Harbor** *(800) 776-2628, (916) 238-2383, fax (916) 238-2102.*
• **Packers Bay Marina—Holiday Flotels** *(800) 331-3137, (916) 275-5570, fax (916) 275-5570.*
For more information on this area contact:
Shasta-Cascade Wonderland Association. See page 361.

THE DELTA
• **Herman & Helen's Marina** *(800) 676-4841, (209) 951-4634, fax (209) 951-6505.*
• **Paradise Point Marina** *(800) 588-7100, (209) 952-1000, fax (714) 588-7400.*
For more information on this area, see page 243.

Rafting Trips

The adventure of rafting down a changing and unpredictable river offers a real escape for the harried, city-weary participant. But don't expect it to be relaxing. Participants are expected to help with setting up and breaking camp, and they are sometimes mercilessly exposed to the elements. While usually not dangerous when done with experienced guides, an element of risk is involved. Still, most participants walk away ecstatic and addicted to the experience.

The outfitter will provide shelter, food, and equipment for the trip. Participants need only bring sleeping gear and personal items. Costs range from $185 to $590 per person for an overnight run. Some day trips are available. Seasons and rivers vary with each company.

Most outfitters offer special trips for families with young children. The minimum age requirement for children ranges from 4 to 8. For details, contact the tour operators directly.
• **The American River Touring Association** *Groveland, (800) 323-ARTA, (209) 962-7873, fax (209) 962-4819.*
• **ECHO: The Wilderness Company** *Oakland, (800) 652-ECHO, (510) 652-1600, fax (510) 652-3987.*
• **Mariah Wilderness Expeditions** *Point Richmond, (800) 4-MARIAH, (510) 233-2303; fax (510) 233-0956.*
   This is California's only woman-owned and operated white water raft and wilderness company. Special mother-child trips are scheduled, as well as father-child trips (with both female and male guides). A professional storyteller accompanies all family trips.
• **O.A.R.S.** *Angels Camp, (800) 3-GO-OARS, (209) 736-4677, fax (209) 736-2902.*
• **Outdoor Adventures** *Point Reyes Station, (800) 323-4234, (415) 663-8300, fax (415) 663-8617.*
   This company caters to children with campfire games and songs and other activities.
• **Turtle River Rafting Company** *Mt. Shasta, (800) 726-3223, (916) 926-3223, fax (916) 926-3443.*
   Among the special trips are personal growth workshops.
• **Whitewater Connection** *Coloma, (800) 336-7238, (916) 622-6446, fax (916) 622-7192.*
• **Whitewater Voyages** *El Sobrante, (800) 488-RAFT, (510) 222-5994, fax (510) 758-7238.*
   Several bargain half-price Clean-Up Trips are scheduled each year. Participants get the same amenities as on any other trip, but they are expected to pick up any debris they encounter.

For information on more California river outfitters, contact **California Outdoors** at (800) 552-3625.

Pack Trips

Packing equipment onto horses or mules allows for a much easier and more comfortable trek into the wilderness than does backpacking.

Campers need simply choose the type of pack trip desired. On a spot pack trip the packers will load the animals with gear, take them to a prearranged campsite, unload the gear, and return to the pack station with the pack animals. They return to repack the gear on the day campers are scheduled to leave. Campers can either hike or ride on horses to the campsite. If riding, campers usually have a choice of keeping the horses at the campsite or of having the packers take them back out. If keeping the horses, campers need to arrange in advance for a corral and feed, and they should be experienced with horses. Children who haven't had at least basic riding instruction should not be included on such a trip.

A more rugged trip (where the campsite is moved each day) or an easier trip (with all expenses and a guide included) can also usually be arranged with the packer.

This is not an inexpensive vacation. Prices will vary according to which of the above options are selected. Often there are special rates for children, who must be at least 5 years old. Trips are usually available only in the summer.

For general information and a list of packers, contact the **Eastern High Sierra Packers Association** *(690 N. Main St., Bishop 93514, (619) 873-8405), fax (619) 873-6999)*.

One of the biggest and most organized packers is **Red's Meadow Pack Station** *(Mammoth Lakes, (800) 292-7758, (619) 934-2345, fax (619) 934-8785)*, which schedules a large number of pack trips each summer. Horses, saddles, and meals are included, and discounts are available for children

under 15. Day rides can also be arranged, and occasional horse drives and wagon rides are scheduled.

Guided pack trips can also be taken with llamas. They're familiar with this chore, having been used as pack animals for over 2,000 years in the Andes. And they are so gentle even a 4-year-old can lead one. For details, contact **Sierra Llamas** *(13325 Peninsula Dr., Auburn 95602, (916) 269-2204)*, which schedules trips in the Sierra and at Point Reyes National Seashore.

Camping

Because there are excellent resources available on campgrounds, this book mentions only briefly those that fit into the text. For convenience, they are also included in the index under "campsites." For more complete information, consult the following references:

• *The California-Nevada Camp Book.* This book and its companion maps list camping facilities and fees. They are available free to California State Automobile Association members.

• *The California State Parks Guide.* This informative brochure includes a map pinpointing all state parks, reserves, recreation areas, historic parks, and campgrounds. It is available free by calling (800) 444-7275.

Reservations are advised at most state park campgrounds. For a small service fee, they can be made by phone as early as seven months in advance. For general information on state park campgrounds and to make reservations, call (800) 444-7275.

Miscellany

American Hiking Society *Washington, D.C., (301) 565-6704, fax (301) 565-6714.*

This group organizes vacations using teams of volunteers for work trips in remote back country areas. Their annual directory, *Helping Out in the Outdoors,* tells how to get a job as a state park or forest volunteer—hosting a campground, helping improve trails, collecting data on wildlife, or explaining an area's history to visitors. Very few of these jobs reimburse travel and food costs or provide accommodations. Opportunities are available in all 50 states; most are not appropriate for children. For a copy of the directory, send $7 to: American Hiking Society, P.O. Box 20160, Washington, D.C. 20041-2160.

American Youth Hostels *San Francisco, (415) 863-1444, fax (415) 863-3865.*

The idea behind hosteling is to save money, so accommodations are simple. Women bunk in one dormitory-style room, men in another. Some hostels have separate rooms for couples and families. Guests provide their own bedding and linens (sleepsheets can be rented), and bathrooms and kitchens are shared. All guests are expected to do a chore. Hostels are closed during the day, usually from 9:30 to 4:30, and lights go out at 11 p.m. Fees are low, ranging from $10 to $16 per person per night, and children under 18 with a parent are half of that. Members receive a discount at most hostels and get a newsletter and handbook describing U.S. hostels. Package tours are available. Call for a free brochure detailing the hostels in Northern California.

Backroads *Berkeley, (800) GO-ACTIVE, (510) 527-1555, fax (510) 527-1444.*

Weekend bicycle trips include the Wine Country, Russian River, and Point Reyes Seashore. Many more trips are scheduled in other states and countries. The emphasis is not on endurance but on getting some exercise. Two or three tour guides accompany bikers, and a support vehicle transports equipment and tired cyclists. Allowing for different ability levels, several routes are available on each trip. Accommodations are in either interesting hotels or comfortable campgrounds, and meals are included. Special family trips are available. Children are welcome on most other trips as well, and they qualify for discounted rates. Walking and cross-country ski trips are also available.

Bed & Breakfast International *Burlingame, (800) 872-4500, (415) 696-1690, fax (415) 696-1699. $$-$$$+; 2-night min. Children under 2 free. Continental or full breakfast.*

This B&B reservations service books travelers into over 350 private homes, inns, and vacation homes throughout California. Many of the host homes are appropriate for children. Though most cannot accommodate more than two people in a room, a discount is given for children staying in a second room. Amenities, of course, vary with the property.

Bike California *Oakland, (800) 827-2453, 510-638-5864, fax 510-638-8984.*

Sponsored by the American Lung Association of California, these bicycle trips are fully supported and are led by an experienced staff. Vans carry gear, and mechanics are available for repairs. Camping accommodations and both breakfast and dinner are provided. Though prices are reasonable, it is possible for participants to raise pledges for the organization and go along for even less.

Cal Adventures *Dept. of Recreational Sports, University of California, Berkeley, (510) 642-4000, fax (510) 642-3730.*

Adventure trips include rock climbing, backpacking, cross-country skiing, river rafting, kayaking, sailing, and wind surfing. Day classes and a special program for children in grades 3 through 12 are also available.

California Academy of Sciences *San Francisco, (415) 750-7098, fax (415) 750-7346.*

These nature study trips are led by members of the academy staff. On some trips participants camp out and cook their own meals. On other less strenuous trips, motel lodging and restaurant meals are included. Destinations include Lava Beds National Monument and Santa Cruz Island. The Junior Academy offers similar one-day and weekend trips for children ages 6 through 16.

Coastwalk *Sebastopol, (707) 829-6689, same fax.*

Since 1983, Coastwalk has organized summer hikes in California's coastal counties. Hikers can sign up for walks ranging from four to six days, with camping gear shuttled by vehicle. Participants bring and prepare their own food. It is possible to join a walk for just a day, or for a shorter portion of the trip. The goals of this non-profit organization are to nurture an awareness of the coastal environment and to promote development of a continuous California Coastal Trail.

Green Tortoise *San Francisco, (800) TORTOISE, (415) 956-7500.*

Travel on this laid-back alternative bus line is enjoyed at bargain rates. The clientele tends to be the under-30s crowd, but all ages are welcome. Trips are available to almost anywhere on this continent. There are cross-country trips with stops at national parks, and there are river rafting trips to Baja. Usually the scenic route, which is not necessarily the most direct route, is followed. Overnight accommodations are often arranged in hostels, but sometimes riders must bring their own bedding. The jack-of-all-trades bus drivers often organize cookouts, and they get out and fix break-downs themselves. Passengers have also been known to get out and push when necessary. All in all, a trip on this bus line is really a *trip*.

Junior Rangers Program *At California State Parks, (916) 653-8959.*

Children ages 7 through 12 can participate in a program designed to help them discover the rich natural and cultural heritage in California's state parks. Sessions last about an hour each day for several days, and awards are presented as the kids progress. A child can begin the program at one park and continue at a later date in another location.

Sierra Club *San Francisco, (415) 977-5630, fax (415) 977-5795.*

Nature appreciation trips, special family trips, and service trips that take participants to remote wilderness areas to maintain trails and clean up trash are all scheduled. All trips are one or two weeks long and are described in the January/February issue of *Sierra Magazine*, which is sent free to all club members. Shorter day and overnight trips are scheduled through the local chapter; for information, call (510) 653-6127.

University Extension and Research Programs.

Many state colleges and universities have travel/study programs.

• **San Jose State University** *(408) 924-2625.*

On location natural history programs are offered through the Extension Division. Special programs that include children 6 through 16 are scheduled in summer.

• **University of California** *(510) 642-6586.*

These research expeditions are not appropriate for children under 16.

Annual Events

January

AT&T Pebble Beach National Pro-Am, Pebble Beach, 108

Chefs' Holidays, Yosemite National Park, 306

Chinese New Year Celebration & Parade, San Francisco, 8

Sierra Sweepstakes Sled Dog Races, Truckee, 379

Zoo Run, San Francisco, 72

February

Chinese New Year Festival, Isleton, 244

Pacific Orchid Exposition, San Francisco, 8

Valentine's Day Sex Tour, Zoo, San Francisco, 72

March

Bouquets to Art, San Francisco, 60

Camellia Festival, Sacramento, 336

cherry blossoms bloom, San Francisco, 70

Daffodil Hill, Volcano, 291

Family Ski Challenge, Alpine Meadows ski area, Tahoe City, 376

Mendocino Coast Whale Festival, Mendocino, 148

Russian River Wine Road Barrel Tasting, Russian River area, 200-201

Snowfest!, North Lake Tahoe, 377

Spring Wild Flower Excursion, Western Railway Museum, Suisun City, 335

St. Patrick's Day Parade, San Francisco, 8

Victorian Easter Parade and Egg Hunt, Columbia S.H.P., 283

wildflower display, Grass Valley, 298

April

Apple Blossom Festival, Sebastopol, 201

Butter & Egg Days, Petaluma, 194

Cal Day Open House, Berkeley, 329

Cherry Blossom Festival, San Francisco, 8, 76

Easter Egg Hunt, Roaring Camp & Big Trees Narrow-Gauge Railroad, Felton, 241

Fisherman's Festival, Bodega Bay, 141

International Teddy Bear Convention, Nevada City, 299

John Druecker Memorial Rhododendron Show, Fort Bragg, 152

San Francisco Decorator Showcase, San Francisco, 8

San Francisco International Film Festival, S.F., 8

Sheep Shearing, Petaluma Adobe S.H.P., Petaluma, 196

South Shasta Model Railroad, Gerber, 362

spring bloom, Kruse Rhododendron State Reserve, Jenner, 144

Steam Donkey Days, Fort Humboldt S.H.P., Eureka, 230

Victorian Home Tour, Pacific Grove, 105

wildflower display, Independence Trail, Nevada City, 303

Wildflower Show, Pacific Grove, 108

May

Bay to Breakers footrace, San Francisco, 9

Carmel Art Festival, Carmel-by-the-Sea, 109

Carnaval, San Francisco, 9

Chamarita, Half Moon Bay, 84

Chocolate Festival, Oakdale, 307

Cinco de Mayo Festival, San Francisco, 9

Civil War Encampment and Battles, Felton, 241

Fireman's Muster, Columbia S.H.P., 283

Jumping Frog Jubilee, Angels Camp, 287

Living History Day, Petaluma Adobe S.H.P., Petaluma, 196

Mother's Day Rose Show, San Francisco, 71

Roses of Yesterday and Today, Watsonville, 89

Sacramento Jazz Jubilee, Sacramento, 336

Seamen's Memorial Cruise, San Francisco, 63

West Coast Antique Fly-In & Airshow, Watsonville, 89

World Championship Great Arcata to Ferndale Cross Country Kinetic Sculpture Race, Ferndale, 224

World Croquet Championship Finals, Windsor, 207

June

Arcata Bay Oyster Festival, Arcata, 228

Bluegrass Festival, Grass Valley, 297

Cable Car Ringing Championships, San Francisco, 9

Dipsea Race, Muir Beach, 134

Early Days at San Juan Bautista, 172

Fiesta, Mission San Antonio de Padua, King City, 175

Great Isleton Crawdad Festival, Isleton, 244

International Street Performers Festival, San Francisco, 77

Italian Picnic and Parade, Jackson, 289

Live Oak Park Fair, Berkeley, 317

Mountain Play, Muir Beach, 134

North Beach Festival, San Francisco, 9-10

Open House, Dry Creek Vineyard, Healdsburg, 209

Open Studios, Berkeley, 317

Stern Grove Midsummer Music Festival, San Francisco, 10

Summer Concert Series, Lakeport and Clearlake, 215

Ugly Dog Contest, Petaluma, 194

Union Street Fair, San Francisco, 78

West Coast Cherry Pit-Spitting Championships, Placerville, 294

July

Adobe House Tour, Monterey, 97

Bohemian Grove, Russian River area, 201

California Rodeo, Salinas, 173

California Wine Tasting Championships, Philo, 212

Carmel Bach Festival, Carmel, 109

Fortuna Rodeo, Fortuna, 224

4th of July Parade, Nevada City/Grass Valley, 299-300

Fourth of July Waterfront Festival, San Francisco, 10

Independence Day Humboldt Bay 4th of July Festival, Eureka, 226

Lights on the Lake, South Lake Tahoe, 344

Living History Day, Fort Ross S. H. P., Jenner, 144

Marin County Fair, San Rafael, 190

Mendocino Music Festival, Mendocino, 148

Music at Sand Harbor, North Lake Tahoe, 351

Music from Bear Valley, Bear Valley, 284

Night Tour, zoo, San Francisco, 72

Categorical Index

Alphabetical Index

More Great Books from Carousel Press

MILES OF SMILES:
101 Great Car Games & Activities

Anyone who has ever been trapped in a hot car with bored kids is well aware that the world needs a sure-fire way of easing the resulting tensions. This clever book fills that need. In fact, according to one enthusiastic user it just "may be the ultimate solution for back seat squabbling." The book is filled with games and activities that have travel-related themes. Ninety-seven require just your minds and mouths to play, and the other four need only simple props: a penny, a pencil, and some crayons. A helpful index categorizes each game and activity according to age appropriateness, and humorous illustrations that kids can color add to everyone's enjoyment. *128 pages. $8.95.*

THE ZOO BOOK:
A Guide to America's Best

Detailed descriptions of the top 53 U.S. zoos are included. The author has visited each zoo, and his review includes hours and admission fees, driving and bus directions, don't-miss exhibits, touring tips to make a visit easier and more efficient, and details on the entertainment available. Each zoo's featured exhibits are highlighted—plus other exhibits are described, special attractions for the kids are noted, and what's new at the zoo is discussed. Smaller zoos, aquariums, and other places that display animals are also described, as are noteworthy zoos in Canada, Mexico, Europe, and other areas of the world. An entire chapter is devoted to descriptions and photos of interesting zoo animals. *288 pages. $14.95.*

THE FAMILY TRAVEL GUIDE:
An Inspiring Collection of Family-Friendly Vacations

These meaty tales from the trenches promise to help you avoid some of the pitfalls of traveling with children. Information is included on hot spots of family travel (California, Hawaii, Washington D.C., Europe) as well as on lesser-touted havens (Las Vegas, New York City, Belize, Jamaica), and how-to-do-it details are provided on home exchanging, RVing, selecting souvenirs, and traveling with teens. The New York Times says this "is clearly the book for parents who prefer their reading to be more National Geographic than 'Hints from Heloise.'" *432 pages. $16.95.*

DREAM SLEEPS:
Castle & Palace Hotels of Europe

Designed to make fairy tales come true, this book details the exciting castles and palaces in Europe that are open to the public for lodging and dining. Using the positioning maps included for each country, readers can easily determine which hotels potentially fit their itinerary. All information needed to make an informed decision (driving instructions, rates, food services, family amenities, on-site recreation, nearby diversions) is included along with the basic phone and fax numbers and U.S. booking representatives. The author, who has personally visited each hotel, includes a fascinating history for each and an enticing description of the present-day facilities. *304 pages. $17.95.*

WEEKEND ADVENTURES UPDATE:
The Newsletter

Updates to this 6th edition of *Weekend Adventures in Northern California*, and completely new adventures, are published periodically. To receive the most recent edition, send $1 (to cover postage and handling) along with your name and address to: Carousel Press, Weekend Adventures Update, P.O. Box 6038, Berkeley, CA 94706.

TO ORDER DIRECT
call Carousel Press at (510) 527-5849